PUBLICATIONS OF THE GERMAN HISTO

The German Historical Institute is a center for advanced stu
is to provide a permanent basis for scholarly cooperation am
Republic of Germany and the United States. The Institute conducts, promotes, and supports research into both American and German political, social, economic, and cultural history, into transatlantic migration, especially in the nineteenth and twentieth centuries, and into the history of international relations, with special emphasis on the roles played by the United States and Germany.

Other books in the series.

Hartmut Lehmann and James J. Sheehan, editors, *An Interrupted Past: German-Speaking Refugee Historians in the United States after 1933*

Carole Fink, Axel Frohn, and Jürgen Heideking, editors, *Genoa, Rapallo, and European Reconstruction in 1922*

David Clay Large, editor, *Contending with Hitler: Varieties of German Resistance in the Third Reich*

Larry Eugene Jones and James Retallack, editors, *Elections, Mass Politics, and Social Change in Modern Germany*

Hartmut Lehmann and Guenther Roth, editors, *Weber's Protestant Ethic: Origins, Evidence, Contexts*

Catherine Epstein, *A Past Renewed: A Catalog of German-Speaking Historians in the United States after 1933*

Hartmut Lehmann and James Van Horn Melton, editors, *Paths of Continuity: Central European Historiography from the 1930s to the 1950s*

Jeffry M. Diefendorf, Axel Frohn, and Hermann-Josef Rupieper, editors, *American Policy and the Reconstruction of West Germany, 1945–1955*

Henry Geitz, Jürgen Heideking, and Jurgen Herbst, editors, *German Influences on Education in the United States to 1917*

Peter Graf Kielmansegg, Horst Mewes, and Elisabeth Glaser-Schmidt, editors, *Hannah Arendt and Leo Strauss: German Emigrés and American Political Thought after World War II*

Dirk Hoerder and Jörg Nagler, editors, *People in Transit: German Migrations in Comparative Perspective, 1820–1930*

R. Po-chia Hsia and Hartmut Lehmann, editors, *In and Out of the Ghetto: Jewish–Gentile Relations in Late Medieval and Early Modern Germany*

Sibylle Quack, editor, *Between Sorrow and Strength: Women Refugees of the Nazi Period*

Mitchell G. Ash and Alfons Söllner, editors, *Forced Migration and Scientific Change: Emigré German-Speaking Scientists and Scholars after 1933*

Manfred Berg and Geoffrey Cocks, editors, *Medicine and Modernity: Public Health and Medical Care in Nineteenth- and Twentieth-Century Germany*

Stig Förster and Jörg Nagler, editors, *On the Road to Total War: The American Civil War and the German Wars of Unification, 1861–1871*

Norbert Finzsch and Robert Jütte, editors, *Institutions of Confinement: Hospitals, Asylums, and Prisons in Western Europe and North America, 1500–1950*

David E. Barclay and Elisabeth Glaser-Schmidt, editors, *Transatlantic Images and Perceptions: Germany and America since 1776*

The Treaty of Versailles

A REASSESSMENT AFTER 75 YEARS

This book on the Treaty of Versailles constitutes a new synthesis of peace conference scholarship. It illuminates events from the armistice in 1918 to the signing of the treaty in 1919, scrutinizing the motives, actions, and constraints that informed decision making by the French, American, and British politicians who bore the principal responsibility for drafting the peace settlement. It also addresses German reactions to the draft treaty and the final agreement, as well as Germany's role in the immediate postwar period. The findings call attention to diverging peace aims within the American and Allied camps and underscore the degree to which the negotiators themselves considered the Versailles Treaty a work in progress. A detailed examination of the proceedings from the point of view of the main protagonists forms the core of the investigation.

Manfred F. Boemeke is chief editor at the United Nations University Press in Japan.

Gerald D. Feldman is a professor of history and the director of the Center for German and European Studies at the University of California at Berkeley.

Elisabeth Glaser is a former senior research fellow of the German Historical Institute in Washington, D.C. She currently is a German Marshall Fund fellow.

The Treaty of Versailles

A REASSESSMENT AFTER 75 YEARS

Edited by
MANFRED F. BOEMEKE
GERALD D. FELDMAN
and
ELISABETH GLASER

GERMAN HISTORICAL INSTITUTE

Washington, D.C.

and

CAMBRIDGE
UNIVERSITY PRESS

CAMBRIDGE UNIVERSITY PRESS
Cambridge, New York, Melbourne, Madrid, Cape Town, Singapore, São Paulo

Cambridge University Press
The Edinburgh Building, Cambridge CB2 2RU, UK

Published in the United States of America by Cambridge University Press, New York

www.cambridge.org
Information on this title: www.cambridge.org/9780521621328

© The German Historical Institute, Washington, DC 1998

First published 1998
This digitally printed first paperback version 2006

A catalogue record for this publication is available from the British Library

Library of Congress Cataloguing in Publication data
The Treaty of Versailles : a reassessment after 75 years / edited by
Manfred F. Boemeke, Gerald D. Feldman and Elisabeth Glaser.
p.   cm. – (Publications of the German Historical Institute)
Includes bibliographical references and index.
ISBN 0-521-62132-1
1. Treaty of Versailles (1919) – History.   2. World War, 1914–1918
– Peace – History.   I. Boemeke, Manfred F. (Manfred Franz)
II. Feldman, Gerald D.   III. Glaser, Elisabeth.   IV. Series.
KZ186.2   1919
940.3′142–dc21   98-15770
                                            CIP

ISBN-13 978-0-521-62132-8 hardback
ISBN-10 0-521-62132-1 hardback

ISBN-13 978-0-521-62888-4 paperback
ISBN-10 0-521-62888-1 paperback

Contents

vii

Acknowledgments

This book has been a collaborative effort, and we would like to acknowledge the help of all those who participated. The Gerda Henkel Foundation provided generous financial support. The Center for German and European Studies at the University of California at Berkeley and the German Historical Institute in Washington, D.C., participated in the funding of the conference and the expanded version of the proceedings. Patricia La Hay and her colleagues on the staff of the Center at Berkeley provided invaluable help in organizing the conference; Joel Berg, Vicky Macintyre, and Daniel S. Mattern patiently and expertly prepared the manuscript for publication.

The Treaty of Versailles: A Reassessment After 75 Years is dedicated to the memory of William C. McNeil, whose tragic and sudden death on April 18, 1993, at the age of forty-six, deprived the history of international relations and political economy of one of its most promising practitioners. Professor McNeil, who was chairman of the History Department at Barnard College at the time of his death, was a beloved teacher and a fine scholar. He received his Ph.D. in history at the University of California at Berkeley for a dissertation subsequently published as *American Money and the Weimar Republic: Economics and Politics on the Eve of the Great Depression* (New York, 1986). He was always a lively and enthusiastic participant in conferences such as this one, and he would certainly have loved to return to Berkeley on such an occasion.

Tokyo, Berkeley,
and Charlottesville

Manfred F. Boemeke,
Gerald D. Feldman, and
Elisabeth Glaser

Contributors

Manfred F. Boemeke is chief editor at the United Nations University Press, Tokyo.

Gerald D. Feldman is a professor of history at the University of California at Berkeley.

Niall Ferguson is a fellow and tutor in modern history at Jesus College, Oxford University.

Carole Fink is a professor of history at the Ohio State University.

Antoine Fleury is a professor of history at the University of Geneva.

David French is a reader in modern history at University College, London.

Michael Graham Fry is a professor of international relations at the University of Southern California, Los Angeles.

Lawrence E. Gelfand is a professor of history at the University of Iowa.

Elisabeth Glaser is currently a German Marshall Fund fellow.

Erik Goldstein is a professor of international studies at the University of Birmingham.

Jon Jacobson is a professor of history at the University of California at Irvine.

William R. Keylor is a professor of history at Boston University.

Fritz Klein is a professor emeritus in the Academy of Sciences of the former German Democratic Republic.

Thomas J. Knock is a professor of history at Southern Methodist University, Dallas.

Diane B. Kunz is an assistant professor of history at Yale University.

Antony Lentin is a professor of history at the Open University, Faculty of Art, Milton Keynes.

Sally Marks is an independent historian in Providence, Rhode Island.

Gordon Martel is a professor of history at the University of Northern British Columbia, Prince George, B.C.

Wolfgang J. Mommsen is a professor of history at the Heinrich Heine University, Düsseldorf.

Stephen A. Schuker is a professor of history at the University of Virginia in Charlottesville.

Klaus Schwabe is a professor of history at the Rhineland-Westphalian Technical University, Aachen.

Alan Sharp is a professor of history at the University of Ulster.

Georges-Henri Soutou is a professor of history at the Sorbonne, University of Paris.

Ronald Steel is a professor of history at the University of Southern California, Los Angeles.

David Stevenson is a reader in international relations at the London School of Economics.

Piotr S. Wandycz is a professor of history at Yale University.

William C. Widenor is a professor of history at the University of Illinois at Urbana-Champaign.

Introduction

MANFRED F. BOEMEKE, GERALD D. FELDMAN, AND ELISABETH GLASER

I

This book brings together the proceedings of an international conference on the Treaty of Versailles. The 1919 peace treaty left an enduring mark on twentieth-century historiography. Even now, the reason for the ultimate collapse of the Versailles system remains disputed. A detailed examination of the motives and making of the treaty, as undertaken here, goes a long way toward explaining whether that failure stemmed from inherent weaknesses of the treaty or from postwar revisionism and economic instability. There exists a solid basis for this reevaluation: multiarchival studies that have appeared in the past twenty-five years have minimized national bias, although most have treated a specific national problem or taken a particular national perspective.[1] Furthermore, no effort has been made to produce an international research-oriented synthesis.

A group of German and American historians concluded in 1992 that a reassessment of the peace settlement from an international perspective after seventy-five years would therefore be particularly timely. In May 1994 experts from France, Germany, Great Britain, Switzerland, and the United States gathered to reconstruct the making of the treaty by discussing the latest archival evidence and the extant literature. The conference took place under the auspices of the Center for German and European Studies of the University of California at Berkeley and the German Historical Institute in Washington, D.C.

The resulting reappraisal, as documented in this book, constitutes a new synthesis of peace conference scholarship. The findings call attention to divergent peace aims within the American and Allied camps and underscore the degree to which the negotiators themselves considered the Versailles Treaty a work in progress. Many of the essays here situate the peace

1 See the historiographical survey later in this chapter and the bibliography at the end of the book.

1

settlement in the context of postwar conditions in Europe. World War I had produced human suffering, destruction, and economic and political up-heaval on an unprecedented scale. Europe in 1919 struck many observers as being closer to another war than to a prolonged peace. Dealing with the sequelae therefore seemed analogous to the process that Tacitus described so aptly: "They make it a wilderness and call it peace."[2] The peace treaty with Germany had to solve the most pressing material questions arising out of the war and simultaneously had to lay the groundwork for a stable inter-national system. Far from aiming at a punitive settlement, as several chap-ters in this book show, the United States and the Allies sought to preserve Germany, but to contain its power to fight future wars. At the same time, they tried to establish a ring of independent states around the Reich – and to ensure the existence and economic viability of those states.

In the following pages, these proceedings are investigated from the view-point of the protagonists. The analysis is limited mainly to France, Ger-many, Great Britain, and the United States as players or the objects of delib-erations. The contributors seek to reconstruct the complex reality of peacemaking; the confluence of diplomacy, domestic pressures, alliances, and political ties; and the problems of material destruction, human loss, and political disruption in Europe.[3] Indeed, the arrangements concluded in 1919 affected every aspect of European life.

As a result, many analysts, beginning with John Maynard Keynes, have blamed the treaty for Germany's subsequent vindictiveness and revisionism. Some see its harsh indemnity provisions as the cause of the German eco-nomic and financial crisis of 1929–33, and even of the Depression itself. Others claim that the treaty helped the National Socialists gain power in 1933. And a few even think that it contributed to the outbreak of World War II.[4] Those criticisms reflect two main themes: first, that the Versailles Treaty

---

2 Tacitus, *Agricola,* chap. 42.
3 This book does not cover Italy's role at the peace conference, nor the questions of Tirol or the Adri-atic. On these subjects, see René Albrecht-Carrié, *Italy at the Paris Peace Conference* (Hamden, Conn., 1934); Daniela Rossini, *L'America riscopere l'Italia: L'Inquiry di Wilson e le origini della questione adriat-ica, 1917–1919* (Rome, 1992).
4 Public criticism started with John Maynard Keynes, *The Economic Consequences of the Peace* (New York, 1920), chap. 4. The scholarly debate in Germany is summarized in Hagen Schulze, *Weimar: Deutsch-land, 1917–1933* (Berlin, 1982); and Karl-Dietrich Erdmann, *Die Zeit der Weltkriege* (Stuttgart, 1973). A. J. P. Taylor viewed World War II as a conflict over the Versailles settlement and argued that the treaty lacked moral validity and failed to solve the German problem. See A. J. P. Taylor, *The Origins of the Second World War* (London, 1963), 16, 28, 32, 44, 190. See also Gordon Martel, "The Revi-sionist as Moralist: A. J. P. Taylor and the Lessons of European History"; Sally Marks, "1918 and After: The Postwar Era"; and Stephen A. Schuker, "The End of Versailles" – all in Gordon Martel, ed., *The Origins of the Second World War Reconsidered: The A.J.P. Taylor Debate After Twenty-Five Years* (Boston, 1986), 1–16, 17–48, 49–72. Marion Gräfin Dönhoff ("Von Weimar kann keine Rede sein," *Die Zeit,* no. 48, Nov. 20, 1992) asserts that the Allied and American reparations policies based on the Versailles Treaty ruined Germany's economy, which was already weakened by the war.

reduced Germany's chances of improving its social, economic, financial, and political situation; and, second, that Germany's revisionism weakened the postwar European system. Consequently, the treaty proved unworkable and finally failed. George F. Kennan has recently argued that the "vindictiveness of British and French peace terms" helped pave the way for National Socialism and a renewal of hostilities. World War II resulted, in Kennan's view, from "the very silly and humiliating punitive peace imposed on Germany after World War I."[5]

Such revisionist judgments have held sway for several generations.[6] In recent years, however, detailed archival research has underscored the successes of the German peace compact. Whatever its shortcomings, the treaty lent itself to future revision and eventually led to an era of temporary stability between 1924 and 1931. By 1932 the reparations dispute was largely resolved, the Rhineland occupation had come to an end, and Britain and the United States had signaled their readiness to enter into negotiations for a new settlement of the Polish Corridor. By contemporary standards, in short, the treaty did not prove an inflexible instrument. Had a worldwide depression not supervened, the process of peaceful readjustment might have gone further. The peace settlement and its subsequent revisions, viewed from this perspective, represented the most stable arrangement that could have emerged from the contentious peacemaking process in Paris.

Scholars, although remaining divided, now tend to view the treaty as the best compromise that the negotiators could have reached in the existing circumstances.[7] The delegations in Paris and their entourages had to work quickly. Troops had to be sent home, food shipments needed to enter blockaded ports, and revolutionary movements required containment. None of those endeavors allowed for delay. Still, the labors of the conference proceeded haltingly, owing to the involuted bureaucratic structure of the gathering. The progress of the deliberations – from the preliminary preparations to the organization of the League, and from the draft treaty to the final version of the compact – made heavy demands on the organizational skills, patience, mental and physical health, and political survival skills of the participants.[8] Yet the broader public, to judge from newspaper opinion and text-

---

5 George F. Kennan, "The War to End War," originally published in the *New York Times,* Nov. 11, 1984, reprinted in George F. Kennan, *At a Century's Ending: Reflections, 1982–1995* (New York, 1996), 17–19; and George F. Kennan, "Historical Inevitability and World War (1890–1914)," talk given at the Kennan Institute, Washington, D.C., Apr. 2, 1985, reprinted in Kennan, *At a Century's Ending,* 20–9. For a discussion of the revisionist accounts of the treaty, see chapters 23 and 26 in this book.
6 For an insightful analysis of this question, see chapter 26.
7 Alan Sharp, *The Versailles Settlement: Peacemaking in Paris, 1919* (New York, 1991).
8 On the organization of the peace conference, see Frank S. Marston, *The Peace Conference of 1919: Organization and Procedure* (London, 1944).

book treatment, clings to the impression of a Carthaginian settlement that gave the French too much leeway to play a predominant role in Europe at Germany's expense.[9] Recently, Hagen Schulze, in a book that seeks to set the tone for German postunification historiography, has denominated the Versailles Treaty "a dictated peace." He describes the compact as a "destructive middle course" that "put Germany under special laws, took away its military power, ruined it economically, and humiliated it politically."[10] Nevertheless, the position taken in this book is that it is heuristically preferable to analyze the strengths and weaknesses of the peace settlement by distinguishing between long-range economic and political factors and the immediate domestic and diplomatic developments that inevitably loomed so large in the consciousness of the negotiators and their contemporaries.

II

Archive-based research treating the Paris Peace Conference from an international perspective took off in the 1960s when the main belligerents abandoned the fifty-year rule for opening diplomatic records. The resulting works built on a felicitous confluence of new materials and methods.[11] The following selective overview highlights these trends.

Historical studies on the Paris Peace Conference started in World War II, at a time when a reassessment of the earlier peace required no justification. Previous accounts coming from the desks of participants had offered subjective reflections, but rarely systematic analysis. With few exceptions, those memories of the peace severely criticized the motives, making, and execution of the accord. John Maynard Keynes's cleverly written account of the Council of Four commanded lasting attention among popular writers, although neither enlightened contemporaries nor historians considered it fair-minded or well-informed. Wartime historical investigations provided valuable groundwork for systematic research and included a substantial source publication on the German delegation in Paris as well as a retrospective assessment that became the standard account of the conference used during World War II.[12]

9 William R. Keylor discusses these negative assessments in chapter 19 in this book. Recent critical German comments include those of Klaus Hildebrand, *Das vergangene Reich: Deutsche Aussenpolitik von Bismarck bis Hitler, 1871–1945* (Stuttgart, 1995), 383–412; and Heinrich Klümpen, *Deutsche Aussenpolitik zwischen Versailles und Rapallo: Revisionismus oder Neuorientierung?* (Münster, 1992).
10 Hagen Schulze, *Kleine deutsche Geschichte* (Munich, 1996), 166.
11 A recent synthesis on the making of the Versailles Treaty that outlines the historiography and provides a useful starting point is Sharp's *Versailles Settlement.* For postwar developments, see Sally Marks, *The Illusion of Peace* (New York, 1989).
12 Robert Skidelsky, *John Maynard Keynes: A Biography,* vol. 1: *Hopes Betrayed, 1883–1920* (New York, 1986); Paul Birdsall, *Versailles Twenty Years After* (London, 1941); Alma Luckau, *The German Delegation at the Paris Peace Conference* (New York, 1941).

Post-1945 research on Germany's role at the peace conference, resting on the captured records of the Wilhelmstrasse, set the problem of the Reich's response to peacemaking in 1918–19 within a comparative framework and employed German as well as non-German sources. A lucid portrait of German diplomacy during the conference provided fresh insights while passing a critical judgment on the treaty provisions.[13]

Fritz Fischer's revisionist evaluation of German World War I war aims, first published in 1961, triggered an impassioned controversy in the Federal Republic about the country's responsibility for the war. That seminal work shaped the subsequent debate on the justice of the Versailles Treaty.[14] Fischer's revelations followed a pioneering work on the Reich's western war aims that had won considerable acclaim in the United States. Nevertheless, those findings had escaped notice by the general public in West Germany, and Fischer's study met with ferocious criticisms at home.[15] But reviews from abroad tended to be positive. As a whole, the Fischer controversy promoted fresh research in all the former belligerent countries.

Beginning in the 1970s, German historians began to exploit the German records dealing with Versailles more fully. The resulting studies treat German reparations policy, the Reich's conference diplomacy in May and June 1919, the fate of the emperor and the German military, as well as the debate about the treaty within the emerging political class of the Weimar Republic. These books provide a balanced review of Germany's difficulties in 1918 and 1919. The authors stress the continuity of Germany's foreign-policy aims as well as the constraints on German diplomacy that were imposed by domestic upheaval, the Allied blockade, and resulting isolation.

Some revisionist accounts have emerged as well. An acerbic monograph on French plans for the settlement with Germany concludes that Paris's ambitious territorial aims limited Germany's options for domestic political reform. The critical debate about the treaty in the Federal Republic in the wake of the Fischer controversy became more nuanced. Historians sought an open exchange with their colleagues in other countries.[16] A landmark

---

13 Klaus Epstein, *Matthias Erzberger and the Dilemma of German Democracy* (Princeton, N.J., 1959), 284–327. For the work of other émigré historians on problems of World War I and postwar Europe, see Hartmut Lehmann and James J. Sheehan, eds., *An Interrupted Past: German-Speaking Refugee Historians in the United States After 1933* (New York, 1991).

14 Fritz Fischer, *Germany's War Aims in the First World War* (London, 1967).

15 Hans Gatzke, *Germany's Drive to the West: A Study of Germany's Western War Aims During the First World War* (Baltimore, 1950).

16 See the contributions in Helmut Rössler, ed., *Ideologie und Machtpolitik 1919: Plan und Werk der Pariser Friedenskonferenzen 1919* (Berlin, 1966). See also Peter Krüger, *Deutschland und die Reparationen, 1918–1919: Die Genesis des Reparationsproblems in Deutschland zwischen Waffenstillstand und Versailler Friedensschluss* (Stuttgart, 1973); Peter Krüger, *Die Aussenpolitik der Republik von Weimar* (Darmstadt, 1985), 1–76; Udo Wengst, *Graf Brockdorff-Rantzau und die aussenpolitischen Anfänge der Weimarer*

study of German and American policies from the armistice to the peace
exploited archives on both sides of the Atlantic with equal diligence and
delineated the divergence between German expectations of the Fourteen
Points and the practical demands of *Realpolitik* that confronted President
Woodrow Wilson at the end of World War I. Those studies of German reactions to the armistice and the peace complemented an array of investigations
that had concentrated on Germany's domestic situation in 1918–19 at the
expense of diplomatic background.[17] An important monograph treated
the response of official German historiography to the military defeat and the
peace settlement. The author explained why German historians embraced
revisionism and how they shaped public opinion during the 1920s.[18] Problems pertaining to German demobilization have been examined in an essay
collection. A massive study of the German inflation analyzes social and economic problems of demobilization and views them in the larger context of
wartime and postwar financial instability. And a recent work traces the diplomacy of Bavaria from the armistice to the peace.[19]

The reevaluation proceeded apace in the former Allied nations during
the 1960s. The first generation of international histories of the peace conference used American official records and British private collections. They
studied British and American war aims and yielded insights about the transition from war to peace diplomacy.[20] A revisionist interpretation of the

Republik (Berne, 1973); Leo Haupts, *Deutsche Friedenspolitik, 1918–1919: Eine Alternative zur Machtpolitik des Ersten Weltkrieges* (Düsseldorf, 1976); Peter Grupp, *Deutsche Aussenpolitik im Schatten von
Versailles, 1918–1920: Zur Politik des Auswärtigen Amtes vom Ende des Ersten Weltkrieges und der
Novemberrevolution bis zum Inkrafttreten des Versailler Vertrags* (Paderborn, 1988).
17 Klaus Schwabe, *Deutsche Revolution und Wilson-Frieden: Die amerikanische und deutsche Friedensstrategie
zwischen Ideologie und Machtpolitik, 1918–1919* (Düsseldorf, 1971); Klaus Schwabe, *Woodrow Wilson,
Revolutionary Germany, and Peacemaking, 1918–1919: Missionary Diplomacy and the Realities of Power*
(Chapel Hill, N.C., 1985); Walter Schwengler, *Völkerrecht, Versailler Vertrag und Auslieferungsfrage: Die
Strafverfolgung von Kriegsverbrechen als Problem des Friedensschlusses 1919/20* (Stuttgart, 1982); Reinhard Rürup, "Demokratische Revolution und 'dritter Weg': Die deutsche Revolution von 1918/19
in der neueren wissenschaftlichen Diskussion," *Geschichte und Gesellschaft* 8 (1983): 278–301, discusses the literature on Germany's domestic situation in 1918–19.
18 Heinrich August Winkler, *Von der Revolution zur Stabilisierung: Arbeiter und Arbeiterbewegung in der
Weimarer Republik, 1918–1924* (Bonn, 1985), 206–27; Peter Krüger, "German Disappointment and
Anti-Western Resentment, 1918–1919," in Hans-Jürgen Schröder, ed., *Confrontation and Cooperation: Germany and the United States in the Era of World War I, 1900–1924* (Oxford, 1993), 323–36;
Ulrich Heinemann, *Die verdrängte Niederlage: Öffentlichkeit und Kriegsschuldfrage in der Weimarer Repub-
lik* (Göttingen, 1983).
19 Henning Köhler, *Novemberrevolution und Frankreich: Die französische Deutschlandpolitik, 1918–1919*
(Düsseldorf, 1980); Wolfgang J. Mommsen, ed., *Die Organisierung des Friedens: Demobilmachung,
1918–1920* (Göttingen, 1983); Siegfried Sutterlin, *Munich in the Cobwebs of Berlin, Washington, and
Moscow: Foreign Policy Tendencies in Bavaria, 1917–1919* (New York, 1995); Gerald D. Feldman, *The
Great Disorder: Politics, Economics, and Society in the German Inflation, 1914–1923* (New York, 1993),
99–155.
20 Seth P. Tillman, *Anglo-American Relations at the Paris Peace Conference* (Princeton, N.J., 1961);
Lawrence E. Gelfand, *The Inquiry: American Preparations for Peace, 1917–1919* (New Haven, Conn.,
1963); David F. Trask, *The United States in the Supreme War Council: American War Aims and Inter-*

period as a clash between Anglo-American efforts to reconstitute the liberal economic and social order and the "forces of movement" represented by socialism and Soviet communism broadened the scope of inquiry, yet confined analysis of diplomatic sources largely to printed documents.[21]

Owing to the sophisticated development of cabinet machinery by Sir Maurice Hankey and the long traditions of the Foreign Office, British records on the armistice and the peace conference were richer than those of other countries and allowed a detailed reconstruction of decision making. The release of the official British files at the end of the 1960s stimulated a series of investigations of David Lloyd George, the British delegation, and Foreign Office and Treasury planning and responses to the conference. A number of meticulously researched studies analyzed the evolution of British war aims, plans for the League of Nations, and the work of the Council of Four. Not surprisingly, controversial interpretations of Lloyd George's stand on reparations emerged (which are reflected in this book as well).[22] Together, those works led to a deeper understanding of British policy and the qualified success of the British Empire at the peace conference. A recent two-volume study provides a definitive account of British political, military, and naval strategy in the last two years of the conflict.[23]

France, the staunchest defender of the Versailles peace, stood at the forefront of international scholarly inquiry. Paris's postwar quest for security

Allied Strategy, 1917–1918 (Middletown, Conn., 1961); Harold I. Nelson, *Land and Power: British and Allied Policy on Germany's Frontiers, 1916–19* (London, 1963).

21 Arno J. Mayer, *Policy and Diplomacy of Peacemaking: Containment and Counterrevolution at Versailles, 1918–1919* (London, 1968); see also *The Political Origins of the New Diplomacy, 1917–1918* (New Haven, Conn., 1959); for a searching critique of Mayer, see Lloyd E. Ambrosius, "The Orthodoxy of Revisionism: Woodrow Wilson and the New Left," *Diplomatic History* 1 (1977): 199–214.

22 See chapters 5, 10, and 24 in this book.

23 Victor H. Rothwell, *British War Aims and Peace Diplomacy, 1914–1918* (Oxford, 1971); George W. Elcock, *Portrait of a Decision: The Council of Four and the Treaty of Versailles* (London, 1972). A careful edition of Sir James Headlam Morley's peace conference memoirs provides indispensable documentation on British decision making: Agnes Headlam Morley, Russell Bryant, and Anna Cienciala, eds., *Sir James Headlam Morley: A Memoir of the Peace Conference, 1919* (London, 1972). See also George W. Egerton, *Britain and the Creation of the League of Nations: Strategy, Politics, and International Organization, 1914–1919* (Chapel Hill, N.C., 1978); Robert E. Bunselmeyer, *The Cost of War, 1914–1919: British Economic War Aims and the Origins of Reparations* (Hamden, Conn., 1975); F. Gregory Campbell, "The Struggle for Upper Silesia, 1919–1922," *Journal of Modern History* 42 (1970): 361–85; Michael Dockrill and Zara Steiner, "The Foreign Office at the Paris Peace Conference in 1919," *International History Review* 2 (1980): 55–86; Michael Dockrill and J. Douglas Goold, *Peace Without Promise: Britain and the Peace Conferences, 1919–1923* (London, 1981); Antony Lentin, *Lloyd George, Woodrow Wilson, and the Guilt of Germany: An Essay on the Pre-History of Appeasement* (Baton Rouge, La., 1985); Lorna Jaffe, *The Decision to Disarm Germany: British Policy Towards Postwar German Disarmament, 1914–1919* (London, 1985); Gerard de Groot, *Blighty: British Society in the Era of the Great War* (London, 1996). See also Arthur Marwick, *The Deluge: British Society and the First World War* (London, 1991), 2; Erik Goldstein, *Winning the Peace: British Diplomatic Strategy, Peace Planning, and the Paris Peace Conference, 1916–1920* (Oxford, 1991); David French, *The Strategy of the Lloyd George Coalition, 1916–1918* (Oxford, 1995); and chapter 2 in this book.

8   *Manfred F. Boemeke, Gerald D. Feldman,* and *Elisabeth Glaser*

received widespread attention in the scholarly community. The opening of
French archival records on the peace conference in the 1960s and 1970s
stimulated works on war aims, the armistice, and public opinion, as well as
a broadly gauged investigation of French politics and society during the war
and the peace settlement. As early as 1962, a pathbreaking book on French
policy toward Czechoslovakia and Poland appeared.[24] New studies since the
late 1970s, based on records in several countries, likewise explored postwar
alliance diplomacy. Those publications set Franco-German and French-
American relations within the broader context of wartime conditions and
the evolution of postwar economic, financial, and political relations. A
monograph that examines domestic and foreign factors in French reparations policy leading to the Dawes Plan offers a model for international history in the postwar era.[25] A recent multiarchival study on German and
Allied material war aims has set a new standard for comparative historical
investigation that emphasizes political and economic motives as well as
decision-making processes in Paris, London, Washington, and Berlin. On
the whole, those bilateral or multilateral works provide valuable case studies on France's role in the making and execution of the treaty.[26] Future
research on the peace conference will profit from a new edition of Paul
Mantoux's notes of the Council of Four.[27]

Studies on the American role in the peacemaking, with the exception of
a monograph on economic peace planning, have concentrated biographi-

24 Pierre Renouvin, "Les Buts de guerre du gouvernment français, 1914–1918," *Revue historique* 235
(1966): 1–37; Pierre Renouvin, *L'Armistice de Réthondes, 11 novembre 1918* (Paris, 1969); Pierre
Miquel, *La Paix de Versailles et l'opinion publique française* (Paris, 1972); Piotr S. Wandycz, *France and
Her Eastern Allies, 1919–1925: French–Czechoslovak–Polish Relations from the Paris Peace Conference to
Locarno* (Minneapolis, 1962); Jean-Baptiste Duroselle, *La France et les Français, 1914–1920* (Paris,
1972).
25 Karlevo Hovi, *Cordon sanitaire: The Emergence of the French East European Alliance Policy, 1917–1919*
(Turku, 1975); Jacques Bariéty, *Les Relations franco-allemandes après la Première Guerre Mondiale, 11
novembre 1918–10 janvier 1925: De l'exécution à la négociation* (Paris, 1977); André Kaspi, *Les temps
des Américains: Le concours américain à la France en 1917–1918* (Paris, 1976); Stephen A. Schuker, *The
End of French Predominance in Europe: The Financial Crisis of 1924 and the Adoption of the Dawes Plan*
(Chapel Hill, N.C., 1976). See also John F. V. Keiger, *Raymond Poincaré* (Cambridge, 1997).
26 David Stevenson, "French War Aims and the American Challenge, 1914–1918," *Historical Journal* 22
(1979): 877–94; David Stevenson, "Belgium, Luxembourg, and the Defence of Western Europe,
1914–1920," *International History Review* 4 (1982): 504–23; David Stevenson, *French War Aims Against
Germany, 1914–1919* (Oxford, 1982); Marc Trachtenberg, *Reparations in World Politics: France and
European Economic Diplomacy, 1916–1923* (New York, 1980); Marc Trachtenberg, "'A New Economic
Order': Etienne Clémentel and French Economic Diplomacy, 1916–1923," *French Historical Studies*
10 (1977): 315–41; Walter A. McDougall, *France's Rhineland Diplomacy, 1914–1924: The Last Bid for
a Balance of Power in Europe* (Princeton, N.J., 1978); Gitta Steinmeyer, *Die Grundlagen der französischen
Deutschlandpolitik, 1917–1919* (Stuttgart, 1979); Michael J. Carley, *Revolution and Intervention: The
French Government and the Russian Civil War, 1917–1919* (Kingston, Ont., 1983); Georges-Henri
Soutou, *L'Or et le sang: Les buts de guerre économiques de la Première Guerre Mondiale* (Paris, 1989).
27 Paul Mantoux, *The Deliberations of the Council of Four (March 24–June 28, 1919): Notes of the Official
Interpreter,* trans. and ed. Arthur S. Link, with the assistance of Manfred F. Boemeke, 2 vols. (Prince-
ton, N.J., 1992).

cally on Wilson and to a lesser extent on Edward House, Wilson's chief adviser. A first work on the president was written in the heat of World War II, and the experience of the war may have influenced the critical assessment of his diplomacy. After 1945 the tone of interpretations became markedly more positive. A series of exhaustively researched biographical studies based on the Wilson papers followed, including detailed volumes on the president's diplomacy during the early stages of the war. Out of those endeavors grew a publication of Wilson's papers that by general acknowledgment sets the standard for scholarly manuscript editions.[28] Recent biographies of the president and his role in the peacemaking process include some studies that depart from the hagiographic tradition in Wilson biography. However, one notable account reaffirms the positive evaluation of Wilson's aims for the League of Nations and the peace.[29]

A selective edition of House's diary in the 1920s first depicted his role in the negotiations. A later study, though based on careful research, adopted an uncharitable tone, and House still awaits a dispassionate biographer. Likewise, the role of other American delegates and their advisers remains underresearched. A recent monograph, however, has outlined the role of American historians in peace planning. German–American relations after 1919 form the subject of a detailed account that analyzes mutual diplomatic ties, changing economic interests, and America's role in solving the reparations question. An examination of the German–American peace treaty of 1921 characterizes it as an attempt by the State Department to secure the substantive advantages of the treaty after the Senate had rejected that document.[30]

28 Carl Parrini, *Heir to Empire: United States Economic Diplomacy, 1916–1923* (Pittsburgh, 1969); Thomas A. Bailey, *Woodrow Wilson and the Lost Peace* (Chicago, 1944); Thomas A. Bailey, *Woodrow Wilson and the Great Betrayal* (New York, 1945); Arthur S. Link, *Wilson, the Diplomatist: A Look at His Major Foreign Policies* (Baltimore, 1957); Arthur S. Link, *President Wilson and His English Critics* (Oxford, 1959); Arthur S. Link, *Wilson,* 5 vols. to date (Princeton, N.J., 1947), particularly *Wilson: The Struggle for Neutrality* (Princeton, N.J., 1960); Arthur S. Link et al., eds., *The Papers of Woodrow Wilson,* 69 vols. (Princeton, N.J., 1966–92); Arthur S. Link, *Woodrow Wilson: Revolution, War, and Peace* (Arlington Heights, Ill., 1979); Arthur S. Link, ed., *Woodrow Wilson and a Revolutionary World, 1913–1921* (Chapel Hill, N.C., 1982); Schwabe, *Woodrow Wilson, Revolutionary Germany, and Peacemaking.*

29 Arthur Walworth, *America's Moment, 1918: American Diplomacy at the End of World War I* (New York, 1977); Arthur Walworth, *Wilson and His Peacemakers: American Diplomacy at the Peace Conference* (New York, 1986); John M. Cooper, "The British Response to the House-Grey Memorandum: New Evidence and New Questions," *Journal of American History* 59 (1973): 958–71; John M. Cooper and Charles E. Neu, eds., *The Wilson Era: Essays in Honor of Arthur S. Link* (Arlington Heights, Ill., 1991); Lloyd E. Ambrosius, "Wilson, the Republicans, and French Security After World War I," *Journal of American History* 59 (1972): 341–52; Lloyd E. Ambrosius, *Woodrow Wilson and the American Diplomatic Tradition* (Cambridge, 1987); Thomas J. Knock, *To End All Wars: Woodrow Wilson and the Quest for a New World Order* (New York, 1992).

30 Charles Seymour, ed., *The Intimate Papers of Colonel House* (New York, 1928); Inga Floto, *Colonel House in Paris: A Study of American Policy at the Paris Peace Conference, 1919* (Aarhus, 1973); Jonathan M. Nielson, *American Historians in War and Peace: Patriotism, Diplomacy, and the Paris Peace Conference, 1919* (Dubuque, Iowa, 1994); Werner Link, *Die amerikanische Stabilisierungpolitik in Deutschland,*

Germany's neighboring countries and the League of Nations, vital subjects of the Paris deliberations, take a prominent place in the historical literature on Versailles. A revealing account of Belgian diplomacy during the Paris Peace Conference inspired further multiarchival research on the smaller powers and newly erected states.[31] Several studies have dealt with plans for the League of Nations.[32] Meanwhile other international bodies that emanated from the peace treaty have not received much scholarly attention. A lucid account of the Conference of Ambassadors constitutes an exception.[33]

III

Our reexamination of the peace starts in part one with an analysis of American and Allied war aims and the making of the armistice. It then portrays in part two the leading peacemakers and their interaction with domestic interlocutors during the conference. The shaping of the territorial, economic, and financial provisions of the treaty forms the subject of the next part. The treaty's impact on Poland and Russia, as well as its consequences for the postwar international system, receive attention in the fourth part. The last part deals with contemporary reflections and reactions to the peace conference.

The opening part compares the original American, British, and French schemes for a settlement with Germany. It emphasizes the haste with which the belligerents concluded that the armistice left critical issues, except for military and naval provisions, unresolved. As a consequence, the peace conference faced an immense workload.

1921–1932 (Düsseldorf, 1970); Elisabeth Glaser-Schmidt, "Von Versailles nach Berlin: Überlegungen zur Neugestaltung der deutsch-amerikanischen Beziehungen in der Ära Harding," in Norbert Finzsch and Hermann Wellenreuther, eds., *Liberalitas: Festschrift für Erich Angermann* (Stuttgart, 1992), 319–42.

31 See Carole Fink's essay on the Polish Minority Treaty (chapter 11) in this book; Sally Marks, *Innocent Abroad: Belgium at the Peace Conference of 1919* (Chapel Hill, N.C., 1981); Hovi, *Cordon Sanitaire;* Kai Lundgreen-Nielsen, *The Polish Problem at the Paris Peace Conference: A Study of the Great Powers and the Poles, 1918–1919* (Odense, 1979); Kai Lundgreen-Nielsen, "The Mayer Thesis Reconsidered: The Poles and the Paris Peace Conference 1919," *International History Review* 7 (1985): 68–102; Betty Miller Unterberger, *The United States, Revolutionary Russia, and the Rise of Czechoslovakia* (Chapel Hill, N.C., 1989); Wandycz, *France and Her Eastern Allies,* and chapter 13 in this book.

32 Egerton, *Great Britain and the League of Nations;* Knock, *To End All Wars;* Gelfand, *Inquiry.* For subsequent developments, see chapter 20 in this book.

33 Jürgen Heideking, *Areopag der Diplomaten: Die Pariser Botschafterkonferenz der europäischen Hauptmächte und die Probleme der europäischen Politik, 1920–1931* (Husum, 1979); Jürgen Heideking, "Vom Versailler Vertrag zur Genfer Abrüstungskonferenz: Das Scheitern der alliierten Militärkontrollpolitik gegenüber Deutschland nach dem Ersten Weltkrieg," *Militärgeschichtliche Mitteilungen* 28 (1980): 45–68.

Klaus Schwabe's essay in chapter 1 depicts Brockdorff-Rantzau's diplomacy in 1918–19 against the background of continuing unrest at home. Schwabe explains that the Reich, as the defeated belligerent, had to accept an imposed peace settlement. Wilson's Fourteen Points became the basis on which Berlin hoped to attain a lenient settlement. Failure of the negotiators in Paris to consult the Reich during the making of the treaty left Germany with a single realistic option: economic revisionism. In Schwabe's view, the resort to economic resistance reflected Germany's lack of choice rather than a purposeful continuity of pre- and postrevolutionary foreign policy aims.[34] Alan Sharp, in commenting on Schwabe (see chapter 5), observes that the conversion of German officials to Wilsonianism did not spring from genuine conviction but rather from the desire to salvage something from the jaws of defeat. In the second part of his argument, Schwabe delineates Brockdorff-Rantzau's attacks on the treaty. He maintains that Brockdorff's polemics represented the successful start of a campaign to undermine the treaty's legitimacy. The time was simply not ripe in 1919, Schwabe concludes, for reconciliation among the erstwhile foes.

In his discussion of French peace planning from December 1918 to February 1919, David Stevenson takes a different approach (chapter 3). As he demonstrates, security against future German attacks figured as the foremost French goal. The longing for security surpassed even the demand for reparations in importance. Stevenson makes clear that the French instrumentalized reparations to obtain a joint Allied occupation of the Rhineland and with it the promise of a future alliance against Germany. He calls attention to the traumatic quality of the French experience with German aggression and thereby explains French insistence on security during the conference.[35] If the Allies had perpetuated their wartime alliance to ensure French security, Stevenson concludes, the treaty might have achieved more durable results.

The fact that victory came in 1918 instead of 1919 had important implications for the peace. David French's discussion of the armistice in chapter 2 indicates that the sudden end of the war surprised the War Cabinet and left Whitehall little time to prepare Great Britain's terms.[36] The theme is further underlined in Alan Sharp's comment. Both present arguments that

---

34 Schwabe expands arguments developed by him in *Deutsche Revolution und Wilson-Frieden*, as well as by Krüger, *Reparationen*, and by Helmut Rössler, "Deutschland und Versailles," in Rössler, ed., *Ideologie und Machtpolitik*, 210–43. On Wilson's Fourteen Points, see also chapter 4 in this book.
35 Stevenson here elaborates arguments made in his *French War Aims*, and in *First World War*, 89–137, 236–305.
36 This theme is also discussed in French's *Strategy of the Lloyd George Coalition*, 260–85.

put British strategy during the peace conference into the perspective of insufficient preparation for peace.[37] Notwithstanding the element of surprise, the naval provisions of the armistice rated as an unqualified success for Great Britain. Better military and financial terms, as French points out, had to be obtained at the peace conference.

Thomas J. Knock describes American diplomacy leading to the armistice in chapter 4. Here Wilson emerges as a skillful leader, whose advocacy of the Fourteen Points in the pre-armistice negotiations proved a qualified success. The president further served as the indispensable proselytizer for the League covenant and thus promoted what Knock defines as the substance of Wilsonianism.[38]

Part Two turns to the relationship between home fronts and negotiators, a topic that inevitably opens up the controversy surrounding the merits of the treaty itself. The authors indicate how domestic pressures influenced proceedings in Paris at various stages. Yet they also show that in no case did domestic concerns determine the final outcome. As Antony Lentin observes in chapter 10, public opinion at home produced more sound and fury than decisive impact in Paris. Georges Clemenceau and Lloyd George emerge as quasi-sovereign interlocutors who negotiated on the basis of their countries' long-term interests and remained mindful of the requirements of international cooperation as well as domestic support to enforce the treaty. Wilson, as Lentin points out, neglected to mobilize Democratic legislators to defend the treaty's provisions and thereby contributed to its failure.[39]

In chapter 6 Erik Goldstein examines Lloyd George's stand toward peace negotiations in Paris as well as toward his home front. Undoubtedly the Welsh wizard's pledges in the Khaki Election of 1918 shaped the treaty's war guilt and reparation clauses to some degree. Yet, as Goldstein emphasizes, Lloyd George was able gradually to insulate himself from domestic pressures. By the end of the conference, he stood ready to heed the advice of Keynes and others to leave the amount of reparations for future determination. The outcome of the reparations imbroglio, as Goldstein asserts, did not correspond to Lloyd George's original intentions in 1919. Lloyd George emerges here in a more positive light than in contemporary comments that likened him to a sharpshooter.[40]

If the peace treaty led to a less propitious outcome for France than portended in 1919, as Georges-Henri Soutou sees it (chapter 7), Clemenceau

37 In their respective chapters, Fry (chapter 24) further elaborates these arguments and Lentin (chapter 10) presents the countercase against Lloyd George.
38 For the German reactions to Wilson's Fourteen Points and peace program, see chapter 1 in this book.
39 See also Ambrosius, *Woodrow Wilson and the American Diplomatic Tradition.*
40 André Tardieu, *La Paix* (Paris, 1921), 113.

hardly deserves the blame. Soutou depicts "the Tiger," as the French premier was known, as a resourceful negotiator who compromised on small issues and achieved his essential economic and strategic aims. If the ultimate outcome belied the assurances of the treaty, the fault lay with later divergences of opinion between Paris, London, and Washington, which rendered the Anglo-American guarantees for France inoperable. Antony Lentin does not concur and faults the Tiger for his attempt to promote Rhenish separatism as a way of controlling domestic events in Germany.[41]

German illusions in the period between the armistice and the publication of the draft treaty form the subject of Fritz Klein's essay (chapter 9). Klein describes the "dreamland" in which Germany chose to live during this period of uncertainty. The political and psychological motives for the retreat from reality were manifold. Conservative and nationalist forces did not wish to face military defeat; the German Left expressed disappointment that the visionary Wilson proved to be a Realpolitiker in the end. Klein discerns a path from Versailles to Hitler, but he turns that familiar interpretation on its head. That such a path was taken seems by no means inevitable. Germany's fate sprang from the country's failure to face the consequences of defeat and from the implicit national consensus for revisionism.[42]

As Lawrence E. Gelfand argues in chapter 8, political participation in the peace settlement lay in U.S. national interest. Gelfand's depiction of the American delegation at the peace conference underscores the seriousness with which the United States envisioned the task of helping to construct a multilateral settlement on the other side of the Atlantic. If American concepts for the League of Nations failed to materialize, he maintains, that should not be attributed to a weakness in Wilson's leadership in 1919. Gelfand's discussion of memoirs from the American delegation supplements other essays here that examine contemporary reactions to the conference.[43]

Part three deals with the financial and economic provisions of the treaty and with the French pursuit of security. French dependence on continued support from Britain and America, as well as the provisional character of the treaty, emerge as the main themes. In chapter 12, Stephen A. Schuker analyzes the French quest for strategic control of the Rhineland during the peace negotiations. He contrasts French losses during the war with superior German economic and demographic strength. According to Schuker,

41 Although working with different sources and in a different argumentative pattern, Lentin here touches on themes developed by Köhler in *Novemberrevolution und Frankreich*. See also Stephen A. Schuker's positive evaluation of Clemenceau's strategy in chapter 12 in this book.
42 In chapter 8, Lawrence E. Gelfand develops themes first discussed in his work on the preparation of the peace conference. See Gelfand, *Inquiry*. See also chapters 4, 10, and 23.
43 See also chapters 3 and 7 in this book.

Clemenceau agreed to scale back French plans for a Rhineland detached from Germany to a temporary joint occupation of the left bank because he recognized French weakness after the war and understood how badly his country needed Anglo-American security guarantees.[44] Schuker emphasizes that Colonel House expressed an open mind about the idea of detaching the Rhineland from Germany, but that the other Anglo-American principals flatly rejected such schemes. The emergent compromise, embodying the Guarantee Pact and the temporary Rhineland occupation, ultimately proved inadequate when Wilson failed to secure ratification of the peace and the treaties of guarantee and when the wartime alliance broke down. Standing outside the narrow prism of Wilsonian hagiography, Schuker rehabilitates House as a protean figure in the tradition of realistic American internationalism and involvement in European affairs.[45]

Elisabeth Glaser traces the economic clauses of the treaty back to divergent war aims (chapter 15). She interprets French peace plans in this area as a quest for economic security against Germany and links those plans to French reparation demands. Because of their dependence on outside help, the French could not take a stand against the Anglo-American resolve to encourage liberal trade rules after a transitory period of five years. Thus the economic clauses of the Versailles Treaty constituted a compromise between the American Open Door Policies and the more restrictive schemes promoted by the Europeans during the war for political control of trade.

The evolution of the Polish settlement is taken up by Piotr S. Wandycz in chapter 13. He identifies France as the main champion of a strong Poland, links French promotion of a viable Polish entity to Paris's security concerns, and concludes that geopolitical considerations, not preoccupations with self-determination, dominated the decision making on Poland's borders. Wandycz defends the territorial settlement in the east as the minimum necessary to provide defendable Polish borders and underscores the depth of German opposition to a genuinely independent Poland. He suggests that the loss of Upper Silesia did not seriously hurt the German economy and that the Polish Corridor figured as a sine qua non for a viable Polish state.

In her historical reconstruction of the Polish minorities treaty (chapter 11), Carole Fink looks at the tangled nationalities problem of eastern Europe from a different point of view. Elaborating a curious parallel to Wandycz's analysis of the Polish political settlement, Fink shows how the contradictory pressures on America and the western European Allies led to

44 For another view on House, see chapter 4.
45 See also Fritz Klein, ed., *Deutschland im Ersten Weltkrieg* (Berlin, 1968).

an unhappy compromise on the minority treaty that ultimately weakened the prospects for meaningful enforcement of minority rights in eastern Europe. Although the Comité Juive lobbied vigorously for minority rights and even autonomy in Paris, the final outcome fell distinctly short by Wilsonian standards of self-determination.

The fate of the League of Nations and the consequences of Versailles are taken up in parts four and five. Part four opens with Jon Jacobson's analysis of the Soviet response to Versailles during the 1920s (chapter 18). He distinguishes between cautious official diplomacy carried out through the Narkomindel and Comintern sponsorship of class antagonism in postwar Germany. Although the Soviet Union polemicized against Versailles and promoted revision through the 1922 Treaty of Rapallo, the Moscow regime simultaneously championed revolutionary opposition to the Weimar Republic by the German working class. Jacobson suggests that the dual policy of Communist leadership limited Russia's room to maneuver and ultimately undermined Soviet security.

The fundamental flaw in the compact, some critics contend, was that Germany was excluded from drafting the armistice and negotiating the peace treaty. The armistice left the Reich without effective military defense. Germany was then forced by an ultimatum to subscribe to a formula attributing to it sole responsibility for the damages of war. In their respective chapters, Fritz Klein, Klaus Schwabe, Wolfgang J. Mommsen, and Niall Ferguson trace the situation in Germany from the armistice to the signing of the treaty.

In chapter 22 Wolfgang J. Mommsen challenges established wisdom about German options in June 1919 through his depiction of Max Weber's reactions to the treaty. Weber served as an adviser to the German delegation. The politician-diplomats consulted the famous sociologist about possible responses to the draft treaty. Weber urged the delegation to risk Allied invasion rather than subject the Berlin government to domestic attack by accepting the treaty's crushing financial obligations. As Mommsen suggests, this rejectionist attitude was widespread among the German elites. The fervor of this hatred for Versailles would later contribute to the fall of the Weimar Republic.[46]

46 In chapter 22, Mommsen expands themes developed in previous works on German intellectuals in World War I. See Klaus Schwabe, *Wissenschaft und Kriegsmoral: Die deutschen Hochschullehrer und die politischen Grundfragen des Ersten Weltkrieges* (Göttingen, 1969); and Wolfgang J. Mommsen, ed., *Kultur und Krieg: Die Rolle der Intellektuellen, Künstler und Schriftsteller im Ersten Weltkrieg* (Munich, 1996). See also Wolfgang J. Mommsen, *Max Weber und die deutsche Politik* (Tübingen, 1974). For a comparative perspective on France, see Martha Hanna, *The Mobilization of Intellect: French Scholars and Writers During the Great War* (Cambridge, Mass., 1996).

As other essays in this collection make clear, a consensus existed among the Allies that Germany should not be formally consulted before the parties assembled in Paris had agreed on a common draft. That consensus reflected a pragmatic resolution to maintain Allied–American unity in dealing with the former enemy. Perhaps an Allied invasion of Germany at the end of the war would have preserved the winning coalition and eased the task of imposing peace conditions. Such at least was the retrospective analysis commonly made in 1945.[47]

But the ambiguous outcome of the 1918 armistice accurately reflected the complications of coalition warfare and the wide divergence of Allied war aims. Under the circumstances, the decision to reach consensus on the draft treaty before its presentation to Germany seemed prudent strategy. Given the pressures to repatriate and demobilize front-line forces, the work of the peace conference had to be concluded as soon as possible. Wilson and Lloyd George felt impelled to return home to deal with myriad domestic problems. This, too, rendered it urgent to wrap up the proceedings expeditiously. Finally, the diverse threats of Bolshevism and the influenza pandemic led many negotiators to prefer a flawed settlement to further delay.

Pragmatic requirements characteristically influenced the shaping of the much misunderstood Article 231. That paragraph reflected the presumed legal necessity to define German responsibility for the war in order to specify and limit the Reich's obligations. The chapters in this book about German reactions to the peace relate the opposing views to different individual and group expectations and divergent perceptions of national interest rather than to a search for objective historical truth.

In chapter 19 William Keylor examines negative popular perceptions of the Treaty of Versailles alongside the growing scholarly consensus that the treaty constituted a workable instrument, albeit one needing reinforcement by its signatories to endure. Keylor reviews Wilson's policy aims and contrasts these with the implementation of his objectives in Paris. He faults the president for raising excessive expectations through his high-flown rhetoric and offers a counterpoint to Knock's interpretation.[48] Like Fink and others, he emphasizes the unresolved problems inherent in the settlement for eastern Europe.

Antoine Fleury praises the work of the League of Nations in the 1920s as a beneficent and potentially revolutionary element in international poli-

47 Cf. Harry R. Rudin, *Armistice 1918* (New Haven, Conn., 1944), with Herbert Feis, *Churchill, Roosevelt, Stalin: The War They Waged and the Peace They Sought* (Princeton, N.J., 1957); and Ann Armstrong, *Unconditional Surrender: The Impact of the Casablanca Policy upon World War II* (New Brunswick, N.J., 1961).
48 For a another critical evaluation, see Lentin, *Lloyd George, Woodrow Wilson, and the Guilt of Germany,* and chapter 10 in this book.

tics (chapter 20). Diane B. Kunz, by contrast, faults the treaty for failing to make the League an effective instrument for international security (chapter 21). Kunz agrees with those who conclude that it was not the treaty itself, but rather its negative reception that increased the likelihood of future war. Long-term considerations of international security likewise inform Ronald Steel's prologue to this book. Steel compares the peace settlements of 1919 and 1945 with the end of the Cold War in 1989. His multifaceted discussion emphasizes the insoluble problems resulting from the breakup of the Austro-Hungarian Empire into small states without adequate minority protection under the dispensations of 1919.[49]

At the core of the persistent controversy over the Versailles Treaty lies the question of German war guilt. This book does not address the long-term sequelae of the war-guilt controversy. Nevertheless, the ongoing debate over the origins of the war cannot fail to influence assessments of how the victors treated the losers. The documentary record confirms that Germany bore the main responsibility for starting the conflict. The Reich's civil and military leaders, fully aware of the potential risks, supported an offensive strategy in August 1914 that made a limited war impossible.[50] The German Empire's prosecution of total war in violation of nineteenth-century norms of conduct, its uniquely ambitious war aims, and the startling realization of those aims in the Brest-Litovsk peace treaty suggest that Germany, by any reasonable measure, bore a substantial responsibility for war damages.

The question was to what extent Germany should and could be obliged to pay reparations to the Allied countries, and whether a German reparations levy could be fashioned so as to contribute to a recovery in western and Central Europe. The burdens imposed by the treaty and the 1921 London Schedule of Payments are a key issue of the debate on the Versailles Treaty, which continues despite some important findings on reparations in the past two decades. The disagreements derive not only from the different perspectives of the authors, but also from their respective concentration on Allied or German records. This book looks further into the origins of the reparation stipulations, their relation to other treaty provisions, and their justification in wartime destruction and in projects for European reconstructions.[51]

49 See also chapter 11.
50 James Joll, *The Origins of the First World War* (New York, 1984); Volker R. Berghahn, *Germany and the Approach of War in 1914* (New York, 1973); Stephen Van Evera, "The Cult of the Offensive and the Origins of the First World War" and Marc Trachtenberg, "The Meaning of Mobilization in 1914," both in Steven E. Miller, Sean M. Lynn-Jones, and Stephen Van Evera, eds., *Military Strategy and the Origins of the First World War* (Princeton, N.J., 1991), 59–108, 195–225, respectively.
51 See chapters 3, 14, 16, and 17 in this book. For a recent antireparations synthesis, see Bruce Kent, *The Spoils of War: The Politics, Economics, and Diplomacy of Reparations, 1918–1922* (Oxford, 1989). The different positions are summarized in Peter Krüger, "Die Reparationen und das Scheitern einer deutschen Verständigungspolitik auf der Pariser Friedenskonferenz im Jahre 1919," *Historische*

Sally Marks stresses the contrast between original treaty provisions and eventual outcomes of the reparations clauses (chapter 14). She contrasts the comparative moderation of the initial payment mechanisms with Germany's unmeasured resentment of the reparations and war-guilt clauses. Marks suggests that the reparations provisions, though neither perfectly rational nor easy to fulfill, were less onerous in reality than German reactions made them appear. Yet the conflict between Germany and the Allies over reparations, as Marks observes, went beyond perceptions. Reparations would govern the distribution of monetary wealth and with it the balance of power. Marks does not view National Socialism as an inevitable outcome of the treaty provisions. But she follows Klein and others in identifying German resentment of the treaty as one cause of Hitler's rise.

Gerald D. Feldman, taking issue with Marks's views, claims that reparations fed the German inflation (chapter 17). Indeed, Feldman argues that the treaty's reparations provisions exerted a baleful influence on the economy and society through 1932, although he also calls attention to other structural and policy failures that retarded effective reconstruction during the postwar years.[52]

Niall Ferguson also describes contemporary German reactions to the reparations clauses of the treaty (chapter 16). German bankers originally viewed inflation, as Ferguson suggests, as an apt way to soften the effects of a reparations levy.[53] In contrast to Marks, Ferguson concludes that reparations became too burdensome for Weimar's economy, particularly when inflation spiraled out of control.

Reparations, both territorial and financial, emerged as an early focal point for criticism of the treaty. The debates at first took place within the delegations, but soon dominated the news media as well. Keynes's *Economic Consequences of the Peace,* which appeared at the end of 1919, rehearsed familiar objections to the territorial and financial provisions of the peace and used them as a basis for a personal condemnation of the statesmen responsible for it. Keynes's treatment set the tone for an array of subsequent publications of lesser literary quality.

Zeitschrift 221 (1975): 326–72; Peter Krüger, "Das Reparationsproblem der Weimarer Republik in fragwürdiger Sicht: Kritische Überlegungen zur neuesten Forschung," *Vierteljahrshefte für Zeitgeschichte* 29 (1981): 21–47; Sally Marks, "The Myth of Reparations," *Central European History* 11 (1978): 231–55; Stephen A. Schuker, "Origins of American Stabilization Policy in Europe: The Financial Dimension, 1918–1924," in Schröder, ed., *Confrontation and Cooperation,* 377–408.

52 See also Feldman, *Great Disorder,* 385–97, 414–28, 821–35, 854–8.

53 This theme had first been developed by Stephen A. Schuker, "Finance and Foreign Policy in the Era of German Inflation," in Otto Büsch and Gerald D. Feldman, eds., *Historische Prozesse der deutschen Inflation, 1914–1924* (Berlin, 1978), 343–61; and Agnete von Specht, *Politische und wirtschaftliche Hintergründe der deutschen Inflation, 1918–1923* (Frankfurt am Main, 1982).

Part five examines contemporary views about peacemaking. The contributions here trace the genesis and dissemination of revisionist thinking. As some of the authors demonstrate, the treaty formed merely a starting point for a subsequent reshaping of the international system.[54] Changing economic and political conditions in the United States and the Allied countries, after the peace treaty was signed, precluded the envisioned restructuring of the international system. Not only did the United States fail to ratify the treaty, the Allied coalition fell apart. Each country focused on its domestic difficulties. Meanwhile, in Weimar Germany, revision of the treaty became the most important foreign policy goal. The means to achieve that end evolved over the coming fourteen years, but the principle was never questioned. Those destabilizing impulses did not originate with the treaty texts, and they cannot be attributed to defects in the treaty terms. They nevertheless shaped revisionist criticism of the treaty for generations. World War I in 1917 and 1918 had become a war of attrition. Throughout Europe public expectations of large indemnities, social benefits for veterans, and national grandeur had run high. Given the magnitude of suffering and sacrifice during the war, postwar resentment and disappointments seemed inevitable.[55] Still, scholars do not yet fully understand how those negative reactions shaped the subsequent public debate on the treaty.

The evolution of Wilson's views on Germany is the subject of Manfred F. Boemeke's essay (chapter 25). Boemeke shows that Wilson's hostility at the outset of the war shifted to a more balanced view in the following months. Only the Treaty of Brest-Litovsk, writes Boemeke, finally persuaded the president that the German people at large, and even the Social Democratic Party, supported the Reich's aggressive pursuit of the war. Accordingly, Wilson's perception of German war guilt tilted sharply in a negative direction after Brest-Litovsk, yet it still could not be regarded as irrational hatred. In Paris the president sought due punishment for the Reich within the confines of a just settlement.[56]

In chapter 23, William C. Widenor discusses published accounts of the treaty by Americans who participated in the conference, such as Ray Stannard Baker, Bernard M. Baruch, George Creel, Robert Howard Haskins, Edward M. House, Robert Lord, David Hunter Miller, and Joseph P. Tumulty. Their descriptions, Widenor notes, were influenced by their political preferences and personal loyalties and thus shed light on the clashes

---

54 See, e.g., chapters 4, 10, and 19.
55 See, e.g., Stuart I. Rochester, *American Liberal Disillusionment in the Wake of World War I* (University Park, Pa., 1977).
56 In chapter 25, Manfred F. Boemeke challenges Lentin's interpretation put forth in *Lloyd George, Woodrow Wilson, and the Guilt of Germany.* See also chapter 10.

between idealistic and pragmatic approaches. The American approach to peacemaking, he concludes, was neither as homogeneous nor as overbearing as critical commentary would suggest.[57]

Michael Graham Fry looks at reactions to the draft treaty within the British delegation (chapter 24). He registers the group's sharply critical mood and distinguishes between its tactical and ideological revisionism. Proposals to soften the treaty were partly motivated by British perceptions of the Bolshevik threat. Negative comments grew so insistent that Lloyd George had to struggle to keep the dissenters from going public. Since he knew that the United States would not support a march on Berlin, the premier worked assiduously to get Germany to sign the draft treaty. Ultimately the desire to revise the peace settlement became the new orthodoxy in Whitehall, Fleet Street, and Oxbridge. Fry's discussion adds substantially to our knowledge about Lloyd George's troubles with his colleagues.

Gordon Martel's commentary in chapter 26 elaborates on the dissemination of revisionist thinking. Martel underlines the prevalence of hostile interpretations in the United States and Britain as opposed to France. A better understanding of the events and interests that shaped the treaty, he points out, can be reached through further research on the lower-level officials who defined and promoted war aims.

As several contributors to this book suggest, the limitations of time and the requisites of procedure for drafting the treaty did not allow the framers of individual sections to examine the document as a whole before it went to press.[58] Ultimately, however, conflicting national interests fed revisionism in Great Britain and the United States and underscored the familiar problems of making peace after coalition warfare.[59] The devastations of the war, moreover, produced long-term economic and financial dislocation in all European countries. That dislocation stirred anticapitalist sentiment and ultimately proved impossible to cure through state intervention on the economic level alone. As Keynes correctly discerned, Lenin was right when he said that there was no subtler means of overturning the existing basis of society than to debauch the currency.[60] Still, Keynes failed to recall a further doleful insight about the origins of the postwar crisis: *Krieg ist der Vater aller Dinge.*

---

57 His account supplements that of Gelfand. For the subsequent debate on the treaty in the U.S. Senate, see Widenor's *Henry Cabot Lodge and the Search for an American Foreign Policy* (Berkeley, Calif., 1980).
58 See chapter 15 in this book.
59 Donald Kagan, *The Fall of the Athenian Empire* (Ithaca, N.Y., 1987), 416–17.
60 Keynes, *Economic Consequences,* 236.

Prologue: 1919–1945–1989

RONALD STEEL

There have been three great wars in this century. Each concluded with hopes, even blueprints, for transcending ancient rivalries of states and peoples. In 1919, after World War I, came the Fourteen Points and the League of Nations. In 1945, after World War II, the world welcomed the United Nations and the principles of the Atlantic Charter. In 1989, which saw the end of the Cold War, the breaching of the Berlin Wall, and the crumbling of the communist bloc, there was neither treaty nor ceremony. But the air was filled with the heady promise of liberation. All of these promises are embodied in the vision of Woodrow Wilson: the prophet scorned, and now once again redeemed. Today, Wilsonianism is triumphant. Everywhere leaders pay obeisance to his vision. The principles he championed – democracy, collective security, self-determination – are extolled as the building blocks of a new world order (itself another Wilsonian construct). Wilson, having periodically been criticized as a dreamer or a failure, is once again hailed as a visionary whose ideals can light the way to a brighter future.

Although Wilson initially hoped to keep America out of the European war and as late as January 1917 was proposing a compromise peace, a "peace without victory," he also sought, as he said a few months later, a "right more precious than peace." That right, he declared in his message to Congress, was "democracy, the right of those who submit to authority to have a voice in their own government, for the rights and liberties of small nations, and to make the world itself at last free."

Ultimately, there was a victory and a peace of sorts. But it was not the kind that Wilson had envisaged, and within a generation war had erupted again. Near the end of that war, in 1945, Franklin D. Roosevelt, on returning from the Yalta Conference, told Congress that the agreements he had reached with Churchill and Stalin "ought to spell the end of the system of unilateral action, the exclusive alliances, the spheres of influence, the balances of power, and all the other expedients that have been tried for cen-

21

turies – and have always failed." But the new expedients also failed, and the result was the Cold War.

It, too, ended with the dawning of a more rational and equitable future based on the principles Wilson expressed so memorably. For the third time in this century, the world has seen a great war waged and a great victory won. Again, there are hopes, even blueprints, for transcending ancient rivalries and smothering conflicts among states and peoples. Again, victory has brought neither peace nor resolution, just as the treaty signed at Versailles failed to make possible a just and lasting peace, despite the great expectations of Wilson and others. Democracy, self-determination, and collective security were viewed as instruments with which to attain this goal. The way to eliminate many of the causes of war, Wilson believed, was to let each citizen have a meaningful vote, each people a land to call its own, each nation friendly allies that would look on its sovereignty as essential to theirs.

Beyond that, Wilson sought to sketch a blueprint for a peaceful capitalistic world order under international law. Rejecting both traditional imperialism and the dangers of revolutionary socialism, he hoped "to end all wars" by overcoming the conditions that gave birth to them. A generation later, Roosevelt inherited Wilson's mantle but not his idealism. Rooted in practical politics and with a keen sense of power and interests, he made a bow to Wilsonianism by affirming the Atlantic Charter, which spoke of the "right of all peoples to choose the form of government under which they will live."

But Roosevelt had little respect for the League of Nations and – despite British entreaties – refused to include any reference to an international organization in the Atlantic Charter. Such a reference would only confuse people; "the time had come to be realistic."

(Roosevelt was, of course, an enemy of colonialism, at least of the European variety. The British colonial secretary, Oliver Stanley, related a 1945 encounter with the president. Roosevelt: "I would not want to be rude, but in 1841, when you acquired Hong Kong, you did not acquire it by purchase." Stanley: "Let me see, Mr. President. That was about the time of the Mexican War, wasn't it?")

To organize his world order, Roosevelt proposed a consortium of great powers known as the Four Policemen, who were to guarantee peace. As public support for an international organization grew, FDR harnessed it in such a way as to ensure approval for an active American role in the postwar world. His plan yoked a Wilsonian peace, through the General Assembly, to a great power peace, through the Security Council. Yet in his mind there was never any question as to where the emphasis lay.

Roosevelt had his own vision of how the world should be organized: Four Policemen, but only one Sheriff. He sought to replace great-power spheres of influence with a more integrated and centralized world system resting on American power.

Nearly five decades later, after a second failed peace and a war that for millions took a toll equal to that of previous conflicts, another American president, George Bush, proposed his formula for global peace. The demise of communism offered the opportunity to build what he called a "New World Order" based on democracy and market capitalism. The testing ground of this order would be in the Persian Gulf, where Iraq's invasion of Kuwait posed a challenge to America's claim to leadership in the post–Cold War world. To have let Iraq's aggression go unchallenged might not have affected the price or availability of oil to the industrialized states, but it would have threatened the power balance in the Gulf and the role of the United States as the holder of that balance. Not surprisingly, Bush chose not to define the stakes in those terms, but rather to put them in a neo-Wilsonian framework. It is only within such a framework that a nation such as the United States, with no direct stake in the quarrel between two Arab states, could justify intervention. For this reason, the sanction of the United Nations, and the participation of other nations – whether in the form of military forces or of financial support – was considered to be essential. Thus was the spirit of Wilson invoked to sanction what was for most purposes a unilateral intervention.

Yet the Gulf intervention is unlikely to be a model for the future: either for the United Nations acting in concert, or for the United States acting unilaterally. An international society is still more an aspiration than a reality. The benevolent hegemony exercised by the United States after the collapse of the Soviet Union is at best only temporary. It is being undermined not only by the rise of other major powers, but by America's relative economic decline. This decline, reinforced by a growing reliance on foreign capital, makes it increasingly difficult to finance and carry out the operations required of an international hegemon in such a New World Order. The cost of this role inevitably erodes the ability to perform it. Thus the New World Order ostensibly ushered in by the Gulf War has already become a historical footnote. Not only is the international police authority increasingly constrained from within and without, but the notion of an international society is under assault. Potential at best, that society is breaking down into component ethnic, national, and religious parts. Long-submerged and resentful groups are rediscovering, and sometimes violently asserting, their demands. The fragmentation of what only a few years ago seemed to be a politically stable world is taking place at an alarming rate. Indeed, it is one of the ironies of our time that notions of world order are gaining vogue at the precise moment that the world is becoming increasingly fragmented. The gap between universalist ambitions and political realities will be as difficult for theorists as for diplomats to bridge.

What momentarily seemed to some the dawn of a New World Order has already dissipated. The Gulf War appears not as a model for the future, but as an aberration. This world order is said to rest on the foundation of the Wilsonian principles of self-determination and collective security. But at the first real test – the collapse of Yugoslavia into a rerun of the wars of religion – these principles have been revealed as inadequate and perhaps detrimental. In the years since 1989, as in the years following 1919 and 1945, rhetoric and hope have conflicted with passions and reality. Euphoria has been followed by disillusion and resignation. Was it the hopes that were romantically exaggerated? Was it the execution that was faulty? Or were the principles flawed?

Wilson and Roosevelt attempted to address the greatest problem of their times: the instability and violence between nations. The League and the United Nations were designed to deal with that problem. But the League turned out to be inadequate, and the United Nations was essentially irrelevant during the half century of the Cold War. It is widely assumed that, had the United States been a member of the League, German and Japanese aggression would have been blocked. That is possible. But the European nations showed little interest in blocking Nazi Germany even when they had the power. They thought they could tame it, or even use it to their purposes, as they tried to do with fascist Italy. Experience with the United Nations also belies the assumption that the League, with American participation, would have been able to block aggression. For the United Nations, the problem was the abandonment of Roosevelt's scheme of the Four Policemen. The importance of this scheme was certainly recognized at the time. As Walter Lippmann wrote in 1943 of the need of the wartime allies to remain united after the defeat of the aggressors: "The failure to form an alliance of victors will mean the formation of alliances between the vanquished and some of the victors." Russia, he argued, must be brought into the alliance with Great Britain and the United States.

For a complex of reasons, this alliance did not endure. The resultant conflict known as the Cold War was a classic struggle of state systems. This was a conflict fully within the parameters that Wilson and Roosevelt had addressed, and that each, in his own way, had thought to remedy. The Policemen fought among themselves. But the greatest challenge to stability today is not conflict between nations, but conflict within them. The most violent disputes of the past few years lay outside the state system: in ethnic, religious, and tribal struggles. Many of these long antedate the Cold War, or even this century. This is exemplified by the war among the peoples of the former Yugoslavia. This conflict is not a bizarre anomaly of today's presumably rational era, but rather a continuation of ancient grievances unresolved – and even exacerbated – by the settlements of 1919 and 1945. In 1919 the great powers of the day tried to deal with the problem of ethnic and religious disputes by formulas based on the principle of self-determination. They sought to give each people its own state. But national borders did not correspond to ethnic ones. Woodrow Wilson dealt with this problem by pretending that it did not exist. A similar problem arose when two or more peoples claimed the same land – each for reasons they considered not only valid, but indisputable. The peacemakers also wanted to create viable states. So they forged multinational entities of semiautonomous units, like Yugoslavia. States of this nature are based on the assumption that there is no conflict between the ethnic nation and the constitutional state. Indeed, the peacemakers assumed that both these entities could be harnessed to construct a wider and more harmonious international order. Unfortunately, this has proved to be a totally false assumption. Wilsonian formulas that inspired such intense arguments, and on which the fervent hopes of millions everywhere were riding, proved quite inadequate to deal with loyalties predating and going beyond the constitutional state.

Just as Wilsonian principles have proved inadequate to cope with this problem, so have traditional methods of great power diplomacy. Those methods – sanctions, embargoes, threats, or even force – have been singularly ineffective in dealing with the internal collapse of states and the brutal passions of ethnic warfare. The international order – or disorder, as the case may be – that emerged so unexpectedly in 1989 is now revealed to be completely different from that of 1945 or 1919. What it marks is not the attempt to repair or reconstitute the systems of Yalta and Versailles. Rather, it demonstrates the complete breakdown of those systems, which at least provided the illusion of control over anarchy through the eminence of the nation-state. Not the nation, but the state; not the *nation*-state, but the nation-*state*. But today the very concept of order based on a system of territoriality and the sovereignty of states – in short, the system of Westphalia – has been called into question. Instead of a complex, but usually ordered, international system of states invoking the highest allegiance of peoples, now there is a perplexing multiplicity of actors. Each one of these is beholden to its own particular god. The concept of an overriding loyalty to the sovereign state is everywhere being overridden by powerful and competing loyalties.

This is true even in the advanced industrial states, as can be seen in Canada. In the United States the concept of a single people pledging allegiance to an all-inclusive state is being eroded by the competing claims of nationality, culture, and ethnicity. The national motto of *E Pluribus Unum* is in danger of being reversed. It would surely be folly to predict with any confidence that within a decade the borders of Russia, China, and India – not to mention those new entities in the Caucasus and beyond – will be what they are today. Most uncertain of all are the borders within the old multinational states once under rigid communist control. These new entities are fragile and often prone to violence today – just as some of their predecessors were in 1919 – only in part because they are unused to governing themselves.

Equally important is the notion that citizenship in this area – an area that begins in Germany and extends everywhere to the east – is based not on residence or loyalty, but on ethnicity or religion. Community is defined not by an affirmation of will, but by the accident of blood. Citizenship is often equated with racial purity. In order to make such states cohesive, only those within the bloodline receive the full benefits of citizenship. Others are often discriminated against with perfect legality.

This creates the bizarre situation in which those born in a country can be denied its full rights of citizenship (such as the Turks in Germany), whereas those who, with their ancestors, have been citizens of another country for centuries (such as the Volga Germans) are welcomed to "return" as lost tribe members. Attempts at racial purification, which is now taking place in some of the successor states of the Soviet Union, will almost certainly lead to intercommunal and intrastate warfare. Yet this lies quite beyond what the settlements of Versailles and Yalta envisaged, and what the United Nations – set up as an instrument to resolve international conflicts – is capable of coping with.

The world seems to be reaching the end of an era of cohesive nation states. Yet such states are the building blocks of the international system. Without them the system falls apart. Of course, state power can often be abused. Nonetheless, the protection of constitutional rights and of minorities can best be ensured by a strong state supported by a popular consensus. If the state itself is riven by ethnic or religious rivalries or becomes the instrument of a single group, the notion of loyalties beyond those of blood or faith will be eroded. This is what has happened so tragically in the former Yugoslavia.

The undermining of the order of Westphalia comes not only from loyalties based on ethnicity, religion, and tribalism but also from the penetration of borders once considered to be impermeable. There are at least two reasons for this: first, economic integration, whether through trade accords such as the North American Free Trade Agreement or through quasi-political structures such as the European Union; and second, waves of migration fed by ethnic wars, poverty, and human rights abuses. The West will not be spared this penetration of borders; indeed, the West is particularly susceptible to it because of the relative tranquility and economic opportunity it offers. The kind of ethnic and economic problems that have so afflicted the former Soviet Empire will continue to spread into the hitherto tolerant nations of the West. The United States can no more insulate itself from the disorder, oppression, and poverty of Mexico and Central America than can western Europe from similar conditions in the former communist lands and on the southern shores of the Mediterranean.

The end of the Cold War – by opening up eastern nations to Western contacts and influence – has also swept away the basis of their economies and undermined their social structures. The attempted transition to market economies and democracy has, in all but the most fortunate of these nations, intensified instability, ethnic tensions, and migration. Where conflict has broken out in areas once sealed off and tranquilized by the Cold War, the media have been quick to respond. The most terrible images of violence now enter every living room in the West. These images spur the demand to "do something" to redress the grievances in areas that hitherto were inaccessible and ignored. Indeed, the opening of borders and the weakening of central control have made possible outbreaks that otherwise would not have been allowed to take place. Yet the divorce of this violence from traditional Cold War security considerations removes the most compelling reason to intervene. Why become involved if one's own security is not at stake? Why become involved if the issues are muddy and the cause of justice is uncertain? This is particularly true if the very act of outside intervention may further spread the violence and increase suffering. The wars in the former Yugoslavia are a sobering object lesson in the difficulty of determining a "just" solution to a tribal war. The war of states against states had at least a primitive clarity. But how do North Americans and western Europeans judge the rival claims of Serbs, Croats, and Bosnian Muslims, or of Macedonians, Albanians, and Bulgarians? How do they decree a workable compromise on what are perceived as questions of survival? The collapse of strong multinational states – such as the Soviet Union or Yugoslavia – has increased both freedom and its handmaiden, instability. It has done this by reviving issues that were never resolved either by the settlement of Versailles, which shattered imperial structures, or the settlement of Yalta, which created new, but unstable, ones.

Two central principles of Wilsonian diplomacy were enunciated at Versailles, reaffirmed at Yalta a quarter century later, and celebrated nearly a half century after that in the collapse of Soviet authority in 1989. These two principles are self-determination and collective security. These were the building blocks on which Woodrow Wilson sought to construct his just international order – principles to which even Franklin Roosevelt, a most skeptical Wilsonian, paid allegiance. These principles were hailed by George Bush during the 1991 war in the Persian Gulf when he sought international approval, and financial support, for an American-led military intervention to uphold the New World Order. The concept of collective security was, to Wilson's mind, the raison d'être for the League of Nations. It was to preserve the League that he sacrificed so much else at Paris. He believed that it was crucial to prevent another war even more terrible than that from which a battered Europe had only just emerged. Collective security calls for nations to band together to punish aggressors under the authority of a wider military organization, such as the North Atlantic Treaty Organization (NATO), or, in the Wilsonian formulation, a wider political one, such as the League, or its successor, the United Nations.

The presumption is that nations easily agree on who the aggressor is and who the victim in any dispute. They can then be counted on quickly to reach judgment and, by joint action, dispense punishment accordingly. Warlike nations – knowing they would face a unified and militant world community – would presumably refrain from aggression. This is the principle on which such Cold War alliances as NATO were ostensibly based, although in practice these alliances were simply arrangements by which a great power pledged to protect its allies and dependencies. Now that the former allies have become economic rivals, and military power has declined in value as a currency, a broader and more traditional notion of collective security is once again in vogue. This is, within limits, a policy well-suited to the present situation of the United States. It can permit a great power to set the agenda and deputize others in the effort. With its declared links to universal democracy, such a policy is rooted in American political traditions. Yet even tyrants can subscribe to it when it suits their interests. For its guiding principle is the sanctity of borders. Even on its own terms there are problems with this doctrine. It presumes that an act of aggression anywhere is a threat to peace everywhere. Indeed, it assumes that there is such a thing as "world peace." This is the hyperinflated language of Woodrow Wilson.

It is also the language of Harry Truman. In defending his decision to intervene in Korea in 1950, Truman declared that "if history has taught us anything, it is that aggression anywhere in the world is a threat to peace everywhere in the world." Indeed, as historians well know, history has taught us precisely the opposite. Peace is, and always has been, divisible. Otherwise every border squabble and every remote conflagration would immediately be inflated into global war. Such universalism obscures the way the world really works. It turns every dispute into a crusade for the soul of mankind. By phrasing disputes between states in moral terms, as those between good and evil, it can justify the most extreme means in pursuit of debatable, and often only marginally moral, ends. For the self-serving cynicism of raison d'état it substitutes a self-deceiving reign of virtue. If all aggression is a crime, there is little room for compromise. Yet most international violence is rooted in ambiguity. By demanding military action against aggressors as a matter of principle, the doctrine of collective security could embroil the great powers in wars everywhere. Rather than reducing the recourse to war, collective security can – by raising local quarrels to the level of regional, or even global, ones – in some cases make it more likely.

The Cold War, for all its irrationalities, was based on real military, political, and economic issues. The issues may have been misunderstood by leaders, but they were at least grounded in concepts of security. With the Cold War behind them, nations are now drawn into conflict in pursuit of virtue. However desirable this standard may be for individuals, it is not suited to nations. It can lead either to unending wars for peace in the name of morality, or to a reputation for hypocrisy and empty rhetoric. The Wilsonian doctrine of self-determination is equally troublesome. The notion that every ethnic group or nationality should have its own state sounds eminently sensible – especially if it is argued that this will promote not only justice but international tranquillity. However, the closer the principle comes to home, the less it is appreciated. Anglo-Canadians would not apply it to Quebec, the French and Spanish to the Basques, the Russians to Chechnya, the Chinese to Tibet, the Indonesians to East Timor, the Nigerians to Biafra, the Iraqis and Turks to the Kurds. Nor in the war between the American states did the North apply it to the South. Abraham Lincoln was not an apostle of self-determination.

This principle lies at the heart of much of the disorder that has swept Europe since 1989. Its seeds were sown in 1919. The decision at Paris to break up the Austro-Hungarian Empire created a host of nation-states that ostensibly corresponded to the placement of the tribes that inhabited them. If these tribes had had the good grace to coalesce into neatly defined areas, the task of drawing and maintaining frontiers might have been less compli-

cated. But such borders did not previously exist. Ethnic groups spilled mess-
ily along trade and migratory routes into one another's supposed territories.
Nonetheless, these tribes, or at least their leaders, demanded that they be
constituted into independent states. So borders were drawn and countries
were created. The unhappy result was predictable. Millions of people found
themselves living in territories deemed by hostile majorities to be ethnically
not "theirs" – Hungarians in Romania, Romanians in Russia, Germans in
Czechoslovakia and Poland. The decisions made in 1919 in the name of
ethnic self-determination compromised an already shaky peace and have
lived on to haunt the world with the collapse of the multinational Soviet
Empire, just as it did with the earlier dismemberment of the Austro-
Hungarian one. Wilson, of course, did not intend a vindictive peace or a
heritage of ethnic bitterness. In his Fourteen Points address of January 1918
he called for a "liberal policy toward revolutionary Russia," for limitations
on French and Italian territorial claims, for a consideration of the "interests
of the populations concerned" in all colonial settlements, and most interestingly, he resisted the breakup of the Austro-Hungarian Empire.

Although he supported internal autonomy for the groups within the
empire (what he called their "autonomous development"), he assured
Vienna that "no dismemberment of the empire is intended." He was driven
from that position by the British and French, who sought political influence
in the region; by pressure from émigré groups; and by the argument that a
promise of independence would spur rebellion by the various nationality
groups within the empire. The destruction of the empire contributed, it
seems likely, to the collapse of the political balance in Central Europe that
ultimately led to World War II. It is a curious fact that today some parts of
the old empire – Austria, Slovenia, Hungary, the Venezia-Giulia region of
Italy – like detached parts of a single organism, seek to rejoin themselves in
a regional organization. The victorious Allies proceeded to carve up the
empire in the name of self-determination. But the principle was also
observed in its breach, as millions of Hungarians, Germans, and Austrians
were put under alien rule. One can conclude from this that Wilson gave way
to necessity, that the demands of statecraft triumphed over his idealism, and
that idealism in practice cannot easily be purchased without compromise.

Franklin Roosevelt's formulation, the Atlantic Charter, suffers from the
same infirmities. Despite the verbal commitment of Roosevelt and Winston
Churchill to self-determination during World War II, the settlement was
marked above all by its denial: in eastern Europe, in Germany, in Korea, in
Indochina, and in colonial Africa. The Soviet Union was not alone in
denying full self-determination to the peoples it ruled. Such behavior, how-

ever deplorable, also corresponded – perhaps not incidentally – to a period of political stability in Europe. If self-determination has been flawed in practice, especially in eastern Europe, it is also open to question in principle. Its central premise is that peoples of different faiths and ethnicities cannot live together in harmony. It is a principle based on tribal loyalties, the suppression of internal differences, and, all too often, intolerance. It is atavistic and frequently prone to violence. It is a principle that has been used to promote the destruction of existing states, by fomenting violence on the part of one nationality group against another – as Hitler showed in Czechoslovakia, Yugoslavia, Austria, Poland, and Russia – and more recently as the world's democracies demonstrated in their handling of the breakup of Yugoslavia.

Self-determination can be, as Walter Lippmann wrote more than fifty years ago, a "license to intervention and aggression," inviting majorities to be intransigent, and leading to the atomization of human societies. It is also a contradiction of the very principles on which the United Nations – and indeed the United States – is founded. Wilson and Roosevelt advanced the notion of self-determination on the assumption that it would be a stabilizing force. They believed that peoples neatly tucked into their own homelands would refrain from coveting the lands of others and would instead bucolically pursue peaceful endeavors. They did not anticipate violent outbursts of resentment and revenge based on ancient religious and tribal quarrels. Both Wilson and Roosevelt, like virtually all statesmen, were concerned with the relations among states. Wilson put his faith in the League, Roosevelt in his Four Policemen. Neither took serious account of the force of ethnic, as distinct from civic, nationalism. Managers of the post-1989 industrial world eschew nationalism of all forms. The market itself is the object of the highest loyalty. In many realms it commands allegiances greater than that of the state itself. If the market has no citizenship, neither, so it often seems, do the global executives and traders who seek the highest return wherever it can be found. The quest for profit and efficiency knows neither loyalty nor frontiers. The American–Soviet quarrel of the past half century ignored ethnic considerations. It was primarily a great power conflict: one intensified, but not subsumed, by competing ideologies.

The Soviet Union was viewed in the West primarily as an ideological, not an ethnic, state. Yet the ideology only papered over the ethnic chasms of a multinational empire – just as, in George Kennan's words in 1946, it was the "perfect vehicle for the sense of insecurity with which Bolsheviks, even more than previous Russian rulers, were afflicted." When the center collapsed, the ideology, imposed from without but ignored largely from within, dissipated in a puff of smoke, and the world's largest multinational state reverted to its ethnic parts. Ethnicity became the shelter in which fearful groups could seek protection. New states were formed from the ruins of this empire. Many of these states lacked the fundamental necessities for an independent existence, other than the ethnicity of the majority of their inhabitants. To maintain the cohesion of these ethnically based new states, age-old conflicts with neighbors were resurrected, and differences hardly apparent to the outside observer were magnified. Thus wars erupted between Armenians and Azeris, between Georgians and Ossetians, and, in that other collapsed multinational state, Yugoslavia, wars took place among Catholic Croatians, Muslim Bosnians, and Orthodox Serbs.

In these ruined empires, the exaltation of the Volk and the nation, including the forging of its identity through violence, has become the crucible for the formation of the state. In this sense, to extend Charles Tilly's dictum about the state and war, it could be said that the ethnic state makes war, and war makes the ethnic state. The ethnic state became inherent in the notion of self-determination as nationalism spread into eastern Europe, and the notion of a "people" was redefined to mean those sharing ethnic traits. Woodrow Wilson, of course, contributed to this definition. As he lectured Congress in February 1918: "No people must be forced into a sovereignty under which it does not wish to live. No territory must change hands except for the purpose of securing those who inhabit it a fair chance of life and liberty."

The intent was noble. But how could such states be built without creating national minorities, which, in the insecurity of their new status, would not elevate ethnic identity over civil rights? Wilson stated that self-determination is "an imperative principle of action which statesmen will henceforth ignore at their peril." He was certainly right. Yet, interestingly, the Covenant of the League of Nations never mentions self-determination. Indeed, in a dispute concerning the Aaland Islands between Finland and Sweden, a League commission ruled that "international law does not recognize the right of national groups, as such, to separate themselves from the state of which they form a part by the simple expression of a wish, any more than it recognizes the right of other states to claim such a separation."

Self-determination fell on hard times in the interwar period, with the failure of the League to halt great power aggression, and has had mixed results since that time. The Atlantic Charter declared that there should be "no territorial changes that do not accord with the freely expressed wishes of the peoples concerned." Yet the United Nations limited self-determination to non–self-governing and trust territories. Furthermore, boundary changes took place in Palestine and Ethiopia without the consent of the inhabitants, as in Biafra, Tibet, and East Timor. And it was the United Nations itself that suppressed self-determination in the Katanga province of the Congo. In 1970, U Thant, then secretary-general, made the position clear: "As an international organization the UN has never accepted, does not accept, and I do not believe will ever accept the principle of secession of a part of its member states." As U Thant recognized, the Wilsonian assumption that the self-determination of states leads to greater stability in the international arena is problematical at best. The tragic sequence of events in the former Yugoslavia demonstrates the dangers inherent in his doctrine. As Alfred Cobban has written: "The history of Self-Determination is a history of the making and the breaking of states."

The collapse of the Yugoslav federation raises questions that go to the heart of notions of self-determination. Among these one must ask: Which groups in a multinational federal state should have a right to self-determination? Where does the process of dividing a state end? What is the effect on international stability and human rights of the indefinite disintegration of states? To what degree should economic and political viability be a factor in the granting of international recognition? When should recognition of ethnic claims for independence imply international protection? Is there an inalienable right to self-determination if the likely result is the suppression of minority rights? Do recent events indicate that self-determination is a stimulus to violence rather than to stability? There are times and places where the ethnic or religious separation of peoples may be unavoidable. It may even be the only hope of long-term peace. Yet if democracy means the equality of citizens and the protection of minorities, must not national self-determination – at least in its ethnic or religious form – often be profoundly antidemocratic?

The record of European self-determination during the interwar period – and more recently in the wake of the collapse of the multinational communist empires – makes such a conclusion difficult to escape. If similar catastrophes are to be avoided in the future, the world must take a more restricted view of the right of self-determination. Unless the international community is willing to engage in military action to enforce one side's claims, or simply to stand by as states disintegrate into ethnic violence, there must be conditions for the recognition of political self-determination. It must be made clear that no ethnic or civic group has the absolute right to self-determination, but only the right to bargain for it and to demonstrate that it is capable of dealing with it responsibly. Otherwise it cannot expect international protection. Woodrow Wilson thought that the role of the state, which he believed to be egotistical, could be overcome by the collective will of mankind operating through just institutions. The League of Nations was his alternative to the state.

Yet today, after the lessons of the past five years and the collapse of the post-1989 euphoria, the evils of the state system seem less naked than in 1919 or 1945 – and the alternatives appear less appealing.

The history of this century has demonstrated the need for individuals to free themselves from the control of an all-powerful state. Yet, under proper controls, the state is also a guarantor of rights. Civic nationalism and constitutional democracy are the means by which freedom is found within the state. Wilson's formulas for self-determination, like those that came into vogue at the end of the Cold War, show an insufficient understanding of this reality.

In multinational societies there is no other effective arbiter of conflicting rights than constitutionally restrained state authority. Where there are only group rights, as in ethnic states, there is little room for individual rights. There is perhaps no greater conformity than that demanded by the ethnic state. This is the baleful lesson learned from the 1989 settlement – a settlement that was supposed to correct the injustices suffered in Europe in 1945, but instead reverted to the illusions and well-meaning failures of 1919. Blueprints for a just world order require a just and powerful enforcer. The dilemma of these times is that there is no international society to make the rules of a post–Cold War world – or to provide the military means to enforce them. Without superpower rivalry, there is less reason to fear cataclysmic war – but also none of the order that the superpowers were able to impose on weaker states.

How order, let alone tolerance, will be protected in a world where ethnic, tribal, and religious loyalties are becoming ever more powerful is an issue that none of the architects who sought to build a new order from the ruins of war – in 1919, 1945, and 1989 – thought necessary to resolve. It is now an inescapable task. And it requires not only conviction, which such visionaries as Wilson had in great abundance, but also a hard respect for the power of passionate reasons that reason itself does not always know.

PART ONE

Peace Planning and the Actualities of the Armistice

I

Germany's Peace Aims
and the
Domestic and International Constraints

KLAUS SCHWABE

Germany's peace policy both before and during the Versailles peace conference has been dealt with rather harshly by recent historiography. The Berlin
government has been criticized for, among other things, its lack of realism,[1]
its failure to develop a European perspective in its program,[2] its insincerity
in the war-guilt question, and, generally, its traditionalist attachment to the
policies of its Wilhelmine predecessor.[3] Briefly, it has been blamed for not
having been attuned to the historic break achieved by the revolution of
November 1918.

This chapter reassesses Germany's peace policies of 1918–19 in the light
of these judgments. It takes stock of the merits of those policies, their drawbacks, and the international and domestic constraints that limited Germany's
options. An attempt of this sort requires, first, a chronological review of the
major developments in the conception and implementation of Germany's
peace program, and second, a reevaluation from a long-term perspective.

I

The roots of the peace program that Germany presented at Versailles have
been justly traced to the final phases of World War I or, more precisely, to
the resolution passed by the German Reichstag on July 19, 1917, more than
a year before Germany was proclaimed a republic.[4] This resolution was the

1 Hans Mommsen, *Die verspielte Freiheit: Der Weg der Republik von Weimar in den Untergang* (Berlin,
  1990), 85.
2 Peter Krüger, *Die Aussenpolitik der Republik von Weimar* (Darmstadt, 1985), 52, 74.
3 Heinrich August Winkler, *Weimar, 1918–1933* (Munich, 1993), 87–8, 97.
4 Krüger, *Aussenpolitik*, 19–20.

culminating point of a debate over Germany's war aims that had begun soon after the outbreak of the war and was responsible for a widening split in Germany's home front. On the one side was a movement in favor of far-reaching annexationist and expansionist economic aims that were attainable only if Germany won a decisive victory. Such "annexationists" were to be found among right-wing parties and associations such as the Pan-Germans, the military, and numerous members of all bourgeois parties. On the other side was a slowly emerging countermovement that tended to view a peace of accommodation as the only realistic way out of the carnage of the war. It drew support mainly from labor organizations, left-wing liberals, and some commercial interests.[5]

The government of Chancellor Theobald von Bethmann Hollweg attempted to steer a middle course between these extremes and not to commit itself in public to a specific set of war aims. The dispute came to a head in the spring of 1917, after Russia's czarist monarchy had been overthrown and the Bolsheviks had come out in favor of a peace of accommodation. Their call for a "peace without annexations and indemnities" left a particularly strong impression on the two socialist parties in Germany, the Social Democrats (SPD) and the Independent Social Democrats (USPD), whose members and supporters were among the growing number suffering material deprivation. Some bourgeois politicians also began turning in this direction when they saw Germany's chances for a victory dwindle.

Matthias Erzberger, a leading member of the Center Party, became a spokesman for this disillusioned segment of the population.[6] In early June 1917 he created a sensation by questioning the validity of the German navy's calculations of its chances of prevailing in submarine warfare against Allied supply routes. Erzberger argued that Germany had to try to reach a peace of compromise while it still had the resources and the military standing to negotiate from a position of relative strength. Germany's Reichstag deputies, Erzberger believed, had to break the ice for such negotiations by passing a resolution in favor of a peace of understanding and by trying to commit the German government to it.

The Center leader found support for this policy among all parties except the far Left (the USPD) and the far Right (the Conservatives). This group set up an informal committee of SPD, Progressive, and Center Reichstag deputies, which foreshadowed the composition of the future "Weimar coalition." It prepared the peace resolution adopted by the Left–Center majority of the Reichstag on July 19, 1917.

5 Leo Haupts, *Deutsche Friedenspolitik, 1918–19: Eine Alternative zur Machtpolitik des Ersten Weltkrieges* (Düsseldorf, 1976), 120.
6 Klaus Epstein, *Matthias Erzberger and the Dilemma of German Democracy* (Princeton, N.J., 1959), 189.

The resolution was the first public statement of peace aims shared by the entire moderate Left in Germany, which late in 1918 was to assume responsibility for Germany's foreign policy. Eager to defuse possible criticism from the military High Command, it did not subscribe verbatim to the Bolshevik formula of a peace "without annexations and indemnities" but came close to it, stating that Germany's primary aim was to defend its independence and its territorial integrity. Within these limits Germany strove for a peace based on a permanent reconciliation between peoples. "Forced territorial acquisitions" and "political, economic, and financial oppressions" were declared incompatible with that goal. In addition, the resolution favored free trade and freedom of the seas and promised support for "legal institutions" capable of guaranteeing peace after the war.

Significantly, this proposal was coupled with a demand for a parliamentary system. If the German Empire adopted such a system, so the argument went, the German plea for peace would appear more credible to the masses in enemy countries and, above all, to American President Woodrow Wilson. The inclination to view changes in Germany's political system as final proof of the sincerity of Germany's pledge to a peace of understanding, a proof that might establish a claim for a defeated Germany, anticipated Berlin's later peace policy.[7]

In the months following the adoption of the peace resolution, the German government became more and more the tool of the High Command and pursued a highly ambivalent course in its peace policies. After Lenin's takeover in Russia, it entered into negotiations with the Bolshevik regime for a peace that sharply differed from what the Reichstag majority had envisaged. This was one reason why the German far Left was by this time (January 1918) also beginning to press for a peace without annexations and indemnities.

II

This was the situation when, on January 8, 1918, the American president proclaimed his famous Fourteen Points as the basis for a future "peace of justice." His program foreshadowed some territorial cessions at Germany's expense, both to its west (Alsace-Lorraine) and to its east (in favor of a free

---

7 Erich Matthias and Rudolf Morsey, *Der Interfraktionelle Ausschuss 1917/18* (Düsseldorf, 1959), 1:6, 9–10, 93; Epstein, *Erzberger*, 182–90, 203–4. In passing the resolution, the Reichstag majority had Russia, in particular, in mind, which seemed most inclined to negotiate a compromise peace. For the perspective of the SPD, see Susanne Miller, *Burgfriede und Klassenkampf: Die deutsche Sozialdemokratie in Ersten Weltkrieg* (Düsseldorf, 1974), 304, 309; and Friedhelm Boll, *Friede ohne Revolution? Friedensstrategien der deutschen Sozialdemokratie vom Erfurter Programm 1891 bis zur Revolution 1918* (Bonn, 1980), 222, 228.

Poland). But basically, Wilson let it be known that the Western powers had "no jealousy of German greatness" and did "not wish to injure" Germany "or to block in any way her legitimate influence or power." He demanded to know, however, for whom Germany's spokesmen stood "when they speak to us, whether for the Reichstag majority or for the military party and the men whose creed is imperial domination."[8]

Wilson's Fourteen Points did not fail to impress the parties that had passed the Reichstag resolution; some of their spokesmen went so far as to consider them a result of their own peace propaganda, and they requested that the German government offer peace parleys based on Wilson's program.[9] To an extent and in a highly qualified manner, the imperial chancellor, Georg von Hertling, yielded to this pressure in his public statements. In addition, in early March he began behind the scenes to sound out more or less self-appointed American intermediaries, intimating that Germany was prepared to discuss any peace issue in confidence, except the integrity of its territory.[10]

This is not the place to go into the details of the exchange of views that went on during the following months and, on the German side, that involved agents of the German Foreign Office as well as emissaries of the German Left, who got in touch with American and a few British intermediaries. Suffice it to say that there were indeed members of the German Foreign Office who genuinely believed that "America, just because it does not fight for its existence, might be the first country to be inclined toward peace and be prepared to influence its allies in that sense."[11] On the other hand, it was only in September 1918, after Germany's failure to win the war in the West had become evident, that German emissaries were authorized to commit the empire to a restoration of Belgium. All along, the American president's peace program had been considered merely the starting point of negotiations, never a binding basis for a "peace of understanding."[12]

This situation changed in late September 1918, when Germany's High Command conceded defeat and demanded the immediate conclusion of an armistice and the initiation of peace negotiations. At this critical juncture it was primarily the Foreign Office that insisted Germany should appeal to the

---

8 Ray Stannard Baker and William E. Dodd, eds., *The Public Papers of Woodrow Wilson*, vol. 3: *War and Peace* (New York, 1927), 161–2.

9 Klaus Schwabe, *Deutsche Revolution und Wilson-Frieden: Die amerikanische und die deutsche Friedensstrategie zwischen Ideologie und Machtpolitik, 1918–1919* (Düsseldorf, 1971), 78–9.

10 Klaus Schwabe, "Die amerikanische und die deutsche Geheimdiplomatie und das Problem eines Verständigungsfriedens im Jahre 1918," *Vierteljahrshefte für Zeitgeschichte* 19 (1971): 1–32.

11 Ibid., 19. See also Karl Heinrich Pohl, *Adolf Müller: Geheimagent und Gesandter im Kaiserreich und in der Weimarer Republik* (Cologne, 1995), 200–5.

12 Schwabe, "Die amerikanische und deutsche Geheimdiplomatie," 16.

American president and should base its appeal on an unqualified acceptance of the Fourteen Points. In view of German sentiment a few weeks later, it is significant that at that early stage a number of voices both inside and outside the government were warning that acceptance of Wilson's peace program might lead Wilson to call for the German emperor's abdication and for dire territorial and other sacrifices.[13] The Foreign Office defended its new policy partly under the pressure of an apparently desperate military situation, but also out of tactical considerations. It admitted that Germany needed to change its political system, in accordance with Wilson's presumed demands, by making the majority parties of the Reichstag responsible for foreign policy. It conceded that the ultimate peace terms might turn out not to be in harmony with the moderate peace aims the American president had proclaimed. But even in this worst-case scenario, Germany's secretary for foreign affairs, Paul von Hintze, emphasized, the Fourteen Points would provide a platform for Germany's future foreign policy, which would demand a revision of the peace treaty.[14]

Aside from this calculation, opportunist as it was farsighted, there did exist, especially among Germany's left-wing parties, a genuine belief that Wilson's program was the only sure path to a lasting peace. Matthias Erzberger, for one, fell into this camp, and in 1918 he published a brochure that pictured a future League of Nations as the only alternative to the "unrestricted individualistic national life" that had been responsible for so many wars.[15] Cool diplomatic reasoning as well as genuine conviction clearly lay behind the German appeal for an armistice and peace negotiations issued on October 3, 1918. It was sent to the American president – and only to him – by a German government headed by the moderately liberal Prince Max von Baden and supported by the left-center Reichstag majority; thus it was in line with what Wilson had demanded in his Fourteen Points speech.

It took Wilson and his European Allies a whole month to agree on a response to the German request. The delay was due in part to Wilson's own doubts about the credibility of the new German government's claim to represent the democratic forces in their country, but even more to the inability of the military experts to agree on a list of armistice terms. On the face of it, the German government succeeded in its new peace policy. On November 5, Secretary of State Robert Lansing sent a note to the German government that agreed, in the name of the Western powers, to negotiations

13 Krüger, *Aussenpolitik,* 41; Schwabe, *Deutsche Revolution,* 99.
14 Klaus Schwabe, *Woodrow Wilson, Revolutionary Germany, and Peacemaking, 1918–1919: Missionary Diplomacy and the Realities of Power* (Chapel Hill, N.C., 1985), 37.
15 Quoted in ibid., 34.

for an armistice and a peace treaty based on Wilson's Fourteen Points. In German eyes, this opened the door to a peace of understanding and spared Germany the humiliation of an unconditional surrender for which spokesmen of the Right in both the Allied countries and the United States were vociferously clamoring.

In reality, it was a highly qualified success for Germany. The American note reserved the right of the Allies to interpret the freedom of the seas in accordance with their own interests and demanded that "compensation . . . be made by Germany for all damage done to the civilian population of the Allies and their properties by the aggression of Germany."[16] In addition, the armistice terms agreed on by the Allies were so severe that Germany would not even be able to contemplate military resistance to any peace terms the victors might wish to impose on it. Having, in fact, surrendered, Germany was further reduced to military helplessness by the revolutionary turbulence that led to the overthrow of its monarchy in early November 1918.

Despite such crippling military conditions, the advocates of Germany's new peace policy remained moderately optimistic about the chances of a peace that would observe the Fourteen Points both in procedure – negotiation, not dictation – and in substance by respecting the right of the German people to self-determination. Insiders at the Foreign Office and some leading representatives of the new Social Democratic elite felt confident that a moderate interpretation of the Fourteen Points had, indeed, served as the basis for the Paris armistice negotiations. It had been written by the young Walter Lippmann, then serving the American government as an ardent admirer of Wilson's liberal war aims program. This interpretation had been intercepted by the German intelligence service and continued to serve as a reference for peace planning in the Wilhelmstrasse.[17] So prepared, Germany's policy planners entered what Ernst Troeltsch referred to as the "dreamland of the armistice period."[18]

III

Germany's preparations for peace negotiations did not begin in earnest until January 1919, by which time the Social Democrats had emerged as the strongest party of the postrevolutionary German government. Like their predecessors, the Social Democrats were committed to peace terms based on the Fourteen Points. Friedrich Ebert, the de facto president of the new

16 Ibid., 85.
17 Ibid., 82–3, 110, 187, 302.
18 Ernst Troeltsch, *Spektator-Briefe,* ed. Hans Baron (Tübingen, 1924), 69.

German republic, sounded the keynote of Germany's ensuing peace propaganda: Germany, having become a republic and thus espousing Wilson's democratic ideology, had, he said, established its claim to be treated as an equal by its former adversaries. Hence it was entitled to membership in the League of Nations. Time and again during the following months, spokesmen of the moderate Left based Germany's insistence on a peace of justice (*Rechtsfrieden*) – that is, a peace in accordance with the Fourteen Points – on its conversion to democratic republicanism.[19] As subsequent events showed, this position was to create serious problems for Germany's peacemakers.

As far as the implementation of this peace program was concerned, the Social Democratic leadership deferred to the supposed experts and left this task largely to the Foreign Office and its new head, Ulrich Graf Brockdorff-Rantzau, who had been appointed in early December 1918.[20] This scion of the old Holstein nobility, successor to Wilhelm Solf (who had served in the cabinet of Max von Baden), had been Germany's minister in Copenhagen during the war. He was a career diplomat of the old school and, at the same time, an ardent nationalist who adhered to an idealistic and aristocratic code of honor. Still, he had succeeded in winning the respect and confidence of the moderate Left in Germany, including leading Social Democrats such as Ebert and Phillip Scheidemann, because he had been a critic of the old regime, had favored moderate liberal reform in Prussia, and had proved an advocate of a compromise peace by his opposition to the government's decision in early 1917 to launch unrestricted submarine warfare and thus to risk involving the United States in the war.

In fact, this high-strung and rather class-conscious aristocrat had developed a certain attachment to liberal beliefs. But to him it was only partly a matter of conviction. He was also influenced by what might be called an enlightened opportunism. From his observation post in Denmark, he had developed an awareness of the liberal and democratic spirit that had been generated by the war and that had provided Germany a potent weapon in its attempts at revolutionizing czarist Russia, thereby opening opportunities for a peace of compromise with its eastern adversary. The peace soundings he had engaged in with Russian emigrants, some of them socialists, such as Parvus Helphand, had introduced him to the Social-Democratic party elite in his own country.[21] After the armistice, a peace of accommodation

19 Schwabe, *Woodrow Wilson*, 124–5.
20 Susanne Miller, *Die Bürde der Macht: Die deutsche Sozialdemokratie, 1918–1920* (Düsseldorf, 1978), 194, 248.
21 Haupts, *Deutsche Friedenspolitik*, 407–9; and Leo Haupts, *Graf Brockdorff-Rantzau: Diplomat und Minister in Kaiserreich und der Republik* (Göttingen, 1984), 50–60.

seemed to Brockdorff-Rantzau the obvious guiding objective of Germany's peace policies.[22]

Did the new foreign minister deserve his reputation as a liberal? To what extent was he really an exponent of a new German diplomacy inspired by the Wilsonian ideal of a long-term peace of reconciliation between wartime adversaries? In his public statements during his first weeks in office, he went out of his way to profess progressive values: like Ebert, he considered the American president's peace program the only basis for a viable and enduring peace and, at the same time, the "legally binding maximum" to which the German republic had committed itself. What was at stake at the peace table, in his eyes, was the victory of morality and the final worldwide vindication of democratic principles, after Germany had transformed itself into a democracy as a "concession in advance" to its adversaries.[23] In this sense, he also strongly advocated the creation of a League of Nations, which would establish international relations on entirely new principles, among them the right to self-determination, free trade, universal disarmament, the renunciation of the obsolete rule of a balance of power, and international arbitration of conflicts between nations.[24]

Looking more closely at his declaration, however, one cannot fail to notice that all of his principles happened to serve the supreme purpose he pursued in preparing Germany's peace strategy: which was to maintain Germany's status and "dignity" as one of the leading world powers regardless of its military defeat – a great power, to be sure, that was cooperative in its foreign policy and thus acceptable to the rest of Europe and the world, because, as he admitted, Germany had no more military trump cards left. In this, he differed from the sponsors of the July 1917 Reichstag resolution and from some in the military who continued to cling to their illusions even after the armistice.[25]

As was to be expected, Brockdorff-Rantzau demanded Germany's immediate admission to the League of Nations and a seat on its executive council; "a free people," he argued, "can be asked to cede a large portion of its sovereignty only if it participates in [the League's] executive and thus pro-

---

22 Udo Wengst, *Graf Brockdorff-Rantzau und die aussenpolitischen Anfänge der Weimarer Republik* (Frankfurt am Main, 1973), 15–17.
23 Ibid., 17–18.
24 Ulrich K. Graf Brockdorff-Rantzau, *Dokumente und Gedanken um Versailles* (Berlin, 1925), 40–1, 57–8.
25 Ulrich K. Graf Brockdorff-Rantzau, "Die nächsten Aufgaben der deutschen äusseren Politik," Jan. 21, 1919 (memorandum), in *Akten zur deutschen auswärtigen Politik, 1918–1945* (hereafter *ADAP*), Serie A: *1918–1925*, 14 vols., vol. 1: *Nov. 1918–May 1919*, ed. Peter Grupp (Göttingen, 1982), 204–7.

vides means for the enforcement [of peace]. We cannot join a League of Nations in which we would be only an object of the executive."[26]

Close scrutiny of the foreign minister's confidential and public statements shows that his entire peace strategy – his appeal for American support, the adoption of the Fourteen Points, his anti-Bolshevism, and his reliance on the Left inside and outside Germany – was actually directed toward this single purpose. As he clearly stated, Germany's recent reorientation toward the West – this meant, above all, toward the United States – could continue only if the peace treaty permitted Germany to return to the club of the big world powers. If it did not, then (and only then) would Brockdorff-Rantzau want Germany to abandon the newly adopted anti-Bolshevik direction of its foreign policy and seek an alignment with Soviet Russia and the forces of social protest against the capitalist (i.e., the victorious) powers all over the world.[27]

Two crucial questions remain: How did Brockdorff-Rantzau define the peace terms that would guarantee Germany's comeback as a great power? What tactics did he propose to have such terms accepted by Germany's adversaries?

In the German foreign minister's written and confidential peace program, territorial questions figured most prominently. Such questions would have to be settled in accordance with the right of national self-determination. Therefore a plebiscite would have to be held in Alsace-Lorraine if France was not prepared to permit its future eastern border to coincide with the existing language border. Any further territorial claims France might make against Germany, he stressed, could not be considered – either with regard to the Saar basin or the Rhineland at large. On Germany's eastern border, only those areas that plebiscites had determined to be unquestionably Polish were to be ceded. The vote would not take place until after the peace had been concluded; only areas in which at least two-thirds of the population voted for incorporation in the new Polish state were to be ceded. Free access to the sea would be assured to the Poles on the basis of international conventions; the province of West Prussia would thus remain German. Overseas, Germany would keep its colonies, but it would accept supervision of its colonial activities by the League of Nations. Finally, Brockdorff-Rantzau

---

26 Ulrich K. Graf Brockdorff-Rantzau, "Deutschlands auswärtige Politik: Programmrede vor der Verfassungsgebenden Deutschen National-Versammlung," Feb. 14, 1919, in Brockdorff-Rantzau, *Dokumente*, 58–9. See also Schwabe, *Woodrow Wilson*, 185–7.

27 Wengst, *Brockdorff-Rantzau*, 37, 40; Haupts, *Friedenspolitik*, 57–63, 74–5; Krüger, *Aussenpolitik*, 153; Peter Grupp, *Deutsche Aussenpolitik im Schatten von Versailles 1918–1920* (Paderborn, 1988), 67.

claimed that the right of self-determination demanded that the longing of the German Austrians to be united with Germany be fulfilled.

As for reparations, Brockdorff-Rantzau insisted on the letter of the Lansing note. That is, Germany was obliged to reconstruct the areas of Belgium and northern France that had been occupied by German troops and make compensation for other material losses neutral Belgium had suffered as a consequence of Germany's invasion. Germany was under no obligation to make reparations for damage inflicted by German submarine warfare.

In his public statements, the foreign minister added proposals for improvements in international law, such as a League of Nations, for the protection of national minorities, and for labor legislation.[28] At the time the peace treaty was presented to Germany, the German government had already published a league covenant of its own, which had been prepared by eminent experts in international law and pacifists such as Walther Schücking; in providing for a world parliament, it was more radical than Wilson's own draft covenant.[29]

For the most part, Brockdorff-Rantzau's program reflected opinions prevailing in the Foreign Office. It was discussed with various experts without being fundamentally altered. The treatment of the reparation issue in the final version of the "directives" for the peace delegation of April 21, 1919, was a case in point.[30] Not only was any claim for reparation as a result of Germany's submarine warfare considered to be of doubtful legality, there was general agreement that Germany, immediately after the signing of the peace, could make no reparation at all without destroying its credit. What it could do was participate in the reconstruction of Belgium and northern France by furnishing equipment and raw material and offering labor on a voluntary basis. Reparation payments could not begin before Germany had revived its export industries.[31]

There was one major difference between Brockdorff-Rantzau's drafts and the final "directives": the latter allowed for a plebiscite in the province of Posen exclusively and, moreover, only in those parts of the province

28 "Richtlinien für die deutschen Friedensunterhändler," Jan. 27, 1919, in Susanne Miller, ed., *Die Regierung der Volksbeauftragten 1918/19*, Quellen zur Geschichte des Parlamentarismus und der politischen Parteien, 1. Reihe, Bd. 6, 2 vols. (Düsseldorf, 1969), 2:319–23; Brockdorff-Rantzau, "Deutschlands auswärtige Politik," Feb. 14, 1919, in Brockdorff-Rantzau, *Dokumente*, 44–61; Schwabe, *Woodrow Wilson*, 186–7; Hagen Schulze, ed., *Das Kabinett Scheidemann: 13. Februar bis 20. Juni 1919*, Akten der Reichskanzlei, Weimarer Republik (Boppard am Rhein, 1971), 205 (hereafter *AR Kabinett Scheidemann*).
29 Schwabe, *Woodrow Wilson*, 306–8, n. 47.
30 "Richtlinien für die deutschen Friedensunterhändler," Apr. 21, 1919, in *AR Kabinett Scheidemann*, 191–204.
31 Schwabe, *Woodrow Wilson*, 304–6.

located to the east of the border between Germany and Poland that had been drawn in the last extension of the armistice in late February 1919. The remaining part of the province, as well as West Prussia and Upper Silesia, were thus considered unquestionably German. In limiting the use of plebiscites, the experts, most of them administrative representatives of the areas involved, had won out over Brockdorff-Rantzau's own more flexible interpretation of the Fourteen Points.[32]

Brockdorff-Rantzau then had to determine by what tactics he could best reach his goal of restoring Germany's great power status. The German foreign minister believed, correctly, that Germany's peace strategy needed to identify areas of common concern, sufficiently persuasive to Germany's adversaries to transcend the clash of interests that existed between them and the defeated Germany. In other words, German diplomacy had to distract them from the pursuit of purely nationalistic aims at Germany's expense.[33] The Foreign Office and other German policy makers found it relatively easy to develop a dialog of common concerns with the United States.[34] At the same time, they knew that this would be much more problematic with regard to Great Britain,[35] and exceedingly difficult with respect to France.

As already mentioned, German peace diplomacy banked on the ideological commonality of German and American peace aspirations. Germany, as a new democracy, seemed to deserve peace terms that stayed within the limits of Wilson's Fourteen Points. The United States, for the sake of its own vision of a world order that would ensure peace, was believed to have every interest in seeing its peace program put into effect. Thus, from more than just a tactical point of view, the Fourteen Points, as perceived in Berlin, remained the bedrock of the common ground between Germany and the United States. The bits and pieces of information about Wilson's own position that leaked out at the peace conference, though increasingly at odds with the German point of view, failed to affect this basic orientation of Germany's peace policy.[36]

The reliance on the Fourteen Points was the reason why the Foreign Office brought up the war-guilt issue as early as the latter part of November 1918.[37] The office's policy makers reasoned that Germany would jeopardize the protection it enjoyed under the Fourteen Points if it left unchallenged the Allied claim of German responsibility for the outbreak of the war and

32 Ibid., 303.
33 Grupp, *Deutsche Aussenpolitik*, 74–6; Krüger, *Aussenpolitik*, 43; Haupts, *Brockdorff-Rantzau*, 72–3.
34 Wengst, *Brockdorff-Rantzau*, 17, 20.
35 Ibid., 30.
36 Schwabe, *Woodrow Wilson*, 186.
37 Fritz Dickmann, *Die Kriegsschuldfrage auf der Friedenskonferenz von Paris 1919* (Munich, 1964), 62–7.

thereby tacitly admitted German "war guilt." They feared that Germany's alleged responsibility for the war would cause the Allies to broaden the relatively restrictive meaning of the term "reparations" to be found in the Lansing note and serve as the legal basis for unlimited reparation claims.[38] These are the basic reasons that Brockdorff-Rantzau himself decided to challenge the negotiators on this issue.[39] This policy, however, had one glaring drawback: In refusing to acknowledge Germany's "war guilt," the new German government implicitly exonerated the old monarchical order. Most important, by failing to dissociate itself from the old regime, it undermined its claim that postrevolutionary Germany was a historic new democratic beginning deserving credit at the peace conference. Moderate party leaders and the Scheidemann government, which defended Germany against all war-guilt allegations, were further embarrassed by the radical left-wing USPD, which continued to stress the need for the new republican government to draw a clear distinction between itself and the discredited imperial leadership, in order to see Wilson's position strengthened at the peace conference.[40]

A cabinet meeting devoted to this issue (held on March 22, 1919), revealed that some Social Democrats, such as Eduard David and Eduard Bernstein, were of the same mind on this issue. Both men urged the present government to clearly dissociate itself from the old regime, since this appeared to be the only way to enhance the reputation of the new German republic in the eyes of Germany's former enemies, above all, in the eyes of Wilson himself. But the cabinet majority, and certainly the financial experts, were of a different opinion. They looked at the problem from a thoroughly legalistic point of view. For them, the heart of the matter was not the change that had taken place in Germany but the assets and liabilities that – under international law – the new Germany had assumed from the old.

The cabinet majority and its supporters had good reason to stress this legal continuity, for the Lansing note, which provided the legal basis for a peace according to the Fourteen Points, had been addressed to the imperial government. A clear-cut dissociation from the old regime, they feared, would create two serious problems. First, it would call into question the republican government's claim to act as the successor of the imperial government and its internationally recognized titles and, thereby, would under-

---

38 Krüger, *Aussenpolitik*, 62–3.
39 Ulrich K. Graf Brockdorff-Rantzau, "Rechtsfrieden, Schuldfrage, Völkerbund. Ansprache an die Vertreter der ausländischen Presse," Jan. 24, 1919, in Brockdorff-Rantzau, *Dokumente*, 40–3.
40 Grupp, *Deutsche Aussenpolitik*, 95–6. The issue was related to the question of whether Germany should proceed with the publication of diplomatic records dealing with its role in the July crisis of 1914. Winkler, *Weimar*, 87–9. See also Schwabe, *Deutsche Revolution*, 337.

mine the validity of the *pactum de contrahendo* contained in the Lansing note. Second, by making a confession of guilt, the government would provide the enemy with a new legal basis for the peace negotiations that was far less advantageous for Germany, particularly on the reparation issue. For this reason, Brockdorff-Rantzau and Erzberger, in a rare moment of unanimity, prevailed over the objections of David and Bernstein and made sure that the "directives" instructed the German negotiators to reject all Allied accusations of Germany's war guilt.[41]

In insisting on the legally binding character of the Lansing note, the German foreign minister also rejected all attempts of the Allied military command to prejudge the results of the peace conference in territorial or economic questions by creating accomplished facts when the armistice was to be extended. The Allies never questioned the basic legality of this position, and the American president explicitly supported it.[42]

Brockdorff-Rantzau emphasized not only that the United States and Germany shared an ideological platform but also that the two countries had common political and material interests that would help to overcome the antagonism between Germany and all of the Western powers. The strongest of these bonds was, of course, the desire to contain Bolshevism. "Above all," Brockdorff-Rantzau wrote, "the Western powers need a central European power able to keep Bolshevism out of Western Europe. . . . If law and order exist in Germany, the character of the German people will guarantee that the spark of the extremist theory and practice of Bolshevism will not ignite the West."[43] The foreign minister hoped the reference to Bolshevik Russia would persuade the Western powers of the advisability of "realistic" economic terms that would not crush the German economy, create chaos, and thus pave the way for a Bolshevik takeover. He also hoped that the Allies and the United States might favor the creation of a common German, British, and American border guard (not a military crusade), coupled with a united propagandistic counteroffensive – in other words, measures that promised first to contain Bolshevism in Russia and then to prepare for its ultimate downfall by totally isolating it.[44] If this program of defensive military action

41 Cabinet meeting, Mar. 22, 1919, in *AR Kabinett Scheidemann*, 85–90; Schwabe, *Woodrow Wilson*, 305–6; Wengst, *Brockdorff*, 34. For a parallel discussion on March 27, 1919, among experts of the Geschäftsstelle für die Friedensverhandlungen, see Peter Krüger, *Deutschland und die Reparationen 1918/19: Die Genesis des Reparationsproblems zwischen Waffenstillstand und Versailler Friedensschluss* (Stuttgart, 1973), 148–9.
42 Ulrich K. Graf Brockdorf-Rantzau, "Deutschlands auswärtige Politik," Feb. 14, 1919, in Brockdorff-Rantzau, *Dokumente*, 45; Wengst, *Brockdorff*, 27; Schwabe, *Woodrow Wilson*, 212, 218–19.
43 Ulrich K. Graf Brockdorff-Rantzau, "Die nächsten Aufgaben der deutschen äusseren Politik," Jan. 21, 1919, *ADAP*, Serie A, vol.1, 205, 207.
44 For more ambitious plans of the German army (General Wilhelm Groener), see Schwabe, *Woodrow Wilson*, 222–3.

combined with a political offensive succeeded, Brockdorff-Rantzau reasoned, the moment for an international program for reconstructing the Russian economy and developing Russia's economic potential would have arrived. Such a program would provide Germany, the United States, and Great Britain (and possibly France as well) with a common objective.[45]

The Bolshevik bogey (which, one must not forget, did have a temporary and tenuous foothold in reality in the spring of 1919, for example, in Hungary) was the most effective, but not the only, trump card Brockdorff-Rantzau hoped to play at the peace table. In addition, he was convinced that the former enemies, for the sake of the reconstruction of Europe's economy and the revival of world trade, could not ignore the economic and demographic potential of a country with seventy million inhabitants.[46] For a moment, Brockdorff-Rantzau even entertained the idea that the United States might be interested in maintaining Germany's power in Europe as a counterweight against its historic enemy, Great Britain.[47]

Confident that economic reason would prevail at least among the Anglo-Saxon powers, the German government continuously pleaded for a loosening of the blockade, which was initially established by the armistice. Providing food imports for the starving masses in Germany, the German government argued, would serve two purposes: it would keep Germany's general economy running and thereby prevent further dislocations; and it would prevent social unrest and hence deflate communist influence.[48] Encouraged by confidential contacts, the German government again counted primarily on American support in this matter, as the Americans seemed to be most keenly aware of the dangers of Bolshevism in Central Europe. Such hopes turned out to be wellfounded, as American (and ultimately British) pressure resulted in an agreement, concluded in Brussels on March 15, 1919, that provided for American food exports to Germany in return for immediate cash payment.[49] This was the only major success German representatives could claim in the context of the implementation of the armistice. As a result, the German government became somewhat over-

45 Wengst, *Brockdorff-Rantzau,* 29–30; Schwabe, *Woodrow Wilson,* 188; Grupp, *Deutsche Aussenpolitik,* 79–83.
46 Ulrich K. Graf Brockdorff-Rantzau, "Aufzeichnung," Apr. 29, 1919, in *ADAP,* Serie A, vol. 1, 453; see also Krüger, *Aussenpolitik,* 51, 71; Haupts, *Friedenspolitik,* 415; Leo Haupts, "Zur deutschen und britischen Friedenspolitik in der Pariser Friedenskonferenz: Britisch-deutsche Separatverhandlungen in April/Mai 1919?" *Historische Zeitschrift* 217 (1973): 64–5.
47 Ulrich K. Graf Brockdorff-Rantzau, "Die nächsten Aufgaben der deutschen äusseren Politik," Jan. 21, 1919, *ADAP,* Serie A, vol. 1, 206.
48 Haupts, *Friedenspolitik,* 282–96.
49 Schwabe, *Woodrow Wilson,* 191–208.

confident and was led to underestimate the severity of the peace terms Germany could expect.[50]

Brockdorff-Rantzau's very rigid definition of the essential and nonnegotiable German interests made any agreement with the enemy exceedingly difficult. Was this rigidity simply the result of not knowing what sort of terms the German negotiators could expect? As we know today on the basis of all relevant sources, this was not the case at all. Secret contacts between the German government and American, British, and French intermediaries gave Berlin a fairly clear notion of the territorial and, to some extent, the economic, sacrifices that were to be imposed on Germany.[51]

Especially during the second half of April, American and other Allied intermediaries clearly indicated to Brockdorff-Rantzau and other German representatives that Germany would have to accept harsh terms without much discussion, for the simple reason that the German people and the rest of the world needed peace soon.[52] American sources also intimated that German hopes of Wilson's siding with Germany were unfounded and that the president stood solidly behind the treaty he had negotiated personally with the European Allies.[53] In reality, as noted earlier, the German foreign minister had abandoned this particular illusion soon after he had been appointed.[54] And yet, in spite of this disillusionment and in spite of all secret information he had received afterward, Brockdorff-Rantzau and the German delegation never once considered lowering Germany's conditions for what they considered a "just peace," which they alone were prepared to sign. This was true, in particular, with regard to the territorial demands, which to Brockdorff-Rantzau were nonnegotiable, as they touched on the very existence and future of the German state. By this, Brockdorff-Rantzau, of course, implied that his position on the financial and economic terms would *not* be quite the same.[55]

But would there be negotiations at all? Brockdorff-Rantzau was skeptical, as he feared from early January 1919 on that the peace would simply be

---

50 Ibid., 301.
51 Ibid., 300–2, 313–15.
52 Ibid., 313–15, 318–19. It is true that a British source, which had established contacts with the German minister in The Hague, suggested that the German government indicate which of the peace terms were acceptable and which parts were not and thus hinted that there might be room for some negotiation. But this suggestion was ultimately dismissed by Brockdorff-Rantzau, who did not want such secret exchanges to substitute for the official oral negotiations he desired. See Haupts, "Zur deutschen und britischen Friedenspolitik," 73–5; Wengst, *Brockdorff-Rantzau,* 45–6. For French contacts, see n. 102 to this chapter.
53 Schwabe, *Woodrow Wilson,* 329.
54 Ibid., 302, 308.
55 Brockdorff-Rantzau, "Aufzeichnung," Apr. 27, 1919, *ADAP,* Serie A, vol. 1, 450.

dictated.[56] Even before his appointment he had therefore demanded a free hand to reject a peace treaty that did not conform to his program. He reminded Ebert of this request on the eve of the presentation of the Allied terms at Versailles. The provisional German president remained evasive.[57]

Was the German foreign minister, then, determined from the outset to break with the victorious powers without bothering much about chances for negotiations with them? Such a conclusion would not quite do justice to the strategy that Brockdorff-Rantzau had developed during the long period of waiting for his departure to Versailles. He was indeed prepared, as he assured Ebert before he left, to respond to the victors' peace terms with counterproposals designed to demonstrate that the Allied conditions were legally and morally untenable and, at the same time, impracticable.[58] The primary purpose of this procedure, however, was to gain time and, most important, to draw the Allies into oral negotiations, an aim that in Brock-dorff-Rantzau's opinion was both a question of prestige for Germany as a great power and a matter of practicality in opening the road to mutual concessions. One strategy in face-to-face meetings might be for the German delegation to offer generous economic concessions in an effort to buy its way out of territorial losses that would otherwise be unavoidable. In addition, he felt, a common front against the spread of Bolshevism could prepare the ground for a "reunification" of Germany with the Western powers. In any event, before accepting a treaty that in his view would ruin Germany, Brockdorff-Rantzau would rather resign. These tactics received the cabinet's blessings.[59]

IV

Whatever tenuous hopes Brockdorff-Rantzau may have had were dashed on May 7, 1919, when he was handed the draft of the peace treaty with the provision that no negotiations, only written observations, were permitted. To Clemenceau's terse remarks on that occasion, he reacted with a defiant rejoinder.[60] On studying the terms, the German delegation realized that even its worst fears had been exceeded. The German foreign minister thereupon immediately began an exercise in open diplomacy (after all, "open

---

56 Brockdorff-Rantzau, "Aufzeichnung," Jan. 14, 1919, *ADAP*, Serie A, vol. 1, 184.
57 Brockdorff-Rantzau, "Aufzeichnung," Apr. 27, 1919, *ADAP*, Serie A, vol. 1, 449–50.
58 Haupts, *Friedenspolitik*, 362.
59 Schwabe, *Woodrow Wilson*, 329–30. It was in line with these tactical considerations that Brockdorff-Rantzau, before leaving for Versailles, issued a directive demanding that all feelers coming from Soviet Russia be turned down.
60 Wengst, *Brockdorff-Rantzau*, 48–9.

covenants of peace openly arrived at" had been the first of Wilson's Fourteen Points) by having the numerous German notes criticizing the various
peace provisions turned over to the press. In line with his "grand design," his
primary goal was to arouse the Left all over Europe, especially within the victorious countries, against this "capitalist" peace treaty. He expected that pressure from the Left would gradually soften the attitude of the victorious powers, that this pressure would mount if Germany rejected the peace treaty as
it stood, and that, as a consequence, conflicts among the Western powers
would flare up. In an effort to lend more credibility to the German government's attempt to employ such Trotskyite tactics, Brockdorff-Rantzau
extended feelers to the USPD with a view to forming a wholly socialist government to replace the Scheidemann cabinet.[61] Apparently, he saw that the
chance for oral negotiations and an agreement on terms acceptable to Germany as a great power would come only after the position of Germany's
opponents, under the impact of growing left-wing pressure, had sufficiently
weakened. He thus banked on a more long-term success for his peace strategy; as far as the written negotiations were concerned, which the Allies had
permitted, he accepted the calculated risk of a failure.[62]

During the first weeks of May, however, he had not yet arrived at that
point, as he had not yet fully discarded the possibility that a generous financial offer might pave the way for oral negotiations and for modifications of
the victors' peace terms. At the moment, this was indeed the most realistic
course for the militarily crippled Germany to adopt – the course it was to
choose during the 1920s – namely, to use its economic capacity as a bargaining chip. The Berlin cabinet concurred in principle. Brockdorff-
Rantzau thus felt authorized to embark on a policy that would not hesitate
to incur the long-term indebtedness of Germany vis-à-vis the victorious
powers, if the Allies, in exchange for such financial concessions, were willing to mitigate the territorial terms of the treaty.

Carl Melchior, a German banker and financial expert, was willing to
pursue this course to its logical conclusion. Since early April 1919, he had
been engaged in German-Allied negotiations related to financial aspects of
the armistice. These contacts with enemy experts had made him fully aware
of the severity of the peace terms. It was then that he hit on the idea of making the victors an attractive financial offer that would induce them to take
a softer stand at the peace conference. He suggested that Germany commit
itself to an interest-free payment of 100 billion gold marks, its payment

---

61 Haupts, *Brockdorff-Rantzau*, 64.
62 Ibid., 75; Wengst, *Brockdorff-Rantzau*, 50–1.

schedule being linked to Germany's annual budget receipts. Melchior and Max Warburg, his business partner, supported this idea once they had seen the draft treaty and formulated the terms of their offer so as to ensure the immediate rebuilding of Belgium and northern France.[63]

There were two tactical considerations behind this offer. First, the terms of the long-term debt that Germany would incur were likely to be modified by the victors in the foreseeable future, once moderate forces became stronger and chauvinist sentiments subsided in their societies. Second, and even more important, the Western powers could hardly refuse oral negotiations after receiving such a generous financial offer – if for no other reason than the complexity of the technical problems that the German offer would raise. To Warburg, this offer seemed the only alternative to an outright rejection of the treaty. The spirit in which he suggested it is reflected in a letter in which he discussed the great international task that lay ahead for his generation. International economic agreements, he wrote, will

ultimately reduce ethnic and national borders to matters of relative insignificance and . . . will lead to the formation of a "supreme parliament" to which the individual nations will send their delegates by way of the League of Nations. . . . It will be a task worthy of noble minds to solve, within this supreme parliament, the world's financial and economic problems – much more important than the traditional business of major statesmanship, which will be at least partially submerged by this work. It is my hope that we will succeed to a great extent, if not totally, in wiping out secret diplomacy, militarism and dominance of the seas.[64]

Warburg and Melchior's plan deviated from Germany's previous policy in that it was conceived as a practical compromise without bothering about legal and ideological niceties, such as references to the German definition of the term "reparation" or the Lansing note and the Fourteen Points.[65]

This innovative offer met with a more positive response in the German delegation than in the cabinet, which objected to the amount of money offered and to the deemphasizing of the legal basis provided by the Lansing note. Brockdorff-Rantzau, acting as mediator between the delegation and the authorities in Berlin, was able to persuade the government to include the financial offer as conceived by Melchior in the final German counterproposals. A central condition of this offer, however, was that Germany would maintain its territorial integrity as of 1914 – unless German territory was reduced "as a consequence of the right of self-determination of the

63 Peter Krüger, "Die Reparationen und das Scheitern einer deutschen Verständigungspolitik auf der Pariser Friedenskonferenz in Jahre 1919," *Historische Zeitschrift* 221 (1975): 330–2.
64 For the quotation and the preceding paragraph, see Schwabe, *Woodrow Wilson*, 358–9.
65 Ibid., 359–60.

inhabitants of Alsace-Lorraine, of Schleswig, and of parts of the province of Posen." In other words, Germany was prepared to accept the votes of the populations of those areas in favor of separation from Germany, but, in compensation for its reparation offer, it was not willing to go any further. At the same time, the counterproposals explicitly reaffirmed Germany's legal position, regarding the limitation of its obligation to compensate for war damage in Belgium and northern France. Warburg justly pointed out that this legalistic reasoning was inconsistent with the more pragmatic original intent of Germany's reparation offer and was thus bound to reduce its attractiveness, but he was overruled.[66]

As a result, the German government, in its counterproposals, argued its legal case as strongly as it had previously done. Under the influence of Schücking, the final German answer went so far as to condemn the peace treaty as the "last dreadful triumph" of a "moribund conception of the world, imperialist and capitalist in tendency."[67] Clearly, this argument responded less to the demands of a peace that had to be concluded here and now than to the desire to arouse the public and prepare the road for a future revision of that peace.

The appeal to financial reason helped the German cause no more than the attempt to mobilize left-wing forces against the governments that were responsible for the terms of the treaty. The Western powers yielded to the German appeals to a limited extent – their most important concession being that Upper Silesia was not to be ceded to Poland outright, as the draft treaty had provided, but was to be submitted to a plebiscite that would decide its future national allegiance. But these modifications fell far short of what the German counterproposals had demanded.

The question that had to be decided was whether Germany should carry out its threat not to sign the treaty. The foreign minister urged the government to reject the treaty. He enjoyed the unreserved support of the German peace delegation. Apparently, it shared his conviction that "because the adversaries are not satisfied with the reasonable German propositions, reaching the limits of the practicable as they did, the population of the enemy countries, deeply impressed by the German covering note, will be disappointed and rise against their own governments and will soon thwart violent action [by their governments], even though such action may not be averted initially."[68] He predicted that, once chauvinism had subsided in the

---

66 Krüger, *Deutschland und die Reparationen*, 204–6; Schwabe, *Woodrow Wilson*, 360–1.

67 Schwabe, *Woodrow Wilson*, 361. Even the banker Max Warburg ascribed the harshness of the treaty to the Allies' intention to cripple the German republic because of its socialist makeup. See Krüger, "Die Reparationen," 339.

68 Brockdorff-Rantzau to Ebert, June 9, 1919, quoted in Wengst, *Brockdorff-Rantzau*, 81–2.

enemy countries, successor governments would offer oral negotiations, and
the moment for a genuine accommodation with the Western powers would
have arrived. At the same time, Brockdorff-Rantzau and his advisers
opposed any military resistance to the Allied occupation of Germany and
were quite willing to let the Allies take over its administration, as they were
confident that the Allies would be unable to carry out that task. As soon as
they realized it, the Allies would enter into negotiations with Germany.[69]

Brockdorff-Rantzau and the German delegation were convinced that by
refusing to sign the treaty Germany would become the herald of the "ideas
of the future," spokesmen of the socialist Left all over the world. Time and
again, they expressed their confidence that within a few months the present
enemy governments would be unseated by their legislatures, that dissension
would break out between the victors, and that negotiations under much
improved conditions for Germany were "around the corner."[70]

The ensuing discussion on the pros and cons of rejecting the treaty
showed that even the most powerful arguments put forth by those German
political leaders who favored signing no longer had anything to do with the
contents of the peace treaty. They now had solely to do with tactical aspects
and the presumed long-term effects on Germany if it did not sign. Brockdorff-Rantzau and his adversaries both despised the treaty. Erzberger, the
foreign minister's most influential political rival, preferred to lure the Western powers with the attractive prospect of Germany's signature on the treaty
rather than frightening them with its potential rejection. Erzberger and a
growing number of political leaders in Berlin did not share the foreign minister's optimism as to the consequences of Germany's refusal to accept the
peace terms. Instead, they foresaw further suffering of the German population, a disruption of the empire, and, in the end, the imposition of still
harsher peace terms.[71] The decisive voice in this debate probably belonged
to General Wilhelm Groener, the commanding general of Germany's
remaining military forces, who declared military resistance against the
imposition of the peace terms was simply out of the question. To the foreign minister, this was beside the point, but, apparently, it impressed other
political leaders. Brockdorff-Rantzau, in any event, was overruled. He
resigned, as did the entire Scheidemann government. A new (Center-
Socialist) government was formed and authorized by a majority of the
Reichstag to sign the treaty. On June 28, 1919, the German plenipoten-

---

69 Ibid., 85.
70 Wengst, *Brockdorff-Rantzau*, 81–90; Schwabe, *Woodrow Wilson*, 382–4.
71 Epstein, *Erzberger*, 315–16; Schwabe, *Woodrow Wilson*, 385–6.

tiaries' signatures sealed Germany's defeat, which the majority of the German people still refused to acknowledge.

V

Recent scholarly discussion has suggested that these events of seventy-five years ago will not be fully understood until the following questions are answered.

1. To what extent and in what way was Germany's foreign policy planning during the war linked with its peace policy after the November revolution and the armistice?
2. Was Germany's postrevolutionary leadership sincere in its profession of a new and progressive foreign policy?
3. Were Germany's peace program and the efforts to implement it successful, and if so, in what sense?
4. Were there preferable alternatives to the peace policy of the Ebert-Scheidemann-Brockdorff government?
5. Do the answers to the preceding questions provide any clues to the domestic and international constraints that limited the German peacemakers' options?

Thus far, this chapter has clearly shown the *lines of continuity* between the programs developed in wartime Germany and the policies pursued after the collapse of the empire. This said, it must be emphasized that the campaign for a peace of understanding launched by the Reichstag majority in the summer of 1917 was not the policy of the government but the attitude of the forces that were opposed to the prevailing official view, especially among the influential military. Those forces persisted in pursuing an all-out victory and a peace with annexations. In contrast to such chauvinism, the moderate Left continued to adhere to the ideal of a peace of accommodation, with no regard to the changing military condition from 1917 to 1919.

As for the peace program of the Reichstag majority, some of its key proposals – notably, the call for free trade and for a peacekeeping institution after the war – likewise survived the November revolution. By and large, the supporters of the Reichstag majority under both the empire and the republic felt that Germany's peace program should be in line with the aspirations of the American president. As a result, many in this group tended to associate progress in implementing democratic reforms within Germany with improved possibilities for a "peace of understanding." What had been the attitude of a quasi opposition in 1917 became the program of Germany's government in October 1918.

As mentioned earlier, after the revolution Germany began to think that
it had earned the right to expect a lenient peace based on the Fourteen
Points precisely because it had undergone a revolution. This was a distortion of the record, in that the shift toward a professed Wilsonian peace program occurred when Prince Max became chancellor, which was before the
German republic was proclaimed, a fact that only helps to underline the
continuity between the last phase of the empire and the early republic.

Still, one should not exaggerate such lines of continuity. When the international situation is taken into account, it seems misleading to consider
Germany's peace policies during the period after the revolution, as Peter
Grupp has done, as a mere continuation of the official policy of Germany's
imperial governments.[72] In 1917 it was still possible for Germany to offer a
peace without victory; in 1919, however, there could not be the slightest
doubt that the Allies had won the war militarily. The all-important question here concerns political means. Contrary to what Grupp states, it was
more than a question of degree that caused the new German peace policy
to rely solely on economic means rather than military ones in order to
achieve its aims. At the same time, these aims cannot justly be summarized
as a German hegemony over Europe similar to what the annexationists had
demanded during the war.

Closely related to the continuity question is the issue of whether the government was *sincere* in promising to transcend the rivalries of power and
empire that lay at the root of recent wars and accept the tenets of a new international world order. Such a new world order could be perceived as an
implementation of the program that the American president had propagated
during the war. In a more general sense, it could also be understood as the
definition and successful application of principles of universal interest, and
the willingness to subordinate specific national goals to such principles.

In order to avoid meaningless generalizations, individual personalities
will have to be brought into the picture. It must be remembered, for example, that Germany's initial appeal to Wilson had originated in the Foreign
Office of Imperial Germany and was based on cool Machiavellian reasoning, at least on the part of Secretary Hintze, the head of the Wilhelmstrasse.
The same seems to be true in the case of the real designer of Germany's
peace program and policies, Brockdorff-Rantzau. As was proved at Versailles, there was really only one value to which he felt personally attached:
the rank and the prestige (he said "dignity") of Germany as a great power.
All other popular ideologies were to him subordinate to this single purpose.

72 Grupp, *Deutsche Aussenpolitik,* 45.

The Russian example – that is, the exploitation of the Bolshevik movement by Germany as a means to end the war with that country – had taught him the advantages of a policy that instrumentalized mass movements. Having grown aware of the impact of Wilson's concept of an organized peace on the European Left, he did not hesitate to subscribe to it. He knew, of course, that Wilson's Fourteen Points were Germany's only protection against the European Allies' imperialist ambitions. Sublime opportunist that he was, he did not hesitate at Versailles to agree to the capitalist "deal" that German financial experts had proposed. At the same time, he condemned the treaty as a capitalist concoction and had no qualms about advocating the resumption of relations with the Bolshevik regime in Russia if the peace terms were not satisfactory to Germany. His numerous memoranda show that he unreservedly acted on the premise of the primacy of foreign policy. Foreign policy to him was limited to the exercise of power, although in Germany's case this could not mean military power; he had no illusions about Germany's military helplessness and the need in the foreseeable future to replace military leverage with political and diplomatic skill and economic clout. Remember, too, that for all his bloated rhetoric, this nationalist was still being sharply criticized by some military diehards and the German Right, who accused this "public-relations count" (*Reklamegraf*) of cringing "dishonesty" in his public utterances.[73]

Clearly, Brockdorff-Rantzau's political and professional environment cannot be judged in the same light as the foreign minister himself. It is true that most of the diplomats, experts, and business representatives such as Melchior, with whom Brockdorff-Rantzau had to deal in preparing Germany's peace program, adored him personally, believed in the soundness of his demand for a greater Germany (which included German Austria and most of its former overseas possessions), and supported his policy to the bitter end.[74] There was also a singular lack of awareness of the nightmares that a greater Germany of some eighty million inhabitants would generate in Germany's neighbors, especially France. And yet, the Germany that most German Social Democrats, as well as liberal business representatives like Warburg, envisioned was a Germany imbued with the good intention of making itself acceptable to the other nations of Europe by cooperating with

73 Wengst, *Brockdorff-Rantzau*, 63.
74 Even the convention of the German Workers and Soldiers Councils held in Berlin in mid-December 1918 passed a resolution that claimed "that only the unified greater German democratic and socialist state would guarantee the cultural and economic development of the German people." Quoted in Miller, *Die Bürde der Macht*, 189. See also Max Warburg's defense of Germany's status, including its colonial possessions, in Warburg to Bernstorff, Dec. 30, 1918, in *ADAP*, Serie A, vol. 1, 154–6.

them within the framework of the League of Nations and by contributing
to the common international endeavor of rebuilding Europe's economy.[75]
The same could be said of the Catholic Matthias Erzberger, in spite of his
notorious opportunism.[76] Germany could not be expected to submit a
blueprint for its specific role in Europe, as all German peace planning rested
on the expectation of American leadership in international life once peace
returned, and on the need for Germany to take this into account.[77] It was
this expectation, in particular, that made Germany's loyal cooperation in the
future League indispensable. Thus, the establishment of a League as a guarantee against the recurrence of another world conflict had become an article of faith to most of Brockdorff-Rantzau's advisers, such as the pacifist
Schücking. There also existed a real hope for international economic
understanding as a vehicle of ultimate political reconciliation. To all these
German progressives, some of whom deserve to be called genuine and sincere Wilsonians, Germany's exclusion from international life and world
trade, and above all its nonadmission to the League of Nations, as spelled
out in the treaty, came as a bitter disappointment.[78] Surely, the treaty intellectually disarmed some of Germany's most sincere liberals and advocates of
international and economic accommodation and thus discredited them in
their own country, as some of them had begun to fear at Versailles.[79]

The sincerity or disingenuousness of Germany's representatives as such did
not guarantee the *success* of their peace diplomacy at Versailles. A consistent
strategy as well as a clear insight into the political psychology of Germany's
opponents was equally necessary. Much blame has been heaped on Brockdorff-Rantzau and the German peace delegation for their lack of such qualities. And indeed, if Brockdorff-Rantzau wished to create a climate of
accommodation with the enemy governments – there remain some doubts
that he really did – then a number of his tactical decisions, such as the
provocative language he chose when he received the text of the treaty, clearly
were counterproductive. The same must be said with regard to his overem-
phasis on the war-guilt issue, his efforts to mobilize the Left against the vic-

---

75 Krüger, "Die Reparationen," 363–6.
76 Epstein, *Erzberger,* 254–5.
77 This seems to explain the omission of specifically European aspects in the German peace program,
a lack that Peter Krüger has criticized. See Krüger, *Aussenpolitik,* 74.
78 For this reason, it is not entirely correct to claim that representatives of Germany's peace policy never
bothered to analyze the Fourteen Points and their implications for Germany. See Peter Grupp, "Vom
Waffenstillstand zum Versailler Vertrag: Die aussen- und friedenspolitischen Zielvorstellungen der
deutschen Reichsführung," in Karl Dietrich Bracher, ed., *Die Weimarer Republik 1918–1933* (Düsseldorf, 1988), 292. For economic "progressives" such as Melchior, see Krüger, "Die Reparationen,"
349.
79 Krüger, "Die Reparationen," 329, 345, 365–6. See also n. 97.

torious powers, and his attempt to substitute a "genuinely" – that is, pro-German – Wilsonian peace program for the actual peace treaty, to which, as he knew perfectly well, the American president himself had substantially contributed. Similarly, the submission of a League plan as an alternative to the covenant, a part of the peace treaty and largely the American president's brainchild – in other words, the attempt to "out-Wilson" Woodrow Wilson wherever possible – was certainly not conducive to endearing the representatives of the new Germany to the American president and to winning his support for Germany's claims.[80] In fact, Wilson's attitude toward Germany hardened during the course of the Versailles conference.[81] It is no surprise, therefore, that Brockdorff-Rantzau failed to achieve his primary tactical goal of involving his opponents in oral negotiations.

Whether the policy of desperation he advocated at the end of the conference, regardless of Germany's refusal to sign the treaty, would have led to the predicted success of Germany's peace policy, remains a hypothetical question, as he did not have the opportunity to carry his strategy to the end. It was for this reason that he personally continued to consider his mission at Versailles ultimately to have failed.[82]

Viewed from today, the question of whether the rejection of the treaty would have brought about the vindication of Germany's peace policy, as Brockdorff-Rantzau optimistically prophesied, can be assessed on the basis of at least circumstantial evidence. As is now known, he was mistaken, for example, in expecting European labor to rise up in protest against the treaty.[83] On the other hand, he was probably right in doubting that the victors would be able to shoulder the burden of an all-out occupation and administration of Germany.[84]

But this did not mean that the victors were unable to impose the treaty on a recalcitrant Germany. There were other means of subjugation at their disposal: They could have dealt, for example, with the various German states separately. This was explicitly agreed on by the Allies and held out a definite promise of success. In retrospect, it also seems highly likely that the

80 Antony Lentin, *Lloyd George, Woodrow Wilson, and the Guilt of Germany: An Essay on the Pre-history of Appeasement* (Leicester, 1984), 87–8, 101.
81 Arthur Walworth, *Wilson and His Peacemakers: American Diplomacy at the Paris Peace Conference, 1919* (London, 1986), 393, 410.
82 Brockdorff-Rantzau, *Dokumente*, 119, 125; Wengst, *Brockdorff-Rantzau*, 97.
83 Miller, *Die Bürde der Macht*, 280, 289–90.
84 I would like to make this point despite the arguments in favor of such a policy that Alan Sharp puts forward in his book, *The Versailles Settlement: Peacemaking in Paris, 1919* (London, 1991), 128–9. Allied rule over Germany after 1919 may have had a salutary effect on the Germans, but it does not seem to have been practicable and was, as far as I can see, never seriously considered by the Allies, who even postponed all plans for a direct march to Berlin. Apparently, the Russian example was a deterrent.

62   *Klaus Schwabe*

United States, Great Britain, and France, in defense of the work of the peace conference against German defiance, would have been able to put aside their differences and close ranks.[85] The foreign minister's strategy of refusing to sign the treaty thus would in all probability not have led to a collapse of the Entente, but instead to the disruption of the German republic, as Erzberger had predicted. In addition, it would have annulled the Lansing note as the legal basis for Germany's claims.[86]

And yet, in order to introduce a fresh approach into a somewhat outworn debate, I would venture to argue that, judged by its own standards, that is, in the light of a pure foreign policy conducted with the goal of maintaining Germany's status as a great power, Brockdorff-Rantzau's strategy was indeed successful in the long run. This success was threefold. First of all, at the very beginning of the Versailles "negotiations," the German delegation induced the Western powers to reaffirm their commitment to the Fourteen Points and thus forced them to claim that the Versailles Treaty conformed with Wilson's program.[87] This was bound to renew controversies, at least within the British and the American delegations, where the prevailing opinion was that some provisions of the treaty were in fact not in line with the Fourteen Points and that in the reparations question the Germans indeed had made a far-reaching concession, which deserved to be considered seriously by the Western powers.[88]

Lloyd George adopted this view and threatened to break away from the war alliance if the victors did not try to accommodate Germany to a certain extent. At the height of that dispute, he personally challenged Wilson for not remaining faithful to his own Fourteen Points; he also vaguely alluded to the possibility of labor protests.[89] The German foreign minister's propagandistic counteroffensive at Versailles thus created a crisis of confidence both in the British and in the American delegations, and among the

---

85 Schwabe, *Woodrow Wilson,* 386–91. Jean Baptiste Duroselle (*Clemenceau* [Paris, 1988], 766) is misleading at this point in implying that plans for separate negotiations with the south German states were "rejected" by the Big Four, who, following Clemenceau's examples, disliked meddling in Germany's internal affairs. As the record shows, the Big Four actually had committed themselves to that very policy on June 20, 1919, in case Germany did not sign the treaty. See Paul Mantoux, *Les Délibérations du Conseil des Quatre (24 Mars–28 Juin 1919): Notes de l'officier interprète,* 2 vols. (Paris, 1955), 2:465–7 (hereafter *PMCQ*).
86 Schwabe, *Woodrow Wilson,* 389–90. I would like to make this point despite the arguments put forth by Wolfgang J. Mommsen in chapter 22 of this book supporting Germany's refusal to sign the treaty.
87 Schwabe, *Woodrow Wilson,* 343, 346; Peter Krüger, *Versailles: Deutsche Aussenpolitik zwischen Revisionismus und Friedenssicherung* (Munich, 1986), 29.
88 Howard Elcock, *Portrait of a Decision: The Council of Four and the Treaty of Versailles* (London, 1972), 270–7.
89 June 3, 1919, in *PMCQ,* 2:266, 278–9.

three Allied and associated powers.[90] This, the *second* aspect of his success, contributed to concessions that were more significant than Brockdorff-Rantzau was willing to admit, especially the provisions for a plebiscite in Upper Silesia. Beyond that, Melchior's offer of 100 billion gold marks left a deep impression on American experts Norman Davis and Thomas Lamont and, taken by itself, also on John Maynard Keynes, their counterpart on the British side; as is known today, his offer nearly resulted in the oral negotiations for which Brockdorff-Rantzau was aiming.[91]

But Brockdorff-Rantzau was successful, above all, in a more comprehensive way. The essential purpose of the campaign that he launched against the peace treaty, signed or not, had been to discredit it legally and morally. In this he may not have succeeded at Versailles in comparison with the victorious peacemakers, but succeed he did with regard to progressive opinion inside and especially outside Germany, certainly in the long run – and this seems to be the *third* and most important aspect of his "victory."[92] Keynes's scathing indictment of the treaty in *The Economic Consequences of the Peace*, written immediately after the peace conference, was only the beginning of a quick erosion of the international prestige the Versailles Treaty was supposed to enjoy. Germany's policy of a revision of the treaty could be carried out under an increasingly favorable climate of opinion, especially on the left. As Secretary Hintze had predicted when he advocated Germany's appeal to Wilson and his program, Germany, by basing its own peace program on the Fourteen Points, did not essentially gain much during the Versailles peace conference as such, but it managed to build up a strong and increasingly convincing case for a revision of the peace treaty and, thereby, gradually to isolate France from Great Britain.[93] In this sense, it seems fully justified to identify Versailles with the prehistory of appeasement, as Antony Lentin has done in his recent monograph.[94] This strategy was all the more effective as Germany's peace policy from the Armistice to Versailles had

90 Lentin, *Lloyd George, Woodrow Wilson, and the Guilt of Germany,* 93–4; Schwabe, *Woodrow Wilson,* 339–43.
91 Schwabe, *Woodrow Wilson,* 371; Krüger, *Die Reparationen,* 360. John Maynard Keynes, *The Economic Consequences of the Peace* (London, 1920), 146, 201, 204–7. On the basis of this evidence, Sally Marks's observation that the "highly contingent German reparations offer . . . fooled nobody" needs to be qualified. Lamont states that the German offer went "further . . . than we ever expected," and all American financial advisers pleaded strongly in favor of accepting this German proposal of a fixed sum. See Schwabe, *Woodrow Wilson,* 363–4.
92 In this sense, Brockdorff-Rantzau's policy was not a policy of "all or nothing," as Grupp contends in "Vom Waffenstillstand," 295. Whatever consequences for his policy that Brockdorff-Rantzau foresaw, the public disqualification of the treaty, in his eyes, was an ineluctably positive result of his strategy.
93 For a contemporary prediction of this development (in the SPD *Hamburger Echo,* May 11, 1919), see Müller, *Die Bürde der Macht,* 279.
94 Lentin, *Lloyd George, Woodrow Wilson, and the Guilt of Germany.*

coupled its denunciation of a dictated victors' peace with appeals to the principle of international cooperation and reconciliation. This policy simply had to be continued, and, in fact, revision of the peace treaty in the name of international reconciliation soon became the basic tenet of the foreign policy of the Weimar Republic, a foreign policy that, in spite of initial difficulties, soon would lead to remarkable achievements.[95]

VI

This said, the fact cannot be denied that Germany had to pay a heavy price for this long-term foreign policy success. At the time Germany was forced to accept the treaty, the policy of international accommodation and progressivism and a general pro-Western orientation, for which the German government had publicly come out, evidently had borne no fruit. In the eyes of a large section of the German public, this immediate failure counted for more than the possibility of long-term success. It discredited not only this cooperative foreign policy, but its advocates as well – left-wing bourgeois liberals, Social Democrats, pacifists – on whom the future of the Weimar Republic depended.[96] It was the very thing that the German peace delegation feared in case a peace of accommodation should not be achieved; Walter Simons, one of its most eminent members, predicted that, if Germany were confronted with an unacceptable treaty, "the German Nationalist movement will immediately gain strength, *and a leader, as yet undiscovered, would be found to head a great popular uprising.*"[97]

The Reichstag election of June 6, 1920, which drastically reduced the number of Liberal-Democratic as well as Social-Democratic voters, proved that the majority of Germany's electorate no longer supported the "Weimar coalition" (or what in 1917, roughly speaking, had been the Reichstag majority). There is no doubt that the apparent failure of Germany's peace policy at Versailles contributed to this first defeat of the pro-republican forces at the polls in Germany: Brockdorff-Rantzau's long-term propaganda success at Versailles helped to undermine the foundations of the Weimar Republic soon after they had been laid.[98]

95 This hypothesis tries to revise the rather somber view of the effects of Germany's peace policy that is found in Krüger, *Versailles,* 67. This is not to deny the difficult start Weimar's foreign policy had, but it takes a little more of a long-range view and shows that only five years later Germany was able to commit France to a basically cooperative attitude. The problem this hypothesis does leave open is the domestic costs that had to be paid as a result of the setbacks that Germany's diplomacy *initially* suffered.
96 Krüger, "Die Reparationen," 329.
97 Schwabe, *Woodrow Wilson,* 315 (italics added).
98 Krüger, "Die Reparationen," 366, 371.

Could this internally portentous diplomatic strategy have been avoided? Was there an *alternative* to Germany's peace policy? The arguments brought forward by the proponents of a simple rejection of the treaty have already been dealt with. On the other hand, one must ask whether a more flexible policy would have yielded better results. Critics of Germany's official policy at Versailles who share this view, such as Peter Grupp and, to some extent, Hans Mommsen, often point to the bourgeois pacifists or the USPD as exponents of a more realistic, more credible, and ultimately more promising peace program and policy.[99] There is much to be said in support of this hypothesis: these radical progressives or socialists, many of them convinced Wilsonians, were the only ones prepared to make a clear break with Germany's past and its former reactionary regime; they were the only ones prepared to deal in a candid way with the question of Germany's war guilt; and they alone refrained from creating illusions about the severity of the peace terms that could be expected.[100] Thus, on the face of it, they appear to be the German representatives who were ideally suited to bring about a genuine reconciliation with the country's former enemies.

What substantially weakens this hypothesis, though, is that it is impossible to prove these pro-Western radicals would have been able to obtain a better treaty than Brockdorff-Rantzau did. In fact, a number of factors make this seem rather doubtful. To begin with, there is the example of German Austria. It was a pleasant surprise to the Allies that the Austrian delegation displayed a much more accommodating attitude than had Brockdorff-Rantzau. However, as much as the Austrians' politeness and humility were appreciated, in the end it helped them to arrive at oral negotiations no more than did the Germans' defiance.[101]

Two additional factors would have hindered the USPD or pacifist German negotiators from doing any better at Versailles than Brockdorff-Rantzau had. First, the early prestige that the USPD had enjoyed in Allied circles dwindled during the peace conference. After all, the inclination of

99 Grupp, *Deutsche Aussenpolitik*, 290–4; Hans Mommsen (*Die verspielte Freiheit*, 83–4) remarks that a clear break with the old regime, as advocated by Eisner, might have made it more difficult for France to sustain its maximal demands for peace terms at the expense of Germany. I cannot see any palpable evidence to sustain this hypothesis. On the contrary, there is a possibility that the German government might have undermined the credibility of its basically pro-Western foreign policy orientation if it had yielded to USPD influences. After all, the USPD maintained a highly ambivalent attitude between Western and Leninist values. Brockdorff-Rantzau himself overlooked this when he considered an SPD-USPD government on the eve of Versailles. See Heinrich August Winkler, *Von der Revolution zur Stabilisierung: Arbeiter und Arbeiterbewegung in der Weimarer Republik, 1918–1924* (Berlin, 1985), 252–5; and Klaus Schwabe, "Äussere und innere Bedingungen der deutschen Novemberrevolution," in Michael Salewski, ed., *Die Deutschen und die Revolution* (Göttingen, 1984), 344–5.

100 Winkler, *Weimar*, 87–90.

101 *PMCQ*, 2:273; Arthur Walworth, *Wilson and His Peacemakers*, 451.

the USPD to accept the treaty in the hope that a world revolution would soon sweep it away could not have been particularly enticing to the Allied peacemakers and Wilson. Thus, the USPD came to be regarded as no more than a convenient vehicle to break Germany's resistance to signing the treaty.[102] Above all, whether or not German spokesmen wanted to draw a clear line between the old regime and the republic, the Western powers, adhering to precedents in international law, were not prepared in any way to honor such a distinction. As they declared in their note of May 19, there could not be any doubt as to the legal continuity that linked the "two Germanys" of before and after the revolution, with the result that obligations undertaken by the "German nation" could not be "extinguished" "by a modification of its political regime."[103]

But above all, the German government felt unable, for domestic reasons, to consider alternatives to its actual peace policy. This finally introduces the issue of the *international and domestic constraints* limiting Germany's options in 1919. The single and most important of the international constraints was the fact that the compromises that had been worked out during the long sessions of the inter-Allied peace negotiations were so tenuous and fragile as not to permit major concessions to Germany, concessions that were sure to upset the whole brittle edifice. This left little room for whatever peace strategy German representatives might have chosen.[104]

The domestic constraints that explain why the Social Democrats did not follow the example of their fellow socialists on the left, the USPD, in contritely dissociating themselves from the old regime were equally compelling: during the war the SPD had finally succeeded in integrating into the mainstream of German politics and society. The result of this process was that they tended increasingly to identify themselves with the basic interests of the German nation-state. During the war this meant supporting Germany's war effort on the premise that a defensive war was being fought for which Germany was not responsible. As the war progressed, it also meant striving for a peace without victory.

In November 1918 the SPD felt that for the sake of Germany's national interest it should step forward and assume leadership, and thus ensure a Wilsonian peace for Germany. The SPD could not disavow that policy and

102 For French contacts, see Henning Köhler, *Novemberrevolution und Frankreich: Die französische Deutschland-Politik, 1918–1919* (Düsseldorf, 1980), 281–3.
103 Allied reply to the German note of May 13, 1919, in *Papers Relating to the Foreign Relations of the United States: The Paris Peace Conference, 1919* (Washington, D.C., 1945), 5:730.
104 Klaus Schwabe, "Versailles–nach sechzig Jahren," *Neue Politische Literatur* 24 (1979): 473. This was recognized in the German government as well. See Krüger, "Die Reparationen," 340.

admit that it had been wrong without losing face.[105] To concede Germany's defeat, admit its "war guilt," and supinely accept a victors' peace may very well have conjured up a domestic disaster for the SPD worse than the set-backs suffered by it in the following years; it may have led to worse defeats at the polls and to an open break with the military and attendant coups less harmless than the Kapp Putsch. Thus the Social Democratic leadership chose to follow Brockdorff-Rantzau's example: to defend Germany's immediate interests to the utmost and to dismiss any reflection about possible advantages the Versailles peace settlement held in store for Germany, advantages that, from today's perspective, are only too evident. To emulate the USPD's and some pacifists' type of internationalism seemed to jeopardize the domestic gains the SPD had made during the war. Such a policy course, it was feared, would lead to a reversal of the SPD's integration into national politics, to which the war had contributed. It threatened to permit right-wing forces to monopolize German nationalism. As the future would reveal, such concerns were well-founded. The Social Democrats and the bourgeois Left thus had powerful reasons for pursuing a peace policy that qualified them as good German patriots.[106]

In conclusion, under the circumstances only slight modifications of Germany's policy at Versailles seem imaginable – alternatives that were more promising, however, than the course chosen by the German government under Brockdorff-Rantzau's guidance. Possibly the Melchior-Warburg initiative in the reparation question, if followed up more consistently than was actually the case, might have yielded some slight additional tactical advantages for Germany. And yet, even such gains would hardly have changed the basic course of events at Versailles. Time was not yet ripe in Germany (nor in France or Great Britain) for a genuine reconciliation between the former enemies, a reconciliation for which contemporary progressive voices all over the world so eloquently pleaded.[107]

---

105 Miller, *Die Bürde der Macht,* 277.
106 See ibid., 276–8; and Winkler, *Von der Revolution,* 212–13, 225; also Winkler, *Weimar,* 89, 602.
107 Arno J. Mayer, *Politics and Diplomacy of Peacemaking: Containment and Counterrevolution at Versailles, 1918–1919* (London, 1968), 875–93.

2

"Had We Known How Bad Things Were in Germany, We Might Have Got Stiffer Terms": Great Britain and the German Armistice

DAVID FRENCH

In 1914 British policy makers began the war determined to enhance their postwar security against both their enemies and their allies. Britain went to war against Germany in August 1914 ostensibly to liberate Belgium from German military occupation. But British war aims soon assumed an ideological dimension that continued to color them throughout the war. Even before 1914 many British politicians had been suspicious of Germany's growing power, fearing that it might be dangerous because it was unchecked by a democratic electorate.[1] Once the fighting began, British policy makers quickly conceived of the war as a crusade. Britain was fighting not to crush the German people, but to bring about a change in Germany's constitutional arrangements. They were engaged in a war to destroy the control of the Prussian military caste over the German state.[2] As Lord Kitchener, the secretary of state for war, remarked in March 1916, "The only really satisfactory termination of the war would be brought about by an internal revolution in Germany."[3]

I am grateful to the following for permission to quote from material to which they own the copyright: the controller, Her Majesty's Stationery Office (Crown Copyright material); the clerk of the records, the House of Lords Record Office (Lloyd George papers); the master and fellows of Churchill College, University of Cambridge (Hankey and Wemyss papers). The quotation in the title of this chapter can be found in a letter from Sir Eric Geddes to Sir David Beatty, Nov. 12, 1918, 116/1809, Public Record Office (hereafter PRO).
1 Paul M. Kennedy, *The Rise of the Anglo-German Antagonism, 1860–1914* (London, 1980), 157–66.
2 David French, *British Strategy and War Aims, 1914–1916* (London, 1986), 22–3.
3 Arthur S. Link et al., eds., *The Papers of Woodrow Wilson* (hereafter *PWW*), 69 vols. (Princeton, N.J., 1966–94), 36:437.

The British kept an equally wary eye on their allies. At the beginning of September 1914 it was the czarist government, worried lest the Germans should occupy Paris and the French capitulate, that insisted on transforming the Triple Entente into a military alliance. But although the British Cabinet was content to accept the Russian proposal, its members entered one important caveat: when the time came to decide upon detailed peace terms, no member of the alliance should be allowed to insist upon terms to which they had not first agreed with their partners.[4] This was symptomatic of British policy makers' understanding that, although each partner shared the common aim of defeating the Central Powers, their visions of a desirable postwar settlement were markedly divergent, and premature discussion of peace terms might tear their alliance asunder.

Nothing better illustrated this than the tangled discussions that led to the signing of the Constantinople Agreement in March 1915. On March 2, 1915, the British accepted a Greek offer of assistance in the Dardanelles, subject to Russia's agreement. But the czarist government had no intention of allowing the Straits to fall under Greek control. It insisted that the British promise that Constantinople and the Straits would come under Russian domination at the end of the war. Reluctantly, the British agreed, and ministers then began, in secret, to consider Britain's own postwar objectives. Two concerns underlay these and later deliberations: the contingent nature of the existing alliance system and a marked desire not to crush Germany utterly lest it make the creation of a stable postwar balance of power in Europe impossible. Lord Kitchener and Winston Churchill were agreed that Britain itself would be secure against Germany if the German fleet were destroyed, if the Kiel Canal were no longer under German control, and if a large indemnity were imposed on Germany so that a future German government would not be able to rebuild its naval power. But in the light of its great economic strength, a moderately powerful Germany in the center of Europe was inevitable. Indeed it might, under some circumstances, actually be something to welcome, for, as David Lloyd George explained, "It might eventually be desirable to have her in a position to prevent Russia becoming too predominant."[5] The nightmare that haunted Kitchener, the man who did more than anyone in 1914–15 to shape British strategic policy, was the possibility that in the postwar world Great Britain might find itself sharing a common land frontier with the czarist empire in Asia. Such an out-

4 Sir Arthur Nicolson to Sir Edward Grey, Sept. 2, 1914, British Foreign Office (hereafter FO), 371-2173/46060, PRO; Sir George Buchanan to Foreign Office, Sept. 1, 1914, FO 371-2173/45394, PRO; Grey to Buchanan, Sept. 3, 1914, FO 371-2173/46456, PRO.
5 John Grigg, *Lloyd George: From Peace to War, 1912–1916* (London, 1985), 211.

come would be a major strategic disaster for the British, as it would compel them to maintain a much enlarged and very expensive army in Asia. To avoid this, he was determined that, if the Russians secured Constantinople at the end of the war and the French gained control of Syria, the British should maintain a Turkish buffer state stretching from the Persian frontier to Anatolia.[6] Similarly, other ministers argued that the British might find it desirable to annex Palestine to provide a buffer between British-controlled Egypt and the Suez Canal and French-dominated territory to the north.[7]

The theme that the war would have profited Britain little if it had eliminated Germany as a threat to its security only to have it replaced by Russia, France or, after April 1917, the United States, recurred throughout the war when British policy makers considered their war aims. In the summer of 1916, for example, when for a brief period they could convince themselves that the Somme offensive might be on the point of forcing the Germans to negotiate, the War Office and the Foreign Office produced detailed memoranda on war aims. Both agreed that the preservation of a strong, but not overmighty Germany in the center of Europe, shorn of its navy but able to act as a counterweight in the European balance of power, would be a necessary component of a stable postwar world.[8]

In 1914–15 British policy makers hoped to achieve these objectives by withholding their own supreme military effort until early in 1917, when they expected that the French, Russian, German, and Austro-Hungarian armies would have fought themselves to a standstill. Britain would then be able to intervene decisively in the continental land war and Kitchener's New Armies would ensure that Britain not only won the war but was also the arbiter of the peace settlement. But by the spring of 1917 several of the major pillars of this strategy – the ability of the French and Russian armies to continue fighting and Britain's own ability both to control the world's sealanes and act as paymaster to the Entente – began to crumble. At the end of 1917 the War Cabinet had decided to postpone Britain's supreme effort against Germany until 1919, when it hoped that a large American army would have arrived in France capable of sharing the cost of defeating the Germans. That would ensure that, when the fighting stopped, Britain

6 Lord Kitchener, Alexandretta and Mesopotamia, Mar. 16, 1915, British Cabinet Office (hereafter CAB) 42/2/10, PRO; Kitchener, The future relations of the Great Powers, Apr. 21, 1915, CAB 37/127/34, PRO.
7 Herbert Samuel, The future of Palestine, Jan. 21, 1915, 37/123/43, CAB, PRO; Samuel, Palestine, Mar. 11, 1915, 37/126/1, CAB, PRO.
8 Sir Ralph Paget and Sir George Tyrrell, Suggested basis for a territorial settlement in Europe, Aug. 7, 1916, CAB 42/17/4, PRO; Sir William Robertson, General Staff memorandum submitted in accordance with the prime minister's instructions, Aug. 31, 1916, CAB 42/18/10, PRO.

would still retain sufficient military and economic strength to be one of the dominant powers at the peace conference.[9] The sudden collapse of the Central Powers in the autumn of 1918, therefore, happened a year before the British expected it, and caught them off balance. Even so, as the deliberations of British policy makers in the autumn of 1918 demonstrated, they were not caught so far off balance that they forgot their fundamental objectives: to secure the benefits accruing to Great Britain and its empire from the collapse of the Central Powers, and to maximize its postwar security against both its existing enemies and its existing friends.

In October 1918 it was not inevitable that the War Cabinet would look favorably on Germany's request for an armistice. On September 12, 1918, Lloyd George, prime minister since December 1916, told the British people:

> Victory is essential to sound peace. Unless you have the image of victory stamped on the surface the peace will depreciate in value. As time goes on the Prussian military power must not only be beaten, but Germany itself must know it. The German people must know that if their rulers outrage the law of nations the Prussian military strength cannot protect them from punishment.[10]

Prince Max von Baden's "revolution from above" did not convince either the Foreign Office or the prime minister that a stable democratic government had ousted "the Prussian military power."[11] Lloyd George feared that "if peace were made now, in twenty years' time the Germans would say what Carthage had said about the First Punic War, namely, that they had made this mistake and that mistake, and that by better preparation and organization they would be able to bring about victory next time."[12] "Was it," he mused on October 13, "really worth stopping the fighting unless Germany was really badly beaten?"[13] It was only after lengthy deliberations that the War Cabinet decided that it was.

Almost until the armistice negotiations were concluded, the War Cabinet and General Headquarters (GHQ) in France believed that the Germans retained the ability to retire slowly to the Rhine and to make a stand there

9 David French, *The Strategy of the Lloyd George Coalition, 1916–1918* (Oxford, 1995), passim.
10 *Times* (London), Sept. 13, 1918.
11 Sir Horace Rumbold to Foreign Office, Sept. 13, 1918, and minute by Sir Lancelot Oliphant, Sept. 22, 1918, FO 371/3434/160478, PRO; Political Intelligence Department, memorandum on the Prussian franchise bill, July 24, 1918, CAB 24/59/GT5224, PRO; Political Intelligence Department, memorandum on the coming German peace offensive, Aug. 28, 1918, CAB 24/62/GT5539, PRO; Political Intelligence Department, memorandum on German war aims, Sept. 5, 1918, CAB 24/63/GT5615, PRO.
12 Minutes of a conference held at Danny, Sussex, on Sunday, Oct. 13, 1918, CAB 24/66/GT5967, PRO.
13 Ibid. See also War Cabinet, Oct. 25, 1918, CAB 23/14/WC491A, PRO; Sir Charles Callwell, *Field-Marshal Sir Henry Wilson: His Life and Diaries* (London, 1927), 2:143.

throughout the winter of 1918–19. Many ministers and officials who recognized that the German successes in the spring of 1918 had not forced the British to sue for peace, assumed that the Germans would show similar resolution when confronted by the Allied counteroffensive. Although British intelligence reported indications of the serious plight into which Germany had fallen, after so many bitter disappointments in 1916–17 policy makers in London hardly dared to hope that the Allied advances since mid-July had reduced the German army to the point of collapse.[14] Even Sir Douglas Haig, who was the commander of the British armies helping to drive the Germans back toward the Rhine and whose predictions about the impending collapse of the German army in 1916–17 had been shot through with an unrealistic optimism, now shared in this general estimation. His pessimism can be explained by three factors. In August 1918 the accidental death of his chief intelligence officer had seriously disrupted the work of GHQ'S intelligence section.[15] He was also conscious of the growing weaknesses of the British army, which was by then seriously short of manpower.[16] And finally, the British Expeditionary Force (BEF) was confronting an increasingly serious logistical problem. After breaching the Hindenburg line, the British troops found themselves trying to advance across a wasteland in which the retreating Germans had destroyed all means of communication; by early November it was likely that autumn rains would soon make a further advance on the western front impossible. Consequently, on October 16, in the opinion of the chief of the Imperial General Staff, Sir Henry Wilson, "there was nothing to warrant the assumption that the present military situation justified the Germans in giving-in."[17] Thus by mid-October British policy makers believed that if they wanted to impose unconditional surrender on the Germans, they would have to carry on fighting into 1919. They opted instead for a quick armistice. They did so because, after weighing Britain's relative power both in the autumn of 1918 and in the summer of 1919 against that of their partners and enemies, they calculated that the cost of continuing the war would be greater than the benefits Britain would gain from continuing the fighting.

14 GHQ Intelligence, Summary of information, Sept. 1918, British War Office (hereafter WO), 157/35, PRO; Lt. Col. George Macready, Maintenance of the German army, Oct. 4, 1918, CAB 25/123/SWC329, PRO; Robertson to Foreign Office (marked "Special Distribution"), Oct. 8, 1918, FO 371-3444/168249, PRO; Lord Kilmarnock to Foreign Office, Oct. 7, 1918, FO 371-3444/168247, PRO; X-committee, June 17, 1918, CAB 23/17/X14, PRO; Summary of intelligence, GHQ. Entries for Oct. 11, 12, 18, 20, 22, 23, 25, 27, and 31, 1918, WO 157/36, PRO.
15 Sir James Marshall-Cornwall, *Wars and Rumours of Wars* (London, 1984), 38–9.
16 X-committee, Oct. 19, 1918, CAB 23/17/X-29, PRO; Robert Blake, ed., *The Private Papers of Douglas Haig, 1914–1918* (London, 1952), 333–4.
17 War Cabinet, Oct. 16, 1918, CAB 23/8/WC487, PRO; Callwell, *Field-Marshal Sir Henry Wilson,* 2:137.

By the summer of 1918 both Lloyd George and Haig believed that the French were trying to do what the British themselves had aspired to achieve since 1914: to exploit their allies' resources to achieve their own national ends. After General Ferdinand Foch's appointment as generalissimo in the spring, the British began to fancy that Prime Minister Georges Clemenceau was bent on exploiting his position vis-à-vis Foch to ensure that France alone controlled operations on the western front and wanted to bleed the BEF dry in achieving French war aims. Henry Wilson thought that he detected "numberless signs of increasing [French] interference" and that "the French mean to take us over body and soul."[18] During the battles of March and April 1918, the grudging manner in which Foch sent French reinforcements to support the BEF convinced Haig that Foch was ready to sacrifice British soldiers to preserve Pétain's divisions.[19] When Foch suggested rotating tired British divisions to quiet sectors of the French front in April, Wilson suspected that he sought to break up the BEF and so reduce Britain's influence over the final peace settlement.[20] When Lloyd George heard that the French were determined to concentrate the whole of the American army on their sector of the line, he was convinced that this was part of the political game that General Foch was playing at Clemenceau's instigation. The whole object of it was, by depriving Britain of the support of the American troops, to force it to keep up its present total of fifty-nine divisions regardless of the effect upon its industries and national life in general.[21]

He became even more suspicious of French ambitions in August and September when Foch deliberately withheld any advance warning of his counteroffensives from the War Cabinet. Ministers only learned of the Amiens offensive some hours after it had begun.[22] On August 12 they sent their formal congratulations to Haig but coupled it with a message that underlined their unease. Although they were willing to agree to operations like "the third battle of the Somme, short of duration and productive of far-reaching results at comparatively low cost, while inflicting heavy losses on the enemy in men, material, and morale,"[23] they insisted that major opera-

18 Callwell, *Field-Marshal Sir Henry Wilson*, 2:99; Army Council to Lord Milner, May 15, 1918, Lloyd George papers (hereafter LGP), F/38/3/38, House of Lords Record Office (hereafter HLRO).
19 War Cabinet, May 14, 1918, CAB 23/6/WC411, PRO.
20 Callwell, *Field-Marshal Sir Henry Wilson*, 2:94, 99; Diary of Sir Maurice Hankey (hereafter Hankey diary), May 13, 1918, HNKY 1/3, Hankey papers, Churchill College, Cambridge.
21 X-committee, July 26, 1918, CAB 24/17/X-25, PRO.
22 Brigadier Charles Grant, Some notes made at General Foch's headquarters, Aug. 7, 1918, WO 106/1456, PRO; Keith Jeffery, ed., *The Military Correspondence of Field Marshal Sir Henry Wilson, 1918–1920* (London, 1985), 48; Committee of Prime Ministers, Aug. 8, 1918, CAB 23/44A/IWC29A, PRO.
23 Sir Maurice Hankey, Report of the Committee of Prime Ministers, Aug. 20, 1918, CAB 27/8/WP72, PRO; Committee of Prime Ministers, Aug. 12, 1918, CAB 23/44A/IWC29B, PRO.

tions likely to involve heavy losses, which Britain could no longer sustain, must first be submitted to them for approval.[24] In practice, as their major concern remained the defeat of the German army in France, the War Cabinet did not interfere in Foch's conduct of operations in the autumn. But Lloyd George recognized that Foch was intent on preserving the French army at the expense of the BEF, and hoped that "the French would take a big share in the battle, as he did not want the British army to be so reduced that next year we should find ourselves the third Military Power on the Western front."[25]

That was a worrying possibility, for since the beginning of the war British policy makers had believed that Britain's influence over the peace settlement would be in direct proportion to the size of its army. They were therefore eager to bring the war to a close before the end of 1918, if at all possible, for they realized that if the war continued into 1919, the BEF was certain to shrink. In late July, Wilson had warned Haig that so short was Great Britain of manpower that in 1919 the BEF would have to be cut from its current size of fifty-nine divisions to between thirty-nine and forty-four divisions.[26] The War Cabinet took this decision even though they knew that it would have major consequences for Britain's influence within the alliance. Foch left the British in no doubt about what would be the implications in 1919 if they allowed the BEF to wither. "If when the time for discussion of peace arrives we [i.e., Britain] have reduced the number of our divisions while they have not, we shall not have the same weight in council."[27] That was a doubly unappealing prospect, for there was little enthusiasm among British policy makers to continue fighting just so that the French could invade Germany "to pay off old scores."[28] Foch believed that the war could be won only by attacking and defeating the German army in the west, and both he and Clemenceau intended to do so by making the maximum use of British and American manpower, thus saving what was left of France's own forces.[29] When the British claimed that they should be allowed to reduce the size of their army in order to continue supplying their allies with economic assistance, they met a frosty reception in France.[30] In an attempt to placate their ally, the War Cabinet even permitted a represen-

24 Hankey, Report of the Committee of Prime Ministers, Aug. 20, 1918, CAB 27/8/WP72, PRO.
25 X-Committee, May 16, 1918, CAB 23/17/X-2, PRO.
26 Wilson to Sir Douglas Haig, July 26, 1918, WO 256/33, PRO.
27 Sir Charles Sackville-West to Hankey, Aug. 27, 1918, LGP, F/23/3/10, HLRO; Lord Reading to Lloyd George, Sept. 3, 1918, FO 800-222/Fr/7, PRO.
28 Blake, *Private Papers of Douglas Haig*, 334.
29 Trevor Wilson, *The Myriad Faces of War: Britain and the Great War, 1914–1918* (Oxford, 1986), 568.
30 Hankey to Lloyd George, June 22, 1918, LGP, F/23/3/43, HLRO.

tative of the French War Ministry to inspect Great Britain's manpower budget.[31] It was to no avail. The French wanted men *and* supplies, and they believed the British could provide both.

The full force of Anglo-French suspicions was revealed during the armistice negotiations with Bulgaria and Turkey. Furious that the French had agreed to armistice terms with Bulgaria without consulting the British, Lloyd George was determined to repay Clemenceau in his own coin by excluding the French from the Turkish armistice negotiations. The negotiations demonstrated that, following the collapse of the czarist and German empires, the War Cabinet identified France as Britain's most potent colonial rival. But the ministers did not perceive the French to be a real threat to Great Britain's status as a world power. By contrast, they feared that the United States might be both. Any faint hope that Woodrow Wilson might remain aloof and allow the European allies to impose their terms on the Central Powers was crushed on January 8, 1918, when he announced the Fourteen Points of his peace program.[32] Lloyd George and Foreign Secretary Arthur James Balfour publicly supported the president's program, claiming that his ideas were very similar to the British program the prime minister had announced only three days earlier. In fact, there were serious discrepancies between their proposals. Several of Wilson's points, particularly those concerned with the freedom of the seas, the future of enemy colonies, and postwar trade policy, were just not acceptable to the British.[33]

Until October, the War Cabinet agreed that the best way to maintain good relations with the United States was to avoid highlighting these disagreements.[34] But the German request for an armistice and a peace settlement based upon the president's program meant that they could no longer remain silent. Lloyd George was angry with Wilson's initial reply. He had sent it without first consulting his partners, he had made no mention of Alsace-Lorraine, and Lloyd George rejected Wilson's assumption that the United States's European partners accepted his program in its entirety. But according to Sir Rosslyn Wemyss, the First Sea Lord, the doctrine of the freedom of the seas was abhorrent because it was a "step [that] was directed absolutely against the British Navy. If it were adopted we should lose enormously in

31 Colonel Henri Rouré, Report on mission, n.d. [circa July 30, 1918], CAB 24/59/GT5277, PRO.
32 James B. Scott, ed., *Official Statements of War Aims and Peace Proposals, December 1916 to November 1918* (Washington, D.C., 1921), 237–8.
33 Arthur James Balfour to the British ambassador to the United States, Sir Cecil Arthur Spring Rice, Jan. 12, 1918, FO 800-209/478, PRO; War Cabinet, Jan. 14, 1918, CAB 23/5/WC321, PRO.
34 Lord Bertie, British ambassador to France, to Foreign Office, Jan. 10, 1918, FO 371-3435/6103, PRO; Department of Intelligence Information Bureau, Weekly report on France, Jan. 17, 1918, CAB 24/39/GT3386, PRO.

prestige, and enormously in power."[35] He remained insistent that Britain could not surrender on this point and remain a great imperial power, for "on this basis the British Empire has been founded, and on no other can it be upheld."[36] Similarly, those ministers particularly concerned with imperial questions – Lord Curzon (minister without portfolio), Edwin Montagu (secretary of state for India), and Walter Long (colonial secretary) – were determined, despite Wilson's wishes for an impartial settlement of colonial differences, that Great Britain and its dominions would retain the German colonies and Turkish possessions they had captured.[37]

But the War Cabinet also recognized that the longer the war lasted, the greater would President Wilson's ability be to bend Great Britain to his will. The United States had not hesitated to use its economic strength as a lever to force the British to comply with its wishes. In September 1917, for example, by threatening to stop further loans, they forced the British to accept the establishment of the Inter-Allied Council for War Purchases and Finance to supervise all Allied spending in the United States.[38] By threatening export embargoes, the Americans similarly forced the European allies to agree to join similar councils organizing the flow of American food to the Entente countries.[39] The creation of these bodies marked the end of Great Britain's pretensions to be the economic powerhouse of the Entente.[40] Henceforth, Great Britain could no longer exercise power over its allies through its control of allied finance.

35 Minutes of a conference held at Danny, Sussex, on Sunday, Oct. 13, 1918, CAB 24/66/GT5967, PRO.
36 Sir Rosslyn Wemyss, An inquiry into the meaning and effect of the demand for freedom of the seas, Oct. 17, 1918, CAB 24/76/GT6018, PRO; Michael G. Fry, "The Imperial War Cabinet, the United States, and the Freedom of the Seas," *Journal of the Royal United Services Institute* 110 (1965):353–5.
37 Lord Curzon, Conditions of armistice, Oct. 15, 1918, CAB 24/66/GT5980, PRO; Curzon, Basis of policy concerning German colonies and Turkish possessions, Oct. 16, 1918, CAB 23/67/GT6015, PRO; Hankey diary, Oct. 18, 1918, HNKY 1/5, Hankey papers; Edwin Montagu, The future of the German colonies, Oct. 18, 1918, CAB 24/67/GT6028, PRO; Hankey to Lloyd George, Oct. 18, 1918, LGP, F/23/3/17, HLRO; War Cabinet, Nov. 1, 1918, CAB 23/14/WC495A, PRO; Imperial War Cabinet, Nov. 5 and 6, 1918, CAB 23/43/IWC36 and IWC37, PRO.
38 David Lloyd George, *War Memoirs of David Lloyd George*, 6 vols. (London, 1938), 2:1006–8; Sir William Wiseman, memorandum on Anglo-American relations, Aug. 1917, CAB 1/25/12, PRO; Lord Northcliffe to Lloyd George, Aug. 16, 1917, CAB 24/23/GT1780, PRO; War Cabinet, Aug. 10, 1917, CAB 23/3/WC210, PRO; Curzon, Inter-Allied Council, Sept. 18, 1917, CAB 24/26/GT2065, PRO; Hankey, Inter-Allied Council, Oct. 16, 1917, CAB 24/29/GT2309, PRO; War Cabinet, Sept. 26, 1917, CAB 23/4/WC239, PRO.
39 Louise M. Barnett, *British Food Policy During the First World War* (London, 1985), 173–4.
40 Ibid., 170; Kathleen M. Burk, *Britain, America, and the Sinews of War, 1914–1918* (London, 1985), 147–8; War Cabinet, June 8, 1917, CAB 23/3/WC159, PRO; Curzon, Purchases by the European allies in the USA, June 30, 1917, CAB 24/18/GT1228, PRO; War Cabinet, July 5, 1917, CAB 23/3/WC176, PRO.

And the longer the war lasted, the more serious would be the American economic challenge in the postwar world. In August 1917, in order to prevent the British from possessing a large merchant fleet able to compete with American carriers after the war, the United States government requisitioned all merchant ships being built in American shipyards for the Allies.[41] Sir Joseph Maclay, the shipping controller, could only ruefully remark that "the United States were out for post bellum development, of which they always suspect us."[42] In the spring of 1918, Maclay's suspicions were only heightened by the American government's reluctance to transfer American merchant ships from civilian trades to transport troops bound for Europe in an effort to hasten the arrival of General John Pershing's soldiers. Maclay and others also suspected that the Americans were using their political influence in Latin America to increase their own trade at Great Britain's expense.[43] This was a matter of serious concern for the British, for the region was a major center for British foreign investment, and Great Britain's postwar economic recovery would depend in part on the wealth it could generate there.[44] During the crisis in France caused by the German spring offensive, concern for the long-term stability of the British economy took second place to the need to get every possible American soldier to France as quickly as possible. But by July, when the German offensive had been stopped, the War Cabinet agreed that it was a mistake for the British to continue to sacrifice their export trade for the sake of the American army. On August 2 the cabinet decided to reduce the tonnage allocated to the American army.[45]

The longer the war went on, the greater would be the military and economic strength the Americans could exert, and the better placed they would be to cheat Great Britain of its colonial spoils and postwar markets. In January 1918 Haig had hoped for an early peace, for if the war contin-

---

41 Burk, *Britain, America,* 161; Lord Robert Cecil to War Cabinet and enc., Aug. 20, 1917, CAB 24/23/GT1790, PRO.

42 War Cabinet, Oct. 10, 1917, CAB 23/4/WC253, PRO.

43 Edward B. Parsons, "Why the British Reduced the Flow of American Troops to Europe in August–October 1918," *Canadian Journal of History* 12 (1977–8): 177; Naval Staff, Naval weekly appreciation, Apr. 4, 1918, CAB 24/47/GT4155, PRO; Naval Staff, Naval weekly appreciation, Apr. 11, 1918, CAB 24/48/GT4219, PRO; Sir Eric Geddes, World's losses and output of merchant tonnage, May 8, 1918, CAB 24/50/GT4478, PRO; Political Intelligence Department (PID), memorandum on war trade organization in the USA, n.d. [circa Aug. 2, 1918], CAB 24/60/GT5318, PRO; Sir Albert Stanley, Naval effort, Great Britain and the US, Note, Aug. 6, 1918, CAB 24/60/GT5341, PRO; Committee of Prime Ministers, Aug. 6, 1918, CAB 23/44A/IWC28A, PRO.

44 Sir Eric Drummond to Wiseman, Mar. 6, 1918, FO 800/222/LA/1, PRO; War Cabinet, Oct. 2 and 19, 1917, CAB 23/4/WC243 and WC253, PRO.

45 War Cabinet, July 26, 1918, CAB 23/7/WC452, PRO; Hankey diary, July 26, 1918, HNKY 1/5, Henkey papers; July 26, 1918, CAB 23/43/IWC29, PRO.

ued, "America would get a great pull over us."[46] But it was the South African defense minister and member of the War Cabinet, J. C. Smuts, who was the most articulate exponent of the view that Great Britain should sign an armistice in the autumn of 1918 in order to prevent the United States from dominating the peace settlement. On October 24 he predicted that if the burden of fighting the Germans over the next few months fell upon the British because the French were exhausted and the American Expeditionary Force (AEF) was not yet ready for battle, the BEF would melt away before the treaty was signed. But

if peace comes now, it will be a British peace, it will be a peace given to the world by the same Empire that settled the Napoleonic wars a century ago. We have moved forward slowly, but now at the supreme crisis of the war we are at the height of our power; on land and sea and in the air we have the most prodigious forces of all the Allies; the great knock-out blow to the German power on the Western front has just been administered by us.[47]

If, however, the British government insisted on continuing the war into 1919, Germany might be completely devastated, but Britain "would have lost the first position; and the peace which will then be imposed on an utterly exhausted Europe will be an American peace."[48] If the fighting continued, in 1919 the United States "will have taken our place as the first military, diplomatic and financial power of the world." The British Empire had to look to its future, and ministers were urged to remember "that our opponents at the peace table will not only be our enemies; and the weaker we become through the exhaustion of war, the more insistent may be the demands presented to us to forgo what we consider necessary for our future security."[49]

Smuts also warned his colleagues that "the grim spectre of Bolshevist anarchy is stalking to the front." But in October 1918, before the armistice terms were agreed upon between the members of the Entente, few senior British policy makers believed that the need to prevent Bolshevism from spreading from Russia to Central Europe was a good reason to stop the war before the German army had been defeated. Two exceptions to this generalization were Haig and J. W. Headlam-Morley of the Political Intelligence

46 Larna S. Jaffe, *The Decision to Disarm Germany: British Policy Towards Postwar German Disarmament, 1914–1919* (London, 1985), 58; Hankey to Lloyd George, Jan. 22, 1918, LGP, F/23/2/11, HLRO; Blake, *Private Papers of Douglas Haig,* 294.
47 Jan C. Smuts, A note on the early conclusion of peace, Oct. 24, 1918, 24/67/GT6091, CAB, PRO.
48 Ibid.
49 Ibid. See also Winston Churchill, Man-power, 1918 and 1919, Sept. 25, 1918, CAB 24/65/GT5827, PRO.

Department. In mid–October the latter believed that "the danger of a collapse of society seems to me greater than that of a reassertion of the military supremacy."[50] Haig disliked the notion of fighting the war to depose the Kaiser, because to do so "would leave Germany at the mercy of Revolutionaries, and . . . if disorder started in Germany it would spread to France and Britain."[51] But at the Foreign Office, Sir Eyre Crowe cared little about the danger that a collapse of the established order in Germany might pose to Great Britain. He insisted that "we do want to weaken, if not shatter the system of government identified with the Junker regime in Prussia." Lord Robert Cecil was even more insistent that events in Germany be allowed to take their course: "I cannot imagine any conditions in which our intervention in the internal affairs of Germany would be wise."[52] Wemyss cynically dismissed talk on the part of the German armistice delegates of Bolshevism as no more than "part of their game."[53] It was not until November 10, when ministers had already agreed on their armistice terms, that they accepted the Political Intelligence Department's argument that "our real danger now is not the Bosches but Bolshevism."[54] And they preferred to counter it not by proposing lenient terms to the German government, but by confining its influence to Russia and Ukraine and by lending support to anti–Bolshevik movements in Siberia, the Caucasus, and the Baltic states.[55]

On October 26, after considering the advantages and disadvantages of ending the war in 1918 or continuing fighting into 1919, the War Cabinet decided to seek an early armistice on the grounds that the British were likely to achieve better terms sooner rather than later. Certain that if the belligerents agreed to armistice terms it would be impossible to persuade British troops to begin fighting again if the armistice broke down, the War Cabinet also agreed that it was essential that the armistice cripple Germany's ability to continue the war.[56] Great Britain had gone to war in 1914 because Germany threatened the European balance of power on land and British maritime security at sea. Consequently, it insisted that "the naval conditions of the armistice should represent the admission of German defeat by sea in

50 John W. Headlam-Morley to Tyrrell, Oct. 12, 1918, FO 371/3444/172800, PRO.
51 Blake, *Private Papers of Douglas Haig,* 252.
52 Minutes by Tyrrell, Crowe, and Cecil on Headlam-Morley to Tyrrell, Oct. 12, 1918, FO 371-3444/172800, PRO.
53 Wemyss to Balfour, Nov. 11, 1918, CAB 23/14/WC500B, PRO.
54 Callwell, *Field-Marshall Sir Henry Wilson,* 2:148; Robert Bruce-Lockhart to Balfour, Nov. 7, 1918, CAB 1/27/18, PRO; PID, The growing danger of Bolshevism in Russia, Oct. 25, 1918, CAB 24/68/GT6106, PRO.
55 Sir Eric Drummond (Balfour's private secretary), memorandum, Oct. 20, 1918, FO 800/329/Rus/18/7, PRO; Imperial War Cabinet, Nov. 6, 1918, CAB 23/43/IWC37, PRO.
56 Imperial War Cabinet, Oct. 11, 1918, CAB 23/43/IWC484, PRO.

the same degree as the military conditions recognize the corresponding admission of German defeat by land."[57] It had to preserve the domination of the Royal Navy and prevent the Germans from doing what the German High Command had hoped to do when it asked for an armistice, to secure a breathing space so that Germany could resume fighting after a few months.

The final armistice terms to be imposed on Germany and Austria-Hungary were agreed upon in a series of meetings in Paris beginning on October 29. The participants were Lloyd George; Balfour; Clemenceau; Colonel Edward Mandell House, President Wilson's emissary; and the Italian foreign minister, Baron Sidney Sonnino. On October 13 the British had already made their negotiating position clear by warning Wilson that, although they were in general agreement with his Fourteen Points and his subsequent pronouncements, the European members of the Entente had never discussed them and that furthermore some of them could be interpreted in ways that ran counter to Great Britain's own interests. Nor would they be bound by an armistice agreement that deprived them of their freedom of action at the final peace conference.[58] The ensuing discussions in Paris were all the more difficult because some of the most senior British delegates were unable to understand French. According to Wemyss, "The ignorance of French on the part of Englishmen is very deplorable; P.M. frankly ignorant – every word has to be interpreted for him. Derby ditto. Bonar Law speaking with a broad Glasgow accent. Reading translation word by word and nobody really understanding."[59] When Colonel House threatened that the United States would make a separate peace if the European Allies did not subscribe to Wilson's program, the British and French insisted that they would nonetheless continue fighting. But their united front quickly crumbled when Lloyd George accepted the president's program subject to two important provisos: the question of the "freedom of the seas" was to be set aside for further discussion at the peace conference, and the European Allies reserved the right to extract compensation from Germany for the material damage it had done to them.[60] Some of his colleagues had other reservations. When the terms being considered at Versailles were relayed to the War Cab-

---

57 War Cabinet, Oct. 26, 1918, CAB 23/14/WC491B, PRO.
58 Minutes of a conference held at Danny, Sussex, on Sunday, Oct. 13, 1918, CAB 24/66/GT5967, PRO; Hankey diary, Oct. 13, 1918, HNKY 1/5, Hankey papers.
59 Wemyss diary, Oct. 30, 1918, WMYSS 5/7, Papers of Lord Wester Wemyss, Churchill College, Cambridge.
60 Hankey diary, Oct. 29, 1918, HNKY 1/6, Hankey papers; Procès-verbal of the second meeting of eighth session of the Supreme War Council, Nov. 1, 1918, CAB 25/123/SWC350, PRO; House to Wilson, Oct. 30, 1918, in *PWW,* 51:511–12, 515–16, and 581.

inet in London, Curzon, Long, and William Morris Hughes, the Australian prime minister, expressed concern that Wilson's program left the future of the German colonial empire uncertain.[61] Hughes refused to be bound by the Fourteen Points, and Lloyd George had to work hard to reassure him that he would protect Australia's interests at the peace conference and that the German colonies the Dominions had captured would not be returned.[62]

Along Germany's eastern marches, there was never any question of allowing the Germans to retain the gains they had made since 1914. To have done so would have been to perpetuate the very German threat to Britain's Asiatic empire that the British had been fighting so hard to stem. The Germans were to be compelled to withdraw from occupied territory and retreat behind their 1914 frontiers and to abrogate the treaties of Brest-Litovsk and Bucharest. What the British could not do was make any immediate provision for who would fill the resulting vacuum. Balfour was left worrying that "as soon as the Germans left, the people in the evacuated areas would become prey to Bolshevism, as they were devoid of both Army and Police. We, therefore, ran the risk of delivering them to an even worse regime than the German, and much as they hated the Germans they might prefer their rule to that of Bolshevism."[63] In fact, the British were to be little more than interested spectators.

The armistice terms at sea and along Germany's western frontier were the target of considerably more discussion. When they came to consider with their partners the precise terms to be imposed on Germany, some British policy makers, notably Lloyd George, showed qualms about asking for too much, lest the Germans prefer continued resistance to abject humiliation. To ensure that the German army could not resume fighting if the armistice broke down, Foch insisted that it surrender 5,000 artillery pieces, 30,000 machine guns, 3,000 mortars, 2,000 aircraft, 5,000 locomotives, 150,000 wagons, and 10,000 trucks. And to enable France to secure the military frontier on the Rhine that it had long coveted, the Germans were to be required to evacuate not only all of the Allied territory they had occupied in France and Belgium, including Alsace-Lorraine, but also all territory on the left bank of the Rhine. Allied troops were to occupy the major crossing points over the Rhine together with bridgeheads of a 30-kilometer radius on the right bank. If the armistice collapsed, the Entente armies

61 War Cabinet, Nov. 1, 1918, CAB 23/14/WC495A, PRO.
62 Imperial War Cabinet, Nov. 5 and 6, 1918, CAB 23/43/IWC36 and IWC37, PRO.
63 Procès-verbal of the third meeting of eighth session of the Supreme War Council, Nov. 2, 1918, CAB 25/123/SWC351, PRO.

would be fighting on German, not French or Belgian soil.[64] At sea the Royal Navy planned to exploit the armistice terms to secure what it had failed to win by fighting. Sir David Beatty, the commander in chief of the Grand Fleet, insisted that "we have got to take the H[igh] S[eas] F[leet] either by surrender or as a result of Fleet action."[65] It was essential for Great Britain's postwar security to eliminate the German naval menace, for "the existence of the Empire depends on our Sea Power, [so] we must ensure that no Fleet in being is left which can threaten our supremacy."[66] The Board of Admiralty wanted to destroy "both the military and the naval power of Germany."[67] By August 1918 it was confident that it had overcome the submarine threat to Britain's maritime lines of communication; but it also knew of the German navy's plan to begin a new U-boat construction program and was determined to nip it in the bud.[68] On October 16 the board decided that the Germans must surrender all of their U-boats, together with ten battleships, six battle cruisers, eight light cruisers, and fifty of their most modern destroyers.[69]

As late as October 30 the General Staff in London was still receiving intelligence reports indicating that the German High Command was determined to continue resisting rather than accept humiliating armistice terms and that the German army in the west might be able to delay the knockout blow until the spring of 1919.[70] Consequently, when Sir Eric Geddes, the First Lord of the Admiralty, presented the admiralty's terms to Britain's partners on November 1, he encountered criticism, both from Foch and the politicians, including his own prime minister. They thought the terms were

64 General Ferdinand Foch, Conditions of an armistice with Germany, Oct. 8, 1918, CAB 23/43/IWC484, PRO; U.S. Department of State, *Papers Relating to the Foreign Relations of the United States: The Lansing Papers, 1914–1920* (hereafter *FRUS: LP*), 2 vols. (Washington, D.C., 1940), 1:170–1; Procès-verbal of the second meeting of eighth session of the Supreme War Council, Nov. 1, 1918, CAB 25/123/SWC350, PRO; Hankey diary, Nov. 1, 1918, HNKY 1/6, Hankey papers.
65 Sir David Beatty to Wemyss, Oct. 2, 1918, WMYSS 11, Wemyss papers.
66 Beatty to Hankey, Oct. 23, 1918, and enc., HNKY 4/10, Hankey papers.
67 Wemyss, Naval conditions of armistice, Oct. 19, 1918, CAB 24/67/GT6042, PRO; Wemyss, Memoirs, WMYSS 11, Wemyss papers; War Cabinet, Oct. 21, 1918, CAB 23/14/WC489A, PRO.
68 Geddes to Sir Edmund Allenby, Aug. 5, 1918, Admiralty papers (hereafter ADM), 116/1808, PRO; X-committee, Sept. 3, 1918, CAB 23/17/X-28, PRO; Hankey diary, Sept. 3, 1918, HNKY 1/5, Hankey papers; War Cabinet, Sept. 27, 1918, CAB 23/14/WC479A, PRO; Geddes, Some important aspects of the naval situation and the submarine campaign, Sept. 25, 1918, CAB 24/64/GT5783, PRO.
69 Wemyss, Naval conditions of armistice, Oct. 19, 1918, CAB 24/67/GT6042. PRO; Wemyss, Memoirs, WMYSS 11, Wemyss papers.
70 Sir Charles Harrington, Appreciation of the situation, Oct. 30, 1918, CAB 24/68/GT6153, PRO; Lord Kilmarnock to Foreign Office, Oct. 30, 1918, FO 371-3435/180960, PRO; Lord Acton to Foreign Office, Nov. 1, 1918, FO 371-3435/181808, PRO; Lord Kilmarnock to Foreign Office, Nov. 1, 1918, FO 371-3435/181212, PRO.

so severe that, coming on top of the military terms, the Germans would rather continue fighting than accept such humiliation. Foch agreed that the Allies should insist that the Germans surrender their U-boats but believed that it would be sufficient if the High Seas Fleet were confined to the Baltic and if the Allies occupied Heligoland and Cuxhaven.[71] Wemyss and Geddes therefore turned to Balfour to stiffen the prime minister's resolve. The foreign secretary forcefully reminded Lloyd George that, just as French interests demanded a victory on land, so British interests demanded a victory at sea. The internment of German ships might give Britain security during the armistice; but, if they were then returned to Germany, Britain would once again be locked into a naval race in the North Sea.[72]

Lloyd George procrastinated. On November 2 he decided that if Austria-Hungary surrendered, the Allies could stiffen the terms they imposed on Germany. But, if Austria-Hungary rejected the armistice, "we should have to decide whether we wished to conclude peace immediately, or whether we wished to continue fighting for another year."[73] He did not have to wait long. The Austro-Hungarians signed an armistice the next day. The Supreme War Council then agreed that the German navy must surrender 160 U-boats and agree to the internment in a neutral port – or, failing that, an Allied port – of most of its battleships and battle cruisers. Wemyss still wanted the outright surrender of the German vessels, but Lloyd George was able to calm him with the assurance that none of the interned ships would ever be returned to Germany.[74]

The German armistice was signed at 5:10 A.M. on November 11 and hostilities ended on the western front at 11 A.M.[75] Five minutes before the conclusion of hostilities the crowd outside 10 Downing Street began to sing the national anthem. It was a performance, one Unionist member of Parliament remarked, that was "politically though not musically quite satisfactory."[76] It is debatable, however, whether the terms of the German armistice

71 Wemyss diary, Nov. 1, 1918, WMYSS 5/7, Wemyss papers; Arthur J. Marder, *From the Dreadnought to Scapa Flow: The Royal Navy in the Fisher Era, 1904–1919,* vol. 5: *Victory and Aftermath (January 1918–June 1919)* (Oxford, 1970), 180–2.
72 Balfour to Andrew Bonar Law, Nov. 1, 1918, 800/201, GB FO, PRO; Balfour to Lloyd George, Nov. 1, 1918, 800/199, GB FO, PRO.
73 Procès-verbal of the third meeting of eighth session of the Supreme War Council, Nov. 2, 1918, CAB 25/123/SWC351, PRO.
74 Balfour to Foreign Office, Nov. 3, 1918, FO 371-3445/182550, PRO; Marder, *From the Dreadnought to Scapa Flow,* 5:183–4; Procès-verbal of the fourth meeting of eighth session of the Supreme War Council, Nov. 4, 1918, CAB 25/123/SWC353, PRO; Wemyss, Memoirs, WMYSS 11, Wemyss papers.
75 Wemyss to Admiralty, Nov. 11, 1918, LGP, F/47/4/7, HLRO; Wemyss diary, Nov. 8, 1918, WMYSS 5/7, Wemyss papers; Scott, *Official Statements of War Aims and Peace Proposals,* 477–83.
76 John Barnes and David Nicholson, eds., *The Leo Amery Diaries,* vol. 1: *1896–1929* (London, 1980), 243.

were politically satisfactory. They did not amount to unconditional surrender. The German army did not march into captivity. The British, therefore, left one of the tasks they had set themselves in 1914 only half completed. The abdication of the Kaiser and the proclamation of a republic on November 9 may have symbolized the destruction of Prussian militarism. But the fact that the German army could march back into Germany meant that its supreme embodiment remained partly intact. In the 1920s, right–wing propagandists could claim that the German army had not been defeated in battle. Rather, it had been stabbed in the back by the forces of democracy. It is a matter of speculation, however, whether the Weimar regime might have been able to democratize the postwar officer corps and so rob the Reichswehr of its intention and ability to organize a militarized Germany that would once again be capable of waging industrialized warfare, had the Entente invaded Germany in 1919.[77] Such an outcome would have required the political leaders who guided the destinies of the Entente powers to have demonstrated the same political sagacity as their descendants thirty years later.

This is not to suggest that the collapse of the Weimar Republic and the rise of Hitler were inevitable because the Entente failed to press home its military advantage. But it is important to recognize that it was not inevitable that the war had to end in November 1918 in the way it did. If the War Cabinet had been better informed about events inside Germany in the last week of October and the first few days of November, it might have reconsidered its decision to sign an immediate armistice. Confident that in a short time the Entente could complete the destruction of the German army, ministers might have been willing to ignore President Wilson's strictures and instead have advanced into Germany. That might have had incalculable results for the subsequent history of Europe.

However, by the time that British policy makers recognized how close to disintegration Germany had come, it was too late to reverse their decision. It was only on November 5, a day after the last wartime session of the Supreme War Council had ended, that the British began to understand that both the German Empire in central and eastern Europe and the German state itself were dissolving. On November 4 seamen's leaders combined with factory workers to establish a local soviet in Kiel. Two days later similar revolutionary organizations appeared in Hamburg, Bremen, and Lübeck. By

---

77 Manfred Messerschmidt, "German Military Effectiveness Between 1919 and 1939," in Alan R. Millett and Williamson Murray, eds., *Military Effectiveness*, vol. 2: *The Interwar Period* (Boston, 1988), 220–1; Martin Kitchen, "Militarism and the Development of Fascist Ideology: The Political Ideas of Colonel Max Bauer," *Central European History* 8 (1975): 199–220.

November 7 they had spread to many other cities in the Reich. But the first
real indication that British intelligence obtained that a revolution might soon
break out in Germany did not reach them until November 2, when an agent
employed by the British military attaché in Berne reported that soviets were
planning a revolution in Berlin and other cities.[78] And it was not until the
evening of November 5 that the admiralty's code-breakers in Room 40
began to decode signals implying that discipline had collapsed in the High
Seas Fleet. And it took another three days for the British to discover that
soviets had been organized as far apart as Bremen, Hanover, Oldenburg, and
Rostock.[79] It was this news that finally convinced Lloyd George that "the
Germans must accept them [the armistice terms] in view of our menace
through Austria, the internal conditions of Germany & the revolt of the
German fleet."[80]

A qualified success for the British, the armistice safeguarded Great
Britain's maritime supremacy and confirmed that if the German army did
resume fighting, it would do so at a distinct disadvantage and on its own
soil. The armistice also ensured that decisions on the issues of reparations
and the freedom of the seas could be postponed for what the British hoped
would be a more auspicious occasion. What it did not do was establish a new
balance of power in Europe that would promote Great Britain's postwar
interests by ensuring stability on the continent. That was something that
would have to be left to the peace conference. But it was a measure of just
how confusing British policy makers found the situation in Germany that
Henry Wilson could still inform the War Cabinet as late as November 7:
"From a purely soldier point of view [*sic*], there did not appear to be any
actual need yet for the Germans to accept the [armistice] terms."[81] In reality there was every need for the Germans to accept the Entente's terms, but
the British recognized this only after the fighting had stopped. On the day
after the armistice was signed, Sir Eric Geddes wrote ruefully to Beatty:
"Had we known how bad things were in Germany, we might have got
stiffer terms; however, it is easy to be wise after the event."[82]

78 Acton to Foreign Office, Nov. 2, 1918, FO 371/3445/182491, PRO.
79 Memorandum, Nov. 8, 1918, ADM 137/3891, PRO.
80 Phillip Williamson, ed., *The Modernization of Conservative Politics: The Diaries and Letters of William Bridgeman. 1904–1935* (London, 1988), 135.
81 War Cabinet, Nov. 7, 1918, CAB 23/8/WC499, PRO.
82 Geddes to Beatty, Nov. 12, 1918, ADM 116/1809, PRO.

3

French War Aims
and Peace Planning

DAVID STEVENSON

INTRODUCTION

This chapter centers on the negotiating position that the French government of Georges Clemenceau disclosed to its allies between December
1918 and February 1919. Because it was a negotiating position, one should
not take it at face value or assume that all its elements were advanced with
equal conviction. Its fate in the crucial sessions of the peace conference is
discussed elsewhere in this book. The purpose here is to explain the position, the reason it came into being, the concerns that shaped it, and the historiographical controversies that have revolved around it since the French
archives were opened. Perhaps the best place to begin is with a survey of the
historiography.

French policy at the peace conference was contentious from the outset
and was denounced by interwar British and American memoirists ranging
from John Maynard Keynes and Ray Stannard Baker to Harold Nicolson
and David Lloyd George.[1] It was defended by its authors, including
Clemenceau himself, and most persuasively by André Tardieu.[2] It then suffered a generation of neglect, although in the 1940s there was a riposte to
Keynes from Etienne Mantoux, and Philip Mason Burnett and Etienne
Weill-Raynal made major contributions to historical understanding of the
dispute over reparations.[3] The publication of the British minutes of the

---

I am indebted to Karen Partridge for assistance in the word processing of this chapter.

1 John Maynard Keynes, *The Economic Consequences of the Peace* (London, 1920); Ray Stannard Baker,
   Woodrow Wilson and World Settlement, 3 vols. (London, 1923); Harold Nicolson, *Peacemaking 1919*,
   new ed. (London, 1937); David Lloyd George, *The Truth About the Peace Treaties* (London, 1938).
2 Georges Clemenceau, *Grandeurs et misères d'une victoire* (Paris, 1930); André Tardieu, *La Paix* (Paris,
   1921). See also Jean Mordacq, *Le Ministère Clemenceau: Journal d'un témoin*, 4 vols. (Paris, 1930–1).
3 Etienne Mantoux, *The Carthaginian Peace, or the Economic Consequences of Mr. Keynes* (Oxford, 1946);
   Philip Mason Burnett, ed., *Reparation at the Paris Peace Conference (from the Standpoint of the American*

Council of Four and of the much fuller French minutes made possible a new and more informed consideration, which began with studies by Jere Clemens King and Harold Ira Nelson in the early 1960s. Up to that point, however, with a few exceptions such as a study by Albert Pingaud, the wartime antecedents of French policy toward Germany were wholly ignored.[4]

Since the mid-1960s the historiography has been transformed, under the dual impact of a surge of evidence and a general reorientation of debate about the international politics of the First World War and its aftermath. The archives of the relevant Paris ministries, particularly War, Commerce, and Foreign Affairs, have been made available, and the latter enriched by the return from Germany of the A "Paix" series on peace preparation. In addition to the departmental files, there are personal papers, particularly the Tardieu papers at the Quai d'Orsay, the Fonds Clemenceau at Vincennes, the papers of Etienne Clémentel at Clermont Ferrand, and the diaries of Raymond Poincaré in the Bibliothèque nationale.[5] Further evidence about French policy has been released in other national archives, particularly those of the United States, Great Britain, and Belgium, and is contained in the German Foreign Ministry documents edited by Jacques Scherer and André Grunewald.[6] The starting point for the new literature, however, was Pierre Renouvin's groundbreaking essay on French war aims published in 1966, which relied primarily on published sources.[7] Renouvin was moved to write less by the prospect of access to the archives than by the example of Fritz Fischer's study of German objectives, and he mapped out "a vast plan of research, of which I have wished here only to sketch in the canvas."[8]

Since 1966 French war aims and peace planning have indeed formed the object of an international research effort, although much of the investigat-

Delegation), 2 vols. (New York, 1940); Etienne Weill-Raynal, *Les Réparations allemandes et la France,* 3 vols. (Paris, 1947).

4 The British minutes appear in U.S. Department of State, *Papers Relating to the Foreign Relations of the United States 1919: The Paris Peace Conference* (hereafter *FRUS-PPC*), 13 vols. (Washington, D.C., 1942–7), vol. 5. For the French minutes, see Paul Mantoux, *Les Délibérations du Conseil des Quatre (24 Mars–28 Juin 1919): Notes de l'officier interprête,* 2 vols. (Paris, 1955); Jere Clemens King, *Foch Versus Clemenceau: France and German Dismemberment, 1918–1919* (Cambridge, Mass., 1960); Harold I. Nelson, *Land and Power: British and Allied Policy on Germany's Frontiers, 1916–1919* (London, 1963); Albert Pingaud, *Histoire diplomatique de la France pendant la Grande Guerre,* 3 vols. (Paris, 1938–40).

5 Published as Raymond Poincaré, *A la recherche de la paix, 1919,* ed. Jacques Bariéty and Pierre Miquel (Paris, 1984).

6 Jacques Scherer and André Grunewald, eds., *L'Allemagne et les problèmes de la paix pendant la Première guerre mondiale,* 4 vols. (Paris, 1966–78).

7 Pierre Renouvin, "Les buts de guerre du gouvernement français, 1914–1918," *Revue historique* 235 (1966): 1–37.

8 Ibid., 37.

ing has been done by French scholars. In Finland, Kalervo Hovi has reexamined French policy toward the emerging eastern European successor states;[9] in Germany, in addition to the contributions of older historians such as Erwin Hölzle and Ludwig Zimmermann, Gitta Steinmeyer has studied the economic and ideological underpinning of Clemenceau's policy, and Henning Köhler has examined French reactions to the German revolution of 1918–19.[10] In Great Britain, apart from David Watson's biography of Clemenceau and my own analysis of French war aims, Christopher Andrew and Sidney Kanya-Forstner have researched French colonial objectives, and Alan Sharp has produced a new survey of the peace conference.[11] In Canada, Michael Carley has studied French intervention in Russia, and, in the United States, Walter McDougall and Marc Trachtenberg have reappraised the Rhineland and reparations issues.[12] In France itself, Renouvin followed up his essay with a book on the armistice and several further essays, and Jean-Baptiste Duroselle provided a history of wartime France and a new Clemenceau biography.[13] Credit for the largest harvest of French research, however, goes to a younger generation of historians, mostly under Renouvin's and Duroselle's guidance, who completed and published their *thèses d'état* during the 1970s. Among the most significant were those of Pierre Miquel on French public opinion in 1919, Jacques Bariéty on postwar Franco-German relations, André Kaspi on France and the United States, and Guy Pedroncini on Pétain.[14] Particularly noteworthy is the work of Georges-Henri Soutou, most notably a reassessment in 1978 of Renouvin's original contribution and a subsequent analysis of French, German, British,

---

9 Kalervo Hovi, *Cordon sanitaire or barrière de l'est? The Emergence of the French Eastern European Alliance Policy, 1917–1919* (Turku, 1975).

10 Erwin Hölzle, *Die Selbstentmachtung Europas: Das Experiment des Friedens vor und im Ersten Weltkrieg* (Frankfurt am Main, 1975); Ludwig Zimmermann, *Frankreichs Ruhrpolitik von Versailles bis zum Dawesplan*, new ed. (Göttingen, 1971); Gitta Steinmeyer, *Die Grundlagen der französischen Deutschlandpolitik, 1917–1919* (Stuttgart, 1979); Henning Köhler, *Novemberrevolution und Frankreich: Die französische Deutschlandpolitik, 1918–1919* (Düsseldorf, 1980).

11 David Watson, *Georges Clemenceau: A Political Biography* (London, 1974); David Stevenson, *French War Aims Against Germany, 1914–1919* (Oxford, 1982); Christopher Andrew and Sidney Kanya-Forstner, *France Overseas: The Great War and the Climax of French Imperial Expansion* (London, 1981); Alan Sharp, *The Versailles Settlement: Peacemaking in Paris, 1919* (Basingstoke, 1991).

12 Michael Carley, *Revolution and Intervention: The French Government and the Russian Civil War, 1917–1919* (Kingston, Ont., 1983); Walter McDougall, *France's Rhineland Diplomacy, 1914–1924: The Last Bid for a Balance of Power in Europe* (Princeton, N.J., 1978); Marc Trachtenberg, *Reparation in World Politics: France and European Economic Diplomacy, 1916–1923* (New York, 1980).

13 Pierre Renouvin, *L'Armistice de Rethondes, 11 novembre 1918* (Paris, 1969); Jean-Baptiste Duroselle, *La France et les Français, 1914–1920* (Paris, 1972); Jean-Baptiste Duroselle, *Clemenceau* (Paris, 1988).

14 Pierre Miquel, *La Paix de Versailles et l'opinion publique française* (Paris, 1972); Jacques Bariéty, *Les Relations franco-allemandes après la Première Guerre Mondiale* (Paris, 1977); André Kaspi, *Le Temps des Américains:Le concours américain à la France en 1917–1918* (Paris, 1976); Guy Pedroncini, *Pétain: Général en chef, 1917–1918* (Paris, 1974).

and American war aims in the most massive *thèse d'état* of all.[15] The publication of Soutou's thesis in 1989 brought down the curtain on a generation
of activity, and many of the historians mentioned here have shifted their
attention to the Second World War or after, taking the rising generation of
doctoral students with them. It is a good moment, therefore, to attempt a
review.

FRANCE'S NEGOTIATING POSITION IN 1919

The French negotiating claims against Germany were presented to the
British and Americans in the opening stages of the peace conference.[16] For
clarity of exposition, they may be divided into territorial, economic, and
security elements, although this division obscures their interconnectedness.
Although the French had claims on Germany's African colonies in the
Cameroons and Togoland, the territorial starting point within Europe must
be Alsace-Lorraine, the province and a half that in 1871 they had forfeited.
The Clemenceau government successfully insisted that it be allowed to
regain Alsace-Lorraine without a plebiscite, and with the authority to expel
German immigrants and liquidate German holdings in mining and heavy
industry. The protection for minorities that qualified other territorial transfers decided at the conference did not apply here.[17] The northern frontier
of Lorraine, however, had changed on many earlier occasions, and
Clemenceau asked not for the line of 1870 but that of 1814–15, which
included two salients round Saarbrücken and Landau. The former would
give him most of the Saar coal basin, but he also wanted to occupy the
remainder of the coalfield situated beyond the 1814 line, to exploit its mines
and to incorporate the whole of the Saar into the French monetary and customs zone.[18] Farther to the north lay the German territories on the left
bank of the Rhine, which the French contended should be divided into one
or more nominally independent states, to be disarmed, made neutral, and
given their own central bank and note issue. They would be included, however, in the "Western European customs zone," and both the left bank and
the Rhine bridges would remain indefinitely under Allied occupation.

15 Georges-Henri Soutou, "La France et les marches de l'est, 1914–1919," *Revue historique,* no. 578
(1978): 341–88; Georges-Henri Soutou, *L'Or et le sang: Les buts de guerre économiques de la Première
Guerre Mondiale* (Paris, 1989). See also chapter 7 in this book.
16 The following is based on Stevenson, *War Aims,* chaps. 6–7.
17 Tardieu, *La Paix,* 768–76.
18 Meeting of Feb. 6, 1919, recorded in two undated memoranda by Tardieu, both entitled "Sarre,"
Tardieu manuscripts (hereafter MSS) 51 and 52, Ministère des Affaires Etrangères (hereafter MAE).
The Tardieu papers have been recataloged since I consulted them.

Should this program be rejected, Clemenceau and his advisers intended to demand the annexation of a glacis inhabited by one million Germans to the north of the 1814 frontier.[19]

This security system would be incomplete if it excluded the Low Countries, and the French hoped for military cooperation with Belgium, as well as closer economic integration. They supported Belgium's territorial demands on Germany and its pretensions to territory from the Netherlands, which latter would be "compensated" at Germany's expense. In Luxembourg, however, which the Belgians hoped to annex, the Clemenceau government refused Brussels a free hand. The Versailles treaty confirmed Luxembourg's departure from its prewar customs union with Germany but transferred the Grand Duchy's principal railway system from German to French control.[20]

In the remaining territorial questions, French policy moved to weaken Germany as much as possible, disregarding both a scrupulous adherence to self-determination and sometimes the wishes of Germany's neighbors: Denmark, for example, wanted less of Schleswig than Paris wished to see assigned to it.[21] Similarly, France denied the legitimacy of Austrian aspirations for union with Germany, and the peace treaty required the Germans to respect Austrian independence in the absence of a contrary decision by a League of Nations in which France would have a veto.[22] The new authorities in Prague, by contrast, wished to maintain control over the German-speakers of the Sudetenland, and as early as June 1918 the French had publicly supported the Czech National Council's desire for independence "within the historic limits of your provinces." The French conference delegates agreed that the Sudetenland was strategically and economically indispensable to the Czechoslovak republic and fended off American challenges to Czech claims on it.[23]

In September 1918 Clemenceau had made a similar public promise to the Polish National Committee that "on the day of our victory . . . France . . . will spare nothing in order to revive a free Poland corresponding to the

19 Tardieu, memorandum of Jan. 20, 1919, Tardieu MSS 49, MAE; and Feb. 25, 1919, in Tardieu, *La Paix*, 165–84. Tardieu conversation with Philip Kerr and Sidney Mezes, Mar. 11, 1919, Lloyd George papers (hereafter LGP), F/89/2/40, House of Lords Record Office (hereafter HLRO).

20 On the Low Countries, see Sally Marks, *Innocent Abroad: Belgium at the Paris Peace Conference of 1919* (Chapel Hill, N.C., 1981); David Stevenson, "Belgium, Luxemburg, and the Defence of Western Europe, 1914–1920," *International History Review* 4 (1982): 504–23.

21 David Hunter Miller, *My Diary at the Conference of Paris*, 22 vols. (New York, 1924), 10:94–6, 99ff.

22 "Note relative à l'Autriche allemande," Mar. 17, 1919, Service historique de l'armée de terre, Vincennes (hereafter SHA), 6.N.7.

23 Eduard Beneš, *Souvenirs de guerre et de révolution*, 2 vols. (Paris, 1928–9), 2:231–2. Undated meeting on Czechoslovak frontiers, Tardieu MSS 77, MAE.

latter's national aspirations and bounded by its historic limits." These limits
the French Foreign Ministry understood to be the Polish frontiers of 1772,
giving the country a broad land corridor to the Baltic at Germany's expense,
as well as the port of Danzig.[24] During the armistice negotiations the ministry tried unsuccessfully to stipulate that German forces should retreat
behind the 1772 frontier, and an interdepartmental meeting on January 29
reaffirmed support for a strong Poland with a broad land corridor as a "buttress against German expansion," although the "internationalization" of
Danzig and the corridor might, in deference to Britain and America, have
to be accepted as a second best. Farther to the south, in contrast, the French
supported Polish claims to the whole of Upper Silesia, which contained the
second largest German coalfield, and, although of mixed population, had
not been part of Poland in 1772.[25]

To territorial amputations would be added economic restrictions. The
preconference memoranda of the Finance Ministry required Germany to
make restitution in cash and in kind for the damage it had done in the occupied northeastern provinces of France. In addition, it was to reimburse the
French government for disablement and widows' pensions, and for the entire
cost of the war, as well as repaying with accumulated compound interest the
indemnity imposed in 1871.[26] In the opening sessions of the conference's
Commission on the Reparation of Damage, the finance minister, Louis-
Lucien Klotz, upheld this position. Etienne Clémentel's Commerce Ministry, on the other hand, wished to avoid large cash payments, which it feared
would fuel inflation and make French exports less competitive by depreciating the German mark. If the wartime inter-Allied agreements for pooling
raw materials could be preserved, it would demand only reparation for the
damage in the occupied regions, together with protection against dumping
and other unfair trading practices. But in the absence of such agreements it
would seek an "enormous" German debt burden, as well as coal deliveries of
up to 35 million tons annually for twenty-five years.[27] If combined with Germany's loss of the iron ore, coal, and steel of Upper Silesia, Lorraine, and the
Saar, such terms would place its heavy industry at a lasting disadvantage and
go far to redress the Franco-German imbalance that had grown up in the
prewar years.

24 Clemenceau to Zamoyski, Sept. 5, 1918, MAE Europe 1918–29, Pologne 65. G. Degrand, "Note
   pour le Ministre," Sept. 4, 1918, ibid.
25 Armistice negotiations, Nov. 2, 1918, J. de Launay, *Secrets diplomatiques, 1914–1918* (Brussels,
   1963), 132–3. Meeting on Poland, Jan. 29, 1919, MAE Europe 1918–29, Pologne 68.
26 Finance Ministry memoranda, Nov. 18 and Dec. 27, 1918, Tardieu MSS 3, MAE.
27 Commerce Ministry memorandum with covering letter, Dec. 31, 1918, F12 8104, Archives
   Nationales (hereafter AN).

Both the territorial and economic elements of the French position, then, had strategic implications. They must be considered in conjunction with the Clemenceau government's wider security demands. It did not ask that Bismarck's work be undone and German unity broken up, although it encouraged Rhenish and Bavarian separatism and unsuccessfully challenged the Weimar government's legal authority to sign the Versailles treaty.[28] It did favor drastically reducing the German army's personnel and weaponry, although Clemenceau resisted domestic pressure to disarm Germany completely, apparently in part because he feared that as a corollary the Allies would have to guarantee the country's integrity.[29] He allowed his League of Nations expert, Léon Bourgeois, to advocate a strong League, exercising surveillance over armaments and possessing a military and naval planning staff, but a League from which Germany was debarred.[30] In contradistinction to American thinking, such a body would be a disguised continuation of the wartime coalition, and in the Chamber of Deputies on December 29, 1918, Clemenceau served public notice that he still saw value in the defensive system, now condemned by "certain high authorities," of strategic frontiers, armaments, and alliances. Nonetheless, his "directing thought" in the negotiations would be that "nothing must happen which might separate after the war the four Powers that were united during it. To this unity I will make every sacrifice."[31]

THE SOURCES OF FRENCH POLICY

In large measure, the French negotiating demands had been drawn up since the fighting stopped. This is not to say that events before the armistice were irrelevant, and their influence will be considered later in the chapter. But on November 11, 1918, the French leaders knew in outline the settlement they wished for, without having reached a detailed or collective position. The program just described crystallized during the weeks that followed, and it is important to remember how it came into being. The French delegation to the peace conference comprised Clemenceau; his foreign minister, Stephen Pichon; the armaments minister, Louis Loucheur; the former high commissioner in the United States, André Tardieu; and the secretary-general of the

28 Jules Cambon, note, May 2, 1919, in "Mermeix" [G. Terrail, pseud.], *Le Combat des Trois,* 10th ed. (Paris, 1922), 168–71.
29 Tardieu, *La Paix,* 146n.
30 A. Geouffre de Lapradelle, ed., *La Paix de Versailles: La conférence de paix et la Société des nations (la documentation internationale),* 12 vols. (Paris, 1929–36), 1:169.
31 *Journal officiel de la République française, Débats parlementaires: Chambre des députés,* 1918, 3732–3 (hereafter *JO: Chambre des députés*).

Foreign Ministry, Jules Cambon. Cambon was largely a technical adviser, and Pichon, who normally behaved as a loyal subordinate of the premier, contributed little of note. Tardieu after the armistice, however, and Loucheur early in 1919, became Clemenceau's chief territorial and economic advisers, respectively. The delegation therefore included the leading French decision makers but seems not to have deliberated in a formal or collegial way. Nor did it take instructions from the Council of Ministers, which appears to have met rarely and been poorly informed, being left to register a series of faits accomplis. Poincaré, the president of the republic, whose personal relations with Clemenceau were venomous, was kept better briefed, but his contributions were liable to be brusquely rejected. In contrast, Marshall Ferdinand Foch, the Allied commander in chief, had considerable influence between the armistice and the peace conference, despite the friction that developed later between him and the premier. For all the ostensible similarity between the French and British governmental systems, Clemenceau's position was more akin to that of Woodrow Wilson than that of David Lloyd George. An embattled political veteran of seventy-eight, he was less sensitive than the American president to criticism, and found it easier to consult, but he did so among trusted intimates on conditions of his choosing and was spared Lloyd George's need to coexist with independent political heavyweights.

Clemenceau's dominance within the French elite was paralleled by relative immunity from outside lobbying. As *Père-la-victoire* – the father of victory – he enjoyed a personal prestige that only Foch might rival and commanded a dependable Chamber majority. To neither Parliament nor the press, however, did he give much of his negotiating position away. The evidence of Pierre Miquel's exhaustive survey of French public opinion is that, in most matters, the majority of the articulate public and the prime minister and his lieutenants were moving in a similar direction. There was only limited support for breaking Germany up and annexing the left bank; conversely, enthusiasm for Woodrow Wilson had cooled by February 1919, and few outside the Socialist Party would have supported him in a confrontation with Clemenceau. Over disarmament and reparations the government may have been more moderate than majority opinion seemed to be. On the Rhineland, however, its initial demands had support from Foch and Poincaré and were also in line with the prevalent unofficial view. Only after March, when Clemenceau retreated from them, did conflicts arise with Parliament and in civil–military relations.[32]

Although the French negotiating position was never consolidated in a single statement or approved by Clemenceau's cabinet, it developed in part

32 Miquel, *L'Opinion publique,* passim.

from regular position papers submitted by the Paris bureaucracy. This, as has been seen, was true of the initial economic and financial claims; colonial objectives emerged from contributions by the Colonial and Foreign Ministries. League of Nations policy, however, seems to have been delegated to Bourgeois, and that on Germany's frontiers to have been decided by Tardieu after liaison meetings with representatives of Foch, the Quai d'Orsay, and an academic study group set up in 1917, the Comité d'études. The losers in this process were the Ministries of War and Foreign Affairs, and, after Loucheur replaced Clémentel as the leading economic adviser, the Finance and Commerce Ministries were similarly marginalized. On the central complex of questions, concerning the northeastern frontier, reparations, and the security relationship with London and Washington, Clemenceau and his circle took the lead before the opening of the conference and retained it until the treaty was signed.

Tangible economic and security requirements meshed with more elusive ideological and sentimental needs. The starting point for comment on the government's approach, however, must be security, in the sense of safeguarding France against renewed attack by a neighbor that was judged inherently stronger and incorrigibly malevolent. Both axioms need fuller consideration. In population and industrial capacity, the two contestants in the war of 1870 had been approximately balanced, but since the 1890s Germany's superiority in manpower and in strategic industries had been imprinted on French consciousness.[33] The imprint was the more indelible because German strengths seemed the obverse of French weaknesses, and French commentators interpreted declining fertility and poor commercial competitiveness as the litmus of decadence and malaise. Before 1914 a European war had been expected to be one of movement, over within months, and fought with forces in being. But in the battle of attrition that had just ended, Germany's superior resources, as well as its efficiency and cohesiveness, had counted more than ever, and France unaided had no chance of matching them. With a few maverick exceptions, French official planning documents in 1914–18 lacked the hope of the integral nationalists of the *Action Française* that Germany could be repartitioned. It could be weakened, and the postwar revolutionary ferment exploited to undermine central authority; but the underlying imbalance would remain.

The second axiom pertained to German malevolence. The American administration seems at first to have seen the November 1918 revolution as

33 C. Digeon, *La Crise allemande de la pensée française, 1870–1914* (Paris, 1959), provides a discussion. See also R. Tomlinson, "The Disappearance of France, 1896–1940: French Politics and the Birth Rate," *Historical Journal* 28 (1985): 405–15.

a decisive break in Germany's development, which installed a potentially peace-loving and trustworthy regime, even if Wilson subsequently hardened his view.[34] The British were probably more skeptical, although Lloyd George believed, or said he believed, that a suitably crafted treaty might satisfy Allied needs while commanding Germany's voluntary compliance.[35] Both the U.S. and British governments feared that Germany would go Bolshevik, and wished to avoid this, Lloyd George doing so by advocating concessions at other people's expense rather than his own.[36] As for the Clemenceau ministry it was decidedly anti-Bolshevik: it obstructed efforts to negotiate a compromise with Lenin, and in December 1918 sent an expedition to Odessa as part of an ambitious strategy to overthrow him by means of military intervention and economic boycott.[37] The government took seriously the danger that the German revolution might be radicalized but seems to have viewed this as an opportunity to encourage Rhineland separatism. From the start, French statesmen suspected that the revolution was a smoke screen designed to moderate Allied terms.[38] At the peace conference they resisted arguments in favor of undercutting communism by conciliation, and Tardieu and Clemenceau emphasized the continuity between the Second Empire and its "so-called" democratic successor.[39] The Germans had not changed – they were as aggressive and unscrupulous as ever, and there was no purpose in appealing to the sense of justice of a barbarous people who respected only power and firmness. Although the ministry made overtures to Germany for economic cooperation, these were one-sided and limited. Clemenceau did not rule out all chance of an eventual partnership, but he saw it as a prospect, if at all, only for the distant future. His public warning that Versailles was a treaty of "vigilance," that would "bring us burdens, troubles, miseries, difficulties . . . for long years" faithfully reflected his private forebodings.[40]

From the premises of German malevolence and French weakness, Tardieu and Clemenceau proceeded to two possible "systems" for ensuring their security.[41] One would coerce the former enemy through the treaty's territorial, military, and economic clauses. The other would preserve the

---

34 Klaus Schwabe, *Woodrow Wilson, Revolutionary Germany, and Peacemaking, 1918–1919: Missionary Diplomacy and the Realities of Power* (Chapel Hill, N.C., 1985), 5.
35 Notably in the "Fontainebleau memorandum" of Mar. 25, 1919, reprinted in part in Lloyd George, *Truth,* 1:404–16.
36 Ibid.
37 Carley, *Revolution and Intervention,* chap. 7.
38 Köhler, *Novemberrevolution,* 324–7; Stevenson, *War Aims,* 142.
39 Tardieu, *La Paix,* 174, 176.
40 Watson, *Clemenceau,* 361.
41 Tardieu, "Note sur la conversation du 14 mars," Tardieu MSS 51, MAE.

wartime alliance as a deterrent threat to Germany, which if it invaded France would embroil itself with a coalition that had now demonstrated its superior power. The preceding outline of the French negotiating program highlights the first of these two systems, but it must be qualified by the priority Clemenceau gave to the second. The dilemma confronting him – and the weakness at the heart of the settlement – was that the two were potentially in conflict. In practice he attempted to secure as much of the first system, of direct controls on Germany, as was compatible with keeping the alliances in being.

There was nothing new for France in depending on alliances for its security. The *grande nation* of Louis XIV and Napoleon had not needed them, but the Third Republic did. Clemenceau and Poincaré remembered the years of diplomatic isolation that had followed the defeat of 1870 as well as the relief and confidence that followed the Russian alliance of 1891–94 and the Entente with Britain a decade later. France had fought better in 1914 than in 1870, but without assistance it would most likely have suffered another defeat. For the first half of the war czarist Russia had been France's principal land ally, and Nicholas II was more or less willing to endorse whatever demands French politicians chose to make on Germany, even if he had his own embarrassing demands that he expected them to approve in exchange. The spring and summer of 1917, however, were a watershed. Military and civilian morale faltered and never fully recovered; manpower neared exhaustion; and economically, as well as militarily, on both land and sea, the French war effort grew ever more dependent on foreign aid. Russia's provisional government pressed for Allied war aims to be revised, and the Bolsheviks published the inter-Allied secret treaties, expropriated French investments, and unilaterally left the war. By the spring of 1918 the French had abandoned hope that the Habsburg monarchy would break free of its alliance with Germany and replace Russia as a counterbalance to Berlin, and they looked instead to a new "eastern barrier" composed of emergent Poland, Czechoslovakia, and Romania to be established at German, Austrian, and Russian expense.[42] But neither this combination in the east nor military cooperation with Belgium in the west could substitute for the lost continental great-power ally, and it might prove as easily a liability as an asset. An even less plausible replacement for the Romanovs were the Italians, whom the French cordially disliked and whose military performance had seemed mediocre.

This left Great Britain and the United States. Until Lloyd George's Caxton Hall and Wilson's Fourteen Points speeches in January 1918 – and

42 For the fullest discussion of this point, see Hovi, *Cordon sanitaire.*

arguably not then – neither power supported publicly and unambiguously even the claim to the Alsace-Lorraine of 1870, let alone more far-reaching demands, and French diplomatic soundings gave no hint that either would endorse a Rhenish settlement that violated a strict interpretation of self-determination. While hostilities continued, Clemenceau let sleeping dogs lie; however, with the definition of his negotiating aims that followed the armistice he could do so no longer, and he appears to have succumbed to what turned out to have been wishful thinking. When Wilson arrived in Europe he seemed more manageable than had been expected, and Tardieu pointed to the possibility of eliciting an American security commitment by humoring the president over the League of Nations.[43] In London, meanwhile, at the beginning of December Clemenceau had agreed to modify the Sykes–Picot agreement of 1916 on the Middle East in order to give Mosul and Palestine to Britain, in exchange, as Tardieu later asserted, for a promise of support over the left bank of the Rhine.[44] He followed up this conversation by notifying the British, though not the Americans, of his desire for a Rhenish buffer state under international guarantee.[45] In fact, the British cabinet decided to cooperate as far as possible with Wilson rather than with Clemenceau.[46] And if the latter had expected Lloyd George's backing, by March 1919 he was disabused and bitterly resentful.[47] Dismissing as ineffective the Anglo-American blueprint for the League adopted in February, and lacking any more explicit guarantee, the Clemenceau ministry pressed its Rhenish program for all it was worth.

France's military and territorial demands must be judged within this context. Clemenceau was indifferent to his political career prospects and at liberty to disregard French officialdom. An authoritarian leader of forceful intellect, he defended his decisions by talking the language of priorities: *Gouverner, c'est choisir.* He went into the conference with his own ideas on "two or three essential points" and little patience for the remainder.[48] In this scheme of things, colonies or the League of Nations ranked low; and, over Poland, Clemenceau was willing to yield when he encountered a united Anglo-American front. He and Tardieu cast doubt on German disarmament as a safeguard, pleading that enforcement difficulties would undermine it. But they differed relatively little from the British and Americans on

---

43 "L'Opinion française et le Président Wilson," Nov. 26, 1918, SHA 6.N.137.
44 Christopher Andrew and Sidney Kanya-Forstner, "The French Colonial Party and Colonial War Aims, 1914–1918," *Historical Journal* 17 (1974): 104.
45 Earl of Derby to Arthur Balfour, Dec. 14, 1918, LGP, F/52/2/52, HLRO.
46 George W. Egerton, *Great Britain and the Creation of the League of Nations: Strategy, Politics, and International Organization, 1914–1919* (Chapel Hill, N.C., 1978), 106–9.
47 Poincaré, *Recherche,* 245; Watson, *Clemenceau,* 345.
48 Jules Cambon, "La Paix (notes inédites, 1919)," *Revue de Paris,* Nov. 1, 1937, 1.

the issue, and complete disarmament would have weakened the case for their Rhineland claim. Even over the northeastern frontier and the Anglo-American alliance, which were at the heart of Clemenceau's concerns, there was room for negotiation. For instance, the "strategic frontier" north of the 1814 line, initially proposed by Foch, became for Tardieu a fallback if the Rhineland occupation should prove unobtainable.[49] In the Saarland, Clemenceau was sentimentally attached to the 1814 frontier, but Tardieu considered it a "third-rank gain" and was willing to trade it for de facto control of the coalfield.[50] Even in Clemenceau's left-bank proposals there was an element of opportunism, and he subsequently rationalized his buffer state demand as in itself undesirable and in conflict with republican principles, but justifiable as a lever to obtain the Anglo-American guarantee of French security.[51] What mattered to Clemenceau was less the Rhineland's political separation from Germany than the Allied military presence there, and although he dropped the buffer state proposal after the guarantee was offered on March 14, five more weeks of bargaining were necessary before a separate agreement with Woodrow Wilson isolated Lloyd George in his opposition to the occupation and gave the French prime minister what he desired. While keeping the security pledge and a demilitarized 50-kilometer strip east of the Rhine, he obtained a fifteen-year Allied occupation of the left bank "as a guarantee of the execution by Germany of the present treaty," with a right of reoccupation if the treaty was not executed and a right of prolongation if after fifteen years the Allied leaders still considered France inadequately protected.[52] "Now," telephoned Clemenceau to Poincaré after striking his deal with the American president, "I consider that the peace is made."[53] If he could combine the Anglo-American alliance with an extended Rhenish occupation, Clemenceau would obtain the security "essentials" that he wanted.

French economic demands can be interpreted similarly. Trachtenberg and Soutou have shown that here, too, the French were ready to moderate their demands on Germany if their requirements could be met by inter-Allied cooperation, and France's preference for a multilateral solution over going it alone. Clémentel wanted less in reparation if Britain and America would provide cheap raw materials for reconstruction; Klotz, under severe domestic pressure, was more intransigent, but, in the negotiations among experts in March on Germany's capacity to pay, Loucheur was more will-

49 On disarmament, see Poincaré, *Recherche*, 245; on the Saar, see the Tardieu-Haskins-Mezes conversation of Mar. 11, 1919 LGP, F/89/2/40, HLRO.
50 Tardieu, "Note sur la conversation du 14 mars," Tardieu MSS 51, MAE.
51 Watson, *Clemenceau*, 353.
52 Texts agreed on Apr. 20, 1919, Tardieu MSS 49, MAE.
53 Poincaré, *Recherche*, 337.

ing than the British to consider moderate figures.[54] There were two obstacles to the triumph of a conciliatory approach, however. First, by the middle of the conference it was clear that no multinational solution was on
offer. The Americans would agree neither to continued raw material and
shipping pools nor to remission of Allied debts, and assistance during the
postwar economic transition would be brief and limited. If the French were
to redress their mountainous budget and balance-of-payments deficits, they
would be obliged to extract more from the defeated enemy. Second,
Clemenceau notoriously lacked expertise in economic questions and was
slow to impose a consistent line. Reparations mattered less to him than did
territory and security, and he instructed Loucheur to be more and less conciliatory according to the Allies' forthcomingness over the political issues.[55]
By April, however, the two had come together in his mind, and the "execution" of the treaty, which was likely to entail principally its reparation and
disarmament clauses, had become the pretext for a prolonged Rhineland
occupation. Whereas in the previous month Loucheur had seemed close to
agreement with the Americans on a low fixed sum, Clemenceau now
backed the British in including war pensions in Germany's liability, opposing the inclusion of a figure in the treaty, and overturning the previously
accepted principle of a thirty-year time limit. Keynes alleged at the time
that the French demanded reparations in order to stay in the Rhineland, and
Clemenceau told Maurice Barrès that "Germany will not pay, and we will
remain."[56] To his ministers he was still more emphatic: "I shall make a prediction: Germany will default and we shall stay where we are, with the
alliance. Remember that, so that you can remind me of it on my tomb."[57]

It might seem that French policy at the peace conference can be narrowed down to the single imperative of security against Germany, even
reparations being subordinate to this goal. The French leaders, however,
were neither so purely reactive and defensive as this suggests, nor so cere-
bral. Two days before the armistice, Clemenceau and his *chef de cabinet* at the
War Ministry, General Jean Mordacq, had conversed with Foch. "We spoke
naturally of 1870, of the revenge at last obtained, the supreme object of our
existence, the dream so often cherished."[58] Victory over Germany was a
reassertion of a national greatness that had seemed to be receding, and
Tardieu viewed the Versailles Treaty against the backdrop of 150 years of
decline.[59] It was not fortuitous that official memoranda harked back to the

54 Trachtenberg, *Reparation*, 59–60.
55 Watson, *Clemenceau*, 348.
56 Ibid., 354.
57 Bariéty, *Relations*, 62.
58 Mordacq, *Ministère Clemenceau*, 2:345–6.
59 Tardieu, *La Paix*, 423.

Revolution and the Napoleonic Empire, when France had occupied its "natural frontiers" and supposedly fought as the champion of the national principle. Clemenceau and his advisers sought not only to deter and weaken Germany but also to reinvigorate their own country and help it grow. Thus, although they dropped their claim to the 1814 frontier, they hoped a French administrative and economic presence in the Saarland would allow them to win the region permanently in the plebiscite scheduled in fifteen years.[60] Clemenceau and Pichon supported Foch's efforts to use the occupation to encourage separatism on the left bank, particularly by promoting Franco–Rhenish trade.[61] And Clemenceau told a delegation from the Senate, "In reality, we shall occupy until the country is willing to unite itself with France."[62] In other words, even if the premier doubted the feasibility of a buffer state or annexation now, a French occupation, which would neutralize the Prussian and Bavarian administrations in the region, would keep open possibilities for expansion in the long run. Similarly, in Luxembourg, as has been noted, the French took control of the main railway system, and the local French commander was censured when he protected the Grand Ducal government against an insurrection.[63] In the economic sphere, Versailles might enable France to overtake Germany as the leading continental European industrial center, provided the transitional problems created by the reabsorption of Alsace-Lorraine could be surmounted successfully. Clemenceau's warning that the treaty was one of vigilance thus contained an exhortation as well as an admonition. "The treaty . . . will only be worth what you are worth; it will be what you make it." The occupation, he told Lloyd George, was essential to nurture the "will power" of the French people while they rebuilt their ruins. It was a shield behind which vital forces could revive. If the French failed to produce more children, he warned the Chamber, it would be useless. It gave them an opportunity to arrest their long-term relative decline, but there was no guarantee that they would succeed in doing so.[64]

THE PROBLEM OF CONTINUITY

This exposition of Clemenceau's negotiating program may shed some light on the two main historiographical debates arising from the new research on French war aims and peace planning. The first concerns wartime objectives,

60 "Note sur la question de la Sarre," Mar. 29, 1919, in Tardieu, *La Paix*, 294–6.
61 Bariéty, *Relations*, 44–5.
62 Alexandre Ribot, *Journal d'Alexandre Ribot et correspondances inédites, 1914–1922*, ed. A. Ribot (Paris, 1936), 259.
63 Report by General Roques, Feb. 8, 1919, SHA 6.N.148.
64 Watson, *Clemenceau*, 352, 361.

on which the balance struck between the reactive and assertive elements of French policy has a bearing. Fritz Fischer has argued that Berlin exhibited a "monolithic" continuity in its wartime objectives, and that those objectives were consistent with policy before the First World War, and even, perhaps, with policy in the Second. Furthermore, he finds that Germany's expansionist consensus united civilians and the military with the unofficial "war-aims movement" in the political parties, the business community, and the academic world.[65] The French situation, Renouvin contends, was quite different: France was far more cautious and less consistent in its aims. France's wartime governments, Renouvin notes, were more reserved than the general population, and "in the present state of historical research, it therefore seems that the restitution of Alsace-Lorraine without a plebiscite was the sole claim on Germany to be continuously asserted by the French Government between August 1914 and November 1918."[66] In fact, he says, France had not even attempted to define its war aims before July 1916; then by January 1917 it had adopted an extensive program that included annexing the Saar coalfield and establishing independent states on the left bank; but "from March 1917 and until the very last weeks of the conflict it limited its ambitions," even if individual parliamentarians and statesmen continued to support wider objectives.[67]

Soutou provides a rather different interpretation:

The Rhineland was not a fleeting preoccupation for the French leaders: it was at the heart of their reflections on the country's political, economic, and strategic future from the beginning of the war. The whole of the political, administrative, and military class was in agreement from the autumn of 1914 that the simple return of Alsace-Lorraine would not suffice to modify fundamentally in Paris's favor the Franco-German imbalance. Naturally, it was necessary first to win: but one is rightly struck by the continuity [*permanence*] of the war aims, despite the variations in the military position.[68]

To some extent Soutou stands Fischer on his head. The consistency and ambition of French economic objectives, and the degree to which government policy reflected the concerns of unofficial pressure groups, Soutou argues, make Allied, and especially French, economic war aims appear more purposeful and aggressive than those of Germany. By implication, the French negotiating program at the peace conference was the latest manifes-

---

65 Fritz Fischer, *Germany's Aims in the First World War* (London, 1967).
66 Renouvin, "Buts de guerre," 35–6.
67 Ibid., 2.
68 Soutou, "Marches de l'est," 387.

tation of ambitions that extended back unbroken to the first months of the war.[69]

Soutou's corrective to Renouvin's preliminary interpretation is largely justified. Other writers, such as Köhler, have echoed it.[70] The problem, as Renouvin and Soutou both concede, is partly one of definition and emphasis. "War aims" are elusive entities, predicated on the assumption of military success, some negotiable in a compromise solution, others absolute goals to be conceded only in utter defeat. Moreover, what constitutes official government "policy" may not coincide with the personal and private aspirations of statesmen and bureaucrats. Alsace-Lorraine, which was repeatedly demanded in ministerial statements and incorporated in Chamber and Senate resolutions in June 1917, was unambiguously an official objective, although its northern frontier remained undefined, as were the economic aims agreed at the inter-Allied Paris conference in 1916 (though never ratified by all the signatories) and the public undertakings given by Clemenceau in 1918 to the Czechs and Poles. The status of French wartime policy toward the Saar and Rhineland, however, rests largely on the interpretation placed on the Cambon letter of January 2, 1917, a confidential dispatch to Paul Cambon, the French ambassador in London, from Aristide Briand, the premier and foreign minister, and on the secret Doumergue agreement, concluded with the czar by Briand's minister of colonies, Gaston Doumergue, and approved by the prime minister in March 1917.

During the first two years of the war, unofficial publicists and political and economic associations had called for territorial expansion beyond the frontier of 1871, and many officeholders, including Poincaré and Briand, had sympathized with them. In 1915 the Russian government had given, or so the Quai d'Orsay supposed, a blank check for France to demand whatever it chose on Germany's western borders, which Doumergue's mission was to fill out.[71] Until 1917, however, no written diplomatic agreement about the northeastern frontier was negotiated, and the Council of Ministers gave no collective endorsement to more than Alsace-Lorraine. Both Briand and Poincaré had hinted publicly that "guarantees" of French security would be needed beyond that, a codeword that indicated the direction of their thinking but whose significance was not clarified.[72] However, the Cambon letter, which was approved by most of Briand's cabinet, called for Alsace-Lorraine with its frontier of 1790 (marginally more extensive

69 Soutou, *L'Or et le sang*, 847–9.
70 Köhler, *Novemberrevolution*, 190–1.
71 Stevenson, *War Aims*, 27; Soutou, "Marches de l'est," 348–9.
72 Stevenson, *War Aims*, 17; Soutou, "Marches de l'est," 359.

than that of 1814) and for an end to German sovereignty over the left bank. "Neutrality" and "provisional occupation" were envisaged for the region, but a reference in an early draft to buffer states was omitted and the central demand was that in settling the question France must have the "preponderant voice."[73] The Doumergue agreement, in contrast, envisaged "at the very least" the 1790 frontier, including the entire Saarland, and autonomous left-bank states that France would occupy until the peace treaty had been executed in full, Russia's "complete liberty to fix its western frontiers" being recognized in return.[74] The Cambon letter, which asked essentially for a free hand, matched the spectrum of opinion among Briand's ministers, who ranged from moderate socialists to conservative annexationists, better than did the Doumergue agreement. If the cabinet had been consulted over the latter, it is doubtful that they would have approved it. Nonetheless, when Briand's successor, Alexandre Ribot, examined the dossier in May 1917, he decided that despite the overthrow of Nicholas II in the interim the French government remained bound, and it was the Bolsheviks who eventually repudiated the accord.[75]

The similarity between the Cambon letter, the Doumergue agreement, and Clemenceau's and Tardieu's negotiating program is clear. Both of the earlier documents were kept in the Foreign Ministry files and were read out in the secret sessions of the Chamber and the Senate in June 1917. The Doumergue agreement was one of the secret treaties published by the Bolsheviks and reprinted in the Western press. Allowing for minor discrepancies (for example, between the 1790 and 1814 frontiers), there is powerful prima facie evidence here for continuity between French war aims and peace conference planning. The evidence to the contrary is twofold. First, official planning on economic, colonial, and eastern European questions has left a continuous archival trail from Briand through the Ribot and Painlevé ministries in 1917 to Clemenceau, but such a trail does not exist for the northeastern frontier. Second, certain episodes in 1917–18 – particularly the secret committee of the Chamber of Deputies in June 1917, the French reaction to the Fourteen Points, and the armistice agreement – suggest the policy of the Cambon letter and Doumergue agreement had been repudiated. Closer inspection, however, reveals this repudiation to be largely a matter of appearances.

Neither Ribot in 1917 nor Clemenceau and Pichon in 1918 abandoned the coded language of "guarantees." Nor did the Chamber and Senate res-

73 Aristide Briand to Paul Cambon, Jan. 12, 1917, Pichon MSS 4, MAE.
74 Exchange of letters between Maurice Paléologue, French ambassador to Russia, and Nikolai Pokrovsky, Feb. 14, 1917; Briand to Alexander Izvolsky, Mar. 10, 1917, A "Paix" 164, MAE.
75 Ribot to Albert Thomas, French special representative in Petrograd, May 20, 1917, ibid.

olutions of June 1917. Although the Chamber denied that France intended to "conquer" foreign populations, Ribot told the Senate that a neutral and autonomous buffer state between France and Germany "cannot be considered a conquest: it is a protective measure." In the course of the debates, he criticized the "rigidity" of the Doumergue agreement and indicated that he might be willing to abandon it but made no such criticism of the Cambon letter.[76] In any case, the Bolshevik takeover nullified the Doumergue agreement, but in the Chamber on December 17, 1917, Pichon continued to stand on the June resolutions.[77] After the Fourteen Points address he told the Chamber that "all the Allies' declarations are in accord" and that the 1870 frontier was all the ministry wanted.[78] The government quickly followed this, however, by bidding unsuccessfully for an Allied commitment to seek more solid "guarantees" than the Central Powers' signatures could provide.[79] As victory approached, French public pronouncements continued to be restrained, but in September 1918 Pichon acknowledged to Poincaré that he hoped for the frontier of 1790 and the neutralization of the left bank of the Rhine.[80] There is little doubt, in other words, that the French leaders still aspired to more than the Alsace-Lorraine of 1870; during the emergency created by the Treaty of Brest-Litovsk and General Erich Ludendorff's Western Front offensives they were biding their time.

All the same, Pichon's reference to left-bank neutralization rather than autonomy betrays the hiatus in official planning between 1917 and the armistice. Even after the ceasefire, an "Examination of the Conditions of Peace" approved by Clemenceau and presented by the ambassador in London to the British on November 26, 1918, envisaged a prolonged occupation of the left bank but no change in its political status.[81] It was only in the following month that Clemenceau unveiled his buffer-state scheme. To this extent, although Tardieu was evidently cognizant of the wartime context, he was making a fresh start when he pulled together the French negotiating position. This conclusion bears on the final wartime antecedent that needs to be considered: the armistice. For when Germany laid down its arms on November 11 it ostensibly did so on the basis of the Lansing note, an undertaking by Britain, France, and Italy, as well as Germany and America, to make peace, with two reservations, upon the lines set out in the Fourteen Points and President Wilson's later speeches. The discrepancies between this

76 Stevenson, *War Aims*, 69–70; Soutou, "Marches de l'est," 370–2.
77 *JO: Chambre des députés*, 1917, 3626–31.
78 Ibid., 1918, 39–44.
79 Drafts by Pichon and Clemenceau, Jan. 27 and 28, 1918, Pichon MSS 4, MAE.
80 Poincaré, *Au service de la France: Neuf années de souvenirs*, 10 vols. (Paris, 1926–33), 10:336.
81 "Examen des conditions de paix," Nov. 26, 1918, FO 371/3446, PRO.

peace program and the treaty signed seven months later loomed large in interwar polemics.

Germany's request to Wilson for a cease-fire and a peace based on his program took the French government by surprise, at a moment when its aims on the northeastern frontier had still to be precisely defined. Clemenceau was willing to negotiate rather than reject the approach outright, but he was slow to perceive the implications of the armistice clauses for French objectives, and, when he agreed to a proposal by Lloyd George that Germany should evacuate Alsace-Lorraine and the left bank, he did not insist that Allied forces should replace them.[82] It was Foch's intervention that led to French insistence on the occupation of the left bank of the Rhine and of bridgeheads east of the river. The cease-fire clauses, in the marshal's words, must "put in our hands sureties that will guarantee that in the peace negotiations we obtain the conditions that we wish to impose upon the enemy . . . [T]he only definitive territorial sacrifices will be those conceded by the enemy when the armistice is signed."[83] Clemenceau and Pichon confirmed that "the necessary guarantees of the peace must have *points d'appui* in the clauses of the armistice."[84] From the start, therefore, the occupation of the Rhineland, though masquerading as a technician's solution, betrayed the French authorities' renewed concern with "guarantees" and their willingness to modify the region's political status. This was immediately suspected by Lloyd George, but the American negotiator, Colonel Edward Mandell House, failed to support the British premier's challenge to Foch's proposals. Given that the French authorities expected troop movements on the ground to anticipate the peace settlement, and that the armistice gave Clemenceau control over what would be one of his main peace conference objectives, his acceptance of the Lansing note takes on a different coloring. Clemenceau had no love for the American program, which he considered dangerously vague, but when Lloyd George abandoned resistance to it he followed suit, probably assuming that with the acceptance of Foch's military clauses he was conceding nothing of significance.[85] Indeed, for two months after the armistice the French continued to behave as if the Fourteen Points could be ignored, and only in January 1919 did they confirm that they accepted Wil-

82 Minutes of Paris Conference, Oct. 7, 1918, F. Rés. 16313, Dossiers Mantoux, Bibliothèque internationale et contemporaine, Nanterre.
83 Foch to Clemenceau, Oct. 16, 1918, in Foch, *Mémoires pour servir à l'histoire de la guerre de 1914–1918,* 2 vols. (Paris, 1931), 2:276–8.
84 Pichon to Clemenceau, Oct. 21, 1918, and Clemenceau to Foch, Oct. 23, 1918, in René Lhopital, *Foch, l'Armistice, et la Paix* (Paris, 1938), 33–9.
85 Stevenson, *War Aims,* 125–7.

son's program as the peace conference's terms of reference.[86] It made little difference to their subsequent conduct.

CONCLUSION

To recapitulate: although the French 1919 program of territorial, economic, and security objectives against Germany appears drastic and comprehensive, Clemenceau and his advisers were willing to compromise on much of it in exchange for continuing inter-Allied economic cooperation and an Anglo-American security guarantee. Apart from German disarmament and the return of the Alsace-Lorraine of 1870, which his negotiating partners did not contest, his leading concerns were an extended Rhenish occupation and continuing means of influence over the Saarlanders' political allegiance. French policy, however, was not merely security-conscious and defensive, but included elements of anti-German imperialism fired by a conviction of cultural superiority and memories of historic greatness. Had it not been for the imperative to reach agreement with London and with Washington, these undercurrents would have flowed more freely. Although there is little evidence of similar imperialist designs on Germany in the foreign policy of the Third Republic during the generation before the war, demands for expansion at Germany's expense quickly surfaced after war broke out, and at the beginning of 1917 they were incorporated into official policy. Thereafter, although there was continuity in planning in most aspects of French war aims, there was an interruption in planning for the northeastern frontier, not because France had renounced its goals but because the diplomatic and military terrain was temporarily unfavorable for progressing toward them. The pace of official preparation, however, was quickening even before the unexpected advent of the armistice negotiations galvanized ministerial planning. Although there was a break in bureaucratic continuity between the Rhineland program of 1917 and that of 1919, the similarity between the two was no accident.

The remaining and more speculative problem raised in the new historiography is that of the appropriateness of French solutions to the German question. The Clemenceau government achieved its objectives at the peace conference less completely than did the British and suffered major disappointments over inter-Allied cooperation. Nonetheless, it got much of what it wanted. It was sidelined over the League of Nations Covenant, which it

86 Tardieu note of Jan. 5, 1919, in Tardieu, *La Paix,* 97–101.

viewed as secondary, but did well in the commercial, financial, and disarmament clauses. It took the initiative in, and defined the terms of, the negotiations over Germany's frontiers, even though it made substantial concessions over Poland, the Saar, and the left bank of the Rhine. Hence the French negotiating program set the agenda for much of European politics between the wars, and liberal critics of the settlement condemned French influence as pernicious. Only recently, and in the light of the more enduring settlement with Germany after 1945, has it been argued that French policy offered better prospects for European stabilization than did its British and American rivals.[87]

There is a danger of anachronism here. Comparisons with the settlement after 1945 are intellectually stimulating, but they are made with hindsight. The intellectual and political universe inhabited by Clemenceau and Loucheur differed in many ways from the one familiar to Robert Schuman and Jean Monnet. The 1919 leaders had never known a peaceful partnership with a united Germany, even one so precarious as that of the 1920s, and they seem not to have expected it in their political lifetimes. Total war had forced them into unprecedented international cooperation and made them favor sweeping impositions on German sovereignty, but they had no intention of accepting comparable impositions on themselves. So far from envisaging friendship and equality with Germany, Clemenceau distinguished himself from British and American leaders in his stark acceptance of the need for a continuing exercise of power. If French policy is judged more likely than British or American to have achieved an eventual partnership and Germany's willing self-limitation, this reflects an assessment of its probable objective consequences rather than its authors' subjective intentions.

A frequent starting point for criticism of the Versailles Treaty, nonetheless, is Jacques Bainville's aphorism that it was "trop douce pour ce qu'il y a de dur" – too gentle for what is in it that is harsh.[88] It fell between the stools of repression and conciliation, with the result that it first inflamed German nationalism and then failed to protect Europe from the consequences. This approach is superficially attractive, but it falls short on two counts. First, the treaty did cripple Germany militarily, and even in 1933, as Hitler recognized, it was incapable of waging war successfully against a country such as Poland, let alone a major power. The critical failure came not in 1919 but in the abandonment of the disarmament clauses fifteen years later, admittedly, in part, because of the erosion of the Versailles enforcement clauses and of French

87 See, especially, Walter A. McDougall, "Political Economy Versus National Sovereignty: French Structures for German Economic Integration After Versailles," *Journal of Modern History* 51, no. 1 (1979): 4–23.
88 Miquel, *L'Opinion publique*, 404.

political will during the years between the Ruhr occupation and the Great Depression. Second, if the post–1945 experience is relevant, however, its lesson is that both coercion *and* conciliation were needed to resolve the "German question," as well as to effect a transformation of German mentalities and social structures much more thorough than that of 1918–19. The Soviet Union failed in the Berlin blockade crisis to prevent the creation of the Federal Republic and later failed to prevent its limited rearmament, but for forty years it maintained Germany's division and occupation, and subjected it to far more draconian territorial losses than those envisaged by Clemenceau. Unlike France a generation earlier, it was an independent enforcing agent, which had no need of British and American cooperation. The economic rehabilitation and democratic political stabilization of the western half of the former Germany proceeded on the basis of a heightening of the country's vulnerability and a dramatic weakening of its power.

In contrast to Stalin, who may have wanted a united, communist-dominated Germany but settled for a divided one, French governments after 1945 began, if anything, with harsher demands than Clemenceau but after 1947–8 reoriented their policy toward rapprochement with West Germany on favorable terms. By the mid-1950s they had found one, although probably conceding more coercive powers in the process than they would have preferred. It was only the Cold War, and the greater Anglo-American acceptance of continental involvement that it elicited, that allowed the Franco-German conflict to be so transcended, and it may yet be that Franco-German rapprochement will fail to survive the Cold War's end. In the interwar period also, American economic involvement (the Dawes loan) and British political involvement (the Locarno guarantee) were required to blunt the edges of Franco-German antagonism; and the resurgence of American and British isolationism in the early 1930s helps explain the disasters of the following decade. Probably what was required in 1919 was a combination of financial leniency toward Germany and strictly enforced security clauses. Such a combination, however, was unrealizable without continuing cooperation among the victors. At the peace conference, Clemenceau had no vision of German stabilization and no strategy for achieving it. Although his government pursued closer economic and political integration with the Rhineland and the Low Countries, it had no interest in supranational solutions. He did perceive, however, that the German problem required not a firefighting operation but a long haul, and that a successful settlement would be neither cheap nor self-regulating. On the contrary, it would require continuing inter-Allied solidarity and effort in both the economic and security spheres. It was this perception, for a time at least, that went down to defeat.

4

Wilsonian Concepts
and International Realities
at the End of the War

THOMAS J. KNOCK

In coming to grips with the international realities at the end of World War I, a few preliminary observations about "Wilsonian concepts" are in order. That term can mean many things, of course; but at its core sits the League of Nations idea. If this is the shorthand sum and substance of Wilsonianism, it should be pointed out that the League idea had many authors and that the concept was in a constant state of metamorphosis. Wilson's most important contributions to it were grand synthesis and propagation.

At a fairly early stage in the war, a new internationalist movement had come into being in the United States. This movement consisted of two divergent aggregations of activists – "progressive internationalists" and "conservative internationalists." Wilson's relationship with each group was consequential, but fundamentally so with the progressive internationalists.[1] Among other things, the genesis of that relationship has important implications not only for Wilsonian concepts and international realities at the end of the war, but also for the domestic political struggle of 1919–20. As Gilbert Hitchcock, the Democratic leader in the Senate, declared at the start of the great debate over the Treaty of Versailles, "Internationalism has come, and *we must choose what form the internationalism is to take.*"[2] No one ever put the matter more succinctly.

Conservative internationalism was first advanced systematically in June 1915, by the founders of the League to Enforce Peace (LEP). Led by former president William Howard Taft and other Republicans prominent in the

---

1 For an extended discussion, see Thomas J. Knock, *To End All Wars: Woodrow Wilson and the Quest for a New World Order* (NewYork, 1992), 48–69.
2 *Congressional Record* (hereafter *CR*), 65th Cong., 3d sess., Feb. 27, 1919, 4414–18.

field of international law, the LEP's platform, "Warrant from History," called
for American participation in a world parliament that would assemble periodically to make appropriate changes to international law and employ arbitration and conciliation procedures to settle certain kinds of disputes. While
more or less endorsing the general principle of collective security, most conservative internationalists also believed that the United States should build
up its military complex and reserve the right to undertake independent coercive action whenever the "national interest" was threatened. The LEP did
not concern itself with self-determination; nor did it advocate disarmament
or even a military standoff in Europe. These internationalists were openly
proAllied; in fact, the slogan, "The LEP does *not* seek to end the present war,"
appeared on its letterhead in the autumn of 1916.[3]

Progressive internationalism was different in both subtle and conclusive
ways. Like its conservative counterpart, progressive internationalism
evolved within the context of American neutrality – coincidentally, during
an extended interlude in American political history when many liberal
reformers and many American socialists seemed to agree on more things
than they disagreed on. Frederick Jackson Turner once called the Progressive Era "the age of socialistic inquiry."[4] It was an apt description. Beginning in 1914, and continuing roughly into the first months after the United
States entered the war, Wilson regularly sought the counsel and political
support not only of progressives outside the Democratic Party, but also of
individuals and groups of pronounced leftist tendencies. His communion
with the American Left, as well as with the liberal Left, exerted a profound
impact on his foreign policy – especially on the League movement. Moreover, organizations such as the Woman's Peace Party, the American Union
Against Militarism, and various elements of the Socialist Party of America
made up the most intellectually vital part of the historically crucial left-of-
center coalition that elected Wilson to a second term in 1916. These groups
were at once the advance guard of the so-called New Diplomacy in the
United States and the impassioned proponents of an Americanized version
of social democracy. From this heady welter emanated most of the salient
components of Wilson's blueprint for a new world order (and for a program
for social and economic justice at home).[5]

3 The major study is Ruhl Bartlett, *The League to Enforce Peace* (New York, 1944); but see also Sondra
   Herman, *Eleven Against War: Studies in American Internationalist Thought, 1898–1921* (Stanford, Calif.,
   1969), 24–33 and 64–5. The quotation is from C. Roland Marchand, *The American Peace Movement
   and Social Reform* (Princeton, N.J., 1972), 157.
4 See Turner's 1891 essay, "The Significance of History," republished in Fritz Stern, ed., *The Varieties of
   History: From Voltaire to the Present* (New York, 1957), 197–208.
5 The literature on early twentieth-century peace movements, pacifism, and internationalism is quite
   large; for an introduction, see Charles Chatfield, *For Peace and Justice: Pacifism in America, 1914–1941*

For progressive internationalists, the search for a peaceful new world order provided a logical common ground. Peace was indispensable to change itself – to the survival of the labor movement, to its campaigns on behalf of women's rights and the abolition of child labor, and to social justice legislation in general. If the war in Europe were permitted to rage on indefinitely, they believed, then the United States could not help but get drawn into it; not only their great causes, but also the very moral fiber of the nation would be destroyed should its resources be diverted from reform to warfare. During the "preparedness controversy" of 1915–16, progressive internationalists helped to steer Wilson toward the conclusion that the reactionary opponents of domestic reform and the advocates of militarism, imperialism, and balance-of-power politics were twins born of the same womb.[6]

Wilson won the enthusiastic support of most liberals, a large bloc of socialists, and of many in between, when, on the eve of his reelection campaign in 1916, he pushed through Congress an impressive array of social justice reforms. In addition to appointing Louis Brandeis, the "people's lawyer," to the Supreme Court, Wilson secured measures to restrict child labor and to establish the eight-hour day for railroad workers, the first such federal legislation of its kind; he signed into law a Revenue Act, a progressive income tax weighted heavily against corporations and the wealthy; he not only kept the country out of war but also proposed membership in an international organization that he hoped to see bring about disarmament among the great powers; and he won the public endorsement of Jane Addams, Max Eastman, John Reed, and Mother Jones! On Election Day, large numbers of Socialists and former Bull Moose Progressives swelled the normal Democratic vote for president; the returns suggested that a left-of-center coalition, with Wilson as its pivot, held the balance of political power in the United States.[7]

Wilson cemented the alliance with progressive internationalists, however, by drawing together the strands of their thought on foreign policy and by focusing world attention on the idea of a league of nations during the campaign of 1916. According to Amos Pinchot, the deeper meaning of his victory was unmistakable. "The President we reelected has raised a flag that

(Knoxville, Tenn., 1971); Warren F. Kuehl, *Seeking World Order: The United States and International Organization to 1920* (Nashville, Tenn., 1968); and Marchand, *American Peace Movement.*

6 See, e.g., an account of Wilson's meeting with a delegation from the Socialist Party of America, in January 1916, in Morris Hillquit, *Loose Leaves from a Busy Life* (New York, 1934), 160–2; and a transcript of a White House colloquy with a delegation from the American Union Against Militarism, on May 8, 1916, in Arthur S. Link et al., eds., *The Papers of Woodrow Wilson* (hereafter *PWW*), 69 vols. (Princeton, N.J., 1966–94), 36:634–48; and another account by Max Eastman, "The Masses at the White House," *The Masses* 8 (July 1916), 16–17.

7 See Knock, *To End All Wars*, 85–104.

no other president has thought or perhaps dared to raise," he submitted. "It is the flag of internationalism." And it was at this juncture that the League began to take on a strongly ideological and partisan complexion, a development that owed in part to the failure of conservative internationalists to secure even a vague endorsement of their position in the Republican party platform. The LEP's regrettable omission, in tandem with Wilson's campaign slogan, "He Kept Us Out of War," allowed the Democrats to lay claim to the League idea.[8]

Shortly afterward, the broader concept of "Wilsonianism" itself was born. Fortified by reconfirmation at the polls, the president decided on a bold stroke. In a climactic attempt to end the war, he went before the Senate, on January 22, 1917, and called for "peace without victory." In this manifesto, for the first time, Wilson launched a comprehensive, penetrating critique of European imperialism, militarism, and balance-of-power politics – which were the root causes of the war, he said. In their stead, he held out the promise of a "community of nations" – a new world order sustained by procedures for the arbitration of disputes between nations, a dramatic reduction of armaments, self-determination, and collective security. The chief instrument of this sweeping program was to be, of course, the League. Thus Wilson began his ascent to a position of central importance in the history of twentieth century world politics.[9]

The peace without victory formulation met with an unprecedented outpouring of praise from progressive groups at home and abroad. Even so, the governments of both warring coalitions in Europe still hoped for a decisive victory and either ignored the speech or greeted it with contempt. Then, a week later, Germany announced the resumption of unrestricted submarine warfare, beginning on February 1, 1917. By the end of March, Wilson had concluded that war had thus been thrust upon the United States. In his war address, however, he said that his goals were the same as before and implied that Americans would be fighting to establish some measure of "peace without victory," a program attainable now, apparently, only through the crucible of war.

In exchange for American belligerency, Wilson did not impose any conditions on the Allies; in light of their self-aggrandizing territorial ambitions, then, considerable divergence in avowed purposes remained unreconciled as Congress voted on the war resolution. Though a day of reckoning was inevitable in any case, the problem would soon become exceedingly vexa-

8 Theodore Roosevelt would not permit Taft such an interposition. See Bartlett, *League to Enforce Peace*, 56–60.
9 See "Peace Without Victory Address," in *PWW*, 40:533–9; and Knock, *To End All Wars*, 111–15.

tious owing to epochal upheavals in Russia. By the end of 1917, the Bolshevik leaders, Vladimir Lenin and Leon Trotsky, had pulled their ravaged nation out of the war. They thereupon issued proclamations on behalf of a democratic peace based on self-determination and summoned the peoples of Europe to demand that their governments – the Allies and the Central Powers alike – repudiate plans for conquest. (Their program was not unlike the "peace without victory" formulation.) To tell the unholy lie on Allied war aims, the Bolsheviks also published the secret treaties to which Nicholas II had been a party. Shortly afterward, Russian representatives engaged the Central Powers in peace negotiations at Brest-Litovsk. For all practical purposes, Russia had left the war.[10]

Many progressive groups within the Allied countries were now experiencing grave doubts about their governments' motives. In the circumstances – not the least of which being the Allies' persistent disinclination to embrace ideologically progressive war aims – Wilson really had no choice but to respond to the Bolshevik challenge. In his Fourteen Points address of January 8, 1918, the most celebrated utterance of his presidency, he reiterated much of the anti-imperialist "peace without victory" formula and once again made the League of Nations the capstone. He also argued, against Lenin's entreaty to stop the war, that German autocracy and militarism must be crushed first, before humanity could set about the task of creating a new and better world. Wilson's endeavor to remove the suspicions hanging over the Allied cause and rally doubting liberals and socialists to see the war through to the bitter end succeeded magnificently. The popular approbation that greeted the Fourteen Points in both Europe and America approached phenomenal proportions. (Even Lenin hailed the address as "a great step ahead towards the peace of the world.") But as before, the Allied *governments* declined to endorse or comment on Wilson's progressive war aims.[11]

At the same time, Wilson's own immediate priorities at home had inexorably shifted toward the exigencies of war mobilization. And, in part owing to stinging Republican criticism of "peace without victory" and, later, the Fourteen Points as the basis for the postwar settlement, he refused to discuss his plans for the League in any concrete detail throughout the period of American belligerency. He also neglected to lay essential political groundwork for it at home. By the autumn of 1918, important segments

---

10 For these developments, see George F. Kennan, *Russia Leaves the War* (Princeton, N.J., 1956), 16–26, 71–84, and 92–3; and Arno J. Mayer, *Political Origins of the New Diplomacy, 1917–1918* (New Haven, Conn., 1959), 78–80, 167–8, 245–66, 278–80, and 315–24.

11 See Wilson's Fourteen Points Address, in *PWW*, 45:534–9; Knock, *To End All Wars*, 142–7; Lenin quoted in Mayer, *Political Origins of the New Diplomacy*, 373.

among both conservative and progressive internationalists had grown disenchanted with Wilson, albeit for entirely different reasons.

This development would prove to be as unfortunate as the partisan opposition led by the president's arch-nemeses, Theodore Roosevelt and Henry Cabot Lodge. For example, Wilson grievously offended Taft by frustrating the wartime efforts of the League to Enforce Peace and other conservative internationalists, who wanted to make formal plans for the League in cooperation with the British government. (There were, of course, serious ideological differences between his and Taft's conception of the League, but Wilson might have found a way to use the Republican-dominated LEP to defuse some of the incipient senatorial criticism.)[12]

Perhaps just as consequential, Wilson failed to nurture the left-of-center coalition of 1916, a dynamic political force that, if it had remained intact, might have made it possible for him to secure and validate American leadership in a peacekeeping organization intended to serve progressive purposes. But he began to lose his grip on his former base of support as a tidal wave of anti-German hysteria and superpatriotism swept over the country in 1917–18. Sanctioned by federal legislation, innumerable acts of political repression and violence were committed practically everywhere against not only German-Americans, but also pacifists and radicals. (To cite but one, and perhaps the most famous, example, Eugene Debs, the Socialist leader, was sentenced to ten years' imprisonment for making a speech against American participation in the war.) The majority of progressive internationalists steadfastly supported the war effort, but they could not countenance such patent violations of basic First Amendment rights, for which, ultimately, they held the president responsible. Because he acquiesced in the suppression of civil liberties, Wilson himself contributed to a gradual unraveling of the coalition of 1916.[13]

The circumstances surrounding the congressional elections of autumn 1918, coupled with Germany's coincident request for an armistice, greatly compounded the larger problem. By late summer, the Republicans had launched a fiercely partisan, ultraconservative campaign against the Democrats and the Wilsonian peace plan. This time around, endorsements on behalf of the administration by leading progressives outside the Democratic party hardly matched those of the 1916 contest. Even so, the centralization of the wartime economy and the core of Wilson's foreign policy placed him far enough to the left to make all Democrats vulnerable to Republican charges that they were "un-American."

12 Knock, *To End All Wars*, 126–8 and 149–51.
13 For a discussion, see ibid., 131–7 and 157–60.

Senator Lodge struck the keynote on August 23. Because Germany faced almost certain defeat, the time had come to state precisely the kind of peace that all patriotic Americans desired. "It cannot be a peace of bargain," Lodge declared on the floor of the Senate. "The only peace for us is one that rests on . . . unconditional surrender. No peace that satisfies Germany in any degree can ever satisfy us. . . . [We] must go to Berlin and there dictate peace." Roosevelt, for his part, was no less ardent in echoing Lodge's theme at every opportunity, even going so far as to liken Wilson's leadership to "fighting the Civil War under Buchanan."[14] Undoubtedly, fate and the American political calendar rendered the timing of Max von Baden's overture of October 6 exceedingly inauspicious.

In any case, Wilson approached the proposition of an armistice with the reserve of both a victorious leader and a would-be mediator. What he was still striving to achieve was some practicable measure of "peace without victory" – a settlement that "would prevent a renewal of hostilities by Germany yet . . . be as moderate and reasonable as possible."[15] As he stepped upon this narrow crossing, Wilson was at last confronted head-on by the contradictions of fighting a common enemy for reasons significantly different from those for which the Allies were fighting. His speeches on progressive war aims – in many ways, as much arraignments of the Allies as of the Central Powers – surely had a penetrating, if delicate logic to them; but, until now, the implications of that logic had been sedulously avoided by all diplomatists concerned.

Moreover, to arrive at the point where his speeches might have practical application had required "force without stint or measure," as Wilson himself had declared during the war. The very act of girding the sword had sanctioned for some nineteen months the incessant portrayal of the enemy as the most evil and autocratic power the world had ever known and had created a political environment that allowed no variance. If he hoped to achieve a settlement based on the Fourteen Points and a league of nations, Wilson had also somehow to quell, or satisfy, the demands of the American public and the Allied governments that Germany acknowledge military defeat and political bankruptcy. That this was the case was made abundantly clear after October 6, both in the debates that took place in the Senate and in the numerous diplomatic communications that flashed between Washington and the Allied capitals.

14 See *CR*, 65th Cong., 2d sess., 9393–4. See also William C. Widenor, *Henry Cabot Lodge and the Search for an American Foreign Policy* (Berkeley, Calif., 1980), 280–7. On Roosevelt, see Seward Livermore, *Politics Is Adjourned: Woodrow Wilson and the War Congress, 1916–1918* (Middletown, Conn., 1966), 212.
15 Wilson to Edward M. House, Oct. 28, 1918, *PWW*, 51:473.

Republican Senator Miles Poindexter, inspired by fears of a "compromise peace," initiated debate in the upper house on October 7. "The only condition of an armistice ought to be an allied victory," he said. "Anything else would be approaching in a degree the betrayal of the great cause for which we are fighting, and would be action along the line of what the Bolsheviki of Russia perpetrated in a larger degree." Poindexter also said he counted on Clemenceau and Lloyd George "to protect their countries and ours from the results of any such unwise step." He commended not fourteen terms, but one, for an armistice – "unconditional surrender."[16]

No one was surprised that Lodge, too, rose at this time to demand a peace of retribution. More illuminating for Wilson, however, were the comments of several Democrats. "A wide pathway of fire and blood from the Rhine to Berlin should be the course our Army should take," declared Henry F. Ashurst of Arizona, "and when our armies have reached Berlin, . . . the German Government will be told what the peace terms will be." After other Democrats expressed similar views, Senator Hitchcock, chairman of the Committee on Foreign Relations, acknowledged that a suspension of hostilities just now was "absolutely abhorrent" to the sensibilities of the entire chamber.[17]

Wilson read portions of this debate aloud to Colonel Edward M. House on the following day. "He did not realize how war mad our people have become," House noted, nor the extent to which the country was "against anything but unconditional surrender."[18] Yet, Germany had turned to Wilson because he had promised some degree of fairness. He could not, of course, dismiss the possibility that Germany's request for an armistice represented a devious feint; but neither could he responsibly let pass the opportunity to end the war without testing the enemy's sincerity.

Thus, in a noncommittal reply on October 8, he sought to ferret out Germany's true intentions. Before entering into actual negotiations, his note said, the president first must have assurances that the German government accepted the terms of his Fourteen Points. Second, he could not propose a cessation of hostilities until the German armies had evacuated Allied territory. And finally, by asking whether the imperial chancellor was speaking "merely" for those who had conducted the war, Wilson implied that he would deal only with a civilian ministry.[19]

Initial Republican reaction could almost be predicted. Lodge cited Ulysses S. Grant as the example whom Wilson should emulate in dealing

16 See *CR*, 65th Cong., 2d sess., 11155–8.
17 Ibid., 11158–63.
18 Diary of Edward M. House, Oct. 9, 1918, in *PWW,* 51:278.
19 For the text, see Secretary of State Robert Lansing to Friedrich Oederlin, the Swiss chargé d'affaires, Oct. 8, 1918, in *PWW,* 51:268–9.

with a defeated foe. Roosevelt dismissed the diplomatic exchange as "an invitation to further note-writing" apt to hamper the advance to Berlin. Senator Poindexter said that any peace based on the Fourteen Points would be tantamount to the Allies losing the war.[20] Yet Wilson's detractors were temporarily countered by sober journalistic commentary, particularly in some Republican newspapers, and by the absence of criticism in the Allied press. For instance, the Chicago *Tribune* (no admirer of Wilson) praised the "masterly skill with which he parried the German thrust." Even so, the administration's most dependable editorial supporters believed that Wilson must demand the Kaiser's abdication as the minimum condition of peace.[21]

As for Allied opinion, the London *Westminster Gazette* affirmed that Wilson "fulfills the hopes and expectations of the Allies in Europe." In Paris, the *Journal des Débats* emphasized that Wilson's question about who spoke for Germany was "a blow in the Kaiser's face."[22] On the golf links outside Paris, Lloyd George and Robert Cecil read the note apparently with such equanimity that they saw no reason not to finish their game.[23] From the British Foreign Office, Lord Reading sent the following communication to Washington: "The President's message in answer to Germany has been extremely well received here."[24]

Nonetheless, many leading Democrats seemed as apprehensive as the Republican leadership. What, they wondered, would Wilson's next step be? On October 14, Senator Ashurst requested an audience at the White House. The Senate, the press, and the people all expected "that you demand an 'unconditional surrender' of the German armies," he said to the president. "If your reply should fail to come up to the American spirit, you are destroyed." Could it be, Wilson rejoined, that the people did not remember the Fourteen Points and the League? "I am thinking now only of putting the US into a position of strength and justice. I am now playing for 100 years hence." As for his being destroyed, he said, "I am willing if I can serve the country to go into the cellar and read poetry for the remainder of my life." Wilson's assurances failed to comfort. If he came up short of unconditional surrender, Ashurst warned, "the cyclone of the people's wrath" would, indeed, force him into the cellar.[25]

By this juncture, Wilson realized that he could no longer hold all the cards in his own hand. For one thing, despite Lord Reading's agreeable message,

20 See *CR*, 65th Cong., 2d sess., Oct. 10, 1918, 11171–2; *New York Times*, Oct. 12, 1918; and "The President's Reply and the People's Reply," *Literary Digest*, Oct. 19, 1918, 7–8.
21 *Literary Digest*, Oct. 19, 1918, 8–9.
22 Quoted in ibid., 10.
23 Henry F. Hollis to Wilson, Oct. 11, 1918, in *PWW*, 51:298.
24 Reading to Sir William Wiseman, Oct. 10, 1918, in *PWW*, 51:295.
25 Ashurst diary, Oct. 14, 1918, in *PWW*, 51:338–40.

the Allies were voicing legitimate concerns. Before he answered the German response of October 12, the prime ministers of Great Britain, France, and Italy conveyed to him their unanimous judgment: measures must be taken to prevent Germany from fortifying its defensive position; the terms of the armistice must square with the recommendations of Allied and American military and naval experts – and, in this, the Germans could have no say.[26] Wilson personally vouchsafed to French Ambassador Jean Jules Jusserand that he understood these concerns perfectly well. A German evacuation was "only a condition to be met, so that one could *speak* of an armistice," he said.[27] All the same, the Allies remained uneasy, for Wilson also told Sir Eric Geddes that "undue humiliation [of Germany] would be inexcusable."[28]

Wilson sent a second note to Berlin on October 14. Though far from a demand for abject surrender, it conformed to the wishes of the Allies and reflected the mood of American public opinion. The conditions of an armistice were matters to be determined exclusively by Allied military advisers; neither the Allies nor the United States could accept any arrangement that did not guarantee the military supremacy of their armies in the field. The note closed by implying that the whole process of peace would depend upon the further democratization of Germany.[29]

Wilson's sharper tone received nearly unanimous approval on both sides of the Atlantic. As one of his advisers commented, when the text was read in the Senate, "it spoiled everything that had been said all day long by everybody." Even Lodge hesitated to criticize it.[30] For the same reasons, the note fell heavily in Berlin. Wilson had not only rejected the "mixed commission" to supervise the evacuation of Belgium and France; he was also presuming to interfere in Germany's internal affairs. A defiant response, however, was not a practical alternative. Germany's military position had further disintegrated and political conditions teetered on the brink of revolution. More-

26 See, e.g., Cecil's three telegrams (all on October 9) to the British embassy in Washington, D.C., in *PWW,* 51:288–90; Lloyd George to Sir Eric Geddes, Oct. 12, 1918, in *PWW,* 51:313; Reading to Wiseman, Oct. 12 and 13, 1918, in *PWW,* 51:313–14 and 324–5; Balfour to the British chargé (two telegrams), Oct. 14, 1918, printed as enclosures with Lansing to Wilson, Oct. 14, 1918, in *PWW,* 51:334–6.
27 See Jusserand's account of this interview, printed as an enclosure with J. J. Jusserand to C. A. de R. Barclay, Oct. 11, 1918, in *PWW,* 51:307–9.
28 Geddes to Lloyd George, Oct. 13, 1918, in *PWW,* 325. See also Wiseman to Reading and Drummond, Oct. 13, 1918, in *PWW,* 328.
29 See Lansing to Oederlin, Oct. 14, 1918, in *PWW,* 51:333–4. For a discussion of the drafting process, see House diary, Oct. 15, 1918, in *PWW,* 51:340–2. See also Klaus Schwabe, *Wilson, Revolutionary Germany, and Peacemaking, 1918–19: Missionary Diplomacy and the Realities of Power* (Chapel Hill, N.C., 1985), 50–5.
30 Memorandum by Homer S. Cummings, Oct. 20, 1918, in *PWW,* 51:392. For a review of opinion in the American and Allied press, see *New York Times,* Oct. 15, 1918; and *Literary Digest,* Oct. 26, 1918, 14–16.

over, Max von Baden took some solace in the first sentence of Wilson's note, which had finally acknowledged the sincerity of his government's acceptance of the Fourteen Points. Thus a third German note, dispatched on October 20, capitulated to Wilson, trusting that he would "approve of no demand which would be irreconcilable with the honor of the German people." In addition, the Germans gave assurances that fundamental constitutional reforms were under way – the choosing of a Reichstag through universal franchise, for example. The request for an armistice, then, came from a government "free from arbitrary and irresponsible influence . . . [and supported by] the overwhelming majority of the German people."[31]

Two days later, the British foreign secretary conveyed an admonitory message to Wilson. The German note still assumed "an undisturbed retreat," Balfour wrote, which would give the enemy the opportunity to reorganize defenses should some diplomatic impasse arise. The evacuation of France and Belgium was not enough. Any armistice must contain absolute guarantees against a resumption of hostilities, and that end could be attained only by providing for Allied occupation of some enemy territory and preventive measures against German naval warfare.[32]

On the afternoon of October 22, Wilson called his cabinet together. According to Franklin K. Lane, the secretary of the interior, the president appeared "manifestly disturbed" as he described Senator Ashurst's visit and alluded to his second note to Germany, pointing out that it "had no pacifism in it." Now he had not only to respond again, but also to decide whether to recommend to the Allies the commencement of formal negotiations.[33]

Only Postmaster General Albert Sidney Burleson counseled unconditional surrender. William Gibbs McAdoo, secretary of the treasury, countered by saying that the United States could not finance the war indefinitely; it would be a terrible responsibility to carry on if the war could be ended on the president's terms and the Allies made secure by ironclad guarantees against a renewal of hostilities. William B. Wilson, secretary of labor, observed that the press clamored for "all kinds of punishment for the Germans, including the hanging of the Kaiser"; but, in his opinion, labor "opposed war for what imperialistic England desired." Secretary Lane then emphasized the risk of calling for an armistice over Allied objections; this

31 The complete text is printed in *Correspondence Between the Governments of the United States and Germany, October 23, 1918* (Washington, D.C., [1918]), 5–6. For a discussion of the German decision, see Harry R. Rudin, *Armistice 1918* (New Haven, Conn., 1944), 133–65; and Schwabe, *Wilson, Revolutionary Germany, and Peacemaking*, 55–8.
32 Telegram from Balfour, Oct. 21, 1918, conveyed to Wilson on Oct. 22, in *PWW,* 51:411–12; see also Rudin, *Armistice 1918,* 168–70.
33 Memorandum by Franklin K. Lane, Oct. 23, 1918, in *PWW,* 51:413–14.

would amount to coercion, he said. The president replied that the Allies "needed to be coerced, that they were getting to a point where they were reaching out for more than they should have in justice."[34] David F. Houston, secretary of agriculture, agreed. As Germany's collapse appeared to be imminent, the Allies simply would "have to be held in check."[35]

Two hours of discussion seemed to confirm Wilson's misgivings about unconditional surrender. If his next note embodied Balfour's latest communication, then no one could accuse him of not being alive to the security concerns of the Allies. At the same time, by endorsing the German request for sounding leading to an armistice – that is, the commencement of negotiations to discuss the application of the Fourteen Points – the Allies could then be "held in check." If Wilson accepted the Allies' basic *military* terms, then, would they not at last have to accept his *political* terms, especially if Germany accepted a Wilsonian compound of both sets of conditions?

Wilson cabled Berlin on October 23. His note reiterated the German government's previous assurances about his terms for peace. It also contained Balfour's proviso that the armistice must leave the Allies "in a position to enforce any arrangements that may be entered into and to make a renewal of hostilities on the part of Germany impossible." Finally, Wilson required further guarantees that he was dealing with "the veritable representatives of the German people who have been assured of a genuine constitutional standing." It was his duty to say that if the United States must continue to deal with Germany's military masters, "it must demand, not peace negotiations, but surrender."[36]

Simultaneously, Wilson transmitted to the Allies all of his correspondence with the Germans, along with his recommendation that formal negotiations with the enemy begin at once. Germany would not respond to the third American note for almost a week; already, however, Colonel House was on his way to Paris for direct talks with Lloyd George, Clemenceau, and Vittorio Emmanuele Orlando, the Italian premier. The question remained as to whether the president had gained the essential and irreducible leverage that would give him the opportunity to resolve the monumental political conundrums of the war to end war. The key seemed to lay in an armistice itself, or, put another way, in removing the serpent's fangs without actually destroying the beast. Keeping the German state intact (even as it underwent fundamental political reform) would prolong the

<hr>

34 Ibid., 415.
35 David F. Houston, *Eight Years with Wilson's Cabinet, 1913–1920*, 2 vols. (New York, 1926), 1:316.
36 See Wilson to Lansing, with enclosures, Oct. 23, 1918, in *PPW,* 51:416–19. For the German government's reaction, see Schwabe, *Wilson, Revolutionary Germany, and Peacemaking,* 95–117.

Allies' material reliance upon the United States throughout the entire process of peace. Moreover, an armistice based on the Fourteen Points would invigorate European liberals and the moderate Left. That, too, could provide leverage. An unconditional "peace without victory" was perhaps no longer a possibility, but, neither was an unconditional surrender.

At this juncture, Colonel House vied for center stage, in an ornate salon in the Trianon Palace, at Versailles.[37] Into this, the most exacting test of his career, he carried no specific instructions. "I feel you will know what to do," the president had said as his emissary departed.[38] Indeed, the colonel well understood his paramount task – to get the Allied governments formally to adopt the Fourteen Points. "If this is done," his diary entry for October 28 reads, "the basis for the peace will already have been made."[39] The Allied prime ministers and foreign secretaries, also, understood this to be the case. None of them was unmindful of the plain fact that Germany was suing for peace based on the Fourteen Points; should they fail now to obtain specific reservations, they would be bound permanently to Wilson's program.

On October 27, Clemenceau presented House with a draft armistice prepared by Marshall Ferdinand Foch. It included the following recommendations: the surrender by Germany of 35,000 pieces of heavy artillery and machine guns, 5,000 locomotives and 150,000 railroad cars, and 160 submarines; the internment of its entire surface fleet; the evacuation of all invaded countries; and the occupation by Allied and American forces of the left bank of the Rhine and the establishment of bridgeheads on the right bank.[40]

In the ensuing discussions, the main source of acrimony, in keeping with American priorities, proved to be the president's famous address, rather than the military condition of the armistice per se. During House's first meeting with the Allied statesmen, on October 29, Clemenceau claimed unfamiliarity with the Fourteen Points and said that Wilson had never solicited his opinion of them. "I have never been asked either," Lloyd George added disingenuously.[41] House then produced a detailed commentary on the

37 The most detailed studies of these negotiations are Inga Floto, *Colonel House in Paris: A Study of American Policy at the Paris Peace Conference, 1919* (Copenhagen, 1973; reprint, Princeton, N.J., 1980), 38–60; Schwabe, *Wilson, Revolutionary Germany, and Peacemaking*, 81–94; Arthur Walworth, *America's Moment, 1918: American Diplomacy at the End of World War I* (New York, 1977), 32–73; and Rudin, *Armistice 1918*, 177–92 and 266–319. Charles Seymour, ed., *The Intimate Papers of Colonel House*, 4 vols. (Boston, 1926–8), 4:89–200, is an indispensable published source (hereafter *IPCH*).
38 *IPCH*, 4:88.
39 House diary, Oct. 28, 1918, in *IPCH*, 150–1.
40 See House to Wilson, Oct. 27, 1918 (No. 2), in *PWW*, 51:463. Foch's memorandum, dated Oct. 26, 1918, is in *IPCH*, 4:143–5; all of his conditions would be incorporated into the armistice virtually without alteration.
41 *IPCH*, 4:162.

address that Walter Lippmann had prepared the night before.[42] Lloyd George stopped at Point Two. In no circumstances, he declared, could Great Britain accept "freedom of the seas," a doctrine that impinged upon his country's chief means of defense. When the French and Italians compounded this objection by voicing scepticism about the League of Nations, House warned that President Wilson might be compelled to conclude a separate peace with the Central Powers.[43]

House had not misspoken. Wilson, upon receiving his report of the day's interchange, cabled that the exclusion of "freedom of the seas" would mean the substitution of British navalism for German militarism. "Neither could I participate in a settlement which did not include league of nations," he went on, "because peace would be without any guarantee except universal armament which would be intolerable. I hope I shall not be obliged to make this decision public."[44]

Lloyd George had meanwhile worked out a solution, couched in the language of compromise, and showed a draft of it to House moments before their meeting with Clemenceau on the following morning. The British government would make peace with the enemy on the president's terms, subject to two reservations. First, the question of "freedom of the seas" must be deferred until the peace conference. (Should he herein concede more, he claimed, he would be forced to resign "in a week's time.") And, second, Germany must make compensation for all damage it had inflicted upon Allied civilians and their property.[45]

The revised British position, though hardly a retreat, struck House as reasonable. However, it soon appeared that the French and the Italians were preparing their own list of reservations. If they persisted, House announced, he would have to advise the president to lay before Congress all of their conditions, not to mention the prospect of having to continue the war in order to fulfill them. Unlike the previous threat, Lloyd George and Clemenceau seemed to take this one seriously. With amazing suddenness, the French premier yielded, ostensibly because of the prevailing Anglo-American unity as well as House's ultimatum. That evening, House notified Wilson of the

42 The so-called Cobb-Lippmann memorandum is in House to Wilson, Oct. 29, 1918, in *PWW,* 45:495–504. See also Ronald Steel, *Walter Lippmann and the American Century* (Boston, 1980), 149–50.
43 See House to Wilson, Oct. 30, 1918 (no. 8), in *PWW,* 51:511–13; see also Rudin, *Armistice 1918,* 266–71; and Floto, *Colonel House in Paris,* 50–1.
44 Wilson to House, Oct. 30, 1918, in *PWW,* 51:513. See also Wilson to House, Oct. 29, 1918, in *PWW,* 51:504–5.
45 The British memorandum is in House to Wilson, Oct. 30, 1918 (no. 12), in *PWW,* 51:515–16. See also Wilson to House, Oct. 31, 1918, and House to Wilson, with enclosure, Nov. 4, 1918 (no. 41), in *PWW,* 51:533 and 569–70.

breakthrough and recommended that he accept the British proposal together with Foch's terms for the military settlement.[46]

By virtue of their dissent, House believed that the Allies had undercut their own ability to challenge Wilson any further. "I am glad the exceptions were made, for it emphasizes the acceptance of the Fourteen Points," the Colonel wrote in his diary.[47] With the final draft of the armistice in hand, he sent word, on November 5, that "a great diplomatic victory" had been won, telling his chief that he doubted whether the Allies "realize how far they are now committed to the American peace programme."[48]

House's contribution to the so-called Pre-Armistice Agreement remains a historical ambiguity. Klaus Schwabe and Inga Floto have argued that he won Allied acceptance of the League and the remaining eleven points only at considerable cost — that is, in the trade-off with Lloyd George and, more important, in his endorsement of Foch's plan to occupy the Rhineland. (Floto speculates that Clemenceau had secretly offered to abandon opposition to American war aims in exchange for House's support of French security interests, in particular, Allied occupation of the Rhineland. The theory is certainly plausible, and it perhaps best explains Clemenceau's sudden turnabout.)[49] But the Allies thereby gained a stranglehold on Germany that weakened Wilson's future bargaining position. Schwabe has characterized House's "victory" as "at best, a partial one," while Floto maintains that he "failed miserably."[50]

Without question, Colonel House paid too little attention to the military aspects of the negotiations. Even so, it was not House's alleged bungling, but, rather, the unanticipated collapse of the German state and the onset of revolution after the armistice that snapped the diplomatic lever Wilson hoped to use against accelerating Allied demands. Moreover, the president himself, in his determination to make the Fourteen Points the basis of peace, pursued a strategy that emphasized the political over the military dimensions of the armistice. To be sure, on October 28, he had cautioned House that "too much success or security on the part of the Allies will make a genuine peace settlement exceedingly difficult if not impossible." And, in a dispatch to Gen-

---

46 House to Wilson, Oct. 30, 1918 (no. 12), in *PWW,* 51:515–17.

47 House diary, Nov. 4, 1918, *IPCH,* 4:188.

48 House to Wilson, Nov. 5, 1918, in *PWW,* 51:594. For a detailed discussion of the actual drafting of the armistice terms, see Rudin, *Armistice 1918,* 285–319.

49 See Schwabe, *Wilson, Revolutionary Germany, and Peacemaking,* 90–2; and Floto, *Colonel House in Paris,* 44–7, 53. Keith L. Nelson apparently was the first scholar to analyze House's performance along these lines, in "What Colonel House Overlooked in the Armistice," *Mid-America* 51 (Apr. 1969): 75–91.

50 Schwabe, *Wilson, Revolutionary Germany, and Peacemaking,* 92 (see also 94); and Floto, *Colonel House in Paris,* 60. Arthur S. Link, *Woodrow Wilson, Revolution, War and Peace* (Arlington Heights., Ill., 1979), 87–8, basically agrees, but is not nearly as harsh in his assessments.

eral John Joseph Pershing, the commander of the American Expeditionary
Force, on the same day, he doubted the advisability of taking up positions
east of the Rhine, "as that is practically an invasion of German soil."[51] But
never again, in his ten subsequent cablegrams to House, did the president
question Foch's terms, much less make an issue out of them.

In considering the efficacy of both Wilson's and House's diplomacy at the
end of the war, it is also important to note that Great Britain and France
had suffered, respectively, some 900,000 and 1.4 million battle deaths – or
forty-seven times as many as the United States. Unlike Roosevelt and
Lodge, who seemed to yearn to spill blood on German soil, the Allied
statesmen were acutely sensitive to the hazards of confronting a wounded
animal, of demanding unconditional surrender from a flagging enemy perhaps still capable of a *levée en masse*. On this issue (albeit for different reasons), the Allies were as one with Wilson, and he quickly discerned it once
the negotiations got under way.

Only in the provision for bridgeheads east of the Rhine did Foch expand
the general scope of Wilson's third note to Berlin. Of all the subjects that he
addressed in his cables, however, Wilson maintained comparative silence on
the Rhineland occupation. (Even Lloyd George worried over the severity
of this condition.) But then, as House reported, Clemenceau had given "his
word of honor that France would withdraw after the peace conditions had
been fulfilled."[52] In these circumstances, Wilson evidently did not consider
a *temporary* occupation unwarranted – not if the Allies were willing to comply in the main with the Fourteen Points and the League. All things considered – not least his domestic difficulties – Wilson, and House in his stead,
had not, perhaps, done so badly.

Meanwhile, the congressional campaign (which would turn out to be
more important than most presidential elections in American history) had
entered its most intense phase. That Wilson was virtually demanding Germany's submission to Allied military terms impressed few Republicans. On
October 22, Senator Poindexter submitted a resolution to make it "unlaw-
ful" for the president to enter into negotiations "before such time as the
German armed forces shall have surrendered to the allied nations," on pain
of impeachment if he did not observe this stricture.[53] On October 24,
Theodore Roosevelt, in a published telegram to Lodge, Poindexter, and
Hiram Johnson (Republican senator from California), urged the Senate to

---

51 Wilson to House, Oct. 28, 1918, and Peyton C. March (Army chief of staff) to Pershing, Oct. 27
    1918, enclosure with N. D. Baker to Wilson, Oct. 28, 1918, in *PWW,* 51:473 and 471–2, respectively.
52 See House to Wilson, Oct. 30, 1918, in *PWW,* 51:516.
53 Poindexter, quoted in the *New York Times,* Oct. 22, 1918.

demand Germany's unconditional surrender and to "declare against the adoption in their entirety" of the Fourteen Points which, he said, held the potential to bring about "the conditional surrender of the United States."[54]

Most historians maintain that Wilson, in countering the Republicans' attacks, committed the worst blunder of his presidency – by making an ostensibly partisan appeal to the public to maintain the Democrats' control of Congress.[55] Whether or not the results constituted a response to his request for a vote of confidence, November 5 transformed Democratic majorities in the House and Senate into Republican majorities of forty-five and two, respectively; Wilson's opponents could now claim that he stood repudiated.

Although the election created new and formidable obstacles to American participation in the League of Nations, it did not, at this point, necessarily render the League a lost cause. Nor was the campaign responsible for making the League a partisan issue; that, as already mentioned, had occurred some time ago. The election of 1918 was the tentative resolution (if not the climax) of a sequence of events set in motion in 1915–16, at the very inception of the progressive internationalist movement – in the politics of neutrality and preparedness and, especially, in the forging of the Wilsonian victory of 1916.

Yet one thing was clear. Whether the midterm elections might be explained away by local and regional issues, or as the consequence of Wilson's appeal to the voters, most progressive internationalists believed that this turn of events owed something, one way or another, to the giant wrecking machine called "One Hundred Percent Americanism." George Creel of the Committee on Public Information (to cite but one of many entreaties to Wilson) had no doubts about the veracity of this interpretation. "All the radical, or liberal friends of your anti-imperialist war policy were either silenced or intimidated," he told the president. "The Department of Justice and the Post Office were allowed to silence and intimidate them. There was no voice left to argue for your sort of peace. The Nation and the Public got nipped. All the radical and socialist press was dumb." The situation was not utterly hopeless, but there was only one way to repair it. "The liberal, radical, labor and socialist press will have to be rallied to the President's support. You will have to give out your program for peace and reconstruction and find friends for it. Otherwise, the reactionary patrioteers will defeat the whole immediate future of reform and progress."[56] Thus, unless

---

54 Roosevelt to Lodge, Oct. 24, 1918, printed in the *New York Times,* Oct. 25, 1918.
55 For a discussion, see Knock, *To End All Wars,* 178–81.
56 Creel to Wilson, Nov. 8, 1918, in *PWW,* 51:645–6. For other examples, see Knock, *To End All Wars,* 185–7.

he was prepared to take steps to revitalize his once-ascendant coalition, the new configurations on Capitol Hill would simply overwhelm him.

As for other realities, across the Atlantic, it is worth mentioning that, among most of the war-weary peoples of Europe, the Fourteen Points had acquired the status of sacred text, and the word "Wilson" was now becoming something more than simply the name of a president. Italian soldiers were placing his picture in their barracks. An old woman said she heard that in America "there was a great saint who was making peace for us."[57] French Nobel Laureate Romain Rolland designated him the greatest "moral authority" in the world, "the only one who can speak alike to both the proletariat and the middle classes of all nations and be listened to by them."[58] Then, too, whereas the League was not at the center of their concerns, Lloyd George, Clemenceau, and Orlando, by virtue of the political terms of the Armistice, had all but agreed to make it a priority at the peace conference – this in the face of Roosevelt's repeated reminders that "Mr. Wilson has no authority to speak for the American people at this time."[59] The Allied prime ministers well knew that their countrymen regarded the president – even under the cloud of his political setback, or perhaps because of it – as "our Wilson." (And when millions of people poured into the streets and piazzas of Paris, London, Rome, and Milan to hail "the Moses from across the Atlantic," the prime ministers were right to be alarmed. Public demonstrations of such historic proportions transcended mere pageantry; an articulate expression of mass political opinion, they strengthened Wilson's hand during the early stages of the conference and helped to insure the inclusion of the Covenant of the League as an integral part of the treaty of peace.) Nor were Europeans in general "impressed at all by the thousands of American ward bosses who feel superior to him," George Bernard Shaw observed, "and that fact must be accepted for the moment unless American democracy wishes to be set down as a political failure which has accidentally produced a greater individual success than it is capable of appreciating."[60]

Indeed, if the League of Nations represented the hopes of millions in Europe and America and now seemed nearer fruition, and if those who condemned it could not ignore the League even in its present abstract form, then it was because of Wilson's incomparable ability to communicate to an international constituency – "to evoke, by open speech, the latent sanity of

57 Thomas Nelson Page, American ambassador to Italy, to Wilson, Nov. 5, 1918, in *PWW,* 51:601.
58 Quoted in *Literary Digest,* Dec. 14, 1918, 11.
59 Quoted in the *New York Times,* Nov. 27, 1918.
60 Bernard Shaw, *Peace Conference Hints* (London, 1919), 49–50.

mankind," as H. N. Brailsford put it.[61] And, as he had done in the past, Wilson would continue (perhaps too much) to rely upon the appeal to principle, upon the judgment of "the people." It was not without justification that, in his final address to Congress on the eve of his departure, he evinced a feeling of personal responsibility for the creation of the League of Nations:

The gallant men of our armed forces on land and sea have consciously fought for the ideals which they knew to be the ideals of their country; I have sought to express those ideals; they have accepted my statements of them as the substance of their own thought and purpose, as the associated Governments have accepted them; I owe it to them to see to it, so far as in me lies, that no false or mistaken interpretation is put upon them, and no possible effort omitted to realize them. It is now my duty to play my full part in making good what they offered their life's blood to obtain. I can think of no call to service which could transcend this.[62]

With this penitential invocation, Wilson joined the ranks of those Americans who went across the sea to fight the war to end all wars.

---

61 Brailsford in *The Herald* of London, Jan. 4, 1919, quoted in Arno J. Mayer, *Politics and Diplomacy of Peacemaking: Containment and Counterrevolution at Versailles, 1918–1919* (New York, 1969), 193.
62 Annual Message on the State of the Union, Dec. 2, 1918, in *PWW,* 53:285.

5

A Comment

ALAN SHARP

The chapters of part I each provide interesting and valuable analyses. David Stevenson (chapter 3) offers an appraisal of French war aims and objectives from 1914 through to the end of the conference. Klaus Schwabe (chapter 1) begins his survey slightly later, with the early stirrings of the peace movement within Germany. He, too, follows the process through to what was a bitter end for the socialists and left-wing liberals who had passed the Peace Resolution in the Reichstag and whose belief in Woodrow Wilson's ideals was deep and genuine. David French (chapter 2) analyzes the British military and political desiderata, arguing that part of the objective for the British, as for Wilson, was an ideological one, as can be seen in their effort to bring about a decisive change in Germany's system of government – an aim also pursued by the Germans who opposed the regime and supported the Peace Resolution. Yet it was clear that Britain did not wish to see Germany destroyed if this meant it was merely to be replaced by a new danger to British interests. The possible candidates varied with the changing fortunes of war: first it was Russia, then France, and finally the United States. Like French, Thomas J. Knock (chapter 4) has been more literal in his interpretation, ending his discussion of Wilson's ideas and their domestic political fate more or less as the guns fell silent.

These four chapters raise a number of significant questions about the peace process. How well organized and prepared for peace were the participants by the end of the war? Did they know what they wanted? Did they know how to get what they wanted? Did the governments want the same things as their electorates? How well integrated were the military and naval demands of the Armistice with the political objectives of the Allies? To what extent were the national priorities of the different allies reflected in the terms demanded, and did these priorities indicate serious differences of purpose? Was the Armistice premature? Did the Allies miss the opportunity to bring home to Germany the extent of its defeat? Some technical and legal questions can be added to this list as well. How well-informed were the various parties about the aims and intentions of the others? In several instances the chapters suggest that who knew what and when and how that information was acquired could shed light on the negotiations and their outcome. What were the legal and constitutional implications of the armistice? How should the success of the Armistice be judged? Some of these issues are taken up in the following comments.

What these chapters and earlier works by the four contributors and other participants show is the important role that historians (albeit often ancient or medieval historians) played in official or quasi-official think tanks like the Comité d'études in France, The Inquiry in the United States, and the Political Intelligence Department in Britain. Yet despite the substantial number of briefing papers these bodies produced it is clear that, although Britain and France did have a grasp of their broad strategic aims, neither had really worked out the details of its peace program before the Armistice.[1] This is not so surprising, for the end of the war came more quickly than most people expected. Moreover, until the outcome was known, it was difficult to determine which war aims would be worth pursuing and which would be impractical. Stevenson's discussion of how far French war aims changed between 1914 and 1918 suggests a possible area for consideration in the German context. As the chapters also emphasize, the October and November negotiations took place under extreme pressure. Decisions had to be made rapidly not only about the military and naval terms which, in the end that amounted to a German surrender, but also about political issues, where the Germans obtained certain guarantees. The European leaders had to make snap judgments about what items they found unacceptable on an agenda they had not set. They had then to consider the consequential costs: whether, at its most extreme, they would fight on without the United States.

Why did the Allies conclude the armistice when they did? Clearly and overwhelmingly, they thought that if Germany was ready to meet their demands, then the war was won. As Ferdinand Foch declared to Edward

---

1 On this issue, see: David Stevenson, *French War Aims Against Germany, 1914–1919* (Oxford, 1982); Klaus Schwabe, *Woodrow Wilson, Revolutionary Germany, and Peacemaking, 1918–1919: Missionary Diplomacy and the Realities of Power* (Chapel Hill, N.C., 1985); V. H. Rothwell, *British War Aims and Peace Diplomacy, 1914–1918* (Oxford, 1971); Thomas J. Knock, *To End All Wars: Woodrow Wilson and the Quest for a New World Order* (New York, 1992); Lawrence E. Gelfand, *The Inquiry: American Preparations for Peace, 1917–1919* (New Haven, Conn., 1963); Erik Goldstein, *Winning the Peace: British Diplomatic Strategy, Peace Planning, and the Paris Peace Conference, 1916–1919* (Oxford, 1991); Alan Sharp, "Some Relevant Historians: The Political Intelligence Department of the Foreign Office, 1918–1920," *Australian Journal of Politics and History* 34 (1989): 170–88.

House on October 31, 1918, "I am not waging war for the sake of waging war. If I obtain through the Armistice the conditions that we wish to impose upon Germany, I am satisfied. Once this object is obtained, nobody has the right to shed one more drop of blood."[2] Both Georges Clemenceau and David Lloyd George were concerned about the terms demanded by Foch and Sir Wester Wemyss, which they thought were too severe and would provoke Germany into fighting with renewed vigor. Germany's acceptance of the terms came as something of a surprise but also indicated that the Allies had failed to assess just how desperate the German situation had become. Indeed, both Sir Douglas Haig and Henry Wilson believed the German army was not yet broken, while leading British decision makers expected to find in Berlin the same spirit that had prevailed in London and Paris in the dark days of March 1918. Above all, the Allied camp perceived the armistice as a victorious end to the war – there might be other objectives that they wished to obtain but none merited a continuation of a war that, as French points out, somewhat to their own surprise, they had won sooner than they expected.

Other considerations also moved them toward an armistice. Given that the United States had been approached by Germany, what would have happened if the European allies had refused to countenance Wilson's exchanges with Germany and had split from the United States over this issue? Could they have fought on alone, as they threatened to do during their negotiations with House? In view of what is now known about Germany's plight, the answer is yes, but to what extent were Clemenceau and Lloyd George basing their position on bravado rather than confidence? The need to maintain good relations with the world's major economic and financial power must have been a major consideration in the minds of the European decision makers in October and November 1918.

In "Oh! What a Lovely War," Douglas Haig prays that he can win the war before the Americans arrive. Clearly that moment had passed, but Jan Smuts still believed that Britain could dominate a peace conference, provided that the war ended immediately. This advice reinforced the assessment of the British military, which had decided that Foch was anxious to fight to the last drop of blood of the last Englishman. The fear of becoming the third military power on the western front with the subsequent loss of political leverage was a powerful inducement to quit while still ahead. America's growing economic strength added further weight to this argument. As French's compelling evidence shows, Britain thought an armistice

2 Ferdinand Foch, *The Memoirs of Marshal Foch,* trans. Colonel T. Bentley Mott (London, 1931), 541.

to be a more cost-effective way of achieving its aims than pursuing the war to an unconditional surrender.

For its part, the government of the United States showed little inclination to fight on: the costs were too high, unconditional surrender would merely unleash even more immoderate demands by the Europeans, and the United States was not engaged in a crusade to extend British dominion over palm and pine. This was not necessarily a reflection of domestic opinion, firmly in the grip of "One Hundred Percent Americanism." The persecution of radicals and pacifists raises the fascinating question of whether it was easier for alternative policies to be advanced in the autocratic Germany described by Schwabe in chapter 1 than in the democratic America that Knock analyzes in chapter 4. Knock makes a strong case that Wilson's neglect of the liberal and socialist elements of the coalition that had secured his reelection in 1916 precipitated the Republican gains in the 1918 midterm elections that undermined his credibility in the later negotiations.

This raises the more general question of the security of the position of all the main players at the forthcoming conference. In contrast to Wilson, the British and French leaders seemed to be operating from positions of strength. Lloyd George had won an overwhelming electoral victory immediately after the war, but the manner in which the election was fought and the political complexion and inexperienced personnel of the new Parliament represented potential hostages to fortune.[3] Clemenceau enjoyed political preeminence, reinforced by the euphoria of success. He was able to win a parliamentary mandate for his peace strategy in December 1918, but the Third Republic was not noted for its consistent support of its political leaders. Furthermore *Père-la-Victoire* was seventy-seven years old, so there was less certainty about the longer term. For Germany, facing military defeat, the abdication of the Kaiser, and the threat of more serious revolutionary disturbances, nothing was certain. Domestic issues and short-term electoral and parliamentary considerations would clearly be important elements in the forthcoming negotiations. The democrats of Paris might be less detached than the aristocrats of Vienna.

Wilson cabled to House on October 29:

My deliberate judgement is that our whole weight should be thrown for an armistice which will not permit a renewal of hostilities by Germany, but which will be as moderate and reasonable as possible within that condition, because lately I am certain that too much severity on the part of the Allies will make a genuine peace

---

3 See Robert Bunselmeyer, *The Cost of the War, 1914–1919* (Archon, 1975), 121–70; Harold Nicolson, *Peacemaking 1919* (London, 1933), 18–20.

settlement exceedingly difficult if not impossible. . . . Foresight is better than immediate advantage.[4]

This comment supports Knock's argument that the United States' perception of its aims was clouded by the ambiguity of Wilson's own thinking. Was he going to approach peacemaking as an impartial arbitrator or as the apostle of democracy, triumphantly scourging the sins of autocracy? What, in fact, was the armistice supposed to achieve? Wilson's instructions reveal that he was aware of the political and wider implications of an armistice, although its primary function in this instance was to ensure Allied military and naval superiority under conditions that would not permit Germany to resume hostilities. Given that the European partners were concerned that Germany should not merely be given a breathing space to consolidate its crumbling positions and to organize a more effective resistance, the paradox was how to avoid an armistice that amounted to a military surrender. How and where could moderation be built into such an armistice, which, if it succeeded in leaving Germany incapable of resuming the war, ultimately left it at the mercy of whatever terms its enemies chose to impose? That the military and naval terms were crippling is beyond question; the final proof came in June 1919 when the German High Command scuppered any thought of fighting to avoid signing the treaty, but Wilson made little detailed comment on them. He made a mild protest about the most controversial of the military terms, the occupation of the left-bank Rhineland and the right-bank bridgeheads, but, Knock points out, he did not persist.

In this respect, it is interesting to speculate whether Foch had a clearer sense of the political implications and realities of the armistice than Wilson or Clemenceau. It was Foch who insisted that German troops should not merely evacuate Alsace-Lorraine and the left bank of the Rhine but that they should be replaced by the Allies. And, says Stevenson, it was Foch who argued (ultimately incorrectly) that "the only definitive territorial sacrifices will be those conceded by the enemy when the armistice is signed." In any event, if there was to be moderation, it would have to be built into the broader context of the pre-armistice agreement.

Why did Germany seek an armistice? It was hardly from a deep-felt desire to see Wilsonian ideas being put into practice. Germany faced the unenviable truth that it had to reassess its position in the light of its military collapse. Although, as Schwabe amply demonstrates, there was a strong and growing body of German opinion that sincerely favored a Wilsonian approach to

4 Charles Seymour, ed., *The Intimate Papers of Colonel House,* 4 vols. (Boston, 1926–8), 4:112–13 (hereafter *IPCH;* all references are to vol. 4).

peacemaking, the German "official mind" was undoubtedly more concerned with salvaging something from the disaster. Once again, "The questions of the day [were] not decided by speeches and majority decisions . . . but by blood and iron."[5] A key question that remains is how important would the Reichstag resolution have been if Germany had won? The answers suggested by Brest-Litovsk and Bucharest would appear to cast serious doubt upon any claim that the influence of the liberals and socialists would have been anything other than negligible, no matter how sincere their internationalism.

Despite European indignation that Germany had approached Wilson rather than its enemies of longer standing and their fears that he might throw the game in its dying moments, Wilson was clearly not soft on the Germans. His insistence on allied military superiority after any armistice disarmed his domestic critics and mollified the Europeans, argues Knock. But there was now the question of his political program becoming part of the armistice contract. It is clear that Clemenceau and Lloyd George resented this deeply: "Have you ever been asked by President Wilson whether you accept the Fourteen Points?" Clemenceau caustically inquired. "I have not been asked." "I have not been asked either," replied Lloyd George.[6] But inexorably the philosophical and moral agenda for the forthcoming peace settlement was being set by Wilson, whose manifesto for the peace of the world had captured the imagination of liberals and radicals on both sides. Wilson was not personally presenting the program, however. He had despatched his friend and confidant, Edward House, to Europe with the splendidly vague exhortation, "I have not given you any instructions because I feel you will know what to do."[7] House's mission was to obtain European consent to the president's pronouncements forming the agenda and the basis of the final treaty. Henry Wilson could rail at Woodrow Wilson:

As regards Wilson, we agreed that we would wire to say that he must make it clear to the Boches that his fourteen points (with which we do not agree) were not the basis for an armistice, which is what the Bosches pretend they are. As regards the Press, we agreed that they should be told that Wilson is acting on his own, that the War is not over, that the fourteen points are not an armistice, and that an armistice is not a peace. It was a very interesting afternoon. Everyone angry and contemptuous of Wilson.[8]

But with the German request for an armistice public knowledge, and with the president now asking his partners for a decision, the British and French

5 Bismarck to the Budget Commission, Sept. 29, 1862. Helmut Böhme, *The Foundation of the German Empire* (Oxford, 1971), 116.
6 *IPCH*, 167.   7 *IPCH*, 88.
8 Sir Charles Callwell, *Field-Marshal Sir Henry Wilson: His Life and Diaries*, 2 vols. (London, 1927), 2:136.

leaders were firmly on the spot. The consequences of a continuation of the war after the German requests to Wilson were incalculable, but to what extent could they accept Wilson's package and still obtain their own main aims and fulfill the various promises and pledges delivered during the war to their own people and to one another?

Two issues dominated the subsequent discussions: "the freedom of the seas" and reparations. Italian murmurings about the limitations on their aims implied by Wilson's pronouncements on national self-determination were quietly ignored. Freedom of the seas appeared to be a matter on which no compromise was possible. "I cannot consent to take part in the negotiation of a peace which does not include freedom of the seas," Wilson cabled to House on October 30, while Great Britain, according to Lloyd George, would "spend her last guinea to keep a navy superior to that of the United States or any other power" and was not prepared to surrender the weapon on whose "basis the British Empire has been founded, and on no other can it be upheld."[9] Characteristically, House did compromise, by accepting phrasing advanced by Lloyd George, which conceded little beyond agreeing that the matter could be discussed at the peace conference. In the event, it was not. Thus, although Sir William Wiseman declared that "the 'Freedom of the Seas' nearly broke up the conference," the crisis blew over, although some scholars argue that this was only because House did not truly represent the president's policy and accepted an unsatisfactory deal. Was it a genuine crisis, or was Wilson protecting his domestic position and equipping himself with a bargaining chip when he threatened to outbuild the British navy?[10]

Reparations proved to be a much hotter and more enduring problem for the conference and subsequent history. The Europeans were determined, at the very least, to define Wilson's term "restoration" so as to ensure that Germany would be liable to repair all the damage it had caused to their civilian nationals and their property. They recognized, however reluctantly, that Wilson would not agree to include any of the wider costs of waging the war. Thus the formula that they agreed on did implicitly exclude any claim for war costs. The final draft read: "By it [restoration] they understand that compensation will be made by Germany for all damage done to the civilian population of the Allies and their property by the aggression of Germany by land, by sea, and from the air." This definition was passed to Ger-

9 *IPCH*, 173. See also Seth P. Tillman, *Anglo-American Relations at the Paris Peace Conference of 1919* (Princeton, N.J., 1961), 49.
10 See Tillman, *Anglo-American Relations*, 44–52; and *IPCH*, 171, n. 1. For later developments, see John R. Ferris, "The Symbol and the Substance of Seapower: Great Britain, the United States, and the One-Power Standard, 1919–1921," in B. J. C. McKercher, ed., *Anglo-American Relations in the 1920s: The Struggle for Supremacy* (London, 1991), 55–80.

many in the Lansing Note of November 5, drawn up by the American secretary of state, but the preamble to Paragraph 19 of the armistice stated: "With reservation that any future claims and demands of the Allies and the United States remain unaffected, the following financial conditions are required: Reparation for damage done." This "lamentably obscure" wording had been taken from a draft prepared by Louis-Lucien Klotz, the French finance minister, before the definition of "restoration" was agreed upon.[11] Given that France and Great Britain would move between November 1918 and January 1919 to claim their full war costs, which wording took precedence? In the minds of John Maynard Keynes and James Headlam-Morley, there was no doubt that any attempt to claim war pensions and allowances, much less war costs, was impossible under the terms of the Pre-Armistice Agreement, and it is difficult to imagine that any serious scholar could disagree.[12] Whether Lloyd George always intended, nonetheless, to advance such a claim must remain a matter of speculation.

More interesting is Ulrich Graf Brockdorff-Rantzau's argument, explained by Schwabe, that the strict letter of the Lansing Note would exclude damage inflicted by German U-boat warfare while the final instructions to the German peace delegation would concede no more than that any such claim would be "legally doubtful." There can be little doubt that when the British amended the original wording of the definition of "restoration" to substitute "the aggression of Germany" for "invasion of Allied territory" it was precisely German shipping losses and the need to make some provision for the claims of the Dominions that it had in mind. Was the new wording sufficient to justify a claim that merchant shipping losses were legitimate civilian damage when, presumably, the vast majority of the ships lost were carrying war material?[13] Although the question is somewhat academic, it is still worthy of discussion since it encapsulates the wider problem of the legal and moral standing of the pre-armistice agreement as a whole.

House believed that he had ensured the triumph of Wilson's principles in the October and November negotiations, though both Knock and Stevenson dispute this claim. Yet how well prepared was Wilson to translate the high principles of the Fourteen Points, the Four Principles, the Four Ends, and the Five Particulars into practical policies? Skeptics in Europe

11 H. W. V. Temperley, ed., *A History of the Peace Conference of Paris,* 6 vols. (Oxford, 1920–24; reprinted, 1969), 2:44. Klotz's note, Oct. 19, 1918, in Fonds Clemenceau, 6N73, "Armistice," Service Historique de l'Armée de Terre at Vincennes.
12 John Maynard Keynes, *The Economic Consequences of the Peace* (New York, 1920), 113–19. See the James W. Headlam-Morley papers, ACC 688, box 4, Churchill College, Cambridge.
13 Keynes certainly thought so. *Economic Consequences,* 117.

doubted this. Sir Eyre Crowe's minute in the Foreign Office for November 30, 1918, states: "I do not believe President Wilson has thought out his nebulous proposals." But astute observers believed that this was an advantage, especially when they were told by Colonel House that it was possible to "establish almost any point that anyone wished against Germany" from Wilson's speeches.[14] Indeed, it is clear that France, Britain, and Germany all planned to use Wilson's ideas to their own ends; the Germans, notes Schwabe, were hoping at least to snatch "dignity" from the jaws of defeat by pushing to have his program made the starting point of negotiations; the British and the French, convinced that Wilson would do anything to ensure the birth of the League of Nations, were determined not to offer their support without substantial concessions. Both André Tardieu, Clemenceau's main political adviser, and Lloyd George shared the view that "the League was the only thing which he [Wilson] really cared about" and that cooperation in this matter would bring rich rewards elsewhere.[15] This would have appealed particularly to Lloyd George because, with skill, he could both have his cake and eat it. All were confident that the withholding of consent to Wilson's wishes over the League could prove a major weapon in obtaining their own programs in Paris.

Was the armistice premature? It is scarcely strange that bemused German citizens could not comprehend the true nature of the situation in November 1918; a war that Germany had dominated in terms of territorial advantage from the outset was now declared to be over, but without either a German victory or an Allied soldier on German territory. David French demonstrates how Lloyd George's perceptive, if belligerent, enthusiasm for bringing home the realities of defeat to the German people was dissipated by Douglas Haig's and Henry Wilson's assessment that Germany was not yet ready to collapse – a judgment that was hardly likely, in the light of immediately subsequent events, to have caused the prime minister to revise his distrust of the capacity of soldiers to make accurate forecasts. As French points out, that leaves one with the wistful hindsight of Sir Eric Geddes. Although General John Pershing did, rather late in the day, object to any kind of armistice, he was the most recently arrived of the Allied commanders and his military reputation was not high in October 1918.[16] Indeed, some in Allied government circles blamed him for the failure to achieve a

---

14 Crowe minute in British Foreign Office, 371/4353, Public Record Office, London. See also *IPCH,* 194.

15 George Egerton, *Great Britain and the Creation of the League of Nations: Strategy, Politics, and International Organization, 1914–1919* (Chapel Hill, N.C., 1979), 106.

16 *IPCH,* 95.

more evident victory. David Lindsay, the Earl of Crawford and Lord Privy Seal in Lloyd George's government, predicted that this could lead to a German myth of a stab in the back: "Thanks to Pershing's incompetence Foch was unable to bring off a great and conclusive coup. This war did not end with a Sedan as it might and should have done. To that extent Germany can argue that her armies though pressed back were never broken still less annihilated."[17] In discussing this point, Schwabe is skeptical about whether the final treaty would not have been better if Germany had been occupied and disarmed and if reparations had been extracted rapidly in a short sharp operation, rather than a long drawn-out one.[18] Lloyd George's speech of September 12, and his question to the cabinet in October as to whether it was not legitimate to lash Germany as it had lashed France does suggest that there was some sympathy for the idea of continuing the fighting until the overwhelming nature of their defeat became apparent to the German people. French argues that it was not inevitable that the British government would accede to Germany's request in October 1918, and Stevenson's conclusion raises some interesting speculations about this and related matters. Nonetheless, there was no enthusiasm for unconditional surrender nor any plan for an extensive territorial occupation of Germany.

What makes Schwabe's discussion particularly fascinating is its revelation of the "dreamworld" inhabited by German decision makers in the aftermath of the Armistice. Two cartoons, one published in Germany in November 1918 and the other in November 1919, illustrate this dreamworld and the harsh reality. In the first, published in *Lustige Blätter,* President Friedrich Ebert escorts Gretchen to the European ball where she is received in open harmony by Marianne and Clemenceau and her other erstwhile enemies. The second cartoon, published in *Der wahre Jakob,* has two parts: the upper part shows three German generals imposing peace upon Russia at Brest-Litovsk, and one of them is pounding the table with his huge fist, shouting, "We are the victors"; the lower part shows Clemenceau, flanked by Wilson and Lloyd George, pounding the table with an even larger fist and saying, "No, we are the victors!" The caption reads: "When two [parties] do the same thing, it is not the same thing."[19] Brockdorff-Rantzau and his colleagues probably saw the first cartoon as nothing but a fantasy, but the second showed the extent of their failure to obtain favorable terms. As Schwabe explains, the main weapons they hoped were in their armory were

17 John Vincent, ed., *The Crawford Papers* (Manchester, 1984), 398–9.
18 Alan Sharp, *The Versailles Settlement: Peacemaking in Paris, 1919* (London, 1991), 128.
19 W. A. Coupe, "German Cartoonists and the Peace of Versailles," *History Today* 32 (Jan. 1982): 46–53, 46–7.

the Allied fear of Bolshevism spreading to Germany, the necessity of a prosperous Germany to the economic well-being of Europe, and the expectation that they could engage the Allies in face-to-face negotiations.

The Bolshevik threat was certainly something Headlam-Morley in the British Foreign Office took seriously, says French, and this theme was prominent in Lloyd George's Fontainebleau memorandum. Despite Hungary and Munich, however, no one was prepared to make great concessions to avert the danger and, as the peace conference progressed, the threat became devalued by overuse: any disappointed power pointed to the risk of contagion if their wishes were not granted. Thus, whereas Bernard Partridge's cartoon in *Punch* on April 2, 1919, showed Bolshevik wolves prowling outside the temple of peace, Testevuide's drawing in *Le Ruy Blas* on April 13 portrayed Bolshevism as a mask, to be worn by Germany whenever convenient.[20] The economic argument had more success both in the short and the long term, leading to some concessions to Germany in March 1919, and certainly striking a chord with a Britain that equated the long-term unemployment of the 1920s with the collapse of its Central European markets. Where Britain saw sixty-five million customers, however, France saw a nation-in-arms, and this was one of the perceptions that divided the two as they came to enforce the treaty.

The German strategy of direct negotiations with the Allies represented a potentially fruitful policy but the prospects faded as the conference in Paris got under way. The various stratagems and devices that Brockdorff-Rantzau, Carl Melchior, and Max Warburg advanced in the hope of establishing a dialogue with the Allies did not succeed but were not necessarily ill-conceived. In January, even after the conference had begun, it was not clear what form it would take, and many of the Allied territorial commissions made their recommendations in the expectation that these represented bargaining stances that would be modified by negotiations with Germany. Each of the preceding chapters offers helpful insights into the wartime suspicions and fears of the powers about their partners. As the negotiators revealed their hands, the Allies realized that they would have difficulty reaching some sort of accommodation with one another and that it would be unwise to allow the Germans around the same table.[21] Brockdorff-Rantzau might be no Talleyrand but he hardly needed to be, and the Allies

---

20 *Punch* (London), Apr. 2, 1919; Testevuide's cartoon is reproduced by Paul Ducatel, *Histoire de la IIIe République vue à travers l'imagerie populaire et la presse satirique,* vol. 4: *La Grande Guerre,* 5 vols. (Grassin, 1978), 164.

21 Nicolson, *Peacemaking 1919,* 95–100.

were sufficiently aware of the history of the Vienna negotiations to avoid taking the risk.

The new German government was faced with a further dilemma. One of the major advantages in trying to create some sort of rapport with the United States, perceived as being the most sympathetic of its enemies, was that such a move represented a clean break with the imperial German past, a new democratic beginning. Yet Germany's major safeguard arising from the Armistice was the Lansing Note, the pre-armistice agreement, delivered to the Kaiser's last government. The debate was fierce, but those who urged Germany to maintain the insurance of November 5 won, and thus, as Schwabe points out, the new regime found itself the reluctant apologist for the old, a situation that was exacerbated by the later need to refute Article 231. Whether this was, in 1919, a good bargain seemed doubtful. A cartoon in *Lustige Blätter* in June showed the paint of Wilson's promises running to form two new words, "Hate" and "Scorn." Given the journal's progressive but politically uncommitted position, this cartoon suggests that the disappointment of the "new" Germany was likely to be dangerous for the future.[22] Headlam-Morley, unlike many of his colleagues in the Foreign Office who seemed more at home with the old German elite, despite wanting to see them overthrown, commented on January 24, 1919: "We must win the confidence of the Liberal and Socialist Left."[23] The conference did not advance this cause very far.

There are tantalizing reminders in the preceding chapters that the history of the conference has yet to be written from the point of view of the intelligence available to the participants: the incomplete and inaccurate assessments of the German military and political situation at the end of the war, the Allied interception of the German request for an armistice, the German knowledge of the Cobb–Lippmann commentary on the Fourteen Points, or the advance warning they received concerning some of the territorial provisions of the treaty. Although it is possible to show how Britain used secret intelligence information at the Lausanne conference in 1922–23 by gathering material mainly from the papers of Sir Horace Rumbold, George Curzon, and the published documents, the Paris negotiations are an altogether more complex affair and would entail a massive amount of excavation.[24] The French could make a valuable contribution by releasing File 359 in the *Ministère des Affaires Etrangères* series, "1914–1920": "Plenipotentiaires

22 Coupe, "German Cartoonists," 49.
23 Minute, Jan. 24, 1919, on 41/1/1, in British Foreign Office 608/9.
24 Keith Jeffery and Alan Sharp, "Lord Curzon and Secret Intelligence," in Christopher Andrew and Jeremy Noakes, eds., *Intelligence and International Relations, 1900–1945* (Exeter, 1987), 103–26.

Allemands: télégrammes interceptés avril–décembre 1919." The records of the intercepted telephone conversations between members of the German delegation and Berlin are available in the Fonds Clemenceau at Vincennes but are useful only in revealing the mood of the delegation.[25] There is clear scope here for an international research project that should yield fascinating and valuable results.

Was the armistice a success? It did end the fighting on the western front, it did ensure that Germany would not be able to resume the war, and it did enshrine the Allied superiority of 1918 to the degree that Germany had no alternative but to sign the treaty on June 28, 1919. At the same time, it created a new set of problems as well as opportunities, and the early signs were not encouraging for those on both sides of the Atlantic, and on both sides in the recent war, who hoped that Wilson's program for world peace could be translated from speeches into actions. In the east the situation was more ambiguous. The alarming lack of authority of the victors in central and eastern Europe and the ensuing chaos were also ominous. By January 22, 1919, Lansing was recording in his diary, "The Great War seems to have split up into a lot of little wars."[26]

The Europeans now had to motivate themselves to take up the task of peacemaking, but it was difficult to shrug off the exhaustion and tension of the past four years, which may have been the reason that so many of the key figures contracted the terrible influenza that descended on the world at the end of the war. Maurice Hankey records that "at the eleventh hour of the eleventh day of the eleventh month of the year 1918, when the German Armistice was signed, I was bedridden in my home in Limpsfield, Surrey, stricken down by that deadly type of influenza that was sweeping the world, and which is said to have caused more deaths than the war itself."[27] In any case, there was inevitably a relaxation of pressure, even though everyone was well aware that the job was only half done. Peace planning now had to be translated into peace, but the question remains, how fit and prepared were the participants, after such a grueling struggle? The whole war had been a learning process, about the organization and deployment of mass armies, and the rethinking of industrial practices and economic theories to meet the exigencies of total war. The record of the generals, the admirals, the politicians, and the industrialists and bankers during the war showed that, on the

25 Alan Sharp, "'Quelqu'un nous écoute': French Interception of German Telegraphic and Telephonic Communications During the Paris Peace Conference, 1919," *Intelligence and National Security* 3 (Oct. 1988): 124–7.
26 Quoted by D. Perman, *The Shaping of the Czechoslovak State: Diplomatic History of the Boundaries of Czechoslovakia, 1914–1920* (Leiden, 1962), 105.
27 Sir Maurice Hankey, *The Supreme Control at the Paris Peace Conference, 1919* (London, 1963), 9.

whole, this was a slow and difficult business in which success was reached partly through the experience of past mistakes and partly through luck. Would the process of peacemaking prove to be different, and how lucky would the peacemakers be?

The last word must go to the Welsh wizard. It is instructive to compare the Lloyd George of September 12, 1918, emphasizing, "Victory is essential to a sound peace," with the Lloyd George of October 1936, writing in his *War Memoirs:*

Beyond question it was a disaster that we had to lay Germany prostrate before we could reach a peace settlement. Had Ludendorff retreated earlier to strong lines within the German frontier and there held out against us, a peace settlement might have been reached that contained fewer roots of bitterness than one dictated to a foe who even in defeat clung with his claws to the foreign lands he had invaded and devastated and in the process of liberating his hold increased the desolation. Unhappily, for the peace of the world, the hostile armies were still on the soil of France and Belgium when the end came, and the surrender had to be complete enough to guarantee the aims for which we fought.[28]

Lloyd George was never one to miss an opportunity to have it as many ways as possible!

28 David Lloyd George, *The War Memoirs of David Lloyd George,* 2 vols. (London, 1936), 2:1973–4.

PART TWO

The Peacemakers and Their Home Fronts

6

Great Britain: The Home Front

ERIK GOLDSTEIN

The settlement with Germany generated much sound and fury in Britain in the months between November 1918 and June 1919. After a war that had such a profound effect on the life of the country, the home front was a factor that could not be ignored by the government in the negotiation of the final peace terms with Germany. There were many facets to the British home front: the populace with its broadened franchise, active pressure groups, members of Parliament (MPs), and, more important, the members of the ruling coalition parties, as well as the empire.[1] The views of all these groups, in varying degree, had to be taken into account by the peacemakers. Between the end of the war and the conclusion of peace, the government's reactions to the home front dimension passed through three periods. The first stretched from the November 1918 Armistice to the December general election, in which all the pent-up emotions of war were released and views on the nature of the settlement vociferously expressed across the political spectrum. Here the requirements of political expediency led the government to pander to public opinion in order to secure a majority in the House of Commons. The second period ran from the general election to mid-April 1919. These were the months in which Lloyd George grew increasingly aware of the dangerous direction being taken in the drafting of terms but was constrained (and therefore British diplomacy was constrained) by the uncertain support of his own backbenches. The third phase encompassed the final stage of the peace conference and saw Lloyd George confident of his political base, less concerned than in any previous phase about his home front, and in the negotiations pushing for a more moderate settlement.

---

1 As a result of the Representation of the People Act, the electorate was now three times what it had been at the last general election in 1910, the vote now including most men over twenty-one and women over thirty.

For four years, between August 1914 and November 1918, the largest British army ever raised, combined with a mighty naval blockade, confronted the German Empire. For the first time Great Britain saw conscription used to raise its army, an army that suffered a higher casualty rate than any army in its history. The war front and the home front thereby became inextricably linked in the minds and emotions of the British people, even if Great Britain suffered less than other European states. Societies do not view such events from a comparative point of view. For Britain the casualties amounted to 702,410 on all fronts, 512,564 of these dying on the western front, and many writers have pointed to the emotional impact of this toll.[2] Correlli Barnett concluded, "The truth was that the Great War crippled the British *psychologically* but in no other way."[3] The emotional dimension, however, almost crippled Great Britain diplomatically as well. The last and most critical campaign of a war is that waged by the negotiators at the green baize–covered table. It is here that a war is ultimately won or lost.[4] The emotional anguish in Great Britain, made vocal and magnified by key figures in political life, acted as a serious distraction to the peacemakers, who either had to alter objectives or organize diversionary campaigns against the hecklers. According to Harold Nicolson, in his well-known account of the Paris Peace Conference, "Given the atmosphere of the time, given the passions aroused in all democracies by four years of war, it would have been impossible even for supermen to devise a peace of moderation and righteousness."[5] Nicolson goes on to remark that since it was necessary for the leaders of the democracies to find solutions that took account of the desires of their people, compromises were inevitable, and he wonders how "human nature, having but recently indulged in the folly of the Great War, could suddenly manifest the calm serenity of almost superhuman wisdom."[6] The emotions unleashed by the war proved to be a fickle factor in the peacemaking.

PRESSURE GROUPS

A variety of pressure groups existed by the war's end, some more organized than others, some no more than individuals with similar views who can conveniently be grouped together under a common label. These groups span the political spectrum, and the Foreign Office files are replete with quanti-

2 *Statistics of the Military Effort of the British Empire* (London, 1922), 238, table (i) (9G).
3 Correlli Barnett, *The Collapse of British Power* (London, 1984), 425–6.
4 Erik Goldstein, *Winning the Peace: British Diplomatic Strategy, Peace Planning, and the Paris Peace Conference, 1916–1920* (Oxford, 1991).
5 Harold Nicolson, *Peacemaking 1919* (Boston, 1933), 7.
6 Ibid., 7.

ties of letters, memorials, and pamphlets advocating every possible solution to every imaginable question likely to arise at the peace conference. Looking across the political spectrum, it is possible to identify three serious and influential exemplar pressure groups, the Union for Democratic Control, the New Europe group, and the anti-Germans. The Union for Democratic Control (UDC) on the left had the least direct influence, though Lloyd George had to keep a wary eye on it because of the Left's growing popular support. The New Europe group represented the Gladstonian liberal tradition and succeeded in achieving some significant input into the details of the final settlement. The anti-Germans were a more inchoate grouping of those who wished to punish Germany, most practicably by making it pay for the war and by trying its leaders. It was a group that was to have a highly negative impact on British statecraft at the Paris Peace Conference. These three groups provide a sense of the diversity of opinion on the forthcoming peace treaty.

The Union for Democratic Control was established in 1914 with a view to promoting more popular input into foreign policy and a lasting postwar peace.[7] It enjoyed strong support from the radical wing of the Liberal Party as well as from the Labour Party. Its followers were believers in rationalism and internationalism and included Bertrand Russell, Norman Angell, Ramsay Macdonald, and E. D. Morel. Within the domestic political schema it was a facet of the growing transfer of political support from the Liberal Party to the Labour Party and was a vocal wartime opponent of government policies. The UDC took the view that the Anglo–German conflict was the result of traditional secret diplomacy and therefore apportioned Britain an equal share of the responsibility for the war. Its members did not therefore seek to penalize Germany in the settlement. A growing wartime convergence of the UDC with the Labour Party brought about a blending of the UDC's radical-liberal view of international relations with Labour's socialist policies.[8] Lloyd George was aware that there was little he could do to satisfy those whose ambition was to replace him in power. One supporter of the UDC recalled of the Versailles settlement, "We denounced it, at the time; we were indeed bound to do so, whatever it had been."[9] The UDC came to occupy a distracting position on Lloyd George's peripheral vision as a potent symbol of the threat on his immediate political left.

7 Marvin Schwarz. *The Union for Democratic Control in British Politics During the First World War* (Oxford, 1971).
8 Kenneth E. Miller, *Socialism and Foreign Policy: Theory and Practice in Britain to 1931* (The Hague, 1967).
9 Mary Agnes Hamilton, *Remembering My Good Friends* (London, 1944), 105, cited in Schwarz, *Union for Democratic Control*, 219.

The New Europe group was heir to a particular strand of Gladstonian liberalism in foreign affairs. Its supporters can be seen as adherents of Gladstone's ideal of "the enthronement of the idea of Public Right as the governing idea of European politics."[10] While the New Europe is often associated with the ideas of Woodrow Wilson, himself a transatlantic Gladstonian, some important distinctions need to be drawn. The New Europe was not a pressure group for Wilsonian ideas, but rather the European product of the same ideas that had stimulated the American president. Wilson was concerned with global issues; the New Europe was Eurocentric. The New Europe group saw Europe, given the war, as a *tabula rasa*, ripe for constructing a new order.[11] In the words of Thomas Masaryk, who was part of the group, Europe was "a laboratory sitting atop a vast graveyard."[12] Europe would have to be redesigned if a repetition of the carnage of this apocalyptic war was to be avoided. The New Europe did not seek to exculpate Germany for its actions during the war, nor did it wish to penalize it. Its views on reparations were grounded on what Germany could reasonably pay for damage inflicted, while on the territorial settlement it followed the New Europe ethos of removing what it saw as one of the chief causes of European war by establishing well-defined nation-states. Hence the redrawing of German frontiers to leave significant numbers of Germans under foreign rule was opposed.

The driving force behind the New Europe was R. W. Seton-Watson, who in 1917 established the journal *New Europe* and associated with it a distinguished set of European "collaborators." The journal lasted until 1920 and served during the period in which the postwar order was being shaped as a focal point for an important group of like-minded individuals, inside and outside of government, British and non-British alike. Contributors to the *New Europe* included Oscar Browning, Erskine Childers, Anatole France, Sir James Frazer, Samuel Hoare, Thomas Masaryk, Bernard Pares, and Leonard Woolf. A movement that attracted such notable support would inevitably have had some influence on the final shape of British policy, but its influence was magnified by the presence of a group of its supporters at the very heart of British policy planning in the Political Intelligence Department (PID) of the Foreign Office. Nicolson, a member of the PID, recalled that he went to the Paris Peace Conference "overwhelmingly imbued" with the doctrines of the *New Europe,* "the concepts 'Germany,' 'Austria,' 'Hungary,' 'Bulgaria,' or

10 Quoted in Gilbert Murray, *The Foreign Policy of Sir Edward Grey, 1906–1915* (Oxford, 1915).
11 This phrase was used explicitly in "The *Tabula Rasa* in Central Europe," *New Europe* 9 (Nov. 14, 1918): 98–102.
12 Quoted in Maurice Baumont, *La faillite de la paix, 1918–1939*, 2d ed. (Paris, 1946), 8.

'Turkey' were not in the forefront of our minds. It was the thought of the new Serbia, the new Greece, the new Bohemia, the new Poland which made our hearts sing hymns at heaven's gate."[13]

In October 1918 the PID was charged with preparing the British brief for the Paris Peace Conference and eventually provided the expert advisers to the prime minister and the British delegation at Paris. Seton-Watson went over to Paris for the duration of the peace conference and there remained in almost daily touch with the PID staff. Seton-Watson had great faith in the group's influence through the PID, noting just after the armistice that "we are pretty sure . . . that the policy of the Government will ultimately be found to reflect the sobriety of the Political Intelligence Department of the Foreign Office rather than the excesses of Fleet Street gutters."[14] He had every reason to be assured of their views, for as Nicolson later recalled, he and his colleague Allen Leeper "never moved a yard without previous consultation with experts of the authority of Dr. Seton-Watson who was in Paris at the time."[15] Leeper and Nicolson, with advice from Seton-Watson, did indeed influence the settlement, as the historian and assistant director of the PID, James Headlam-Morley, noted in a letter from the conference, "Self–determination is quite *démodé*. Leeper and Nicolson determine for them what they ought to wish, but they do it very well."[16]

The third pressure group advocated harsh treatment for Germany. A factor that influenced popular British thinking about the settlement has to be the exponential growth in anti-Germanism as the war continued. Anglo-German relations had been on the decline at least since the beginning of naval rivalry in 1898, and the war had transformed this earlier animosity into hatred. Public opinion was influenced by the remarkably successful wartime propaganda effort, which did much to blacken the view held of Germany.[17] The sinking of the *Leinster* in October 1918, as armistice negotiations were under way, reinforced this feeling, even infuriating the normally unflappable Arthur Balfour, who was led to declaim of the Germans, "Brutes they were, and brutes they remain."[18] Nicolson later noted that the impact of this incident was "deeper, more immediate, than is to-day remembered."[19] After the final German push in 1918 Great Britain saw a

13 Nicolson, *Peacemaking 1919*, 33.
14 "The Prime Minster's Mandate for Versailles," *New Europe* 9 (Dec. 19, 1918): 231–4.
15 Nicolson, *Peacemaking 1919*, 126.
16 Headlam-Morley to Edwyn Bevan, Mar. 5, 1919. Reprinted in Sir James Headlam-Morley, *A Memoir of the Paris Peace Conference, 1919* (London, 1972), 44.
17 Philip Taylor and Michael Sanders, *British Propaganda During the First World War, 1914–18* (London, 1982).
18 Nicolson, *Peacemaking 1919*, 24.
19 Ibid.

remarkable upsurge in anti-Germanism, reinforced by tales of those returning from a devastated continent. There would be no respite in this anti-
German tide until many months had elapsed from the armistice and the
emotions of war finally began to abate.[20] Indeed, the armistice with Germany was not an event necessarily welcomed by all. On Armistice Day,
Admiral "Jacky" Fisher expressed the wish "to hang the Kaiser and sack
Berlin, [and] was almost black with fury," adding "I am damned if *I* will give
thanks to God for this ignominious and disgraceful surrender of all that we
have fought for!"[21] Fisher reflected the mood of popular frustration that a
final, conclusive battlefield defeat of Germany had not occurred. The transference of this desire to the final engagement of the war, the peace settlement, is not surprising. Leo Amery noted this mood, while out campaigning on November 26: "The great British people are not in the least
interested in Social Reform or Reconstruction, but only in making the
Germans pay for the war and punishing the Kaiser."[22] And he wisely
adapted his electioneering oratory to this reality. Many MPs found it convenient to fan the flames of anti-Germanism. The most infamous of this lot
were undoubtedly the Independent MPs Horatio Bottomley and Pemberton Billing.[23] The latter in 1918 became notorious for his claim that Germany had a black book listing 47,000 important Britons whose sexual
weaknesses made them prey for German agents.[24] Claude Lowther, a
Unionist MP, expressed the desire during the campaign to "put the Kaiser
in an iron travelling cage and show him in every town and village."[25] Given
the popular climate, King George V tried unsuccessfully to dissuade Lloyd
George from calling an immediate election.[26]

The anti-Germans were greatly assisted by the newspaper magnate Lord
Northcliffe, who had an almost pathological hatred of Germany and was in

20 An important account of the growth of anti-Germanism is to be found in Robert E. Bunselmeyer, *The Cost of the War, 1914–1919: British Economic War Aims and the Origins of Reparation* (Hamden, Conn., 1975), 106–20.
21 Alan Clark, ed., *"A Good Innings": The Private Papers of Viscount Lee of Fareham* (London, 1974), 183.
22 John Barnes and David Nicholson, eds., *The Leo Amery Diaries* (London, 1980), vol. 1: *1896–1929* (hereafter Amery diary), 246.
23 Horatio Bottomley (1860–1933): founder of the *Financial Times* (1888) and *John Bull* (1906); defended himself from charges of fraud but declared bankrupt, 1911; MP (Lib.), 1906–12 and MP (Ind.), 1918–22; imprisoned for fraud 1922–7; declared bankrupt, 1931. Noel Pemberton Billing (1881–1948): founder and first president of Vigilantes, a society with the object of promoting purity in public life; MP (Ind.), 1916–21.
24 His allegations were made in his paper *Vigilante*. See also Robert Blake, *The Unknown Prime Minister: The Life and Times of Andrew Bonar Law, 1858–1923* (London, 1956).
25 *Northwestern Daily Mail*, Nov. 29, 1918, cited in Bunselmeyer, 216. Bunselmeyer provides an analysis of Lowther's campaign, 159–60. Col. Claude Lowther (1872–1929): chairman of the Anti-Socialist Union; MP, 1900–1906, 1910–22; in 1921 withdrew support from coalition to support Horatio Bottomley's Independent Group.
26 Harold Nicolson, *George V* (London, 1952), 328–30.

a position to give vent to his spleen through his control of such newspapers as the *Times* and the *Daily Mail*. On the eve of his death in 1922 he complained that he had been "poisoned by the Germans by ice cream."[27] Lloyd George had unsuccessfully attempted to co-opt him during the war by making him director of propaganda in enemy countries, as well as a viscount. During the period of the Paris Peace Conference, Northcliffe used his papers to mount a vitriolic campaign against the prime minister. At the height of the conference an exasperated Lloyd George complained of his irritation at these attacks, which he saw as branding him a pro-German.[28] The anti-Germans bent on revenge struck a sympathetic chord with many of the electorate in the immediate aftermath of the war. Although their influence would ebb in the first months of 1919, they were able to force the government to commit itself to a more severe course than it had wished to adopt. Anti-Germanism emerged as a potent political weapon in time to be wielded in the 1918 general election, and Lloyd George had to ensure that it would not be wielded against himself.

THE GENERAL ELECTION

Lloyd George badly needed an electoral victory to help legitimize his leadership. One of the constraints on Lloyd George was his tenuous position as leader of a coalition government. Having come to office through what amounted to a palace coup, he was dependent on the support of Unionist MPs. The Unionist leader, Andrew Bonar Law, in addressing his fellow Unionist MPs on November 12, 1918, observed of Lloyd George's predicament, "It is not his Liberal friends, it is the Unionist Party which has made him Prime Minister."[29] Lloyd George was at the height of his personal popularity, however. As one observer reporting his arrival at the London Guildhall on the eve of the armistice noted, "The whole company went nearly mad with enthusiasm and I thought they would never stop cheering."[30] The Liberal Party was meanwhile disintegrating under Lloyd George's extremely agile political feet, the majority of Liberal MPs having remained loyal to Asquith, and many of the radical wing of the party deserting to Labour.[31]

27 Cited in Christopher Andrew, *Secret Service: The Making of the British Intelligence Community* (London, 1985), 39.
28 Lord Riddell, *Lord Riddell's Intimate Diary of the Peace Conference and After, 1918–1923* (London, 1933), 46, Apr. 5, 1919.
29 Bonar Law papers, 95/3, House of Lords Record Office, London; also cited in Blake, *Unknown Prime Minister,* 387–8.
30 Diary entry, Nov. 9, 1918, Clark; *"A Good Innings,"* 183.
31 Asquith had retained the support of 160 Liberals, while 100 Liberals supported Lloyd George. Notable defections included Noel Buxton (chairman of the Liberal Foreign Affairs Group in Parliament), E. D. Morel (founder of the UDC), and C. R. Buxton.

By calling an election almost immediately, he clearly hoped to benefit from his postarmistice popularity, as did the Unionists who agreed to remain in coalition with the Lloyd George Liberals.[32] The domestic imperatives of electoral politics dismayed the diplomats, causing Lord Hardinge, the Foreign Office's permanent undersecretary, to exclaim of the impact on the negotiating process, "The whole thing is badly organised from the point of view of conversations and exchanges of views, but it must be admitted that the formation of a Government is a convincing reason for delay, although the delay has been too far prolonged."[33]

Lloyd George's early views on the German settlement, as expressed in his Caxton Hall speech in January 1918, were notably moderate. In speaking to Liberal Party workers at Downing Street the day after the armistice he reiterated these moderate views:

No settlement which contravenes the principles of eternal justice will be a permanent one. . . . We must not allow any sense of revenge, any spirit of greed, any grasping desire, to over-ride the fundamental principle of righteousness. Vigorous attempts will be made to hector and bully the Government to make them depart from the strict principles of right and to satisfy some base, sordid, squalid ideas of vengeance and of avarice.[34]

He was already aware, however, that among his coalition partners some members held more extreme views. On October 28 a group of Unionist MPs, calling themselves the National Party, had placed an advertisement in the *Times* with the message, "Germany Can Pay. Germany Must Pay."[35] Such views were not confined to the Unionists. Lloyd George's own Liberal supporters were sending back reports from the constituencies indicating strong support for harsh action against the Germans, including heavy reparations, the trial of leading Germans, and the expulsion of German nationals from Great Britain. Jan Smuts observed that he had besought Lloyd George "not to commit himself, told him he was bound to win easily and that he need give no pledges. But letters came pouring in from election agents all over the country declaring that people were caring about nothing but punishments and indemnities and Lloyd George gave way."[36]

32 Lloyd George announced the calling of a general election on Nov. 12, Parliament was dissolved on Nov. 25, the election was held on Dec. 14, and the results declared on Dec. 28, 1918.
33 Hardinge to Rodd, Jan. 11, 1919, box 20, First Lord Rennell of Rodd papers, Bodleian Library, Oxford.
34 Nicolson, *Peacemaking 1919,* 21.
35 A faction of the Conservative MPs formed in September 1917. See Henry Page Croft, *My Life of Strife* (London, 1948).
36 Trevor Wilson, ed., *The Political Diaries of C. P. Scott, 1911–1928* (London, 1970) (hereafter C. P. Scott diary), 375, diary entry recording conversation with Smuts, July 5, 1919.

Lloyd George later recalled that at the time his government was threatened by conspiracies from both right and left. "Had he proceeded to Paris with both flanks thus continuously exposed, he would have been hampered and uncertain in his every decision. It was essential for him to provide himself with an unassailable mandate."[37]

Lloyd George opened his campaign on November 23 with a notably moderate speech focusing on domestic issues with the theme, "To make Britain a fit country for heroes to live in." The audience, however, wanted to hear about his plans to punish the Germans, much to his discomfiture.[38] Lloyd George was not slow to respond to the political climate. On November 29 he dramatically and publicly adopted a much harsher line toward the German settlement, stating to an enraptured audience that "Germany must pay the cost of the war up to the limit of her capacity to do so," as well as supporting the view that the Kaiser had committed indictable offenses.[39] The *Times* observed with some satisfaction of this development, "Mr. Lloyd George showed a sounder instinct for political strategy when he endeavoured . . . to satisfy the public demand on the[se] two fundamental questions."[40] On December 5 he issued a Statement of Policy that included the phrase, "The Kaiser must be prosecuted."[41] It also reiterated the policy of exacting reparations up to the capacity of Germany to pay. In all of these statements Lloyd George was careful to leave room for maneuver as to what actually would be done. He was clearly reluctant to tie himself with iron-clad public promises, as he would not want to go to the negotiating table with his position thus restricted. Lloyd George's careful attempts to avoid specific commitments, however, were noted and criticized in the press, and on December 11, in a speech at Bristol, he felt obliged to name a reparations figure. He stated that the British estimate of damage was £24,000 million, though he added that this was known to exceed German capacity to pay. What would be remembered from this speech, though, was the figure stated.[42] Both Lloyd George and Bonar Law were clearly skeptical of the higher figures being bandied about in electoral oratory, but neither did they publicly attack them. Many of their coalition colleagues gave vent to less restrained rhetoric. George Barnes, one of the Labour members of the government, launched the slogan "I am for hanging the Kaiser," while Eric

37 Nicolson, *Peacemaking 1919*, 19.
38 *Times* (London), Nov. 25, 1918, reporting speech at Wolverhampton, Nov. 23, 1918.
39 *Times* (London), Nov. 30, 1918, reporting speech at Newcastle-upon-Tyne, Nov. 29, 1918.
40 Ibid.
41 Antony Lentin, *Lloyd George, Woodrow Wilson, and the Guilt of Germany: An Essay on the Pre-history of Appeasement* (Leicester, 1984), is the best account on this aspect.
42 *Times* (London), Dec. 12, 1918, reporting speech at Bristol, Dec. 11, 1918.

Geddes made the famous promise, "The Germans, if this Government is returned, are going to pay every penny, they are going to be squeezed as a lemon is squeezed – until the pips squeak."[43] All these politicians were careful to hedge their statements round with warning caveats, but the "news bite" that was headlined and recalled were these hardline statements.

Some of the leading figures on the political left despaired at the turn the campaign had taken, with Beatrice Webb writing, "I feel physically sick when I read the frenzied appeals of the Coalition leaders . . . to hang the Kaiser, ruin and humiliate the German people – even to deprive Germany of her art treasures and libraries. . . . It may be all election talk, but it is mean and brutal talk degrading to the electorate."[44] Many contemporaries, and most subsequent historians, saw this shift as a direct result of the necessities of electoral life. C. P. Scott, editor of the *Manchester Guardian,* noted, "George who at the start meant very well (he spoke to me of his determination to stand for a just peace with obvious sincerity) has gone downhill under stress of the election."[45]

The election was a resounding success for the coalition, winning a majority of over 340, the largest majority in history. Among those who lost their seats were the leading antiwar members of the Independent Labour Party, including Ramsay Macdonald and Philip Snowden. The result also revealed darker domestic fears, with the head of Scotland Yard's Special Branch warning that "the sweeping defeat of pacifist and revolutionary candidates, such as W. C. Anderson, Miss Mary MacArthur, Mr. Jowett, Mr. Snowden, Mr. Ramsay Macdonald and others at the recent Election will probably result in a recrudescence of underground revolutionary agitation for 'direct action,' on the plea that the House of Commons has ceased to represent the nation as a whole."[46] Nicolson observed that the result certainly had "returned to Westminster the most unintelligent body of public-school boys which even the Mother of Parliaments has known."[47] Lloyd George was under no illusion as to the trustworthiness of his own backbenchers. During the campaign he wrote to his wife, "candidates are pretending support who mean murder."[48] C. P. Scott informed President Wilson that the election result was

---

43 *Times* (London), Dec. 2, 1918, reporting Barnes speaking at Netherton, Nov. 29, 1918. *Cambridge Daily News,* Dec. 11, 1918, reporting Geddes speaking at Cambridge, Dec. 9, 1918.
44 Margaret I. Cole, ed., *Beatrice Webb's Diaries, 1912–1924* (London, 1952) (hereafter Webb diary), 139, Dec. 12, 1918.
45 C. P. Scott to J. L. Hammond, Dec. 4, 1918, C. P. Scott diary, 362.
46 "Fortnightly Report on Revolutionary Organisations in the United Kingdom and Morale Abroad," Dec. 30, 1918, 24/73/GT 6603, GB CAB 24, Public Records Office.
47 Nicolson, *Peacemaking 1919,* 19.
48 Lloyd George to Margaret Lloyd George, Dec. 13, 1918, in Kenneth O. Morgan, ed., *Lloyd George: Family Letters, 1885–1936* (Cardiff, 1973), 189.

"due to a great wave of emotion thrown up by the war and was at the bottom an expression of pure anti-Germanism inflamed by Lloyd George's appeals."[49] Lloyd George had finally won his own popular mandate, but at the cost of seemingly committing himself to an uncongenial course of action. His position, however, remained tenuous. Walter Long, a Unionist member of the cabinet, observed of the result, "George thinks he won the election. Well he didn't. It was the Tories that won the election, and he will soon begin to find that out."[50] Lloyd George was prime minister by the grace of the Unionist Party, the majority partner in the coalition. If they withdrew their support, as they eventually would do in 1922, he would immediately fall from office. Lloyd George the peacemaker would have to act cautiously in negotiating a settlement and continue watching his home front.

WHITEHALL

This leads to a consideration of how Great Britain's policies for the German settlement actually evolved, as not all fell within the sphere of popular debate. Most people were ignorant of the minutiae of the territorial questions. Lloyd George pointed out to the Commons, "How many Members have heard of Teschen? I do not mind saying that I had never heard of it."[51] Much of the detailed planning was therefore left to the Whitehall bureaucracy, in which a number of centers of policy development can be identified. The Foreign Office played a role on territorial questions, particularly through its Political Intelligence Department; the Treasury and Board of Trade influenced to some extent the financial clauses; while the Admiralty and War Offices helped to shape the military provisions. All of these offices were inevitably influenced by the wider popular feeling about the nature of the peace settlement. All their recommendations had to be fed up the political chain of command to the cabinet and Lloyd George. The entire process was made all the more difficult by Lloyd George's well-known suspicion of the established bureaucracies and a fondness for creating ad hoc parallel structures.

The Foreign Office had been preparing, ever since the return of Lord Hardinge as permanent undersecretary in 1916, to play a leading role in determining Britain's diplomatic strategy and in implementing that strategy

---

49 C. P. Scott diary, Dec. 29, 1918, 366. Scott was generally a supporter of Lloyd George, but during the 1918 campaign he had vociferously opposed Lloyd George's coalition with the Tories.
50 A. J. P. Taylor, ed., *Lloyd George: A Diary by Frances Stevenson* (London, 1971), 169, entry for Mar. 5, 1919.
51 *Hansard,* 5th ser., vol. 114, Apr. 16, 1919.

at a postwar peace conference.[52] With this end in mind, Hardinge had
worked out an elaborate structure and brought together a trained staff to
service this role. Already 180 background reports had been prepared. Lloyd
George, however, had other plans. To begin with, he intended to attend the
conference in person, a decision that undoubtedly surprised Hardinge, who
assumed that the foreign secretary would oversee the lengthy negotiations.
Lloyd George's decision to attend the conference must have been as great a
shock to the Foreign Office as was Wilson's decision to attend in person.
Lloyd George saw no reason why the arrangements for a diplomatic conference should be left to the Foreign Office and instead assigned this function to the secretary to the cabinet, Maurice Hankey. The drawing up of a
peace brief for the British delegation was likewise not assigned to the Foreign Office, but rather to Jan Smuts, on October 21, 1918. It was a remarkable choice when one considers that it had been only fourteen years since
Smuts had been on the other side of the negotiating table from Britain at
the end of the Boer War. Smuts, however, had no significant staff at his disposal, and inevitably had to rely on the existing machinery. Hardinge
offered Smuts the cooperation of the Foreign Office, of which Smuts made
full use. As a result, Smuts's peace brief essentially consisted of reports prepared by the PID, together with reports from the Board of Trade and the
Treasury. Since it was widely used in Paris by the staff that attended Lloyd
George, these departments played a role in determining the contours of
Britain's diplomatic strategy.

On the issue of reparations, Lloyd George also went outside Whitehall by
appointing on November 26, 1918, Billy Hughes, the Australian prime
minister, as chairman of the cabinet committee on the subject. Hughes's
views did not converge with more temperate opinion in London, and this
post was in part an attempt to co-opt the irascible Australian, who had
already made a row over London's failure to consult the dominions in settling the armistice terms.[53] It was an attempt Lloyd George must subsequently have regretted, as Hughes became the most vocal exponent of a
Carthaginian peace among the British delegation at Paris. The appointment
of both Smuts and Hughes to such key roles in the peace process must also
be seen as part of the necessity to assuage the dominions' feeling that they
were being ignored now that their wartime sacrifice had been made. The
future relationship of the self-governing dominions to Great Britain was yet
another of the many domestic issues Lloyd George had to keep in mind.

52 See Roberta Warman, "The Erosion of Foreign Office Influence in the Making of Foreign Policy,
    1916–1918," *Historical Journal* 15 (1972): 133–59.
53 Amery diary, Nov. 8, 1918.

At Paris the election pledges continued to haunt British diplomacy. Lloyd George in negotiating over reparations found himself engaged in a two-front struggle. On one side, he had to consider this issue as part of the overall negotiations at Paris, and how the issue formed part of Great Britain's strategic objectives vis-à-vis other countries. On the other hand, he was aware that it was the issue that attracted the greatest attention from his home front. He was clearly unhappy with the pressure of the hardliners, such as Hughes and his colleague Lord Sumner, and was looking for ways to escape their strictures and regain diplomatic flexibility. A month into the conference he noted, "That stunt about indemnities from Germany that *they* [Hughes and Sumner] started during the election was a very foolish business."[54] Hankey remarked on March 5, 1919, "I fancy that the economic and financial conditions are going to be our bottle neck. Reparation is especially a difficulty. I am afraid that those Election pledges will be like a millstone round our neck."[55] So events were to prove. The speed with which the conference came to grips with the key questions has frequently been criticized, but from the point of view of easing the domestic pressures on the negotiators it was undoubtedly a benefit, allowing the emotions of war to recede.

From the perspective of British negotiating strategy, the problem of reparations has to be seen as forming part of the concerns over the future Franco-German balance in western Europe. At Paris, British policy toward western Europe desired the continuance of its traditional policy of maintaining a balance of power. In applied terms, for Great Britain a balance-of-power system was one that prevented any one power from dominating the continent opposite it and thus posing an invasion threat. This not only meant rolling back German power but also blocking France's mor expansionist plans. Great Britain had no intention of replacing a German threat with a French one. The eastern European settlement was envisaged on lines similar to those espoused by the New Europe group, who through their presence in the PID and as expert advisers at Paris, had unusual influence in the negotiations. Eastern Europe's part in the balance of power was to remain stable and thereby avoid causing consequential disturbances to the western European balance. It was thought this could best be achieved by the

54 Webb diary, Feb. 22, 1919. Lloyd George, during a visit to London to deal with the threat of a miner's strike, asked Haldane to arrange a dinner with the Webbs, much to their bafflement. It was probably intended not only to try to build bridges with Labour over the miners but also to try to indicate Lloyd George's attitude to the German settlement.
55 Hankey to Jones, Mar. 5, 1919, in Thomas Jones, *Whitehall Diary* (London, 1969), vol. 1: *1916–1925* (hereafter Jones diary), 80–1.

creation of reasonably well-sized nation-based states, thereby reducing the causes for dispute to a minimum.

As the negotiations played themselves out at Paris, the reparations question came to be debated as part of the western European settlement. The British during the early months of the conference had seen the French make a reflexive bid for supremacy, which included a substantial territorial rearrangement in western Europe and the creation in eastern Europe of allied states, in particular Poland, which was to benefit greatly from German territory. Lloyd George's expert advisers were bringing increasingly to his attention the dangers posed for British security if French dominance was allowed on the continent. Allen Leeper was warning by mid-March that the French "are obsessed by the dream of a great Poland which could and should never exist."[56] Likewise, penal reparations were seen as part of a French program to keep Germany weak, and as John Maynard Keynes had already observed in December, the "French demand for a huge indemnity was to be the basis for continued occupation and ultimate acquisition of the Rhine provinces."[57] Keynes opposed heavy reparations on several grounds, but he was also among the first to perceive the linkage between financial instability and the balance of power. Increasingly the concerns of Keynes and his Treasury colleagues over the future financial stability of Germany meshed with the worries of the territorial advisers over French aims, and this brought about a shift of attitude at the highest level. As concerns grew in the British delegation about French aims, so British thinking on reparations began to alter during the critical month in which the conference considered the linked issues of the Rhineland and reparations.

The linkage of economic consequences to future diplomatic development was only just coming to be seen as an integral part of statecraft. The perception of reparations as a serious problem to those primarily engaged on the territorial settlement grew but slowly within the British delegation as its impact on the continental balance became more evident. Assessing punitive reparations on Germany might have been a popular domestic proposal that offered the illusion not only of penal punishment but also of less domestic financial strain. Some negotiators, though, sensed the danger that harsh reparations might weaken Germany to the extent that it would cease

56 A. W. A. Leeper to R. W. A. Leeper, Mar. 17, 1919, A. W. A. Leeper papers, Churchill College, Cambridge.
57 Quoted in Howard Elcock, *Portrait of a Decision: The Council of Four and the Treaty of Versailles* (London, 1972), 49. A strong argument that reparation demands were not a function of France's Rhenish policy is made by Marc Trachtenberg, *Reparation in World Politics: France and European Economic Diplomacy, 1916–1923* (New York, 1980).

to be an effective counterweight against France, an eventuality that suited French but not British plans.

The pivotal month of the conference was between March 25 and April 22, when it almost collapsed over the question of reparations and the Rhineland. This period also coincides with a demonstrable shift in public opinion in Great Britain and with Lloyd George consolidating his position in the Commons. This critical month followed Wilson's return to Paris and the decision to establish the Council of Four, and began with Lloyd George's Fontainebleau Memorandum. In the preparation of this document, Lloyd George had his advisers role-play characters from the various home fronts, with Hankey acting as the average Englishman.[58] Lloyd George concluded in the memorandum that the envisaged settlement was of Carthaginian proportions, and that it was probably unworkable in the short term and certainly in the long term. He therefore opposed transferring more Germans from German rule than could be helped, and he argued that Germany could not be both crippled and expected to pay. As a former chancellor of the exchequer he had a good grasp of financial issues and their political ramifications. He aptly noted that "injustice, arrogance, displayed in the hour of triumph will never be forgotten or forgiven." Lloyd George was clearly paving the way to distance himself from earlier, hardline statements. Smuts indeed had "advised him for the sake of his own future and the future of the world to stand by the great human democratic things, even if it meant temporary defeat and eclipse."[59]

The British attempt to avoid agreeing to high payments began on March 28 with a proposal to separate the issues of what Germany owed and what it could pay. Lloyd George argued that if a single assessment was made, whatever sum was named, "many people in England, as well as in France, will exclaim at once: 'It is too small!'"[60] The *New Europe* supported the growing view that the amount of reparations to be paid had to be set at a realistic level, observing that as such it held "a middle position between the fantastic endeavour to extract twenty-five milliards out of Germany and the positively traitorous tendency to 'let the Germans down easy.'"[61] After fur-

58 Lord Hankey, *The Supreme Control at the Paris Peace Conference, 1919* (London, 1963), 100–1.
59 Smuts to A. Clark, Mar. 28, 1919, in W. K. Hancock and Jean van der Poel, eds., *Selections from the Smuts Papers* (Cambridge, 1966), vol. 4, doc. 921.
60 Paul Mantoux, *The Deliberations of the Council of Four (March 24–June 28, 1919): Notes of the Official Interpreter* (hereafter *DCF*), trans. and ed. Arthur S. Link, with the assistance of Manfred F. Boemeke, 2 vols. (Princeton, N.J., 1992), 1:59.
61 Cited in Hugh Seton-Watson and Christopher Seton-Watson, *The Making of a New Europe: R. W. Seton-Watson and the Last Years of Austria-Hungary* (London, 1981), 352.

ther negotiations, it was agreed on April 7 to establish an inter-Allied reparations commission to set the sum owed no later than May 1921.

Lloyd George still had to face the hardliners in his own camp. Toward the
end of March, Claude Lowther circulated a note to all MPs claiming Ger-
many could easily pay £25,000 million, an amount close to what Lloyd
George had suggested during the election campaign was owed by Germany.
The incident forced a special debate in the Commons on April 2. Bonar
Law did his best to deflect Lowther and the hardliners, but as he wrote to
Lloyd George, "I had a bad time about indemnities last night. I do not think
I convinced anyone and probably nine out of ten, of the Unionist members
at least, were disgusted."[62] The pressure on the British peacemakers contin-
ued to mount, and on April 8 a group of 233 Unionist MPs issued a joint
letter, published in the *Times* the following day, demanding that Germany
be made to pay the full cost of the war. The situation was grave enough for
Bonar Law to fly to Paris to discuss it with the prime minister. Lloyd
George, sensing his antagonists closing in on him, opted to take the offensive. He decided to return to London and confront his opponents in Parliament. He was careful to lay the groundwork for this action, requiring of
the Council of Four that before he confronted Parliament the date be
announced when the treaty would be presented to the Germans. Hankey
recalled that to this announcement Lloyd George "attached the utmost
importance, in order to improve the atmosphere."[63] It was therefore arranged that this be announced the day before his speech. First, however, he
dealt with the hardliners in the British Empire Delegation, bludgeoning
them into submission, with Bonar Law's assistance, at a meeting on April
11.[64] Just before he departed for London he told his colleagues in the
Council of Four, "I will return on Friday, unless the House of Commons
refuses me its confidence – in which case it will be with Lord Northcliffe
or with Horatio Bottomley that you will continue these discussions."[65]
Lloyd George was aware, though, that British public opinion was already
beginning to shift to new, more domestic concerns, and away from the
issues that had dominated the general election, as shown by two recent
coalition by-election losses. On March 14 an Asquithian Liberal took a seat
from the Unionists at West Leyton, while on April 11 Hull likewise
changed hands. After the former result, Lloyd George wrote to Lord

62 Bonar Law to Lloyd George, Apr. 3, 1919, 101/3/39, Bonar Law papers, quoted in Blake, *Unknown Prime Minister,* 407.
63 Hankey, 117.
64 F/28/3/24, Lloyd George papers (hereafter LGP), House of Lords Records Office, London.
65 *DCF,* 1:226.

Birkenhead that he hoped "the result of the West Leyton election will suffice as a warning to those who have drawn wrong deductions from the overwhelming majority of the last election. . . . The country is in no mood to tolerate reactionaries, high or low."[66]

At a cabinet meeting held on April 14, Lloyd George reported on the current state of the reparations negotiations, which he believed would give France £5,100 million and Britain £2,200 million. Given that the hardliners had been demanding £24,000 million, Bonar Law asked nervously, "What will our lunatics at home say to this?"[67] Lloyd George, however, had an answer ready for them. On April 16, he made one of his greatest speeches in the Commons, and in it he demolished his opponents. Seton-Watson observed that Lloyd George had in this confrontation succeeded in extracting "a blank cheque from the House of Commons for the remainder of his activities in Paris."[68] Lloyd George himself thought that he had gained "complete mastery of the House, while telling them absolutely nothing about the peace conference."[69] Lloyd George's demolition of his parliamentary opponents and his seizure of the political initiative was a virtuoso performance and shows the Welsh wizard at his most effective.

Lloyd George was now able to return to Paris with a sense of greater stability on his home front. As a result, he could push for moderating the reparations terms, which would in turn help to establish a better equilibrium between France and Germany as well as help to block French hegemonic aspirations. By the end of April the Council of Four had agreed on the text of the peace treaty, which was presented to Germany on May 7. Public opinion is notably volatile and forgetful, and in some quarters surprise was expressed as to the harshness of the treaty. Those on the political left, such as Beatrice Webb, branded it, not surprisingly, a "hard and brutal peace," though her more perceptive husband noted that on examining the details it was better than might have been expected. He saw that the open reparations amount and projected war crimes trials were an elegant way of putting them off to a later date when they could be overthrown.[70] C. P. Scott, more importantly for Lloyd George, wrote in the *Manchester Guardian,* "The fundamental question is whether we desire a peace of appeasement or a peace of violence."[71] George Barnes, the token Labour member of the British delegation, observed, "The terms seem to be out of character with the aims

66 F/3/5/1, LGP.
67 Jones diary, 84. This meeting is not recorded in the run of Cabinet Minutes in GB CAB 23.
68 "The Cup and the Lip," *New Europe* 11 (Apr. 24, 1919): 25.
69 Taylor, ed., *Lloyd George: A Diary by Frances Stevenson,* entry for Apr. 17, 1919.
70 Webb diary, May 10, 1919.
71 *Manchester Guardian,* May 10, 1919.

of the mass of our people."[72] The *New Europe,* while unhappy with the potential difficulties over the open reparations, focused on raised popular expectations: "At the time of the General Election we said that someone was being duped. Now we know who it is. Colonel Claude Lowther and his friends may shout a little while longer, but the facts of the case will drown their tumult, and the deceived peoples will demand a reckoning with those who so wantonly misled them."[73] Harold Nicolson, as usual, put his finger on the greatest point of discontent when he wrote to his wife, "The great crime is in the reparation clauses, which were drawn up solely to please the House of Commons, and which are quite impossible to execute."[74]

It has been observed, "Once alive to the resurgence of moderate feeling and the extent of support which it commanded, Lloyd George was in a fever of anxiety to accommodate it."[75] As a result, Lloyd George took the unusual step of summoning the cabinet to a meeting in Paris on June 1, where it decided that the treaty was indeed too harsh and gave Lloyd George a free hand to attempt further modifications. The British public had by now lost interest in the negotiations, and, as Robert Graves recalled, public interest now "concentrated entirely on three home-news items: Hawker's Atlantic flight and rescue; the marriage of England's reigning beauty, Lady Diana Manners; and a marvellous horse called The Panther – the Derby favourite, which came in nowhere."[76] By this stage, however, the complex interlocking components that comprise an international settlement were no longer easily played with, and no significant modifications could now be achieved.

CONCLUSION

The difficulties facing the peacemakers at Paris in 1919 were immense, and not the least of these were their own home fronts. Lloyd George, in reporting to Parliament, observed, "I am doubtful whether any body of men with a difficult task have worked under greater difficulties – stones clattering in the roof, and crashing through the windows, and sometimes wild men screaming through the keyholes."[77] Largely as a result of his domestic situation, Lloyd George's views and pronouncements on the terms of peace with Germany and his actions during the negotiations follow a convoluted

72 Barnes to Lloyd George, May 16, 1919, F/4/3/15 LGP.
73 "First Thoughts on the Treaty," *New Europe* 11:135 (May 15, 1919): 102.
74 Letter to VSW, May 28, 1919, in Nicolson, *Peacemaking 1919,* 350.
75 Lentin, *Lloyd George, Woodrow Wilson, and the Guilt of Germany,* 94.
76 Robert Graves, *Goodbye to All That,* new ed. (London, 1960), 236.
77 *Hansard,* 5th ser., vol. 114.

and often confusing course, but tracking them against developments on the home front does help to clarify much about British statecraft during the Paris Peace Conference.

Lloyd George was a politician, not a diplomatist, and was therefore open to different pressures. The tactical approach of a politician often differs from that of a professional diplomat, and as Harold Nicolson noted after observing the prime minister at Paris, "Mr. Lloyd George taught me that apparent opportunism was not always irreconcilable with vision, that volatility of method is not always indicative of volatility of intention."[78] Nicolson remarked of the problems posed by the home front for the diplomacy of the conference, "It must be recognised that a Prime Minister, with his attention diverted, and his absence frequently entailed, by the requirements of domestic politics, does not in fact possess the detachment essential in a negotiation requiring flawless concentration and unruffled placidity of mind."[79]

Aside from the distractions being caused by the hardliners in Parliament, Lloyd George faced a plethora of critical domestic issues, among them industrial unrest and strikes among miners, dockers, and shipyard and utility workers in localities around the country. A member of the cabinet secretariat observed, "The conclusion of peace is really becoming very urgent from a trade and labour standpoint."[80] The miners' crisis in particular forced the prime minister to be absent from Paris for a month, from February 8 to March 6. Lloyd George told his Council of Four colleagues, "I know something about the Bolshevik danger in our countries; I have fought it for several weeks now."[81] Ireland likewise remained a volatile issue, while the year 1919 also saw revolts in Egypt and India, and a war with Afghanistan. Lloyd George's hypersensitive awareness of the precariousness of his own political base, a characteristic in marked contrast to that of Woodrow Wilson, was an important factor in his actions in the negotiations. As he became more confident of his position, so too did he feel better placed to act on the advice he was receiving on the problems of the envisaged settlement. It was Keynes who proposed the mechanism of leaving the reparations sum blank in the treaty, and leaving its determination to an inter-Allied commission, and thus holding it over for discussion in a calmer atmosphere. As is well known, subsequent events conspired to allow this process to result in a high amount being set, not at all Lloyd George's intention in 1919. Lord Blake has commented, though, "It is also true that no Prime Minister could have

78 Nicolson, *Peacemaking 1919,* 209.
79 Ibid., 64.
80 Jones to Hankey, Feb. 27, 1919, in Jones diary, 79.
81 Meeting of Mar. 27, 1919, *DCF,* 35.

survived a day if he had submitted to the House of Commons as a final figure for reparations even the highest sum that was actually within Germany's
power to pay."[82] The expedient of this unspecified amount was forced upon
British peacemakers by the combined demands of France and their own
home front. Individually, each of these could probably have been dealt with,
but jointly they prevented any British attempt to set achievable terms at the
conference. The inevitable cooling off of British public opinion shows
Lloyd George's acumen in attempting not to be tied by a reparations figure
while emotions ran high. Nicolson doubted "whether any British statesman
then alive could, given the state of public opinion at home, have achieved,
or rather, have avoided, so much."[83] The virtuosity of British statecraft is
seen, even in adversity, in its successful maneuver to leave open the way to
achieving its preferred figure.

It is questionable if the public's views had much influence after the general election, though MPs' views remained significant until Lloyd George
successfully confronted them on April 16. Lloyd George acknowledged at
the end of March 1919, "If our terms seem too moderate I will have great
difficulties in Parliament, but they won't come from the common people."[84]
In retrospect, the home front had its greatest impact on the treaty in the two
areas of reparations and war guilt, and it is the eventual imposition of harsh
terms in these areas that has most often been assailed as having fatally cor-
rupted the Versailles settlement. The experience of the impact of the home
front on the requirements of statecraft during the Paris Peace Conference
raises the consideration, how healthy is public or parliamentary pressure for
diplomacy during a period of negotiation?

82 Blake, *Unknown Prime Minister,* 405.
83 Nicolson, *Peacemaking 1919,* 63–4.
84 *DCF,* 35.

7

The French Peacemakers and Their Home Front

GEORGES-HENRI SOUTOU

David Lloyd George is usually considered to have lived up to his reputation for wiliness at the Paris Peace Conference. Woodrow Wilson remains the principled man, despite having succumbed to the tricks of corrupt Europeans. And Georges Clemenceau is generally believed to have led France well during the war, but to have been no more than an ineffective and irritated old man during the peace conference. I would like to revise this judgment and to argue that Clemenceau, the man who coined the phrase "politicians never resign and seldom die," was, on the contrary, at the height of his political and intellectual power and extracted probably the most that could have been expected for France, a country among the victors, on the one hand, but, on the other, exhausted far more than its allies or enemies.

FRENCH WAR AIMS

It is first of all necessary to keep in mind French war aims as they had evolved since the beginning of the war and been agreed upon by the government during the autumn of 1916. Apart from the return of Alsace-Lorraine, there was general agreement that German geopolitical, military, and economic power should be drastically reduced. Germany was widely considered to have striven for, and largely achieved, a hegemonic position in Europe. Thus it would be necessary to reduce its territory: Russia would take the Polish part of Prussia; France would retake Alsace-Lorraine and annex the Saar. There was no complete agreement in government circles on the Rhineland. Some favored annexation. Others thought this went too far and suggested that it should instead be cut off from Germany and transformed into two states closely linked to France and Belgium. At the very least it would be permanently occupied by French forces. But everyone

167

agreed that France's allies should let Paris decide the matter when the time came. As for the rest of Germany, it might be transformed into a loose confederation, in place of the Bismarckian Reich.[1]

The only discussion that took place in Parliament about war aims was in June 1917. Under the influence of the Russian Revolution, the failure of the Nivelle offensive in April, and America's entry into the war, a majority agreed that there should be no annexation of the Rhineland. Nevertheless, a very large majority wanted "security guarantees on the left bank of the Rhine," which meant either permanent occupation or even separation from Germany.

French war aims included a drastic reduction of German economic power, entailing Allied control of raw materials imported by Germany and of German exports, as envisioned at the Allied Economic Conference of June 1916. At the same time, the return of Alsace-Lorraine, the annexation of the Saar and possibly Luxembourg (which would at the very least be closely linked to France), and trade agreements with Belgium and Italy would make France the center of a large, new industrial grouping in western Europe.

These war aims, in conjunction with colonial aims in Africa, such as the seizure of Togo and Cameroon and the establishment of a French presence in the Middle East, implied a complete victory over Germany and were widely shared among political circles, economic groups, and numerous lobbies. But there were dissenters. In 1917 Joseph Caillaux, an influential radical leader, pleaded that the best security for France would be the democratization of Germany; Aristide Briand, prime minister until March, and Paul Painlevé, war minister and prime minister from September to November, believed it might be necessary to come to a compromise peace with Germany, which would balance German concessions in the west (restoration of Belgium, return of Alsace-Lorraine, potential security arrangements involving both Alsace-Lorraine and the Rhineland) with German advantages in the east, at the expense of Russia. They made contacts with Germany and Austria-Hungary to that end. Both Briand and Painlevé believed it might not be in France's interest to reduce German power too drastically in face of the Russian Revolution and the evident ascendancy of England and the United States.[2]

---

1 For French war aims, see Georges-Henri Soutou, "La France et les Marches de l'Est, 1914–1919," *Revue historique,* no. 528 (Oct.–Dec. 1978): 341–88; David Stevenson, *French War Aims Against Germany, 1914–1919* (Oxford, 1982); Soutou, *L'Or et le Sang: Les buts de guerre économiques de la Première Guerre mondiale* (Paris, 1989).

2 George-Henri Soutou, "Briand et l'Allemagne au tournant de la guerre (septembre 1916–janvier 1917)," in *Media in Francia . . . Recueil de mélanges offerts à Karl Ferdinand Werner à l'occasion de son 65ème*

Clemenceau put an end to those speculations and secret dealings when he became prime minister in November 1917 and restored French war aims to the shape they had taken during the discussions of autumn 1916 and spring 1917. Those aims inspired his policies during and after the war much more than has been generally admitted, and I do not share the oft-held view that he disregarded them. But, even if the greater part of public opinion, without necessarily agreeing in all the details of the government's aims, shared the main idea that German power, both geostrategic and economic, should be curtailed, there was still a current of dissent within France. In particular, large banks and heavy industry, which had had close links to the Central Powers before the war, preferred a resumption of those links to the punitive and, in their view, detrimental economic war aims of the government and the reorientation toward Great Britain that they entailed. Some conservative circles did not like the prospect of French alignment with England and the United States. They preferred a more balanced postwar order, one less punitive toward Germany and Austria-Hungary, which they considered useful bulwarks against the consequences of the upheaval in Russia and the threat of social revolution in Europe after the war.[3] On the left, many believed that democratization of Germany would be more useful than the enforcement of traditional territorial peace terms. To some extent, Clemenceau discreetly took these views into account.

CLEMENCEAU THE PEACEMAKER

There is no question that Clemenceau was in full control of peacemaking on the French side. He worked with a close inner group, which included Georges Mandel, Philippe Berthelot at the Foreign Ministry, André Tardieu, and Louis Loucheur for reparations and economic questions. But he was, at the same time, war minister, and as such he had direct control over the army and the Secret Service, both of which played major roles, for example, in the Rhine question and in the problems affecting central and eastern Europe. Furthermore, his extensive net of relations formed over the years since 1871 gave him access, outside of the political world, to the press and to economic circles, either directly or through the inner group I have mentioned.[4] One

anniversaire (Paris, 1989); Georges-Henri Soutou, "Poincaré, Painlevé et l'offensive Nivelle," forthcoming.

3 See Gabriel Hanotaux, *Carnets (1907–1925),* published by Georges Dethan in collaboration with Georges-Henri Soutou and Marie-Renée Mouton (Paris, 1982).

4 See Jean-Baptiste Duroselle, *Clemenceau* (Paris, 1988); David Robin Watson, *Georges Clemenceau: A Political Biography* (London, 1974); Général Mordacq (Clemenceau's chef de cabinet at the War Ministry), *Le Ministère Clemenceau: Journal d'un témoin,* 4 vols. (Paris, 1930).

should not be misled by the often sorry state of French archives for that period; one must remember that most clerical work at the Foreign Office was performed by retired diplomats or very young men unfit for service at the front, and at the War Ministry by wounded officers.[5] Present-day historians, surrounded by the comforts of their universities, often have some trouble comprehending the actual state of affairs in a country that was exerting all of its resources to win, or perhaps I should say not to lose, the war. But Clemenceau was at the controls, and he received all the necessary information.

Clemenceau had little interference to fear. Raymond Poincaré, the president of the republic, lost most of his influence the minute Clemenceau came to power. The majority of Parliament, across the political spectrum, was solidly behind Clemenceau, even if sometimes he had to bow to its wishes, as, for instance, when it came to the self-determination of eastern European countries. The only opposition came from the socialists and the unreconciled Caillautist radicals.

Thus in simultaneous and full control of all the necessary levers and encountering little opposition in France, Clemenceau could embark upon an active and complex peace strategy that had a profound inner logic and was closely related to French war aims, even if, owing to its secrecy and complexity, its logic escaped many contemporaries who criticized it as indecisive and haphazard. His strategy was three-tiered. First, he hoped to achieve a basic and permanent alliance with Great Britain and the United States, because of common values and genuinely shared views on some problems, because Clemenceau considered this to be the best guarantee of French security, and because such an alliance was necessary to encourage both London and Washington to accept French war aims. The second tier was, under the cover of the first and to the greatest possible extent, to implement French war aims as they had developed since the beginning of the war. The third tier was very secret: it entailed conversations with the Germans concerning political and economic issues. These conversations, from spring 1919, were thought necessary in order to encourage Germany to sign the treaty and accept its reduced status. Moreover, France would have to live with Germany even after the peace treaty and could not expect to rely entirely on Anglo-American support, especially in economic matters.

---

5 For a vivid description of the Foreign Office at the time, see Jean Barbier, *Un Frac de Nessus* (Rome, 1951).

THE FIRST TIER OF CLEMENCEAU'S PEACE: THE UNION OF WESTERN DEMOCRACIES

There is no reason to dispute Clemenceau's liberalism and his deep ideological and sentimental sympathy for the democratic way of life in Great Britain and the United States. He was convinced France shared those values with its Anglo-American friends, and that was for him one (but only one) pillar essential to France's security in the future. That is why he was convinced that peace should be not only victorious but also just. That is why he was not against the Fourteen Points even if he considered them too abstract.[6] That is also why he was willing to sacrifice major French war aims, such as a separate Rhenish entity, in order to achieve the two treaties of guarantee with Great Britain and the United States.[7]

In fact, the most important positive features of the Versailles Treaty from a German point of view, features that ran against expectations in France but also in Great Britain, were the confirmation of German unity and the non-annexation of territories undisputably German. These were not just concessions on Clemenceau's part to Anglo-American views; they corresponded to his deep-seated conviction that German unity was final and that France should abandon its old dream of the "frontières naturelles," that is, of annexing the Rhineland.[8]

Finally, although Clemenceau was less sanguine than Wilson or Lloyd George about the prospects for democracy in the new Germany, the French did follow most closely internal events in that country in 1919. Some of their agents there supported the Independent Socialists, believed to come closest to the French Jacobin model.[9] Clemenceau himself considered the occupation along the Rhine as a sort of democratic school for the inhabitants of the Rhineland and, by extension, the whole Reich.

Clemenceau also personally and directly supported Commerce and Industry Minister Etienne Clémentel's views on economic cooperation of the Allies after the war in order to share scarce raw materials, expedite reconstruction, and expand trade. Although there were ulterior motives, such as to control the German economy and to force Germany, through economic blackmail, to respect the terms of the peace treaty, there was also the genuine wish to rationalize the world economy along liberal lines,

6 Duroselle, *Clemenceau,* 721ff.
7 André Tardieu, *La Paix* (Paris, 1921), is, in fact, an extended justification of this choice.
8 See Duroselle, *Clemenceau,* 727.
9 See Henning Köhler, *Novemberrevolution und Frankreich* (Düsseldorf, 1980).

involving a modicum of government control and international cooperation in order to regulate market forces so that the price and flow of commodities would not vary too wildly after the war. Let it be said at the outset that the resolute opposition of first the United States and later on Great Britain to this typically French proposition led in the summer of 1919 to a reorientation of French policy.[10]

THE SECOND TIER: FRENCH GEOSTRATEGIC AND ECONOMIC INTERESTS

It has been frequently said, at the time and since then, that Clemenceau gave absolute priority to the alliance with England and the United States as the principal basis of French security and that he sacrificed other French war aims to achieve that end, especially territorial ones, such as autonomy for the Rhineland, in which he supposedly did not really believe.[11] But the facts appear to have been more complex and must be seen in the context of a multitiered policy.

For instance, the whole territorial complex of the Rhine regions was very much on Clemenceau's mind. As for the Saar, he had to abandon, against the adamant opposition of Lloyd George and Wilson, the claim of the 1814 border, which included one-half of the territory, although this was one of the few war aims he had precisely stated. It is often not clearly recognized that the French were at the time convinced that they would win the 1935 plebiscite. They owned the mines and all the schools, housing, and social services that came with them and hoped to use them to win hearts and minds. Further, they were preparing a penetration of the Saar economy by French firms and decided very early to introduce the franc in the expectation that prosperity in the Saar, in contrast to the ruin of Germany, would influence voters in France's favor. As early as July 1919 a special committee, under the direct supervision of Clemenceau and Tardieu, began to devise this policy, the avowed aim of which was to influence the 1935 plebiscite so that the voters would choose union with France (or part of them would do so: the vote would take place precinct by precinct and the Saar territory could be divided along the results of the vote; this frequently overlooked disposition of the treaty is for me proof that the French meant

10 See Soutou, *L'Or et le Sang,* 490ff., 816ff.; and Georges-Henri Soutou, "Guerre et économie: Le premier projet français de nouvel ordre économique mondial," *Revue universelle* 31 (Apr. 1977).
11 With strong qualifications and in a positive presentation, it is still Duroselle's thesis in his *Clemenceau,* 720ff., esp. 758.

business and that the English and the Americans realized that little could be done to hinder them once the treaty had been signed).[12]

As for Luxembourg, Clemenceau, Berthelot, and a very powerful lobby of important radical politicians were keen to support, or at least to do nothing to prevent, Luxembourg republicans from toppling the monarchy, which they vainly attempted on January 9, in the knowledge that a new regime would seek close ties to France. Clemenceau officially renounced the aim of an economic union between France and Luxembourg (which would have resulted in a kind of disguised protectorate) solely in order not to antagonize the Belgians, who sought such a union for themselves. But this renunciation was disingenuous. In fact, the union between France and Belgium, the basis for which had been laid in 1915, would absorb the union between France and Luxembourg. Thus, the French insisted on gaining control of Luxembourg's railways, much to the chagrin of the Belgians, to whom Clemenceau's true motives were quite clear.[13]

As for the Rhineland, in March and April Clemenceau had to abandon first its separation from Germany and the creation there of an independent state, then permanent occupation, and to content himself instead with a fifteen-year occupation in exchange for the two treaties of guarantee with London and Washington.[14] But Clemenceau's resolution in this matter has been underrated. His frequent collisions with Ferdinand Foch have distorted historians' views on this.[15] These collisions had less to do with the principle of the Rhineland's separation from Germany than with Clemenceau's touchy views on military–civilian relations and Foch's continuing to argue for the separation of the Rhineland after Clemenceau had decided it was an aim both useless and harmful to retain, at least openly. But Foch's note to the Allies of January 10 asking for the creation of autonomous states in the Rhineland linked with France and Belgium had in fact been drafted in Tardieu's own handwriting![16]

Clemenceau certainly did not abandon his Rhenish aims. The French designed the treaty in such a way that if Germany did not pay reparations, the occupation of the Rhineland could be prolonged. Clemenceau stated his belief before the council of ministers, on April 25, that Germany would not

12 Soutou, *L'Or et le Sang,* 786–8.
13 Ibid., 794–800; and Georges-Henri Soutou, "Le Luxembourg et la France en 1919," 39 *Hémecht* (1987).
14 Duroselle, *Clemenceau,* 751–3.
15 Jacques Bariéty, *Les Relations franco-allemandes après la première guerre mondiale* (Paris, 1977), 26–63; and Pierre Miquel, *La Paix de Versailles et l'opinion publique française* (Paris, 1972), 281ff.
16 Soutou, "La France et les Marches de l'Est."

be able to pay and that the French would remain along the Rhine.[17] Here one encounters the heart of France's ulterior motives at the Paris conference.

Furthermore, Clemenceau kept a very close watch on autonomist movements in the Rhineland. He was kept fully informed by the military and the secret service about their dealings with those movements.[18] And he met with General Charles Mangin, commanding officer of French occupation forces in the Rhineland, at least three times to discuss the situation there.[19] Did he, on such an occasion, tell Mangin to encourage the autonomist movement, as J. A. Dorten has asserted?[20] Conventional wisdom suggests that he did not, citing as proof his anger at Mangin for supporting the autonomists and his sending a member of the government, Jules Jeanneney, to the Rhineland in order to inquire into the matter.[21] This is further supported by what Clemenceau himself wrote in his 1930 book *Grandeurs et misères d'une victoire,* but his assertion does not have to be taken at face value. The matter is probably more complicated. Clemenceau certainly believed Mangin had been imprudent, but he also had to discipline the general in order to placate the English and the Americans (Lloyd George wanted to reduce the fifteen-year period of occupation of the Rhineland because of these incidents) and because the involvement of the French military had been too obvious.[22] But it is evident that Clemenceau did not exclude the possibility of manipulating Rhenish separatist sentiment.

French authorities in the Rhineland and Clemenceau himself were aware of the divisions among the Rhinelanders (even if they could not understand all of their intricacies) and recognized that there were basically two kinds of separatism. The first was the moderate and "legal" one led by Konrad Adenauer.[23] This movement sought the creation of a Rhenish republic separated from Prussia but inside the Reich, in agreement with Berlin and in the framework of the new German constitution, in the hope of achieving better terms at Versailles. The second was more extremist and wanted, in fact, to gain independence from Germany through a quick and illegal "coup," even if no one other than Dorten stated it publicly. This important distinction most probably explains Clemenceau's attitude at the time. The

---

17 Bariéty, *Les Relations franco-allemandes,* 62.
18 See 6-N-116, Fonds Clemenceau, Service historique de l'armée de terre, Vincennes (hereafter SHA); and Rive Gauche du Rhin, vols. 1 and 2, Ministère des Affaires Etrangères (hereafter MAE), Europe 1920–40.
19 Notes of July 16 and Sept. 12, Rive Gauche du Rhin, vol. 1, MAE.
20 Dr. J. A. Dorten, *La Tragédie rhénane* (Paris, 1945), 77ff.
21 Duroselle, *Clemenceau,* 757–8.
22 Tardieu, *La Paix,* 418.
23 See Hans-Peter Schwarz, *Adenauer: Der Aufstieg, 1876–1952* (Stuttgart, 1986), 202ff.

Secret Service and the Deuxième Bureau of the General Staff of the Army generally favored the first option. It had wider support, from more important Rhenish personalities, and would lead to deeper, if less spectacular, results than the "coup" contemplated by Dorten and his friends.[24] Commanding officers on the spot, such as General Marie Fayolle, tended to support more radical autonomists.[25] Mangin himself probably kept both options open, as he suggested to the Foreign Ministry on July 16, 1919.[26] There is reason to believe that Clemenceau, while not wanting to go so far as to support the more extremist Dorten concept, especially after his clumsy attempts of May and June 1919, did contemplate the idea of a Rhenish republic inside the Reich. All the Secret Service and General Staff reports quoted here (which reached Clemenceau's cabinet) frankly stated that the French army of occupation was supporting the Rhenish republic (inside the Reich) scheme, which had a good chance of succeeding without outside interference. On May 17 Mangin met in Mainz with leaders of the Rhenish republican movement, who presented their ideas for a republic independent of Prussia but inside the Reich, provided that a softening of the peace terms made such a solution politically feasible.[27] On May 19 Mangin apparently told one autonomist leader, Dahlen from Aachen, that the French government would be willing to consider peace terms more favorable toward Germany and to renounce the Saar if a Rhenish republic were established, even if it remained inside the Reich.[28] Other French officers were expressing similar ideas at the same time; evidently they were maneuvering to facilitate both the acceptance of the treaty in Germany and a rearrangement of western Germany beneficial to French aims.[29]

Clemenceau was informed of these maneuvers and did nothing to stop them: a Secret Service report of May 20, addressed only to him, the Foreign Office, and Marshall Foch (and which in fact reached Clemenceau's cabinet) clearly stated the Rhinelanders' aim of establishing a Rhenish republic inside the Reich in exchange for French concessions regarding the Saar and Silesia. The report stated that the French High Command had

24 Secret Service reports of May 20 and particularly of May 26, MAE, Rive Gauche du Rhin, vol. 1.
25 Report from General Fayolle on March 30, advocating an independent Palatinate instead of a bigger Rhenish republic remaining inside the Reich, Rive Gauche du Rhin, vol. 1, MAE.
26 Ibid.
27 Secret Service note of May 20, ibid.; and Frohberger report of May 31, WK Pol 8m, Politisches Archiv des Auswärtigen Amtes, Bonn (hereafter PA-AA).
28 WK Pol 8m and Pol 8m Beiband, PA-AA.
29 Notes of May 15 and 19 (IA Deutschland 182, PA-AA) from the German general staff officer in Cologne; these same notes also mention a Captain Rostan who evidently was the liaison between Mangin and the Adenauer group; telegram sent by Brockdorff-Rantzau from Versailles on June 2, opposing Adenauer's ideas and proving that Rantzau suspected such a French ploy.

been apprised of this project and added that "the intervention of the French High Command is decisive; execution (of this project) will be presently pursued."[30] Thus there is no reason to doubt what Mangin himself told Berthelot about Clemenceau's position: "He had approved [Mangin's] line of conduct consisting in letting the minds orientate themselves towards the Rhenish Republic, of which he realized the advantages, provided that the French military authorities could not be accused of interfering." (Mangin added that he had also spoken with Mandel, who was against the idea of a Rhenish republic because it would preclude any future annexation by France, an illuminating insight about the real state of the discussions inside Clemenceau's team.)[31] Hence one can understand Clemenceau's reaction to the French army's obvious support of Dorten's sudden coup; it was both a departure from the policy evidently cleared by Paris and an irritant to the British. Clemenceau was not against Rhenish autonomy as such, but he was against the option represented by Dorten. It was considered in Paris to be ill-advised, without sufficient support in the Rhineland, and dangerous for France's relations with its allies. Mangin himself may have been confused by the complexity of the matter, by the internal rivalries among the autonomists, sometimes following personal rather than political lines, and by the fact that the autonomist leaders he saw on May 17 were deeply divided. Although they pretended on that day to be united, some supported Adenauer's prudent approach and considered the formation of a Rhenish republic inside the Reich a way to achieve better peace terms, whereas others, such as Dorten, were already contemplating a coup.[32]

After Dorten's attempt to establish a Rhenish republic failed in early June, the matter, contrary to current wisdom, did not come to a rest, least of all in Paris. At the beginning of June, Adenauer met two French officers and explained how a Rheno-Westphalian republic, separated from Prussia but remaining in the Reich, would solve France's security problem, provided that France agreed to revise the peace terms.[33] Adenauer sent the French a memorandum along those lines once again on June 16.[34] On June 19 two French agents, one from the Secret Service and one from the propaganda center of the prime minister's office, saw Froberger, a moderate autonomist, who told them that he still considered the formation of a

30 This report is to be found in both the quoted files at the MAE and the SHA.
31 Berthelot's note of July 16, 1919, Rive Gauche du Rhin, vol. 1, MAE.
32 Report of the German staff officer in Cologne, May 19, IA Deutschland 182, PA-AA; note of May 26, WK Poll 8m; see also Dorten, *La Tragédie,* 68–9.
33 Note of June 5 from the Administration des Territoires rhénans, Rive Gauche du Rhin, vol. 1, MAE.
34 Schwarz, *Adenauer,* 225.

Rhenish republic inevitable.[35] At the beginning of July Mangin met with the minister president of Hesse, who discussed with him the prospects of a smaller central Rhenish state, which would include the Palatinate and Hesse and remain inside the Reich.[36] On June 8 Paul Tirard, chief of the French administration in Rhineland and a major figure in the administrative world of the Third Republic, reported to the Foreign Ministry that Clemenceau "was himself following closely all the questions linked with the prospect of a Rhenish republic more or less independent" of the Reich. On June 9 Tirard advised the Foreign Ministry to take very seriously the possibility that Adenauer might realize his plans with the agreement of Berlin and the British authorities in Cologne.[37]

It is true that there was discussion and disagreement in Paris after Dorten's fracas in Wiesbaden. Some major diplomats, like Cambon in London, urged utmost caution, at least before the signing of the treaty.[38] But Tirard insisted that Dorten's failure did not mean that Adenauer and his group had abandoned the idea of a Rhenish republic, in agreement with Berlin and with the support of British authorities, and argued that Paris had to decide what position France would take in case Adenauer's ideas came to fruition.[39] Berthelot and Foreign Minister Stephen Pichon reaffirmed on June 10 a policy that was not inconsistent with what is known of Clemenceau's position: there was a strong movement for the separation of western Germany from Prussia and the formation of a separate entity for the Rhenish provinces inside the Reich; this movement was in France's interest, and France should, without appearing to support separatism, prevent Berlin from forcibly suppressing the expression of the Rhinelanders' free will.[40]

Of course, the signing of the treaty on June 28 without any major change from the original May 7 text, apart from the Silesian plebiscite, dealt a serious blow to Adenauer's ideas. But apparently this was not realized in Paris, and Clemenceau finally clarified his Rhenish policy at a meeting with Foreign Ministry officials and Tirard on December 20. It was decided that Tirard (who was to become high commissar in the Rhenish provinces and chairman of the Inter-Allied Commission on January 10, when the treaty would come into force) would follow a policy on two levels. He would try

---

35 Note of June 22, ibid., MAE.
36 Note from the Prussian minister in Darmstadt, July 2, IA Deutschland 182, PA-AA.
37 Rive Gauche du Rhin, vol. 1, MAE.
38 Cambon's letter from June 12, ibid.
39 Tirard's note on June 6, ibid.
40 Note of June 10, ibid.

to foster goodwill toward France, through various sorts of political and cultural propaganda, and to draw the Rhinelanders toward democratic values
on the French model, in the hope of thus influencing the evolution of the
whole Weimar Republic. But he would also "keep in constant and discreet
touch with all autonomist leaders," so that France could eventually choose
to support the group most useful to it.[41] All eventualities were thus covered.
No matter how long the occupation of the Rhineland lasted, whether or
not it resulted in the Rhineland's separation from Prussia or the Reich, it
would at least serve as a powerful means to influence positively the development of the young republic, through the attraction of French republican
values. But if the occasion arose, France would be well placed, provided its
actions were kept hidden, to promote separation from Prussia or even from
the Reich, to the extent, in the manner, and with the leaders that would
best suit it. Thus Clemenceau could reconcile his deep liberalism, his conviction that any annexation of German territory was out of the question,
and his desire to consolidate French security.

Clemenceau had a clear perception of French geopolitical and economic
interests in central and eastern Europe but has been frequently accused of
having wanted to destroy Austria–Hungary for ideological reasons. This is
not true: he did not want to recognize Czech aspirations in June 1918 but
was obliged to do so by the radical left in the Chamber.[42] Rather, he was,
in October 1918, secretly negotiating with Vienna in an attempt to save the
empire and prevent its German-speaking part from linking with Germany.[43]
After the Austrian Empire disappeared and Russia became incapable of
playing the role of counterweight to Germany, Clemenceau, Foch, and the
French military missions in eastern and central Europe played a major role
in drawing the frontiers of the new or enlarged states, which were supposed
to help France keep Germany in check ("la Barrière de l'Est"), frequently
without excessive regard for the rights of self-determination and largely
along lines of geopolitical expediency.[44] Meanwhile, Paris was preparing a
thorough economic penetration of those countries.[45] As for Russia,

41 Clemenceau note of Dec. 20 and penciled marginalia from Berthelot, ibid.; report from Tirard on
    Feb. 14, 1920, ibid., vol. 2. Tirard's far-reaching ideas about French occupation as an opportunity
    to export the French republican model to Germany can be seen in Pierre Jardin, "La Politique rhé-
    nane de Paul Tirard (1920–1923)," *Revue d'Allemagne* (Apr.–June 1989).
42 Soutou, "Jean Pélissier et l'Office Central des Nationalités, 1911–1918: Renseignement et influ-
    ence," *Relations internationales* 78 (1994).
43 Louis-Pierre Laroche, "L'affaire Dutasta: Les dernières conversations diplomatiques pour sauver
    l'empire des Habsbourg," *Revue d'histoire diplomatique* (1994).
44 See Stevenson, *French War Aims.*
45 Soutou, "L'Impérialisme du pauvre: La politique économique du gouvernement français en Europe
    centrale et orientale de 1918 à 1929," *Relations internationales* 7 (1976).

Clemenceau's policy, clumsy as it was, was to construct a powerful and democratic Russian federation. He hoped this federation would serve as a counterweight to Germany and break with czarism and Bolshevism, both of which he loathed. He did not believe, nor did his aides, in Ukrainian independence and recognized Baltic aspirations at the end of 1918 only under strong pressure from Parliament.[46]

French negotiators, with Clemenceau's support and despite his disregard of details, did not abandon French economic war aims in regard to Germany. The treaty included very important clauses concerning deliveries of German coal and chemicals to France and its allies. Although the reparations in general were not fully settled, these clauses were very precise and final and were essential to the realization of French industrial ambitions. Germany lost its patents and its oceanic telegraphic cables, its rivers were internationalized, its tariff freedom was suppressed for at least eighteen months, and it lost the benefit of the most-favored-nation clause for at least five years. That was, almost word for word, the program of the inter-Allied economic conference of 1916. Clemenceau himself successfully negotiated with Lloyd George to gain French access to Mesopotamian oil: he was not interested in economic details, but he understood perfectly well the paramount importance of oil for a country poor in natural resources, as was France.[47]

THE THIRD TIER: SECRET DEALS WITH GERMANY BUT FROM A POSITION OF STRENGTH

Professor Haguenin, chief of the so-called Press Bureau of the French embassy in Berne and in fact chief of the French Secret Service in Switzerland, which dealt with Germany during the war, arrived with his aides in Berlin in March 1919 as an unofficial representative of the French government. From that time began a series of secret Franco–German conversations, which were continued in Versailles after the German delegation arrived there. For the French, the first objective of these conversations was to persuade the Germans, through vague promises of alleviation in the future if they complied with it, to sign the treaty. But these conversations were not just tactical; they were substantive, and to some extent the French took German views into account. The Germans, as their archives testify, took the conversations very seriously. They knew Haguenin quite well; he had been a professor at Berlin University before the war (probably with links

46 See Soutou, "Jean Pélissier."
47 See Soutou, *L'Or et le Sang*.

even then to the French Secret Service) and had had very important secret talks in Switzerland with high-level Germans in 1916 and 1917.[48] To judge from these conversations, Silesia (and the 44 million ton of coal extracted there each year) was even more important to the Germans than the Saar or the Rhineland. The second major preoccupation of the Germans was the extensive power of the Reparation Commission – which amounted to full control over the German economy. Their third wish was to be allowed to submit a reparation proposal to the Allies, which would include a fixed sum for the settlement, rather than wait for a full evaluation of the damages. Thus a sort of tacit deal evolved: the Germans would accept settlement of the Saar and Rhineland issues (essential to the French) and the French would in turn agree to modify the treaty. And that is what happened! First, Clemenceau reluctantly agreed with Lloyd George to oppose Wilson and hold a plebiscite in Silesia rather than give it immediately to Poland. Although this was the only important modification to the treaty conceded to the Germans, it was of major importance to them. Second, Clemenceau agreed to the wording of the Allies' letter to the Germans on June 16 and of their declaration of June 28, both of which promised that the Reparation Commission would respect Germany's sovereignty and allow it to submit a proposal for affixed settlement.[49] One should add here that the French did not consider reparations as solely a restorative and financial matter, but also as a means to develop French industry. On this matter, they were less resistant to rational arguments than John Maynard Keynes at the time and many historians since have believed.[50]

After the signing of the treaty, in July and August, Loucheur suggested to the Germans that a series of Franco-German cartels be created, for steel, potash, and dyes. These cartels were considered a way to encourage the Germans to carry out the coal and raw materials deliveries called for by the treaty. France, according to Loucheur, would be the leader of the cartels, and in this way the industrial power base the treaty provided would be enlarged. But it went beyond that. An important segment of French industrial and economic elites, disillusioned by the Anglo-American refusal to endorse France's postwar economic plans, was fully prepared to rebuild Europe's economy on the basis of Franco-German cooperation and in competition with America and England, as the cartel proposals implied. These

---

48 See Soutou, "Briand et l'Allemagne."
49 Soutou, "La France et l'Allemagne en 1919," in J. M. Valentin, J. Bariéty, and A. Guth, eds., *La France et l'Allemagne entre les deux guerres mondiales* (Nancy, 1987).
50 See my essay in Marta Petricioli, ed., *Une Occasion manquée? 1922: la reconstruction de l'Europe* (Berne, 1995). See also Marc Trachtenberg, *Reparations in World Politics* (New York, 1980).

proposals were shelved not because of the German government (which was interested) but because of German industrialists, who did not want to deal from a position of inferiority.[51]

This discussion suggests a more complex view of Clemenceau's peace-making than is normally held. Without a doubt, he had principles and objectives and could be as obstinate as the next politician. But he also knew how to deal, even with the Germans.

PUBLIC OPINION: DISILLUSIONED AND DIVIDED

At the beginning of 1919, French public opinion tended to rally behind President Wilson and Wilsonianism, although for a variety of reasons. The Right believed that, after a bout of what Clemenceau had nastily called "noble candeur," which is not the same as "noble candor," and having been exposed to Germany's attitude throughout 1918, Wilson was approaching the French view of peace, namely, that the League of Nations would be a club of the victors, a traditional alliance against Germany, and that America would help France maintain a new European order restricting Germany. The Left clung to an idealistic view of Wilsonianism and counted on Wilson to impose a fair settlement in Europe, to support, or at least to tolerate, the Russian Revolution and to build a lasting peace along internationalist lines.[52]

When Wilson arrived in France at the beginning of 1919, he was greeted by some of the most enthusiastic demonstrations the country has ever recorded. But by the end of February hopes on both sides of the political spectrum had evaporated. The Right soon realized that the American president was not going to align himself with French positions and concluded that he would oppose them, an excessively pessimistic swing in my view. The Left was bitterly disillusioned after the failure of the Prinkipo Conference and of the socialist meeting in Berne. From that time, Wilsonianism as such had only a few supporters left in France.

During the ratification proceedings before the Chambers, lasting from July to October, Parliament and the press were very critical of the government, even in those circles that constituted its political base. Clemenceau was accused of having negotiated independently, without taking the advice of the Chambers. The treaty was considered to be lacking on two major counts: reparations, of which the amount was not even fixed and the collection problematic to say the least; and security. Several speakers regretted

---

51 Ibid. See also Soutou, *L'Or et le Sang,* and "L'année 1922."
52 Miquel, *La Paix de Versailles.*

the failure to impose a permanent occupation along the Rhine; some warned that the U.S. Senate might not ratify the treaty, which would jeopardize the treaties of guarantee with the United States and Great Britain. Clemenceau responded that he believed the Senate would ultimately ratify and argued that a refusal to do so would not weaken the treaties of guarantee. This was probably disingenuous of him, as Tardieu's book *La Paix* shows that Clemenceau was very much aware of the problem and spent the last week of April discussing it with Wilson. The result of all this concern and discussion was the final paragraph of article 429, which provided for an extension of the occupation of the Rhineland if, in 1935, security guarantees were deemed insufficient and covered the consequences of the United States' possible failure to ratify. In fact, Clemenceau alluded to article 429 in such a context before the Chamber.[53] This concession would seem farfetched today but was considered a very real and valuable asset by French political, diplomatic, and military circles until the Hague Conference of 1929.[54]

The treaty was finally carried by a vote of 372 deputies for, 53 against, and 72 abstentions. The tally was not an expression of enthusiastic support, but of the realization that it was too late to refuse the treaty unless France was prepared to launch a major crisis of uncertain outcome. The optimism of November 1918 was gone. France would have to continue its involvement in order to receive reparations and achieve security. The treaty was only a framework and would not resolve those problems by itself. Clemenceau himself was convinced of that. He told the Chamber on September 25 that the treaty was "not even a beginning, but the beginning of a beginning."[55] But if a majority of public opinion grudgingly accepted this view, it did not realize to what extent Clemenceau had managed to salvage French war aims. Thus the treaty engendered fierce opposition from both the Right and the Left.

JACQUES BAINVILLE AND THE *ACTION FRANÇAISE*, MAURICE BARRÈS AND THE RHINE

For the most part, the ideas of the royalist right, recalling a Bourbon tradition (largely reconstructed after the royalist revival of the late nineteenth century), were developed by Jacques Bainville in the newspaper *Action*

53 Tardieu, *La Paix;* and Duroselle, *Clemenceau,* 771.
54 Soutou, "L'Alliance franco-polonaise (1925–1933) ou comment s'en débarrasser?" *Revue d'histoire diplomatique* (1981/2-3-4).
55 Quoted in Duroselle, *Clemenceau,* 773.

française. Their influence extended far beyond royalist circles and became a sort of common gospel for large segments of the French elite after the war.[56] By 1919 Bainville had more influence than he is frequently given credit for; he possessed extensive contacts in government, administrative, and military circles. Consistent with the spirit of the time, the *Action française* was considered more of a patriotic movement, effective against pacifism and treason in 1917, than an extremist political group.

The major issue for Bainville was German unity. A stable balance of power in Europe resulting in security for France was possible only if Germany were once again divided along its historical fault lines. Bainville believed that the right time to achieve that would have been the period right after the armistice, when the Germans were in shock and some parts of the country might have been willing to escape the consequences of defeat by abandoning the Bismarckian Reich (in that respect he was not at all afraid of a Spartacist revolution in Berlin, which could only draw conservative Germans to the Allied Powers). Anytime afterward was probably too late. By the time of the January elections in Germany, the new republic had gained the breathing space necessary to combat separatism and to give a democratic content to the concept of unity, endowing it with a strength of which Bismarck could hardly have dreamed. The treaty was the consequence of this lost opportunity; for Bainville, its primary flaws were its confirmation and reinforcement of German unity and its division of eastern Europe into small states, which invited German expansion.

The idea of suppressing German unity was, at the time, not so far-fetched as it would seem today. At the end of 1916 Poincaré and the government seriously considered the possibility of concluding separate peace treaties with the several German states, arguing that the European Powers had not been properly notified of the creation of the Reich in 1871.[57] Clemenceau, on the other hand, was too deeply steeped in the Romantic tradition of the nineteenth century to take such ideas seriously.

In eastern Europe, Bainville believed that the Russian, Austro-Hungarian, and Ottoman empires had played a vital role in maintaining the balance of power and bringing civilization to an otherwise underdeveloped region. He regretted their demise, all the more so as they had been counterweights to German influence. He stressed that the new states were still ethnically mixed, contained large German minorities, and, as a result, were

---

56 See William R. Keylor, *Jacques Bainville and the Renaissance of Royalist History in Twentieth-Century France* (Baton Rouge, La., 1979), 126ff. One can easily follow Bainville's ideas at the time in his collected works: *Journal 1901–1918, Journal 1919–1926, L'Allemagne*, vol. 2 (Paris, 1939, 1948, 1949).
57 Soutou, "Briand et l'Allemagne," 490.

unstable. The folly of self-determination, he and Charles Maurras agreed, was the worst instance of Wilsonian ideology.[58]

Although Bainville did not advocate annexation of the Rhineland, he believed that those provinces, once separated from the German states to which they belonged, would succumb to the "influence and penetration" of France, through a combination of "time, prestige and . . . circumstances."[59] It was, in fact, what the monarchy had always done in that part of Germany.[60] Thus the preferred option was separation of the Rhineland from Germany; to this end, Bainville wrote in support of Dorten's movement in May 1919. But it seems that he did not believe that France would lose any influence over the outcome if separation did not occur quickly. It was more a matter of applying a constant and consistent policy to an evolving situation. Autonomy for (as distinguished from separation of) the Rhenish provinces from Prussia and Bavaria, even in a German framework, might be an acceptable and useful opening.[61]

From 1919 on, Maurice Barrès, famous writer, well-known proponent of royalist ideas, and member of the Chamber, defended a similar policy on the Rhine, although in a more prudent manner. He was against both annexation and, in contrast to Bainville, an independent Rhenish state. Rather, he favored separation from Prussia and autonomy within the Reich, in order that French influence could permeate the Rhineland and establish it as a pacific link between the two countries and a beneficial cultural and political influence on the rest of Germany.[62] Barrès's influence at the Chamber and in the country at large, thanks to the wide circulation of the *Echo de Paris* to which he contributed regularly, was probably greater than that of Bainville.

Bainville's and Barrès's ideas about French options in the Rhineland did not differ significantly from those of Clemenceau and Tirard. They all considered that, in the long run, penetration and influence were preferable to, because less difficult than, outright annexation by France, or even complete separation from Germany, and could be equally effective in promoting French security. And Clemenceau did try to help the autonomists sever ties with Prussia, more so than Bainville, despite his frequent contacts with general Mangin, realized at the time. But there was one major difference. For Clemenceau, and even more so for Tirard, proper French policy along the Rhine should help promote democratic and federalist values in the rest of

58 Charles Maurras, *Les Trois idées du Président Wilson* (Paris, 1919).
59 Quoted in Keylor, *Jacques Bainville,* 129.
60 Hermann Weber, "Richelieu et le Rhin," *Revue historique* 486 (1968).
61 See the Oct. 3, 1919, entry in his *Journal.*
62 Maurice Barrès, *La Politique rhénane* (Paris, 1922).

Germany, thus reinforcing French security. For Bainville, such a democratic evolution would only make German unity even more popular, hence stronger and more dangerous.

For the sake of completeness, one should mention the fact that the notion of Anglo-Saxon finance's willingness to support Germany and Russia at the expense of France, a notion that would be among the most frequently discussed topics of the French Right after the war, was also present in Bainville's articles, as early as April 1919.[63]

THE SOCIALISTS

From the outset of the Paris conference, the socialists were largely against what was to become the Versailles treaty.[64] Even if, by June 1917, a small segment of the socialist group in the Chamber remained willing to contemplate security "guarantees" for France on the Rhine,[65] the mood, especially after Lenin's victory and the rising influence of the Left inside the party, was quite different. The party was united against the prospect of an "imperialistic" peace; its leaders told the Germans as much at the Berne meeting in February 1919, where the different socialist parties tried to hold a congress of the Second International and where the French socialists met Germans for the first time since the war had begun.[66] If one is to believe the German minister in Berne, Adolf Müller, the socialist leader Longuet was even contemplating, at the beginning of June, a general strike against both the Allied policy in Russia and the peace settlement itself.[67] Most socialists were united in the belief that a European reconstruction along peaceful and internationalist lines, with a meaningful role for the League of Nations, would be impossible if Germany were excluded from it, a possibility that a harsh interpretation of the treaty most decidedly did not rule out. And socialist opposition to the treaty certainly played a major role in the widespread rejection of it in intellectual and "progressive" circles, thus laying the foundations of a postwar pacifist movement in France.[68]

Still, as already mentioned, the treaty was susceptible to more than one interpretation; the socialists were not fully agreed upon theirs and would

63 *Action française,* Apr. 6, 1919.
64 For the depth of their opposition, see Bariéty, *Les Relations franco-allemandes,* 327ff.
65 Soutou, "Les Marches de l'Est."
66 See Jacques Droz, *Histoire du socialisme démocratique* (Paris, 1968), 179; and the report of Adolf Müller, a German socialist sent as minister to Berne also for the purpose of unobtrusively meeting other European socialists, Feb. 10, 1919, Deutschland no. 137 Geheim, vol. 8, PA-AA.
67 WK, Deutsche Friedensdelegation Versailles, Pol. no. 1b, vol. 2, PA-AA.
68 See Jean-François Sirinelli, *Génération intellectuelle: Khâgneux et Normaliens dans l'entre-deux-guerres* (Paris, 1994); and Patrick de Villepin, *Victor Margueritte* (Paris, 1991).

not be during the whole interwar period, even after splitting with the communists. Some of them evidently believed that the treaty could be implemented in a tolerable way. Although forty-nine socialist deputies voted against the treaty, thirty-three abstained when it was passed in the Chamber on October 2. In fact, most socialists did not dispute the need for security and reparations. What they opposed was the way the government had tried to solve those problems, spending too much time and political capital for dubious territorial gains and not enough for a sound reparation settlement and true security. Vincent Auriol, who gave one of the most cogent criticisms of the reparations clauses of the treaty at the time, argued that it should have settled the question of French priority payments from Germany and the reduction of inter-Allied debts. This was not renunciation. But the guiding principle of the socialists was that, in the long run, it was both necessary and possible to achieve better relations with a democratic Germany, where socialists had held power since the revolution. That is why they opposed the treaty clauses that would jeopardize improved relations, without, in their view, significantly enhancing French security. But public opinion in France was not supportive of that policy before 1924, and then only reluctantly.

CONCLUSION: AN ASSESSMENT OF CLEMENCEAU'S PEACEMAKING

Clemenceau's tactics at the Paris Peace Conference, to negotiate first on secondary matters and make early concessions to the Allies in order to be paid back later when issues of more significance to France were discussed, have been frequently criticized, probably correctly. But he did manage to salvage more French war aims than has been usually recognized. The economic terms were often exactly what the French had devised in 1916. Germany's economic, military, and geopolitical power was greatly reduced. In the Saar and the Rhineland, France was presented with extensive opportunity for action over a long period of time, provided the populations were ready to modify their relationships with the Reich or Prussia. But realistically, how could France, in the world as it was then, have opposed in the long run the will of the populations? The reparations provisions of the treaty, coupled with the economic terms and the active policy pursued by Clemenceau toward coal and oil, improved France's access to energy sources, its weakest point since the eighteenth century. Thus, between 1914 and 1929, when the provisions of the treaty in that respect reached their peak, France's steel production doubled and its chemical production tripled.

Clemenceau's main failure was to have put too much faith in the Allies. The treaties of guarantee and many provisions of the treaty could work only if Paris, London, and Washington agreed.[69] In Paris, many warned that the U.S. Senate might not ratify the treaty. Poincaré, in his discussions with Clemenceau, stressed this fact; for instance, he advised Clemenceau to refuse any definite limit on the occupation along the Rhine as long as the alliance treaties with London and Washington were not fully ratified and completed by military conventions.[70] This was not a radical notion and would have prevented the collapse of France's security policy when the Senate did indeed refuse to ratify. As for the other major failure of the 1919 treaties, setting an unstable eastern and central Europe next to a Germany that could rise again was not something that Clemenceau had promoted; on the contrary, he tried to prevent it.

On a higher level, Clemenceau's flexibility toward both the Allies and the Germans made the treaty an instrument of European peace, which, despite its faults, possessed some merit and did not preclude the restoration of a European order. Above all, it was flexible. The occupation of the Rhineland could last fifteen years, or more, or less. As for reparations, Germany could always ask to pay less, or suggest more convenient means of discharging its debt. The economic clauses were due to last five years, but could be prolonged. Germany could remain excluded from the League, or be admitted. In other words, the treaty allowed for a harsher or more lenient treatment of Germany, depending on the way it evolved. And in fact, the treaty accommodated as well Poincaré's policy in 1923, the London Conference and the Dawes Plan in 1924, the Locarno Agreements of 1925, the Young Plan and the evacuation of the Rhineland in 1929 and 1930, and Germany's equality of rights in armaments in 1932. The treaty could even have accommodated some territorial revisions, as was frequently discussed between Briand and Stresemann. It took Hitler to destroy the treaty. After such an upheaval, such passions, so many dead, the destruction of three European empires and the turmoil of a fourth (Germany), the emergence of American power and of a revolutionary ideology of unprecedented zeal and attraction, and the ruin of the world economy, it would not have been easy to do much better.

But the French did not recognize the extent of Clemenceau's achievements. Their disillusionment became a contributing factor to several ideologies, from the extreme left to the extreme right, concerning interna-

69 Duroselle, *Clemenceau*, 758.
70 Note from Poincaré on Apr. 23, 1919, in Raymond Poincaré, *A la Recherche de la Paix* (Paris, 1974), 363–7.

tional relations in the interwar period: revolutionary internationalism and pacifism on the left, anti-Americanism and hostility to Anglo-Saxon finance on the right. The spirit of Munich may well have been a late off-shoot of the disillusionment of 1919.

8

The American Mission
to Negotiate Peace:
An Historian Looks Back

LAWRENCE E. GELFAND

On December 9, 1919, the remnant of the American Mission to Negotiate Peace closed its books in Paris, and its personnel prepared to embark for the homeward voyage. Less than a year earlier, President Woodrow Wilson had led the mission to Europe, greeted by enthusiastic crowds in every city visited on the eve of the Paris Peace Conference. The importance of the conference was underscored by the attendance for nearly six months of the president of the United States as one of the five American commissioners plenipotentiary. At its height, the mission numbered nearly 1,300 civilian and military members, constituting what may have been the largest national delegation ever to attend an international conference.[1] Besides the numerous clerks, orderlies, security officers, and other service personnel, a good many members of the American mission, drawn from the regular and wartime bureaucracies in Washington and New York, served as advisers to the American plenipotentiaries and often served as negotiators themselves on the fifty-eight committees into which the peace conference was organized. For six months following the signing of the Versailles treaty with Germany on June 28, the United States had maintained a detachment of delegates who participated in the work of the remaining peace treaties with Austria, Hungary, Bulgaria, and Turkey. The passing of the American mission ended a notable episode in American history.

Frank Polk and his colleagues had sufficient cause to feel despondent as they made their way back across the Atlantic. The idealism and dream of creating a comprehensive world order devoid of further military bloodshed

---

1 U.S. Senate, *Expenditures of the American Commission to Negotiate Peace,* 66th Cong., 3d sess., 1920, S. Doc. 330.

that permeated the mission a year earlier had turned sour, replaced by a bitter cynicism. Now, after nearly a full year of peacemaking, this collective enterprise seemed doomed, maybe even a waste of time.

In hearings conducted by the Senate Foreign Relations Committee during the previous summer, successive witnesses testified about their objections to different sections of the Treaty of Versailles.[2] None expressed enthusiasm for the peace with Germany; none seemed very pleased with the outcome of the peace conference. President Wilson's tour of the western states in August and September, intended to build public America's support for ratifying the treaty of peace and becoming an active partner in the new world order now seemed a futile effort. The strain of hectic travel and frequent speech making that came so soon after his exertions at the peace conference took a toll on the president's health. Wilson's paralysis left him unable to contend effectively in the climactic struggle over the treaty in the Senate chamber. In November, the U.S. Senate failed to approve the treaty.

America's leadership, both moral and political, which had offered so much hope for the new world order, now seemed only a faint voice. The promise made by the victors in the "war to end all wars" appeared empty, unfulfilled. The Allied secret treaties, Shantung, Fiume, Danzig, and reparations were sharply drawn symbols of American compromise, concession, even failure. The League of Nations, the World Court, and the International Labour Organisation, along with the Mandate System and the various security arrangements that President Wilson and the American delegation had worked to make real might possibly flounder in the absence of support and participation by the United States. Polk, Colonel Edward House, General Tasker Bliss, and Henry White were anxious to return home after the rigors and frustrations of the year spent in Paris.

Many questions must surely have passed through the minds of America's returning delegates. For the next generation, veterans of the conference would publish memoirs explaining their peacemaking experiences and commentators would offer plausible speculations. The question remained: what had gone wrong at Paris? In explaining the American withdrawal from leadership in the world community during the 1920s and 1930s, a hypothesis might well be advanced that the literary war fought over the peace conference exercised as profound an influence on the American withdrawal from international leadership in those decades as the simultaneous debate over the wisdom of American military intervention in 1917. In

2 U.S. Senate Committee on Foreign Relations, *The Treaty of Peace with Germany Signed at Versailles on June 28, 1919, and Submitted to the Senate on July 10, 1919, by the President of the United States*, 66th Cong., 1st sess., 1919, S. Doc. 106.

both situations, revisionists maintained that American actions had been ill advised. At least for those politicians and publicists who sought justifications for an American retreat from world leadership, the nation's failures to achieve complete satisfaction at the peace conference could be advanced.

The Americans had hardly settled down to await the presidential election, the "solemn referendum of 1920," when the first salvo of criticism was fired against the treaty by John Maynard Keynes.[3] A liberal economist, Keynes had served with the British delegation at the peace conference. He had arrived at the judgment that Wilsonian principles, however idealistic and moderate in intent, were wrongly conceived. Too much emphasis had been placed on a League of Nations and suitable boundary arrangements; too little regard had been given to the economic realities. Moreover, Keynes had reached the conclusion that the Treaty of Versailles, by allowing Carthaginian terms to be imposed on Germany in the form of severe financial burdens and cessions of territory, threatened Europe's entire financial equilibrium. Such economic strangulation also threatened to prolong needlessly European recovery from the war. Through his general criticism of the peace negotiations, Keynes singled out Wilson for special opprobrium. In his view, the American president had never thought through any of his idealistic rhetoric. Wilson had shown himself to be muddleheaded and unsystematic, for he had not bothered to work out in a coherent fashion any of his program prior to the opening of the peace conference. And when the conference did convene, Wilson was simply no match for the quick, alert, crafty, and shrewd Lloyd George and Clemenceau. Thus Wilson, inept in the art of diplomatic bargaining, threw his trump card and his compromises on the table.

Perhaps Keynes's polemic was as widely read and discussed in England and America during the 1920s because Keynes had articulated reasons for supporting views that many persons had already formed. By their refusal to accept and support the treaty, which they believed fell short of implementing the Wilsonian program, many liberals were willing to believe, with Keynes, that Wilson had sold out everything that really mattered in order to salvage his cherished League of Nations.

No sooner had Keynes's broadside begun to elicit a response, than various individuals who had themselves served on the American Mission to Negotiate Peace began to prepare their own versions for publication. American writing about the conference during the 1920s and 1930s was dominated by veterans of the conference. At a time when there was a paucity of hard-core

3 John Maynard Keynes, *The Economic Consequences of the Peace* (New York, 1920).

documentation, persons who could speak from experience held a decided advantage. In addition, there were staff members of the American mission who had entered the delegation by way of academic careers via the Inquiry and other agencies of the federal bureaucracy. For scholars such as Charles Seymour, Robert H. Lord, Isaiah Bowman, James T. Shotwell, Charles Haskins, Archibald Cary Coolidge, and David Hunter Miller, their involvement in the peace settlement had begun not at Paris but many months before the armistice.[4] Some had been inspired by the rhetoric; others appear to have been persuaded that the president's program for a League of Nations and World Court offered the best chance for a peaceful world order. Still others, it would seem, saw Wilson as the president who had brought America to the pinnacle of leadership among the Allied and associated coalition during the war. Withdrawal from leadership into some posture approaching isolation represented to them a move in the wrong direction.

Writings by the academic and professional advisers were unavoidably part memoir, part history. Only incidentally did they address the actual processes of peacemaking. By and large, this genre emphasized what may have been the most fundamental innovation of Wilsonian "new diplomacy," namely, the making of a rational or scientific peace settlement. By using presumably disinterested historians and social scientists rather than seasoned diplomats to guide the delegation's work, Wilson put the emphasis on a new kind of international politics. The application of ethnic self-determination was to be based on objective historical, geographical, and ethnological data, not on narrow territorial self-interest of either the parties immediately concerned or the interests of the victorious Allied and associated governments. Economic statistics and population censuses were intended to provide the persuasive justification for the location of boundaries and the disposition of territories, even the clauses designating indemnities and reparations.

Not an academic scholar, Ray Stannard Baker had been a liberal journalist before the war. Prior to the armistice, Wilson had sent Baker on a mission to Allied countries in Europe for the purpose of discovering what liberal organizations and their spokesmen regarded as the important issues of war and peace. Baker succeeded so well that at the outset of the peace conference, Wilson appointed him to direct the press bureau and public relations for the American mission. From notebooks in which Baker scrawled daily accounts of his activities, it seems reasonably clear that as the president's relations with Colonel House cooled, Baker succeeded as Wilson's

---

4 Lawrence E. Gelfand, *The Inquiry: American Preparations for Peace, 1917–1919* (New Haven, Conn., 1963).

closest confidant. A year later, it was to Baker that Wilson entrusted exclusive access to his peace conference files and ultimately to his entire papers when Baker was commissioned to serve as Wilson's authorized biographer.

Any reader of Baker's volumes will observe the extensive quotations drawn from the Wilson papers. What is not so apparent is the fact that Baker conducted extensive correspondence with many former members of the American mission. In his innocence, Baker perceived the conflict at the peace conference as one between liberals and reactionaries. The Wilsonian cause had not been mistaken, as Keynes maintained; it had been sabotaged by Allied statesmen who in turn had received assistance via concessions allowed by Colonel House. During the president's return to the United States in late February and early March, House had sabotaged the Wilsonian program by eliminating the League Covenant from the Preliminary Treaty of Peace. Despite the stinging criticism that his books received, Baker persisted in holding to this version.

Just as Wilson had deputized Baker, so Colonel House found an advocate in Charles Seymour, who was made custodian of the House papers at the Yale Library. In 1928, the last two volumes of the *Intimate Papers of Colonel House,* containing House's version of the peace settlement, appeared. As editor, Seymour had carefully selected the documents and excerpts from House's voluminous manuscript diary that would not detract from the Colonel's image. In spite of this careful screening, the *Intimate Papers* provided a major breakthrough in private documentation of the conference.[5] It must be remembered that House was still alive and exercised an active editorial interest in the publication of his papers. Clearly, what must have rankled Baker when the volumes appeared was the persistent view that it was House who had acted as the truly important architect of the country's foreign policy. House was the man who pulled the strings, giving valuable advice that Wilson invariably followed. Baker had insisted, and in this most historians concur, that Wilson maintained tight control over foreign policy at least during American belligerency and later during the conference.

Rivalry between custodians of the Wilson and House collections continued during the 1920s and well into the 1950s, even after Baker's death. To quote from a letter that Charles Seymour wrote to Baker in 1938:

As you know, I have been troubled by your interpretation of Colonel House's policy and advice to Wilson in various instances. . . . But it seems to me fair that the

---

5 Charles Seymour, ed., *The Intimate Papers of Colonel House,* 4 vols. (Boston, 1926–8), vols. 3, 4; Ray Stannard Baker, *Woodrow Wilson and World Settlement,* 3 vols. (Garden City, N.Y., 1923).

letters of Colonel House should not be cited as evidence in favor of an interpretation which I as curator of the letters would not regard as reasonable; for since I am
unable to publish the Wilson side of the correspondence I should be hampered in
an effective presentation of my point of view. I should be entirely satisfied if you
felt willing to permit me to see the pages of your manuscript in which there is interpretation of the House material and to make comment upon it before publication.
This was the method which we followed in the case of Dr. [Harley] Notter's work
and in that of several other scholars who have used the House Collection.[6]

Management of literary rights and access rights apparently conferred a
license to censor unfriendly interpretations.

In the 1920s, when Keynes's polemic and Baker's and House's versions of
the peace conference appeared, David Hunter Miller, who had served as an
officer of the Inquiry and later as adviser on international law to the American mission, privately published his diary and appended documents in a
series of twenty-one volumes.[7] This series provided the most comprehensive documentation to that date covering the plans and procedures used at
the conference, richly supplementing the papers selected for their volumes
by Baker and Seymour. Miller's diary, like much that was written about the
conference in the 1920s and 1930s, reflected the tensions and the generally
chaotic atmosphere in which the conference operated.

Although much writing on the peace conference during the 1920s and
the 1930s came from former delegates, one exception was the work of
Robert C. Binkley, the first American student of the peace negotiations.
Young, energetic, and very versatile in his interests, Binkley had gone to
Paris in 1919 on a mission to gather documents for the recently proposed
Hoover Institution planned for the campus of Stanford University. Later,
Binkley proceeded to graduate study at Stanford, choosing for his disserta-
tion a study entitled "Reactions of European Public Opinion to Woodrow
Wilson's Statesmanship from the Armistice to the Peace of Versailles."[8]
Completed in 1927 and never published, this dissertation, along with Bink-
ley's critical historiographical articles, continue to offer useful insights for
students of the peace conference.

In 1939 Harold Nicolson, a veteran of the British delegation and already
a notable diplomatist, brought out his part memoir, part diary, part severe
critique, entitled *Peacemaking 1919*.[9] He emphasized that the intense con-

6 Letter from Seymour to Ray Stannard Baker, Oct. 7, 1938, Baker MSS, Library of Congress. Harley
   Notter, *The Origins of the Foreign Policy of Woodrow Wilson* (Baltimore, 1937).
7 David Hunter Miller, *My Diary at the Conference of Paris,* 21 vols. (New York, 1924).
8 Robert C. Binkley, "Reactions of European Public Opinion to Woodrow Wilson's Statesmanship
   from the Armistice to the Peace of Versailles," Stanford University Library. See also Max Fisch, ed.,
   Selected Papers of Robert C. Binkley (Cambridge, Mass., 1948).
9 Harold Nicolson, *Peacemaking 1919: Being Reminiscences of the Paris Peace Conference* (Boston, 1933).

fusion had had a detrimental effect on negotiations at Paris. Although he heaped praise on the scholars who staffed the American mission for their impressive mastery of the vast data, Nicolson insisted that more could have been accomplished at Paris had seasoned diplomats, applying a realistic view of national interests, been more widely utilized as American negotiators. Like Keynes, he challenged the effectiveness of the Wilsonian program, both as means and ends. Nicolson also commented that, from the outset, Wilson's effectiveness had been seriously undermined by the American electorate's repudiation of the Democratic leadership in the congressional elections of November 1918.

With a profound sense that personnel at the peace conference were engaged in "making history," numerous members of the American mission were inspired to keep a diary. Ray Stannard Baker commented in his own diary on the American compulsion to keep diaries. He observed:

The President is the only one of the Commissioners here who never stands aside to look at himself or consider this moment as one of historic importance. . . . It is amusing, going about as I do to discover them all more or less surreptitiously keeping diaries. Lansing writes in a small neat book in a small neat hand. House dictates, sitting on his love couch with his legs coddled in a blanket, to his stenographer and secretary, Miss Denton. He speaks in a soft, even voice of the celebrities he has had in confidence. . . . As for the others who keep diaries in this vast Crillon establishment [where most members of the American mission were housed] they are like the sands of the sea and the sound of the pens is like the waves on the beach. And I too! Though perhaps as a writer I may have some faint excuse.[10]

Perhaps another motive weighed with members when deciding to keep diaries. Joseph Grew may at least have been thinking of this other reason when he wrote to William Phillips at the State Department on January 1, 1919: "Whatever course we steered there was bound to be criticism, and I was fully prepared for it. I entered on this job [as secretary-general of the American mission] with the definite assumption that a congressional investigation would some day take place and have continually held that assumption in view."[11] It suffices to say there are at least thirty American diaries, most unpublished, that lie extant in libraries and archives across the United States. Some members of the American mission who did not keep formal diaries, such as Charles Seymour and Tasker Bliss, provided an almost daily record in letters sent to family members in America, even though they were

10 Ray Stannard Baker MSS, Apr. 28, 1919, box 124, Library of Congress.
11 Letter from Joseph Grew to William Phillips, Jan. 1, 1919, quoted in Grew, *Turbulent Era: Diplomatic Record of Forty Years, 1904–1944*, ed. Walter Johnson (Boston, 1952), 1:368.

aware that letters written by members of the mission were subject to censorship.[12] Many alumni of the mission who lived on into the 1950s and
beyond have also left oral histories, many of which have now been tran-
scribed. A good many of these personal accounts contain severe criticism of
the conference and the procedures followed by the American mission. Criticism is often directed against President Wilson, who, writers alleged, either
failed to consult the personnel of the mission sufficiently or failed to heed
their advice. Comments of the youthful Adolf Berle are probably more
extreme than typical. Near the end of May 1919, Berle stated in a letter:

[A report in the London *Daily Herald*] says that practically the whole membership
of the American Commission at Paris are [*sic*] disgusted and disappointed with the
peace treaty. You will not find a half dozen [members] who approve it. They are
convinced that so far from being a basis for lasting peace, the Treaty will be the
direct and certain cause of further wars. . . . They find they have assisted in the
making of a peace based, not on the ideals for which America fought, but upon
the greed and ambitions of European imperialists. The general feeling in the delegation is that they have been duped. They resent keenly the manner in which the
peace has been framed; the secrecy, the autocratic methods of the Big Four, the
refusal to listen to criticism; the contemptuous flouting of the will of the people.[13]

Diarists and letter writers in the American mission were often most critical
of how their own recommendations were altered by the Supreme Council
when the Treaty of Versailles was drafted.

Even before the twentieth anniversary of the conference was reached in
1939, the territorial status quo formed by the treaties of 1919 had become
severely impaired. A muffled observance coincided with a new military
conflagration. The United States, which had failed to ratify the Treaty of
Versailles, was nevertheless a party to the articles of that treaty relevant to
the disarmament of Germany: these articles were incorporated word for
word in the Treaty of Berlin of August 1921, which became the official
peace settlement for the United States.[14] Yet, when the Nazi government
in Germany repudiated those disarmament clauses, there was hardly a
whimper of protest heard in Washington.

12 Charles Seymour, *Letters from the Paris Peace Conference,* ed. Harold B. Whiteman Jr. (New Haven,
   Conn., 1965). See also letters by Tasker H. Bliss to his wife and other family members in the Bliss
   MSS, Library of Congress.
13 Letter from Adolf Berle to his sister, May 8, 1919, and report of article that appeared in the Lon-
   don *Daily Herald* on May 17, 1919, both in Adolf Berle, *Navigating the Rapids, 1918–1971: From the
   Papers of Adolf A. Berle,* ed. Beatrice B. Berle and Travis B. Jacobs (New York, 1973), 12–13.
14 "Treaty Between the United States and Germany Restoring Friendly Relations," Aug. 25, 1921, in
   Papers Relating to the Foreign Relations of the United States: The Paris Peace Conference (hereafter *FRUS-
   PPC*), 13:22–8.

In the midst of the Second World War, there was a widespread resurgence of interest among Americans in Wilsonian internationalism. Books, articles, and even a feature-length biographical film of Wilson, emphasizing his political battle for the League, appeared. Not all of this attention was sympathetic to the former president, but there was a decided view that America in 1919 had taken the wrong fork in the road when it veered away from the treaty with the League Covenant attached. Paul Birdsall and Thomas A. Bailey published interpretive and critical analyses of American participation in the peace conference. Birdsall's *Versailles Twenty Years After* and Bailey's *Woodrow Wilson and the Lost Peace* differ in many ways, but both authors were concerned with drawing lessons from the experience of 1919 that would guide the American public and their leaders in a future peace settlement.[15] Birdsall attempted to write a comprehensive history of the negotiations based on existing monographic literature and his reliance on certain papers of House, Bliss, Lansing, and Henry White. Although Birdsall acknowledged certain faults, he concluded that the peace settlement, on balance, was supportive of the Wilsonian agenda. The first group of Wilson's papers had only recently been opened to scholars at the Library of Congress, but not in time for Birdsall to avail himself of them.

In one sense, Bailey's study is an elongated essay; in another, it becomes a guide to what an American statesman should or should not do at a peace conference. Throughout, Bailey focused his spotlight directly and almost exclusively on Wilson. By the end, the pitfalls, plain errors in judgment, inconsistencies, and poor administration have made such a cumulative effect that the reader may well wonder how any decent treaty could have been ready for signature in the Hall of Mirrors at Versailles on June 28, 1919.

In both Bailey's and Birdsall's renditions, as with many American studies of the conference prepared during the interwar decades, there seems to be an assumption that the ideal peace settlement followed the principles set forth by President Wilson. American writers differed not so much on the nature of the ideal as with the reasons why the ideal failed to materialize. Following the Second World War, these pat formulas changed significantly. Inasmuch as the settlement had already been wrecked on the stormy seas of the Second World War, the familiar issues of *why* the peace of 1919 had failed lost practical relevance. American historians could begin the next phase of peace conference historiography: to direct their attention to the fundamental Wilsonian premises.

---

15 Paul Birdsall, *Versailles Twenty Years After* (New York, 1941); Thomas A. Bailey, *Woodrow Wilson and the Lost Peace* (New York, 1947).

American writers had not unleashed a critical attack on the fundamentals of Wilsonian diplomacy until Hans Morgenthau and George F. Kennan began publishing their critiques of moral idealism in American diplomacy during the late 1940s and 1950s.[16] Wilson became the prime target for these critics because he, more than other leaders, had articulated the idiom and principles as his goals. Morgenthau best summarized the realist's arguments against moral diplomacy as applied to the peace settlement with the following statement:

Faced with the national interests of the great allied powers, Wilson had nothing to oppose or support them with but his moral principles, with the result that the neglect of the American national interest was not compensated for by the triumph of political morality. In the end Wilson had to consent to a series of uneasy compromises, which were a betrayal of his moral principles – for principles cannot, by their very nature be made the object of compromise – and which satisfied nobody's national aspirations. These compromises had no relation at all to the traditional American national interest in a viable European balance of power. Thus Wilson returned from Versailles a compromised idealist, an empty-handed statesman, a discredited ally. In that triple failure lies the tragedy not only of Wilson, a great yet misguided man, but of Wilsonianism as a political doctrine.[17]

Had Morgenthau consulted the Wilson papers, he might have softened his statement. He would have found evidence that, while Wilson was a moralist, he also possessed a keen appreciation of national interests and even a pragmatic strategy, which took numerous forms: Wilson's insistence on maintaining American diplomatic separateness from the Allies within the wartime coalition; his establishment in 1917 of the Inquiry to discern whether America's co-belligerents were interested in the same objects in the war as the United States; his adroit handling of the prearmistice negotiations by first winning a commitment from the German government to accept an end to the war on Wilsonian terms, and only then proceeding to obtain assurances of support for his program from the Allied governments at the Supreme War Council meeting at Paris in late October 1918. What the critics of the president's diplomacy could not readily explain was why Wilson had acquiesced in so many compromises; why he failed to defend the moral principles that he had so eloquently articulated before the armistice in his negotiations at the peace conference. Historians, particularly those writing in the 1960s, were beginning to perceive a Wilson not so exclusively draped in the attire of moral idealism.

16 Hans Morgenthau, *In Defense of the National Interest: A Critical Examination of American Foreign Policy* (New York, 1951); George F. Kennan, *American Diplomacy* (Chicago, 1951).
17 Morgenthau, *In Defense of the National Interest*, 27.

Since the 1960s, students of the peace conference have had the satisfaction of knowing that virtually all American documentation, including archival and private records, are open to their inspection. Not only have the 537 bound volumes of State Department records been opened but relevant documentation from the War and Navy Departments, the Commerce Department, and the independent bureaus whose representatives served in the American mission have become accessible. When one takes into account the many private collections of papers at the Library of Congress, the Hoover Institution, and at such centers as Yale, Harvard, Columbia, and Princeton universities, along with smaller collections at institutional libraries across the United States, the vastness of the literary documentation can be regarded as a mixed blessing for the researcher. When one adds to this the accumulation of British documentation in the Public Record Office and elsewhere in the United Kingdom, along with documentation in French, Italian, Japanese, Belgian, and other national archives – all of which are germane to the work of the American mission, scholars may become more discouraged than encouraged by this superabundance.

The relationship of the First World War to national revolutions in Russia, elsewhere in Europe, Asia, and Africa was broached by Elie Halevy in his celebrated Oxford essays of 1928.[18] Since then, historians such as N. Gordon Levin, Arno Mayer, John Thompson, and George F. Kennan in the United States have published important studies of how the peace settlement related to the turbulent national revolutions throughout the world.[19] America's statesmen were extremely sensitive to the potential of revolution for stirring disruptive anarchy that would be detrimental to the liberal-capitalist order they sought for stability in the peaceful new world. Wilson sought to support policies that would thwart revolutionary expansion. He saw revolutionary Bolshevism as essentially tyrannical and inimical to democratic institutions. According to Mayer, Wilson supported the broad use of economic weapons against the Bolsheviks. It was the spread of the Bolshevik virus in Europe and Asia that needed to be combatted. Mayer has observed: "America's use of the economic weapon was particularly noteworthy. She had a vast reservoir of instantly available capital, food, and manufacturers, and her delegation had a precocious understanding of economic

18 Elie Halevy, "The World Crisis of 1914: An Interpretation," in Elie Halevy, *The Era of Tyrannies: Essays on Socialism and War,* trans. R. K. Webb (Garden City, N.Y., 1965), 209–47. See also N. Gordon Levin, *Woodrow Wilson and World Politics: America's Response to War and Revolution* (New York, 1968); Arno Mayer, *Political Origins of the New Diplomacy* (New Haven, Conn., 1959); and Arthur S. Link, ed., *Woodrow Wilson and a Revolutionary World, 1913–1921* (Chapel Hill, N.C., 1982).
19 George F. Kennan, *Soviet–American Relations, 1917–1920* (Princeton, N.J., 1956–8), vols. 1–2; John M. Thompson, *Russia, Bolshevism, and the Versailles Peace* (Princeton, N.J., 1966).

power as an instrument of control in the international politics of this dawning era of civil war."[20]

Even from the distance of seventy-five years, the sheer magnitude of the
Paris Peace Conference and the activities of the American mission defy easy
comprehension. The communications network of the American mission
required coding and decoding of nearly every one of the hundreds of mes-
sages that passed daily between Washington and Paris and between the mission's headquarters in Paris and its numerous agents throughout Europe.
The gathering of intelligence data from nearly all parts of the political world
was all the more remarkable when one realizes that, prior to 1917, the
United States had little that could rightly be called an intelligence capability. Food relief, coordination of the huge U.S. delegation, and the process
of keeping members of the mission informed of the current status of the
conference added to the strains on the administrative apparatus.

At the top of President Wilson's agenda was the creation of the League
of Nations, a World Court, a mandates system, and such other international
machinery as might be needed. The League was to be something special,
and its covenant, Wilson insisted, must be incorporated into the treaties of
peace. With support from its constituent members, the League was designed
to rid the world of the scourge of war through a community of power.
"Selling" this concept of collective security was no easy feat for Wilson. In
an increasingly interdependent world, America could no longer remain
politically aloof from the changes affecting Europe, Asia, Africa. Wilson
recognized that wars occurring anywhere in the world would adversely
affect the interests of the United States; therefore, America must assume a
leading role in the League of Nations.

Failure of the U.S. Senate and public to embrace collective security and
the new universalism preached by Wilson cannot be explained simply in
terms of the personal enmity between the president and Henry Cabot
Lodge, then chair of the Senate Foreign Relations Committee. Nor can
partisan opposition by Republicans anxious to defeat a Democratic president's program explain adequately the failure of the Senate to approve the
treaty during 1919–20. After all, a good many members of the American
mission at Paris had expressed disappointment and dissatisfaction with the
products of their labors. Barely ten years before, in 1906, the Senate had
attached an interpretive statement to a most modest treaty negotiated at
Algeciras, Spain, under the aegis of a Republican president and concerned
solely with Morocco:

20 Mayer, *Political Origins,* 17.

That the Senate, as part of the ratification, understands the participation of the United States in the Algeciras Conference . . . was [with] the sole purpose of preserving and increasing its commerce in Morocco . . . and without purpose to depart from the traditional American foreign policy which forbids participation by the United States in the settlement of political questions which are entirely European in their scope.[21]

Wilsonian universalism called for the United States to assume obligations for maintaining collective security that transcended whatever the League of Nations or other international organizations might request of member states. While at the peace conference, Wilson also accepted a commitment for the United States to guarantee French security against any resurgent German aggression.[22] Although this agreement was never submitted to the Senate, its existence shows the extent to which he was willing to expand the country's foreign policy.

In a very real sense, Wilson's paradigm of universalism and collective security established the nature of American discourse about foreign policy for the remainder of the twentieth century. American membership in the United Nations, the debate over the Truman Doctrine for Greece and Turkey, American occupation forces in Germany after 1945, American leadership in the North Atlantic Treaty Organization, American military intervention in the Korean War, and even the rationale for the military presence of the United States in Vietnam may be included in the legacy of Wilsonianism.

One achievement of the peace conference, influenced markedly by the American mission, had to do with what is commonly called humanitarian services and, in more recent years, human rights. I shall refer here to only a few examples. In its adaptation of the principle of ethnic self-determination to the establishment of viable international boundaries and to the creation of the new nation–states in east–central Europe, there was a widely recognized need to protect minorities inhabiting these territories. Guarantees were inserted into international treaties for minorities in Germany, Poland, Czechoslovakia, and other states in Europe. Although the principle of international protection for minorities was no novelty in the treaties following the First World War, no previous international accord applied this principle so extensively. Even so, at the peace conference of 1919 and in the years following, objections to these provisions protecting minorities were frequently raised, chiefly on the grounds that such instruments infringed on the sover-

21 William Malloy, comp., *Treaties, Conventions, International Acts, Protocols, and Agreements Between the United States of America and Other Powers, 1776–1909* (Washington, D.C., 1910), 2:2183.
22 Agreement Between the United States and France, June 28, 1919, in *FRUS-PPC,* 13:757–9. See also Louis R. Yates, *The United States and French Security, 1917–1921* (New York, 1957).

202 Lawrence E. Gelfand

eign rights of those nation-states where minorities resided. Protection of ethnic and religious minorities from persecution and exploitation was a further means for preserving peace and security.[23]

Humanitarian concerns were necessarily combined with American universalism when the peace conference addressed the plight of the Armenian community residing within the Ottoman Empire. For many years, the Armenian population in Turkey had been subject to violent persecution at the hands of the Turkish state, often with the police and army participating in the ruthless slaughter of this minority. Turks complained that the Armenians were plotting to overthrow the established government, and the treatment accorded by the Turks constituted righteous retaliation for high crimes against the state. The plight of the Armenians touched the liberal conscience everywhere to the extent that, during the course of the peace conference, the proposal was made to establish an American mandate for an Armenian state. President Wilson was dubious about whether the American people would support their country's assumption of responsibilities so far removed from the western hemisphere, but he believed that safeguarding the Armenian Christian community from annihilation by the Turks would eventually move Americans to accept the mandate. In the end, nothing came of the American mandate for Armenia; but the concern for human rights and a concerted desire to intervene on behalf of a distant minority was evident in this failed endeavor.[24]

In retrospect, the Paris Peace Conference of 1919 held a special quality for the United States. For the first time, the United States was accorded parity with the principal European powers at an international conference. For the first time, the United States government participated fully in the comprehensive arrangements for peace not only in Europe but also in Africa, the Middle East, East Asia, and Oceania. Wilsonian foreign policy had extended the perimeter of American national interests to embrace the entire political world of which America would become a full partner. Trade could not proceed in the absence of political participation in this postwar world. And American national interests, defined in this manner, demanded a peaceful world order. To ensure that end, America had to become an active participant in the new international community. That this conception failed to materialize is not necessarily an indictment of Wilsonian leadership in 1919.

23 *FRUS-PPC*, 13:116–19, 123, 203, 207, 222–7, 813–15, and 800–1.
24 James B. Gidney, *A Mandate for Armenia* (Kent, Ohio, 1967). For interpretations of Herbert Hoover's food relief program and the economic reconstruction program in Europe during the course of the peace conference, see several essays in Lawrence E. Gelfand, ed., *Herbert Hoover: The Great War and Its Aftermath, 1914–1923* (Iowa City, Iowa, 1979), esp. the papers by Murray Rothbard and Robert Van Meter Jr.

9

Between Compiègne and Versailles: The Germans on the Way from a Misunderstood Defeat to an Unwanted Peace

FRITZ KLEIN

Walter Rathenau evocatively summoned images of catastrophes in an open letter to Colonel Edward House in December 1918 when it became clear that Germany would have to reckon with a hard peace. Never in the history of the world, he wrote, had three countries and three men – Woodrow Wilson, Georges Clemenceau, and David Lloyd George – wielded such power to decide the fate of a talented, healthy, and industrious people:

> If in future decades and centuries the thriving German cities become desolate and fall apart, commerce is destroyed, the German spirit in science and art dries up, and millions of German people are torn from their native land and driven out; will history and God judge that this people has been dealt with justly and that these three men have carved out that justice? What we are threatened with, what hatred proposes to do to us, is destruction, the destruction of German life, now and for all times.

Similarly, the appeal to "all nations" was wildly exaggerated. "We will be destroyed," Rathenau lamented, and painted a bleak picture of German misery twenty years after the peace accord. "The cities . . . half dead blocks of stone, still partly inhabited by wretched people, the roads are run down, the forests cut down, a miserable harvest growing in the fields. Harbors, railways, canals in ruins, and everywhere the sad reminders standing, the high, weather-worn buildings from the time of greatness. . . . A folk lives and is dead. . . . The border to Asia now lies at the Rhine, the Balkans now extend to the North Sea."[1]

This chapter was translated by Robert Lumer.

1 Walter Rathenau, *Nach der Flut* (Berlin, 1919), 62–70. Both appeals were published in newspapers of neutral countries.

The creator of that apocalyptic vision was not a man of rash nationalism and was not anti-Western on principle, as were so many in the upper classes of the Kaiser's Reich. On the contrary, in his appeal to House he explicitly emphasized his sympathy for the political constitutions of the Western countries, stating that he saw German guilt in the fact that the Germans, unlike the people of the Western countries, had never been able to carry out a revolution. The German revolution now in progress had Rathenau's approval – provided it did not move too far to the left. As he wrote in a private letter in 1918 in a much calmer tone than in the open letter to House, the destruction of the old, military-feudal system was so important that all its disadvantages had to be accepted.[2] And his conviction, expressed in December 1918, "that a great victory would have done us harm,"[3] merely echoed his certainty of 1914 that the time would never come "when the Kaiser would parade through the Brandenburg Gate with his paladins on white horses. . . . On that day world history would lose all meaning."[4]

After the signing of the peace treaty, things turned out exactly the way Rathenau had bleakly predicted. On May 31, 1919, in an article appropriately titled "Das Ende," published in Maximilian Harden's *Zukunft*, he had not only urged Germany to refuse to sign the treaty but also called for the simultaneous dissolution of the National Assembly, the resignation of the Reich president and the government, and the turning over of all rights of sovereignty to the victorious countries.[5] But after the treaty was signed, he – unlike many others – faced up to reality and tried to reach an understanding with the victors and negotiate on the means of complying with the treaty, which could only be amended – if at all – in this way.

This drastic change in Rathenau's attitude could be explained by his eccentric personality, for such behavior was typical of this unusual man. The war years in particular provide examples of Rathenau's activities and views that hardly fit neatly together. One could simply attribute all of this to Rathenau's personality if his extreme outbursts between the defeat and the peace treaty did not sound like so many other complaints by people of various political and social leanings.

2 Rathenau, *Politische Briefe* (Dresden, 1929), 214.
3 Ibid., 223.
4 These words, taken from a private talk in 1914, were made public by Rathenau in his brochure "Der Kaiser," published in March 1919 in Berlin. Quoted in Rathenau, *Schriften aus Krieg und Nachkriegszeit* (Berlin, 1929), 305.
5 As he wrote in a letter on June 3, 1919, with this proposal Rathenau was counting on the Entente soon becoming convinced that the demands of the peace treaty could not be met and recognizing that a "healthy government" would have to be installed in Germany to make the country productive. See Harry Graf Kessler, *Walter Rathenau: Sein Leben und sein Werk* (Berlin, 1928), 283. This idea, which sounded rather adventurous in 1918–19, suggests that some attention should be given to the relationship between Germany and its opponents at the end of World Wars I and II.

During the armistice period, Ernst Troeltsch has observed, people were in a "dreamland," "where everyone, without grasping the conditions and real consequences, could portray the future in fantastic, pessimistic or heroic terms."[6] This description crops up again and again in historical writing. It therefore seems useful to examine more closely the conditions under which the political and social illusions, fear, anger, and desperation sprang up, all of which were so far from reality that it seemed as though the terrible sacrifices and efforts of the war had destroyed people's ability to judge their place in history realistically.

Another great German intellectual – Thomas Mann – was beside himself with indignation over the godforsaken behavior of the victors.[7] His denunciation, as sharp as Rathenau's, was different on one important point, however. The philosophizing industrialist was disappointed with the imposed peace since it was not in keeping with the more democratic conditions – superior to those in Germany – in the Western countries, especially in the United States under Wilson. The poet, on the other hand, in his verbal frenzy against the rape of Germany, continued the passionate polemic against Western civilization and democracy, in which he had engaged so painfully in his just published "Betrachtungen eines Unpolitischen." At the beginning of February 1919, Rathenau, although increasingly skeptical, placed his greatest hopes in the Americans, whom he considered "the least blind." The American delegates, he thought, behaved with animosity toward the French and seemed friendly toward the Germans. House, to whom Rathenau had written in December with the serious hope of support, had thanked him and said a few soothing words.[8] Thomas Mann reacted differently. He contemptuously characterized a long speech by Wilson on the League of Nations as "disgustingly oily." Subsequently he showed somewhat more understanding of Wilson's special role in Versailles, which he called "desperately tragicomic," but he hardly distinguished the American president from the other victors in his exalted outbursts.[9]

Clemenceau, "that poisonous old man . . . with *oval* eyes," Mann wrote on May 12, stands out as the real devil. This feature was, in his opinion, a sign that the French prime minister might possess the blood stock giving

---

6 Ernst Troeltsch, *Spektator–Briefe* (Tubingen, 1924), 69.
7 "The Entente peace demonstrates that the 'victors have been forsaken by god' [die Gottgeschlagenheit der Sieger]." This was Thomas Mann's answer to a newspaper poll after the draft treaty was submitted at the beginning of May 1919. Thomas Mann, *Tagebücher, 1918–1921* (Frankfurt am Main, 1979), 235.
8 Taken from a letter of February 2, 1919, to Wilm Schwander, which Martin Sabrow (Berlin) was friendly enough to point out to me and which will be published in one of the next volumes of the complete works of Rathenau.
9 Mann, *Tagebücher,* 152, 165.

him a hereditary right "to carry Western civilization to its grave and create Kirghizian conditions."[10] This utterly senseless image pleased the poet so much that, having first used the expression in a private letter, he repeated it shortly after at the end of May in an article on the imposed peace that appeared in several newspapers, except that he replaced "Kirghizian conditions" with a "Slavic Mongolia."[11] As extreme as this characterization of the victor was, equally extreme were the means of deliverance that Mann temporarily sought.[12] But the thoughts he noted in the middle of March appear balanced in comparison with what was to come. It was necessary for Germany "to invent something new in politics." This could not be Western-style parliamentarianism. The soviets, Mann continued vaguely, would probably play an important role as a kind of class representation, although he categorically rejected the rule of the proletariat.[13] But shortly afterward, on March 22, he recorded a thought in his diary that would be on his mind for several weeks: "I feel a growing sympathy with that which is healthy, human, national, anti-Entente, antipolitical in spartacism, communism, bolshevism." And only two days later, under the influence of increasing left-wing tendencies in Hungary, Austria, and Italy, all seen as directed against the Entente's imperialism, Mann was audacious enough to speculate in a way that can only be called adventurous coming from a man like him. He wrote: "Rejection of the peace by Germany! Rise up against the demagogical bourgeois! A national uprising after allowing oneself to be worn down by the fraudulent phrases of the riffraff, even in the form of communism – a new August 4, 1914! I am perfectly willing to take to the streets and yell 'Down with the lie of Western democracy! Long live Germany and Russia! Long live communism!'" There are similar statements in his diary in the following weeks, the last on April 30: "How can one not go over to communism with bag and baggage, seeing as it has the great advantage of being antagonistic to the Entente? It is senseless by nature and a kind of Hottentottenism. But in Germany it would not stay like that for long."

It was the direct observation of an attempt at communist rule that led Mann, who lived in Munich, the capital of the Bavarian Soviet Republic, to go so far in his speculative thinking. But these ideas did not last long, were never without a certain critical distance, and finally gave way to an attitude of decided anticommunism when the soviet republic was brought

---

10 Thomas Mann, *Briefe, 1889–1936* (Frankfurt am Main, 1961), 162.
11 Thomas Mann, *Aufsätze-Reden-Essays* (Berlin, 1986), 3:14.
12 Mann, *Tagebücher,* 233, 223.
13 Mann, *Aufsätze,* 3:12.

down by troops loyal to the government. The battles between the "reds" and "whites" in and around Munich were not completely over when the author called Bolshevism "the most appalling cultural catastrophe" that ever threatened the world in a talk on May 22 with his wife Katja. It was Germany's destiny, he said, to prevent this catastrophe, this "mass migration from below," and stop the fall of Western civilization. His criticism of the Entente now was that the blind rage of the victors did not allow them to grasp this role of Germany and the conditions of the peace treaty hindering Germany from playing it.[14] One has, he wrote later, "looked down into an abyss. The Entente is detestable, but Western civilization must be saved from a mass migration from below." There is no trace of sympathy for communism anymore. The author explicitly approved of the military dictatorship's "cleanup" by firing squad, and made fun of his mother-in-law, for whom things were too militaristic.[15]

With the return of bourgeois normalcy to the world around him, Mann became calmer in his judgments. He remained opposed on principle to the signing of the peace treaty, but considered the possibility at the end of May, when German counterproposals were sent, that it might be more astute to sign the unfulfillable Entente peace treaty than Germany's own, which could not be kept.[16] Mann apparently increasingly recognized – at least his diaries give that impression – that signing the treaty was unavoidable. The news of the cabinet's agreement to an unconditional acceptance of the agreement was met by a laconic "All right, in God's name." He did not bother to comment on the signing at Versailles and consoled himself with the remark that things otherwise would be terrible. The French had moved up to Frankfurt am Main earlier and had warships on the Main ready to attack the city if the signing did not take place.[17]

Like Rathenau, Thomas Mann faced reality once the die was cast. It is remarkable how tirelessly he reconsidered everything and arrived at new, critical evaluations of the war and a more sober – if resigned – opinion of the results. "This war increasingly appears to me (insofar as it was not a social revolution from the very beginning, but that is another matter) to be immensely

---

14 In the same conversation, Thomas and Katja Mann also vented their feelings about that "Russian Jewish type of leader of the international movement, an explosive mixture of Jewish intellectual radical and Slavic visionary." In their opinion, "All possible energy and a hasty firing squad" were necessary for the world to deal with these types (*Tagebücher*, 223). This outburst of hatred apparently was directed at the leader of the Bavarian soviet movement, Eugen Leviné, the son of a wealthy Jewish merchant in St. Petersburg born in 1883, who settled in Germany in 1897 and studied there, writing his dissertation at Heidelberg University.
15 Mann, *Tagebücher*, 227.
16 Ibid., 253.   17 Ibid., 273.

quixotic, a final mighty preparation and a final, powerful blow by the Germanic middle ages, which survived astonishingly well before coming to a rattling halt. What will follow is the Anglo-Saxon rule of the world, i.e., the perfection of civilization."[18] New insights became apparent. A new path would lead the writer within a few years to the role of spokesman and ever more decisive defender of the German republic. In light of this, one could ask whether the ideas so intensively considered for a time – of opposing rape by the Entente with the transition to communism – was ever anything more than a kind of feverish dream, at best a brief flirtation with an unusual, experimental idea. Certainly this is true to a degree, and one should be careful not to make Thomas Mann a partisan of communism or to take his thoughts in this direction too literally or seriously. But precisely because this is so, his ideas on the subject merit some consideration. They were a reflex response to the fact that all relations had been deeply shaken by the catastrophe of the world war. They show how strong, widespread, and radical the feeling was that it was necessary "to find something new in politics." From the ashes of defeat, as Stefan Zweig feared, hate and nationalism were being spawned. The peace, he felt, would poison the atmosphere for a hundred years. And he also saw only one solution: "The only hope left is the world revolution, and there are signs of it everywhere."[19]

The signs were deceptive. The world revolution – hoped for or feared – never happened. This is not the place for a critical evaluation of the concept of world revolution. But it should be included in one's observations of the epoch as an influential current in a time of misery, want, and destruction in a war of unprecedented dimensions. The idea of radically changing the status quo was understandable in a world of lost ideals and great uncertainty, other than the one conviction held by many: things would not and should not be the way they had been before the war.[20] Hindsight about the mistakes and final failure of that experiment begun in 1917 does not make superfluous an objective study of its effect on the months between war and peace. But of course it forces one to look more closely at the illusions and

18 July 5, 1919, in a letter to Gustav Blume (Mann, *Briefe*, 165).
19 Stefan Zweig to Romain Rolland, Jan. 2, 1919, in *Romain Rolland–Stefan Zweig: Briefwechsel, 1910–1940* (Berlin, 1987), vol. 1: *1910–1923*, 418.
20 This was true of the whole political spectrum. Peter Fritzsche has made an informative and instructive analysis of the strong tendencies of German conservatism not to react to the defeat and the November revolution with nostalgia for the world of the Kaiserreich, but to deal positively with these events, to be stimulated by them to move in new directions. "Conservative Revolution" – this both vague and characteristic term – has its origins in these considerations. See Peter Fritzsche, "Breakdown or Breakthrough? Conservatives and the November Revolution," in Larry Eugene Jones and James Retallack, eds., *Between Reform, Reaction, and Resistance: Studies in the History of German Conservatism from 1789 to 1945* (Providence, R.I., 1993), 299–328.

misjudgments, as well as at the political and moral weaknesses, that from the very beginning were part of the undertaking of a "world revolution."

The peace program presented by the Communist Party of Germany – the German party whose program committed it to world revolution – was a truly great illusion. On May 18, 1919, the party published "Basic Principles of Peace," which stated that the acceptance and rejection of the peace treaty were equally catastrophic.[21] Signing, the document said in agreement with bourgeois politicians and journalists and the majority of the Social Democrats, would lead Germany into "endless misery." Not signing would lead to a fatal blood-sucking by Entente capitalism, facilitated by occupation. "The only possible and unavoidable solution is the overthrow of this government and of bourgeois rule altogether, the establishment of a proletarian dictatorship . . . and so the participation in the world revolution." This program was a logical consequence of seeing the war as an imperialist undertaking, equally unjust on the part of all participants. The radical, undifferentiated damnation of the policies of the ruling classes of all countries participating in the war led, in the abstract logic of this thinking, to the demand that the existing forms of government be done away with in general.

But the authors of this program greatly misjudged existing realities. They spoke of the armed proletariat, the free and united workers combining "solidarity and enthusiasm in the production process, who would become the masters of their own fate because they ran the factories and the country," as the basis for the soviet dictatorship. The German Red Army, it stated with a darkly threatening undertone, would "sooner or later" break down the barrier against revolution created by the Polish, Czechoslovakian, and Southern Slav states – all vassals of the Entente. As if the course and results of all attempts to push the revolution forward had not shown that the great majority of the workers could not be won over to it, goals were set based on nonexistent conditions. Not only domestic but also international conditions were miscalculated. Strengthened by the moral support of the working classes of the Entente countries, as the communist peace program promised, a soviet government would confront the victors with much greater authority than the government of a bankrupt imperialism. Certainly, it is difficult to speculate about things that never happened, but this suggestion is highly questionable. There can be no doubt about the will and determination of the victorious powers to prevent the revolution begun in Russia from moving into Germany. And as for the attitude of the workers

---

21 *Die revolutionäre Arbeiterbewegung im Kampf um den Frieden, 1848–1964: Dokumente* (Berlin, 1964), 58–65.

in the Entente countries, there is no convincing reason to assume that the majority of them would have ended their patriotic support for their governments, which they had amply demonstrated during the war. Arno Mayer's observation is worth quoting here: "Victory in war provides a welcome tonic for the forces of order and reaction; defeat in war presents a perilous opportunity to the forces of reform and revolution."[22]

The importance of anticommunism at Versailles is still debated. Mayer, for one, suggests that finding a proper reaction to revolutionary movements emanating from Soviet Russia was the overriding purpose of the peace conference. Klaus Schwabe qualifies this, especially in relation to Woodrow Wilson's policies, by asking, "Was Wilson primarily an anti-Bolshevist at the peace conference? Was he prepared to let all other possible peace objectives take second place behind his desire to incorporate the new Germany into the ranks of the anti-Bolshevist states and to *integrate* it into the community of non-Bolshevist states? Was he willing, for the sake of this shared anti-Bolshevist interest, to treat the Ebert–Scheidemann government more as future allies than as former enemies and therefore meet them halfway in working out the peace terms?"[23] Schwabe's answer to these suggestive questions is, of course, negative. Delving deeply into his subject on the basis of a rich selection of source materials, he examines the complicated web of domestic constraints and international conditions within which the American president acted, making the anti-Bolshevist motive only one among many.[24]

The problem of Germany's possible radicalization and its importance for the peace negotiations were constant themes during the period under consideration and were discussed among the different factions and parties in Germany, among the victorious powers, and between Germany and the Allies. The precise role this question played is difficult to determine, however. The hopelessness of the second revolution in Germany was by no means as obvious to contemporaries as it is to later historians. There were constant uprisings. Hunger, want, and unemployment were the lot of many people, and no improvement was in sight. Everything seemed unstable and nothing seemed impossible. Thomas Mann, made uncertain by the experi-

---

22 Arno J. Mayer, *Politics and Diplomacy of Peacemaking: Containment and Counterrevolution at Versailles, 1918–1919* (New York, 1969), 90.

23 Klaus Schwabe, *Woodrow Wilson, Revolutionary Germany, and Peacemaking, 1918–1919: Missionary Diplomacy and the Realities of Power* (Chapel Hill, N.C., 1985), 4.

24 The books by Mayer and Schwabe are not comparable insofar as they deal with the problem in totally different frameworks. Mayer is involved with the whole complex of the Versailles negotiations, whereas Schwabe concentrates on Wilson's policies toward Germany and the German reaction to them.

ence with the soviet republic in Munich, expressed no objections when
Eugen Leviné was put to death by a firing squad on June 6. Such an end
seemed fitting for a "political fanatic." Whether such proceedings were
politically advisable was, in his opinion, another matter. "What will happen
when communism comes again?"[25] The dreamland had become a nightmare land.

It was not just the nervous writers who were worried. As Schwabe has
shown, the large shipments of food to Germany, announced in a speech by
Lansing and confirmed by a formal treaty on March 15, were an expression
of the almost panic-stricken reaction to reports from Berlin and other
industrial centers painting a picture of near civil war.[26] "The real thing with
which to stop Bolshevism is food." Wilson's comment in a letter to Lansing
of January 10, 1919, referred to American policies toward Russia.[27] But it
applied everywhere that Bolshevism threatened or seemed to threaten. This
situation presented the Germans with difficult options. Parties and groups
from the Social Democratic majority to the extreme right were united in
their rejection of a further radicalization of the revolution but differed in
their attitude toward the revolution as such. They tended to agree with the
strictly anti-Bolshevist victors and could therefore highlight this anti-
Bolshevist agreement so as to downplay the opposing interests of the victors
and defeated and thereby win a more lenient peace treaty. The Germans
played this game over and over, generally without success, but often they
were effective on individual questions such as food aid deliveries.

Judging the degree of danger accurately was difficult for both sides. This
uncertainty led the Germans – unconsciously or consciously – to play the
game both ways. They were determined – and this goal was given high priority – to prevent the continuation of the Russian-style revolution and to
suppress all attempts in this direction. But the more successful they were at
this, the less likely they were to impress the Entente with the Bolshevist danger. If this made the anti-Entente forces wish that the Bolshevist danger not
appear too small, interest in maintaining bourgeois rule demanded that they
ruthlessly oppose this movement. In fact, they did so successfully again and
again in Berlin from December 1918 until the defeat of the Bavarian soviet
republic at the end of April 1919. Hagen Schulze, in his discussion of the
protocols of the Scheidemann cabinet, points out that the "internal German
civil war" is mentioned surprisingly seldom in the files of the Reichskanz-

25 Mann, *Tagebücher,* 258.
26 Schwabe, *Wilson,* 192.
27 See Mayer, *Politics,* 424; and Fritz Klein, "Krieg-Revolution-Frieden, 1914–1920," *Zeitschrift für Geschichtswissenschaft* 28 (1980): 544–54.

lei.[28] The government was obviously fairly certain of success in dealing with all attempts at revolution. Insofar as this was true, the German politicians were bluffing when they played up the Bolshevist danger in Germany.

Nonetheless, no one could feel safe in the country during these months, as it remained in turmoil. A revealing demonstration of the governing circles' insecurity about domestic developments and their meaning for the relationship with the victors can be found in the exchange between Foreign Minister Ulrich Graf Brockdorff-Rantzau and General Wilhelm Groener, the chief of the German army command, on April 4.[29] Internal affairs, the worried general thought, would hasten a final peace insofar as "the Entente fears an outbreak of Bolshevism here." The position of Germany would, he felt, be weakened in this case and the following weeks would be of decisive importance. The government therefore could not shy away from a confrontation with the soviet system and could not make any compromises. The foreign minister agreed. He also believed a third wave of revolution, stronger than the previous ones, was still to come. But "when a government had no instruments of power, what should it do? We are not throwing ourselves into the arms of Bolshevism, but rather Bolshevism is inundating us." Brockdorff-Rantzau's comment to an English general are reminiscent of Thomas Mann's fantasies: "It is possible," the minister wrote, "that we cannot save ourselves from Bolshevism, in which case it would appear in a more respectable form than in Russia but would be an all the more infectious disease, and I would make sure that the English caught it."

In the victorious camp opinions differed as to how real the Bolshevist danger was. In a talk with Walter Loeb, Matthias Erzberger's representative, on March 8 and 9, Colonel Conger, the chief of intelligence in the advanced headquarters of the American Expeditionary Forces in Trier, informed the German, with whom he had had close contacts since the days of the cease-fire, that the Allies were of divided opinion. Some felt that a danger really existed and thus made concessions, at least in the question of supplies, necessary. Others were convinced Germany was using a nonexistent Bolshevist danger for propaganda purposes. The Americans for the most part supported the first point of view.[30] Ultimately, the French impression prevailed, namely, that the threat in Germany was more propaganda than reality. In a warning

---

28 Hagen Schulze, ed., *Das Kabinett Scheidemann: 13. Februar bis 20. Juni 1919*, Akten der Reichskanzlei, Weimarer Republik (Boppard am Rhein, 1971), xxxix.

29 The following is taken from the extensive notes by Groener on the talk, in *Akten zur deutschen Auswärtigen Politik, 1918–1945*, series A: *1918–1925*, 14 vols., vol. 1: *Nov. 9, 1918–May 5, 1919*, ed. Peter Grupp (Göttingen, 1982), 394ff.

30 Schulze, ed., *Das Kabinett Scheidemann*, 29.

tone, Reichspresident Friedrich Ebert tried to extract more lenient peace terms, at least with respect to the extradition of war criminals. "If we unconditionally sign, Bolshevism will surely come," he said ominously in a phone call to Ambassador von Haniel on the morning of June 23. There was no reply to this.[31] The reason Ebert gave for his cry of alarm was his fear that the volunteer troops would split up after an unconditional peace was signed and that the country would then be unprotected from radicalism. But he underestimated the realism of the military leadership. On the same day, General Groener declared before the officers of the army high command in Kolberg his belief that revolutionary unrest would not break out in the country. He had come to accept the necessity of signing and called all proposals for military resistance idiocy.[32] On the other hand, just a few days earlier Paul von Hindenburg had spoken up for precisely such idiocy before the high command. In a report to the government, he stated that a favorable conclusion to hostilities would be highly unlikely if fighting were resumed. But he added the high-sounding sentiment that "as a solider he would prefer an honorable downfall to a shameful peace."[33]

Groener's position in June 1919 was more or less similar to that of his predecessor, Erich Ludendorff, in October 1918. In both cases the military had understood the seriousness of the situation and was reasonable enough to advise yielding. In both cases, however, it tried to cover its tracks. The fact that it was the high command, led by Hindenburg and Ludendorff, whose panic-stricken insistence persuaded the government to ask for ceasefire negotiations has been driven out of the memory of most Germans by the dishonest propaganda of the *Dolchstoss,* which claimed that an undefeated army had been betrayed by its country. This shift in blame makes one think of the declaration by Groener on June 23, 1919. Reviling the German people, he spoke with a melancholy promise of future revenge: "The near future lies dim before us. It is still unclear when the German people will rise from their shameful national degradation, will stand together as one man and take up the battle once more against external forces for the honor and dignity of generations to come. I do not believe this will happen soon."

Everyone recognized that it would be hopeless to resist a new military offensive in the west, which the French would certainly begin if the Germans refused to sign. But opinions differed on the implications of this situation. Whereas Groener recommended that the treaty be accepted and that revenge be taken at some future time, Hindenburg dreamed of defeat in a

31 Anton Golecki, ed., *Das Kabinett Bauer: 21. Juni bis 27. März 1919,* Akten der Reichskanzlei, Weimarer Republik (Boppard am Rhein, 1980), 7.
32 Ibid., 12.   33 Ibid., 5.

classical, heroic form. The diplomat Kurt Riezler thought of a third possibility.[34] He had been serving since April as the Reich's representative to the Bavarian government, which had taken refuge in Bamberg. On June 1 he sent a telegram from there insisting that the treaty should be rejected. The French, he thought, would then begin an offensive along the Main line to separate northern and southern Germany.[35] But in the long run the unity of the country would not be in jeopardy. France would bear the burden of collecting heavy taxes and contributions and being an occupier and as such would become an object of nothing but hatred. As soon as the occupation forces left the country, the south would rush to reunite with the Reich. "The final consequence of a French occupation of the south – after what of course would be difficult years – would be a renewal of the belief in the German Reich and would hardly be more dangerous to German unity than signing a destructive peace agreement leading to a misery for which the leadership would bear the blame." Similar arguments were presented by the Prussian chargé d'affaires in Munich, Baron Zech. The brutally enforced sanctions of the Entente would "after the unavoidable decline of Bavaria, make the greatness of the time of unification with the German Reich appear in a rosy light."[36]

The Berlin leadership was sensible enough not to act on such risky speculations. From the very beginning it expected terrible results from renewed fighting for which it could not take the responsibility. Its first concern was the danger from the left. "If war was resumed, the national assembly would break down within two weeks, Spartacism and Bolshevism would come to Germany and the people would go hungry." Ebert and Philipp Scheidemann presented this bleak perspective in February to Brockdorff-Rantzau.[37] In the summer, another danger emerged, and concern about the country's unity ultimately led the cabinet and the national assembly to decide not to risk mil-

---

34 The following is taken from Kurt Riezler, *Tagebücher, Aufsätze, Dokumente*, ed. and introd. Karl Dietrich Erdmann (Göttingen, 1972), 152. See also Schulze, ed., *Das Kabinett Scheidemann*, 398–9, 410–11.

35 Riezler was right in assuming that the Allies planned such an operation if Germany refused to sign the treaty. In a direction from May 20 the commander-in-chief of the Allied Forces, Marshall Ferdinand Foch, gave the orders for a massive operation of thirty-seven infantry divisions and five cavalry divisions (French, American, British, and Belgian). The aim was to contain Germany "by greatly weakening southern Germany, for taking possession of the Main River valley would separate north from south." See Historical Division, Department of the Army, ed., *U.S. Army in the World War, 1917–1919*, vol. 10: *The Armistice and Related Documents* (Washington, D.C., 1948), 1119–23. I would like to thank Gerhard L. Weinberg for passing along this information. However, not every politician and general in France was as eager as Foch to resume hostilities. On this period, see Henning Köhler, *Novemberrevolution und Frankreich: Die französische Deutschland-Politik, 1918–1919* (Düsseldorf, 1980), 309–23.

36 Schulze, ed., *Das Kabinett Scheidemann*, 411.

37 *Akten zur deutschen Auswärtigen Politik*, 1:249.

itary confrontation and sign the treaty. This fear was not without justification. The country, under the shock of defeat and the threat of strict peace terms, was opening at the seams. It was not certain if the German Reich, hardly fifty years after its founding, would hold up under this exceptional strain. The confusing web of movements oscillating between autonomy, particularism, and separatism cannot be analyzed in detail here. But a few examples from a broad spectrum of activities can be mentioned, such as the spectacular proclamation of the Rhine Republic by the prosecuting attorney Dr. Dorten on June 1 in Wiesbaden, or the droll offer of the "Welfen" Party representative, Georg von Dannenberg, to fight actively against the Prussians with the French if the latter advanced to the Weser and armed the "Welfen" freedom fighters."[38] In Bavaria Georg Heim advocated the creation at first of a southern German federation including Austria, later a Rhine-Donau federation.[39] Count Batocki-Friebe, the Oberpräsident of Eastern Prussia, even considered Eastern Prussia's joining Poland if the peace proved disadvantageous for it.[40] Foreign Minister Brockdorff-Rantzau took very seriously the plans of Cologne's Mayor Adenauer and other Rhenish dignitaries to prevent the secession of the Saar region and Eupen-Malmedy as well as a permanent occupation of the left bank of the Rhine by proclaiming some independent republics within the framework of the Reich. In a telegram to the Ministry of Foreign Affairs, the minister called the idea "disastrous" because it would lead the Rhineland into the arms of the Entente. Ebert and Scheidemann agreed completely that Adenauer's plan had to be "prevented by all possible means."[41]

The efforts just mentioned only skim the surface of the attempts at separation or a loosening of ties. Motives and goals differed from movement to movement and within each group as well. Preventing "Bolshevism" – or whatever was understood by that term – in a particular region was a general goal. Hard-core conservatives were neither capable nor willing to make too great a distinction between Liebknecht, Haase, and Scheidemann. The south and west resented Prussian dominance. Other lines of conflict were drawn between the Catholic south and west and the Protestant north, as well as between federalists and centralists. And of course one should not forget the ambitious provincial politicians primarily interested in their own careers.

38 Köhler, *Novemberrevolution und Frankreich,* 320.
39 Ibid., 317–19.
40 Schulze, ed., *Das Kabinett Scheidemann,* xli–xlii, 163–74.
41 *Akten zur deutschen Auswärtigen Politik,* series A: *1918–1925,* 14 vols., vol. 2: *May 7–Dec. 31, 1919* (Göttingen, 1984), 81. The plans of Adenauer and his friends have often been studied and are still a source of controversy. See Hans-Peter Schwarz, *Adenauer: Der Aufstieg, 1876–1952* (Stuttgart, 1986), 202–29; Henning Köhler, *Adenauer und die Rheinische Republik: Der erste Anlauf, 1918–1924* (Opladen, 1986), 15–124.

Eastern autonomy movements played a special role. Antisocialist like the rest, they differed in their consistent attitude toward the victors. Whereas Bavarians, Rhinelanders, and Hanoverians hoped to win a more lenient peace through more or less direct cooperation with the Entente, resistance pervaded in the east. Some dreamed of the eastern provinces becoming the core of a national rebirth, playing much the same role as they had during the time of the wars of liberation. The parallels were, of course, problematic. Eastern Prussia's nobility had found the anti-French alliance with the czar no threat to the internal rule of Germany and much easier to swallow than cooperation with Lenin's and Trotsky's Russia.

The victors' attitude toward attempts to divide Germany varied. France generally viewed them positively and supported them in spite of internal French controversies about whether this or that action was useful and practicable. For Clemenceau, long-term security held priority. If Germany wanted to dissolve itself, he did not want to do anything to stop them, he said, in response to a skeptical point made by Lloyd George in the Council of Four that, if Germany broke up, it would be weaker but no longer able to fulfill the terms of the peace treaty.[42]

Wilson was just as skeptical as Lloyd George. He resisted France's active support of separatist plans, especially in the Rhineland, going beyond coolly observing Germany break apart. Schwabe quite rightly emphasizes that it was largely due to Wilson and his advisers that "Germany emerged from the Versailles conference as an undivided nation state and as a potential major power in the economic sector and in its military potential."[43]

Wilson's role was another theme constantly discussed in "dreamland" Germany in connection with both expectations and fears, hopes and disappointments:

> We bid you welcome, bravest fighters.
> God and Wilson help us further.

This verse could be found on one German city's gate, greeting soldiers returning home from the war.[44] Theodor Hahn took it to be an indication of the extent to which "the people were ready to accept these ideas." The ideas had only to be carried out, he added, "and the world would be at peace."[45] But this enthusiastic admirer of Wilson obviously exaggerated

42 Köhler, *Novemberrevolution und Frankreich*, 320.
43 Schwabe, *Wilson*, 402.
44 Quoted in Theodor Hahn, *Woodrow Wilsons Worte: Als Rechtfertigung der Revision des Versailler Vertrages* (Heilbronn, 1924), 13.
45 Ibid.

German readiness to accept a world order based on Wilson's principles. As Peter Krüger recently showed in an informative study, the fourteen-point program had little support in Germany from the very beginning.[46] After reaching an agreement with people like Colonel Bauer and Hugo Stinnes, who had nothing to do with Wilsonism, Albert Ballin, personally supportive of a peace based on rapprochement and a modernization of the German Reich, suggested to the Kaiser on September 5, 1918, that peace could be obtained through Wilson.[47] For purely pragmatic reasons and without any ideological sympathies at all, the representatives of Germany, facing an unavoidable military defeat and the threat of revolution, chose to go to Wilson. His program at least promised to spare Germany more than the Entente probably would. But that a Wilson peace would also demand great sacrifices from Germany, that there could not be a peace "without winners and losers," was clear to everyone who spoke for a peace mediated by the American president. This was true of Ludendorff as well as of Kurt Hahn, Prince Max von Baden's adviser and the inventor of the nebulous term "ethical imperialism," who came closest to being a Wilsonian.

Given this situation, it is difficult to understand the degree of embittered disappointment over Wilson, who was depicted in the German press as a demonic hypocrite. Krüger considers this part of the right wing's anti-Western resentment. This makes sense, but I think it is necessary to go farther back in history than he does. Certainly the anti-American feelings – and interests – of German agrarians in the last two decades of the nineteenth century were an important factor. Anti-Western resentment was, however, characteristic of the political culture in Germany from the beginning of the nineteenth century and the onset of the national movement, with its two-sided position against the foreign domination of Napoleon and against the influence of the French Revolution. And it was not just a question of rights. The meetings of the leading committees of the majority Social Democracy in the last weeks of the Kaiserreich give a rather mixed impression.[48] A certain affinity to the ideas of Wilson could have been expected from the meetings of the party that was to play a leading role in the following months: a

---

46 See Peter Krüger, "German Disappointment and Anti-Western Resentment, 1918–19," in Hans-Jürgen Schröder, ed., *Confrontation and Cooperation: Germany and the United States in the Era of World War I, 1900–1924* (Providence, R.I., 1993), 323–35.

47 Modernization was considered "more correct and less poisonous" than democratization, according to his notes in preparation for the talks. It was also felt to be the only means "to save the dynasty in the long run." This formulation may have been chosen for tactical reasons in order to make acceptable what were for the Kaiser monstrous proposals. But there is no question that Ballin's ideas about the peace conditions and the necessary internal changes were far less advanced than Wilson's. See Ballin's notes in Walter Görlitz, ed., *Regierte der Kaiser?* (Göttingen, 1966), 417–521.

48 See Erich Matthias and Eberhard Pikart, eds., *Die Reichstagsfraktion der deutschen Sozialdemokratie 1898 bis 1918,* 2 vols. (Düsseldorf, 1966), 2:417–521.

negotiated peace and democratization were points held in common. The meetings of the Reichstag faction from the end of September to the end of October dealt primarily with demands and measures for parliamentarization, in keeping with Wilson's ideas as they were indicated in the American notes, although the changes – those demanded and those achieved – were less radical and slower paced. But Wilson's peace plan met with greater skepticism. The Social Democrats spoke in favor of the Wilson notes without having any great illusions about a "Wilsonian peace." For example, in the opinion expressed by Representative Cohen on October 17, Wilson dictated "the conditions in the interest of the Entente . . . We must save our country from an *invasion*. This is why we must react positively to the *Wilsonian* notes. We have no alternative."[49]

Where, to repeat the question, did this overwhelming feeling, this passionate reproach, come from, this feeling of being intentionally deceived when the peace conditions were the same as had been supposed from the very beginning? This attitude was clearly a result of what is suggested in the title of this chapter regarding a misunderstood defeat. Ludendorff, unfortunately, had every reason to quote with glee the remarks of Konrad Haussmann, the liberal politician and state secretary of the Max von Baden government. Haussmann was the vice president of the national assembly, who, during the famous parliamentary protest meeting against the peace conditions in the assembly hall of Berlin University on May 12, had cried out, "If our army and our workers had known on November 5 and 9 what kind of peace it would be, then our army and even the soldiers' councils would never have laid down their weapons, and our workers would have remained steadfast before they would have let Germany be beaten down in such a way."[50]

It was a strange event. Politicians like Haussmann had had good reasons to refuse in October and November to go along with the abrupt shift in the position of the military leadership. After it became apparent that the defeat would have painful results, the military wanted to hear nothing more about their own realistic appraisal of the situation, which had forced the politicians to ask for a cease-fire in the first place. They suddenly called for holding out. But the politicians of the Max von Baden government, having lost their confidence in the military's promises, had agreed on a cease-fire. The complete peace program, presented in May 1919, was of course much

49 Ibid., 485–6.
50 *Verhandlungen der verfassungsgebenden deutschen Nationalversammlung: Stenographische Berichte: 6. Februar 1919 bis 21. Mai 1920* (Berlin, 1920), 327:1093. See also Erich Ludendorff, *Meine Kriegserinnerungen, 1914–1918,* 4th ed. (Berlin, 1919), 610.

harder than they had expected. Protest or even indignation would have been understandable. This, however, did not change what had made the cease-fire inevitable in November – Germany had lost the war. Its armies were defeated. A continuation of the fighting could only make the situation worse. Haussmann's senseless phrases, for which he received thunderous applause, show how effective the perfidious coverup tactics of Ludendorff and the high army command had been, how deeply their influence went, even into the democratic camp. Many experienced the defeat first-hand, but still felt it was not – could not – be true that a war fought with such great effort and sacrifice, with troops in positions far into enemy territory, could end with the enemy determining the future. Having grown up and been educated in a tradition of almost blind trust in the power, superiority, and intelligence of the German military, people tended to close their eyes and flee from the harsh reality into wishful thinking and imagine that the war had somehow ended differently than it had. The foundation was laid for the permanent bad conscience regarding patriotism and the will to resist that was to paralyze so many liberals and democrats throughout the Weimar republic and contributed disastrously to the final success of audacious, openly revanchist forces.

Troeltsch wrote in June 1919 that the dreamland had come to an end. No one, he continued, could predict the future. One thing, however, appeared certain to him: Germany was no longer a world power. Work, order and moral renewal were necessary. His appeal for sobriety and reason went unheeded.

But it was not only Germans who found themselves in a dreamland. As Pierre Miquel has made clear, the French also had difficulties. Two great disappointments shaped public opinion in 1919: the Left's disappointment with Wilson, who proved not to be a prophet of a better world but an imperialist using power politics, and the Right's disappointment with the war's results, which it felt took French interests inadequately into account.[51] Future comparative research on the different dreamlands should lead to a better understanding of European developments, but the image of a dreamland should not, of course, be worn thin with use. One thing seems abundantly clear, however: the German dreamland did not begin in November 1918 and certainly did not end in June 1919. The mistakes, illusions, and disorientation of those months have historical roots, some extending far back into the past. When a majority of the German people proved unwilling after 1919 to be realistic about the defeat, when people's thoughts were

51 Pierre Miquel, *La Paix de Versailles et l'opinion publique française* (Paris, 1972).

clouded by senseless slogans regarding an "undefeated army," and when the criticism of Versailles was used with growing success to lay the intellectual groundwork for a war of revenge, continued mistakes, illusions, and disorientation proved disastrous. This chapter's criticism of this attitude is not aimed at doing away with all criticism of the treaty. In many ways it was designed to call forth revanchism. There is doubtless a path leading from Versailles to Hitler. But I cannot agree that Versailles made Hitler's takeover of power inevitable. The Germans had a choice when they decided to take this path. In other words, they did not have to. Hitler's victory was not an unavoidable result of Versailles.

IO

A Comment

ANTONY LENTIN

Public opinion is an elusive entity. How, precisely, does one measure its impact on foreign policy? Often, the most one can say is that it exists and that politicians have to respond to it, even if only in the form of lip service. In 1918 politicians were especially sensitive to public opinion after four years of total war, a war of peoples, whose outcome was acclaimed in the three great Western victor-states as the triumph of democracy over autocracy. In all the former warring states, including for the first time Germany, political leaders were directly answerable to public opinion in the form of mass electorates, parties, or coalitions in representative assemblies and had to pay heed to the ever present agitations of the popular press. The Italian delegation, after all, actually walked out of the Paris peace conference for some weeks, in response to perceptions of public outrage on the issue of Fiume. Popular expectations across Europe were stimulated to dangerous heights. Hopes were aroused that the war, with its unprecedented strains, disruptions, and heartaches, would lead to something better. Hence the millenarian appeal, among the victors and defeated alike, of Wilsonian liberalism. Hence, too, the elemental desire that the losers be made to pay, in the widest sense, for the events of the last four years and be rendered harmless to repeat them.

Such was felt to be the unique importance of peacemaking that, in the Allied states, the three supreme elected representatives of the people decided independently not merely to attend the conference, but to lead their delegations and to fulfill in person the national will, while their foreign ministers danced attendance, in each case little more than a cipher. In his democratic scorn for the "old diplomacy," President Woodrow Wilson believed that this peace conference would be "*the first conference in which the decisions depended upon the opinion of mankind,* not upon the previous determinations and diplomatic schemes of the assembled representatives."[1] Was

---

1 I. Bowman, memorandum, Dec. 10, 1918, in Charles Seymour, ed., *The Intimate Papers of Colonel House,* 4 vols. (Boston, 1926–8), 4:291. The italics are in Bowman's original notes.

he correct? The evidence of chapters 6–9 suggests that public opinion as such, though it found frequent and sometimes sensational expression, on the whole produced noise rather than a discernible impact on the decisions reached at Paris.

The British peace program had been decided in outline long before the armistice.[2] Eric Goldstein rightly points out that the New Europe group was a native British growth, not an American implant: "not a pressure group for Wilsonian ideas, but rather the European product of the same ideas that had stimulated the American president." The New Europe group, heir to the tradition of Gladstonian liberalism in foreign affairs and committed to national self-determination and the League of Nations, was well represented in the Political Intelligence Department of the Foreign Office and in the British delegation itself. The enlisting of academics as well as diplomats to prepare expert briefs for their delegates, which Lawrence E. Gelfand calls "the most fundamental innovation of Wilsonian 'new diplomacy,'" was as much a part of British as of American peacemaking. On the other hand, it was the visionary eloquence and moral grandeur of Wilson's pronouncements, backed, as it seemed, by the irresistible power of the United States, which most touched the imagination, in Great Britain as elsewhere, as appearing to raise the possibility that the hopes of the New Europe were about to come true.[3] David Lloyd George, as a Welshman temperamentally sympathetic to small nations struggling to be free, was predisposed to accept the recommendations of the Political Intelligence Department, and, as Goldstein points out, there was no opposition in Great Britain to national self-determination in continental Europe (the line was drawn at Ireland) from the main grouping in public opinion. Their concern was with what the London *Times* called "the two fundamental questions," namely, the fulfillment of the government's pledges to "hang the Kaiser" and to "make Germany pay." Like Lloyd George, the anti-Germans had never heard of Teschen, and they showed little interest in the details of boundary settlements between remote and obscure nationalities.

---

2 Erik Goldstein, *Winning the Peace: British Diplomatic Strategy, Peace Planning, and the Paris Peace Conference, 1916–1920* (Oxford, 1991).
3 Harold Nicolson, *Peacemaking 1919* (London, 1933), 36–42.

Anti-Germanism and the Mythology of the
"Carthaginian Peace"

Goldstein describes the fierce currents of anti-German sentiment prevalent at the close of the war. He instances the sinking of the *Leinster* and the postarmistice press reports of returning prisoners of war, emerging accounts of life under the occupation as French and Belgian towns were liberated, of the willful destruction and looting of national assets by the retreating Germans: the dynamited railway lines, flooded coal mines, the wholesale removal of cattle and industrial plant to Germany. These accounts helped to keep public indignation on the boil well into the new year, fueling popular fervor for reparation and for punishment of those deemed responsible for war crimes, that is, for the coming of the war and all its consequences. The war-guilt clause seemed at the time a statement of unquestionable fact. It also seemed right that an example should be made of the Kaiser, popularly seen, in Lloyd George's words, as "the person supremely responsible for this war."[4]

In general, Goldstein follows the Keynesian line of historiography, which continues to prove remarkably tenacious. He emphasizes the demagogy of the "Coupon Election" and its outcome in an unprecedented government majority of 340 and a "Carthaginian" treaty forced on the prime minister against his better judgment. There can be little complaint against Lloyd George's choosing to hold an election immediately after the armistice. There had been no election since 1910, and the government was entitled to seek a fresh mandate. Like all prime ministers, Lloyd George sought to hold an election at the most opportune moment. Was he really the helpless agent of the legendary Parliament of "hard-faced men" immortalized by John Maynard Keynes? In a thoughtful but little-known book published in 1944, *Public Opinion and the Last Peace,* R. B. McCallum pointed out that the Unionist members of Parliament of 1919, whether or not they were hard-faced, "had nearly all been in the previous Parliament," and argued that

---

4 Speech in House of Commons, July 3, 1919, *Parliamentary Debates,* (Commons), 5th ser., vol. 117 (1919), col. 1127. Leo Maxse, editor of the right-wing *National Review,* described the war-guilt clause as "an unimpeachable statement of an undeniable fact," quoted in Robert E. Bunselmeyer, *The Cost of the War, 1914–1919: British Economic War Aims and the Origins of Reparations* (Hamden, Conn., 1975), 183; H. W. V. Temperley, editor of the standard *History of the Peace Conference of Paris,* 6 vols. (London, 1920), 2:45, agreed that "there is no doubt that the Allies were justified in exacting this confession of a moral obligation." Northcliffe's attitude to Lloyd George was "When he is vigorous in fighting Germany, I support him: when he sings his 'Be kind to poor little Germany' song, I oppose him," Apr. 22, 1919, Add. Mss. 62157/141, Northcliffe papers, British Library. On war crimes, see James F. Willis, *Prologue to Nuremberg: The Politics and Diplomacy of Punishing War Criminals of the First World War* (Westport, Conn., 1982).

British aims at the peace conference would have been much the same, election or no election.[5] The argument gives pause for serious thought. While it is true that Lloyd George was hypersensitive to the vagaries of public opinion and the press – and Goldstein traces this process – Keynes's stereotype of a sublimely irresponsible prime minister and a vindictive British peace policy, dictated to the squelch of squeezed lemons and squeaking pips, may be in need of some revision after seventy-five years.

Reparations

After condemning the provocative unwisdom of the war-guilt clause, Goldstein agrees with Keynes that reparations were among the very worst feature of Versailles.[6] But he does not say why. Were reparations objectionable in themselves? Yet they represented more than just a demagogic response to public clamor. As Lloyd George saw from the start, they were a crucial part of the geopolitical settlement. Unless Germany paid something considerably over and above the making good of material damage, Great Britain and France would be crippled by their war debts to the United States. In economic terms, they would have lost the war, while unencumbered Germany would have an enormous start.[7] Or was the main error in 1919 the failure to settle an agreed amount with Germany? If the latter, one can certainly sympathize. The issue of a fixed sum was one of the main bones of contention between Germany and the Allies in a settlement bedeviled overall by a lack of genuine consensus both between former enemies and former allies. If a sum could have been agreed then and there, the poisoning of the international atmosphere across a dozen years and the obsessive perpetuation of German bitterness over Versailles might have been mitigated. The German offer of an interest-free £5 billion in gold may or may not have been serious. Keynes himself argued that it was not. The evidence seems to me to suggest that it was at least open to negotiation. It should have been followed up. There is no reason to doubt that the new Germany would have

5 R. B. McCallum, *Public Opinion and the Last Peace* (London, 1944), 41.
6 For the use of the expression "the aggression of Germany" in the Pre-Armistice Agreement of Nov. 5, 1918, and in the war-guilt clause, see Antony Lentin, "Philip Kerr e 'l'aggressione della Germania,'" in Giulio Guderzo, ed., *Lord Lothian: Una Vita per la Pace* (Florence, 1986), 63–7; on war guilt in general, see Fritz Dickmann, *Die Kriegsschuldfrage auf der Friedenskonferenz von Paris 1919* (Munich, 1964); Antony Lentin, *Lloyd George, Woodrow Wilson, and the Guilt of Germany: An Essay in the Prehistory of Appeasement* (Leicester, 1984).
7 David Lloyd George, *The Truth about the Peace Treaties,* 2 vols. (London, 1938), 1:463; "British Empire Interests," F/147/3/2, Lloyd George papers.

adhered to an agreement freely entered into.[8] What it would never willingly do was discharge a debt that was acknowledged only under duress and that German opinion regarded as morally invalid, on the thesis of war guilt instead of on the prearmistice agreement. The advantages that bad debtors can exercise over their creditors are well known, and the 1920s revealed the practical difficulties of trying to get blood out of a stone.

And yet the domestic difficulties for Lloyd George – partly, it is true, of his own making – were undeniable. The temptation to postpone a decision on a final sum proved irresistible. Delay averted a multitude of problems. No one really knew how much Germany could afford, least of all his so-called experts, Lords Cunliffe and Sumner. To settle a figure in 1919 was politically elusive, because, as Lloyd George said, however much Germany offered, public opinion would still complain: "It's too little."[9] To that extent the failure may be blamed on public pressures. On the other hand, Lloyd George enjoyed unconditional political support for an immediate settlement from the quarter that mattered most: his own cabinet. With only two dissidents from the dominions (the prime ministers of Australia and New Zealand), the cabinet and British Empire delegation urged him to settle a figure then and there. Andrew Bonar Law, the Unionist leader, promised continuing support whatever the figure. Walter Long, a barometer of Unionist backbench feeling, agreed.[10] Moreover, as Goldstein points out, Lloyd George won a stupendous renewal of his personal mandate on April 16 in one of the greatest Commons speeches of his career. The three hundred backbenchers who had been harrying him with emergency debates and a minatory open telegram about reparations were paralyzed at one blow, leaving him carte blanche to bring home whatever settlement he thought fit.

Why, then, did he continue to stall? Partly, no doubt, for the reasons stated. Having committed himself so publicly, not least in his April 16 speech, to make Germany pay "up to the limit of her capacity," he did not

8 John Maynard Keynes, *The Economic Consequences of the Peace* (London, 1920), 204–7; "Reply of the Allied and Associated Powers to the Observations of the German Delegation on the Conditions of Peace," in Alma Luckau, ed., *The German Delegation at the Paris Peace Conference* (New York, 1941), 387–91, 446; Klaus Schwabe, *Woodrow Wilson, Revolutionary Germany, and Peacemaking, 1918–1919: Missionary Diplomacy and the Realities of Power* (Chapel Hill, N.C., 1985), 357–60. The German offer provoked protests in Germany and demonstrations against Melchior and Warburg: see Victor Schiff, *The Germans at Versailles, 1919* (London, 1930), 109.

9 Minutes of the Council of Four, Mar. 28, 1919, in Paul Mantoux, *Les Délibérations du Conseil des Quatre (24 Mars–28 Juin 1919): Notes de l'officier interprète*, 2 vols. (Paris, 1955), 1:61 (hereafter *PMCQ*).

10 British Empire delegation minutes, May 30, 1919, and June 1, 1919, in Kenneth Bourne and D. C. Watt, eds., *British Documents on Foreign Affairs: Reports and Papers from the Foreign Office Confidential Print*, pt. 2, ser. 1: *The Paris Peace Conference of 1919* (Bethesda, Md., 1989), 91–116; Lentin, *Lloyd George, Woodrow Wilson, and the Guilt of Germany*, 91–2, 96, 126.

wish to eat his words. More important perhaps, as John Hemery argues, he also wanted to leave open his options. There was no point in agreeing to a lump sum for the sake of finality if it turned out that Germany could pay more, perhaps far more, in years to come.[11] Hence, too, Lloyd George accepted that Germany's economic recovery was in British interests and warned Georges Clemenceau against killing the goose that might lay some golden eggs. Yet the fallacy of postponement was still this: that, not having been consulted, let alone having given its approval, Germany would only pay grudgingly and as little as possible, because it denied and resented the basis of the demands. Germany had agreed to pay reparations in the sense of compensation for war damage in occupied France and Belgium, nothing more, under the Pre-Armistice Agreement. And yet Lloyd George insisted that Germany must also pay a significant measure of Allied war costs under the contentious heading of pensions. Otherwise, Great Britain could claim next to nothing by way of war damage.

This also helps to explain the role of Lord Sumner. Whatever Lloyd George's reservations about Sumner as a notorious extremist and German-ophobe – and Keynes argued that Sumner was appointed "for press and parliamentary purposes" – it is also clear that the prime minister relied on this tough lawyer to produce maximalist arguments about Great Britain's share and about pensions.[12] Once Britain decided to put off setting a fixed sum, it was Sumner who devised the constitution and powers of the Reparations Commission to be created to determine and exact the sums eventually agreed. Sumner was not simply an embarrassing appointment later regretted by Lloyd George; he was a key agent in Lloyd George's strategy, from which the prime minister never really deviated: to exact from Germany as large a sum as possible – "somewhere between £5 billion and £11 billion."[13] Goldstein therefore follows a popular error, it seems to me, in arguing that Lloyd George was able to "push for moderating the reparations terms." He did, as Goldstein points out, take the imaginative and politically astute step of summoning the cabinet to Paris for a root-and-branch discussion of the entire treaty. He pushed Clemenceau and Wilson hard to make other concessions to Germany. But these did not include concessions on reparations. Here, as Lord Robert Cecil noted, he was "curiously reluctant to make any

11 John Hemery, "The Emergence of Treasury Influence in British Foreign Policy, 1914–1921," Ph.D. diss., University of Cambridge, 1988, 201–34.
12 Lentin, *Lloyd George, Woodrow Wilson, and the Guilt of Germany*, 114.
13 Hemery, "Emergence of Treasury Influence," 223–6, 233–5, 238–40, 253–5; British Empire delegation minutes, May 30, 1919, *British Documents on Foreign Affairs*, pt. 2, ser. 1, *The Paris Peace Conference of 1919*, 4:96.

changes."[14] On the contrary, as he told his cabinet on June 1, "he did not think that the time had quite come for letting Germany off anything. . . . Why should the Allies surrender any part of their legitimate claim? . . . Somebody had to pay. If Germany could not pay, it meant that the British taxpayer had to pay."[15]

Policy toward France

Goldstein reminds us that a constant aim of British strategy was the maintenance of a balance of power in Europe, and that with the end of the war, "Great Britain had no intention of replacing a German threat with a French one." There were divided and ambiguous counsels about France. On the one hand, Anglo–French relations were generally good, public opinion was pro-French, and individual statesmen were willing to extend the *entente cordiale* into the postwar era. On the other hand, radical differences emerged at the conference, and the two allies found themselves opposed on a number of awkward issues: the Rhineland, the Saar, the Middle East mandates. Furthermore, there was a school of thought, represented by George Curzon, which aimed at isolation and the empire, or at least a loosening of commitments to France.[16] Since the Commons was solidly pro-French, Lloyd George was able to pass unopposed his remarkable bill for a treaty of guarantee to France. On the other hand, by linking the coming into being of that treaty with the ratification by the Senate of an analogous treaty of guarantee by America, Lloyd George contrived, in a characteristic piece of legerdemain, to evade his commitment to France altogether. Once again he kept his options open.[17]

---

14 Lentin, *Lloyd George, Woodrow Wilson, and the Guilt of Germany,* 96.
15 *British Documents on Foreign Affairs,* pt. 2, ser. 1, *Paris Peace Conference of 1919,* 4:111.
16 F. S. Northedge, *The Troubled Giant: Britain Among the Great Powers, 1916–1939* (London, 1966), 160; General Panouse, French military attaché in London, to the chief of the French general staff, Dec. 10, 1919, and Dec. 20, 1919, 7N.1255 Fonds Clemenceau, Archives de l'Armée de Terre, Vincennes; Sir G. Grahame, British chargé d'affaires in Paris, to P. Kerr, Apr. 3, 1920, GD40/17/1368, Lothian papers, Scottish Record Office, Edinburgh. See Alan Sharp, "Standard-bearers in a Tangle: British Perceptions of France After the First World War," in David Dutton, ed., *Statecraft and Diplomacy in the Twentieth Century: Essays Presented to P. M. H. Bell* (Liverpool, 1995), 55–73.
17 Antony Lentin, "The Treaty That Never Was: Lloyd George and the Abortive Anglo-French Alliance of 1919," in Judith Loades, ed., *The Life and Times of David Lloyd George* (Bangor, Me., 1991), 115–28. Lloyd George lent plausibility to his pledge of immediate British aid against a future German aggression by his promise of a Channel tunnel. Clemenceau was "very moved" by this. Tardieu informed the Chamber of Deputies that the tunnel would be completed "in a few months' time": see Emmanuel Beau de Loménie, *Le Débat de Ratification du Traité de Versailles à la Chambre des Députés et dans la presse en 1919* (Paris, 1945), 60. See Antony Lentin, "Several Types of Ambiguity: Lloyd George at the Paris Peace Conference," *Diplomacy and Statecraft* 6 (Mar. 1995): 223–51.

GEORGES–HENRI SOUTOU: THE FRENCH PEACEMAKERS AND
THEIR HOME FRONT

Georges–Henri Soutou presents the latest thinking on Clemenceau and his
policy, or rather policies, at Paris. Let me begin by agreeing that Clemenceau "extracted probably the most that could have been expected for
France" in a very difficult situation. The odds were decidedly against him.
Everything he sought for France can be summed up in the word "security,"
a concept that did not even enter into the thinking of England or the
United States, because, thanks to the Channel, the Atlantic, and the surrender of the German fleet, they already had it. For them, the struggle
ended with the armistice. For France, it was still to be fought. Clemenceau
rightly feared the postwar struggle more than the war itself. Despite a last-
minute military victory, France, both in the long term and even in the short
term, looked set to be the loser after a war that had gravely weakened it.
France, as Soutou points out, was "exhausted far more so than its allies or
enemies." Demographically, economically, strategically, France remained
Germany's inferior, far more disadvantaged in 1918 than in 1914. The prize
of Alsace-Lorraine was heavily outweighed by the destruction of industry
in the war zone, the enormous debts owed to England and the United
States, and the irreparable losses in manpower. One man in four between
the age of eighteen and thirty had perished in the holocaust. How could
France be compensated for its inherent and now aggravated inferiority?

Clemenceau was acutely conscious, more so than his countrymen, that
France had been saved by its allies and would need them more than ever in
the future. With Russia out of the picture, it was all the more vital to forge
closer links with England and the United States. But this being so, he was,
as he said, no more free to make peace on his own terms than he had been
to make war.[18] And on many aspects of peacemaking crucial to France,
Lloyd George and Wilson were against him. This, then, is the first and most
significant conclusion to be drawn about France's predicament at the peace
conference. The obstacles that Clemenceau had to face did not come from
his home front. In the *Chambre bleu–horizon,* as Soutou points out, he stood
on solid ground, winning a huge vote of confidence in December 1918.
His political authority at the conference was unassailable. On April 16, the
same day Lloyd George routed his backbench rebels, Clemenceau beat off
a demand in the Chamber that he divulge the peace terms before they were
yet finalized. Again he secured an overwhelming vote of confidence. The

18 Henri Mordacq, *Le Ministère Clemenceau: Journal d'un témoin* (Paris, 1930), 3:259.

problems that really daunted him were the combined facts of a united Germany of over sixty million inhabitants and an alliance less than solidly pro-French when it came to endorsing French demands. The emphasis of Soutou's discussion lies in its analysis of Clemenceau's peace strategy in the face of these complexities.

First in what Soutou calls Clemenceau's "three-tiered" strategy came the maintenance of the alliance with England and the United States. It is true, as Soutou points out, that Clemenceau was temperamentally and ideologically in the Anglo-Saxon democratic camp. But his policy was based first and foremost on Realpolitik and an avowed belief in the balance of power as an effective deterrent. He hoped to weld England and the United States permanently to France's side because only such a solid bloc could even begin to compensate for the loss of Russia. He made no secret of these aims nor of the fact that he was prepared to make sacrifices in order to attain them, as he told the Chamber in December 1918.[19] The treaties of guarantee from the United States and particularly from Great Britain, he wrote later, were "nothing less than the ultimate sanction of the Peace Treaty" and "the keystone of European peace."[20] They alone could prevent a repetition of 1914 or ensure victory in a future conflict with Germany. Not only would England and the United States come to France's aid, but any German violation of the demilitarized Rhineland zone would constitute a *casus foederis,* bringing about immediate British and French mobilization while German troops were still on their own territory. A German invasion of France would be preempted and then reversed with American help. These were the primary guarantees that Clemenceau accepted, and that he thought he had secured before he signed the Treaty of Versailles. It seems to me that Soutou makes too little of the fact that this "first tier" of Clemenceau's policy, the "keystone" on which he staked so much, came crashing to the ground. It is fair, too, to point out that there were those who predicted at the time that the treaties of guarantee would prove mere "scraps of paper" and that France's concessions would be in vain. Clemenceau's critics included not only Ferdinand Foch, who foresaw exactly what was to happen in 1940, but also President Raymond Poincaré (who, as Soutou indicates, advised that ratification by England and the United States of the treaties of guarantee should be a condition precedent to the formal commencement of the fifteen-year Allied occupation of the Rhineland), the

---

19 *Journal officiel de la Republique française: Débats parlementaires,* Dec. 29, 1918, 3732–6 (hereafter *JO: Chambre des députés*).
20 Georges Clemenceau, *Grandeurs et misères d'une victoire* (Paris, 1930), 208, 210.

veteran diplomats the brothers Cambon, and skeptical opponents in the Chamber.[21] On the right, the Marquis de Baudry d'Asson pointed out Clemenceau's "inexplicable aberration": the paradox of asking the Chamber "to ratify a treaty [the Treaty of Versailles] based on a guarantee said to be essential and crucial; and to do so before it [the guarantee] . . . has even been given."[22] Soutou agrees that "Clemenceau's main failure was to have put too much faith in the Allies." The fact is that he was outmaneuvered, or rather hoodwinked, by Lloyd George and let down by Wilson, who did not even keep his promise to put the treaty to the Senate.

Nowhere were Great Britain and the United States more intransigent in their opposition to Clemenceau's peace aims than over his demands for the detachment of the Rhineland from Germany. "When confronted with the Rhineland question," Clemenceau recalled, "Mr Wilson shook his head in an unpromising fashion, and Mr Lloyd George assumed a determined air of antagonism."[23] Soutou argues that Clemenceau's abandonment of this Rhineland scheme "corresponded to his deep-seated conviction that German unity was final." It is true that Clemenceau gradually became more sensitive to the price of insisting on a strategic frontier on the Rhine and more skeptical of its military value. He questioned whether the Rhine was really an effective barrier to invasion in an age of long-range artillery and aerial attack. He was concerned with the drain on French manpower and resources should France attempt to hold the Rhine singlehandedly. In another war, he believed, the Allies, or at any rate Great Britain, would come to France's assistance with or without a formal alliance, out of straightforward self-interest. He also doubted, as Soutou points out, the feasibility of turning Rhinelanders into Frenchmen or of attempting to unscramble Bismarck's Reich.[24] But all that said, were these not largely justifications after the event, after he had reconciled himself to the fact that, faced with the joint hostility of Lloyd George and Wilson, he was powerless to push through a policy of separation? If he insisted on holding the Rhineland against their wishes, he

---

21 Raymond Poincaré, *Au Service de la France: Neuf années de souvenirs* (Paris, 1974), vol. 9: *A la Recherche de la Paix 1919,* 337, 350, 362, 363; *Le Temps,* Sept. 12 and 13, 1921; P. Cambon to J. Cambon, Mar. 31, 1919, Pichon, 7:63–4, Ministère des Affaires Etrangères; Beau de Loménie, *Le Débat de ratification du Traité de Versailles,* 188; *JO: Chambre des Députés,* 1919, annexe 6657, 305–22.

22 *JO: Chambre des députés,* 1919, 4161. In the words of Jean-Baptiste Duroselle: "Clemenceau a sacrifié la réalisation complète de son programme au maintien d'une alliance – garanties comprises – qu'il croyait plus solide qu'elle n'était en effet," in *Clemenceau et la Justice: Actes du colloque de decembre 1979* (Paris, 1983), 176. For a review of Clemenceau's policy, see Antony Lentin, " 'Une Aberration inexplicable'? Clemenceau and the Abortive Anglo-French Guarantee Treaty of 1919," *Diplomacy and Statecraft* (forthcoming).

23 Clemenceau, *Grandeurs et misères d'une victoire,* 200.

24 Beau de Loménie, *Le Débat de ratification du Traité de Versailles,* 188.

risked exposing France to the very danger he was determined to avoid at all costs: a future war with Germany in which France would fight alone. Until March 14, when Lloyd George produced his ingenious alternative of the treaties of guarantee, Clemenceau and André Tardieu fought as vigorously and passionately for the detachment of the Rhineland as for that of the Saar, straining the conference almost to breaking-point.[25]

The "second-tier" strategy that Clemenceau therefore pursued in tandem with the first was to connive at spontaneous Rhineland separatism. While denying that France had any intention of interfering, he hoped to tempt the separatists with the prospect of exemption from liability for reparations. He was happy to give discreet encouragement to local varieties of self-determination, provided that they appeared to offer a reasonable chance of success, as with Adenauer's scheme for a Rhenish republic within the Reich but independent of Prussia. As far as Clemenceau was concerned, "the more separate and independent the republics were established in Germany, the better he would be pleased."[26] In Soutou's words, "Clemenceau was informed of these maneuvers and did nothing to stop them." What he repudiated as counterproductive, because it alienated Lloyd George, Wilson, and the Rhinelanders themselves, was Charles Mangin's open support for the bungled Dorten coup of July 1919 aimed at outright independence. The difference was over means rather than ends. After Versailles, Clemenceau's policy remained much the same: to maintain contact with the separatists and to hope that French occupation would infuse democratic values both in the Rhineland and in the Weimar Republic generally. Such a policy of divide and rule, in the spirit of Richelieu, Professor Soutou seems to admire. And yet, as Clemenceau himself pointed out afterward, it was a total failure.[27] Admittedly his remarks were aimed at Poincaré's open and disastrous attempts to support separatism by force in 1923. Did he write with benefit of hindsight? Or was he himself a skeptic in 1919? Did he seriously hope to bring about a pro-French climate of opinion both in the Rhineland and also in the Saar, where, Soutou states, he apparently anticipated a vote for union with France in the 1935 plebiscite? This sounds like wishful thinking if, as Soutou maintains, Clemenceau himself accepted in the final analysis the validity of national self-determination and conceded that German blood was

25 6N. 73 Fonds Clemenceau, Archives de l'armée de terre; GD40/17/1173, Lothian papers; Mermeix (G. Terrail), *Le Combat des Trois: Notes et documents sur la Conférence de la Paix* (Paris, 1922), 228–9; Clemenceau, *Grandeurs et misères d'une victoire*, 99; Jean Martet, *Clemenceau: The Events of His Life as Told by Himself to His Former Secretary Jean Martet* (Paris, 1930), 152–3.
26 "Notes of an interview between M. Clemenceau, Colonel House and myself [P. Kerr]," Mar. 7, 1919, GD40/17/1173/6, Lothian papers.
27 Clemenceau, *Grandeurs et misères d'une victoire*, 171–97.

thicker than water. When the notion of appeasing the Rhinelanders through a mild and beneficent French rule was first mooted with the British by Foch in December 1918, Bonar Law replied that England had been trying to do the same thing in Ireland for centuries, without conspicuous success.[28] This is not to deny that the possibilities for France were extremely limited, and that perhaps the most Clemenceau could do was what he did do: keep open France's options by providing in the treaty for a prolongation of the occupation after 1935 or even a reoccupation if French security required it or if Germany failed to meet its reparations obligations.[29]

In his discussion of the "third tier" of Clemenceau's strategy, Soutou argues for the importance of secret Franco-German talks in Berlin and even at Versailles. He contends that "a sort of tacit deal" was struck with Germany whereby the Germans would sign the treaty, including the provisions for a fifteen-year occupation of the Saar and Rhineland, considered the minimum necessary for French security. In return, Clemenceau would consent to a plebiscite in Upper Silesia and would consider a lump-sum settlement of reparations instead of the Reparation Commission, which the Germans resented as an intolerable violation of sovereignty. I do not myself find this thesis of a quid pro quo entirely convincing, to judge at any rate from the minutes of the Council of Four. In the first place, although it is true that Clemenceau did eventually agree to the Silesian plebiscite, it was only under intense pressure from Lloyd George. Until then, Clemenceau had given out-and-out support to Ignacy Paderewski and his maximalist demands for territory at Germany's expense, including Silesia. If that weakened the German economy, so much the better. He seems to have yielded only reluctantly to Lloyd George's logic and persistence.[30] Second, pressure to allow the Germans to offer a fixed sum within four months of signing the treaty came in the first instance not from Clemenceau, but from Wilson, who had always sought a clear-cut solution. Lloyd George and Clemenceau agreed to it because they had, after all, nothing to lose: they could always turn down an offer.[31] In the end, none was forthcoming anyway. Third, the formal Allied reply of June 16 to the German counterproposals contained no concessions on the Reparation Commission, but merely a restatement, drafted by Summer, of its powers, and a denial of German complaints of

---

28 Lloyd George, *Truth about the Peace Treaties*, 1:135.
29 As Soutou points out, Clemenceau predicted that Germany would default and France would remain on the Rhine. Tardieu claimed the force of article 429 to be "pas de traités de garantie, pas d'évacuation en 1935," in André Tardieu, *La Paix* (Paris, 1921), 236.
30 Minutes of Meetings of Council of Four, June 2, 3, and 10, 1919, in *PMCQ*, 2:265–9, 281–3, 380–6.
31 The form of the proposal came from Lloyd George. Minutes of Meetings of Council of Four, June 2, 3, 9, and 10, 1919, in *PMCQ*, 2:273, 283–5, 354–6, 359–64.

unwarrantable interference.[32] One must therefore question whether the "third tier" of Clemenceau's strategy really amounted to much.

I have suggested that Clemenceau had little trouble with French public opinion during the conference. The treaty once signed, however, was subjected to a far more prolonged and searching scrutiny in France than in England or even than in the United States. While Lloyd George, with his usual panache, carried the treaty through the Commons virtually unopposed in a matter of days, formal hearings before the United States Senate were spread across six weeks, while the ratification debates in France, as Soutou mentions, lasted from July to October, though it is also true, as he points out, that in contrast to the United States, France, once the treaty was signed, engaged in essentially academic debates. This does not mean that they were unimportant. The treaty's many weaknesses were skillfully exposed, which added to justified apprehensions of a hollow victory.[33]

LAWRENCE E. GELFAND: AMERICAN MISSION TO NEGOTIATE PEACE

Why, at the end of the day, did the United States reject the treaty inspired, negotiated, and signed by the president and predicated on American cooperation for its enforcement? A variety of answers have been suggested – political, constitutional, even medical and psychological – almost all laying responsibility at the president's door.[34] Gelfand agrees that it was not simply a question of "personal enmity" between Wilson and Henry Cabot Lodge, intense though that enmity was. Serious matters of principle were at stake. Gelfand cites a telling senatorial gloss on the Treaty of Algeciras (1906) to remind us of the Senate's traditional jealousy of its independent treaty-making role. The president, as far as the home front is concerned, committed a succession of incredible and, in the end, irreparable errors of judgment and tactics. They all boiled down to ignoring the simple fact that for the treaty to become binding on the United States, it required the consent of a two-thirds majority in the Senate, not a simple majority, which, in fact, it achieved. As author of the standard textbook on the American constitu-

---

32 "Reply of the Allied and Associated Powers to the Observations of the German Delegation on the Conditions of Peace," in Luckau, *German Delegation at the Paris Peace Conference*, 443–5; *PMCQ*, 2:360–1.

33 Beau de Loménie, *Le Débat de ratification du Traité de Versailles*.

34 Lloyd E. Ambrosius, *Woodrow Wilson and the American Diplomatic Tradition: The Treaty Fight in Perspective* (Cambridge, 1987); Edwin A. Weinstein, *Woodrow Wilson: A Medical and Psychological Biography* (Princeton, N.J., 1981). For a convenient conspectus, cf. Ralph A. Stone, ed., *Wilson and the League of Nations: Why America's Rejection?* (New York, 1967).

tion, no one knew better than Wilson the importance of coming to terms with the Senate, then in the hands of a tiny but crucial Republican majority of forty-nine to forty-seven.[35] A year after Algeciras, however, he had expressed a view of the presidential prerogative in foreign affairs as "very absolute" and thus relegated the Senate's part in treaty-making to that of a rubber stamp.[36] This tendentious but firmly held conviction, which he never repudiated, may help to explain much that followed.

His open contempt for the Republicans caused needless offense. His tactless call for a personal mandate in the congressional elections of November 1918 received its comeuppance: the election of 237 Republicans as against 190 Democrats in the House of Representatives surely entitled former President Theodore Roosevelt to claim that Wilson's claims to represent the will of the American people were not well founded.[37] This was taken up with a vengeance by Cabot Lodge and the irreconcilables. Wilson declined to broaden the basis of his delegation to the peace conference by appointing to it any Republican of real political weight.[38] He offended Cabot Lodge by making triumphalist speeches upon landing at Boston, the power base of the "Senator from Massachusetts." He failed to win over the Republicans who attended the dinner party at the White House on February 26 that Edward House had persuaded him to host for that purpose. He defied Cabot Lodge's "round robin" resolution against the League of Nations. In a speech at the Metropolitan Opera House on the eve of his return to Europe, he insisted that the League was an indissoluble part of the peace settlement, though he was well aware that it was the League, more than anything else in the treaty, that Republicans felt to fly in the face of American tradition in foreign policy.

All this Colonel House, Stannard Baker, and others of Wilson's closest supporters saw and were powerless to redress. The hostility of Secretary of State Robert Lansing and the growing skepticism of the American com-

---

35 Woodrow Wilson, *Congressional Government* (first published in 1885, it ran to fifteen editions by 1900 alone).

36 "The initiative in foreign affairs, which the President possesses without any restriction whatever, is virtually the power to control them absolutely. The President cannot conclude a treaty with a foreign power without the consent of the Senate, but may guide every step of diplomacy, and to guide diplomacy is to determine what treaties must be made, if the faith and prestige of the government are to be maintained. He need disclose no step of negotiation until it is complete, and when in any critical matter it is completed, the government is virtually committed. Whatever its disinclination, the Senate may feel itself committed also." From Wilson's Blumenthal lectures of 1907, in Arthur S. Link et al., *Wilson's Diplomacy: An International Symposium* (Cambridge, Mass., 1973), 12.

37 Arthur Walworth, *Woodrow Wilson*, 2 vols. (Boston, 1965), 2:216–17.

38 Henry White, a veteran career diplomat, was not a Republican activist.

missioners at Paris meant that Wilson had to defend the treaty, as he had negotiated it, almost alone. Unlike Lloyd George and Clemenceau, he failed to make use of the press: five hundred American journalists stood kicking their heels in Paris, fed occasional stale crumbs by Stannard Baker.[39] Given all this, what also calls for explanation is why England and France, who received full warning of mounting opposition in the United States, did not take it more seriously. They could not, however, be expected to foresee that the president would deliberately kill the treaty sooner than compromise on the League. By setting his face against any "reservations" to the League Covenant, he made ratification impossible. Had he not ordered the moderate Democrats to vote against the "reservations" he would have won his two-thirds majority with a dozen votes to spare. His attempt to appeal, in a hectic whistle-stop tour, to the American people above the heads of the Senate, a kind of Midlothian campaign to turn the presidential elections of 1920 into "a great and solemn referendum" on the League of Nations, was a desperate and tragic failure. Although, as Gelfand points out, he had committed himself at Paris to an American guarantee to France, which Cabot Lodge and the Senate were willing to endorse, he failed even to submit it to the Senate. As Lloyd E. Ambrosius writes, "indifference of the Democratic President and Senators, even more than opposition from some Republicans, killed this alliance."[40]

FRITZ KLEIN: BETWEEN COMPIÈGNE AND VERSAILLES: THE
GERMANS ON THE WAY FROM A MISUNDERSTOOD DEFEAT
TO AN UNWANTED PEACE

Fritz Klein's essay is about the psychological trauma of defeat and the effects of Versailles on German public opinion. His approach is impressionistic rather than analytical, and none the worse for that in conveying what Ernst Troeltsch called the "dreamland" flavor of that fluid, eventful half-year between armistice and treaty, punctuated by the birth pangs of parliamentary democracy, the pains of demobilization, the maraudings of the Freikorps, the Spartacist and separatist uprisings, the specter of Bolshevism and world revolution, and the mounting horror, incredulity, and disillusion at

---

39 H. G. Nicholas, in Arthur S. Link et al., *Wilson's Diplomacy,* 82–3.
40 Ambrosius, *Woodrow Wilson and the American Diplomatic Tradition,* 214; William R. Keylor, "The Rise and Demise of the Franco-American Guarantee Pact, 1919–1921," *Proceedings of the Annual Meeting of the Western Society for French History* 15 (1988): 371–3.

the peace terms. He does not discuss the effects of the blockade, which are studied in C. P. Vincent's *The Politics of Hunger,* although he does review the difficult issue of to what extent Bolshevism was considered a serious threat in Germany, to what extent a bluff with which to scare the Allies into moderating the peace terms.[41] The answer seems to be something of both.

From Armistice to Dolchstosslegende

Klein stresses the importance of the *Dolchstosslegende,* the unwillingness, despite firsthand experience, to accept that Germany had lost the war. It began with the disingenuousness of the High Command in first insisting on an armistice because the war was lost, then calling in the civilians to gain a breathing space, and later blaming those same civilians for losing the war. When, in November 1918, the civilians sent a delegation under Matthias Erzberger through the lines with a white flag to treat with Foch, why did they not include among its number a really high-ranking member of the High Command? Instead of Major General von Winterfeldt and naval Captain Vanselow, why not Erich Ludendorff or Wilhelm Groener? The answer, of course, is that the civilians were brought in to get the military off the hook, not the other way round. When the last imperial chancellor, Prince Max of Baden, demurred at the panic in seeking an armistice, the Kaiser put him in his place: "You have not been called in to make difficulties for the High Command."[42] Ludendorff was already off the hook. Ironically, Prince Max had just secured his dismissal as quartermaster-general, thinking that he had thus vindicated the primacy of civilian over military rule.[43]

Neither was Groener, Ludendorff's successor, available. Friedrich Ebert, who replaced Prince Max as head of a provisional government on November 9, next day struck his famous deal with Groener whereby the army agreed to help the new government to keep order against spartacism. Nor was Ebert, that deeply conventional, even deferential Social Democrat, the man to embarrass the High Command by instructing the venerable commander in chief, Paul von Hindenburg, to sue to his Allied opposite number or to endorse the armistice publicly, as he did privately. In any case, it was anticipated that the Allies would refuse to treat with senior representatives of the High Command, since Wilson had warned in his note of Octo-

41 C. Paul Vincent, *The Politics of Hunger: The Allied Blockade of Germany, 1915–1919* (Athens, Ohio, 1985).

42 Max von Baden, *Erinnerungen und Dokumente* (Stuttgart, 1927), 346.

43 Schwabe, *Woodrow Wilson, Revolutionary Germany, and Peacemaking,* 96–7.

ber 23 that in such a case, the United States would demand "not peace negotiations, but surrender."[44]

Thus the High Command was able to evade responsibility for the lost war, for the humiliation of the armistice, and for the *Schandvertrag* of Versailles, and to blame all three on Wilsonism, the republic, and the civilians. In November 1919, Hindenburg and Ludendorff were summoned before a public committee of inquiry. Intended to place the blame for the prolongation of the war fairly and squarely on the High Command, the spectacle had the opposite effect: it revived the prestige of the Reichswehr as the repository of German honor, it lent authority to the *Dolchstosslegende,* and it served to discredit republican and liberal values.[45]

What more could the Allies have done in 1918 to bring home to Germany the reality of defeat? It is conventional wisdom to say that they should have pressed on into the heart of Germany and dictated terms at Berlin.[46] But with the Allies suffering terrible casualties right up to the end, such a course was out of the question once Germany agreed to accept Foch's terms of armistice. In all but name these amounted to unconditional surrender, and perhaps they should have been designated as such, though would even that have necessarily prevented the *Dolchstosslegende?* Why was evacuation of Alsace-Lorraine, military retirement to the east of the Rhine, and Allied occupation of the Rhineland not sufficient proof of defeat? As Klein observes, "People tended to close their eyes and flee from the harsh reality into wishful thinking." There are none so blind as those who will not see. Besides which, there was truth enough to prompt a search for scapegoats in Ebert's claim that the German army, though in retreat, was not defeated in the field.[47] On November 11, in west and east, German troops still stood foursquare on foreign soil. Germany was defeated in the sense that, particularly with the collapse of its allies, its leaders accepted that the odds were

44 Bullit Lowry, *Armistice 1918* (Kent, Ohio, 1996), 40.
45 Ernst Fraenkel, in Arthur S. Link et al., *Wilson's Diplomacy,* 75–6; Peter Krüger, "German Disappointment and Anti-Western Resentment, 1918–19," in Hans-Jürgen Schröder, ed., *Confrontation and Cooperation: Germany and the United States in the Era of World War I, 1900–1924* (Oxford, 1993), 323–35. On early manifestations of anti-Semitism, see Fraenkel, in Arthur S. Link et al., *Wilson's Diplomacy,* 54. The appearance in German of Keynes's *Economic Consequences of the Peace* also served to put the seal on overall German impressions of Versailles as a *Schandvertrag.* On this point, see Fraenkel, in Arthur S. Link et al., *Wilson's Diplomacy,* 66–8. No doubt, as Lawrence E. Gelfand observes in the American context, Keynes confirmed what critics of Versailles wished to hear.
46 See, e.g., Sally Marks, "1918 and After: The Postwar Era," in Gordon Martel, ed., *The Origins of the Second World War Reconsidered: The A. J. P. Taylor Debate After Twenty-five Years* (London, 1986), 23–4. Lloyd George himself had warned against a premature cessation of hostilities, see *Times* (London), Sept. 13, 1918.
47 Friedrich Ebert, *Schriften, Aufzeichnungen und Reden* (Dresden, 1926), 2:127.

impossible. They hoped for better terms by suing for armistice sooner rather than later.

But there is no denying the historical importance of the profound psychological unwillingness to look facts in the face and the "apocalyptic" despair that gripped many German thinkers by no means conservative in outlook. Victims not merely of imperial tradition and wartime propaganda, but of a heady succession of undeniable victories and massive annexation in the east, at the same time convinced that Germany had fought a war of self-defense, they gave little thought to the consequences of defeat and of Allied fears of Germany. This explains perhaps part of the depth of their shock and disillusion. One has the impression that much of Germany was as blinkered intellectually and imaginatively as it was blockaded physically: a "dreamland" indeed. The German delegation was, of course, literally enclosed and palisaded in its quarters at Versailles, and isolated again in the Trianon Palace Hotel, where the treaty was formally presented on May 7.[48] The consequent feelings of self-righteous resentment inspired Ulrich Graf Brockdorff-Rantzau's notorious diplomatic gaffe, when he refused to stand up and delivered a dramatic speech of protest that, while reasonable in content, was defiant and ungracious in tone and manner. "The most tactless speech I have ever heard," said Wilson. Even Lloyd George said that it had made him "more angry than any incident of the war." But Brockdorff-Rantzau also had the home front to consider in his refusal to be placed, as he saw it, in the dock. In the words of Peter Krüger, "es war eine innenpolitische Rede."[49] It was the first (and as it turned out the last) opportunity for anyone at the conference to represent Germany's honor. But it was a lost opportunity, and as disastrous in its effects in hardening Allied attitudes as was, a month later, the burning of the French flags at Berlin and the scuttling of the High Seas Fleet at Scapa Flow.

The "German trauma" – as Versailles has been called by Hans-Joachim Koch – with "post-traumatic stress-symptoms"[50] affecting so many leading German thinkers cited by Klein – Rathenau, Thomas Mann, Ernst Troelsch (and let us, as historians, add Gerhard Ritter)[51] – is the central theme of Klein's essay. When he refers to the intellectuals' revulsion at the treaty and

48 W. Simons, May 8, 1919, in Luckau, *German Delegation at the Paris Peace Conference*, 118–21; Schiff, *Germans at Versailles*, 58–65.

49 Lentin, *Lloyd George, Woodrow Wilson, and the Guilt of Germany*, 87–8; Peter Krüger, *Versailles: Deutsche Aussenpolitik zwischen Revisionismus und Friedenssicherung* (Munich, 1986), 22.

50 Hans-Joachim Koch, "An den deutschen Leser–Versailles, ein deutsches Trauma," foreword to Antony Lentin, *Die Drachensaat von Versailles: Die Schuld der "Friedensmacher"* (Leoni am Starnberger See, 1988), 29.

51 Ibid., 7.

Thomas Mann's cry for Germany to align itself with Bolshevik Russia, he might also mention that playing the Russian card became the policy of Brockdorff-Rantzau, who resigned as foreign minister rather than subscribe to Versailles; and as ambassador to Moscow, he devoted the rest of his life to fostering ties against the Entente. His policy of nonacceptance of Versailles was supported by the entire German delegation. Victor Schiff, a liberal journalist accredited to the delegation, recalled his own reaction to the final, uncompromising Allied note of June 16: "convinced Republicans as we were, what could we feel in face of a rancour so refined, except solidarity even with . . . Imperial Germany?"[52]

The government, on the other hand, could not risk the luxury of the heroic defiance suggested by Hindenburg, who, while admitting that military resistance was hopeless, expressed a preference for going down to defeat sword in hand in Wagnerian grandeur. This, as Klein points out, was romantic escapism. Refusal would certainly have triggered an Allied invasion, with the strong likelihood that the Reich, barely fifty years old, would disintegrate, as its constituent states made separate peace with the Allies. After the resignation of the Scheidemann government over the *Schmachparagraphen,* the Bauer cabinet took the decision to accept, because, as Klein observes, "a continuation of the fighting could only make the situation worse." This decision saved both German unity and German sovereignty.

The German Counterproposals

For the first time in German history, a government was elected to power on a popular franchise. The elections to the National Assembly at Weimar in January 1919 gave a sweeping mandate to the Social Democrats to negotiate a Wilson peace, and it is significant that the country to formulate proposals on the whole most approximate to the Fourteen Points was Germany itself. Klein cites a revealing diary entry by Thomas Mann suggesting that it would be better to sign the Allied *Diktat* than the German counterproposals; the counterproposals themselves provide extremely interesting evidence of one of the great "might-have-beens."[53] Their best point, Lloyd George told his own delegation, could be expressed as follows: "You [the Allies] have a set of principles which, when they suit you, you apply, but which, when they suit us, you deny."[54] Thus the Germans welcomed disarmament

---

52 Schiff, *Germans at Versailles,* 127.
53 The German counterproposals appear in English in Luckau, *German Delegation at the Paris Peace Conference,* 302–411.
54 "British Empire Delegation minutes," May 30, 1919, in *British Documents on Foreign Affairs,* pt. 2, ser. 1, *Paris Peace Conference of 1919,* 4:92.

and asked that it be applied on both sides, but were willing to disarm unilaterally, provided that Germany was admitted immediately to the League
of Nations.[55] They complained of unfair discrimination in Eupen-
Malmédy, the Polish Corridor, Danzig, and Upper Silesia, territories predominantly German, not to mention the fifteen-year loss of the Saar and
occupation of the Rhineland. They were willing to recognize an ethnic
Poland in Posnania with access to German ports. They renounced Alsace-
Lorraine but asked for a plebiscite there for the record, and also, more significantly, in Austria and Bohemia.[56]

The counterproposals made an immediate impression on the British and
could theoretically have constituted ample material for face-to-face discussion. This was put to Lloyd George in a memorandum from a member of
his cabinet: "It seems to me quite natural that [the Germans] should put forward a series of counterpropositions, and we ought to take these up *seriatim*
with patience and goodwill and endeavour to split the outstanding differences. In this way we shall get a genuine German acceptance."[57] The
author? Winston Churchill, then secretary of state for war. Sir Henry Wilson, chief of the imperial general staff, acknowledged that not merely had
the Germans "driven a coach and horses through our terms," but had produced "a much more coherent . . . set of their own, based on the Fourteen
Points." H. A. L. Fisher, like Thomas Mann, declared that the counterproposals "were in themselves the most brilliant treaty that victors had ever
imposed upon conquered."[58] The special meeting of the British Empire
delegation and cabinet, summoned by Lloyd George to consider the counterproposals, marks an important moment, not indeed in the reshaping of
the treaty, since its terms had nearly all been fixed beyond the point of recall,
but in what may be called the "prehistory of Appeasement," a spreading
conviction among liberal and left circles in Great Britain, starting within the
British delegation itself, that Germany had not been fairly treated and that
the treaty would have to be revised at some time or other.

From the four chapters under discussion, the following summary and
tentative conclusions may be drawn. Domestic pressures as such were less

---

55 Germany was willing to renounce not merely the High Seas Fleet, interned at Scapa Flow under the
    armistice, but even such warships as the Allies were prepared to allow it to build under the treaty.
    See Luckau, *German Delegation at the Paris Peace Conference*, 304, 322–3.
56 Left/liberal aspirations for Anschluss with Austria, though consonant with the Fourteen Points,
    failed to consider Allied (especially French) fears of a greatly expanded postwar *Grossdeutschland*
    (Greater Germany) of eighty million inhabitants, "camouflée en démocratie."
57 Churchill, memorandum to Lloyd George, May 21, 1919, in Lentin, *Lloyd George, Woodrow Wilson,
    and the Guilt of Germany*, 93.
58 Wilson diary, May 31, 1919; Fisher diary, May 31, 1919, quoted in Lentin, *Lloyd George, Woodrow
    Wilson, and the Guilt of Germany*, 93, 94.

important in the shaping of the peace than is commonly supposed. Apart from examples like reparations or Fiume, it is difficult to find aspects of the peace where decision making at Paris was diverted by public pressures outside the conference from a course already determined by the peacemakers, their advisers and experts in accordance with objective perceptions of national interest. Personal factors often played a greater role than public opinion. Wilson's apparently arbitrary award of the Brenner Pass to Italy is a well-known example. His championship of the new Poland, it seems, was less the result of pressure from the Polish-American community than from the close friendship between Paderewski and Colonel House.[59] Although keeping public opinion satisfied on particular issues of concern was an occupational hazard for Lloyd George and Clemenceau, both were seasoned politicians, well able to take care of themselves. What really counted was their political power base, their majority in the legislature. It was Wilson's refusal to accept that fact that led to his catastrophic failure on the home front. "Ultimately," as Lloyd George recalled, "a peace could only be negotiated by the accredited representatives of a country's Government."[60] At a time when popular government enjoyed unprecedented prestige after a war fought, in Wilson's words, to "make the world safe for democracy," Lloyd George and Clemenceau could claim beyond dispute to be such accredited representatives. Not so the president.

In England, France, and Germany, the opposition parties counted for little, whether during the negotiations at Paris or during the ratification of the treaty. In England, the Asquithian liberals and the Labour Party, more or less wiped out at the elections, could be ignored in the short term.[61] A fortiori so could the Trade Union Congress and the Union for Democratic Control. In Germany, acceptance of the treaty, recommended by the Bauer cabinet, was sanctioned by the Socialists and Center Party in the National Assembly. It was pressure from the ruling parties that had to be reckoned with. Around what Goldstein calls the "green baize-covered table," public opinion, real or alleged, was frequently invoked and used as a form of bargaining pressure, especially by Lloyd George. When, as Goldstein reminds us, Lloyd George warned Wilson that he might be replaced at that table by Lord Northcliffe or Horatio Bottomley if he did not deliver on reparations, or when he threatened the House of Commons with a fresh general election unless it gave him

59 Derek Heater, *National Self-Determination: Woodrow Wilson and His Legacy* (London, 1994), 76; Louis L. Gerson, "The Poles," in Joseph P. O'Grady, ed., *The Immigrants' Influence on Wilson's Peace Policies* (Lexington, Ky., 1967), 272–86.
60 David Lloyd George, *War Memoirs of David Lloyd George,* 6 vols. (London, 1938), 2:1595.
61 In any case, the Asquithian rump in the House of Commons tended to show itself almost as "hard-faced" as the Unionists.

a free hand, he was certainly bluffing, likewise Clemenceau when he suddenly tendered his resignation to Poincaré. The result, and no doubt the intention of both men, was to strengthen their position at home and at the conference.[62] Lloyd George was too much influenced by domestic pressure, adroit in summoning it up, chasing it, or keeping ahead of it, surfing to victory on its crest;[63] Wilson was too contemptuous of it and too unbending in his conviction that he alone embodied the highest aspirations of the American people; Clemenceau was neither too little nor too much affected by it: geopolitics not home politics was the problem for France. By and large, although the peacemakers themselves were occasionally infected by popular passions and by what Wilson called "exaggerated feelings and exaggerated appearances," the battles they fought concerned genuine national interests. Reparations and the Rhineland were deadly serious issues.[64]

In the final analysis, the constraints on the peacemakers, including domestic pressures, were those inherent in the clash of conflicting geopolitical imperatives arising from the survival of a united Germany in a weakened and fragmented Europe. Germany had come close to subduing the continent and had emerged in 1918 in better shape than its neighbors and most of its late enemies. Goldstein and Klein seem to be right about Bolshevism: notwithstanding the arguments of Arno Mayer, the containment of Germany rather than of Bolshevism was the main impetus behind Allied strategy at Paris. In their attempts to reconcile their disparate national imperatives, the Allies cobbled together in great haste, with great difficulty, and with constant heartsearching a mass of interconnected compromises, which satisfied none of them but which could not be unraveled without undoing the work of the conference. That was why they came to realize that it was no longer open to them to negotiate with Germany, as had been tacitly assumed when the conference began. That was why the conference never became a congress and why it produced only a *Diktat* instead of a true meeting of minds.

This mass of inter-Allied compromises, rather than any readily identifiable domestic pressures, was why the conference was felt to be, and was, so profoundly unsatisfactory. "They should have realised," Nicolson con-

62 *PMCQ*, 1:226; Lentin, *Lloyd George, Woodrow Wilson, and the Guilt of Germany*, 76; G. Riddell diary, Apr. 11, 1919, in J. M. McEwen, ed., *The Riddell Diaries, 1908–1923* (London, 1986), 268; Poincaré diary, Apr. 6, 1919, in *Au Service de la France: Neuf années de souvenirs*, vol. 9: *A la recherche de paix 1919* (Paris, 1974), 315–18. See Alan Sharp, "Lloyd George and Foreign Policy, 1918–1922: The 'And Yet' Factor," in Judith Loades, ed., *Life and Times of David Lloyd George*, 129–42; and Lentin, "Several Types of Ambiguity."
63 Lentin, "Several Types of Ambiguity."
64 Lentin, *Lloyd George, Woodrow Wilson, and the Guilt of Germany*, 115.

tended, "that there was no middle path between a Wilsonian peace and a Carthaginian peace."[65] But compromise was the very essence of peacemaking. "It took many of us to win the war," Colonel House noted at the outset, "and each one of the powers will have to be consulted in winning the peace. In adjusting these different points of view, our principal difficulty will lie."[66] That was also why, as emerges clearly from all four chapters here, there was "embittered disappointment over Wilson," disillusion, mutual suspicion, and cynicism in all the Allied states, feelings reflected, as Gelfand illustrates, in the letters and diaries of members of the various delegations, whether they resigned, as did Keynes and William Bullitt, or stayed on, despite their reservations, to the bitter end, as did Jan Christian Smuts, Jules Cambon, and Colonel House.

The outcome of compromise with every power except Germany made the treaty paradoxical and ultimately unworkable unless the Allies stood foursquare behind it. The treaty was not self-enforcing: it was inherently ambiguous and malleable. As Soutou points out, depending on the will of the victors, it was adaptable to a policy either of enforcement or of appeasement, of a Poincaré line or a Briand–Herriot line. As Clemenceau told the Chamber of Deputies: "It will be what you make of it."[67] The evidence of contemporary letters and journals, many still unpublished, giving the immediate reactions of the participants, and the battle of the books that followed soon after, suggests that Versailles found few defenders in the United States, little will to enforce it from the British side, small confidence in its effectiveness in France, and, on the part of Germany, every incentive to undermine it and every intention of doing so. "The opinion of mankind," which Wilson had invoked as the inspiration of the treaty, revealed its many misgivings at the outcome. This being so, as the *New Statesman* predicted – and it expressed the burgeoning reactions of leftist and liberal opinion everywhere – "the settlement will not last. That, after all, is the test, and the only test, that counts."[68]

65 Nicolson, *Peacemaking 1919*, 95. As C. P. Scott expressed it at the time, "The fundamental question is whether we desire a peace of appeasement or a peace of violence," *Manchester Guardian*, May 10, 1919.
66 Stephen Bonsal, *Suitors and Supplements: The Little Nations at Versailles*, 2d ed. (New York, 1969), 8.
67 Beau de Loménie, *Le Débat de ratification du Traité de Versailles*, 37.
68 *New Statesman*, May 10, 1919. For the spread of Keynesian interpretations of the treaty, cf. observations by Sir Eyre Crowe [1920], 800/243/139, Great Britain, Foreign Office Records, Public Record Office.

Clemenceau en convalescence à Versailles après l'attentat de 1919 (RV 500.817).
Clemenceau relaxing at Versailles after the assassination attempt of 1919. (Reproduced by
permission of Roger-Viollet, Paris.)

Traité de Versailles, 26 juin 1919: Signatures et sceaux des deux delegues de l'Allemagne,
Hermann Müller et le Docteur Bell (RV 357.842). The Treaty of Versailles, June 28, 1919:
Signatures and seals of the two German delegates, Hermann Müller and Dr. Bell. (Repro-
duced by permission of Roger-Viollet, Paris.)

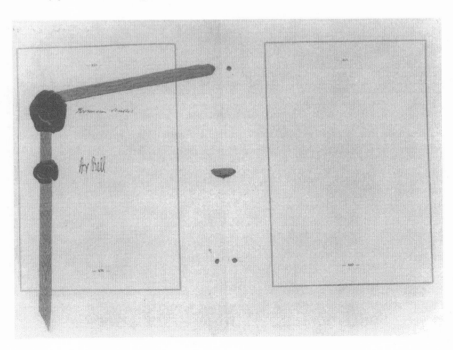

Signature de traité de la paix à Versailles: Clemenceau, Wilson, et Lloyd George, sur la terrasse du château (RV 305.985). Clemenceau, Wilson, and Lloyd George on the terrace of the Palace of Versailles at the signing of the peace treaty. (Reproduced by permission of Roger-Viollet, Paris.)

Signature de la paix: une ronde dans la rue à Paris, le 28 juin 1919 (BRA 107.385). Dancing in the streets of Paris at the signing of the peace treaty, June 28, 1919. (Reproduced by permission of Roger-Viollet, Paris.)

PART THREE

The Reconstruction of Europe and the Settlement of Accounts

II

The Minorities Question
at the Paris Peace Conference:
The Polish Minority Treaty,
June 28, 1919

CAROLE FINK

On June 28, 1919, shortly after Germany signed its treaty in the Hall of Mirrors at Versailles, the two Polish delegates, Ignacy Paderewski and Roman Dmowski, were ushered into an adjoining room. There they signed an agreement with the Allied and Associated Powers that ostensibly heralded a new era in the history of minority rights. The Polish Minority Treaty, one of the notable accomplishments of the Paris Peace Conference, has received mixed reviews from publicists and historians over the past seventy–five years. Proclaimed at the time a "new bill of rights" for minorities, it rapidly lost stature during the ambiguous 1920s and the violent 1930s and 1940s and was buried during the Cold War era, only to be exhumed, with more affirmative assessments, in the ethnically volatile atmosphere of recent years.[1]

In order to appraise the Polish Minority Treaty on its own terms – and *not* by way of its misuse and the lackluster system of implementation that developed afterward – one must examine how it was constructed at the peace conference. This "little Versailles," as the Poles still term their imposed obligation, although decidedly not one of the major undertakings of the Paris Peace Conference, was more than a side show. Between the armistice and the signing, what clash of forces, policies, and individuals, what mixture of political

This chapter was written when I was a senior fellow at the Rutgers Center for Historical Analysis and a participant in the 1993–95 project "War, Peace, and Society in Historical Perspective," under the direction of John Whiteclay Chambers II. I should also like to acknowledge the research support of the National Endowment for the Humanities and the Ohio State University, as well as the helpful comments and suggestions of Ziva Galili, Richard Hamilton, Michael Hogan, and Peter Kenéz.
1 Mark Levene, "Nationalism and Its Alternatives in the International Arena: The Jewish Question at Paris, 1919," *Journal of Contemporary History* 28 (1993): 511–31.

disruption, violence, and publicity, created this novel instrument, with its cautious generosity toward minorities, its judicious encroachment on state sovereignty, and its timid advance in a major realm of international supervision?

Since the dawn of modern diplomacy, minorities have been a highly volatile element in the European state system. Because of the continent's intricate religious, linguistic, and ethnic divisions, no state has been homogeneous, no neighbor has remained disinterested in the fate of its kin, and no outsider has been untouched by the repercussions of minority persecutions or the interventions of minority champions. The long record of international guarantees dating back to the Treaty of Westphalia (1648) testifies not only to the gravity of the minority problem but also to its steadily increasing complexity. The challenge facing the great powers was to reconcile the principle of state sovereignty and the realities of imperial rivalries with minimal security guarantees for minority populations.[2]

International awareness of the minorities issue increased measurably after the French Revolution with the growth of nationalism, industrialization, urbanization, transportation, communication, and, above all, democracy. As new states were formed and older entities expanded, humanitarianism, liberalism, and crusading zeal joined forces with the older interventionist impulses on behalf of minority rights. Thus the treaties signed at the three major peace congresses of the nineteenth century – Vienna (1814–15), Paris (1856), and Berlin (1878) – provided for the rights and security of populations which were to be transferred to a foreign sovereignty. These agreements seemed to signify a generous international commitment to groups destined to be denied their own state.[3]

In fact, these were by and large formal acts that lacked effective tools for enforcement. When tsarist soldiers massacred Polish patriots (in breach of the Final Act of Vienna), when the Turks slaughtered Bulgarian Christians (in contravention of the Treaty of Paris), and when Romania refused to grant citizenship to its Jewish population (in violation of Article 44 of the Treaty of Berlin), the other signatories took no steps to enforce the provisions for minority protection.[4]

2 The most useful source is still C. A. Macartney, *National States and National Minorities*, 2d ed. (London, 1968).
3 Lucien Wolf, "Interventions on Grounds of Humanity," in Lucien Wolf, ed., *Notes on the Diplomatic History of the Jewish Question* (London, 1919), 6–62.
4 See, e.g., Carol Iancu, *Les Juifs en Roumanie (1866–1919): De l'exclusion à l'émancipation* (Aix-en-Provence, 1978).

To be sure, diplomatic intervention on behalf of a minority, however endangered, constituted a risky state policy offering limited benefits to off-set the unpredictable domestic and international consequences. Up to World War I, the inhibition against interference actually grew, even in the face of mounting spoliation, evictions, oppression, and pogroms against minority populations. Liberal constitutional governments, devoted to the principle of national sovereignty, were reluctant to intervene in the internal affairs of other states, even when warfare, whether in the form of local insurrection, civil war, or interstate conflict, created onerous conditions for minorities. Indeed, some of the new borders, governments, and ruling peoples posed greater dangers to minorities than the old multinational empires. Caught up in a dominant system of Realpolitik and lacking any form of supranational organization, minorities remained perpetually at risk.[5]

On the eve of World War I, the persecution of minorities loomed as a genuine threat to international order. Violence and other forms of oppression produced waves of emigrants and refugees who strained the social, religious, political, and economic equilibrium of nearby and distant lands. With a sensationalist press magnifying atrocities and downplaying conciliation, national groups assembled their own publicists who produced propagandistic tracts of ancient settlement versus usurpation, heroism versus perfidy, "us" versus "them." Tensions grew because putative minority champions had few qualms about stirring up and jettisoning minority victims. Allied states were reluctant to restrain their partners' conduct toward their subject populations, and there was no international court of appeal. As their fortunes deteriorated, minorities split apart or vied with other minorities for better positions and official favors. Some attempted to assimilate, some devised programs of cultural or national autonomy, and some turned to universalist solutions, such as socialism and communism, to escape the conundrum of irreconcilable national claims.[6]

World War I, with its mobilization of vast human and material resources, was a watershed in the modern history of nationalism. As the war expanded in time and space it stirred widespread hopes and fears over the future political contours of Europe. When massive combat failed to break the stalemate, the battle moved inside the enemy's territory. By inciting the Irish, Poles, Czechs, Ukrainians, Romanians, South Slavs, Italians, Jews, Arabs, Africans, and Armenians to oust their overlords, form their own states, or join

5 Significantly, the Treaty of Bucharest (1913), negotiated by the combatants after the second Balkan War, contained no minorities clause despite the urging of some of the Western powers.
6 The Habsburg and tsarist empires were fertile seedbeds of all three tendencies. For a particularly poignant instance of disaffection between subject groups, see Stephen D. Corrsin, "Political and Social Change in Warsaw from the January 1863 Insurrection to the First World War: Polish Politics and the 'Jewish Question,'" Ph.D. diss., University of Michigan, 1981.

their brethren, the chancelleries and military chiefs of Europe sparked volatile and competing aspirations that persisted and indeed grew after the armistice of November 11.[7]

When the guns fell silent in western Europe, there was a crucial two-month hiatus during which the victors conducted elections and slowly prepared for the peace conference. The great powers sought order and limits, but their wartime clients sought rewards and satisfaction. Meanwhile, the vanquished foes worked to intensify the turmoil. A struggle of succession erupted in eastern Europe, marked by frontier, religious, and ideological battles, as well as by famine and disease. Although Germany had been halted in its quest for European hegemony, the vacuum created by the collapse of the Romanov, Ottoman, Habsburg, and Hohenzollern empires – together with the compelling Wilsonian and Leninist rhetoric of self-determination – set the stage for the creation of a new configuration of nation-states between the Baltic and the Black and Adriatic seas, and for vast new minority problems as well.

FROM LWÓW TO PARIS

The first sign of trouble appeared immediately after the armistice. Poland, newly liberated from its three defeated ruling powers, insisted on a large and strong state and fiercely opposed any concession to the non-Poles who were about to fall within its borders. When the Jews of Kielce held an authorized meeting on Armistice Day to outline their national claims, they were assaulted by Polish soldiers and civilians. During a two-day rampage in the city, four Jews were killed, one hundred were wounded, and much property was destroyed.[8]

An even more serious incident took place on November 22, 1918, in Lwów.[9] For three weeks, Poles and Ukrainians had clashed in the streets of Lwów in the opening round of a nine-month struggle for Eastern Galicia; both sides claimed the multiethnic, oil-rich province of the former Habsburg monarchy for their own new state. The Jews of Lwów, numbering one-fourth of the inhabitants of Eastern Galicia's capital, had declared their neutrality and thereby incurred the resentment of the embattled Poles. No sooner had they driven the Ukrainians from Lwów on November 22, than

---

7 On World War I and the national/minorities problem, see Fritz Fischer, *Germany's Aims in the First World War* (London, 1967); Z. A. B. Zeman, *A Diplomatic History of the First World War* (London, 1971).

8 Kielce, in Western Galicia, had been the site of anti-Jewish riots in 1915 after the Russians withdrew and before the Central Powers returned. In 1946 Kielce became a notorious pogrom site once again, when there was a systematic attack against returning concentration camp inmates that left forty-two dead and drove the remaining survivors from Poland.

9 The city's Austrian name was Lemberg; its Ukrainian name, Lviv.

the Polish legionnaires headed for the Jewish quarter, where they spent three full days looting, beating, raping, and killing in what the Zionist press termed a "war of extermination" against the Jewish people.[10]

The Allies, startled and dismayed, responded forthwith to the pogrom reports. Britain had already denounced Poland's use of force in Eastern Galicia.[11] The ensuing wave of attacks on Galician Jews, universally censured, provoked warnings from the Western powers that Poland's case before the peace conference would be prejudiced by these reported atrocities.[12]

Poland's representatives countered these protests by blaming the incidents on the military and civilian chaos at the battlefront, where armed bands of demobilized soldiers were wandering about in a daze. The scene they depicted was one of hoarding, starvation, and political anarchy. The new Warsaw government accused the retreating Germans and Austrians as well as the Zionists and Bolsheviks of inventing and disseminating anti-Polish propaganda.[13]

Jewish leaders in Great Britain and the United States had anticipated such consequences of Polish statehood within the larger reconfiguration of borders in eastern Europe, and they were proved right: millions of their coreligionists now faced new forms of religious, social, economic, and political oppression. Throughout World War I, Jewish officials and agencies in the Western democracies had dedicated themselves to relief work and also to lobbying their governments and negotiating with the new states on their people's behalf.[14]

10 The term was first used by the Jewish National Council of Vienna, which issued the initial report of the events in Lwów. See Grant Smith to State Department, Copenhagen, Nov. 23, 1918; Pleasant Alexander Stovall to Robert Lansing, Berne, Nov. 27, 1918; John Work Garrett to Lansing, The Hague, Nov. 29, 1918; and Jacob Judah de Haas to Lansing, Nov. 30, 1918, United States Department of State (hereafter USDS), Record Group (hereafter RG) 59, 860c.4016, National Archives, Washington, D.C. (hereafter NA). See also "Judenmord in Galizien," *Basler Zeitung*, Nov. 28, 1918; and articles in *La Victoire*, Nov. 26, and *Le Matin*, Nov. 30, 1918. The best summary is Jerzy Tomaszewski, "Lwów, 22 listopada 1918," *Przegląd Historyczny* 75 (1984): 275–85.
11 See Foreign Office to Władisław Sobánski, Nov. 8, 1918, in Stanisłas Fiłasiewicz, *La Question polonaise pendant la guerre mondiale* (Paris, 1920); Sobánski to Arthur James Balfour, Nov. 12, 1918, 371/3279, Great Britain, Foreign Office Records, Public Record Office (hereafter GB FO, PRO). The *Jewish Chronicle* of November 27, 1918, reprinted Balfour's public declaration of November 14 that "disorders" in the east would foreclose Western assistance to the new states.
12 State Department to U.S. Embassy, Paris, for Polish National Committee, Washington, D.C., Dec. 2, 1918: "If these reports are true, the sympathy of the American people for Poland's national aspirations will undoubtedly be affected" (USDS, RG 59, 860c.4016, NA).
13 William Graves Sharp [Lansing] to State Department, Dec. 6, 1918, records his meeting with Roman Dmowski, who discounted the reports of Jewish massacres as "exaggerated." USDS, RG 59, 860c.4016, NA; "Les 'pogroms' en Galicie: un démenti polonais," Europe/Russie, 837, France, Ministère des Affaires Etrangères (hereafter France MAE). A full record of atrocity reports and Polish repudiation can be found in Archivio Politico Ordinario e di Gabinetto (1918), 165, Polonia: Pretesi eccidi di ebrei in Polonia, Italy, Ministero dei Affari Esteri (hereafter Italy MAE).
14 The wartime work of Lucien Wolf, head of the Joint Foreign Committee of Great Britain, is documented in the Wolf-Mowschowitch Collection, Yivo Institute for Jewish Research, New York, as

Paradoxically, the Balfour Declaration, the Jews' most spectacular wartime diplomatic achievement, impaired the struggle for minority rights in eastern Europe. It rent the Jewish world into opposing camps of Zionists, non-Zionists, and anti-Zionists. It created the "Palestine priority" among the most active pro-Zionist Jews, who assigned eastern Europe a secondary, if not subordinate, status. Moreover, the official confirmation of a separate Jewish nationality and homeland fueled the arsenal of European anti-Semitism, bolstering the proponents of Jewish conspiracies and Jewish exclusion.[15]

Jewish organizations mobilized for their role at the Paris Peace Conference. Between December 15 and 18, 1918, an American Jewish Congress, representing three million persons, met for the first time in Philadelphia to endorse the Zionist program. Shaken by the events in Lwów, it also passed a nationalist "Bill of Rights" for the Jewish minorities of eastern Europe. More restrained preparations took place in London, Paris, and Rome, where Jewish leaders solidified their ties with government officials and with the press. In eastern Europe, most of the Jewish communities elected national councils to represent them before their new governments and the international community.[16]

To be sure, the issue of minority rights was not solely a Jewish question. During World War I, women's, socialist, and pacifist organizations had expressed support for various forms of equality and national rights.[17] Immediately after the war, the German government grasped the issue as well, seeking out alliances with Jewish, neutral, and left-wing bodies to place the minorities' case prominently before the peace conference.[18]

The portents seemed favorable to minority advocates. In their wartime statements and public contacts with Jewish leaders, the U.S. president, Woodrow Wilson, the British prime minister, David Lloyd George, and the Italian prime minister, Vittorio Orlando, all appeared friendly toward minorities. France had been the first continental nation to emancipate the

---

well as in the Archive of the Board of Deputies of British Jews, Woburn House, London; the work of Louis Marshall, head of the American Jewish Committee, in the American Jewish Archives, Hebrew Union College, Cincinnati.

15 Carole Fink, "Jewish Diplomacy and World Politics: The Minorities Question at the Paris Peace Conference of 1919," paper read at Hebrew University of Jerusalem (Mount Scopus), Mar. 1992.

16 James Parkes, *Emergence of the Jewish Problem, 1878–1939* (London, 1946), 110–11; Ezra Mendelsohn, *Zionism in Poland* (New Haven, Conn., 1981), 91–110.

17 In 1915 the International Congress of Women announced that "autonomy and a democratic parliament should not be refused to any people"; in 1917 the Central Organization for Durable Peace called for an "international treaty on minority rights"; and at conferences in The Hague (1916) and in Stockholm (1917), socialists endorsed minority rights and minority autonomy.

18 See Moritz Sobernheim to Max Warburg, Dec. 4, 1918, L1288/L350393, as well as preceding documents L350158–52, Politisches Archiv des Auswärtigen Amtes, Bonn (hereafter PA-AA).

Jews and had vindicated the falsely accused Dreyfus. However, the truth was that the Allies had concentrated their attention on winning the war and developed no concrete positions on minority rights.[19]

Everything depended on how the minorities' case was presented. The Western democracies recognized that national and religious oppression posed a threat to European peace and stability, but they rejected extreme solutions.[20] They opposed every suggestion that promoted political or cultural autonomy as not only opposing their national values and historical development but also favoring the Germans and the Bolsheviks.[21]

Self-determination, as it was about to be implemented in the lands between Germany, Russia, and in the former Ottoman Empire, was thus conceived in conventional Western terms: the region was to be divided into nation-states whose minorities were to be granted basic religious and civil rights but would not be allowed to exist as a "state within a state." Switzerland, the frequently cited model of a Western, democratic, multinational state, was a superficial, if not negative, example.[22] Since each of the Swiss cantons had a dominant national character, French, German, Italian, and Romansch groups residing outside their national domains had a minimum of political, religious, and linguistic rights. And because Switzerland's diverse population was more influenced by its larger neighbors than by a sense of a common Swiss nationality, its federal structure provided no useful standard for new and fragile states such as Poland and Czechoslovakia, which required some form of national cohesiveness vis-à-vis their stronger, and potentially irredentist, neighbors.[23]

19 The correspondence between two leading members of The Inquiry, a panel of experts appointed in 1917 to work out the details of a future American peace plan, Archibald Cary Coolidge and Walter Lippmann, Mar. 10, 19, and 25, 1918, reveals a lack of preparedness. See Records of the American Commission to Negotiate Peace (hereafter ACNP Records), RG 256, box 3, NA; confirmed in Lawrence E. Gelfand, *The Inquiry: American Preparations for Peace, 1917–1919* (New Haven, Conn., 1963), 205–8. For Great Britain, see E. H. Carr and James W. Headlam-Morley memoranda, Nov. 14, 1918, 371/4353 (PID), PC 33/33, 412–14, PC 23/23, fos. 1–4, GB FO, PRO. For France, see Sylvain Lévi to MAE, Dec. 2, 1918, Papiers d'Agents 166 (Tardieu), vol. 280; and André Tardieu (?), "Questions juives et politique française" (undated, ca. Jan. 1919), Papiers d'Agents 166 (Tardieu), vol. 131, France MAE.

20 Poland's minorities, e.g., were likely to exceed 30 percent of the total population. The figures in the 1926 census, eight years later, were as follows: Poles, 69.2 percent; Ukrainians, 14.3 percent; Jews, 7.8 percent; Belorussians and Germans, 3.9 percent each. Stephen Horak, *Poland and Her National Minorities, 1919–1939* (New York, 1961), 81.

21 In mid-November officials in the British Foreign Office overwhelmingly opposed Jewish demands for cultural autonomy as a claim "extremely difficult to enforce." Memorandum by Sir Lewis Namier and Arnold Toynbee, Nov. 15, 1918, "Conference on the Jewish Question," Nov. 19, 1918, 371–3414/191911, GB FO, PRO.

22 Noted in Coolidge to Lippmann, Mar. 10, 1918, ACNP Records, RG 265, box 3, NA.

23 Frank Hadler, "Peacemaking 1919 im Spiegel der Briefe Edvard Beneš' von der Pariser Friedenskonferenz," *Berliner Jahrbuch für osteuropäische Geschichte* 1, no. 1 (1994): 213–55.

To minority advocates, the new League of Nations seemed an ideal instrument for promoting political equality, religious toleration, and even special rights; it also offered the prospect of substituting solid enforcement for the haphazard behavior of the Concert of Europe. Yet the League's most ardent supporters did not think it should dictate internal policy to sovereign states, new or old. With Bolshevism a menacing new feature of the international scene, the victors were on guard against all forms of revolutionary currents and "subversive" propaganda, which undoubtedly meant curbing even the most generous interventionist impulses.[24]

Although they differed over goals and methods, the great powers agreed that their past efforts to protect minorities or curb their would-be attackers had failed miserably. The minority deliberations in Paris in 1919 were as haunted by Romania's prolonged defiance of the Treaty of Berlin as by the specter of German intervention on behalf of the millions of *Auslandsdeutsche* who were about to be placed in the new and enlarged states of eastern Europe. Aware of the danger of unenforced clauses, the victors were understandably hesitant to commit their power and prestige to a remote, unfamiliar, and seemingly contentious region. At the same time, the Allies had few inhibitions about their right to dictate rules of political conduct, despite their minimal military and political role in the area. The defeat and disappearance of four empires, combined with the emergence of vulnerable dependents and unconstrained new masters, forced on the victors unwonted and unwanted power and responsibility.

Thus the question of minority rights established itself uncomfortably and essentially, prominently and obscurely, at the Paris Peace Conference as one of the paradoxes of the Allied victory. This issue, with all its human, national, and international implications, reflected the precarious intermediary state of eastern Europe – with the political faits accomplis here and official warranty there, with self-determination for some and not for others. Between January and June 1919, the minorities question pervaded the strategic, political, and ideological deliberations over eastern Europe, especially over Poland.

A UNIVERSAL SYSTEM OF MINORITY RIGHTS?

If self-determination could not be granted to all peoples, how were the rights of new and existing minorities to be secured? Given the failure of pre-

24 Alfred A. Zimmern, "Foreign Office Memorandum" [Nov. 1918], in *The League of Nations and the Rule of Law, 1918–1935* (London, 1939), 200–2.

vious efforts to dictate policies of toleration and rights, Wilson sought a panacea in the as yet unborn League of Nations.[25] Instead of inserting specific provisions in the territorial treaties, Wilson devised a more general solution: he proposed, first, that the League's Covenant bind the new states, and all League members, to bestowing equality of treatment on "all racial or national minorities"[26]; second, that it provide a guarantee against interference or discrimination against any creed or belief "whose practices are not inconsistent with public order or public morals."[27]

Wilson's global solution corresponded with France's desire to organize the peace conference around some guiding principles. France recognized the link between self-determination and the rights of minorities in solidifying the new territorial order in eastern Europe.[28] The League's partisans saw its involvement as a promising solution to the dilemma of how to protect the new states against irredentism while establishing a workable apparatus to enforce minority rights.[29]

However, the attempt to internationalize the minorities question was met with strong criticism. Wilson's concept of "national" minorities was considered dangerous. His advisers were dubious about the undifferentiated nature of the "political equality" he propounded and the absence of a specific enforcement procedure.[30] The British, in particular, were alarmed at the thought that the League might be encouraging "American negroes, Southern Irish, Flemings or Catalans" to "appeal over the head of their own government" or that it might be sanctioning propaganda and intervention

25 In his first draft of the League Covenant, written in the summer of 1918, Wilson was silent on the minorities issue. Text in David Hunter Miller, *The Drafting of the Covenant*, 2 vols. (New York, 1928), 2:12–16; his second and third Paris drafts (Jan. 10 and 20, 1919) contained the minority clauses.

26 Wilson's proposal, Part VI of the supplementary agreements in his second, third, and fourth drafts (Jan. 10, 20; Feb. 2, 1919). Quoted in Miller, *Drafting of the Covenant*, 2:91, 105, 153–4: "The League shall require all new States to bind themselves as a condition precedent to their recognition as independent or autonomous States and the Executive Council shall exact of all States seeking admission to the League the promise to accord to all racial or national minorities within their several jurisdictions exactly the same treatment and security, both in law and in fact, that is accorded the racial or national majority of their people."

27 Part VII, reprinted in Miller, *Drafting of the Covenant*, 2:105.

28 See André Tardieu, *La Paix* (Paris, 1921), 97–103. The French representative, Léon Bourgeois, seconded Wilson's proposal on February 10. See Société des Nations 10, France MAE.

29 Zimmern, *League of Nations*, 201: "Instead of . . . haphazard interference by the 'Concert of Europe' . . . a mandate of this kind . . . should provide also for the appointment of a commission of investigation . . . [which] should deliberate and report to the sovereign Power and should have the right to publish any such report."

30 Wilson's legal adviser, David Hunter Miller: "The purpose . . . is beneficent, but . . . general treatment is impossible. Doubtless equal religious and cultural privileges should be accorded in all cases, but it is impossible to suppose that all racial minorities can be entitled, e.g., to have their languages used in official records." Miller, *Drafting of the Covenant*, 2:91.

by the Bolsheviks or other governments in the internal affairs of their neighbors.[31] Great Britain, accustomed to the role of a distant and impartial mediator, upheld the traditional method of writing specific minority provisions in the territorial treaties as opposed to burdening the new League with vague and general precepts that it could neither enforce nor supervise. The threat of injustice and oppression had to be balanced against "the negation of the sovereignty of every state in the world."[32]

Wilson's second clause upholding religious freedom was also greeted with opposition, this time in the League of Nations Commission. Despite its importance to the U.S. president, America's European partners shrank before the political complications as well as the difficulties of defining and enforcing a freedom of religion clause.[33] The coup de grâce was delivered by the Japanese delegate, Baron Nobuaki Makino, who made a fervent plea for racial equality: he asked that all citizens of all members of the League be guaranteed equal treatment everywhere regardless of race or nationality. As recompense for their sacrifices for the common cause and their willingness to make further contributions to collective security, the colored peoples of the world were asking for an equitable commitment from the victors.[34] This disconcerting demand merely hardened British and Australian opposition, with the result that Wilson's prized proposal had to be withdrawn.[35]

The setback was serious. The chance, however remote, to incorporate global provisions for political equality and religious freedom into the League statutes, and thereby give minority rights universal stature, had been lost. Partly to blame were two of the United States' principal partners, who held widely divergent views: the British, on the one hand, thought that international disruption could be reduced by minimizing the League's

31 Between Paris drafts two and three, Wilson expanded its applicability from "all new states" to "all states seeking admission to [the League]," leaving ambiguous whether this applied to founding League members.
32 Lord Eustace Percy quoted in Miller, *Drafting of the Covenant,* 2:130; Sir James Headlam-Morley: "Some general clause giving the League of Nations the right to protect minorities in all countries which were members . . . would give [it] the right to protect the Chinese in Liverpool, the Roman Catholics in France, the French in Canada, quite apart from more serious problems, such as the Irish. . . . Any right given to the League . . . must be quite definite and specific and based on special treaties. . . . Even if the denial of such right elsewhere might lead to injustice and oppression, that was better than to allow anything which means the negation of the sovereignty of every state in the world" (Headlam-Morley, *A Memoir of the Paris Peace Conference, 1919* [London, 1972], 113).
33 Miller diary, quoted in *Drafting of the Covenant,* 1:267–9; Société des Nations 10 (session Feb. 13, 1919), France MAE.
34 Paul Lauren, "Human Rights in History: Diplomacy and Racial Equality at the Paris Peace Conference," *Diplomatic History* 2, no. 1 (1978): 257–78, gives a sympathetic interpretation of the Japanese initiative, which was intermingled with its contested claim to Shantung.
35 Miller, *Drafting of the Covenant,* 2:323–6.

interference in its members' internal affairs; the Japanese, on the other, advocated a global campaign for racial equality. The U.S. delegation backed away from Wilson's fundamental conception of embedding minority protection in the League itself.[36]

By the close of the preliminary debates on the League of Nations in February 1919, no other inclusive solution to the minorities question was pending. Minorities were at even graver risk because of the eruption of fighting in eastern Europe among the Poles, Ukrainians, and Bolsheviks, as well as between the Romanians and Hungarians. In Paris, territorial commissions were established to decide the borders of eastern Europe, and the question of minority rights was buried under historical, strategic, political, and economic considerations.[37] Two months would elapse before the issue resurfaced and, in the meantime, the military situation had changed, frontiers had been assigned, and positions had hardened.

NATIONAL AUTONOMY

Just when the minorities question appeared to have been eclipsed, the old formulas for guaranteeing national rights, cultural autonomy, and political autonomy were revived.[38] In March 1919 pro-Zionist and nationalist Jewish delegations arrived in Paris. Appointed by elected national councils, they came fully prepared to argue their cases against the new states. The claims they made were anathema to the great powers as much as to their own governments.

Earlier, there had been no official, unified Jewish delegation at the Paris Peace Conference. During the first two months, the representative of the British Joint Foreign Committee, Lucien Wolf, and the leaders of the Paris-based Alliance Israélite Universelle, had worked informally and discreetly together, each lobbying their respective governmental delegates. Wolf, who

---

36 Erwin Viefhaus, *Die Minderheitenfrage und die Entstehung der Minderheitenschutzverträge auf der Pariser Friedenskonferenz 1919* (Würzburg, 1960), 118–19, believes that Wilson beat a tactical retreat, only to introduce the same clauses later. The seriousness of the setback is described in Lucien Wolf diary, Mar. 1, 1919, Mocatta Library, University College London.

37 Wilson's absence for one month strengthened the British strategy of awaiting the conclusion of the territorial treaties. In the meantime, Lloyd George urged that they avoid "putting too many Germans in Poland." Apr. 1, 1919, Paul Mantoux, *Les Délibérations du Conseil des Quatre (24 Mars–28 Juin 1919): Notes de l'officier interprête,* 2 vols. (Paris, 1955), 1:107 (hereafter *PMCQ*). France was presumably split between those favoring minority negotiations (Cambon, Tardieu) and those hoping to bury the issue entirely (Pichon).

38 For a brief history and bibliography, see Max Hildebert Boehm, "Autonomy," in *Encyclopedia of the Social Sciences* (New York, 1930), 1:332–6.

was also in active contact with eastern European leaders, had failed to convince anyone of the need for a special committee for minority rights.[39]

When the representatives of the American Jewish Congress arrived in March, the fervent Zionist Julius Mack and the more moderate Louis Marshall quickly overshadowed the leading American Jewish antinationalists, Henry Morgenthau, Oscar Straus, and Cyrus Adler. The Americans then moved to join the Comité des Délégations Juives auprès la Conférence de la Paix, which had just been formed by the Jewish representatives from Romania, Yugoslavia, Czechoslovakia, Ukraine, Lithuania, and Poland. The Americans, insisting on the importance of union, offered to lead the Comité. The British and French stayed resolutely outside.[40]

Underlying the deliberations of the Comité was the belief that the Jewish people constituted a distinct nationality, one that was about to be further fragmented by the new borders of eastern Europe. The new arrivals spurned the cautious demarches of the French and British Jews that had produced no results. The Comité's outlook went well beyond the western European and American concept of individual rights and freedom: it was framed in terms of a collective Jewish identity that included group rights and communal authority. Far exceeding Wilson's goals of political equality and religious toleration, the Comité's aim was to persuade the new governments to grant as large a measure of autonomy as possible to Jewish minorities: this meant the full use of their language and expression of their culture, as well as local self-government and representation on the national level. The Comité drew on the writings not only of Jewish scholars Nathan Birnbaum, Chaim Zhitlowski, and Simon Dubnow but also of the Austrian socialists Otto Bauer and Karl Renner. It maintained that Jewish nationhood could be an asset, not a handicap, to the new states provided that these governments granted minorities sufficient power and resources to maintain a separate and thriving national existence.[41]

The issue of autonomy was of special importance to the three million Polish Jews, who had suffered a prolonged economic boycott, wartime pogroms, and the postwar outbreak of violence. The German Jews of Poznań, on forming their own national council in November 1918, declared: "Present conditions no longer allow one nation to be the sole ruler of a state and to force its language, customs, and culture on the other nationalities."[42]

39 R. W. A. Leeper memorandum, Mar. 1, 1919, 608 151/493/1/1, GB FO, PRO; Wolf diary, Apr. 23, 1919, Mocatta Library, University College London.
40 The history and proceedings of the Comité in A126 (Motzkin papers) 52/34, Central Zionist Archives, Jerusalem (hereafter CZA).
41 Oscar I. Janowsky, *The Jews and Minority Rights (1898–1919)* (New York, 1933), 263–319, 332.
42 "Mitteilungs-Blatt des jüdischen Volksrats Posen, Sonder-Ausgabe," Mar. 1919, Z3/185, CZA.

In addressing the Piłsudski government on November 12, Zionist leaders promised their full collaboration if allowed to maintain their national existence through special voting rights, representative bodies, and a special secretary of state.[43] As the Warsaw Zionists put it:

We have the right to live our own national life in accord with the democratic principles of autonomous administration proclaimed by the allies. And we are firmly convinced that only the realization of this plan, the recognition of the Jewish national minority, will lead the Poles and the Jews towards a durable peace, a peace necessary to both peoples in equal measure.[44]

Despite their forcefulness, the arguments of the eastern European nationalists caused a split in the larger Jewish world. The Jews of central and western Europe, keenly aware of the difficult circumstances of their more numerous eastern brethren, sympathized with the cultural aspirations of the *Ostjuden* but for the most part opposed their political objectives. "The business of the conference," Eugène Sée told a meeting of Western Jewish delegates on March 31, "is to create a sovereign state for Poland, not for the Jews."[45] In contrast, the Americans Mack and Marshall not only collaborated with the Comité but were converted to its goals, including national autonomy.[46]

To be sure, the political debate over autonomy involved more than the Jewish question. The impending treaty with Germany, with its cessions of Reich land and population, was certain to intensify the minority problem all over eastern Europe and encourage aggressive advocates of minority rights in Berlin. Already in World War I, Germany had established a respectable, if not generous, record of attentiveness to minority rights.[47] On January 3, 1919, the German Society for International Law (Gesellschaft für Völkerrecht) proposed that all League members grant minorities proportionate parliamentary representation and permit them to use their languages in schools, worship, and administration.[48] The Weimar Republic clearly

---

43 Max Rosenfeld, *Nationales Selbstbestimmungsrecht der Juden in Polen* (Vienna, 1918); Joseph Tenenbaum, *La question juive en Pologne* (Paris, 1919).
44 "Mémoires" (Jan. 1919), A127/128, 16, CZA. Specifics included a Jewish state secretary and a separate electoral constituency based on a national curia.
45 Adler papers, 84, Mar., 31, 1919, American Jewish Committee (hereafter AJC), New York archive. In a similar vein, the philosemitic Gustave Hervé praised the Jews for their efforts to return to Palestine but warned against "building their own state on someone else's [sic] soil." "Dokola konferencji," Mar. 4, 1919, 1480 (33–4), Ministerstwo Spraw Zagranicznych (hereafter MSZ), Archiwum Akt Nowych, Warsaw (hereafter AAN).
46 See undated memorandum in Akta Leona Wasieliewskiego, 30 (Konferencja Pokojową w Paryzu 1919), 185–9, AAN, summarizing the Comité's program.
47 Egmont Zechlin, *Die Deutsche Politik und die Juden im Ersten Weltkrieg* (Göttingen, 1969).
48 Macartney, *National States and National Minorities,* 216. The German organization called for a League guarantee against violations and also insisted on the duty of loyalty incumbent on minorities.

intended to assume the role of defender of minority rights. In preparing for its negotiations with the Allies over the expected cessions to Poland, the Wilhelmstrasse aimed to guarantee not only the preservation of Deutschtum but also cultural autonomy, if possible.[49]

Among the new minority states, the most vulnerable target was Czechoslovakia, which had a potentially larger and more compact German minority than did Poland. The impending denial of self-determination to the Sudeten Germans (and also to the Hungarians of Transylvania, the Germans of South Tyrol, and the Ukrainians of Galicia and Bukovina) threatened to burden the League with a string of "Alsace-Lorraines."[50] When the Allies decided to maintain historical borders in Bohemia and elsewhere and favor economic, geographic, and strategic factors over nationality – invariably rewarding pro-Allied over former enemy people – the consequences were foreseen. There were proposals to extend some accommodation, particularly in the cultural realm, to peoples who were denied self-determination. In the opinion of at least one investigator, granting autonomy offered a possible antidote.[51]

Archibald C. Coolidge, the Harvard historian who at Wilson's behest directed an investigation of national conditions in east-central Europe, took a different tack. According to Coolidge, Europe's future security depended on a strict application of the principle of self-determination and the creation of as few minorities as possible. Where peoples remained under alien rule, however, they must be assured, through an authoritative, binding declaration of their "human rights," of "life, liberty, and the pursuit of happiness." Coolidge left the specific details to the League of Nations.[52]

There was indeed little likelihood that the great powers assembled in Paris would endorse a system of cultural or political autonomy under the aegis of the new League. First and foremost, their "associated powers," the minority states, were adamantly opposed to such an idea.[53] It was inconceivable that Poles and Romanians, both of whom were struggling against Bolshevism, and that Czechs, surrounded by a large German world, could

---

49 Instructions given to the German plenipotentiaries, Apr. 1919, quoted in Alma Luckau, *The German Delegation at the Paris Peace Conference* (New York, 1971), 202.
50 Report by Archibald C. Coolidge, *Foreign Relations of the United States: The Paris Peace Conference* (hereafter *FRUS-PPC*), 13 vols. (Washington, D.C., 1945–7), 12:273.
51 Kerner Report, in *FRUS-PPC*, 13:340, modeled on Austria's national register law of 1905 for Moravia.
52 David Hunter Miller, *My Diary at the Conference of the Peace, with Documents,* 21 vols. (New York, 1928), 1:267, 7:366ff.
53 Speaking to a conference of Jewish political leaders on February 18, Paderewski declared his support of equality of rights for the Jews but strongly opposed the autonomist program. Pawel Korzec, *Juifs en Pologne* (Paris, 1980), 89–90.

be compelled to make such politically risky sacrifices, to construct and pay for privileges they had never enjoyed as subject peoples.

Moreover, it is not certain that the minorities themselves were sufficiently cohesive or motivated to take responsibility for their own cultural, not to mention, political affairs. In Poland, for example, despite a certain enthusiasm within the Jewish population over the idea of political autonomy, the question of implementation was fraught with controversy. Were the autonomists advocating representative bodies, electoral constituencies, and special state secretaries for each minority? Would national curiae force minorities into open competition with each other, as well as with the Poles for power and resources? Would this "new" form of democracy deny rights and representation to whole groups of people (the assimilated, those in mixed marriages, those without citizenship)? Would separate forms of national development actually reduce, or merely augment, prejudice and violence against minorities? Polish Jewry, with its historical, religious, and cultural divisions, its huge range of political ideologies – from assimilation to socialist internationalism, from folkist and religious beliefs to Zionism and nationalism – was undoubtedly far from ready for self-government. In fact, the huge resources, guidance, and support required to achieve and sustain national autonomy were probably beyond the reach of almost all the minorities in eastern Europe.

The discussions over autonomy in the spring of 1919 sprang from the belief that the minority question had become a significant factor in world affairs. The presence of numerous Jewish and other minority delegations fortified this conviction. Thus some saw the Comité's proposal as an enhanced Wilsonian solution to the problems of dispersed peoples, compact minorities under alien sovereignty, and areas of inextricably mixed populations. For others, however, autonomy epitomized the riskiest of all minority solutions, given the ostensibly pro-German, anti-Entente, pro-Bolshevik, or even politically neutral stance of most of eastern Europe's minorities in 1919.[54] A generous settlement of their grievances and even partial satisfaction of their political aspirations would signify a setback for the Allies as much as for their associates. With domestic concerns never far from their minds, the great powers regarded autonomy as a last resort, a face-saving means of dealing

---

54 Typical Foreign Office views: "The Jews are determined to do everything in their power to prevent the foundation of a great and independent Poland," Kidston minute, Dec. 5, 1918, 371–3419/198168, GB FO, PRO; "If . . . schools are placed under Jewish management, the more extreme national elements . . . may foster the use of the Yiddish language in such a way as to increase the separation . . . between Jews and other citizens of Poland," Headlam-Morley to Maurice Hankey, June 23, 1919, quoted in Headlam-Morley, *Memoir*, 158–9.

with an egregious violation of self-determination, such as the award of Ruthenia to Czechoslovakia.[55]

In mid-April, with the great powers completely absorbed in the German treaty and the work of the territorial commissions,[56] autonomy made its sole appearance on the world stage. Mack and Marshall presented their daring document to the U.S. delegation. It combined the Wilsonian formula of citizenship, equal rights, and religious freedom with the Comité's precept that national minorities should be constituted as "distinct public corporations" endowed with the right to manage their own institutions, obtain proportional representation on the local and national level, and appeal directly to the League of Nations with complaints against their governments.[57] The Mack-Marshall proposal made its way all the way up to Wilson via David Hunter Miller, the legal adviser to the American Peace Commission, and presidential adviser Edward House.

At that point, the issue of minority rights took on a new sense of urgency. The Allies' decision to defer the mandate question concerning Palestine for at least a year had left a key element in the Jewish question unsettled; the unresolved terms of the mandate and the future of Jewish-Arab relations in Palestine directly affected the fate of the Jews of Lwów, Pińsk, and Vilnius. Moreover, the Allies had ignored two important warnings.[58] The Polish territorial commission, recognizing the consequences of its decisions, had urged the Supreme Council to "consider" measures to protect racial and religious minorities within Poland's borders; and Coolidge had pleaded for action "to tranquilize the populations whose destiny is being decided presumably for all times."[59]

Suddenly, but not unexpectedly, from the frontiers of the Polish–Bolshevik conflict came fresh reports of violence against the native population. In early April Polish soldiers shot thirty-five Jewish civilians in Pińsk. Although Poland characterized the incident as an anti-Bolshevik action in a dangerous border region, the Pińsk massacre, which was heavily reported in the press, led to organized mass protests in Western and neutral countries.[60]

---

55 Poland, on the other hand, would refuse the Allies' proposals to grant autonomy or accept a limited mandate over multiethnic Eastern Galicia.
56 Adler diary, Apr. 4, 10–13, 19, 1919, AJC Archives. Cf. E. H. Carr minute, Apr. 24, 1919: 608 61/129/4/1, GB FO, PRO: "Everyone is working in the dark and no one knows how far the Americans who are having strong Jewish influences brought to bear on them may press the question of Jewish rights."
57 Text in Miller, *Diary*, 8:422–4.
58 The number of potential immigrants to Palestine would, of course, be insignificant; nevertheless, the prospect of a Jewish "nationality" in Palestine played a large role in the minority negotiations among the Allies, the Jews, and the Poles.
59 Miller, *Diary*, 7:366ff.
60 Carole Fink, "What Happened in Pińsk?" paper delivered at the Eleventh World Congress of Jewish Studies, Jerusalem, June 1993.

In the midst of the Pińsk clamor, the German delegation arrived in Versailles expecting to negotiate with the Allies – who at that moment were in total disarray over Italy's walkout and over the war in the east. To make matters worse, direct negotiations between Polish and Jewish representatives had reached a dead end.[61]

On May 1, the "Big Three" finally faced the minorities issue. Wilson revived his two tabled clauses with the clear intention of calming the public's apprehensions and silencing the autonomist clamor. By now the Allies had drifted, irrevocably, into supporting a war in eastern Europe in which numerous Jews, Lithuanians, and Ukrainians would fall under Polish control. The U.S. president announced his resolve to impose the principles of minority rights on the new Polish state, but he and Lloyd George also revealed their unyielding opposition to creating a "state within a state."[62] At this crucial juncture of the Paris Peace Conference, the massacre in Pińsk rekindled interest in and anxiety over the minorities question. The response it sparked in the peacemakers was one that neither the Jews nor the Poles desired.

THE COMMITTEE ON NEW STATES

No doubt Wilson's interlocutors, Lloyd George and Clemenceau, were prepared for the president's initiative on May 1. Both were also under pressure from their advisers and their public to confront the political, economic, and human consequences of the borders they were about to draw; and both were aware that the Germans' arrival in Paris made the minorities issue more urgent than ever.[63]

---

61 See report by Jan Ciechanowski, Apr. 10, 1919, 452, Paderewski papers, AAN; Biuro Kongresowy meetings, Apr. 26 and 29, May 5, Komitet Narodowy Polski, 168–9, AAN; Piłsudski delegation session, Apr. 25, 1919, Archiwum Michała Mościckiego (hereafter AMM), 132, Piłsudski Archive, New York; Patek to Piłsudski, Apr. 15 and 28, Akta Adjuntantury Generalnej Naczelnego Dowództwa (AGND), 16/733, Piłsudski Archive, New York; also Morgenthau diary, May 6, 1919, Library of Congress (hereafter LOC). A major difficulty in these talks was due to the differences among the Polish negotiators, who ranged from the rightist and centralist National Democrats (the Dmowski party), which tended to accept the Zionists' national demands – conceivably as a means of isolating Polish Jews – to the more federally minded Left (Piłsudski's forces, supported by Paderewski), which insisted on equal treatment but refused national rights.
62 *PMCQ*, 1:439–41; but not recorded in *FRUS-PPC*, 5:393.
63 See memorandum by E. H. Carr, Apr. 25, 1919, 608/61/96, GB FO, PRO, urging the creation of an inter-Allied minorities commission to consider the whole question of eastern Europe and also to reduce the strong Jewish pressure on the Americans. It was the British who proposed that economic issues also be clarified prior to Poland's official rebirth. The details on the exchange of envoys, trade, and transit were elaborated in seven additional articles and two annexes to the Polish Treaty; they were written at the same time as the minorities articles. The only controversial clause was Article 21, inserted on France's insistence, in which Poland agreed to assume responsibility for its portion of the Russian public debt. Text in *FRUS-PPC*, 13:801–8.

But instead of simply inserting Wilson's modest two-paragraph statement into the treaty with Germany, the Big Three set in motion an extended process that would produce separate and elaborate arrangements with all the new and enlarged states.[64] The instrument was an appointed group of Allied experts, the Committee on New States, which conducted all the private negotiations with minority representatives, minority states, and the powers and completed the first model Polish treaty in time for it to be signed with the Versailles Treaty.[65]

At long last, the minorities had their own committee, whose bland name masked the drama that would unfold during its deliberations.[66] Over the next seven months, notwithstanding its shifting personnel and untold distractions, the committee functioned as the nerve center of all the minorities diplomacy that took place in Paris. Its purview was all minorities, not simply the Jews, and all of eastern Europe, not simply Poland.[67] The committee appropriated the minorities question from the press, propagandists, and amateur diplomats and delivered it to jurists and bureaucrats seeking a balance between justice and political reality. British pragmatism and tenacity overcame American vagueness and inexperience to create a "safe and solid" means of internationalizing the minorities question, without resorting to unenforceable League clauses or provocative autonomy demands.

The Committee on New States was dominated by its British and American members, with France's representative, Philippe Berthelot, looking inscrutable in the chair and suspected of hoping that their labors would come to nought.[68] There was a functional, if not always amiable, balance between the U.S. lawyers Hunter Miller and Manley Hudson and the British Foreign Office specialists Sir James Headlam-Morley, E. H. Carr, and Lord Robert Cecil. Each committee member continued to work on the German treaty, and each functioned independently as emissary to his

64 Wilson: "I would propose to insert in the treaty, along these lines, two articles which would apply not only to Poland, but also to Bohemia and to the other new states. It is a matter of saying that '(1) the state of ____ agrees to grant all racial and national minorities the same treatment in law and in fact as to the majority; (2) the state of ____ agrees to place no obstacle in the way of the practice of any religion, if that practice is not contrary to public order or morals." *PMCQ*, 1:439.
65 [May 3, 1919], *PMCQ*, 1:472–3.
66 "Instead of more or less banal clauses in the Peace Treaty, we shall now have a detailed Statute of Minorities which will probably be the subject of special Treaties with the states concerned," Wolf Paris diary, May 6, 1919, 228, Mocatta Library, University College London.
67 The committee met sixty-four times between May and December 1919; produced treaties with Poland, Czechoslovakia, Romania, Yugoslavia, and Greece; and drafted the articles that were inserted in the peace treaties with Austria, Hungary, Bulgaria, and Turkey. Texts in League of Nations, *Protection of Linguistic, Racial and Religious Minorities* (Geneva, 1927).
68 Italian and Japanese representatives, Giacomo De Martino and Mineichiro Adatci, were added on May 9 and May 29, but neither played a significant role in the proceedings.

government, to minority representatives, and to the minority states. There was Anglo-American sparring on every level: Wolf vying with Marshall, Miller with Headlam-Morley, and Lloyd George with Wilson. If the format was British, the content came primarily from the Americans.[69]

Operating under severe time and political constraints, the committee drafted the model agreement with Poland in a little over two weeks and then proceeded to draft treaties for the new Czechoslovakia and Yugoslavia as well as for the expanded Romania and Greece. The moment was charged with tension, not only over the fate of the German negotiations but also because of reports from the east. The graphic press accounts of further pogroms against the Jews along the Polish trail of conquest, in Lida and Vilnius, aroused renewed public protests and demands for tough treatment of the Poles. Poland responded with its own accusations against German, Zionist, and Bolshevik propaganda.[70]

No longer deliberating only among themselves, the Allied Powers now had to compel signatures from their associates, as well as from their enemies. The moment was highly inauspicious for considered deliberation. On May 21, the day of a massive antipogrom protest meeting in New York, the Allies delivered the minority treaty to the Polish representatives. Ten days later, the victors held a secret plenary session with the minority states, who hotly objected to the proposed treaties.[71] The German delegation, weighing in with its counterproposals to the treaty, castigated the Poles as untrustworthy protectors of the rights of "national or religious" minorities. The Reich's representatives detailed Poland's oppression of the Ruthenians of Eastern Galicia, its cruel treatment of Germans, and the "massacres" of the Jewish population since November 11.[72]

---

69 See Alan Sharp, "Britain and the Protection of Minorities at the Paris Peace Conference, 1919," in A. C. Hepburn, ed., *Minorities in History* (London, 1978), 170–88.

70 A gloomy report from the Polish National Committee office in London on May 26, 1919 (KNP 1936, AAN), noted that this revived "pogrom campaign" coupled with attacks against "Polish imperialism in Lithuania, Galicia, and Ukraine" – both directed from Berlin via the Zionist offices in Copenhagen, Stockholm, and London – occurred just at the moment the great powers had again turned their attention to Polish affairs. The Jewish press offices in the Netherlands, Denmark, Sweden, and Switzerland were indeed subsidized, and fed sensational information, by the German foreign ministry. See Germany, L1288/L350249, L350300, L350315, L350350–L350353–55; Internationale Angelegenheiten 3: Akten betr. die Juden, Bd. 1 (1918–19) K695/K181627–K182188; and Gesandschaft Stockholm, 75/3: Tätigkeit der Zionisten in Schweden, 1916–1919, PA-AA.

71 Plenary meeting, May 31, FRUS-PPC, 3;394–410; see Lansing diary, May 31, 1919, LOC.

72 German Counterproposals, May 29, 1919: "What dangers threaten the national minorities in Poland is shown most clearly by the massacres practiced on the Jewish population since November 11. Reference is made to the letter just published by a member of the American Food Commission concerning the wholesale murders committed in Pińsk, which the local authorities favored and the Government let go unpunished." Quoted in Luckau, *German Delegation at the Paris Peace Conference*, 338.

The Allies were convinced they had the power to coerce the Poles until the moment the German treaty was signed.[73] Indeed, Poland seemed trapped by its economic and military vulnerability, which was magnified during the enforced return to Warsaw of Ignacy Paderewski, Poland's delegate to the conference. The victors had already withheld Danzig and would force Poland to accept a plebiscite in Upper Silesia. Now, in return for their support of Poland's eastern expansion, the great powers intended to impose a treaty based on the ballyhooed demands of its Jewish and German populations.[74]

Paderewski waited almost an entire month to respond, a delay that paralyzed the Committee on New States.[75] Teetering on a frail political base, the Polish leader could neither condemn the pogroms nor reject the demands of the great powers until he had received the indispensable guarantee of support against the Ukrainians and the Bolsheviks. Once this was given, Paderewski delivered a brilliant riposte. His well-crafted letter of June 15 challenged practically every clause of the Allies' draft, warning against the creation of a "Jewish problem" not only in Poland but throughout the world. He shrewdly noted the differential treatment of minorities in Poland and in Germany, which was to be spared an international engagement.[76]

The Allies, racing toward the June 28 deadline for the German treaty, beat an unceremonious retreat.[77] They dreaded losing the opportunity to dictate the official terms for Poland's rebirth as an independent state. Until the last minute they feared that Warsaw, supported by its friends in Paris, would refuse to sign.[78] Polish propaganda, which had painted its minorities as pro-German and pro-Bolshevik, also had its effect.[79]

73 Lloyd George pronounced this twice to the Council of Four on May 3, 1919. *PMCQ,* 1:473.
74 "The Jews do not want a strong Poland at any price; they want a strong Germany. It is the Jews who are winning the war." Unsigned memorandum, "Note on the Present Position of the Polish Question," Apr. 5, 1919, in PA 978, AAN. Ciechanowski Report, Paris, May 30, 1919, MSZ 1480 (95), AAN, linked "German-Jewish propaganda" in the United States and Great Britain over Polish anti-Semitism with the Reich's claims for Gdańsk and Upper Silesia.
75 Headlam-Morley to Hankey, June 15, 1919, expressed suspicions of a Franco-Polish maneuver to sabotage any agreement whatsoever, Headlam-Morley memoir, 145–6; cf. Hudson to Wilson, June 16, 1919, 5B 4626565, Woodrow Wilson papers, LOC. Hankey to Paderewski, June 15, 1919, PA 846, AAN, requested a response.
76 Paderewski to Lloyd George, June 15, 1919, F57/5/2, Lloyd George papers, House of Lords, Record Office; copy in PA 846, AAN. "This protest creates a very serious situation, and I am somewhat concerned as to what may be the outcome of all of these Minorities Treaties," entry 463, June 18, 1919, Manley Hudson papers, Harvard University.
77 Meeting of Council of Five at Wilson's residence, June 16, 1919, *FRUS-PPC,* 6:514. Although Mantoux served as interpreter, there is no record of this important discussion in *PMCQ,* vol. 2.
78 On June 19 Hudson reported to Wilson: "The French delegate, Mr. Berthelot, would have favored an abandonment of the idea of a Treaty, and the substitution of a formal declaration by Poland voluntarily accepting certain obligations for the protection of her minorities. This would necessitate the Council's receding from its decision, now publicly announced, to impose these obligations on the new States. This suggestion was stoutly opposed by Mr. Headlam-Morley and myself." Memorandum in 5B 47/27121, Woodrow Wilson papers, LOC.
79 E.g., Paderewski interview in *Morning Post* [London], June 25, 1919.

Yet the victors could not abandon the treaty entirely.[80] Not only were they morally committed to it, but they had to be prepared to deal with an aroused public opinion. The Jews and the socialists, the pacifists and the feminists in Western Europe and America demanded something more solid and permanent for minorities than the investigatory efforts of the American commission that was about to be dispatched to Poland.[81]

Even though Wilson and Italy's foreign minister, Sidney Sonnino, strove to save the essentials, Lloyd George forced a number of concessions that seriously diluted the Polish Minority Treaty.[82] These were balanced by a stern letter from Clemenceau to Paderewski (drafted by committee members Hudson and Headlam-Morley) that upheld the great powers' right to impose the treaty but assuaged Warsaw's concern over undue and unfriendly interference in its internal affairs.[83]

THE TREATY

As finally constructed, the Polish Minority Treaty addressed three sets of issues: the basic minority rights proposed by Wilson; the remnants of special minority rights advanced by Marshall, Mack, the Comité, and the Germans; and the novel enforcement procedure to be implemented by the League of Nations. The Wilsonian core of the treaty lay in Articles 1–8, which were deemed "fundamental laws" overriding any form of law, legislation, or official action. The Allies made Poland pledge to ensure the "full and complete protection of life and liberty to all inhabitants . . . without distinction of birth, nationality, language, race, or religion." Echoing the U.S. Constitution, it stated that "all inhabitants . . . [were to] be entitled to

80 Morgenthau to Wilson, Paris, June 20, 1919, Morgenthau papers, LOC.
81 On the advice of Herbert Hoover, Paderewski had asked the U.S. president to dispatch a commission to Poland. Over the protests of most of the Jewish leaders present in Paris, Wilson appointed a vocal anti-Zionist, Ambassador Henry Morgenthau, to head the inquiry.
82 Directly related to Paderewski's criticisms: Polish was established as the sole medium of instruction in higher schools; Jews would not be exempt from military service on the Sabbath; the right to establish minority schools and institutions by Germans was limited to former nationals of the German Reich; and in Article 12, involving modifications of the treaty by a majority of the League Council, the Covenant's unanimity rule was suspended. See *FRUS-PPC*, 6:624–8, for the crucial debate over minority schools on June 23. Paderewski to Władysław Skrzyński, Paris, July 1, 1919, MSZ (210), AAN, reiterates the key alterations.
83 Clemenceau to Paderewski, June 24, 1919: "The territories now being transferred both to Poland and to the other States inevitably include a large population speaking languages and belonging to races different from that of the people with whom they will be incorporated. Unfortunately, the races have been estranged by long years of bitter hostility. It is believed that these populations will be all the more easily reconciled to their new position if they know that from the very beginning they have assured protection and adequate guarantees against any danger of unjust treatment or oppression. The very knowledge that these guarantees exist will, it is hoped, materially help the reconciliation which all desire, and will indeed do much to prevent the necessity of its enforcement." Macartney, *National States and National Minorities,* 237.

the free exercise, whether public or private, of any creed, religion, or belief whose practices are not inconsistent with public order or public morals."

This broad grant to all "inhabitants," including large numbers of Jews whom Poles were in the process of classifying as aliens, had another dimension as well. The Allies, recalling tsarist and Romanian discrimination against their nationals, insisted on foreigners' rights as a new form of extraterritoriality; and the Poles recognized it as such.

Four articles were devoted to the knotty issue of citizenship, which had consumed many hours and jars of ink. The Jews and the Germans, fearing expropriation and expulsion if they had fled or had served in one of the three occupiers' armies during the war, pleaded for an August 1914 date of residency; the Poles insisted on as late a date as possible to eliminate as many non-Poles as possible. The result, a compromise that satisfied no one, gave automatic citizenship to those who were residents on the date the treaty was signed, to those born to "habitual residents," and to those born on Polish soil who were not nationals of another state. This left a large gray area of German colonists and Russian-Jewish settlers whose contested status filled court dockets for many years.

Although Poland pledged not to obstruct former inhabitants of Germany, Austria-Hungary, or Russia from acquiring Polish citizenship, the treaty did not solve the old "Romanian problem" of how individuals could be naturalized. There were no provisions for those who were expelled, or had fled, to return and claim their citizenship rights. Wives were covered by their husbands' decisions and children by their parents'. Thus thousands of stateless Jewish and other refugees in postwar eastern Europe remained entirely unprotected by the minority treaty.

Article 7 contained the basic civil, political, and cultural rights agreed on by virtually everyone: all Poles were to be equal before the law and were to enjoy equal rights as citizens and workers. Notwithstanding the establishment of Polish as the national language, minority tongues could be freely used in private intercourse, public meetings, commerce, religion, and the press, and before the courts.

Article 8, the final "fundamental" protective clause, guaranteed equal legal protection to minorities and to all other Polish nationals; allowed them the identical right to establish, manage, and control at their own expense charitable, religious, and social institutions, schools, and educational establishments; and permitted them to use their language and express their religion therein. Paderewski accepted these provisions in the basic, unalterable package as "sensible and positive" conditions.[84] To be sure, this clause priv-

---

84 Skrzyński to Paderewski, Warsaw, July 2, 1919, MSZ 1480 (166), AAN.

ileged wealthy minorities and those with outside resources over impecunious ones. Most important, in this key article the committee deliberately watered down the concept of distinctive national groups. It substituted the palliative phrase "Polish nationals who belong to racial, religious or linguistic minorities" for Wilson's politically explosive term, "national" minority.

The remnants of the autonomist proposals appeared in the next three articles, which clearly lacked the legal and moral force of the first eight. Article 9 dealt with areas inhabited by a considerable proportion of non-Polish-speaking citizens. In these regions the state had to establish primary schools with instruction in the minority tongue and also to fund local religious and charitable institutions. The restrictions, however, were significant: the Polish language would remain obligatory in all schools; no public funds had to be made available above the primary level; and state subsidies for German schools and institutions were restricted to "that part of Poland which was German territory on August 1, 1914."

Articles 10 and 11 dealt specifically with the Jews. This was Marshall's victory over Wolf and the Alliance Israélite Universelle, obtained through hard bargaining among the Americans, British, and French, and over the unalterable opposition of the Poles.[85] Article 10 provided for the establishment of local Jewish committees, "subject to the general control of the State," to disburse public funds to religious schools and other institutions. Article 11 protected the observance of the Jewish Sabbath, except during state emergencies and the performance of military service; Poland also agreed to refrain from elections on Saturday.

The small victories gained in these three articles actually represented a major setback for the advocates of autonomy. The Germans had been rebuffed in both the cultural and political sphere: there would be no national curiae, proportional representation, or special government office for minorities.[86] Moreover, there would be no central Jewish Committee in Warsaw, so dreaded by the Allies and by the Poles, but only virtually powerless local associations.[87] Despite British disdain and Polish antipathy, the Americans engineered a small victory for Yiddish, which was recognized as a legitimate language of instruction; but it would be supported only at the primary school level. Whereas the German minority was virtually certain to

---

85 Wolf considered this a "rump concession" to the reckless and futile crusade for national rights: singling out the Jews for special privileges, according to Wolf, reduced their credibility and influence in the larger movement for minority rights. Wolf diary, Aug. 19 and 24, 1919, Mocatta Library, University College London; *Jewish Chronicle,* Dec. 19, 1919.

86 The possibility of proportional representation was reduced to a private exchange of notes: Wolf diary, Apr. 23, 1919, Mocatta Library, University College London; Viefhaus, *Minderheitenfrage,* 163; Miller, *Diary,* May 9, 1919, 13:76.

87 See discussions over this issue, June 17 and 23, 1919, in *FRUS-PPC,* 5:529–30, 624–8.

receive funds from Berlin to maintain its Deutschtum, Polish Jewish culture was threatened by the prospects of meager state sustenance. Finally, the controversial Sabbath clause, disputed by the British, Americans, and Poles, was silent on the issue deemed essential by Polish Jews and endorsed only by the British-the sanction for Sunday trading.

The final article of the Polish Minority Treaty dealt with enforcement. Breaches in any of its clauses were placed under the responsibility of the Council of the League of Nations. Differences of opinion between Poland and the Council were to be adjudicated by the World Court, whose decisions were to be final.

Article 12 was the most innovative, contested, and revised portion of the Polish Minority Treaty. Almost every Jewish representative had exhorted the great powers to grant minorities direct access to the League. The Committee on New States was deeply split over the degree of access to be granted to individuals or groups; its members searched for a means of implementation that balanced the reality of threatened minorities with the imperative of state sovereignty.[88]

The great powers were extremely reluctant to give minorities, or their defenders, any form of access to the new world organization.[89] Following on Czech and Greek warnings against a minorities crusade in the League, Paderewski's communication provided the crucial reinforcement to the Allies' restrictive instincts.[90] The Big Three decided that only Council members would possess the right and responsibility to call attention to infractions or the dangers of infractions; and only the Council, not the more democratic League Assembly, could take action. Thus the minorities' fate would again depend on the great powers that would, as in the past, undoubtedly be reluctant to take up their case. Was it of great consequence that any such unlikely intervention could no longer be construed as constituting unwarranted or unfriendly interference in another state's internal affairs?[91]

88 See entries 412, 422, 435, 457, on June 3, 6, 10, and 16, 1919, Manley Hudson papers, Harvard University.
89 Lloyd George to the Council of Three, May 17, 1919: "We cannot allow propagandist associations and societies from all over the world to flood the League of Nations with their complaints. The Jews, in particular, are very litigious, and, as we know all too well, unfortunately, the treaty will not make anti–Semitism disappear from Poland overnight. If the Jews of Poland could address the League of Nations directly, there would be ceaseless incidents." *PMCQ,* 2:91.
90 Entry 464, June 18, 1919, Manley Hudson papers, Harvard University.
91 "The principle . . . is that a communication made to the League of Nations by any state, on the subject of an act which it judges to constitute a threat to peace, cannot be considered as an unfriendly act to another state. If they are persecuted, the Jews of Poland will find a member state of the League of Nations to take up their cause." Lloyd George, May 17, *PMCQ,* 2:90. See also James A. Joyce, *Broken Star: The Story of the League of Nations (1919–1939)* (Swansea, 1978), 93–6.

SOME (PRELIMINARY) CONCLUSIONS

On June 28, 1919, a new kind of charter appeared in the international arena. The free and independent Poland that was envisaged in Wilson's Point 13 and emerged between defeated Germany and Bolshevik Russia was a fragile republic encumbered by extraordinary internationally imposed controls on its domestic legislation and administration.[92] This treaty was dictated largely by great powers that had refused to accept, even theoretically, similar obligations; it was imposed on behalf of named and unnamed minorities that had not been consulted and would play no role in the enforcement process; it became the model for thirteen agreements with new, expanded, and defeated states of eastern Europe.

The Polish Minority Treaty represented the culmination of six months of agonizing over the widespread nonfulfillment of self-determination and the political dangers resulting therefrom. The great powers – caught in the contradictions of their economic, strategic, and ideological decisions over eastern Europe; constrained by the limits on their power in the region, except to succor and scrutinize, encourage and castigate; and constricted by their own domestic politics – fabricated a conservative solution to an explosive issue: a treaty solidly grounded in past precedent with the liberal patina of the new League of Nations and the World Court.

The treaty dashed the world's hopes for universal minority rights and for special autonomous regimes. The powers left the minorities disappointed and relatively unprotected and their governments suspicious, resentful, unregenerate in their desire for national uniformity, and largely resistant to outside control or interference. The temporary glare of publicity had been of little benefit, and conceivably damaged, the cause of minority rights.[93] Minority groups were not only denied official status and collective rights but were now endangered by the backlash against their meddling, as well as by the world's declining interest in their suffering. When the United States refused to join the League, the enforcement procedure lost its most ardent advocate.

Moreover, the new international regime that emerged on June 28, 1919, put no real restraints on irredentism, which was one of the main threats to

---

92 "Cependant la convention, ce n'est pas la paix, c'est la guerre à demeure, car une mesure de cette importance, octroyée à l'Etat Polonais et portant atteinte à sa souveraineté et à l'unité de son administration, crée forcément des rancunes qui seront lentes á se dissiper." "Note sur le projet de convention entre la Pologne et des Puissances concernant les droits des minorités," Aug. 12, 1919, KNP 1259, AAN.

93 One bleak portent: Gisela C. Lebzelter, *Political Anti-Semitism in England, 1918–1939* (New York, 1978), documents the "new anti-Semitism" in postwar Britain.

peace and stability. Hence Germany, which had just spent its time at Versailles expressing special interest in the rights of its lost kinspeople and opposing the territorial settlement, aimed its crusade for minority rights at exploiting, not supporting, a system established without its participation or consent.[94]

What conclusions can be drawn about the Allies' decisions at the Paris Peace Conference? In fulfilling their pledge to do something about minority rights, the great powers rejected the extremes of universalization and national rights, but they left other avenues unexplored. The victors might, for example, have sponsored bilateral talks between interested governments or promoted direct talks between governments and their minorities on the local or national level.[95] They might have given serious attention to Henry Morgenthau's proposal to allocate substantial economic aid to eastern Europe. They might have encouraged regional programs of social, cultural, and economic cooperation and discouraged the militarization of the area. And despite the links between the Allies' anti-Bolshevik sentiments and the military efforts of the Poles and Romanians, the great powers might have restrained their clients' expansion and shown more sympathy toward minorities.

Unquestionably, the Polish Minority Treaty bears traces of all the circumstances of the Paris Peace Conference: the peculiar timetable, leisurely start, and frenzied finish; the chaotic organization; the cacophony of reportage, rumors, and leaks; and the notorious secrecy; the concentration of power in three men, who functioned as warlords and peacemakers. The weary victors hesitated to confer on minorities too prominent a status, weaken the new governments, or provide minority defenders with the means to disrupt the new order. The victors hoped that under their tutelage, their treaties, and their League, with a quasi-democratic order and quasi-promising economic prospects, the minorities question in Poland and eastern Europe would be resolved. It was not.

94 Jaffé, "Denkschrift betreffend den Schutz der Deutschen in den an Polen abgetretenen bezw. abzutretenden preussischen Gebieten" (21), Berlin, July 1, 1919, Friedensabteilung, Polen (Schutz religiöser und anderer deutsch. Minoritäten), vol. 1 (1919), PA-AA.
95 One useful example of bilateralism was the German-Polish convention on Upper Silesia, negotiated under League auspices in 1922, which established elaborate local mediation but also direct minority access to the League for a fifteen-year transition period.

12

The Rhineland Question:
West European Security
at the Paris Peace Conference of 1919

STEPHEN A. SCHUKER

I

The solution of the Rhineland question at the Paris Peace Conference of 1919 left no one happy. Here, in practical terms, lay the cornerstone of the whole diplomatic edifice. Could a peace fashioned through the compromise of fundamentally opposing views prevent Germany from breaking out on the world again or developing the ambition to do so?

Jacques Bainville touched on the nub of the difficulty in his disabused apothegm: the treaty appeared "too gentle for all that is in it which is harsh."[1] Notwithstanding the outcome on the battlefield, the disproportion between French and German power loomed almost as large as ever. France had suffered a demographic holocaust. Ten northeastern departments of the country lay devastated. By contrast, Germany retained the most technologically skilled population in Europe. Its formidable industrial resources remained intact. Could military dispositions provide satisfactory containment?

The French obtained a three-stage, fifteen-year occupation of the Rhineland. But that occupation would lose much of its value as a security guarantee when the Allies evacuated the Cologne zone five years after the treaty took effect. It would end at the latest in 1935, when the French faced their greatest manpower deficit and with the planned reparations schedule still only half fulfilled. The United States and Britain undertook in principle to come to France's aid in the event of a new attack. But neither country promised to maintain the forces in being that would enable them to

---

1 *Action Française,* May 8, 1919, quoted in Pierre Miquel, *La Paix de Versailles et l'opinion publique française* (Paris, 1972), 404.

275

redeem that pledge. President Wilson could not guarantee ratification by a Republican-controlled Senate; Lloyd George conditioned British assurances on ratification by America. Wilson maintained his faith that the League of Nations would eventually provide collective security, yet the Covenant of the League as adopted offered scant support for that vision. The treaty provided for German disarmament and the demilitarization of both sides of the Rhine. Still, military men no more believed in the permanent disarmament of a major industrial nation than they gave credence to the tooth fairy. The Germans, not merely the peace-conference delegation but also those of almost all political inclinations at home, nurtured the flames of resentment. They remained equally unreconciled to border changes, occupation, demilitarization, reparations, or indeed to having lost the war at all. Marshall Ferdinand Foch predicted ominously to Finance Minister Louis-Lucien Klotz when the result became public: "With the treaty you have just signed, you can expect to be paid in monkey tricks."[2] And so, indeed, it turned out.

Could one really have expected better? A camel, according to the familiar aphorism, is a horse designed by a committee. The Allied victory of 1918 resulted from coalition warfare. The Supreme War Council provided strategic coordination while the battle raged, but the victorious nations did not coordinate their war aims because they did not really agree on policy objectives. Where there exists no settled policy, there can be no effective policy/strategy match.

During the war, President Woodrow Wilson elected to put the problem off. "England and France have not the same views with regard to peace that we have by any means," he noted with malign candor in July 1917. "When the war is over, we can force them to our way of thinking, because by that time they will, among other things, be financially in our hands; but we cannot force them now, and any attempt to speak for them or to speak our common mind would bring on disagreements which would inevitably come to the surface in public and rob the whole thing of its effect."[3] In his various war-aims pronouncements, Wilson never directly addressed the question of postwar French security. What compromises would prove necessary where the principle of self-determination conflicted with the dictates of national security and economic rationality remained unexplored.

The eighth of Wilson's Fourteen Points declared that all "French" territory should be freed and the wrong done to France by Prussia in 1871 regard-

2 René Michel Lhopital, *Foch, l'armistice, et la paix* (Paris, 1938), 233.
3 Wilson to Colonel Edward M. House, July 21, 1917, quoted in Ray Stannard Baker, *Woodrow Wilson: Life and Letters,* 8 vols. (Garden City, N.Y., 1927–39), 7:180.

ing Alsace-Lorraine "should be righted."[4] What did that mean precisely? In early 1918, no one could say for sure. In fact, we now know that Wilson and his confidential adviser, Colonel Edward M. House, had more difficulty formulating this provision than any other of the Fourteen Points. At first, they inclined toward calling for the freedom and restoration of French territory generally without mentioning Alsace-Lorraine at all. Wilson fretted that this might make a bad impression. Then House suggested the evenhanded formulation: "If Alsace and Lorraine were restored to France, Germany should be given an equal economic opportunity." Yet that wording too, on second thought, seemed likely to suit neither France nor Germany. After reflection, Wilson crafted the final text, following House's counsel to weaken "must be righted" to "should." House's argument for caution was this: "The American people might not consent to fight for the readjustment of European territory; therefore, in suggesting these readjustments, with the exception of Belgium, the word 'should' ought to be used."[5]

Wilson never felt called upon to explain publicly how his homilies would translate into practice. He thought of himself as a sage, using the bully pulpit of the presidency to voice the common aspirations of mankind, not as a legal draftsman preoccupied with mundane details. On the eve of the Armistice, during negotiations among the Allies in Paris, Colonel House assigned the journalists Frank Cobb and Walter Lippmann to prepare an exegesis of the Fourteen Points. No one in the Washington bureaucracy had thought to craft one earlier. Cobb and Lippmann maintained that France should only obtain the boundaries of 1871. Giving that nation the Saar coalfields along with the boundaries of 1814, they noted, would constitute "a clear violation" of the president's principles.[6]

The two journalists correctly interpreted the dispassionate tenor of Wilson's thought. During the Congressional election campaign, the president had cleverly evaded Republican demands for pursuit of the war until the enemy surrendered unconditionally.[7] "Let us dictate peace by the hammering guns and not chat about peace to the accompaniment of the clicking of

4 Great Britain, Foreign Office, *Papers Respecting Negotiations for an Anglo-French Pact,* Cmd. 2169 (London, 1924), no. 7.
5 Edward M. House diary, Jan. 9, 1918, Sterling Library, Yale University; see also Charles Seymour, ed., *The Intimate Papers of Colonel House,* 4 vols. (Boston, 1926–28), 3:328–30.
6 Seymour, *Intimate Papers of Colonel House,* 4:197. The decision-making process under Wilson remained surprisingly casual. Under Secretary of State Frank Polk, e.g., considered the Cobb-Lippmann memorandum wholly unsatisfactory as a legal document and observed that "the restoration of France is a question very different legally from that of Belgium." Polk's scathing criticisms, however, were overtaken by events (see Polk penciled memorandum, Oct. 29, 1918, Frank Polk papers 25/248, Yale University Library).
7 Earl S. Pomeroy, "Sentiment for a Strong Peace," *South Atlantic Quarterly* (Oct. 1944): 325–37; also Seward W. Livermore, *Politics Is Adjourned: Woodrow Wilson and the War Congress, 1916–1918* (Middletown, Conn., 1966).

typewriters," Theodore Roosevelt had thundered.[8] Undeterred by the militant public mood, Wilson consulted only his conscience. He secretly instructed House:

My deliberate judgment is that our whole weight should be thrown for an armistice that will prevent a renewal of hostilities with Germany but which will be as moderate and reasonable as possible within those limits, because it is certain that too much success or security on the part of the Allies will make a genuine peace settlement exceedingly difficult, if not impossible.[9]

The president's reaction to the proposed military conditions foreshadowed his strategic inclinations. He questioned whether the Allies needed actually to occupy Alsace and Lorraine under the armistice. And he strongly doubted the advisability of going so far as to occupy the eastern side of the Rhine, "as that is practically an invasion of German soil."[10]

The French, unsure where negotiations were heading, expressed an initial disposition not to accept the Cobb-Lippmann interpretation at all. They proposed instead to formulate their own; the other Allies expressed scarcely less dissatisfaction.[11] Eventually, however, the Europeans all decided to back off, especially when House intimated that his chief might have to consider afresh whether to fight on for the principles laid down by the Allies.[12] Taking the hardest of lines, Wilson reiterated his resolve "to fight not only to do away with Prussian militarism but with militarism everywhere."[13] The French, like the British, decided that they could not judiciously attack the Cobb-Lippmann exegesis frontally. All the Europeans had compelling reasons for winding up the war. They would settle for what they could get at the moment. Clemenceau could count himself lucky that House finally agreed to a temporary occupation of the left bank of the Rhine as a satisfaction for the Chamber of Deputies, notwithstanding Lloyd George's scruples.[14] In the so-called pre-Armistice agreement that encapsulated several days of haggling, the Allies voiced formal reservations to the Fourteen

---

8   *New York Times,* Oct. 25, 1918; also Elting E. Morison, ed., *The Letters of Theodore Roosevelt* (Cambridge, Mass., 1954), 8:1380–1. For Lodge's call for unconditional surrender, see Lodge to Roosevelt, Oct. 14, 1918, Lodge-Roosevelt correspondence, box 89, Henry Cabot Lodge papers, Massachusetts Historical Society.
9   Wilson to House, Oct. 28, 1918, Arthur S. Link et al., eds., *The Papers of Woodrow Wilson* (hereafter *PWW*), 69 vols. (Princeton, N.J., 1966–94), 51:473.
10 General P. C. March to Pershing (relaying the president's views), Oct. 27, 1918, *PWW,* 51:471–2.
11 House to Wilson, Oct. 30, 1918, *PWW,* 51:511.
12 House to Wilson, Oct. 30, 1918, *PWW,* 51:511–13, 515–17.
13 Wilson to House, Oct. 30, 1918, *PWW,* 51:513.
14 House to Wilson, Oct. 30, 1918, *PWW,* 51:516.

Points only in respect to reparations and freedom of the seas.[15] House called the result "a great diplomatic victory," achieved "in the face of a hostile and influential junta in the United States and the thoroughly unsympathetic personnel constituting the Entente governments."[16] Yet clearly the bargaining had just begun.

II

During the war, a strong current of public opinion in France had called for recovering the borders of 1790, seizing the Saar, limiting Germany to the right bank of the Rhine, and setting up one or more French-dominated buffer states on the left bank of the river.[17] But for more sober policy makers, battlefield realities always tempered such ambitions. Whatever schemes might appear in newspapers or even in government planning documents, military dispositions would prove determinative. The plain fact was that German armies stood on French soil from the beginning of the war to the end. No hope existed of getting them off except through coalition warfare. This meant that France's announced war aims could never be more than tentative bargaining positions. The ultimate outcome would inevitably depend on relative strengths at the end of hostilities and what the principal Allies would then be prepared to endorse or at least to countenance.

In January 1917, the Briand government outlined French war aims informally to the British. The language of the despatch hinted at fairly expansive pretensions. France demanded the return of a greater Alsace-Lorraine including the Saar, as it existed in 1790, "before the successive mutilations of our old frontier." This rectification, the French insisted, would not count as a new acquisition in the settlement of accounts; the French were merely "resuming possession" of what had been torn from them against the wishes of the population. In addition, the question of the left bank of the Rhine would necessarily arise. Many of those attached to "the oldest traditions of

15 Note from Allied governments to president of the United States, Nov. 4, 1918, in *Negotiations for an Anglo-French Pact*, no. 7.
16 House to Wilson, Nov. 5, 1918, *PWW,* 51:594.
17 David Stevenson, *French War Aims Against Germany, 1914–1919* (Oxford, 1982); Georges-Henri Soutou, "La France et les Marches de l'Est, 1914–1919," *Revue historique*, no. 528 (Oct.–Dec. 1978): 341–88; Georges-Henri Soutou, *L'Or et le sang: Les buts de guerre économiques de la Première Guerre mondiale* (Paris, 1989). See also Werner Kern, *Die Rheintheorie der historisch-politischen Literatur Frankreichs im Ersten Weltkrieg* (Saarbrücken, 1973); Walter A. McDougall, *France's Rhineland Diplomacy, 1914–1924: The Last Bid for a Balance of Power in Europe* (Princeton, N.J., 1978), 17–32; Gitta Steinmeyer, *Die Grundlagen der französischen Deutschlandpolitik, 1917–1919* (Stuttgart, 1979); and Henning Köhler, *Novemberrevolution und Frankreich: Die französische Deutschlandpolitik, 1918–1919* (Düsseldorf, 1980).

our national policy" demanded reincorporation of the left bank as the lost heritage of the French Revolution, necessary to round out natural frontiers as conceived by Richelieu. The French government, however, abstemiously conceded that some might look upon this as conquest. It therefore asked only for a guarantee on behalf of Europe and a solution that would afford protection for its own frontiers. Germany should henceforth have "but one foot across the Rhine." In short, the organization of those territories, their neutrality, and their provisional occupation should be discussed among the Allies; but France, as the country most directly involved in the territorial status of those regions, should have the "preponderant voice" in the decision.[18]

The French demand to the Foreign Office was thus delicately phrased and represented the more cautious current of opinion in the French cabinet and the Quai d'Orsay. By contrast, former premier Gaston Doumergue, operating semi-independently, insisted categorically in negotiations with Russia some weeks later on political and economic separation of the left bank of the Rhine from Germany, its organization as an independent and neutral state, and permanent occupation by French troops until Germany had satisfied all its obligations under the treaty of peace.[19]

The several factions in the French government, squabbling ceaselessly with each other, never quite decided how far they ought to push the matter. At any rate, Whitehall determined to take as little notice as possible of these claims. The foreign secretary, Sir Arthur Balfour, describing his conversation with the French ambassador, noted that he had "said nothing to encourage this rather wild project [for the Rhineland], and I do not think that M. Cambon himself had much belief in it."[20] When the Bolsheviks seized power in Russia and published inter-Allied discussions on war aims, Balfour affected to know nothing about Doumergue's conversations with the czar. "Never did we desire, and never did we encourage the idea, that a bit of Germany should be cut off from the parent State, and erected into some kind of independent republic . . . on the left bank of the Rhine." "That was never part of the policy of His Majesty's Government," he assured the House of Commons. "His Majesty's Government were never aware that this was seriously entertained by any French statesman."[21] In May 1918, with the German armies again threatening Paris, Balfour went still further. The idea of a "big-

18 Aristide Briand, president of the council, to Ambassador Paul Cambon (London), Jan. 12, 1917, *Papers Respecting Negotiations for an Anglo-French Pact*, no. 2.
19 Exchanges between Foreign Minister Pokrovski and Russian ambassador in Paris, Jan. 30–Feb. 26, 1917, *Negotiations for an Anglo-French Pact*, no. 4 (i–v). See also Stevenson, *French War Aims Against Germany*, 48–56.
20 Balfour to Lord Bertie, July 2, 1917, *Negotiations for an Anglo-French Pact*, no. 3.
21 Balfour in House of Commons, Dec. 19, 1917, *Negotiations for an Anglo-French Pact*, no. 4.

ger Alsace" with the borders of 1790 or 1814, he insisted, had never become a war aim of the Allies. "It was altogether outside our whole modes of thought on this subject. It was not a subject which we should ever have seriously contemplated, nor do I think it ever was a very fixed or solid part of the foreign policy for any length of time of any French government."[22]

While these public statements failed to represent the whole truth, Balfour did not miss the mark entirely in suggesting that the French position remained fluid. Within months of leaving office, Briand became involved in secret negotiations with the guileful German diplomat, Baron von der Lancken, for a compromise peace that would have left most of Alsace and Lorraine to Germany.[23] Although Briand covered his tracks sufficiently to save his political career, the fact remains that a number of influential Frenchmen, as well as a large fraction of the Belgian political class, were sufficiently discouraged to entertain the idea of peace on the basis of the status quo ante in the fall of 1917. After he took over as premier, in the midst of military emergency, Georges Clemenceau paid little attention to dividing spoils that were not yet won. Clemenceau's strength lay in his single-minded focus on waging war.[24] Accordingly, although the Comité d'Etudes and the various ministries continued to consider the matter, Clemenceau declined to be pinned down specifically on war aims.

Clemenceau's notable reticence reflected no lack of concern or passion about France's eastern frontiers. Ever since the 1870s the "Tiger" had mourned the loss of Alsace and Lorraine and publicly adjured his countrymen to keep their gaze fixed on the blue line of the Vosges. Yet in a generation when most French leaders spoke no foreign language and felt uncomfortable outside the bounds of the hexagon, Clemenceau knew the outside world intimately and had a realistic sense of the relative weakness of France.

Clemenceau had spent four years after the Civil War in America, and at one time thought of settling there. He spoke English fluently. All his life he retained strong friendships with Americans.[25] One admirer had even named an Arizona copper mine in his honor.[26] Free from the ethnocentric provincialism that sustained the optimism of his countrymen in the darkest hours of the war, Clemenceau had a brooding sense of France as a nation close to

---

22 Balfour speech, House of Commons, May 16, 1918, *Negotiations for an Anglo-French Pact,* no. 6.
23 Much, though not all, of the story can be followed in the documents published by J. Scherer and A. Grunewald, eds., *L'Allemagne et les problèmes de la paix pendant la Première Guerre Mondiale,* 4 vols. (Paris, 1966–78), vol. 3.
24 Jean-Baptiste Duroselle, *Clemenceau* (Paris, 1988), 635–728.
25 Ibid., 66–88.
26 See J. S. Douglas–Clemenceau correspondence in box 50, Lewis W. Douglas papers, University of Arizona Library.

collapse, a land devoid of administration, organization, or sophisticated leadership, and without much prospect of acquiring it.[27] France, he felt, could not afford to go it alone in peace any more than it had succeeded in doing so in war. The wartime premier had seen too much of the world to place trust in the lubricious charm of a changeling like Lloyd George, and he remained too much a creature of the nineteenth century to forget how, in the privacy of their clubs and country houses, most Englishmen really regarded Frenchmen. But he nurtured high hopes for the Americans. Woodrow Wilson would doubtless irritate him with the "super-talky talk of his 'League of Nations'" and those "many pointed wisdom teeth that never let themselves be turned aside from their duty."[28] Still, he had confidence in the fundamental good intentions of the Americans. He resolved to go the extra mile to retain the bonds of the wartime alliance.

During the months leading up to the Armistice, Clemenceau developed a particularly high regard for Colonel House. The working alliance between the two men gradually deepened into perdurable friendship: throughout the 1920s, House visited the one time premier every summer at his cottage in the Vendée. "A super-civilized escapee from the barbarities of Texas," Clemenceau later described his friend, "a man who sees and understands everything, and, while acting only as his conscience dictates, knows how to make the whole world listen and respect him." He gave House the highest encomium: "a good American, almost as good a Frenchman, a level-headed mind, in every way the classic gentleman."[29] In his strategy for winning over Wilson and educating leading Americans to the requirements of European diplomacy, the president of the council placed high hopes in that friendship. To the end of his life, Clemenceau maintained that he had never "acquiesced in defeat" on the Rhineland. He had "fought to the bitter end for the strategic frontier that Marshall Foch judged to be best."[30] Yet he did so within the context of a larger strategic design. Unlike the notable Frenchmen who followed him in World War II, indeed quite against the grain of French political thought generally, Clemenceau considered perpetuation of an Anglo-American alliance as the primary objective of policy. Only with such an alliance could a country in demographic and moral decline hope to contain a larger and still menacing neighbor.

---

27 Clemenceau monologue to Loucheur, Tardieu, and Pichon, Mar. 15, 1919, in Louis Loucheur, *Carnets secrets, 1908–1932* (Brussels, 1962), 72.

28 Georges Clemenceau, *Grandeur and Misery of Victory* (New York, 1930), 148–9.

29 Ibid., 148. See also Georges Wormser, *Clemenceau vu du près* (Paris, 1979), 172–90. Lloyd George also expressed high regard for House's character, but tagged him as an adroit salesman rather than an original thinker; see his *Memoirs of the Peace Conference*, 2 vols. (New Haven, Conn., 1939), 1:157–60.

30 Clemenceau, *Grandeur and Misery*, 233.

Unfortunately for the French cause, House found his influence diminished in Paris owing to the president's loss of confidence in his loyalty. House's earlier role in keeping Wilson focused on the practical requirements of statesmanship can scarcely be overestimated.[31] Wilson did not think straightforwardly about American security interests, and, partly as a result, he had trouble conceiving that other countries might have legitimate security needs as well.[32] As late as December 1916, he had purported to believe that the apparent objects of the belligerent governments were "virtually the same."[33] He had made many other pronouncements that stand up poorly in the pitiless light of history. House had long served the president both as a reality check and as a link to the specialists on the Inquiry who had examined the concrete territorial and economic problems that properly formed the central objects of peacemaking. Largely because of his counsel, Wilson had shown a tendency to moderate his flights of ideological fancy during the period of American belligerency in the service of the war effort.[34] With the battlefield victory won, however, Wilson focused ever more obsessively on the empyrean vision that so thrilled the liberal leader-writers who nourished his prodigious self-regard. "In fact," he assured Inquiry members on the ship steaming to Brest, "he could not see how a treaty of peace could be drawn up or how both *elasticity* and *security* could be obtained save under a League of Nations; the opposite of such a course was to maintain the idea of the Great Powers and of balance of power, and such an idea had always produced only aggression and selfishness and war."[35]

Under the American system of government, the president negotiates treaties, but the Senate must advise and consent. The French could have minimized their risks by exploring a contact with Henry Cabot Lodge, incoming chairman of the Foreign Relations Committee in the Republican-dominated Senate. Lodge had known Ambassador Jules Jusserand since

31 Alexander L. George and Juliette L. George, *Woodrow Wilson and Colonel House: A Personality Study* (New York, 1956), esp. 240–67, is still the most balanced source on the break. Inga Floto, *Colonel House in Paris* (Princeton, N.J., 1980), 164–214, is very full but lacks critical distance about the motives animating House's opponents.

32 The classic statement is still the best: Robert E. Osgood, *Ideals and Self-Interest in America's Foreign Relations* (Chicago, 1953).

33 Appeal for a Statement of War Aims, Dec. 18, 1916, *PWW*, 40:273–6; note the ringing defense of this note, emblematic of Wilsonian scholarship, by Thomas J. Knock, *To End All Wars: Woodrow Wilson and the Quest for a New World Order* (New York, 1992), 107–11.

34 In their desperation, visiting French firemen pounced on every stray comment that Wilson made expressing solidarity with France. See, e.g., notes on a meeting with Viviani and Jusserand, Apr. 30, 1917, in *PWW*, 42:173–4.

35 Isaiah Bowman memorandum on remarks by the president, Dec. 10, 1918, Bowman papers, Johns Hopkins University Library. See also *PWW*, 53:353–6. Arthur Walworth, *America's Moment: 1918* (New York, 1977), 130–6, provides a multisource report on Wilson's monologue, skillfully highlighting what he calls the president's "moral arrogance."

their rambles in Rock Creek Park with Theodore Roosevelt fifteen years before. Lodge counted as a realist internationalist squarely in the Roosevelt tradition; he saw the world, much as did the French, in enlightened balance-of-power terms.[36] "The first and controlling purpose of the peace," Lodge wrote to Henry White (the only nonpartisan on the American delegation), "must be to put Germany in such a position that it will be physically impossible for her to break out again upon other nations with a war for world conquest." Lodge favored establishing the Rhine frontier, occupying select provinces until Berlin completed payment of a heavy indemnity, and possibly separating Bavaria and other components of the Reich as well.[37] Nevertheless, the French did not seek to open back-channel relations with Lodge. André Tardieu, the intellectually acute high commissioner in Washington, who returned home to advise Clemenceau on peacemaking, seemed to have no idea how much Wilson disliked him.[38] Nor did Paris fully register the sea change in American politics that had taken place as a result of the Republican sweep in the midterm elections. Clemenceau placed his faith in face-to-face negotiations with House and Wilson. He would stick with that choice to the end.

III

Clemenceau nurtured a healthy skepticism about British goodwill. His intuition served him well. Not that the British spoke with one mind. Britain, more than the other Allies, still operated through cabinet government. Lloyd George could manipulate that cabinet with skill and dissimulation, but he presided over a fissiparous coalition. Moreover, he had to take account not merely of his colleagues' views but also those of empire representatives whose armies had reinforced His Majesty's forces in the field.[39] Right through the war, most British statesmen had expressed greater interest in future dispositions east of Suez and south of Gibraltar than they did in precise arrangements on the Continent.[40] And in the privacy of the cabinet room, they cultivated a practiced disdain for each of their principal allies.

36 William Widenor, *Henry Cabot Lodge and the Search for an American Foreign Policy* (Berkeley, Calif., 1980), is the only study that treats Lodge with a minimum degree of scholarly dispassion.
37 Lodge memorandum for Henry White, Dec. 1, 1918; additional memorandum, n.d. (Dec. 1918); also Lodge to Paul Herbin, Nov. 18, 1918, box 53, Lodge papers.
38 On Wilson's distrust of Tardieu, see Edith Benham diary, Mar. 28, 1919, Library of Congress, also *PWW,* 56:354–5; further *PWW,* 56:86, Grayson diary, Mar. 19, 1919; and House diary, May 6, 1919.
39 John Turner, *British Politics and the Great War: Coalition and Conflict, 1915–1918* (New Haven, Conn., 1992); Kenneth Morgan, *Consensus and Disunity: The Lloyd George Coalition Government, 1918–1922* (Oxford, 1979).
40 Victor H. Rothwell, *British War Aims and Peace Diplomacy, 1914–1918* (Oxford, 1971).

The British believed that they possessed "the most formidable fighting force in the world." They prided themselves on making the major contribution to victory. The French had thoroughly exhausted themselves; the Americans remained so ignorant of modern warfare that they hardly knew how to feed their troops.[41] It followed that Whitehall should also give a lead at the peace table. The objective was to terminate hostilities in such a way as to achieve optimum results for the British Empire. Yet the problem of achieving that "good peace" bristled with difficulty. Lloyd George wondered on October 26, 1918, whether the Allies should "go on until Germany was smashed"; Balfour countered that, if proper terms could be secured now, sacking Frankfurt would not increase the margin of victory. Lord Curzon fretted portentously about the "wreckage of all civilization and order in the east." Jan Smuts of South Africa made the decisive argument for an immediate armistice: "If we were to beat Germany to nothingness, then we must beat Europe to nothingness, too. As Europe went down, so America would rise. In time the United States would dictate to the world in naval, military, diplomatic, and financial matters. In that he saw no good."[42]

Not surprisingly, therefore, British negotiators took a tough line on naval terms and their right to reparation, but expressed misgivings over sending troops across French borders eastward. Lloyd George insisted on October 29 that the military terms were already too severe: "He did not approve of occupying the left bank of the Rhine."[43] He yielded when Clemenceau pledged to withdraw just as soon as Germany complied with peace conditions, but he voiced the suspicion to the War Cabinet that "the French were treating the situation as a revenge for 1870." The real security problem, the prime minister thought, came from a wholly different quarter. "Marching men into Germany was marching them into a cholera area. The Germans did that in Russia and caught the virus, i.e., of Bolshevism." Winston Churchill seconded the alarm. "We might have to build up the German army, as it was important to get Germany on her legs again for fear of the spread of Bolshevism." The Chief of the Imperial General Staff chimed in that the Rhenish provinces, insofar as possible, should be garrisoned by American troops.[44] While the British did occupy the Cologne zone, they

41 Field Marshal Haig's assessment in War Cabinet minutes, Oct. 21, 1918, CAB 23/14, Public Record Office; also appreciation by General Sir C. H. Harrington, Deputy Chief of the General Staff, Oct. 26, 1918, CAB 23/14.
42 War Cabinet minutes, Oct. 26, 1918, CAB 23/14, Public Record Office.
43 House diary, Oct. 29, 1918.
44 War Cabinet minutes, Nov. 10, 1918, CAB 23/14.

continued to view security along the Rhine as a small piece of a larger puzzle. Churchill foresaw a future full of darkling shadows. Absent imaginative policies on the part of the victors, a dissatisfied Reich might join hands with Bolshevik Russia to form "a great combination from Yokohama to Cologne in hostility to France, Britain, and America."[45]

Clemenceau and Marshall Foch arrived in London on November 30, 1918, in order to exchange views with their British counterparts before the Americans arrived. Fresh from a rousing public demonstration in Trafalgar Square, Foch turned up at Downing Street to elaborate maximum French demands. Drawing on his prestige as supreme Allied commander, Foch proposed not merely to separate the Rhenish provinces from Germany, but to imbricate the independent states on the left bank in a permanent scheme of military assistance and economic cooperation linking France, Belgium, Luxembourg, and Great Britain. The British politicians immediately threw cold water on the scheme. Lloyd George asked whether Foch "did not fear the danger of creating a new Alsace-Lorraine on the other side, which would in course of years result in a new war of revenge." Conservative leader Andrew Bonar Law sourly observed that "we ourselves had tried for years to conciliate the Irish" – with no discernible result.[46]

Undeterred, Foch continued to hammer away over the next weeks in conversation with his good friend, Field Marshal Sir Henry Wilson, chief of the Imperial General Staff (CIGS). Both men shared a long-suffering impatience with the blinkered vision of the "Frocks."[47] Foch assumed that the United States would withdraw its troops at the rate of 500,000 a month and that the last doughboys would disappear from European shores by the spring of 1919. To counter German demographic preponderance, the Western countries therefore needed both an impregnable defensive line along the Rhine and also three-year military service for an indefinite period.[48] Wilson joined Foch in considering the League of Nations "idiotic" and believing that the American Wilson's public fatuities betrayed him as both "Boche and Bolshevik," an "academic ass," and either a "knave" or a "fool."[49] Foch

45 War Cabinet minutes, Feb. 13, 1919, CAB 23/15.
46 Lloyd George, *Memoirs of the Peace Conference,* 1:77–80. Foch's formal memorandum of Nov. 27, 1918, and all essential documentation on the French side may be found in vol. 417, Papiers André Tardieu (PA-AP 166), Ministère des Affaires Etrangères (hereafter MAE), Paris.
47 See Foch–Henry Wilson correspondence in HHW 2/24a–b, Field Marshal Sir Henry Wilson papers, Imperial War Museum (hereafter IWM), London.
48 Henry Wilson diary, Dec. 1, 1918, IWM.
49 Henry Wilson diary, Dec. 22, 1918; Jan. 12 and 26, Feb. 1, 1919. C. E. Callwell, *Field Marshal Sir Henry Wilson: His Life and Diaries,* 2 vols. (London, 1927), edits out most of the negative references to Americans that suffuse the original. Keith Jeffery, *The Military Correspondence of Field Marshal Sir Henry Wilson, 1918–1922* (London, 1985), lifts a part of the veil.

suspected that the Americans would "make big Armies and big Navies and then in alliance with the Boches dictate terms to Europe and the world."[50] The CIGS agreed that the only reasonable plan was to "stick to the line of the Rhine . . . until we have secured the fruits of victory."[51]

The British military, however, faced insurmountable problems of their own. In the first week of January 1919, soldiers arriving at Folkestone on leave mutinied and demanded immediate demobilization. The Cabinet dithered. Chaos spread.[52] At length the prime minister, whom the CIGS also placed squarely in the camp of "stupid fools," agreed to keep conscription for the moment. Still, the War Office realized that it had secured but a short reprieve. Eventually public opinion would compel reversion to a volunteer army. Military planners remained preoccupied throughout the winter with industrial strikes at home and troubles in the colonies. With a volunteer army, Britain could scarcely hope to field the forces necessary to garrison India, Malta, Gibraltar, and Ireland, not to speak of the new territories that would land in the British sphere at the peace conference.[53] What would remain for the Rhine? The War Office could scrounge up a dozen white divisions, plus some colonials, to keep a Continental commitment while the Paris conferees completed their labors. When Britain cut its military establishment down to peacetime size, one division and a flag seemed more realistic.[54]

As British army planners mulled over the intractable problem of Western security, they gravitated toward the view that Germany, too, should be forbidden to retain conscription. Henry Wilson agreed with Foch that the Germans could still carry out paramilitary training. "We can no more limit the number of men trained to arms in Germany than the Germans could limit the output of coal in England." Restrictions on German weapons development likewise appeared "impossible" over the long term. On the other hand, cadres without soldiers to command could not do much harm. Finally, despite his affection for Foch, Wilson wanted "a Germany sufficiently strong to be no temptation to the French."[55] In the end, the CIGS and his advisers came down on professional grounds for a long-service German army and demilitarization of both banks of the Rhine but against a prolonged occupation, which would require Allied forces to hold a line

50 Henry Wilson diary, Jan. 26, 1919.
51 Ibid.
52 Ibid., Jan. 4–14, 1919.
53 Ibid., Jan. 12, 26, 1919.
54 Ibid., Jan. 26, 1919.
55 Ibid., Feb. 16, 1919.

eighty miles longer than the Lorraine–Belgian frontier.[56] Endless palaver by the military men at the peace conference produced a compromise that satisfied no one: a long-service German army that "maddened" Foch and a cap of 100,000 men that Wilson derided as "childish." "So I got my principle but not my numbers, and Foch has got his numbers but not his principle," Wilson minuted in disgust. "An amazing state of affairs."[57] The larger security problem remained to be solved at a higher political level.

The grandees of British politics, however, did not focus closely on the Rhineland issue as the peace conference got under way. As seasoned practitioners of *Weltpolitik,* they trained their gaze instead on the difficulties of Egypt and India, the complications of the Ottoman and Habsburg successions, and the implications of chaos in the Russian borderlands for the British position in the East. By comparison, they held, settling Germany's western borders ought to prove comparatively simple. Britain stood amply forewarned not to countenance another sore spot like prewar Alsace-Lorraine. Lloyd George and his amanuensis, Philip Kerr, felt certain that if the Reich remained resentful, no lasting peace could emerge. Edwin Montagu and Smuts opined that only a reasonably satisfied Germany could form a bulwark against Bolshevism. Balfour chimed in that the French should count themselves lucky to recover Alsace-Lorraine without a plebiscite; they were "opening their mouths wide" to ask for anything more.[58]

Owing largely to these preconceptions, top-level British leaders expressed remarkably little curiosity about political ferment in the Cologne occupation zone during the early months of 1919. As we now know, significant elements in the Center Party expressed great fear of the Workers' and Soldiers' Councils and of the radicalization of economic life in Berlin. They also voiced apprehension about the Socialist government's school policy, which Rhineland Catholics interpreted as an assault on their religion and local autonomy. Events came to a head in a notable meeting held at the Cologne city hall, under the chairmanship of Konrad Adenauer, on February 1, 1919. Even as a local notable, Mayor Adenauer figured as a dexterous rider of political tigers. Adenauer felt his way gingerly toward a subtle *combinazione* that would outflank radical separatists, elaborate an autonomous status for the Rhineland within the Reich, shelter the region from Prussian-Socialist

---

56 Henry Wilson to Lloyd George, Mar. 6, 1919, F/47/8/7, Lloyd George papers, House of Lords Record Office.
57 Henry Wilson diary, Feb. 19, Mar. 4–5, 10, 1919.
58 See correspondence of Kerr, Montagu, Smuts, and Balfour with the prime minister respectively in F/89, F/40, F/45, F/3, Lloyd George papers, House of Lords Record Office.

dictation, and possibly offer sufficient security to secure milder peace conditions from the Entente.[59]

While the British maintained a studious neutrality on German "internal affairs," Tardieu and his staff in Paris scrutinized the Adenauer speech and other reports from Cologne intently.[60] Paul Tirard, the brilliant colonial administrator who had organized Marshal Hubert Lyautey's civil services in Morocco, assumed the post of controller-general of the occupied territories and assembled a first-class team at Marshall Foch's Luxembourg headquarters.[61] But Tirard did not make decisive progress in shaping the situation on the ground. The British continued to run the show at Cologne – the administrative and commercial center of the Rhineland and the gateway to the Ruhr – and they would have no truck with separatism. Generals Charles Mangin at Mainz and Augustin Gérard at Landau, who envisioned themselves as latter-day proconsuls destined to rekindle the glorious traditions of Hoche, Beugnot, and Napoleon, controlled only the lightly populated upper Rhine. Relying on inexperienced intelligence officers with more ideological fervor than good sense, Mangin and Gérard vastly overrated the political legitimacy of the extreme separatists and the prospects of their seizing power.[62]

Tardieu and his sharp-eyed military aide, Lieutenant Colonel Edouard Réquin, read the optimistic accounts coming from the field with mounting skepticism. Tardieu minuted his sharp dissent on a report in late March claiming that the moderate parties were "already won over" (acquis dès maintenant) to the idea of separation.[63] Moreover, Tardieu's economic advisers warned that to establish a customs barrier along the Rhine and to turn that region's trade toward France would cause almost insurmountable

59 Karl Dietrich Erdmann, *Adenauer in der Rheinlandpolitik nach dem Ersten Weltkrieg* (Stuttgart, 1966), 21–48, 212–34; cf. the pejorative interpretation by Henning Köhler, *Adenauer und die rheinische Republik: Der erste Anlauf, 1918–1924* (Opladen, 1986), 47–61.

60 See a collection of these reports, mostly annotated by Lieutenant Colonel Edouard Réquin for Tardieu, in vols. 426–7, Papiers Tardieu, MAE.

61 Jacques Bariéty, *Les Relations franco-allemandes après la première guerre mondiale* (Paris, 1977), 34–51. Paul Tirard, *La France sur le Rhin: douze années d'occupation rhénane* (Paris, 1930), 69–101, gives nothing away.

62 J. A. Dorten, "Le Général Mangin en Rhénanie," *Revue des deux mondes* (July 1937): 39–67; J. A. Dorten, *La Tragédie rhénane* (Paris, 1945), 35–85; L.-E. Mangin, *La France sur le Rhin* (Geneva, 1945), 13–68; Guy de Traversay, "La première tentative de République rhénane," *Revue de Paris* (Nov.–Dec. 1928): 404–31, 586–614; Général Mangin, "Lettres de Rhénanie," *Revue de Paris* (Apr. 1936): 481–526; Paul Jacquot, *General Gérard und die Pfalz*, ed. Ritter von Eberlein (Berlin, 1920). Jere Clemens King, *Foch Versus Clemenceau: France and German Dismemberment, 1918–1919* (Cambridge, Mass., 1960), carefully recapitulates evidence available at the time of publication.

63 See Paul Tirard/Max Hermant report, Mar. 29, 1919, with marginal comments, in Papiers Tardieu 426, MAE.

difficulties: even a wider Franco–Belgian customs union could not absorb Rhenish machine tools, textiles, chemicals, and wine without devastating harm to home production.[64] Meanwhile, from December 1918 onward French industrialists loudly complained about unfair competition from Rhineland exporters with costs reckoned in depreciated marks; they eagerly sought licenses to sell their own manufactures in the occupied areas, but resisted reciprocal trade.[65] Marshall Foch and his acolytes might continue to dream about creating a fait accompli on the ground. More sober spirits acknowledged that, given the economic and political impediments, they could not do so alone. They realized from the opening of the peace conference that their best hope of success lay in persuading the British and Americans of the justice of their cause.

IV

During the first month of negotiations in Paris, Woodrow Wilson concentrated his "higher realism" on drafting the League of Nations Covenant, which he envisioned as the heart and soul of the peace treaty.[66] He delegated detailed consideration of such mundane matters as boundaries, military dispositions, reparations, and trade – the possible components of a "preliminary peace" with Germany – to underlings. Nevertheless, he fairly vibrated with indignation when he contemplated French annexationist proclivities. French attitudes were "petty," "stupid," and "insane," the president told a neutral diplomat on February 12; he would "rather be stoned in the streets than give in."[67]

Tardieu did not present his formal paper refining his country's proposals for the Rhine until February 25. But the French left no one in doubt about their desiderata earlier. Indeed, Marshall Foch's memorandum of January 10

---

64 M. Masson, "Etude sur les conséquences économiques de l'autonomie de la Rive Gauche du Rhin," Mar. 1919, Papiers Tardieu 427, MAE.

65 See full documentation on the protests and the meetings at the Commerce Ministry to deal with them in F^{12}/8041, Ministère du Commerce et de l'Industrie, Archives Nationales. American officials repeatedly denounced the preferences that French licensing authorities gave to their own exports – some recalled the comportment of Yankee carpetbaggers after the Civil War – but they focused less intently on the more serious problem of finding markets for Rhineland exports. See Keith L. Nelson, *Victors Divided: America and the Allies in Germany, 1918–1923* (Berkeley, Calif., 1975), 99–110; Arthur Walworth, *Wilson and His Peacemakers* (New York, 1986), 266.

66 I take the phrase from Arthur Link, *The Higher Realism of Woodrow Wilson and Other Essays* (Nashville, Tenn., 1971). Link wrote without apparent ironic intent.

67 William Rappard to Swiss foreign minister Hans Sulzer, Feb. 13, 1919, *PWW,* 55:151–4; cf. Rappard's diary entry in *Centenaire Woodrow Wilson, 1856–1956* (Geneva, 1956), 55–6; reproduced out of place in *PWW,* 63:630–1.

foreshadowed every essential feature of the full-blown Tardieu scheme. The Quai d'Orsay had carefully vetted Foch's draft, and Tardieu himself had recrafted it line by line.[68] Foch denied any wish to annex German territory. However, the democratic countries of Western Europe, hobbled by permanent demographic inferiority, had no choice but to mount the "Watch on the Rhine." The river formed the only possible "natural frontier" to defend against a tank attack as well as the logical maneuvering base to prepare a counter-offensive. After offering a potted history of Prussian wickedness from Frederick the Great through Wilhelm II, the Marshal predicted that a republic built upon the principles of militarism and centralization would prove no less dangerous than a monarchy. The Allies would therefore have to neutralize the right bank of the Rhine, occupy the left bank "under the auspices" of the League, and create autonomous states in the latter area that were self-governing within prescribed limits.

House, the de facto second in the American delegation, met with Foreign Secretary Balfour on February 9. The two statesmen quickly agreed that, once the prime ministers went home, they should put an end to futile plenary sessions and focus constructively on framing a preliminary peace with the Reich. Both self-consciously regarded themselves as eminently pragmatic professionals. Both expressed a "profound sympathy for France and for the unhappy situation in which she finds herself." However, neither could divine a practical way to solve the French security problem. The French did not seem to realize, House recorded, that "to establish a Rhenish Republic against the will of the people would be contrary to the principle of self-determination. . . . If we did such a thing, we would be treating Germany in one way, and the balance of the world in another. We would run the danger of having everything from the Rhine to the Pacific, perhaps including Japan, against the Western powers." House could only hope that the League of Nations would enforce German disarmament and engender a new "spirit" over time.[69] House elaborated this Texas blarney in a talk with Louis Aubert, Tardieu's deputy, two days later. It would be "bad for France" to impose a wrong upon Germany and would "react against us as the German wrong to France in '71 had reacted upon her."[70] Moral lessons like these offered cold comfort to strategic planners at the rue St.-

68 Foch memorandum, Jan. 10, 1919, in *Negotiations for an Anglo-French Pact,* no. 9; memorandum of the French Government on the Fixation of the Rhine as the Western Frontier of Germany, Feb. 25, 1919, ibid., no. 10; also in André Tardieu, *The Truth About the Treaty* (Indianapolis, 1921), 147–67. Cf. also Foch's draft of Jan. 5, 1919, with Tardieu's rewrite in Papiers Tardieu 422, MAE.
69 House diary, Feb. 9, 1919.
70 Ibid., Feb. 11, 1919.

Dominique. At the very same time, Woodrow Wilson and Lord Robert Cecil were fighting like tigers to defeat Léon Bourgeois's scheme for endowing the League with a General Staff and real military capability.[71]

All the same, Clemenceau and his minions longed to turn from debating the Covenant's fine points to making peace with Germany. As Wilson packed his bags for Washington on February 14, House ventured the prediction that he could "button up everything during the next four weeks." He hoped to reduce the German army and navy to a peace footing, delineate boundaries, resolve the fate of the colonies, fix the amount of reparations, and determine economic treatment of the Reich. The president looked startled and alarmed. House quickly backtracked. He planned not to "bring these matters to a final conclusion but to have them ready for him to do so when he returned." House took care to add that it was sometimes necessary to compromise "in order to get things through . . . not a compromise of principle, but a compromise of detail."[72] Wilson did not reply. Here was a single nimbus cloud, scarcely hinting at the hurricane to come.

During the next weeks, House exercised his fabled skills as a conciliator, cultivating warm relations with Clemenceau as he recovered from an assassination attempt, chatting repeatedly with Tardieu, Balfour, and the Italian Sidney Sonnino, and artfully blurring the hard edges of conflict all around. At the same time, he drove his interlocutors forward with the specter of unforeseen troubles that might make rapid settlement imperative. His experts often expressed frustration at the intricacies of the task. "I thought the British were as crazy as the French," the reparations adviser Thomas Lamont complained one day, "but they seem only half as crazy, which still leaves them a good heavy margin of lunacy."[73] House, however, did not despair. He recalled boyhood camping on the wild Texas frontier. "At night I would inevitably tell gruesome stories having to do with murder and lawlessness. I would then roll over in my blanket and go to sleep, feeling quite certain that my companions would be very watchful."[74] Eventually, House discerned a way to bring the French and British closer on the Rhineland. The French might be authorized to hold the Rhine bridgeheads for a limited period until Germany fulfilled the peace treaty. An autonomous republic would be set up on the left bank, but the people there could exercise self-determination in five or ten years, by which time the League of Nations

---

71 Meetings of the Commission of the League of Nations, Feb. 13, 1919, *PWW,* 55:121–40; House diary, Feb. 13, 1919.
72 House diary, Feb. 14, 1919.
73 Ibid., Feb. 21, 1919.
74 Ibid., Feb. 19, 1919.

would provide effective protection against war. Meanwhile, House leaned on Britain to bail out the failing French exchequer, then assembled his financial team to advise "how and when to bring economic pressure" to further American political aims.[75]

While House remained loyal to the president's deeper purposes, he concluded that the political mood in America and the kaleidoscopic threats to stability in Europe required an active search for compromise. "If the president should exert his influence among the liberals and laboring classes," House reasoned at the time, "he might possibly overthrow the governments in Great Britain, France, and Italy, but if he did, he would still have to reckon with our own people and he might bring the whole world into chaos."[76] Looking backward a decade later, House strenuously denied that he had undermined a liberal peace along with Clemenceau. Instead, in his retrospective interpretation, "when the president first went to Paris he thought an American peace should be forced upon Europe. Later he came to the conclusion that there was justice in European claims and changed his position."[77] However one judges House's *apologia pro vita sua,* the adviser certainly came to view himself as indispensable. "There is scarcely a man here in authority, outside the President, who has a full and detached understanding of the situation," he minuted on March 3. "The president himself lacks a certain executive quality which in some measure unfits him for this supreme task."[78] Lloyd George, who rarely missed an opportunity for manipulative panegyrics, flattered House a few days later by remarking oleaginously that "we four prime ministers can quickly finish up the business that is before us."[79]

On March 10, Lloyd George, Clemenceau, and House agreed to set up a committee composed of three trusted associates – Philip Kerr, Tardieu, and House's brother-in-law, Sidney Mezes – with a mission to explore a settlement of Germany's western frontiers.[80] In fact, House had badly misjudged the prospects for compromise. The British had not the slightest intention of yielding on matters of substance. The War Cabinet had discussed the subject twice. On February 28 the ministers seemed inclined to participate in a low-budget Rhineland occupation, provided the United States did likewise. Secretary of State for War Winston Churchill struck the

75 Ibid., Feb. 19, 23, 25, and Mar. 2, 1919.
76 Ibid., Mar. 3, 1919.
77 House to Clemenceau, Mar. 25, 1929, House papers 27/878, Yale University Library.
78 House diary, Mar. 3, 1919.
79 Ibid., Mar. 7, 1919.
80 Ibid., Mar. 10, 1919.

dominant note. "We should show ourselves as sympathetic as possible to the French, for two reasons: first, in order that she might show herself accommodating in regard to our own Eastern policy; and second, to enable us to acquire great influence over France and the peace conference generally, with a view to the adoption of a merciful policy towards Germany."[81]

By the March 4 meeting, the mood had turned. Lord Curzon declared on behalf of the Foreign Office that the idea of maintaining a permanent military force on the Rhine was "intolerable." The British might safely profess interest in the idea of a left-bank buffer state in order to divert the French from colonial enterprises, since the Americans would likely block the scheme as a violation of self-determination. The delegation in Paris, however, seemed to have lost sight of larger considerations in India, Morocco, and elsewhere. Curzon regarded it as "an extraordinary phenomenon that the French, with their greatly diminished population, should yet, while they were imploring their Allies to protect them, unfold the most ambitious projects all over the world." Other ministers, leaving aside such tactical considerations, criticized the French proposal from various points of view. The chancellor of the exchequer worried about the costs of garrisoning a buffer state. The Conservative leader Bonar Law doubted that the French would really shoulder the financial burden in generations to come. Lloyd George suspected that France would prove "quite satisfied" with the alternative of an Anglo-American guarantee, but that seemed impossible since the president would not hear of entangling alliances. "Forty years hence," he slyly observed, "might see a re-shuffling of alliances and a fresh grouping of Allies." The prime minister placed his faith over the long haul in demilitarizing the Rhineland, developing the League, and imposing a huge indemnity that would fill British coffers while coincidentally preventing the Germans from spending money on their army. The Cabinet authorized the CIGS to work up a precise scheme that could be brought forth once the Americans had turned down the "extreme propositions" of the French.[82]

The Kerr-Tardieu-Mezes discussions therefore involved a degree of play-acting.[83] Kerr advised his superiors to "resist the Tardieu proposition to the

81 War Cabinet "A" minutes, Feb. 28, 1919, CAB 23/15, PRO.
82 War Cabinet "A" minutes, Mar. 4, 1919, CAB 23/15. It is amusing to note that on the day before this meeting, Professor James Shotwell of the U.S. delegation conferred with a British counterpart about how to correct American public misapprehensions about the "Machiavellian cunning of secret British diplomacy." See J. W. Headlam-Morley memorandum, Mar. 3, 1919, in Sir James Headlam-Morley, *A Memoir of the Paris Peace Conference* (London, 1972), 38–9.
83 Notes of discussion between P. H. Kerr, M. Tardieu, and Dr. Mezes, Mar. 11–12, 1919, in *Negotiations for an Anglo-French Pact,* no. 12.

end."[84] The British military had no patience for what the CIGS repeatedly derided as Tardieu's "childish" and "ridiculous" paper.[85] War Office analysts pointed out that rivers had never stopped armies during World War I and that future developments in tank and airplane technology appeared wholly unlikely to enhance the value of a narrow security glacis. Holding the bridgeheads would bring little military advantage, concluded the Director of Military Intelligence, but would "plant so many poisoned thorns in an open sore which it is our business to heal."[86] Foreign Office advisers on duty in Paris meanwhile emphasized that Britain could not fully trust France. J. W. Headlam-Morley, the chief specialist on Central Europe in the British delegation, who had spent many formative years in Berlin, recalled that Strasbourg had served in the past as a starting point for military expeditions against the Reich. If Germany were disarmed and the left bank demilitarized, Headlam warned, the Germans might plausibly suggest that "it would be impossible to depend upon the pacific attitude of the French government and nation." Far from entertaining thoughts of yet further sureties along the Rhine, Headlam predicted that Germany would refuse to acquiesce in the military disabilities now proposed "unless similar restrictions are imposed upon all other nations on the Continent of Europe."[87]

House's month of stringpulling thus failed to break the logjam. On the afternoon of March 12, a disabused Clemenceau decided to confront Lloyd George. Despite an extensive spy network, the French premier lacked access to the paper flow in the British delegation, yet at age seventy-eight he could read the tea-leaves as well as anybody. Pressed to the wall, the sinuous Welshman confirmed that he would never consent to a Rhineland republic or agree to maintain an army at the bridgeheads indefinitely. He suggested protection in other directions. For example, England would build a Channel tunnel, and he would pledge that, in the event of an invasion, the British army would at once hasten to the rescue. A practiced cynic like Clemenceau could divine the worth of such undertakings. The Frenchman immediately went round to complain to House that Lloyd George had "broken his word in declining even to discuss the Rhenish Republic and the proper protection of France." House soothed the old man and told him

84 Kerr memorandum for Balfour, Mar. 13, 1919, Paper 457a, FO 608/142 (Records of British Delegation to the Peace Conference), PRO.
85 Henry Wilson diary, Mar. 5 and 12, 1919, IWM.
86 Memorandum of Major General Sir William Thwaites, DMI, for Balfour, Doc. 2868, Mar. 4, 1919, FO 608/142, PRO.
87 Headlam-Morley minute, Mar. 14, 1919, Paper 4211, FO 608/128. See also other minutes revealing the development of Headlam's thought during March and April in his *Memoir of the Paris Peace Conference*, 38–91. Agnes Headlam-Morley discusses the Teutonophile atmosphere in her childhood home with touching delicacy in ibid., ix–xlii.

that "we would straighten it out in some way and not to worry."[88]
Clemenceau remained unappeased. He fumed to President of the Republic Poincaré that Lloyd George was a "swindler" and a "liar."[89] House, too, was whistling past the graveyard. From the USS *George Washington,* President Wilson had sent a perturbed radiogram on March 10: "I hope that you will not even provisionally consent to the separation of the Rhenish provinces from Germany under any arrangement but will reserve the whole matter until after my arrival."[90]

V

Woodrow Wilson disembarked at Brest on March 13 in a truculent mood.[91] What happened precisely when House briefed the president is a subject still shrouded in mystery. House admits that Wilson reproached him: "Your dinner to the Foreign Relations Committee was a failure." He found his chief "very militant and determined to put the League of Nations into the Peace Treaty."[92] Whether the president upbraided House for his German boundary negotiations remains unclear. Edith Wilson later reminisced that when her husband emerged from the briefing, he had said through clenched teeth: "House has given away everything I had won before we left Paris. He has compromised on every side, and so I have to start all over again and this time it will be harder, as he has given the impression that my delegates are not in sympathy with me."[93] Mrs. Wilson and her retainers spent the next twenty years denigrating House and his entourage; hence her account merits skeptical appraisal.[94] Yet Admiral Cary Grayson, Wilson's doctor and golfing partner, also reports Wilson telling the American commissioners that French claims for a buffer state presented an "embarrassment."[95] Wilson could not break sharply with House because he relied so greatly on the

---

88 House diary, Mar. 12, 1919. In suggesting a Channel tunnel, Lloyd George was blowing smoke. When the matter came up for review the next year, the Foreign Office advised that relations with France would probably never be sufficiently stable and friendly to justify construction of a tunnel. See Alan Sharp, "Britain and the Channel Tunnel, 1919–1920," *Australian Journal of Politics and History* 25 (Aug. 1979): 210–15.

89 Raymond Poincaré, *A la recherche de la paix 1919 (Au Service de la France, XI)* (Paris, 1974), 245.

90 Wilson to House, Mar. 10, 1919, *PWW,* 55:472.

91 Lord Robert Cecil diary, Mar. 16, 1919, Add. MSS. 51131, British Library, also *PWW,* 55:539.

92 House diary, Mar. 14, 1919.

93 Edith Bolling Wilson, *My Memoir* (Indianapolis, 1938), 245–6.

94 Mrs. Wilson's secular effort to burnish her husband's memory and to diminish House's place in the tradition of American internationalism forms a central theme of her papers at the Library of Congress, as well as the papers of Ray Stannard Baker (Library of Congress) and Bernard Baruch (Seeley Mudd Library, Princeton University).

95 Grayson diary, Mar. 14, 1919, *PWW,* 55:496–8. See also Cary T. Grayson, "The Colonel's Folly and the President's Distress," *American Heritage* 15 (Oct. 1964): 4–7, 94–101.

administrative apparatus that his chief adviser had created for him. Instead, a growing chill crept into the relationship. The president continued to call on House for specific services, but negotiated with the European premiers on the Rhineland and other matters increasingly on his own.[96]

Lloyd George called on Wilson at his assigned residence on the Place des Etats-Unis at noon of March 14. Contrary to George's prediction to the Cabinet ten days earlier, Wilson did not reject a pact of military guarantee. The Anglo-Saxons therefore presented a united front on the western boundary question in a tête-à-tête with Clemenceau later that afternoon. They told the Tiger that they refused any occupation of the left bank, except as a short-term and provisional guarantee for payment of the German debt. On the other hand, they offered an immediate military guarantee against "unprovoked aggression" by Germany against France.[97] Clemenceau asked for time to reflect, and huddled with his principal aides – Tardieu, Foreign Minister Stephen Pichon, and economics counselor Louis Loucheur – for two agonizing days at the War Ministry.

"We have to choose," the Tiger insisted, "either France on the left bank of the Rhine alone, or France reduced to the frontier of 1814, with Alsace-Lorraine and some if not all of the Saar, with America and England at our sides." Pichon and Tardieu straddled the fence: a paper alliance might not endure, yet who could take the responsibility of refusing? Loucheur favored acceptance: if France maintained three-year military service to guard the Rhine alone, that would mean 250,000 extra men withdrawn from the productive workforce and stifle economic growth. Clemenceau agreed with Loucheur. France needed wholesale reform of its administration and governing structures. He placed no faith in the current political class. A Rhineland occupation stretching onward to the indefinite future posed inordinate risks of clashes abroad and distractions from tasks at home. The best option was to seek a precise commitment from the Anglo-Saxons and

---

96 Floto, *Colonel House in Paris,* 164–214, may err in emphasizing substantive rather than personal reasons for the break. Edith Galt Wilson had long regarded House as a discomforting rival for her husband's attentions. She awaited a plausible opportunity to stick in the knife. In 1915 House had counseled his chief to postpone his engagement to Mrs. Galt for a year. The Republicans had collected evidence about Wilson's dalliance with a Bermuda socialite while his first wife remained alive and about later payments to help the lady buy a fruit farm. House worried that the story might blow before the 1916 election if Wilson married a woman with a Gibson-girl figure and a fourth-grade education. He relented when he grasped the depths of Wilson's loneliness, though he skipped the wedding ceremony. The bride, one of the most rancorous of women in a country that boasted many of them, neither forgave nor forgot. See House diary, June 24, July 31, Sept. 22, Oct. 1, Nov. 22, Nov. 27, Dec. 15, Dec. 18, 1915.

97 Lloyd George, *Memoirs of the Peace Conference,* 1:265–6; Tardieu, *Truth About the Treaty,* 176–8; General J. Mordacq, *Le Ministère Clemenceau, journal d'un témoin* (Paris, 1931), 3:173–4. No one took notes at these meetings.

to bargain for whatever juridical sureties they could save. The premier thus instructed Tardieu and Pichon to draw up a long memorandum "accepting" the offer of a guarantee treaty but setting forth a laundry-list of conditions. France insisted on the boundaries of 1814 including the Saar and Landau, the extension of the guarantee to Belgium, demilitarization of both banks of the Rhine, permanent enforcement by an Inspection Commission, occupation of the left bank and five bridgeheads for thirty years as collateral for the financial clauses, and the right to reoccupy after that time if Germany violated its military pledges.[98]

For the next five weeks Clemenceau and his team carried on the diplomatic equivalent of trench warfare, fighting on a confusing and smoke-filled battlefield to advance the line foot by foot while facing danger from every side. President Wilson could not stand the chivvying and wheedling of his Gallic interlocutors. "It was intolerable talking to them; it was like pressing your finger into an india-rubber ball. You tried to make an impression but as soon as you moved your finger the ball was as round as ever."[99] The president nevertheless made strenuous efforts to keep his preternatural rigidity in check and to examine each specific proposal on its merits, insofar as that proved conciliable with his principles. The British, by contrast, thought the French effort to build a barrier on the Rhine fundamentally misconceived. Balfour encapsulated Whitehall's deepest convictions in a prophetic memorandum.

Everyone admired Balfour's exquisite manners, cultural attainments, and evident goodwill. And yet the foreign secretary also had the defects of his qualities. He approached the world, as Foch's chief of staff observed, like a man peering down from the gondola of a balloon, noticing "the little Allied ants fighting the little German ants and wondering at the curiosity of the scene."[100] Balfour declined to accept the view that arms control would fail, that the League of Nations would prove impotent, or that Germany would organize itself for revenge. In any event, he insisted on March 18, the French were looking through the wrong end of the telescope:

If international relations and international methods are, as the French assume, going to remain in the future what they have been in the past, and if what civilisation has to fear is the renewal without substantial modification of German ambition, it is in the East rather than in the West that the storm will first break; and no attempt to

---

98 Loucheur, *Carnets secrets,* 71–3; Tardieu, *Truth About the Treaty,* 178–82. The text of the French note is in *PWW,* 56:9–14. On Loucheur's influence, see more generally Stephen Carls, *Louis Loucheur and the Shaping of Modern France, 1916–1931* (Baton Rouge, La., 1993), 150–71.

99 Lord Robert Cecil diary, Mar. 18, 1919, Add. MSS. 51131, British Library, also *PWW,* 56:81; similar comment to Grayson in *PWW,* 56:86.

100 Maxime Weygand, *Mémoires: mirages et réalité* (Paris, 1957), 2:26.

guard against the danger of the future can be deemed other than narrow and incomplete which concentrates its whole attention upon bridgeheads and strategic frontiers, upon the Rhine and the Treaty of 1814.... If Germany is ... going again to pursue a policy of world domination, it will no doubt tax all the statesmanship of the rest of the world to prevent a repetition of the calamities from which we have been suffering. But the only radical cure for this is a change in the international system of the world – a change which French statesmen ... regard with ill-concealed derision. They may be right; but if they are, it is quite certain that no manipulation of the Rhine frontier is going to make France anything more than a second-rate power, trembling at the nod of its great neighbours on the East, and depending from day to day on the changes and chances of a shifting diplomacy and uncertain alliances.[101]

Evidently Wilson did not think through the implications of the Treaty of Guarantee at first. He conceived it as a temporary expedient pending the organization of collective security through the League. It "really amounted to very little more than Article 10 of the Covenant," he confessed to Lord Robert Cecil.[102] Here House again jumped into the breach. For several days the president had kept him out of the loop. No one had informed him about the proposed Treaty of Guarantee. As late as March 17, he was still hawking his plan for a provisional buffer state with a League of Nations decision whether to allow self-determination to be postponed for five years.[103] On March 20, Clemenceau reopened this valuable channel to the American delegation, and House undertook to "champion" the security of France.

Clemenceau asked House to work out a satisfactory formula for the still fuzzy guarantee. House's staff crafted language that would cover an "invasion" of France; Clemenceau broadened the wording to provide for an "attack," which by implication might even apply to the demilitarized zone. On the whole the French seemed overjoyed. "A monument ought to be erected to you," the Tiger enthused. House deprecated the result. He had his doubts whether the American Senate would accept the treaty. "It is practically promising only what we promise to do in the League of Nations," he minuted confidentially, "but since Clemenceau does not believe in the League ... it may be necessary to give him a treaty on the outside."[104] The other American commissioners remained wary. They

---

101 Sir Arthur Balfour, "Memorandum Respecting Control of the Rhine," Mar. 18, 1919, *British Documents on Foreign Affairs: Reports and Papers from the Foreign Office Confidential Print*, pt. 2, ser. I/5 (Frederick, Md., 1989), doc. 127. The idea that France remained stuck in the past and that Germany would turn its ambitions eastward rapidly became Foreign Office orthodoxy. See, e.g., Curzon memo of conversation with Paul Cambon, Apr. 2, 1919, ibid., doc. 128.

102 Loucheur, *Carnets secrets*, 73 (Mar. 18, 1919); Cecil diary, Mar. 18, 1919, *PWW*, 56:81–2.

103 Conversation with Sir William Wiseman, House diary, Mar. 17, 1919.

104 House diary, Mar. 20, 22, 1919. Harold I. Nelson, *Land and Power: British and Allied Power on Germany's Frontiers, 1916–19* (London, 1963), 229–32, clarifies the murky diplomacy of these days.

remonstrated that such a pact would compromise the whole structure of the League; Henry White favored "a definite showdown" with France and opined that, failing agreement, the United States should sign a separate peace.[105] Within the next days, however, the British signed on to House's formulation, and on March 27 the president also accepted it. House felt obliged to warn that some would look upon the guarantee "as a direct blow at the League of Nations," but to his pleasure his chief did not recoil. In a moment of enthusiasm Wilson had committed himself to Clemenceau, and he felt bound by his promise.[106] It remained only to clarify the *casus foederis* and the duration of the guarantee.[107]

One vital matter thus approached settlement. Many related ones remained unresolved. Every time the conferees reached an impasse on some issue, an intricate web of previous compromises threatened to unravel. When decisions reached the Council of Four for final disposition, the premiers did not work in harmony.[108] In Bismarck's famous dictum, a statesman is "like a man wandering in a forest who knows his general direction, but not the exact point at which he will emerge from the wood."[109] Wilson and Clemenceau, though often at daggers drawn, at least knew where they wished to head. Lloyd George had no inner compass. That was his fatal flaw. The liberal journalist C. P. Scott had predicted that it would enable Wilson to control events. "George," he wrote, "is not a statesman, he is a pure opportunist, with a good many sound and generous instincts, but an opportunist to the hour. . . . He wants to be nice to France, but at a pinch he will always throw over France for America."[110] This proved an optimistic appraisal. As the conference lurched from one crisis to another during April, Wilson found Lloyd George "as slippery as an eel."[111] House tagged the Welshman "a mischief maker who changes his mind like a weathervane."[112] Yet in truth none of the principals

105 Meeting of the Commissioners Plenipotentiary, Mar. 21, 1919, *Papers Relating to the Foreign Relations of the United States: The Paris Peace Conference, 1919* (hereafter *FRUS-PPC*), 13 vols. (Washington, D.C., 1945–7), 11:131–2.
106 House diary, Mar. 27, 1919.
107 See the conversation of Wilson, Clemenceau, Lloyd George, Orlando, and Tardieu, Mar. 27, 1919, in Paul Mantoux, *Deliberations of the Council of Four (March 24–June 28, 1919): Notes of the Official Interpreter*, trans. and ed. Arthur S. Link, with the assistance of Manfred F. Boemeke, 2 vols. (Princeton, N.J., 1992), 1:39–42. The other American commissioners remained unreconciled to the decision and made no secret of their skepticism. General Tasker Bliss whispered to the British CIGS on March 31 that "it was a scandalous thing that the president did not make it clear that neither he nor the Senate nor the people of U.S.A. would form an Alliance with France." See Sir Henry Wilson diary, Mar. 31, 1919, IWM.
108 *Deliberations of the Council of Four*, passim.
109 Heinrich Friedjung, *Der Kampf um die Vorherrschaft in Deutschland 1859 bis 1866* (Stuttgart, 1905), 2:565.
110 C. P. Scott to House, Mar. 16, 1919, *PWW*, 55:545–6.
111 Grayson diary, Apr. 23, 1919, *PWW*, 58:3.
112 Ibid.

appraised the others charitably. Lloyd George evaluated Wilson as a badly mixed compound of noble visionary, unscrupulous partisan, and bigoted sectarian.[113] Clemenceau told a newsman that Wilson considered himself "another Jesus Christ come upon the earth to reform men."[114] The president classified the Tiger among the "mad men."[115] Even House, while praising Clemenceau as "the ablest reactionary" in Paris, declared that it was almost hopeless to deal with him except in ways that "we hope to make forever obsolete."[116] This personal dissonance at the top assumed vital importance because, as House justly observed, the other delegates "might just as well be in Patagonia."[117]

Lloyd George, who had pushed for high reparations and other punitive clauses to benefit the British Empire, precipitated a first great crisis by reversing himself in late March. After closeting himself for the weekend with liberal advisers at Fontainebleau, he presented an alarmist memorandum. He decried all thoughts of occupying the Reich. He conjured up the specter of "spartacism from the Urals to the Rhine" if the Allies failed to offer an equitable peace. He even predicted "a huge red army attempting to cross the Rhine."[118] The real agenda here became manifest when Lloyd George read out a letter from Smuts to the Council of Four: "The fact is, the Germans are, have been, and will continue to be, the *dominant factor* on the Continent of Europe, and no permanent peace is possible which is not based on that fact."[119] Lloyd George aimed his hardest shafts at the proposed Eastern frontiers; what would wound the Germans most, he said, was the prospect of abandoning millions of fellow citizens to Polish domination. But he also adumbrated a general argument about justice. Clemenceau responded that "what we find fair here in this room will not necessarily be accepted as such by the Germans." The Tiger insisted that the Allies dared not ignore strategic considerations; George retorted in turn that he wouldn't take the advice of a political naïf like Marshall Foch about "how to insure the greatest possible security to nations." The debate went round and round. When the premiers approached specific questions each wound up the gramophone again.[120]

113 Lloyd George, *Memoirs of the Peace Conference,* 1:145–6.
114 Ibid.
115 Vance McCormick diary, May 15, 1919, Yale University Library, also *PWW,* 59:173.
116 House diary, Apr. 1, 1919; also further witticisms in ibid., Apr. 28, 1919.
117 House diary, Apr. 5, 1919.
118 Lloyd George memorandum, Mar. 25, 1919, in *PWW,* 56:259–70; Lloyd George, *Memoirs of the Peace Conference,* 1:266–74.
119 Smuts to Lloyd George, Mar. 26, 1919, in *Selections from the Smuts Papers,* ed. W. K. Hancock and Jean van der Poel (Cambridge, 1966), 1:83–7; *Deliberations of the Council of Four,* Mar. 27, 1919, 1:38.
120 Conversation among Wilson, Clemenceau, Lloyd George, and Orlando, Mar. 27, 1919, in *Deliberations of the Council of Four,* 1:38.

The four came near to a rupture on March 28 in discussing the Saar.
Clemenceau proposed the annexation of the Saarland as well as the strategic salient of Landau to France. Wilson acknowledged that France deserved
the output of the Saar coal mines in compensation for the pits that the
enemy had systematically destroyed in the Nord and Pas-de-Calais, but he
dug in his heels against additional concessions. "If you try to establish borders according to historical or strategic – and, I will add, economic – considerations, there will be no limit to the claims." The Allies should not
interpret their Armistice commitments to self-determination with "a
lawyer's cunning." At one point Clemenceau called the president pro-
German, and the latter threatened to go home.[121] It took two weeks' hard
bargaining until the experts fashioned a compromise giving France ownership of the mines, providing for League government of the Saarland with a
plebiscite in fifteen years, and leaving Landau anchored in the Reich.[122]
Discussions did not go smoothly. As the British expert Headlam-Morley
remarked, the difficulties arose "not so much from the people at the top, but
from the technical experts, who deal with matters of finance and mining
and such things; they bargain like Jews and they generally are Jews, and it is
they who try to insert all these intolerable petty conditions."[123] Yet despite
the excursions and alarms, neither side really contemplated a break over the
Saar. Early on, House forced Wilson to acknowledge that his own experts
advocated a reasonable accommodation of French desiderata, while Tardieu
admitted privately to a publisher that it was "silliness" to hold out integrally
for the borders of 1814.[124]

Ultimately, prospects for a successful resolution of Western frontiers
turned on finding some workable compromise for military defense of the
Rhine. Foch made a dramatic appearance before the Council of Four on
March 31 and renewed his call for permanent occupation of the Rhine line,
on the ground that British and American aid could never arrive quickly
enough to stave off a surprise invasion.[125] Two days later, Tardieu cranked

121 See conversation of Mar. 28, 1919, in *Deliberations of the Council of Four,* 55–68, and the recapitu-
  lation of the harsh words not memorialized in the transcript in ibid., 54–5.
122 See Tardieu, *Truth About the Treaty,* 250–79; Nelson, *Land and Power,* 249–81; Headlam-Morley,
  Memoir of the Paris Peace Conference, esp. 55–75; and C. H. Haskins, "The New Boundaries of Germany," in Edward M. House and Charles Seymour, eds., *What Really Happened at Paris* (New York,
  1921), 56–66.
123 Headlam-Morley to George Saunders (Foreign Office), Apr. 13, 1919, in Headlam-Morley, *Memoir of the Paris Peace Conference,* 74–5.
124 See Wilson's acknowledgment in the House diary, Apr. 2, 1919; and Tardieu's Apr. 2 conversation
  with Jules Sauerwein of *Le Matin* in Poincaré, *A la recherche de la paix,* 310. Note also Wilson's April
  8 appeal "not to let world peace be hung up on this question of the Saar," in *Deliberations of the Council of Four,* 194.
125 Foch memorandum in *PWW,* 56:445–9; appearance before the Council in *Deliberations of the Council of Four,* 1:86–9.

out another memorandum that sought to double the depth of the demilitarized zone, fortify inspection procedures, codify guidelines for League
review of violations, and bring the guarantee pact into operation if Germany contravened a long list of military stipulations.[126] Both Wilson and
Lloyd George remained wholly unmoved. When the president fell ill with
influenza and had to deputize House to sit on the Council of Four, he took
care to have his wife telephone the colonel and order him not to make commitments on the question of the Rhine.[127] On April 12, Wilson despatched
a peremptory message saying that he had already made his maximum concession on French security and telling the Tiger to take it or leave it.[128]

Clemenceau, however, retained one more arrow in his quiver. He let fly
with exquisite timing on April 14. By a great stroke of luck, the targets all
moved into perfect alignment. Reparations discussions had sufficiently
advanced so that the conferees had to decide what sureties to require for
payment. Lloyd George had left for London to quell a domestic squall. And
Wilson had displaced his moral fervor onto the Italians, who were fighting
his preferred solution for Fiume and threatening to go home. The Tiger
called on House for an ostentatious "love-feast." He proposed to accept the
president's terms for protection of France and the west bank of the Rhine.
They were "not what he wanted," but he thought them sufficient. He was
willing to fight Foch and his other marshals provided the president agreed
to a French occupation of three Rhineland zones, the first for five years, the
second for ten, and the last for fifteen years. Foch, he added, had "no sense."
If Wilson closed the deal, he could "beat his marshals in the Chamber of
Deputies and the Senate," and he would praise the president's generosity in
public. Adding frosting to the cake, he also promised to follow the American lead in Asiatic Turkey and in the neutral revictualing of Russia.[129]

Here was an offer that the hard-pressed Wilson, overwhelmed with erup-
tions and obstructions from Fiume to Shantung, could not easily refuse.
The president made a "wry face," but agreed. House prompted that "we had
better do it with a 'beau geste' rather than grudgingly," though graciousness
did not come easily to his sternly puritan chief. House left for the rue St.-
Dominique to bring Clemenceau the happy tidings. The premier immediately gave the order to a dozen newspapers on the government payroll that
"all attacks of every description on President Wilson and the United States
must cease"; relations between the two countries were "the very best."[130]

126 Text out of chronological order in *PWW,* 57:295–6.
127 House diary, Apr. 4, 1919.
128 Wilson memorandum, Apr. 8, 1919, *PWW,* 57:130–1; Wilson to House with message for Tardieu,
   Apr. 12, 1919, *PWW,* 57:295–8.
129 House diary, Apr. 14, 1919.
130 Ibid., Apr. 15, 1919.

By any standard, Wilson had made a remarkable concession. The writer
Rudyard Kipling had quipped disparagingly to Republican friends that the
conference marked the first time he had witnessed an attempt to apply
"the principles of Chautauqua to the practises of Armageddon."[131] The
Rhineland deal suggested otherwise. When push came to shove, Wilson
studied his dossiers carefully and forced himself to deal. Lloyd George
erupted in fury when he returned to Paris, but he failed to shake the president. "You mustn't think that we'll leave British troops in Germany for fifteen years," George warned the Council of Four. Clemenceau shot back: all
he required was "one battalion and a flag." On April 22 the bargain was
sealed.[132]

And yet one ragged loophole remained, through which the British and
Americans would eventually wriggle out of their commitments. The other
American commissioners had never moderated their hostility to the Treaty
of Guarantee. Henry White warned Wilson on April 16 that it would evoke
passionate criticism at home both from opponents of "entangling alliances"
and from advocates of the League. He pleaded with Wilson to separate the
American from the British obligation. Wilson replied that he had never contemplated a joint arrangement with Great Britain and had merely pledged to
"try" to get a separate treaty through.[133] The text approved on April 22, as
opposed to the French first draft, provided for separate treaties.[134]

Three days later, seeking to provide for the eventuality that something
might go wrong with the Anglo-Saxon undertakings, Clemenceau proposed broad new language. If after fifteen years the guarantees against
unprovoked aggression were "not considered satisfactory" by the Allied and
associated governments, Germany must consent to accept "such similar
guarantees as they may require." Lloyd George immediately labeled this
open-ended formulation "dangerous."[135] Nonetheless, with the legal drafting committee already immersed in its labors, the French continued to
push. On April 30, after a discussion so secret that the secretaries Hankey

131 Kipling's views relayed in Prof. Brander Matthews to Henry Cabot Lodge, May 2, 1919, box 54,
    Lodge papers, Massachusetts Historical Society.
132 Lloyd George, *Memoirs of the Peace Conference,* 280–1; Clemenceau memorandum, Apr. 20, 1919,
    in *PWW,* 57:525; *Deliberations of the Council of Four,* Apr. 22, 1919, 318–19.
133 Henry White to Wilson, Apr. 16, and Wilson to White, Apr. 17, 1919, in *PWW,* 57:416–18,
    430.
134 Cf. the wording in *PWW,* 57:525 and *PWW,* 57:592. Mantoux's notes, in *Deliberations of the Coun-
    cil of Four,* 1:318, are vague on this point. However, Sir Maurice Hankey's minutes replicate Wil-
    son's warning that it was "not wise" to have a tripartite treaty and Lloyd George's endorsement of
    that view. See *FRUS-PPC,* 5:114.
135 Notes of a meeting at President Wilson's residence, Apr. 25, 1919, 6:30 p.m., in *FRUS-PPC,*
    5:244–8; omitted from *Deliberations of the Council of Four.* Nelson, *Land and Power,* 243–5, did
    invaluable work in disentangling the paper trail on this subject, since Mantoux's notes of the Coun-
    cil of Four do not delve into the legal boilerplate.

and Mantoux were ordered to leave the room, the conferees agreed that if guarantees were not considered satisfactory fifteen years hence, evacuation might be delayed to "the extent regarded as necessary for the purpose of obtaining the required guarantees."[136]

At this stage in final drafting, the Big Three (Orlando having departed) were flying by the seat of their pants. Not one of them consulted his military advisers about the practical workings of the occupation, still less of the guarantee. Field Marshal Wilson described Lloyd George as totally "out of his depth." The CIGS deemed the occupation wrongly structured, with the most valuable areas scheduled for evacuation first. Foch denounced all the "Frocks" as "mad."[137] But events had bypassed the military. With the German delegation already cooling its heels at Versailles, further discussion focused purposefully on the niceties of drafting.

President Wilson argued on May 9 that the conferees' original intention was to have Article 430 concerning reoccupation apply only to the reparations clauses. Clemenceau wearily gave way. The final formulation authorized reoccupation in the event the Reparation Commission found that Germany "refuses to observe the whole or part of her obligations for reparation."[138] The convoluted drafting history of Article 430 would lead to much debate among legal advisers at the respective Foreign Offices during the coming decade. What did it really allow? At the end of March, Wilson had nobly adjured his colleagues not to "interpret our promises with a lawyer's cunning." Yet in the end, as so often happens in international affairs, naked power and lawyers' cunning is all.[139]

---

136 *FRUS-PPC*, 5:357.
137 Henry Wilson diary, Apr. 27–May 3, 1919, recapitulated with the juicy bits left out in Callwell, *Field-Marshal Sir Henry Wilson*, 2:184–7.
138 Notes of meetings held at President Wilson's House on May 9, 10, and 12, 1919, *FRUS-PPC*, 5:519–20, 541–2, 576.
139 In later years, the participants could not themselves agree on the proper interpretation of their handiwork. For example, in 1928 the Wilhelmstrasse asserted that, because Germany was currently fulfilling the stipulations of the Dawes Plan, the Allies were bound under Article 431 to evacuate the Rhineland forthwith. Article 431 provided textually that "if before the expiration of the period of fifteen years Germany complies with all the undertakings resulting from the present treaty, the occupying forces will be withdrawn immediately." Lloyd George, who by this time had embraced revisionism, volubly supported the German argument. Foreign Secretary Sir Austen Chamberlain disputed it. Privately, Foreign Office professionals who had attended the peace conference joined in outrage against Lloyd George, but bickered about the fine points themselves. Headlam-Morley maintained that Article 431, which the French and Americans had drafted without British input, "has no meaning and probably was intended to have no meaning." Everyone, he insisted, understood that the occupation would continue for a minimum of fifteen years. Legal Adviser Sir Cecil Hurst did not consider the provision meaningless, but read it as requiring the prior discharge of Germany's entire reparations obligation. Notwithstanding a formal opinion by Law Officers of the Crown, the political controversy continued to simmer. See FO 371/12905–12906: C8739/9105/9141/9304/969/18; also House of Commons *Debates*, Nov. 13 and Dec. 3, 1928; and *The Times* (London), Nov. 17, 1928.

VI

From the middle of March onward, Clemenceau had to fight on a second front, one strewn with as many land mines as the perilous Council of Four. President Poincaré, Marshall Foch, and the nationalist wing of the Chamber began to fear that Clemenceau would give too much away and obtain too little in return. The Paris rumor mills worked overtime. Oppressed by the country's sacrifices and sufferings, the critics did not focus gladly on France's economic exhaustion and circumscribed power. Nor did they concern themselves with the need to establish priorities and make disagreeable trade-offs. Anxious and captious pessimists fretted about reparations, trade, Poland, the Habsburg successor states, Syria, and a host of other matters, large and small. Most of all they worried about security on the Rhine.[140]

Clemenceau made little attempt to educate public opinion. There were several reasons for this. The Tiger did not wish to make damaging admissions that might weaken his hand with Wilson and Lloyd George. At his advanced age, he also felt compelled to husband his energies. In any case, he nurtured an undissembled contempt for his long-time colleagues at the Palais Bourbon. Lastly, he habitually played a lone game. When asked which generals he considered the greatest, he promptly replied, "none of them."[141] He pretended not to remember the name of Foreign Minister Pichon.[142] He failed to extend full confidence even to André Tardieu. While he considered Tardieu an "able fellow" and hoped to tap him as his successor, he feared that this faithful deputy had "no knowledge of men." "France is so short of great men," he confessed to Colonel House, "that I cannot think of anyone who would make a suitable president, or one who would be better than Poincaré, bad as he is."[143] Not surprisingly, Clemenceau's numerous enemies traded one animadversion for another. When a diplomat reported that the Council of Four would henceforth treat all major matters, Poincaré found the news terrifying. "Clemenceau, owing to his deafness and ignorance, is incapable alone of defending French interests."[144]

Scrupulously bureaucratic, fustily legalistic, highly respectful of Third Republic precedents and prerogatives, largely oblivious of the world outside the hexagon, Poincaré figured in many respects as the polar opposite of Clemenceau.[145] Rarely consulted by the premier and hobbled by his own

140 See Pierre Miquel's thorough survey, *La Paix de Versailles et l'opinion publique française,* esp. 215–418.
141 House diary, Apr. 14, 1919.
142 Ibid., Apr. 28, 1919.
143 Ibid., Mar. 10, 1919.
144 Poincaré diary, Mar. 25, 1919, *A la recherche de la paix,* 278.
145 Pierre Miquel, *Poincaré* (Paris, 1961).

belief in limited executive power, Poincaré flustered and fumed at the Elysée with little opportunity to affect events. Busily composing his diary in a scratchy, minuscule hand, Poincaré described the Tiger as morally blind, a catspaw of the Anglo-Saxons, a sleepwalker, a scatterbrain, a swelled head, and a blunderer who had signed the Armistice prematurely and might now be leading the country into the abyss. Day by day he cumulated his imprecations, scoring the premier for bureaucratic confusion, secretiveness, vanity, and refusal to listen to others.[146] On more than one occasion, the two men exchanged juvenile insults, calling each other impudent liars and threatening mutually to resign.[147] Poincaré also kept an open door at the Elysée for those who nourished his anxieties, and many were those who crossed the threshold to criticize or complain. Maurice Paléologue attacked the premier as a regular Calamity Jane (homme pour catastrophe).[148] Camille Barrère thought him a soft-headed dodderer who belonged in an insane asylum.[149] Foch denounced the Tiger on April 15 as "a nervous, weak old man" who sought a "lesser France."[150] In the final analysis, however, Poincaré shied away from a *fronde*. Not only did he hold that his constitutional position restricted his maneuvering room. He also feared that, should the Tiger fall, the Chamber might turn to a ministry of "abandonment and liquidation" under Aristide Briand or, perish the thought, Joseph Caillaux.[151]

All the same, Poincaré saw eye to eye with Foch on the importance of the Rhine line. When Clemenceau told the president on March 27 that he considered demilitarization of the right bank more important than occupation of the left, he could scarcely believe his ears.[152] Poincaré expressed similar incredulity at the moment of Clemenceau's greatest triumph. On the evening of April 15, the Tiger phoned breathlessly to announce Wilson's concession on occupation: "I have the fifteen years. Now I consider that the peace is made!" The president remained stonily unmoved. "Where is the alliance? Where are the precise texts?"[153]

In the second half of April, Foch screwed up his courage and crossed the Rubicon. In France, the principle of civilian control over the military had stood inviolate since the ignominious collapse of the boomlet for General

---

146 Poincaré diary, Mar. 27, Apr. 6, Apr. 23–5, 1919, *A la recherche de la paix,* 287, 321, 323–4, 368–77.
147 See Poincaré's scrupulously detailed notes on the mutual screaming fit that took place on Apr. 6, 1919, *A la recherche de la paix,* 315–24.
148 *A la recherche de la paix,* Mar. 27, 1919, 287.
149 Ibid., Apr. 26, 1919, 374.
150 Ibid., Apr. 15, 1919, 335.
151 Ibid., Apr. 2 and 24, 1919, 305, 371.
152 Ibid., Mar. 27, 1919, 285.
153 Ibid., Apr. 15, 1919, 337.

Boulanger in 1887. Sophisticated military men transgressed that principle at
their peril. They knew that Germany had come to grief in part because,
since the days of Moltke the Elder, the Oberste Heeresleitung had thrown
the teachings of Clausewitz to the winds and assumed the prerogatives of
policy makers.[154] Foch, however, burned with inner conviction. The future
of the country hung in the balance. On April 16 he notified the presidents
of the Chamber and the Senate that Clemenceau had become a danger for
France. "He is tired and doesn't understand the questions. He gives way on
everything."[155] Foch demanded convocation of the Council of Ministers
and offered himself, if necessary, for the succession. The next day he spoke
to Poincaré and others of indicting Clemenceau for treason before the High
Court.[156]

During the next eight days plotters and counter-plotters, peacemakers
and rumor-mongers shuttled back and forth between the Palais Bourbon,
the Elysée, and Clemenceau's headquarters on the rue St.-Dominique. This
activity, all the same, held less significance than met the eye. The Tiger
remained the master of the scene. The president of the Republic, to be sure,
sent numerous carping letters to Pichon. After reviewing the texts with a
lawyer's gimlet eye, Poincaré warned that the alliances had at best a moral
value. There was no guarantee that the Anglo-Saxons would ratify, and no
stipulation for the timely despatch of their troops. France risked abandoning the reality of security for its shadow. Moreover, an occupation limited
to fifteen years offered inadequate collateral for a reparation schedule that
would surely last for thirty. Poincaré proposed, in sum, to delay prescribing
any limit for the occupation until the Reich had met all its engagements and
the Allies had devised precise military accords.[157] Yet the long-building
showdown between Foch and Clemenceau ended with a whimper. At the
Council of Ministers on April 25, Foch said his piece and was sent about
his business. Poincaré sat silent. While Foch raged on in an antechamber
about treason, the ministers unanimously backed Clemenceau.[158]

Clemenceau carried the day with a double argument. On the one hand,
he maintained that, with the rapid evolution of aircraft and long-range
artillery, occupation of the Rhine line no longer retained the strategic
importance it had enjoyed in the era of the foot-soldier. On the other, he

154 See Gerhard Ritter, *Staatskunst und Kriegshandwerk: Das Problem des Militarismus in Deutschland,* 4
vols. (Munich, 1968).
155 *A la recherche de la paix,* Apr. 16, 1919, 338.
156 Ibid., Apr. 17, 1919, 343.
157 Memorandum for Clemenceau, Apr. 23, 1919, *A la recherche de la paix,* 363–7.
158 There is a large literature on this meeting, nicely summarized by King, *Foch Versus Clemenceau,*
61–4. For Foch's side of the story, see Weygand, *Mirages et réalité,* 46–8.

predicted that the occupation would go on. Turning to Poincaré, the Tiger proclaimed dramatically: "Fifteen years from now I shall be dead. In fifteen years, the Germans will not have executed all the clauses of the treaty. And in fifteen years, if you do me the honor to visit my grave, I am sure that you will tell me: 'We are on the Rhine, and we will remain there.'"[159]

Some scholars incline to the view that in late May and early June, the premier turned a blind eye to General Mangin's machinations on the Rhine in the hope of creating a buffer state through a coup.[160] Clemenceau strenuously denied the charge, and no evidence has turned up in the French archives to support it.[161] Doubtless Foch had visited the left bank and given Mangin a wink and a nod; Poincaré urged benevolent neutrality as well.[162] Yet Clemenceau focused intently in early June on preventing Lloyd George from undoing what had already been achieved. Playing the card of Allied solidarity at its highest value, he appealed to the Council of Four in terms that contradicted his earlier assurances to the Council of Ministers: "It is obvious that Germany can't fulfill her commitments in fifteen years. But when she has convinced us that she is truly disposed to fulfill them, and when she has given us the necessary guarantees, I will be ready to evacuate the left bank of the Rhine." He had stopped the fractious generals cold, said the Tiger. He would not yield to political opportunism. He asked his colleagues merely to recall that "in the union between France, England, and America, France herself is absolutely essential."[163]

How did Clemenceau really see the future? The Tiger had lived too eventful a life to believe in the predictability of long-term policy planning. International stability derived from continuing efforts over time. Here lay the true meaning of the balance of power. As he explained in his memoirs, France could only hope to make peace through "the agreement of four governments that did not necessarily . . . share the same views on the best way of creating a Europe of Right." The problem consisted not so much in drawing frontiers as in waiting "for future statesmen and for achievements

159 Although there was no official transcript, several ministers took notes. I follow the account in Mermeix (Gabriel Terrail), *Le Combat des trois* (Paris, 1922), 229–30. Bariéty, *Les Relations franco-allemandes*, 62, relying on the record of Jules Jeanneney, offers a variant rendition: "We have the right to reoccupy or prolong the occupation if we are not paid. I will make a prediction: Germany will go bankrupt and we will remain where we are, with the alliance. Take that down and recall it on my gravestone when I die."
160 See Stevenson's carefully hedged account in *French War Aims Against Germany*, 190–2.
161 See Clemenceau's acerbic dismissal of the Rhineland movement in *Grandeur and Misery*, 205–31; also the account by his young staff assistant, Georges Wormser, *La République de Clemenceau* (Paris, 1961), 343–6, 504–7; and the agnostic analysis by King, *Foch Versus Clemenceau*, 73–104.
162 Foch "Cahiers," May 16–31, 1919, Bibliothèque Nationale; Poincaré, *A la recherche de la paix*, May 23, 28, 30, 1919, 449–50, 463, 466–9; Clemenceau, *Grandeur and Misery*, 223–4.
163 *Deliberations of the Council of Four*, June 13, 1919, 438–41.

of will worthy of those that had enabled us to win the war."[164] Clemenceau
had struck the best deal he could for his country under the circumstances.
The deal he had struck did not work out. But so it is with many reasonable
choices – in diplomacy as in life.

VII

As is well known, the U.S. Senate failed to ratify the Versailles treaty. Wilson
could have secured ratification with amendments. But he preferred to see the
treaty go down to ignominious defeat rather than allow a single alteration in
his handiwork.[165] Until he came under pressure from Capitol Hill, the president did not even submit the special treaty with France for senatorial consideration. Democratic partisans ventured the supposition that "isolationists"
would never have accepted the Treaty of Guarantee. Such a claim rests on
pure conjecture. Internationalist Republicans like Root, Taft, and Lodge
were fully prepared to undertake specific and limited responsibilities consonant with the national interest, even though they repudiated the idea of making an open-ended commitment to the League. Senator Lodge, who managed the treaty fight in the Senate, regretted the president's refusal to
disentangle the issues. "It is a great pity that the treaty with France, cutting
out the reference to the League of course, should not be ratified," Lodge
observed in August. "I hope it may be. But the curse of the League is on it
and it is that which has delayed peace, it is that which endangers the treaty
with France, despite the fact that everyone feels as I do the profoundest gratitude to her and every desire to do everything we could for her."[166]

As the tragedy unfolded, Colonel House labored as best he could from
the sidelines for ratification of the treaty with reservations. The collapse of
his aspirations for American involvement in world affairs filled him with
mortification. "Things have gone badly since we were together," House confessed to Tardieu in July 1920, "and I am deeply humiliated over the turn

164 Clemenceau, *Grandeur and Misery,* 256–9.
165 See Lloyd E. Ambrosius, *Woodrow Wilson and the American Diplomatic Tradition: The Treaty Fight in Perspective* (Cambridge, 1987).
166 Lodge to Charles Prince, Aug. 25, 1919, box 54, Lodge papers. Given the depth of bipartisan sup-port for the Treaty of Guarantee, Ambassador Jusserand remained optimistic through the winter of 1920 that the Senate would eventually dissever it from the League and ratify a modified version. Owing to political passions let loose by the larger struggle, that did not happen. William Keylor, the closest student of the subject, describes the deliquescence of the Treaty of Guarantee as "mys-terious." See his "Rise and Demise of the Franco-American Guarantee Pact, 1919–1921," *Proceed-ings of the Annual Meeting of the Western Society for French History* 15 (1978): 367–77.

affairs have taken in our country. However, I still cherish the hope that every-thing will right itself. France has in America staunch and potent friends whose influence is sure to be felt in her behalf in the hour of need."[167] Wilson took a different view. Following the defeat of the League, he sought to have as little contact as possible with Europeans. He declined, to give one characteristic example, to appoint a minister to Bulgaria. "I have found the Bulgarians the most avaricious and brutal of the smaller nations," he notified the secretary of state, ". . . though for a long time my vote was with Rou-mania."[168] After he retired from office, the crippled ex-president withdrew ever more deeply into an isolationist shell. From his comfortable exile on "S" Street, he hurled thunderbolts at misbehaving foreigners. France drew his special ire. That country had become "the marplot of the world."[169] When Poincaré, now president of the council, occupied the Ruhr in 1923 to enforce compliance with the Versailles treaty, Wilson denounced his old nemesis with language fit to print in the *Kreuzzeitung.* Poincaré, he said, was a "skunk" and a "sneak." He hoped that Germany would "wipe [France] off the map."[170] Thus perished meanly the ideals of the Great Crusade.

France's relations with Great Britain also deteriorated in the postwar world. When the United States dropped the Treaty of Guarantee, Whitehall let slide its undertakings as well. In the next three years, the Cabinet fre-quently discussed reviving a pact, but rather as a way to control France, and not to protect that country.[171] Churchill elucidated the problem with his usual perspicacity in 1921: "The French Chauvinists were in the ascendant, and we might be confronted with a French government bent on attacking Germany in her hour of weakness, with the aid of Poland." That was "a very alarming possibility which we should do our utmost to prevent."[172] Lloyd George decided to offer a security pact in January 1922, in return for a long list of counter-concessions, largely to help the "thoughtful section of French opinion . . . fight the Chauvinist party." Yet the Cabinet now envisioned a substantially broader approach to the problem of European security. "Ger-many is to us the most important country in Europe not only on account

167 House to Tardieu, July 15, 1920, House papers 109/3754.
168 Wilson to Bainbridge Colby, Nov. 15, 1920, *PWW,* 66:367.
169 Ibid., Apr. 16, 1922, *PWW,* 68:26.
170 Wilson conversation with John R. Mott, Dec. 19, 1923, *PWW,* 68:502.
171 Sally Marks, "Ménage à trois: The Negotiations for an Anglo-French-Belgian Alliance in 1922," *International History Review* 4 (1982): 524–52. See also Sally Marks, "Mésentente Cordiale: The Anglo-French Relationship, 1921–1922," in Marta Petricioli, ed., *A Missed Opportunity? 1922: The Reconstruction of Europe* (Berne, 1995), 33–45.
172 Cab 40(21), Conclusions of the Cabinet, May 24, 1921, CAB 23/25.

Stephen A. Schuker

of our trade with her, but also because she is the key to the situation in Russia. By helping Germany we might under existing conditions expose ourselves to the charge of deserting France; but if France was our ally no such charge could be made."[173] Thirty-eight months after the last troops climbed from their fetid trenches on the Western front, this was indeed a new way to look at security on the Rhine.

173 Cab 1(22), Conclusions of the Cabinet, Jan. 10, 1922, CAB 23/29.

13

The Polish Question

PIOTR S. WANDYCZ

The term "question" is singularly appropriate when dealing with the sub-ject of Poland at the Paris Peace Conference, for it suggests wider issues than mere territorial demarcations. Indeed, this expression has acquired a special meaning different from the similarly sounding and much discussed Czech question (Česká otázka). The Polish question goes back to the partitions of the Polish-Lithuanian Commonwealth in the late eighteenth century and the demise of the old *Respublica* divided by Austria, Prussia, and Russia. It came to haunt Europe throughout much of the nineteenth century.

Poland's partitions were, in Edmund Burke's words, a "very great breach in the modern political system in Europe." The ensuing territorial changes brought Russia into the center of Europe and created conditions for a series of confrontations between it and the Habsburg monarchy. They paved the way for Prussia's greatness and eventually Germany's hegemony on the con-tinent. The partitions, as a Polish historian put it, "constituted a great up-heaval of the 'European system'; the Poles could recover their independence only within the frame of a new European upheaval on a similar or even greater scale."[1]

Throughout the nineteenth century the Poles were to follow again and again the advice given to them by Jean-Jacques Rousseau in his *Considéra-tions sur le gouvernement de Pologne:* If you cannot prevent being devoured, you must make sure that you will not be digested. The Poles rose up in insurrec-tion in 1794, 1806, 1830, 1846, 1848, and 1863. Most of these uprisings had international repercussions. Indeed, the great powers found themselves repeatedly confronted with the Polish question, and although at times they tried to ignore it, at others they were forced to seek at least a partial solution. The legitimist program of the Congress of Vienna is a case in point. Since Lord Castlereagh's suggestion that the historic commonwealth be recreated

1 Emanuel Mateusz Rostworowski, *Popioły i korzenie* (Cracow, 1983), 193.

in its 1772 borders was not taken seriously, a compromise solution was worked out that amounted to a redistribution of Polish territories. A Kingdom of Poland (unofficially referred to as the Congress Kingdom) was created and linked to Russia but enjoyed a fair amount of autonomy. Yet, in some respects the prepartition borders remained pertinent. At the Congress of Vienna itself, the concept of an independent Poland received lip service, at least, in a provision for free trade and communications within the 1772 frontiers and a recommendation that the partitioning grant recognition to their Polish subjects. Throughout the nineteenth century "Poland" meant the old Commonwealth not only to Poles of differing political persuasions but also to Karl Marx and Friedrich Engels. Both of them insisted, in 1848 and later, on the rebirth of Poland within at least its historic borders. Rejecting the application of the principle of nationality ("a Russian invention concocted to destroy Poland"), they invoked the right of national existence for the historic peoples of Europe.[2]

As for the Poles, their conception of Poland had evolved from a historic Polish state inhabited by Poles (seen in political, *not* ethnic, terms) to that of a unitary or federalized Poland. A sincere democrat and Marx's friend, the great historian Joachim Lelewel believed that the "Ukrainian, Kashubian, Ruthenian, Great or Little Pole, Lithuanian . . . or the son of whatever land of the old *Rzeczpospolita*" was a Pole.[3] This view was held by progressive Poles for a good part of the nineteenth century. After the revival of the Lithuanian, Ukrainian, and to a lesser extent Belorussian national identity, the Polish Left came to believe that Poland could only be resurrected as a voluntary federation of the nations of the old commonwealth. The Polish Right, which toward the end of the century began to subscribe to the ideology of integral nationalism and social Darwinism, saw a reborn Poland as a centralized state in which the process of polonization, interrupted by the partitions, could be brought to completion. The names of socialist leader Józef Piłsudski and national democratic leader Roman Dmowski came to personify these two different approaches.

In the fifty years before the outbreak of the First World War, the Polish question virtually disappeared from the European international agenda.[4]

2 See *Neue Rheinische Zeitung,* Aug. 20, 1848; and *Commonwealth,* May 31, 1866. For their other views on Poland, see Karl Marx and Friedrich Engels, *The Russian Menace to Europe,* ed. Paul W. Blackstock and Bert F. Hoselitz (Glencoe, Ill., 1952); and Marx, *Manuskripte über die polnische Frage, 1863–1864,* ed. Werner Conze and Dieter Hertz-Eichenrode (The Hague, 1961).

3 Cited in Piotr S. Wandycz, *The Lands of Partitioned Poland, 1795–1918* (Seattle, 1974), 148. On the changing notions of Polish patriotism and nationalism, see the numerous writings of Andrzej Walicki, particularly *The Enlightenment and the Birth of Modern Nationhood* (Notre Dame, Ind., 1989), and *The Three Traditions in Polish Patriotism and Their Contemporary Relevance* (Bloomington, Ind., 1988).

4 The disappearance was not complete, and for its continued, albeit greatly reduced, presence in the minds of European statesmen, see the monumental trilogy of Henryk Wereszycki, *Sojusz trzech*

Indeed, it was difficult to say what was Poland and who belonged to the Polish nation after a hundred or so years of its not being on the political map of Europe. To Westerners, Poland came to be identified with and restricted to the Russian-ruled Congress Kingdom. As for the Poles themselves, they differed widely in their vision of Poland, final goals, and possible strategies for achieving them, yet their leaders were determined to raise the Polish question again as the outbreak of the war in August 1914 heralded the end of the prevailing balance of power.

Since this was a war in which two partitioners (the Central Powers) faced the third (Russia), it was bound to internationalize the Polish question, whether Berlin, Vienna, St. Petersburg, and their allies wished it or not.[5] Appealing to the Polish subjects of their enemies, German, Austrian, and Russian commanders began a game in which bids and antes were to be raised, although the belligerents seldom intended to fulfill their promises. The first such move was made by the Russians, and it took the form of an appeal signed by the commander in chief, Grand Duke Nikolai Nikolaievich. Couched in ringing words, it called on the Polish people to become united again under the scepter of the Russian emperor and spoke of autonomy and religious and linguistic freedoms. The appeal seemed to stir the basic hopes of Dmowski and his supporters who believed that Germany constituted the greatest threat to Poland, and who were determined to link Poland's fate with the cause of the Franco-Russian alliance. The French, however, treated the Polish issue timidly, fully aware that Russia's determination would not welcome any interference in what it regarded as its domestic affair. Making grudging and half-hearted concessions only when forced by events to do so, the Russians followed an essentially negative policy. As Nikolai Maklakov put it, the aim was not to satisfy the Poles but to keep them from separating.[6] Deeds failed to follow words, and even the czar's order of the day of December 25, 1916 – the most far-reaching statement concerning the creation of a free Poland "composed of all three now divided parts" – was issued when Russia no longer controlled any Polish lands.

In appraising Petrograd's Polish policy before 1917 one can hardly improve on Alexander Dallin's epitaph for the fallen regime:

The tsarist government passed from the state of history without having fulfilled its modest promises to Poland, without having satisfied the aspirations of those Poles

cesarzy, 1886–1872 (Warsaw, 1965); Walka o pokój europejski (Warsaw, 1971); and Koniec sojuszu trzech cesarzy (Warsaw, 1977).

5 Major treatments of the Polish issues in World War I include: Titus Komarnicki, Rebirth of the Polish Republic (London, 1957); Wiktor Sukiennicki, East-Central Europe During World War I (Boulder, Colo., 1984); and several studies in Polish listed in the bibliographic essay in Piotr S. Wandycz, Polish Diplomacy, 1914–1945: Aims and Achievements (London, 1988).

6 Cited in Piotr S. Wandycz, Soviet–Polish Relations, 1917–1921 (Cambridge, Mass., 1969), 33.

who have been favorably inclined toward it, without having succeeded in keeping the Polish issue an internal Russian problem and without having made use of the issue for its own political advantage.[7]

Small wonder that Dmowski, who left the Congress Kingdom after it was conquered by the Central Powers in 1915, concentrated all his efforts on the Western Allies. His original program of seeking the unification of all Polish lands under Russian control now included demands for complete national independence.

The response this brought from Berlin, which jointly controlled Congress Poland with the Austrians, made it clear that the fortunes of war and not political designs were forcing it to deal with the Polish problem. Chancellor Bethmann-Hollweg admitted that an "advantageous and satisfactory solution . . . does not exist for us at all."[8] The existing options were to return the kingdom (minus a strategic border strip) to Russia or to create an autonomous kingdom closely associated with one of the Central Powers, with compensations for the other. This second alternative became subsequently linked with the *Mitteleuropa* scheme. As one author aptly put it, "the way to *Mitteleuropa* led over Poland."[9] The immense difficulties of reaching an agreement made Berlin and Vienna resort to a palliative that carried with it the possibility of raising a Polish army on their side.

On November 5, 1916, the Two Emperors' Manifesto announced the creation of a self-governing Polish Kingdom, with its exact territorial links to the Central Powers and the nature of its administration to be determined later. An appeal followed calling for a volunteer Polish armed force. While the manifesto was a statement of intentions rather than a political arrangement, it internationalized the Polish question to a point of no return. What is more, it placed the Poles in a position of being courted by both belligerent camps, even if the courting was subordinated to wartime exigencies and did not represent genuine concern for Poland.

While no pro-German option existed among the Poles themselves, Galician Poles had expressed interest in an Austro-Polish program tying the future Poland to a trialist restructuring of the Habsburg monarchy. This solution was blocked from the beginning by Budapest, which was unwill-

---

7 "The Future of Poland," in Alexander Dallin et al., *Russian Diplomacy and Eastern Europe, 1914–1917* (New York, 1963), 74–5.

8 Cited in Werner Conze, *Polnische Nation und deutsche Politik im ersten Weltkrieg* (Cologne, 1958), 80.

9 P. R. Sweet, "Germany, Austria, and Mitteleuropa, August 1919–April 1916," in Hugo Hantsch and Alexander Novotny, eds., *Festschrift für Heinrich Benedikt* (Vienna, 1957), 206. Cf. Fritz Fischer's remark: "Poland was a key to German hegemony in Europe," in *Germany's Aims in the First World War* (New York, 1967), 523. See also Imanuel Geiss, *Der polnische Grenzstreifen, 1914–1918: Ein Beitrag zur deutschen Kriegszielpolitik im Ersten Weltkrieg* (Lübeck, 1960).

ing to abandon the existing dualist arrangement, and by Berlin, which was worried about future Polish claims upon Prussian Poland. At first glance, it seemed that Piłsudski was following the Austro-Polish path. The legions that he commanded fought on the side of the Central Powers; he agreed to head the military department within the Provisional State Council in Warsaw called into existence by Germany and Austria after their November manifesto. Yet, Piłsudski's motive in cooperating with the Central Powers was purely tactical and carried weight as long as Russian might was not broken. He thought that the impossible might happen: a defeat of Russia by Germany and Austria, and the subsequent defeat of the latter by the West. But whatever happened, the three partitioning powers were likely to be exhausted to such a degree that a small and determined Polish force would be able to create a fait accompli. Raising the ante in his political poker game with the Central Powers, Piłsudski opposed the creation of a large Polish army on their side unless and until all Polish political demands aiming at full independence were satisfied.

The outbreak of the February Revolution in Russia meant for Piłsudski that Germany and Austria now constituted the main obstacle to Poland's aims. Indeed, a conflict with the Germans was unavoidable: in July 1917 they arrested and placed him in confinement at the fortress of Magdeburg. But they had to make some further concessions to the Poles in the Congress Kingdom; notably, they established a regency council and a council of ministers. These two bodies and the now sizable Polish army on the side of the Central Powers became a weapon in the hands of Piłsudski's adversary Dmowski in his efforts to gain support for Poland's goals from the West. This was not easy.

Georges Clemenceau frankly admitted that "we had started [the war] as allies of the Russian oppressors of Poland, with the Polish soldiers of Silesia and Galicia fighting against us." It was only toward the end that "our war of national defence was transferred by force of events into a war of liberation."[10] French war aims were largely limited to the recovery of Alsace and Lorraine, and more vaguely to securing strategic and economic advantages on the left bank of the Rhine. As far as Eastern Europe was concerned, French eyes focused on Russia and only through that prism, and to a minor extent, was it affected by sympathies for the Poles.[11] Thus if Paris had wel-

10 Georges Clemenceau, *Grandeur and Misery of Victory* (New York, 1930), 190–2.
11 See Georges-Henri Soutou, "La France et les Marches de l'Est 1914–1919," *Revue historique*, no. 260 (Oct.–Dec., 1978); Ernest Birke, "Die französische Osteuropa–Politik 1914–1918," *Zeitschrift für Ostforschung* 3 (1954): 321–35. See also David Stevenson, *French War Aims Against Germany, 1914–1919* (Oxford, 1982).

comed the Grand Duke Nikolai Nikolaevich's appeal to the Poles it was largely because it would preclude the likelihood of a separate German-Russian peace, something that the French and the British were greatly concerned about.

With the conquest of the Congress Kingdom by the Central Powers, Paris became increasingly interested in the Poles. In January 1916 Aristide Briand mentioned Poland alongside Belgium, Serbia, and Alsace-Lorraine. In November the French Chamber of Deputies expressed the view that the Two Emperors' Manifesto had internationalized the Polish question. It went on to declare that Poland would need to be reconstituted in its ethnic and political entity. And yet, on the eve of the Two Emperors' Manifesto, there had been some thought of a Franco-Russian accord under which Paris would support a postwar transfer of German Polish lands to Russia in exchange for Russian support of French aims on the Rhine. Such an accord did in fact intervene before the fall of czardom and when publicized by the Bolsheviks did some damage to French–Polish relations.

Polish potential within the proposed *Mitteleuropa* further increased French interest in Poland, but Paris did not dare to go beyond timid promptings of Petrograd and took at face value the czar's order of December 25. Although there was as yet no comprehensive plan expressing French wishes concerning Poland's future shape, the country did figure in the so-called Cambon Program as comprising Poznania, Upper Silesia, and an outlet to the Baltic, under Russian sovereignty naturally.

The British were by and large unconcerned with eastern problems. Not unlike Clemenceau, David Lloyd George stated that the struggle was "not a war of liberation for oppressed races." In 1914 London was bent on destroying German militarism and erasing its threat to European balance and stability. It regarded Polish issues (which were little known in any case) as "totally irrelevant."[12] The British government showed no specific interest in redrafting the map of Europe, particularly eastern Europe, and kept an open mind on the subject. Whether the balance of power and stability would be better served by the maintenance or by the destruction of the Austro-Hungarian monarchy, whether national self-determination was worthy of support or not, depended on the course of the war. Any long-range planning seemed premature and was subordinate to strategic necessity of the moment. This consideration affected the nature of the developing British contacts with the Polish political émigrés, mainly of the Dmowski camp, in the West.

12 Kenneth J. Calder, *Britain and the Origins of the New Europe, 1914–1918* (Cambridge, 1976), 16 and 214. Cf. the treatment by Harold I. Nelson, *Land and Power: British and Allied Policy on Germany's Frontiers, 1916–19* (London, 1963).

Although specific suggestions and preferences expressed at that time by individual British officials should not be mistaken for London's policy, they deserve mention. In 1916 the so-called Paget–Tyrrell report took up the Polish issue and suggested as a future possibility the creation of a Polish state (to which Bohemia would be attached) under a Russian grand duke. An independent Poland as a buffer between Russia and Germany seemed a dangerous idea to Balfour, who thought it would deprive France of the benefit of Russian assistance, and indeed spell doom for the Franco-Russian alliance.[13] He expressed this view at a meeting in which Colonel Edward House participated as an emissary of President Woodrow Wilson.

At this point London attached a great deal of importance to developments in the United States and was encouraging pro-Allied Polish and other Slavic groups there to counter the pro-Central Powers propaganda of German- and Irish-Americans. The Polish National Department, whose de facto head was the great pianist Ignacy Paderewski, belonged to that pro-Allied category. Paderewski succeeded in arousing a good deal of sympathy for Poles in the German-occupied Congress Kingdom, whose plight he compared to that of the Belgians. Arising out of a humanitarian concern, political involvement between Paderewski and Colonel House, and subsequently President Wilson, grew. Wilson's general ideas on international matters are too well known to require full consideration here. It is only necessary to recall that they can be subsumed under three categories: belief in the value of Christian tradition as colored by a Presbyterian outlook, belief in democracy, and belief in America's special role in history. As Wilson put it during his 1912 campaign, "God planted in us visions of liberty. . . . We are chosen . . . to show the way to the nations of the world how they shall walk in the paths of liberty."[14] Four years later, the 1916 campaign was largely fought, in the words of Arthur Link, "for progressivism and peace."

Seeking to mediate the war, the president came up in January 1917 with his famous Peace Without Victory address to the Senate. Its underlying key ideas were: nations had a right to live under governments of their own choice and after the war they should create a league of nations that is based not on the balance but on the community of power and that is designed to prevent future wars. This speech, which reflected Wilson's basic philosophy of peace, contained a specific reference to Poland, partly the result of efforts of Paderewski and House, partly because the Polish case provided a useful illustration of the point the president was making. Referring obviously to

13 Komarnicki, *Rebirth*, 61.
14 Thomas J. Knock, *To End All Wars: Woodrow Wilson and the Quest for a New World Order* (New York, 1992), 11.

the Two Emperors' Manifesto and to the czar's statement (possibly even borrowing from them such words as "free," "autonomous," and "united"), he
declared that statesmen everywhere were agreed that "there should be a
united, independent, and autonomous Poland."[15]

In 1917, the year of the two revolutions in Russia and the entry of the
United States into the war, France broached the idea of detaching Austria-
Hungary from Germany. This involved the concept of a large Poland joined
to the Habsburg monarchy. Although the British were still not sure whether
they wanted to see the Dual Monarchy preserved or destroyed, now that
Russia was visibly weakening they became intent on barring Germany from
the road toward the east. The French sought to give a more concrete form
to the same objective. With the collapse of secret talks with Vienna and the
revolution in Russia, the role of a counterweight to Germany would now
fall to a free east-central Europe, an "eastern barrier" in which Poland would
be "le meilleur rempart." On December 17 Foreign Minister Stephen
Pichon announced in Parliament that France desired a Poland that would be
*"une, indépendante, indivisible, avec toutes les garanties de son libre développement
politique, économique, militaire, et toutes les conséquences qui pourront en résul-
ter."*[16]

Plans for a Poland within a French system in postwar Europe thus began
to take shape in Paris. Meanwhile, London's Polish policy, hitherto mainly
an aspect of Anglo-American relations and hardly the result of any desire
for Poland's independence, was increasingly influenced by military concerns. The fear of a Polish army on the side of the Central Powers prompted
Arthur Balfour to send a telegram expressing these concerns to Pavel Mil-
iukov, which played some role in a declaration by the Russian Provisional
Government on March 30, 1917, regarding Poland. It announced that an
independent Polish state composed of territories inhabited by Polish
majorities, but with eastern borders approved by Russia and "united with
Russia by a free military alliance," would be a reliable guarantee of lasting
peace. These restrictions did not appear, however, in a manifesto on Poland
adopted by the Petrograd Soviet, and indeed the Bolsheviks scored a point
by denouncing the Russian government's continued desire to control
Poland.

In the wake of the October Revolution and the mounting fear of a complete collapse of the eastern front, there was increased need for an official

---

15 See full text of address in Arthur S. Link et al., eds., *The Papers of Woodrow Wilson*, 69 vols. (Princeton, N.J., 1966–94), 40:533–9.
16 Cited in Joseph Blociszewski, *La Restauration de la Pologne et la diplomatie européene* (Paris, 1927), 110.
For an insightful treatment, see Kalervo Hovi, *Cordon sanitaire or barrière de l'Est: 1917–1919* (Turku,
1975), and *Alliance de revers, 1919–1921* (Turku, 1984).

statement of Allied war aims; the peace negotiations at Brest-Litovsk added an element of urgency. The Polish question was bound to enter into the discussions. On December 1, 1917, the British government opposed Pichon's idea, as supported by House, of a declaration on Polish independence, on the grounds that the Allies could not push it through under the existing military circumstances. Dmowski's pleas – by this time he was heading the National Polish Committee in Paris, with which Paderewski was also associated – for a binding statement also proved futile. The phrase in Lloyd George's speech to the Trade Unions on January 5, 1918 – "an independent Poland, comprising all those genuinely Polish elements who desire to form part of it, is an urgent necessity for the stability of Western Europe" – did not constitute a commitment. The emphasis on the ethnic composition of the state represented a longstanding view of the Foreign Office, which disapproved of any Polish extension at the expense of Russia, partly at least because it would make Poland dependent on Germany. At the time of the armistice, Balfour protested sharply Pichon's reference to an evacuation of Poland within its 1772 borders and declared that Great Britain never supported the reconstitution of the historic Polish state.

President Wilson, in his famous Fourteen Points, went further than the British: "An independent Polish state should be erected which should include the territories inhabited by indisputably Polish populations, which should be assured a free and secure access to the sea, and whose political and economic independence and territorial integrity should be guaranteed by international covenant." The use of "erect" rather than "resurrect" implied the rejection of historic criteria; "should" rather than "must" was meant to weaken the commitment; and "access to the sea" was understood as involving the internationalization of the Vistula rather than territorial extension. A subsequent declaration by the Allied Supreme Council on June 3 was phrased even less bindingly; the French, trying to persuade the Italians to subscribe to it, intimated that access to the sea might just mean the internationalization of the Vistula River.

With the sudden end of the war, the principal Allies found themselves less than fully prepared for a settlement of the Polish question. The Armistice contained two articles that had a bearing on Poland: Article 16 (which proved inoperative) spoke of freedom of maritime communications through Danzig; article 12 provided for German withdrawal to 1914 borders – which meant the evacuation of Russian Poland – but only when the Allies authorized it. Were it not for the action of Piłsudski's underground military organization and accords with the German soldiers' councils, the Congress Kingdom would not have been cleared of German occupation. Apart from the kingdom, free Poland comprised only Western Galicia (in

Eastern Galicia, Poles and Ukrainians were locked in a struggle for control) and parts of Prussian Poland, where a Polish uprising occurred in December. The situation further east was still fluid, with the former Russian Empire in a state of disintegration amidst the civil war and the Bolsheviks seeking to spread the revolution westward.

On the eve of the peace conference, the Piłsudski and Dmowski camps reached a compromise, largely because of Paderewski's mediation, according to which Piłsudski remained the temporary head of state, Paderewski became premier and foreign minister, and Dmowski was entrusted with representing the Polish cause in Paris. This arrangement did not obliterate the existing differences between the Left and the Right and between Piłsudski's and Dmowski's conception of Poland and its place in Europe. Although both statesmen agreed that between Germany and Russia there was no room for a small and weak state, Dmowski continued to regard Germany as a lasting threat to Poland and feared a weakened Russia (or an independent Ukraine) succumbing to German penetration. Hence, to him an anti-German front in close cooperation with Paris was essential. To Piłsudski's followers, Dmowski's reliance on France appeared excessive, since they felt that the Anglo-Saxon powers were going to play a decisive role in the decision making at the peace conference. Although Dmowski did not wish to overlook the British, whose support he had previously enjoyed, he found cooperation with them after the end of the war more difficult. Lloyd George and the British leaders in turn came to regard Dmowski as the symbol of Polish nationalism and anti-Semitism. The Americans, intent on making the world safe for democracy, doubted Dmowski's democratic credentials. In that sense, the Piłsudski camp seemed to offer a more liberal option; its attitude toward Poland's eastern problems – as explained in the following paragraphs – aroused more sympathy. Paderewski, whose previous association with Dmowski did not signify an identity of views, came to adopt a position closer to that of Piłsudski. All this resulted in a certain dualism in Polish policy, which, not escaping the attention of the peacemakers, weakened Poland's credibility.[17] To add to the uncertainty, as the Allies, and the Poles themselves, began to seek a settlement of the Polish question in Paris, the two absentees, Germany and Russia, cast a vast shadow over the proceedings.

Did the Allies have a clear notion of what constituted Poland and what kind of Poland they wanted to see on the map? A great deal of information

17 The entire issue of the interaction between Allied and Polish politics is treated at great length in Kay Lundgreen-Nielsen, *The Polish Problem at the Paris Peace Conference* (Odense, 1979). See also his "Woodrow Wilson and the Rebirth of Poland," in Arthur S. Link, ed., *Woodrow Wilson and a Revolutionary World, 1913–1921* (Chapel Hill, N.C., 1982).

on the subject can be found in British Foreign Office handbooks, in the reports of the Inquiry, and in the documentation prepared by the Comité d'Etudes. Two memoranda drawn up at the Quai d'Orsay in December 1918 advocated that Poland include German Silesia, Poznania, Western and Eastern Prussia, and parts of Pomerania, on the assumption that "the more we aggrandize Poland at Germany's expense, the more certain shall we be that she will remain her enemy."[18] The memoranda repeated the familiar point about Poland's being a necessary barrier between Russian Bolshevism and a German revolution but were less clear about Poland's eastern borders, except in favoring a Polish–Lithuanian union and a Polish Eastern Galicia. The Inquiry's position on German–Polish borders and on a Polish–Lithuanian union was more open to alternative solutions. The Foreign Office was skeptical about a Polish–Lithuanian link and supported, by and large, ethnic criteria for the drawing of Poland's eastern borders. The application of such criteria, while controversial at best, in the nationally mixed zones would mean either leaving sizable Polish populations outside of the new state or including non-Polish minorities within its borders. It was obvious that, in the final analysis, political preoccupations rather than concern for the inhabitants' wishes would prevail. Here the views of Clemenceau, Lloyd George, and Wilson, as well as the basic assumptions from which they stemmed, were far apart.

The French were determined to ensure that Germany would not be able to threaten their security again and did not share Lloyd George's view that "the Teuton was largely done for."[19] A strategic frontier on the Rhine and a strong Poland with secure access to the sea, without which "it would inevitably be the prey of Germany or Russia" (as Cambon put it), were conditions of a stable peace.[20] To the British, this smacked of French designs for hegemony. "A greater Poland suited French policy – and the greater the better," Lloyd George observed. And General Carton de Wiart, who was basically pro-Polish, commented that Poland "had been earmarked as the French sphere" and the French did not allow this to be forgotten "for one single instant."[21] This colored British attitudes toward the Poles.

The Polish question quickly became the focus of a debate between the French and British that encompassed not only territorial issues but also transportation to Poland and the use there of General Józef Haller's army

18 Cited in Piotr S. Wandycz, *France and Her Eastern Allies, 1919–1925* (Minneapolis, 1962), 22.
19 Cited in ibid., 29.
20 See *Papers Relating to the Foreign Relations of the United States: The Paris Peace Conference, 1919* (hereafter *FRUS-PPC*), 13 vols. (Washington, D.C., 1945), 4:416.
21 Cited in Wandycz, *France and Her Eastern Allies*, 39 and 25, respectively.

(composed mainly of Polish Americans, organized in France, and with French officers in key positions). The British and the Americans worried that these troops, which had been under the umbrella of the National Polish Committee, would be used to advance Dmowski's position in the power struggle within Poland. From a purely military angle, the presence of some six divisions led by Haller was likely to strengthen Poland (then locked in combat in Eastern Galicia) in the east and along the German–Polish demarcation lines.[22] Marshall Foch urged that the army be sent through Danzig, and that Allied troops move to occupy Danzig and the railroad line down to Thorn (Toruń) if the Germans should try to interfere. Lloyd George opposed this proposal on the grounds that Haller's troops might either fight against the Germans or conquer territories in the east. The British feared that the Poles would use the passage of these troops through Prussian Pomerania to repeat what they had done in Poznania, namely, stage an uprising against the Germans and place the area under their control. Lloyd George even thought that this might mean incorporating all of East Prussia in Poland before the final verdict of the peace conference.[23]

Such fears were not completely groundless, and the Germans resolutely opposed the notion of sending Haller's troops by sea. Eventually, with British support playing an important role in the affair, a Foch–Erzberger protocol in April 1919 provided for the transportation of the Haller army by an overland route. The delay meant that Poland was deprived of the use of these well-equipped and trained soldiers for the first five months of its postwar existence.

Of course, the main issue the peacemakers had to deal with in regard to Poland was the tracing of the new state's frontiers, particularly the western border with Germany. The provisions adopted were to become part of the Treaty of Versailles. On January 29, 1919, at a very early stage of the conference, Dmowski was summoned before the Supreme Council because of a Czech–Polish armed clash that had alarmed the Allies. Clemenceau took this opportunity to ask for a presentation on the entire Polish situation, including the territorial demands. Dmowski acquitted himself brilliantly in what one British diplomat described as a "wonderful performance"; even Clemenceau called it "a masterly statement."[24] As a consequence, a fact-finding mission headed by Ambassador Joseph Noulens was sent to Poland

---

22 See a searching analysis of German aggressive plans in the east during the first phase of the Paris Peace Conference in Piotr Łossowski, *Między wojną a pokojem* (Warsaw, 1976).
23 See David Lloyd George, *The Truth About the Peace Treaties*, 2 vols. (London, 1938), 1:287.
24 Cited in, respectively, Sir Esme Howard, *Theatre of Life* (Boston, 1935–6), 2:303; Roman Dmowski, *Polityka polska i odbudowanie państwa* (Warsaw, 1925), 267.

to help put an end to the ongoing German–Polish hostilities in Poznania, and a Commission on Polish Affairs, headed by Jules Cambon, was established in Paris. The latter turned to the preparation of a report on the German–Polish border.

In his "Note on the Western Frontiers of the Polish State" submitted to the Cambon Commission, Dmowski stated that the recreation of Poland should be viewed, first, as an act of international justice obliterating the partitions. Hence, the last legal frontiers of 1772 should be taken as the starting point for an inquiry into the territorial settlement. Second, it was necessary to take into account the question of nationality, as affected by changes that had occurred during the 120 or so years since then. In some cases, Polish ethnic territory had expanded beyond the 1772 frontiers; in others, it had contracted. Third, Poland's rebirth had to be viewed in geopolitical terms and attention given to the economic and strategic needs of the state if it were to remain a truly independent entity between Germany and Russia. Guided by these three considerations, Dmowski demanded that Poznania and Pomerania be incorporated into Poland on historical and ethnic grounds; that the southeastern part of East Prussia be added for strategic, economic, and ethnic reasons; and that Upper Silesia be included mainly on ethnic grounds. The last two regions had not been part of the historic, prepartition Polish Commonwealth. As for the remaining part of East Prussia, Dmowski recommended its demilitarization and neutralization.

From the Allies' perspective, the issue of access to the Baltic coast through Pomerania – which the Germans later dubbed the "corridor" – was basically resolved in Poland's favor. This meant that the older notion of ensuring access to the sea through an internationalized Vistula was dropped. But differences remained concerning the width of this "corridor" and the status of the only harbor, namely, Danzig (Gdańsk).[25] The French pressed, mainly for strategic reasons, for a 200-kilometer-long Polish coastline and the inclusion of Danzig. A demilitarized East Prussia could, in a sense, complement a demilitarized Rhineland. The British were hesitant. During the war, in April, Balfour had suggested to House that Danzig be made a free port. Then the idea was abandoned, only to be revived again by some proponents in the Foreign Office. By March 1919, however, the British had by and large come around to the viewpoint that Danzig should be part of Poland. The Americans also favored Polish access to the Baltic, mainly for economic reasons, arguing that the interests of some twenty million Poles

---

25 For the most recent discussion, see Anna M. Cienciala, "The Battle of Danzig and the Polish Corridor at the Paris Peace Conference of 1919," in Paul Latawski, ed., *The Reconstruction of Poland, 1914–23* (London, 1992).

were more important than those of two million Germans who would find
themselves in the Polish state. In any case, Pomerania had a Polish majority.
There was less agreement on the status of Danzig.

The Polish territorial program vis-à-vis Germany did not appear exorbitant, even if it was not fully acceptable. The amount of disagreement among
French, American, and British members of the commission was relatively
small: a previous accord between the main American and British representatives (Sir Esme Howard and Robert Lord) seemed to ensure a common
Anglo-Saxon line. True, the accord was not honored later, but there was
still a good deal of common ground left. The commission, working through
a smaller body, reduced Polish claims on the side of East Prussia and adopted
the British demand for a plebiscite in Allenstein (Olsztyn), although the
French were unhappy about it. As proposed, the boundaries were acceptable to the Poles. Dmowski commented on the full support of the French,
and regarded the fact that the French and the British had found it possible
to reach an agreement a great achievement.[26]

The agreement among the experts, however, did not correspond to the
views of the Big Three. At the meeting of the Supreme Council on March
19, Lloyd George bitterly criticized the report for assigning nearly two million Germans to Poland. He refused to be swayed by the argument that, in
the case of Danzig and Marienwerder (Kwidzyń), economic and strategic
reasons outweighed ethnic considerations. Lloyd George's opposition,
however, was determined not so much by concern for ethnic Germans – he
did not worry unduly about the three million Sudeten Germans in Czechoslovakia – as by other motives. His main worry, as he put it, was that the
German government would find it impossible to sign a harsh treaty and
might even collapse. But there was even more to it. The peace conference
was entering a critical stage, at which the French, skeptical of the security
guarantees under a League of Nations, demanded a strategic border on the
Rhine that would also offer "indispensable protection" to the new states of
east-central Europe.[27] Lloyd George and Wilson vehemently opposed it,
albeit for different reasons. The details of the moves and countermoves –
notably the Fontainebleau memorandum and the French reply to it – are
beyond the scope of this discussion. In any case, the point of primary interest here is Lloyd George's proposal of an American–British guarantee to
France, which had a direct bearing on the Polish situation. As Robert Lansing perceived, an Anglo–American guarantee of France's western borders

26 Dmowski, *Polityka,* 372.
27 See the French memorandum on the Rhine border, English text in André Tardieu, *The Truth about
the Treaty* (Indianapolis, 1921), 157–67.

would, in effect, encourage Germany to turn eastward and would "increase rather than decrease" Polish "danger from Germany."[28]

The French were in a quandary. Eventually, in the teeth of opposition from President Raymond Poincaré and Marshal Foch, Clemenceau decided to accept the guarantee offer. This opened the door to further French concessions to the British and Americans. The conference delegates ordered a second plebiscite to be held in East Prussia, in Marienwerder, and, after protracted negotiations, decided that a free city of Danzig would be established. These decisions were taken on purely political grounds, and in the case of Danzig harked back to the British and American stand during the war. Thus, it is inexact to speak of Wilson's completely changing his mind or of his capitulation to Lloyd George. If a certain change did occur, in the sense that at first Wilson stood for strengthening Poland and then favored Danzig as a free city, it was due to the president's opposition to French policies. In a letter to R. S. Baker, Wilson commented that the French were constantly trying to gain more territory, to impose heavier indemnities on Germany, and to dominate east-central Europe. "The only, real interest of France in Poland is in weakening Germany by giving Poland territory to which she has no right."[29]

A third major departure from the Cambon report, in this case concerning Upper Silesia, was yet to come. Upon learning the terms of the treaty, the German delegation heatedly challenged the provisions affecting German–Polish borders. In the words of a British historian, "Every possible concession to Poland was refused, every possible territorial claim denied, every possible attempt made to depreciate Polish civilization and capacity."[30] Since Upper Silesia constituted one of the main targets of German criticism, and since Lloyd George and British financial circles considered the industrial potential of Upper Silesia most important for Germany's economic recovery, it was logical to insist on the modification of this part of the settlement.

In arguing for a concession in the form of holding a plebiscite in Upper Silesia, Lloyd George displayed all his talents of persuasion. After all, what better way to ascertain what the people in the area really wanted? A plebiscite, he argued, would guarantee that "no question of a war of revenge would arise." He disingenuously assured the other peacemakers that, according to his "personal view," Upper Silesia "would vote in favor of Poland" – having already told the British delegates exactly the opposite.[31]

28 Robert Lansing, *The Peace Negotiations: A Personal Narrative* (Boston, 1921), 180.
29 Cited in Lundgreen-Nielsen, *Polish Problem*, 244.
30 Harold W. V. Temperley, ed., *A History of the Peace Conference of Paris* (London, 1920–4), 2:4.
31 See *FRUS-PPC*, 6:140.

He said to Wilson that "Upper Silesia would vote Polish," and somewhat later to Paderewski that the area was not Polish and should not be absorbed into Poland.[32]

The French were alarmed. They regarded Upper Silesia as a German arsenal, and although they could keep an eye on what went on in the Ruhr, they could hardly watch developments in that far-off industrial basin. Clemenceau accused Lloyd George of wishful thinking if he believed that Germany could be conciliated: "The more concessions we made, the more the Germans would demand." To weaken Poland by depriving it of the coal basin would mean placing it at the mercy of Germany and would open the way for German expansion in Russia. If this happened, "the blood which had flown for five years would have been spent in vain."[33] Wilson also voiced objections to the German demands and questioned their need for coal. He pointed out that the chances of a fair plebiscite would be small in a region dominated by German magnates and capitalists. Yet, he was eventually outmaneuvered by the British prime minister, finding it hard to oppose a measure grounded in the principle of national self-determination.

The Upper Silesian plebiscite, eventually held in 1921 to the accompaniment of three Polish uprisings – preceding and following it – did nothing to diminish German hostility toward Poland nor help to increase security in the region. Taken together with other provisions of the Treaty of Versailles, it indicated the already visible French dependence on Great Britain. That France had to reconcile its policies out of concern for cooperation with London was also evident in other aspects of Poland's territorial settlement, notably in the east.

The drawing of the German–Polish border under the Treaty of Versailles was obviously of crucial importance for the two states concerned and for the future stability or instability of Europe. This arrangement, however, needs to be seen in conjunction with the other Polish borders. Even if some of them were not established in Paris, they were part of the settlement of the Polish question. Suffice it here to mention the Czechoslovak–Polish border issues, particularly the thorny problem of Teschen (Cieszyn in Polish, Těšín in Czech), which was addressed at virtually all levels of the peace conference, was resolved by the Conference of Ambassadors in 1920, and continued to affect relations between Warsaw and Prague throughout the interwar period. Indirectly, of course, it played an important role in international affairs, but its significance cannot be compared to the settlement of

32 Ibid., 6:151 and 197.
33 Cited in, respectively, ibid., 6:142; Paul Mantoux, *Les Délibérations du Conseil des Quatre (24 Mars–28 Juin 1919: Note de l'officier interprête,* 2 vols. (Paris, 1955), 2:270 (hereafter *PMCQ*).

Poland's eastern borders with the other great power in the region, Russia. The Russian angle was significant even in the case of Eastern Galicia, which had never belonged to the Russian Empire and which was formally dealt with under the Treaty of Saint Germain with Austria.

With the disintegration of the Dual Monarchy, the Ukrainians in Eastern Galicia proclaimed the creation of a West Ukrainian Republic loosely connected with the Ukrainian People's Republic, which emerged out of the Russian Empire. Poles, who constituted a sizable minority and in several areas a majority in Eastern Galicia, found themselves in a struggle with the Ukrainians. Dmowski, whose eastern territorial program was based on the centralist principle – that is, annexation to Poland of those border regions upon which the Poles had made a cultural, social, and economic impression – demanded incorporation of the province and refused any armistice that might favor the Ukrainians. Piłsudski, who considered the Polish–Ukrainian strife unnecessary, was inclined to seek a compromise. This approach was a reflection of his grander idea of creating a bloc in which Poland, Ukraine, Belorussia, and Lithuania linked together would separate Germany from Russia. Here, the contrast between Dmowski and Piłsudski was most striking, with the "annexationist" program of the former clashing with the "federalist" plan of the latter. True, Piłsudski, a pragmatist who believed in creating faits accomplis, had not offered a blueprint of the future structure, whereas Paderewski had laid out in a memorandum for Wilson the design of a United States of Poland composed of Poland, Lithuania, Belorussia, and Ukraine.[34] Piłsudski wanted above all to "turn back the wheel of history" so as to make Poland (linked with the other border nations) a decisive factor in eastern Europe. For that reason he wanted to win the confidence of the Lithuanians, Ukrainians, and Belorussians who were worried that Dmowski's nationalist and annexationist concepts would prevail and determine Polish policy. This polarity harmed the Polish cause in Paris. The Americans and the British were uncertain of the credibility of the "federalist" program and inclined to suspect the Poles of more or less concealed imperialism.

Formally, Eastern Galicia, as mentioned, had nothing to do with Russia, but the Allies, particularly the British, were careful not to prejudge the issue in a way that might adversely affect Russian interests. According to Lloyd George, "no one thought seriously about the country except as being part

---

34 A good deal has been written on this topic. For brief presentations, see Wandycz, *France and Her Eastern Allies,* 118–12; and Lundgreen–Nielsen, *Polish Problem,* 32–47. For a more extensive treatment, see M. K. Dziewanowski, *Joseph Piłsudski: A European Federalist* (Stanford, Calif., 1969).

of Russia."[35] Hence, after lengthy debates first about the Polish-Ukrainian armistice and then about the ties between Eastern Galicia and Poland, the Allies came to advocate some form of an autonomous regime for the province. In the words of Sir Eyre Crowe, "The main idea which had guided the Council in all its discussions on the autonomy of Eastern Galicia had been that a people was being dealt with who had retained marked sympathy for certain of its neighbours, more particularly Russia. . . . No obstacle should be placed in the way of an ultimate union of Eastern Galicia with Russia."[36] Upon British insistence, it was agreed that the following words should be deleted from the preamble of the statute for Eastern Galicia: "Eastern Galicia formed part of the former Kingdom of Poland until the partition of the latter."[37]

Why then did the Supreme Council authorize Poland in June 1919 to "establish a civil government in Eastern Galicia," then occupied by the Polish troops, although with provisions for a future plebiscite? The principal reason was, as the French had put it in their December 1918 memoranda, the province formed a "screen between Bolshevik Russia and Western Europe." The Poles made much of Eastern Galicia's being, in reality, a vital front against the Bolsheviks, and the French military especially favored the Polish case on these grounds. Even Balfour, when the council was showing its displeasure with the Poles for their military operations, remarked that the Allies "were hampering the action of the Poles" while the Bolsheviks were on the offensive.[38]

The Bolshevik threat to the established order, the civil war in the former Russian Empire, and the national aspirations of such peoples as the Ukrainians naturally had a bearing on Allied attitudes toward the eastern borders of Poland. Once again, one had to determine how far east Poland extended. Was the administrative delimitation of the prewar Congress Kingdom on the Bug the proper frontier in the east?

By the large, the British favored an ethnic border with Russia, which meant that the state should encompass as few non-Poles as possible. They worried little about the large Polish minorities that would remain outside of Poland's borders. American views were somewhat more flexible but were colored by traditional respect for the territorial integrity of Russia. As for the French, the secretary of the Polish delegation in Paris summed up their views well when he wrote: "There were elements which were inclined

35 See *FRUS-PPC,* 6:272–3.
36 Cited in Wandycz, *France and Her Eastern Allies,* 115–16.
37 Cited in ibid., 116.
38 Ibid., 113.

to take the disintegration of Russia as a starting point, and strive to replace it by Poland; others, however, did not cease to count on the resurrection of the old United Russia and did not want to injure [French–Russian] relations by supporting Poland to Russian disadvantage."[39] Finally, as Dmowski noted, serious doubt existed about whether the conference "could establish a boundary line between Poland and Russia in the absence of Russia."[40]

It was not surprising that under these conditions the Commission on Polish Affairs, when instructed to study Poland's eastern borders, immediately faced the "difficulty of ascertaining from what States Poland will be separated by these frontiers."[41] Small wonder that the commission felt it was the safest course of action to invoke the stand of the last Russian government, which had insisted on ethnic criteria and had been willing to attribute to Poland merely the Congress Kingdom. The commission, in its report of April 22, recommended the adoption of a line that corresponded roughly to the prewar division between the kingdom and the empire.

The council did not take up the report, which at this point was rather of academic interest. Polish troops were advancing eastward, fighting the Bolsheviks, and the conference did not want, and was hardly in a position, to stop them. A peculiar situation existed. The peacemakers wanted the Bolsheviks to be defeated without the Poles reaping any territorial advantages from their victory. Polish suggestions for plebiscites in the Ukrainian and Belorussian areas were expressly forbidden, the peace conference reserving to itself the right, under Article 87 of the Treaty of Versailles, to determine Poland's eastern borders. All of this was just as unrealistic and inconsistent as the entire Allied policy toward Russia. In the words of Vittorio Orlando at a meeting of the Supreme Council, the choice had been either to intervene and go to Moscow if necessary, or to regard the Bolsheviks as a de facto government and make peace with them. Neither alternative was adopted, and "we have suffered the worst consequences of pursuing both policies at the same time."[42] This attitude persisted later when, in 1920, the Poles were advised neither to make peace with the Bolsheviks nor to wage war against them.

The peace conference, however, had to adopt some resolution, at least, in connection with Poland's eastern borders. Once again seeking guidance from the Russian stand, the commission took the advice of Sergei Sazonov, the president of the émigré Conférence Politique Russe, and in its report of

39 Stanisław Kozicki, *Sprawa granic Polski na konferencji pokojowej w Paryżu* (Warsaw, 1921), 115.
40 Dmowski, *Polityka*, 404.
41 David Hunter Miller, *My Diary at the Conference of Peace*, 21 vols. (New York, 1926), 17:180–1.
42 *PMCQ*, 1:20.

September 25 suggested the old administrative border of the Congress Kingdom as a minimal Polish ethnic frontier. The report stressed, however, that this border was to be provisional; indeed, the French and the Americans believed that it ought to lie further to the east. Some confusion might perhaps have been avoided if more emphasis had been placed on the fact that the report, strictly speaking, was not defining a frontier, but "according certain territories to Poland."[43] The American representative on the council then suggested that Poland be given the choice of either accepting this arrangement without prejudice to a final settlement, or leaving the matter "entirely open" until such time as Russia and Poland considered it possible to make a definite settlement. After lengthy deliberations, the council decided to make a unilateral declaration on December 8. It said that the Allies, desirous to "put a stop to the existing conditions of political uncertainty, in which the Polish nation is placed" and "without prejudging the provisions which must in the future define the eastern frontiers of Poland," declared that they recognized Poland's right "to organize a regular administration of the territories of the former Russian Empire situated to the West of the line described below." As for "the rights that Poland may be able to establish over the territories situated to the East of the said line [they] are expressly reserved."[44] A detailed description and a map, indicating that the line stopped north of the former Eastern Galicia (which had been dealt with under the Treaty of Saint Germain), were enclosed.

The declaration, whose immediate practical value was nil in view of the fact that the Polish–Bolshevik front was hundreds of miles to the east, was to reappear (with the line extended into Eastern Galicia) in the telegram to the Bolsheviks of July 11, 1920, signed by Lord Curzon. The famous Curzon Line was born. Although rejected at this point by the Bolsheviks and described by Georgii Chichérin as drawn under the influence of anti-Polish White Russian reactionaries, it would become, in the Second World War, a handy instrument of Soviet expansionist policies in the hands of Stalin. This gives some idea of the long-range repercussions of the settlement of the Polish question in 1919–20.

There is little doubt that the Polish question was a particularly difficult problem at the peace conference. The reason, in part, was that the Wilsonian principle of national self-determination was applied to areas in which clear-cut ethnic boundaries were a rarity. But, whereas nationalities intermingled throughout much of east-central Europe, in the case of Poland the

43 *FRUS-PPC,* 8:350.
44 Ibid. The declaration was adopted on December 2 and made public on December 8.

borders affected, directly or indirectly, two giant neighbors who, although defeated or in turmoil, were bound to reemerge as European powers. Neither of them, in the final analysis, wanted to see a Polish state on the map of Europe; it interfered with their expansionist or ideological goals. Hence, the enmity of the two powers toward the Polish settlement could be taken for granted, and this was unlikely to be diminished by localized concessions. The question then was whether a small Poland reduced to its ethnic core (the British and partly the American view) or a strong Poland capable of playing a supporting role in the maintenance of the postwar order (the French view) offered a greater guarantee of peace and stability. For President Wilson, the question was above all related to the League of Nations within which the postwar order was to unfold.

The great powers did not come to the peace conference with ready-made plans: their attitudes gradually evolved during the war under the impact of developments often unrelated to Poland. That is to say, Poland did not spring ready-made, like Athena from Zeus's head, out of Allied blueprints but emerged in stages in which the Poles themselves played a considerable role. Poland was already a state of sorts when the peacemakers assembled in Paris.

Polish politicians and historians have long quarreled about the role their leaders played in bringing forth the new state. Did Piłsudski treat the western settlement as secondary, having told Harry Kessler that Poland would not make war on Germany on that score and referring to the ex-German provinces as a "gift" from the Allies? His adversaries certainly said so. But did these remarks not also reflect Piłsudski's realism? Did Dmowski, as his critics asserted, weaken Polish chances at the conference by relying exclusively on French support and antagonizing the Anglo-Saxons with his nationalism and anti-Semitism?[45] Did the dualism in Polish foreign policy harm Polish chances, as Kay Lundgreen-Nielsen concluded, or was there a de facto division of roles between Dmowski, who wielded the diplomatic instrument in the west, and Piłsudski, who wielded the sword in the east, as Komarnicki has suggested? The former opinion appears more convincing, yet it is difficult to escape a somewhat deterministic view, namely, that the Polish stand was at no point a decisive factor; given the alignment of forces in Paris, the settlement could hardly have been different. Did economic factors play any role at all in the settlement of the Polish question? Obviously they had some effect on the issues surrounding the Galician oil

45 See Piotr S. Wandycz, "Dmowski's Policy at the Paris Peace Conference: Success or Failure?" and Paul Latawski, "Roman Dmowski, the Polish Question, and Western Opinion, 1915–18: The Case of Britain," both in Latawski, ed., *Reconstruction of Poland*.

fields, Teschen, Upper Silesia, and Danzig. Economic provisions regarding
Poland figured in the Treaty of Versailles (arts. 89, 90, 92, 93, 254, and
256), in the so-called Minorities Treaty (arts. 14–18), and later in the Upper
Silesian Convention. By and large, they were meant to ensure the right of
transit, most-favored treatment of Allied trade, and privileges for capital.
Some of them, however, were never ratified and remained a dead letter.
Other Franco-Polish economic arrangements came later.[46] Marxist historiography naturally sought to emphasize the economic dimension of the settlement by pointing to the French desire to weaken Germany economically
and analyzing the role of oil in the drawing of borders. Yet, in the final
analysis, political motives proved to be the determining factor in the Polish
settlement.

The question remains, was it a good or a bad settlement? Perhaps the criterion should not be whether it lasted – so many events *after* the conference,
for which the peacemakers were not responsible, determined that it would
not – but how closely it approached equity and political reality. To judge it
solely by "realistic" standards that exclude imponderables would appear
unjustified.

The peacemakers had at their disposal a great deal of factual and generally reliable material to consult in their deliberations. If they sometimes
overlooked it, it was not out of ignorance, but for political reasons. Wilson,
for one, believed that imperfect arrangements would eventually be adjusted
within the framework of the League. The German–Polish border corresponded by and large to the historical frontier, and one must not forget that
a Polish "corridor" had been a fact of life for several centuries until Frederick II eliminated it through the partitions of Poland. Despite a hundred
years or so of Germanization, the majority of the population remained Polish. On economic grounds, access to the sea was vital to the Poles, whereas
neither the loss of this region nor of Upper Silesia crippled the German
economy. At the same time, to the Germans, who had *not* lost the war in
the east, such territorial amputations were obviously incomprehensible, and
the "corridor" was a monstrosity. But there was really no viable alternative.

The borders in the east were finally drawn by the Poles and Soviet Russia; the great powers recognized them only in 1923. Hence, one can hardly
blame the Allies for them. Had it been up to the peace conference, it is
likely that frontiers corresponding to the Curzon Line would have been
imposed. Such a border would have satisfied the national aspirations of the

46 See the illuminating Georges-Henri Soutou, "L'Impérialisme du pauvre: La politique économique
du gouvernement français en Europe Centrale et Orientale de 1918 à 1929," *Relations internationales*
7 (1976).

Ukrainians and Belorussians, although under the existing conditions its main effect would have been to strengthen the USSR. It would also, as mentioned already, had left several million Poles outside the Polish state. Would such a settlement have brought greater security to eastern Europe? Would it have prevented the German-Russian rapprochement and the Rapallo policy? The answer cannot be a definite yes or a no.

It has frequently been asserted that the Treaty of Versailles, particularly its Polish provisions, contained the germs of the future war. It is all too easy to draw such an a posteriori conclusion. French historian Louis Eisenmann agreed with Clemenceau that "at least half a century would be needed for the treaties to enter into the blood stream . . . make part of the European conscience and show all their value."[47] There were many variables in the interwar period that could have produced different results. Hence, the verdict should be neither guilty nor innocent, but, as Scottish law has it, "not proven." From today's perspective, however, one can offer the hypothesis that multiethnic states such as Yugoslavia and Czechoslovakia have not passed the test of time. Poland did, but in a drastically changed shape and at a high cost of population transfers. Paradoxically, the present German–Polish border seems to offer a far greater degree of stability than the compromise frontier of 1919.

---

47 Cited by Antoine Marès, "La Vision française de l'Europe centrale, d'un prisme à l'autre du XIXe au XXe siècle," in Gérard Beauprêtre, ed., *L'Europe Centrale: réalité, mythe, enjeu XVIIIe–XXe siècles* (Warsaw, 1981), 389. For a balanced appraisal, see the chapter "New Nations and Old," in Harold Butler, *The Lost Peace* (London, 1941).

14

Smoke and Mirrors:
In Smoke-Filled Rooms
and the Galerie des Glaces

SALLY MARKS

When the Allied and Associated Powers gathered in Paris in January 1919 for what proved to be the battle of the Seine, one of the most bitter, crucial, and long-lasting conflicts facing them would be that over reparations. "To the victors belong the spoils" is the oldest rule of international law. However, in response to Socialist and Bolshevik propaganda in favor of "no indemnities," Woodrow Wilson had ruled out this conventional approach to a financial settlement. Hence the concept of repairing the civilian damage done, which was written into the Pre-Armistice Agreement with Germany, provided a new method of providing financial relief for debt-burdened victors.

The case for reparations rested primarily on the military verdict of 1918, which was not in dispute at the time among governments, though increasingly forgotten by the German people as time passed, and secondarily on the fact that the absence of reparations would largely reverse that verdict.[1] Initially, until German diplomats made a fateful connection, reparations were not linked to responsibility for the outbreak of the war. At heart, reparations were about two fundamental and closely related questions: who won the war and who would pay for it, or at least for part of the cost of undoing the damage. The war had been fought on the soil of the victors; they were devastated, and Germany was not. Most European belligerents had large domestic war debts; the victors had vast foreign ones as well[2] but Germany did not.[3] In addition, the continental victors had immense recon-

---

1 And increasingly ignored in the 1920–32 reparations debate, although Germany was in part attempting to use reparations to overturn that verdict.
2 Portugal is an exception to most generalizations about Allied belligerents.
3 Carl-Ludwig Holtfrerich, *Die deutsche Inflation, 1914–1923* (Berlin, 1980), 115.

337

struction costs. Somebody would have to pay to clear the fields and provide new plows, rebuild factories, purchase new equipment and tools, reconstruct bridges and railroads, drain and restore coal mines flooded during the armistice negotiations, and revive the economies of thoroughly devastated and denuded territories. If the Allies, and especially France, had to assume reconstruction costs on top of domestic and foreign war debts, whereas Germany was left with only domestic debts[4] they would be the losers, and German economic dominance would be tantamount to victory. Reparations would both deny Germany that victory and spread the pain of undoing the damage done.

Thus reparations concerned the balance of power, which payment or nonpayment could sharply affect. That is why the reparations struggle turned into "the continuation of war by other means."[5] Clearly, despite its financial and technical complexity, this was an intensely political question fraught with fundamental political consequences, both internationally and in the domestic politics of most nations concerned. That was as true in 1919 at Paris as it was thirteen years later at Lausanne. The size and nature of the bill was a major political issue in Germany; it was, especially in 1919, equally important in potential recipient countries. Though Allied politicians had murmured qualifying phrases, their populations had gained the impression that Germany would pay the costs of the war. Allied leaders knew that was impossible, but, being politicians in democracies and thus dependent upon the consent of electorates and parliaments, dared not say so. The fact that popular interest in foreign affairs had been sharply heightened by the war only increased the political dilemma.

For this reason and because the stakes were so high, there were three general rules of reparations that held true with few exceptions: everything was political, nothing was what it seemed, and nothing stayed settled for long. These rules are related, especially the first two: misdirection arose from the need of politicians to obscure reality in order to stay in office, which is the first task of politicians. As a consequence, those who study reparations must cope with technical complexity and political considerations wrapped in great clouds of misdirection and propaganda.

In the postwar era, propaganda took on new importance in matters of international politics and finance. Its role was enlarged by the war, by the new and continuing concern of electorates with foreign affairs and economics, and by the intricacy of reparations. The task of propaganda was to

---

4 Which in the event were eradicated by inflation.
5 The phrase of a German official, in Karl-Heinz Harbeck, ed., *Das Kabinett Cuno: 22. November 1922 bis 12. August 1923*, Akten der Reichskanzlei, Weimarer Republik (Boppard am Rhein, 1968), 192.

mislead. Germany made a large contribution here, early and late, as did John Maynard Keynes, who had concerns of his own.[6] Allied politicians played a role as well in ensuring that nothing was as it seemed. Further, the technical complexity of reparations was an aid to misdirection. Politicians trumpeted clauses that aided the impression they wished to create; those negating or limiting these assertions were buried in obscurity deep in the financial details where the public would not notice them. The combined effect of propaganda, deliberate misdirection, and technical obscurity fooled public opinion, both German and Allied, especially in the English-speaking world, most parliamentarians, and many historians for decades. The history of reparations is replete with sweeping statements that are only words masking a different reality.

Curiously, it was usually in the political interests of both German and Allied leaders to obscure reality and to present reparations demands as more onerous than they actually were. Leaders of continental victor states needed to convince their electorates that they had obtained considerably more than they really had; Weimar politicians equally exaggerated both to tell the German people what they wanted to hear about the horrors of Versailles and to convince world opinion that reparations were unjust and unpayable. Thus the orchestrations of both sides combined to heighten the distortion.

Despite much talk about justice from all concerned, reparations had little to do with the rights and wrongs of the matter in anybody's eyes, except perhaps Wilson's. At the peace conference, only the United States ever attempted to judge reparations issues according to the merits. It could afford to be relatively dispassionate as it had few claims, which lessened the importance of reparations in its domestic politics.[7] But the United States pursued its own interests as determinedly as other powers. Since it wished to sell food to Germany and agricultural surpluses would soon again be a political issue

6 Especially his guilt as a pacifist over having aided Britain's war effort and his passion for Carl Melchior. In 1923 Keynes volunteered to help prepare a key German reparations note and, once back in England, not only publicly praised his own handiwork but also speculated profitably on the basis of his inside information. Robert Skidelsky, *John Maynard Keynes: A Biography*, 2 vols. (London, 1983), 1:356–7, 364, 2:122–9; John Maynard Keynes, *Two Memoirs* (London, 1949); *The Collected Writings of John Maynard Keynes* (hereafter *JMKW*), 30 vols. (London, 1971–), 18:159–60; Melchior to Rosenberg, June 21, 1923, 1526/3116H/D637557, Selected Foreign Ministry Records, T-120, Auswärtiges Amt, Germany (hereafter AA, T-120); Sthamer to AA, May 30, 1923, tel. 272. Rosenberg to Sthamer, June 4, 1923, tel. 439, June 5, 1923, tel. 441, 1527/3116H/D638676, D638687, D638697, AA, T-120; Stephen A. Schuker, review of *JMKW*, *Journal of Economic Literature* 18 (Mar. 1980): 124–6.
7 The United States had reparations claims of $110,668,701 for submarine damage, the Veterans' Bureau, the Shipping Board, and the Railway Administration, as well as larger related claims for occupation costs and mixed claims. Sally Marks, "The Myths of Reparations," *Central European History* 11 (1978): 235.

in America, the United States ensured that purchase of food was among the
permitted uses of the first German payments under the treaty.[8] Equally, it
resisted Allied efforts to impose the burden of their war costs upon it.

America's own war costs were modest and easily paid. Those of European belligerents were neither. None was eager to pay its own bills, let alone
anybody else's. In this respect, Germany was unusual only in its dogged
determination. Thus Germany began in mid–March 1919 to devise ways to
limit its liability[9] and never ceased to do so. France hoped its war costs could
be covered by someone other than its own notoriously unforthcoming tax-
payers and so sought first to continue wartime economic arrangements,[10]
then argued that as France had paid in blood, America should shoulder the
burden in money, forgiving Allied war debts. Britain's David Lloyd George
shouted one message to the historical galleries but murmured another in
inaudible asides to the Allies; in April 1919, Keynes contrived a clever
scheme through which inter-Allied debts to the United States would be
paid in German bonds whose value would probably be minimal at best.[11]
When Wilson rejected all attempts to dump the costs of Europe's war on the
United States, the battle over reparations was joined in earnest. Because the
stakes were so high, the history of reparations from the peace conference on
became an essay in the cutthroat selfishness of self-centered states, each
European power jockeying for maximum benefit.

I

That became evident even before the peace conference during prearmistice
negotiations among the victors. An Allied declaration to Germany on
November 5, 1918, known as the Pre-Armistice Agreement, provided the
contractual basis for reparations.[12] It stated that "invaded territories must be
restored" and that "compensation will be made by Germany for all damage
done to the civilian population of the Allies and their property by the
aggression of Germany by land, by sea, and from the air."[13] An earlier draft

---

8 Versailles Treaty, pt. VIII, annex II, 12c(1).
9 Hagen Schulze, ed., *Das Kabinett Scheidemann: 13. Februar bis 20. Juni 1919* (hereafter *AR Scheidemann*), Akten der Reichskanzlei, Weimarer Republik (Boppard am Rhein, 1971), 78ff.
10 Marc Trachtenberg, *Reparation in World Politics* (New York, 1980), chaps. 1–2. This work should be
   used with caution.
11 For text, see *JMKW,* 6:429–31; or Ray Stannard Baker, *Woodrow Wilson and World Settlement,* 3 vols.
   (New York, 1922), 3:339–43.
12 The Pre-Armistice Agreement was also known as the Lansing note or the Wilson note.
13 Philip Mason Burnett, *Reparation at the Paris Peace Conference from the Standpoint of the American Delegation,* 2 vols. (New York, 1940; reprint, New York, 1965), 1:411. This is the best collection of
   peace conference documents about reparation, together with a competent summary of the peace
   conference history of the question.

had specified "the invasion by Germany of Allied territory," but this was changed at British insistence to the potentially more morally laden phrase, "the aggression of Germany," so that reparations could be claimed for submarine sinkings of merchant ships. Thus the first inadvertent step toward an imputation of war guilt occurred in this crucial document whose validity Germany fully accepted. Indeed, it clung to a narrow interpretation of the prearmistice statement in an effort to limit its liability. The Armistice Convention of November 11 was less clear. It reserved Allied claims and listed "Réparation des dommages." It was not intended to alter the Pre-Armistice Agreement but nonetheless introduced a note of ambiguity on which Britain and France would try later to capitalize.[14]

They were impelled to do so by press campaigns in both countries from the armistice on in favor of claiming the costs of the war from Germany. In Britain, the December 1918 electoral campaign led to pledges which Lloyd George dared not abandon at the peace conference, especially after he had tried to solve his political problem by naming Britain's most ardent supporters of astronomic reparations to his delegation.[15] Thus, though the Pre-Armistice Agreement supposedly limited Germany's liability definitively to civilian damage and excluded war costs, the matter did not remain settled for long. Most Allied nations sought war costs at the peace conference.

Indeed, as Alan Sharp has pointed out, the key questions at Paris were the extent of German liability, the extent also of its capacity to pay, how Germany should pay, and over how long a period. Subsidiary but nevertheless important questions included how much damage had been done and how to evaluate it; what categories of damages were allowable; whether to add up damage claims or to base the reparations bill on Germany's capacity to pay; if the latter, whether to establish a fixed sum in the treaty or to delay; how to estimate German capacity to pay, especially for the future; the mechanics of payment, including forms of payment, interest rate, and term of years; and how to allocate receipts among the victors. The close connections among these questions made them more difficult to settle. If the German debt were decided by totalling claims, the issue of which categories to allow would affect both the total figure and how it was apportioned. If, on the other hand, one set a fixed sum in the treaty, it must to some degree be based on an assessment of German capacity to pay and thus would not cover all damages; then categories allowable would crucially affect allocation of a limited total. Yet if one started by deciding apportionment and

---

14 Ibid., 1:6–8. Only the French text was authentic.
15 Bruce Kent, *The Spoils of War* (Oxford, 1989), 25, 35, 40; Antony Lentin, *Lloyd George, Woodrow Wilson, and the Guilt of Germany: An Essay in the Pre-History of Appeasement* (Baton Rouge, La., 1985), 112–14. Both should be used with caution. See also Burnett, *Reparation,* 1:10–13.

arrived at allocation percentages, categories of damages would cease to matter, however one decided Germany's debt. As the end result would be of explosive importance in the domestic politics of receiver states, Allied leaders wavered among the various approaches, seeking one entailing the least difficulty among themselves and with their respective public and parliamentary opinions. It is little wonder that the statesmen were reluctant to face these issues and that so few of them were resolved at Paris.[16]

Wilson, Lloyd George, and France's Georges Clemenceau, who made most of the key reparations decisions *à trois* or sometimes *à quatre* with Italy's Vittorio Orlando, understood the importance of the matter, the political imperatives, and the urgency of holding the Entente together.[17] These considerations led to awkward compromises, the first and most fateful of which concerned German liability. Wilson thought this had been settled by the Pre-Armistice Agreement; Britain and France, supported by other Allies, sought to reinterpret it and the Armistice Convention so as to incorporate war costs in the German bill. They knew that Germany in fact could not possibly pay such sums, but they knew as well what their electorates and parliaments expected.[18] As it became clear that the concern was far more with appearance than with reality, young John Foster Dulles proposed to make Germany theoretically responsible for all costs but actually liable only for civilian damage. This, together with a threat from Wilson to make a public dissent if the Allies insisted on war costs, dissolved a bitter impasse, and only Belgium, whose invasion was a violation of international law, was awarded war costs.[19] Although this seemed to settle the question, war costs reappeared in one guise or another.

Meanwhile, two clauses were being drafted to establish an unlimited theoretic responsibility and a specific, narrower, actual German liability. What became Article 231 went through several drafts, with Britain and France insisting on affirming a right to integral reparations even if they did not intend to collect war costs. To avoid violating the Pre-Armistice Agreement, to prevent a statement of unlimited German financial liability, and to make the affirmation of Germany's responsibility as oblique and weak as possible, Dulles inserted the word "causing" before "all the loss and dam-

---

16 Alan Sharp, *The Versailles Settlement* (New York, 1991), 78, 86–8. Sharp's chap. 4 provides a useful summary.
17 Paul Mantoux, *Deliberations of the Council of Four (March 24–June 28, 1919): Notes of the Official Interpreter* (hereafter *DCF*), trans. and ed. Arthur S. Link, with the assistance of Manfred F. Boemeke, 2 vols. (Princeton, N.J., 1992), 1:52–3.
18 Ibid., 1:146–7.
19 Technically, Germany assumed Belgium's prearmistice loans (Article 232), which amounted to virtually the same thing.

age." The moral implication escaped the legal and financial experts, who focused upon concocting a politically acceptable compromise and a firm legal basis for reparations. To counter Lloyd George's and Clemenceau's continuing insistence on an explicit German acknowledgment of an obligation for all war costs, a German recognition of responsibility was added.[20] Thus, Article 231 finally read: "The Allied and Associated Governments affirm and Germany accepts the responsibility of Germany and her Allies for causing all the loss and damage to which the Allied and Associated Governments and their nationals have been subjected as a consequence of the war imposed upon them by the aggression of Germany and her allies." In this, the Three were deliberately creating an unlimited theoretic and moral responsibility to pay in the strictly financial sense, while limiting the actual German liability sharply in Article 232.[21] The principle thus established of theoretical debt as opposed to actual liability carried on, invariably with misleading camouflage, throughout the history of reparations, for the political imperative remained, albeit in reduced form.[22] In 1919, however, the Three, whose focus was almost identical to that of their experts, were conscious neither of setting a pattern nor of imputing war guilt to Germany, though they assumed it themselves, for they were not addressing the question of causing the war, which had been assigned to a committee. But the Germans, who addressed reparations nearly simultaneously with the Three, anticipated a war-guilt clause. In their debates from mid-March on, they devoted as much attention to that prospect as to narrowing their liability, for in their minds the two matters were closely linked.[23] Thus they seized upon Article 231; the sequel is well known.

Once war costs had been ruled out and political needs met by the misleading device of Articles 231 and 232, which narrowed Germany's actual financial responsibility to civilian damages as defined in an annex and to Belgium's prearmistice war debts, Wilson sought to write a fixed sum into the treaty both to limit German liability and to restore much-needed stability to financial markets. French experts appreciated that a fixed sum would facilitate commercialization of the bonds Germany would deliver,

20 *DCF*, 1:147, 169.
21 The history of Article 231 can most conveniently be traced in Burnett, *Reparation*, 1: xii–xiii, 66–70.
22 E.g., the London Schedule of Payments of May 5, 1921, imposed a nominal bill of 132 milliard gold marks plus the Belgian war debt and restitutions but limited actual German liability to 50 milliard gold marks ($12.5 billion) by rendering the bulk of the bonds a dead letter. See Sally Marks, "Reparations Reconsidered: A Reminder," *Central European History* 2 (1969): 356–65.
23 For early German cabinet debates over what they routinely called "Guilt Questions," see *AR Scheidemann*, 78–82, 84–90, 146–8.

thereby raising quick cash and eliminating the need for Allied enforcement.[24] Louis Loucheur, who handled reparations for France, was a realist
at heart, but he and Clemenceau faced pressure from the National Assembly and the press.[25] British experts were sharply divided, with Treasury officials favoring some of the lowest figures discussed in Paris and Lloyd
George's appointees to the peace conference Commission on the Reparation of Damage the highest. Lloyd George had hoped in vain that responsibility would tame Prime Minister William Hughes of Australia and the
"Heavenly Twins," Lords Cunliffe and Sumner, so called because they were
inseparable and their estimates were equally astronomic. Lloyd George,
who knew that Germany's capacity had limits, feared the political damage
this trio could wreak, particularly with a restless, demanding House of
Commons "of hard-faced men who look[ed] as if they had done very well
out of the war."[26] When it became clear that he could not achieve a figure
in the treaty meeting his political requirements, he opted for no figure at all.

Recent research indicates that it was Lloyd George more than the supposedly vengeful French who blocked a moderate settlement at Paris.[27] His
reasons were largely political, as he frankly admitted.[28] Delay would defer a
politically painful decision as well as afford time for both passions and price
inflation to subside. Moreover, by the time the matter had to be faced, he
would be rid of Hughes and the Twins. His famous Fontainebleau memorandum of March 25, 1919, seeking concessions to Germany at the expense
of its neighbors, said little very vaguely about reparations (except about the
British share) and was typical of his tendency to straddle the issue.[29]
Throughout the spring, Lloyd George blocked all of Wilson's efforts to write
a fixed sum into the treaty while often simultaneously preaching moderation.[30] Even in June his campaign to revise the draft treaty to Germany's benefit contained expressions of concern about the lack of a definite figure, but
when Wilson tried once again to gain the fixed sum, Lloyd George, with
Clemenceau's support, blocked it.[31]

---

24 Commercializing the bonds entailed a technical change in their status so that they could be mar-
    keted on the world's stock exchanges to private investors. The victors would receive the cash thus
    obtained at once while Germany would pay off the private investors over time. From the German
    point of view, this had the drawback that whereas intergovernmental debts might be reduced by
    negotiation, those to private investors must be honored to preserve Germany's credit.
25 Trachtenberg, *Reparation in World Politics*, 63–4; Burnett, *Reparation*, 1:54.
26 Lentin, *Lloyd George, Woodrow Wilson, and the Guilt of Germany*, 40; see also Sharp, *Versailles*, 90–1.
27 Kent, Lentin, Trachtenberg, and Sharp agree and with reason.
28 Charles Seymour, ed., *The Intimate Papers of Colonel House*, 4 vols. (Boston, 1926–8), 4:356–7.
29 For text, David Lloyd George, *Memoirs of the Peace Conference*, 2 vols. (New Haven, Conn., 1939),
    1:266–73.
30 *DCF,* 1:52.
31 Paul Mantoux, *Les Délibérations du Conseil des Quatre (24 Mars–28 Juin 1919): Notes de l'officier inter-
    prète*, 2 vols. (Paris, 1955), 2:267–71, 283–5 (hereafter *PMCQ*).

It seems clear in retrospect that had the political imperative not been so determining for Clemenceau and Lloyd George, the peace conference could have arrived at a fixed sum somewhere between 60 and 120 milliard gold marks.[32] What this would really have been worth would have depended not only upon the term of years and interest rate for German reparations bonds but also how much camouflage was used to inflate the total by such devices as lavish credits for transferred territories, payment in depreciated paper marks, or creation of purely notional bonds, all of which were contemplated. The best damage estimates were 60 to 100 hundred milliard marks, and the experts agreed that 60 milliard was the maximum one could extract from Germany.[33] However, the decision rested with the Four, of whom three faced political pressure. In deference to that and to the need to preserve Allied unity, Wilson finally yielded on the fixed sum.

The twin but conflicting themes of war costs and the fixed sum ran through the reparations debates at Paris, recurring as other aspects of the problem were taken up, for Lloyd George and Clemenceau repeatedly tried obliquely to revive the one and Wilson the other. American experts hoped that limiting Germany's payments to thirty years would, in effect, restrict its liability. When Wilson accepted that unpaid balances could be postponed, that effort failed.[34] The British and French equally hoped to reinject war costs substantially by enlarging the categories of damage claims allowable for German repayment. Through a long, fruitless Allied wrangle over allocation of future receipts, each tried to maximize its own share, France by seeking a priority for devastation,[35] Britain by campaigning to include pensions for war widows and allowances for dependents of civilians conscripted to military service. Though a solid case could be made for a priority to devastated areas, there was little justification for pensions and allowances. The American delegation was much opposed. However, Lloyd George sent round General Jan Christiaan Smuts of South Africa, whom Wilson liked because of his support for the League of Nations, and the president gave way.[36]

---

32 Burnett, *Reparation*, 2:124, 160, 360. A milliard is the same as an American billion but is a more precise term inasmuch as billion has a different meaning in Britain. Whereas the paper mark depreciated quickly, the gold mark was fixed at roughly four to the dollar and twenty to the pound.

33 Burnett, *Reparation*, 1:25, 49, 54–8; Sharp, *Versailles*, 90. The final damage estimate on May 26, 1919, by Brig. Gen. C. H. McKinstry, U.S. Army Corps of Engineers, put the total amount at 160 milliard gold marks ($40 billion), excluding damage in Russia, Poland, and Czechoslovakia. Burnett, *Reparation*, 2:46.

34 Inga Floto, *Colonel House in Paris* (Princeton, N.J., 1973), 202. The decision is often attributed to House, but Wilson approved it.

35 Burnett, *Reparation*, 1:637–46.

36 For one of innumerable accounts, see Lentin, *Lloyd George, Woodrow Wilson, and the Guilt of Germany*, 56–8. *Why* Wilson ceded remains unclear, but it is widely supposed that he yielded because Lloyd George threatened to leave the conference and reject the treaty. See, e.g., Arthur Walworth, *Wilson and His Peacemakers: American Diplomacy at the Paris Peace Conference, 1919* (New York, 1986), 281.

Pensions and allowances were included to enlarge the share of Britain and its dominions, for Britain had suffered little physical damage and Hughes's Australia none. In addition, inclusion roughly doubled potential claims, which seemed important because the treaty opted for arriving at a total figure by adding up claims.[37] In the end, however, pensions and allowances affected only the ostensible total, not Germany's actual liability, for the Reparation Commission established by the treaty emulated the peace conference's example by adding up claims to create an ostensible total of 132 milliard gold marks for political reasons and then creating a highly technical and misleading payment schedule based on a realistic estimate of German capacity to pay, consigning all but 50 milliard marks to never-never land.[38] There has been considerable debate about whether it was realized at the peace conference that inclusion of pensions would not in fact enlarge a finite reparations pie, and if so by whom.[39] In fact, an American reparations expert had pointed out to the Four on April 5 that because German capacity was limited, only the distribution of receipts would be affected in practice.[40]

The experts and statesmen haggled for months at Paris over these and related matters and produced a prodigiously long reparations section of the Versailles treaty. Yet one is struck by how much of significance they did not settle. The Three were politicians, accustomed to postponing awkward, politically painful decisions, and so once again they put off evil days. Most important, they left it to a new Reparation Commission of victors to decide in two years what Germany's total liability would be and how it would be paid. Both international and domestic politics dictated deferral of the agonizing matter of apportionment of receipts among the Allies. Though the victors had endlessly debated German capacity to pay, they had given little thought to German will to pay, a striking omission considering how dependent upon German cooperation the entire process of collecting reparations was going to be in the absence of actual Allied physical possession of Germany's economic and financial resources. To the extent that the Three debated the matter at all, they assumed German ill will, especially the French, but did not face the implications, notably in terms of the potential unmarketability of German reparations bonds. Finally, in this connection there was a startling absence of enforcement provisions. Except for the potentially problematic commercialization of the bonds, the only guarantee

37 Burnett, *Reparation,* 1:61, 78.
38 On this point, see Marks, "Myths," 232, 236.
39 Trachtenberg, *Reparation in World Politics,* 69–70; Burnett, *Reparation,* 1:64–5.
40 *DCF,* 1:152. Col. House was substituting for Wilson, who was ill.

was provided by the Rhineland occupation, whose duration was explicitly tied to the fulfillment of reparations obligations.[41]

II

Perhaps one reason the treaty contained so little provision for enforcement was that its clauses on the related issues of reparations and the Rhineland owed so much to the 1871 Treaty of Frankfurt. The dictated peace ending the Franco-Prussian war had been a recent round in the unending game of tit for tat that great powers play, and, in fact, the last previous round between France and Germany. Thus it was much on the minds of Europe's leaders, especially those of France.[42] Indeed, during the exchange of correspondence between the Allies and Germany in May, Clemenceau cited the treaties of Frankfurt and Brest-Litovsk, both imposed after revolutions, to refute Germany's suggestion that the German people could not be held accountable for the actions of their former rulers.[43]

Certainly, the treaties of 1871 and 1919 contained striking similarities, not only in the economic and financial clauses but especially in the link between occupation and payment of an indemnity regarded as astronomical in size, with evacuation in stages if the indemnity was paid up to date and prolongation of the occupation if it were not.[44] In both instances, occupation costs of the victors were borne by the loser and were not credited toward the indemnity. The occupation was to serve as guarantee of payment and to encourage speedy discharge of the debt to liberate the national territory. At Paris in 1919, the victors clearly viewed the Rhineland occupation in this light, though Clemenceau, cynical as always about Germany, professed some doubt as to its efficacy.[45] Further, on both occasions the victors required interest on unpaid balances and refused in respect to Alsace-Lorraine to assume prewar state debts of the loser or to credit state properties in the transferred territories, such as railways, toward payment of the indemnity.

Both treaties demoted the loser from continental primacy and generated a desire for revenge, though Germany, unlike France, was soon able to

41 Versailles Treaty, Articles 430 and 431.
42 In 1871 Germans spoke often of Tilsit. Clemenceau became mayor of Montmartre in September 1870. He was elected to the National Assembly in February 1871 and voted against the Treaty of Frankfurt. See David Robin Watson, *Georges Clemenceau: A Political Biography* (London, 1974), 36, 44–5.
43 A. de Lapradelle, ed., *La Paix de Versailles* (hereafter *Paix*), 13 vols. (Paris, 1930–2), 12:14.
44 For the text of the Treaty of Frankfurt, see Robert I. Giesberg, *The Treaty of Frankfort* (Philadelphia, 1966), 283–93.
45 *PMCQ*, 2:270–2, 507–10.

avenge defeat. Both were imposed on precarious new regimes whose survival seemed to be in question. Each was viewed as a humiliation by the
defeated power, which, on each occasion, felt that a moral wrong had been
imposed on it, though in France this chiefly applied to the loss of Alsace
and much of Lorraine. Both treaties produced in the loser the same rapid
economic recovery and lingering emotional sore.

Yet the differences between the two situations were significant, perhaps
decisive. Self-evidently, the size of the indemnity and duration of payment
were of different magnitudes. The Treaty of Frankfurt demanded five milliard gold francs over three years, whereas that of Versailles required unspecified but vast sums over thirty years or more. Clearly, the psychological
effect alone would not be comparable. Yet perhaps the difference is less startling than it seems at first glance. Prussian leaders expected the indemnity
to cripple France for at least ten to fifteen years; its worth in post–World
War I values (by French estimates) was 25 milliard francs or 20 milliard gold
marks, the sum that in 1919 Germany was supposed to provide as an
interim payment within two years, though not primarily in cash nor chiefly
for reparations. Moreover, 20 milliard marks was 40 percent of what Germany was ultimately asked to pay over thirty-six years. To be sure, the
Treaty of Frankfurt contained no equivalent of Article 231;[46] on the other
hand, the truncation was more severe and the occupation more extensive in
both size and troop numbers. And as the French noted, the indemnity
imposed on France was not for repair of damage, of which Germany had
none in 1871, but for war costs, which it covered more than twice over.[47]

Another important difference was that in 1870–71 Death's Head Hussars
spent six months at Versailles; the Prussian king himself was there for five
months and there became "der Kaiser" when the Second Reich was proclaimed on January 18, 1871, in Louis XIV's Hall of Mirrors, and German
troops paraded the Champs Elysées to and through the Arc de Triomphe.[48]
The French nation had a clear appreciation of crushing defeat; surely, this

46 But in 1919 all *Allied* discussion of the war's origin was consistently divorced from the reparations
    section of the treaty (Part VIII) and contained in Part VII concerning penalties (surrender of the
    Kaiser, trial of alleged war criminals).
47 Note, July 3, 1922, Série Z, Grande-Bretagne, file 49, Ministère des Affaires Etrangères, Paris (here-
    after MAE); Holtfrerich, *Deutsche Inflation*, 109; R. Poidevin and Jacques Bariéty, *Les Relations
    franco-allemandes, 1815–1875* (Paris, 1957), 97–101. The 1870–1 war costs of the German states
    amounted to no more than 1.5 milliard marks or about 1.875 milliard French francs. See Ernst
    Samhaber, "Die Kriegsentshädigung," in Wolfgang von Groote and Ursula von Gersdorff, eds.,
    Entscheidung 1870: Der deutsch-französische Krieg (Stuttgart, 1970), 256.
48 N. Sauvée-Dauphin, "L'occupation prussienne à Versailles," in P. Levillain and R. Riemenschneider,
    eds., *La Guerre de 1870/71 et ses conséquences* (Bonn, 1990), 231; Giesberg, *Frankfort,* 116–23;
    Michael Howard, *The Franco-Prussian War* (London, 1961), 449–50.

contributed to its acceptance of the indemnity without undue emotion and to its determination to do what was necessary to end the occupation. This in turn led to oversubscription of two liberation loans, enabling France to pay the indemnity in two years, and thus to early liberation of what remained of its territory.[49] By contrast, though in the spring of 1919 German peace delegates were lodged as virtual prisoners behind protective fencing at Versailles, Allied troops were confined to the Rhineland, and nobody paraded through Berlin except German troops saluted by their chancellor at the Brandenburger Tor as returning undefeated from the field of battle.[50] Surely this partly explains, together with the lack of devastation, why American agents in Germany after the armistice found it necessary to remind German officials about who won the war, why the German people quickly forgot defeat, and why the entire nation believed that justice demanded evacuation of the Rhineland without substantial payment of reparations. Beyond doubt, the Allies failed between November and May to bring defeat home to the German people or to prepare them for the consequences of that defeat. Nor, less surprisingly, did the new German cabinet.[51] Thus the German people entered upon that state of denial that Ernst Troeltsch called "the dreamland of the Armistice period."[52]

III

Despite possession of considerable information, German leaders also engaged in wishful thinking.[53] They proceeded on the assumption that they

49 Klaus Malettke, "Deutsche Besatzung in Frankreich und die französische Kriegsentschädigung aus der Sicht der deutschen Forschung," in Levillain and Riemenschneider, eds., *La Guerre de 1870/71*, 249–83; Giesberg, *Frankfort*, 180, 286–7, 307–8. Malettke calculates that with interest and local levies, France paid 5.55 milliard gold francs in all. Allan Mitchell, *The German Influence in France After 1870* (Chapel Hill, N.C., 1979), 23, includes occupation costs and "contributions" and estimates that the total bill considerably exceeded 6 milliard francs. In the values of fifty years later, this would amount to about 25 milliard gold marks.
50 Robert G. Waite, *Vanguard of Nazism: The Free Corps Movement in Postwar Germany, 1918–1923* (Cambridge, Mass., 1952), 7. At the time of the Armistice, the Allies thought sending troops far into Germany would be risky.
51 *AR Scheidemann*, 28; Dresel reports, Woodrow Wilson papers, 5B/30–32 passim, Library of Congress, Washington, D.C.; Dresel-Osborne report, n.d., ACNP 84.013102, RG 256, Records of the American Commission to Negotiate Peace, NA; Klaus Schwabe, *Woodrow Wilson, Revolutionary Germany, and Peacemaking, 1918–1919: Missionary Diplomacy and the Realities of Power*, trans. R. and R. Kimber (Chapel Hill, N.C., 1985), 314; Marc Ferro, *The Great War, 1914–1918*, trans. N. Stone (London, 1973), 222; Peter Krüger, *Deutschland und die Reparationen, 1918/19* (Stuttgart, 1973), 161; Gerald D. Feldman, *The Great Disorder: Politics, Economics, and Society in the German Inflation, 1914–1924* (Oxford, 1993), 148.
52 See the elaboration of this theme in chapters 1 and 9 in this book.
53 E.g. Max Warburg, who in December 1918 "believed in the full restoration of prewar Germany in a postwar world." Quoted in Ron Chernow, *The Warburgs: The Twentieth-Century Odyssey of a Remarkable Jewish Family* (New York, 1993), 212.

were entitled to full parity and equality and had no expectation that they might in any respect or degree be treated as they had treated others. Sharp Allied remarks about the treaties of Frankfurt and Brest-Litovsk were quickly rebutted on the basis of the Fourteen Points and the armistice,[54] which the Germans used when to their advantage and ignored, declared invalid, or tried to revise when not, thereby initiating a practice that prevailed through the history of reparations, chiefly as to the treaty. Debate on that treaty began even before the German delegation read it, on the strength of premises that the German cabinet had developed during the spring. Throughout, German leaders were united on their goals but divided both within the cabinet and between the cabinet and the German delegations in France on how to pursue them.[55]

In its springtime debates, the cabinet had dwelt primarily on three closely connected issues. The first was how to reduce the anticipated indemnity by arguing either that the Pre-Armistice Agreement was not a contractual obligation or variously that the "aggression" it cited covered only damage to the territory of France and Belgium, despite its reference to the Fourteen Points, which specified restoration of Romania, Serbia, and Montenegro as well.[56] The Germans had fairly accurate information about the figures being discussed at the peace conference, and considered them all unpayable, since German living standards and social gains could not be impaired.[57] But it seemed best to rest on a narrow interpretation of the Pre-Armistice Agreement as a binding contract conferring responsibility only for damage from direct German aggression to Belgo-French soil. Second, there was the question of how to refute the expected charge of war guilt, which German leaders assumed to be the basis of their liability. The favored methods were a discourse on the history of the past forty years or imputation of aggressive intent to Russia, which at present was conveniently preoccupied and isolated. Finally, there was the related but delicate matter of whether to disassociate the new republic and the German people from the imperial regime, on which the cabinet ultimately straddled. Disassociation was invalid in international law and awkward in regard to civilian and military leaders of 1914–18 still in Germany. Also, any attempt to refute war

---

54 Lapradelle, *Paix*, 12:43.
55 Krüger, *Deutschland*, 167. A German financial delegation had arrived at the château de la Villette near Compiègne at the start of April.
56 Thus "by sea" would mean only sea bombardment of northern France and Belgium and would not cover sinkings of Allied ships.
57 Krüger, *Deutschland*, 108–12. They assumed that fulfillment of the treaty terms must be "consonant with the achievements of the Revolution and that social stability and domestic peace had primacy over all other concerns." Feldman, *Great Disorder*, 136.

guilt implied a link to the Second Reich, as did reliance on the limiting features of the Pre-Armistice Agreement, which had been contracted with the Kaiser's last government. Thus the cabinet was divided on this issue. As to tactics, it agreed on loud and constant repetition of its views, numerous countercharges, and maximum propaganda to rouse world opinion, especially socialists, and to split the Entente, which it hoped was crumbling. Further, Germany would insist on absolute equality and an equal voice, demand neutral arbiters, and make an inflated offer, proposing to pay it in paper marks at the 1914 exchange rate or roughly triple their current value on neutral exchanges.[58] In addition, every means was to be used to lure the Allies into negotiation.[59] Thus Germany would ignore the military verdict and the fact that peace without victory had been overtaken by events and try to resume as much of its negotiating strength at the end of 1916 as possible. Clearly, Germany was as concerned with domestic and international politics as the Allies and as adept with smoke and mirrors, if not more so.

Most of these strands in German thinking appeared at once when the treaty was presented on May 7 at the Trianon palace to a German delegation. The German foreign minister, Count Ulrich von Brockdorff-Rantzau, acknowledged defeat and some violations of international law, but declared at the outset, "We are required to admit that we alone are war-guilty. Such an admission on my lips would be a lie." He referred to the past fifty years of European imperialism, then counterattacked: "The hundreds of thousands of noncombatants who have perished since November 11 through the blockade were killed with cold deliberation, after victory had been won and assured to our adversaries." He sought an impartial inquiry into war guilt by a neutral commission and indicated that Germany would contribute so far as was jointly agreed to "the restoration of the territory of Belgium and Northern France" with "the technical and financial participation of the victors," adding that "experts on both sides will have to study how the German people can best meet its obligation of financial reparation without breaking down under the heavy load." He ended by declaring that only a peace of justice could be fulfilled.[60]

The effort to distance the German people from its former rulers was deferred to the diplomatic notes that ensued.[61] For the rest, he laid the basis

---

58 *Papers Relating to the Foreign Relations of the United States: The Paris Peace Conference, 1919* (hereafter *FRUS-PPC*), 13 vols. (Washington, D.C., 1945–7), 6:913; Gerald D. Feldman, *Iron and Steel in the German Inflation, 1916–1923* (Princeton, N.J., 1977), 472–3; Joseph S. Davis, "Recent Economic and Financial Progress in Germany," *Review of Economic Statistics* 3 (1921): 150.

59 For this paragraph in general, see *AR Scheidemann*, passim; and Schwabe, *Woodrow Wilson*, chap. 6, passim.

60 *FRUS-PPC*, 3:417–20.

61 Lapradelle, *Paix*, 12:13.

for explication of Germany's version of recent European history, claimed full equality, demanded neutral arbiters, and tried to narrow Germany's liability to partial restoration of the soil of Belgium and northern France to an extent consented to by Germany. He launched his propaganda campaign with the first of many dramatic references to the "hunger blockade," which in fact did not exist.[62] Moreover, the campaign against "unilateral war guilt" had been launched before Brockdorff-Rantzau had seen the treaty and before it had occurred to its authors to view Article 231 in that light, although at no time did any country other than Germany suggest that guilt was unilateral, sole, or Germany's alone. Thereafter the German delegation consciously emulated Leon Trotsky's performance at Brest-Litovsk, flooding the Allies with notes, publishing them at once, delaying whenever possible, engaging in as much public diplomacy as could be managed, and launching an intense propaganda campaign to engage the world's sympathies.[63]

IV

When the German delegation read the draft treaty, it reacted with shock and indignation to both the procedure and the terms.[64] Germany had recognized in March that the Allies would present a text for acceptance rather than negotiate, but hope had revived in April. Thus cabinet and delegation thought Germany would enter the conference as a great power, negotiate as an equal, and carry the day by a forceful attitude. Though even stiffer terms had been rumored, leaders who understood in November what to expect had entered into a "dreamland" of their own, interpreting Wilson's imprecise Fourteen Points in the most favorable way and convincing each

---

62 Allied ships remained in place but technical continuance of the blockade did not bar food shipments, which were explicitly permitted by the armistice and which the Allies offered thereafter if Germany provided the ships to carry them. But Germany withheld the ships pending resolution of inter-Allied disagreement over how Germany would pay for the food. By the time Brockdorff-Rantzau spoke, American food had arrived in late March in American ships. *FRUS-PPC*, 2:139–42, 12:115; 371–6, GB FO 371/3776, Public Record Office, passim and especially Admiralty to Foreign Office, Apr. 19, 1919, n. 10630. When Ellis Dresel of the U.S. delegation visited Germany in December 1918, he was repeatedly told the food shortage would not become acute until late spring; several German leaders urged the Allies to announce that no food would be sent until a stable, responsible government was assured. Dresel to Grew, Jan. 10, 1919, report & encls., Woodrow Wilson papers, 5B:8, nos. 6318–36, Library of Congress, Washington, D.C. See also chapter 15 in this book. C. Paul Vincent, *The Politics of Hunger: The Allied Blockade of Germany, 1915–1919* (Athens, Ohio, 1985), adds detail despite a startling lack of context.

63 Alma Luckau, *The German Delegation at the Paris Peace Conference* (New York, 1971), 120.

64 See, e.g., Alan Sharp, "'Quelqu'un nous écoute': French Interception of German Telegraphic and Telephonic Communications During the Paris Peace Conference, 1919: A Note," *Intelligence and National Security* 3 (Oct. 1988): 125.

other that they could avoid substantial territorial loss and hold reparations to a minimum.[65]

The bankers and industrialists were also unrealistic, insisting on giving priority to domestic war loans, complaining that the financial terms deviated from the principle of mutuality, and arguing that if shares in German industry were offered to proprietors of devastated French firms, then shares in French enterprises should be accorded to German industry, ignoring the fact that the aim was to transfer real wealth from Germany to the battered victors.[66] However, unrealistic thinking extended beyond the experts. Lack of awareness of Germany's true position as a defeated power and of Allied attitudes tended to increase with distance from Paris, but neither the delegation nor its leader were immune, often thinking only of German needs and political exigencies, not of Allied requirements. Thus German arguments were based on interpretations that had no prospect of acceptance, and their proposals rarely met Allied needs.

In addition, Brockdorff-Rantzau was tactless, inconsistent as a result of pressure from Berlin, and illogical. His open truculence and attacks on Wilson denied Germany his goals of direct negotiations and using Wilson as a counterweight to France.[67] His tactics required a united home front, especially if he decided to reject the treaty, but the home front was ever more divided.[68] And while Brockdorff-Rantzau insisted on the Pre-Armistice Agreement as a binding contract, his notes danced as far as possible away from the "aggression" contained therein, both primarily to limit financial liability.[69]

The German cabinet and delegation were determined to divorce "aggression" from responsibility for causing the war, which they blamed on czarist Russia, and to strip it of any moral connotation (which in fact the Allies had not intended in the pre-armistice note). Germany admitted aggression only in the sense of an invasion of Belgium in violation of international law and of France through Belgium.[70] This eliminated financial responsibility for damage in Russia, Poland, Romania, Serbia, Montenegro,

---

65 Schwabe, *Woodrow Wilson*, 301; Chernow, *The Warburgs*, 212; Krüger, *Deutschland*, 161, 185; Feldman, *Great Disorder*, 146; see also chapter 1 in this book.

66 Krüger, *Deutschland*, 170, 186, 181.

67 Schwabe, *Woodrow Wilson*, 363, 371.

68 Krüger, *Deutschland*, 194.

69 *FRUS-PPC*, 6:802, 792; Lapradelle, *Paix*, 12:13; Burnett, *Reparation*, 2:24. Brockdorff-Rantzau also stressed that the Pre-Armistice Agreement was legally binding territorially to prevent Allied faits accomplis in armistice renewals.

70 Belgium enjoyed a special status under the treaties of 1839, whereby its independence, territorial integrity, and perpetual neutrality were guaranteed by the great powers.

Italy, or on the seas. Further, Brockdorff-Rantzau's notes argued that Germany accepted the obligation to make reparation "independently of the question of responsibility for the war." The German government resisted any imputation of "war guilt" not only in moral terms but also primarily from fear that such an admission would remove the territorial and financial protections of the Fourteen Points and the Pre-Armistice Agreement and thus give the Allies a new legal basis for a more severe peace.[71]

It soon became evident that the flurry of notes to this effect and on other matters was making no desirable impression on the Allies. Thus, German financial experts argued that better treaty terms could be purchased by a dramatic offer. Since Brockdorff-Rantzau agreed, the delegation faced down the cabinet's reluctance and prevailed in a tense meeting at Spa, though the cabinet's views affected the niggling form of the final note.[72] The purposes of the offer were to prevent territorial loss, preserve the economic unity of the Reich, maintain German predominance in the east, and gain direct negotiations, possibly shattering Allied unity to Germany's profit.

Accordingly, the voluminous German Observations on the treaty transmitted to the Allies on May 29 contained a highly contingent offer. Indeed, it was so contingent that it had no prospect of serious consideration, for the conditions amounted to abandonment of the greater part of the treaty. Though claiming to rest on the Fourteen Points, territorially Germany would cede only the greater part of Posen (Poznan)[73] and accept plebiscites in Alsace-Lorraine and in an area on the Danish border smaller than that specified by the treaty.[74] Poland's access to the sea would be assured through use of German facilities, and all ceded territories would assume a share not only of Germany's prewar debts but also of its war debts and reparations. Anschluss would be permitted to the Germans of Austria and Bohemia, and there would be no Rhineland occupation. Germany would cede title to its colonies if it gained immediate entry into the League of Nations (where it expected a large loan) and the mandate for these colonies. It would retain its merchant fleet and full "freedom of economic movement at home and abroad." There would be a neutral inquiry into "the responsibility for the war."[75]

---

71 *AR Scheidemann,* 193, 197, 203–4; *FRUS-PPC,* 6:791–2; Burnett, *Reparation,* 2:32–3, and quotation, 2:6.
72 Chernow, *The Warburgs,* 216; Krüger, *Deutschland,* 179–99; *AR Scheidemann,* 368–9.
73 At most, Poland would gain the demarcation of the third prolongation of the armistice of February 16, 1919. *AR Scheidemann,* 194.
74 That is to say, Germany would retain Eupen-Malmédy, the Saar Basin, more of Schleswig, West Prussia, all of East Prussia, and Upper Silesia. In regard to Schleswig, the German case was solid and ultimately successful.
75 For text, see *FRUS-PPC,* 6:797–9. See also the elaborative documents that follow, especially 854–6, 880–1, 914.

In return for this drastic treaty revision, Germany offered payments to an apparent maximum of 100 milliard gold marks. Twenty milliard would be paid by May 1, 1926, the rest thereafter in annual payments without interest not exceeding 1 milliard per year in the first ten years. The total would include the Belgian war debt and all other claims on Germany. Germany would also assist in the reconstruction of flooded French mines, ship coal in diminishing amounts to France for ten years,[76] deliver chemicals, provide river boats to France and Belgium, and offer Franco-Belgian participation in German enterprises. However, Germany would receive reparations credit in more categories than the treaty provided, the powers of the Reparations Commission would be greatly reduced, and it would make decisions jointly with a German commission.[77]

The figure of 100 milliard marks derived from the treaty requirement to deliver interest-bearing German bonds to that amount, with the prospect that the Reparations Commission could increase the figure later.[78] Recognizing that the Allies cared about the appearance of a large sum rather than the reality, German experts proposed to maintain the Allied sum "at least nominally."[79] Germany would make the Allied minimum its maximum, but without interest, which reduced the value considerably. Further, the Allies wanted the first 20 milliard paid by 1921, whereas Germany thought to pay it in 1926. Most of the remainder would be deferred to the distant future in hopes that the figures would be revised downward before many payments came due.[80]

The German delegation optimistically thought a nominal and deferred offer of the Allied minimum would preserve the Reich's economic and territorial unity, prevent a Rhineland occupation, and eliminate all supervision. The proposal did not have this effect. American experts showed some interest, chiefly in terms of gaining a fixed sum,[81] but Wilson did not, and there was little enthusiasm among the Allies, who recognized that the real value fell far below one hundred milliard.[82] Indeed, Keynes estimated the present value without interest to be 30 milliard.[83] This fact, together with the extensive conditions, ensured that the German offer was not taken up.

---

76 Ten years was the amount of time to German eyes (but not French) needed to clear and reconstruct the French mines.

77 *FRUS-PPC*, 6:798, 853–6, 914–16.

78 Versailles Treaty, pt. VIII, annex II (12).

79 Krüger, *Deutschland*, 198, quoting Warburg.

80 Ibid., 187, 198–9; Schwabe, *Woodrow Wilson*, 358.

81 Which, however, would be 120 milliard marks, and which Loucheur also favored. Burnett, *Reparation*, 1:137–8, 2:124, 160; Schwabe. *Woodrow Wilson*, 362–4, 370.

82 As Matthias Erzberger had warned they would. *AR Scheidemann*, 369. See also *FRUS-PPC*, 6:966.

83 John Maynard Keynes, *The Economic Consequences of the Peace* (New York, 1920), 222–3. Assuming absolute certainty and a perfect market, present value is a calculation based on the future value at

Meanwhile, an extensive correspondence was in progress that elaborated the stated themes in great detail without adding much other than bitterness and emotion.[84] As the exchanges continued and German resistance to signing was evident, Allied language became as intemperate as that of Brockdorff-Rantzau and amounted in the reply to the German Observations on the treaty to an accusation of war guilt.[85] However, these charges were not in the reparations section of the commentary and, more important, not incorporated in the treaty itself. After one final effort to escape Article 231, Germany was obliged to sign the treaty without substantive change to the reparations clauses.[86]

V

It is not surprising that a war-guilt clause preoccupied German leaders so intensely from March through June, for they knew the events of the July crisis cast their country in an unfavorable light and also assumed a connection between war guilt and financial responsibility.[87] It is more surprising, perhaps, that Allied leaders never thought to write one and never, before the encounter in the Trianon, viewed article 231 thus; at Paris, however, the question of responsibility for the origin of the war had never been treated in conjunction with reparations.[88] In their concern about Allied audiences, the Three gave no thought to the effect on another audience, nor to the fact that the leaders of the fragile new German democracy would be beset with political necessities as well.[89]

Allied statesmen assumed that everybody, including most Germans, realized that Germany had lost the war, that it was to a large degree responsible for the onset of the war, and that it had committed a good many sins, starting with the invasion of Belgium. Not only were some of these assump-

maturity of a bond, the interest rate, the term of years, and the frequency of compounding periods. It represents the intermediate worth amount that with interest will accumulate over a given time to a specified sum. As markets are not perfect and risk exists, present value is not necessarily the market value of the bond. For fiscal and monetary reasons as well as political ones, no German reparations bonds were ever marketable.

84 Full texts are in Lapradelle, *Paix*, 12; relevant extracts in English are in Burnett, *Reparation*, 2.
85 *FRUS-PPC*, 6:926–7.
86 Germany also made a final effort to escape delivery of alleged war criminals. Lapradelle, *Paix*, 12:72.
87 E.g., *AR Scheidemann*, 86–8, 146.
88 It had been dealt with in the Commission on the Responsibility of the Authors of the War and on Enforcement of Penalties, which primarily addressed the question of the Kaiser.
89 In the American delegation, only Dresel, who had made a second trip to Germany in April, worried about the effect of the treaty on the new republic. Schwabe, *Woodrow Wilson*, 340. A leading Germanist has written, "The reality was that a domestically troubled and economically disabled Germany confronted a reparations bill which was certainly beyond its domestic political capacities whatever the bill's technical feasibility." Feldman, *Great Disorder*, 406.

tions disputable but they also overlooked the clear fact that most people prefer to forget rather than face unpleasant truths. The Three inflated their figures and their rhetoric to satisfy Allied voters, ignoring both German politics and the historians.

Of course, they did not explain to Brockdorff-Rantzau the true purpose of Article 231 or the distinction between theoretical responsibility and actual liability, for they did not anticipate a war-guilt interpretation of Article 231; perhaps they should have, though neither Austria nor Hungary so interpreted comparable clauses in their treaties.[90] However, after Brockdorff-Rantzau's public challenge at the Trianon ceremony, it was politically impossible for the Allies to say that they did not mean war guilt. To a large extent, German leaders converted Article 231 into a war-guilt clause by their precipitous action on mistaken assumptions, though the Allied reply to the German Observations certainly confirmed that. And once the German delegation had taken that action, domestic politics made it impossible for successive German governments to abandon the issue, which was publicly raised at the most internationally awkward moments throughout the twenties.[91]

A case could be made that it was in Germany's interest to increase its low tax rate, raise domestic liberation loans, pay reparations promptly, and liberate the Rhineland quickly, emulating the French example of 1871–73.[92] France made this case frequently, often with pointed comparisons. A substantial degree of scholarly consensus now suggests that paying what was actually asked of it was within Germany's financial capacity.[93] But this argument ignores the fact that, when issues become political and emotional, people often do not pursue or vote their best interests. The emotional pitch in Germany was soon such that it would have been fatal for any politician to advocate facing reality. Accordingly, German leaders set out to alter reality and perceptions of it abroad. At great cost to their own country and to others, over a decade they succeeded.

But in 1919 that struggle lay ahead. At Paris as well as thereafter, politics, domestic and international, dominated the war-guilt debate. The Germans kept hoping that the Entente was crumbling;[94] it was, but in 1919 this circumstance only made it stiffen in direct confrontation with Germany. And once the Germans had highlighted Article 231, they found it necessary to continue to do so. The German translation of the treaty, while extremely

90 Article 177 of the Treaty of Saint-Germain with Austria and Article 161 of the Treaty of Trianon with Hungary.
91 E.g., shortly before Locarno in 1925.
92 On Germany's tax rate, see Holtfrerich, *Deutsche Inflation,* 115.
93 See, e.g., Stephen A. Schuker, *American "Reparations" to Germany, 1919–33* (Princeton, N.J., 1988).
94 Luckau, *German Delegation,* 131; *AR Scheidemann,* 500.

precise on the whole, was less so for Article 231 and enhanced the impression of a charge of German moral guilt, although the word "Schuld" was not used.[95] When the German version of that clause was made public, there was no possibility that Weimar politicians would abandon the war-guilt crusade.

Clearly, Allied leaders were both oblivious and obtuse in their lack of contemplation of German reactions to the treaty; their lack of concern for the new republic, which Wilson himself had in part evoked; their reliance on Germany to execute the reparations provisions; and their assumption that German reparations bonds would be marketable whatever the German attitude. Perhaps concern for the enemy was too much to expect after a long, bitter war, even when it was in the long-term interest of the Allies. But if one acquits the Three of gratuitous vindictiveness, one must convict them of psychological blindness, particularly as to the sense of humiliation and dishonor, which only caused Germans to lash out bitterly. Germans were almost certain to react to an unlimited theoretical liability, even without direct imputation of war guilt, and the "blank check" gave the Weimar Republic a splendid propaganda weapon, which it utilized to the utmost.[96] The German people were bound to fix on how much they owed, not the finer points of the technicalities of how it was to be paid. Both sides made much of the clause stating that unanimity was required in the Reparation Commission to lower the debt but passed in silence over another effectively restricting it. But generally, Germans focused on shame, humiliation, and injustice as they saw it.[97]

If the Allies were obtuse about German reactions, German leaders were unrealistic about their country's situation, more than ordinarily incapable of putting themselves in the shoes of other nations, and themselves oblivious to their effect on others. Brockdorff-Rantzau's truculent speech at the Trianon outraged the key members of his audience and only harmed the German cause, as did his later repeated attacks on Wilson. Moreover, it was all too evident, especially in the German Observations, that German indignation was based in part on an assumption that Germany should not suffer[98] and that reparation, particularly of livestock and equipment removed and destroyed,

95 *FRUS-PPC,* 13:445.
96 Actually, Germany agreed with the treaty provision that the bill would be fixed by May 1, 1921, and with the provision for payment over thirty years, for it wanted to delay on the former and to gain the longest time frame possible for the latter. Krüger, *Deutschland,* 171, 206.
97 Luckau, *German Delegation,* 120, 131; *AR Scheidemann,* 490, 497, 503.
98 The German cabinet assumed that (1) living standards in Germany should not be reduced, (2) all cultural and social achievements should be maintained, and (3) once one had paid for these and repaid domestic and foreign debts, nothing would be left for reparations. *AR Scheidemann,* 79–80, 84.

could only occur when and to the degree convenient.[99] Evidently capacity to pay was to mean capacity to pay without pain. The reactions of Allied leaders whose nations' economies had been destroyed were entirely predictable. As the Allied reply to the German Observations phrased it, "Somebody must suffer for the consequences of the war. Is it to be Germany, or only the peoples she has wronged?"[100] That indeed was the difficulty.

VI

Since so much has been written about the Versailles "Diktat" and the "Carthaginian peace," especially as to the reparations provisions, it might be more fruitful to take a contrary approach and examine the degree of relative moderation inherent in the reparations clauses. In the English-speaking world, the widespread belief in their draconian nature was a triumph of German propaganda, abetted by Keynes. It rested on the well-founded view that few people would struggle through Part VIII of the treaty and that if they did, the lack of context and the technical complexity would prevent any measured assessment.

Most analyses of the reparation question have proceeded from an inverted angle. They open by contrasting the largest, most unrealistic Allied proposals with the parlous condition of Germany. This is tunnel vision instigated by propaganda and without context; reams have been written about the need for "German economic reconstruction" without appreciation that it was not Germany that required reconstruction.[101] World War I caused a net loss of wealth for all major European belligerents; but Germany, like Britain, was one of the luckier ones in that it emerged with its economy intact, if battered, and was spared invasion, denudation, and devastation. As Stephen Schuker has noted, "Significantly, Germany emerged from World War I despite military defeat less damaged in terms of human and economic resources than the other major European combatants."[102] The inverted approach focuses on what the war did to Germany with little mention of what it did to the victors. Everybody's treasury was empty, but a more balanced picture would note that the devastation in France's ten richest departments was so severe that German delegates en route to Versailles by train could barely endure to look at it; that Germany had waged

99 *FRUS-PPC*, 6:859–61.
100 Ibid., 6:930.
101 For a recent example, see Kent, *Spoils*, 57–66. Vincent, *Politics of Hunger*, is another instance of tunnel vision.
102 Stephen A. Schuker, *The End of French Predominance in Europe: The Financial Crisis of 1924 and the Adoption of the Dawes Plan* (Chapel Hill, N.C., 1976), 3–4.

long-term economic warfare, transferring entire factories into the Reich; that the spinning industries of northern France, Belgium, and Poland had entirely disappeared into Germany; and that France's war-induced national debt was, by American estimate, 94.1 percent of its national wealth while that of Belgium was 96.6 percent.[103]

Moreover, Germans argued, and historians have long echoed them, that a strong Germany could pay reparations whereas a weak Germany could not.[104] The Weimar Republic constantly pleaded weakness and poverty, falsifying its trade statistics to buttress its argument.[105] However, as time would conclusively demonstrate, under the Versailles treaty Germany remained the continent's greatest power, especially economically.[106] As French leaders recognized, its predominance would only increase when the various temporary bonds of Versailles dissolved. Despite the loss of Saar coal and Lorraine iron ore, Germany remained Europe's industrial powerhouse, quickly able to dominate central and eastern European states and prevented from swamping the devastated economies of the victors only by artificial five-year constraints written into the treaty. When those constraints lapsed in 1925, loss of the Lorraine ore fields gave Germany a whip hand against France in negotiations toward a trade treaty, for France was now dependent both on Ruhr coal and on Germany as an outlet for iron ore and metallurgical semi-products.[107] By then, Germany was nearing industrial hegemony.[108]

Weimar also argued early and late that it could pay reparations only by a massive export drive. It convinced not only the historians but also British leaders, who feared for their battered trade balances. In fact, had Germany ever raised its tax rate to that of the victors, as required by the treaty, ample

103 Luckau, *German Delegation*, 115; Samuel G. Shartle, *Spa, Versailles, Munich: An Account of the Armistice Commission* (Philadelphia, 1941), 35, 64; Deuxième Bureau note, Sept. 10, 1918, 6N/127, Service historique de l'Armée, Vincennes; Francis William O'Brien, ed., *The Hoover-Wilson Wartime Correspondence* (Ames, Iowa, 1974), 276–7; Burnett, *Reparation*, 1:1132–3.
104 See *FRUS-PPC*, 6:857, 903.
105 For this reason, analytic studies based on these statistics possess limited utility. See also Feldman, *Great Disorder*, 484–5, 599.
106 Politically and militarily, Germany suffered short-term eclipse but still could dominate all neighbors except France.
107 Although the Saar had vast reserves, only one mine produced bituminous coking coal. The anthracite from other mines was suitable to the coal grates of Paris apartments, not to steel production. In general, the treaty created an acute Franco-Belgo-Italian dependency on Ruhr coal, as was dramatically demonstrated during the Ruhr crisis when French and Belgian blast furnaces were forced to shut down for lack of it. Hoesch to AA, Mar. 14, 1923, tel. 381, 1525/3116H/D636973, AA, T-120; Logan to Strong, Feb. 23 and Mar. 6, 1923, files 2/287, 328, Papers of Col. James A. Logan Jr., Hoover Institution, Stanford, Cal.; Nollet to Poincaré. Mar. 6, 1923, no. 2535, sous-série B, file 186, MAE; de Gaiffier to Jaspar, Feb. 27, 1923, no. 2852/1381, Belgium, Classement B, file 10.071, MAE.
108 As the 1926 steel cartel and the 1927 Franco-German trade treaty demonstrated. Schuker, *French Predominance*, 373.

amounts would have been raised for reparations, as the 1924 Dawes Committee discovered.[109] Beyond that, a fiscal and monetary housecleaning, which Weimar cabinets were from the outset reluctant to undertake both for domestic reasons and in hopes of a reparations write-down,[110] would have facilitated foreign loans; Germany preferred always to pay in borrowed money.[111] And, of course, the French noted that *their* citizenry had subscribed to 1871–2 loans to meet the problem.

There are two other reasons why the reparations picture is often distorted. One is that German leaders from March 1919 on, and increasingly the German people, assumed that their capacity was limited to what could be paid without pain.[112] Those who had suffered disagreed; in fact, the Allies anticipated some decline in German living standards, though perhaps not to the level of the victors. The other is that there is a tendency to suppose that all those milliards had to be paid in cash, when, in fact, relatively few were. Reparations credit was given for kind (coal, timber, chemicals, and dyes), merchant ships as well as river and fishing boats, livestock, agricultural and industrial machinery, locomotives and rolling stock, some art works, and books to replace those burnt at Louvain. In addition, Germany was credited for military equipment, battlefield salvage, and state property in colonies and territories transferred (except Alsace-Lorraine), including the Saar mines. Credit was given for replacements but not for restitutions, that is, return of the same item rather than a substitute. Thus no credit was given for restoring to Belgium a van Eyck triptych seized in the war, but the books for Louvain were replacements and so credited.[113]

Defenders of the Versailles treaty often argue that its exactions were moderate compared with what Germany imposed on Russia and intended to impose on Britain, but many aspects of the reparations clauses could be called moderate in their own right.[114] For example, the Allies decided that occupation costs and the expense of provisioning Germany with food and raw materials could be deducted from the interim payment of 20 milliard

109 About 4.5 milliard gold marks per year by reluctant British estimate. Ibid., 184.
110 Krüger, *Deutschland*, 210.
111 Ibid., 182.
112 Or, on occasion, without pain to their special interest. Workers generally did not object strenuously to reparations provided that big business bore the burden whereas employers were willing to make an effort if the ten-hour day was restored. See, e.g., Feldman, *Great Disorder*, 199, 371, 663, 667.
113 *FRUS-PPC*, 13:525. See also Reparation Commission, *Official Documents*, 13 vols. (London, 1922–30), 4:8–10, 24.
114 Article 8 of the Treaty of Brest-Litovsk imposed on what remained of Russia a disguised indemnity that Russians estimated at 4 to 5 milliard gold rubles. The treaty of August 27, 1918, required a Russian payment of 6 milliard marks. Russia paid 120 million gold rubles in August and September 1918. A prewar ruble equaled two marks. J. W. Wheeler-Bennett, *Brest-Litovsk, the Forgotten Peace* (1938; reprint, New York, 1971), 273, 344–5, 347.

gold marks that Germany was to make before May 1, 1921, rather than being billed separately. Technically, these prior charges did not count as reparations, but the 1921 London Schedule of Payments had the effect of crediting Germany with 8 milliard marks for such payments.[115] In addition, specification of 2.5 percent and 5 percent interest on later German bonds was generous considering that France and Belgium were borrowing in America at 8.5 percent and more to finance reconstruction.[116] The offer to permit use of German labor to rebuild was also generous, given the high feelings and staggering unemployment rates in devastated areas.[117]

Equally, the important provisions for coal deliveries were meant to be moderate. France had lost half its coal production and Belgium a smaller portion of its to German flooding of the mines just before the armistice. The Allies thought the treaty schedules of compensatory coal delivery were well within German export capacity; certainly, the Versailles Coal Protocol of August 29, 1919, was restrained; moreover, coal quotas could be revised downward and repeatedly were. Further, the treaty contained provision for return of both the Saar and its mines to Germany.[118] In the same vein, though the entirety of German shipping amounted to only about half of what the Allies lost, the treaty requirement of Germany was all the larger ships, half the midsized vessels, 25 percent of small boats, and 20 percent of the river fleet.[119] Similarly, the treaty contained no levy on Germany for the industrial equipment and plant that had been removed from France, Belgium, and Poland; immediate levies of agricultural equipment, which also had largely vanished from the three countries, were confined to continuation of deliveries to France alone under the January 1919 armistice renewal.[120]

---

115 Prior charges effectively consumed all Germany had paid. In 1921 Germany was overcredited with 8 milliard marks to avoid argument about the value of battlefield salvage, which had not yet been fully assessed, but in fact it had paid 7.539 milliard gold marks in such items as coal, military materiel, and merchant ships, including 3.143 milliard for the Rhineland occupation and nearly 4 milliard for food and raw materials. *FRUS-PPC*, 13:439; Reparation Commission, *Official Documents*, 1:4–9, 4:10–11, 16.

116 Burnett, *Reparation*, 1:107; Thomas William Lamont, "Reparation," in E. M. House and Charles Seymour, eds., *What Really Happened at Paris* (New York, 1921), 286; Versailles Treaty, pt. VIII, annex II, 12c (2).

117 *FRUS-PPC*, 6:965. At the Armistice, the Belgian unemployment rate exceeded 85 percent because the economy was paralyzed and there was nothing with which to work. In April 1919 it was still 75 percent. Sally Marks, *Innocent Abroad: Belgium at the Paris Peace Conference of 1919* (Chapel Hill, N.C., 1981), 173–4.

118 Kent, *Spoils*, 83; Burnett, *Reparation*, 1:113–4, 122–3; Marks, "Myths," 241. Coal quotas were reduced in 1921 after Germany lost the Silesian coal fields.

119 Burnett, *Reparation*, 1:114–17. The Three had not intended to require transfer of any smaller vessels, but the small states insisted upon partial recompense for shipping losses.

120 *FRUS-PPC*, 13:507–8.

Though Germany claimed it could provide no livestock for some years, the treaty imposed an immediate levy (which was carried out over three years) of 10 percent of the livestock loss sustained in northern France and Belgium, which had been largely denuded of farm animals. Poland did without. Virtually all livestock deliveries received reparations credit because cows and chickens were not generally identifiable, and only a special breed of Belgian horses and a famous French herd, whose acquisition Germany had advertised, counted as restitutions. Even by German estimates, Germany had retained at least two-thirds of its original herds, plus what it had removed from occupied territories, especially at the time of the armistice in contravention of its terms.[121] The entirety of claims for poultry under the treaty by the six countries receiving livestock amounted to substantially less than the loss in Belgium alone.[122] Except for cattle, German deliveries of farm animals totaled less than 2 percent of holdings and did not impede a rapid recovery, by 1920 in most categories; in contrast, Belgian livestock levels attained 1913 figures only after 1930.[123]

Livestock clearly was not the heart of the matter; money was. Even here the treaty was more moderate than advertised, and the mechanics of payment were illuminating. As a sop to Allied public and parliamentary opinion, it specified delivery of German bonds to 100 milliard gold marks as a first installment, with the possibility of more later.[124] However, only 60 milliard of these bonds (including the interim 20 milliard) could be issued at once. Germany was merely to provide a written commitment to issue the remaining forty milliard when the Reparation Commission was unanimously satisfied that Weimar could service them.[125] Clearly, there was considerable inducement for Germany to demonstrate incapacity to service them by creating a poor record on prior issues. Indeed, though this clause owed something to Wilson's concern that commercialization of too many

---

121 Ibid., 6:859–61; Versailles Treaty, pt. VIII, annex IV, 6; Lamont, "Reparations," 283; Bernard Baruch, *The Making of the Reparation and Economic Sections of the Treaty* (New York, 1920), 43–4; Hoover to Wilson, Apr. 29, 1919, Tibbaut to van den Heuvel, n.d., Délégation belge, file 36, BMAE; Shartle, *Spa*, 23, 30, 54–5. The German argument amounted to a claim that to the losers belong the spoils.
122 The amount was 1.74 million as opposed to 2 million. To the end of 1922, Germany delivered 245,688 in all. Reparation Commission, *Official Documents*, 5:240, 136; Bryce D. Lyon, *Henri Pirenne* (Ghent, 1971), 277.
123 Kent, *Spoils*, 63; Davis, "Recent Economic," 154–5; Fernand Baudhuin, *Histoire économique de la Belgique, 1914–1939*, 2 vols. (Brussels, 1944), 1:97.
124 *DCF,* 1:220–1.
125 Versailles Treaty, pt. VIII, annex II, 12 (c). These bonds were superseded by those of the London Schedule of Payments. Krüger, *Deutschland*, 164, argues that the final 40 milliard could be issued only after the prior series had been paid off and that a write-down on the final forty milliard was likely. Both were indeed probable.

bonds might overload the New York market, some experts recognized that it could be used to limit the German debt.[126] Marketing of bonds was not the only way in which reparations could be realized and in the end no monies were raised in this fashion, but at the peace conference it was expected to be the primary way. At the time, American experts assumed that the United States could apply the brake, but the subsequent history of reparations suggests other possibilities, notably Britain, as well as the opportunities created by the dependence of continental victors on American loans and German coal. In short, the American delegation had at last achieved something approaching a fixed sum.

At the peace conference and thereafter, German leaders pointed out that if Germany worked hard and cleared its first debt, its reward was a second heavy burden.[127] This was true not only of the treaty but also of the 1921 London Schedule of Payments. Germans did not point out, however, that the converse was true as well: if Germany failed to pay, its debt would be sharply reduced, as it effectively was. This immense inducement to default arose from the Allied commitment to both the appearance of a vast figure and a more moderate reality.

VII

That commitment became a constant through the history of reparations, as did much else. The degree to which the peace conference set the basic patterns for the entire history of reparations is striking. The themes, schemes, and devices adopted at Paris appeared again and again in one guise or another whereas those considered but rejected by one side or the other in 1919 revived later on. As one penetrates the successive smoke screens employed through the years, the repetition becomes even more pronounced.

From start to finish, Germany understandably did not want to pay and was doggedly determined not to pay. This was one of several major reasons from the outset why no wholehearted effort was made to reform Germany's budget and currency: blaming financial chaos on reparations might yield a reduction of the debt.[128] Another consistent German approach was to stress difficulties: if Germany lost territory or if it were impoverished, it could not pay. Variously, it could pay only by an export drive or – after Weimar's fiscal and monetary shambles made foreign loans unobtainable – by borrowing abroad. Later, much was made of the difficulty of transferring large sums

---

126 Burnett, *Reparation,* 1:chap. 12. See also *DCF,* 1:224–5.
127 *FRUS-PPC,* 6:907.
128 Krüger, *Deutschland,* 182; Skidelsky, *John Maynard Keynes,* 2:117.

from one currency to another; not only was the problem exaggerated, especially considering that so much of reparations was not in cash, but various schemes starting at the peace conference largely circumvented it, and the Dawes Plan demonstrated that one could protect against it.[129] Despite the record, these arguments, all aimed at escaping payment, were repeated so often that they became axiomatic verities, not only for Germans but also for others.

Throughout, Germany strove for oral negotiations as well as mutuality, equality, and full restoration of its former might and great power status. The hope of splitting the Allies was constant, particularly as it increasingly succeeded. Germany always preferred to pay by borrowing and in the longest possible time frame, again in hopes of downward revision. The idea of German participation in French reconstruction was revived in the 1921 Wiesbaden agreement, whereas that of French shares in German enterprises was taken up again by Germany late in 1923. Although Germany always pleaded destitution, the idea of buying its way out of the Versailles treaty revived as well in Gustav Stresemann's proposal at Thoiry in 1926. Funds seemed to be available for that, if not for substantial reparations payments.

Germany never ceased to make the narrowest possible interpretations of key texts and to attack Article 231, both to escape the moral onus it had attached to the clause and to rid itself of reparations. Increasingly, Britain did as well, although generally not in public. Weimar consistently, especially in the early years, prepared schemes and made proposals in terms of what was politically and economically acceptable within Germany without regard to Allied needs and requirements. In those years, Germany was markedly unrealistic about its own position because it absolutely refused to accept it. As Berlin's strenuous efforts steadily improved that position, the attitude became less unrealistic.

There was a constant inability on each side to see the needs of the other, a situation that, as time passed, prevailed within the Entente as well. Again, among the Allies and between the Allies and Germany there were always sharply different interpretations of a text or a key phrase. All agreed that reparations should be geared to German capacity to pay, but no two powers ever agreed for long about what that was, giving rise to interminable haggles. Throughout, there was Allied division, dissension, and surreptitious individual negotiations with Germany, tendencies that only became more pronounced with time. The Allied debate at Paris over allocation revived, particularly in terms of redivision of the shrinking reparations pie, the old theme

129 *DCF,* 1:157. Both the 1920 Seydoux Plan and the 1921 Wiesbaden Agreement were designed to circumvent the transfer problem. The 1921 British Reparation Recovery Act had the same effect.

of giving priority to devastated areas. At heart there were always fundamental power struggles, usually from 1920 on with Britain and Germany aiming to restore their prewar positions in the European balance at the expense of France, which struggled to retain a few shreds of its former eminence.

Throughout the history of reparations, misdirection and propaganda, both designed to conceal reality, remained constant, as did technical sleight of hand, often employing devices that first appeared at Paris in 1919. Bonds of no real value to inflate totals recurred, as did inducements to default. Schemes with low payments in the first years and heavy ones well into the future were a favorite device, with the clear intent, sometimes on more than one side, of achieving a write-down before payments became onerous. In the early 1920s, several schemes were proposed to base payments on an index of German prosperity, a device used in the variable export-based annuity of the short-lived 1921 London Schedule of Payments and again in the 1924 Dawes Plan. In addition to making economic sense, these schemes introduced a fluctuating yield that made it difficult for the public to learn what amounts would be obtained, but they also had the effect of encouraging further falsification of German trade figures.

Such technical intricacy was invariably present, along with great clouds of propaganda from more than one quarter, but principally from Berlin and London. These, combined with deliberate misdirection, misled not only historians but a great many people at the time. Journalists, the public, and the intelligentsia, especially in Britain, accepted constantly repeated statements without real reflection, not pausing to ask how reparations – which in large part were not being paid – could cause so much, confusing *would not* with *could not,* and forgetting that Germany's failure to pay proved nothing about its capacity to do so.[130] Equally important, politicians, diplomatists, officials, and often financiers came to believe and act upon their own endless reiterations.

Always there was the dichotomy between appearance and reality. In the 1921 London Schedule of Payments a debt of 50 milliard marks was disguised as one of 132 milliards by a complex scheme that clearly encouraged default. The 1924 Dawes Plan effectively reduced the total by incorporating occupation and commission costs and other charges into the global figure, induced a certain murkiness by an indefinite duration, and ostensibly demanded commensurate taxation, as required by the treaty, but then quietly rendered that impossible.[131] The 1929 Young Plan provided a high ostensible figure combined with low payments in the first decade, with the unstated

130 See, e.g., Dorothy L. Sayers, *Busman's Honeymoon* (1937; reprint, London, 1957), 107–8.
131 Schuker, *French Predominance,* 184–5.

intent of a future write-down. And in 1932 at Lausanne, a smoke screen concealed the de facto end of reparations. Throughout, there were artfully contrived gaps between appearance and reality, always to conceal comparative moderation in apparent rigor.

VIII

The fact that the reparations clauses were not as harsh as advertised was less significant than the fact that people, especially in Britain and Germany, thought they were and acted on that belief. Politics, propaganda, and misdirection continued to prevail as the pattern set at Paris was maintained throughout the history of reparations. During the peace conference, it was said that the reparations debate had generated "the maximum of financial disturbance with the minimum of actual result."[132] The same could be said of the entire thirteen-year struggle, which generated a mountain of paper but only 21.5 milliard gold marks or slightly more than what the treaty called for Germany to pay by May 1, 1921. Less than a third of this was paid in cash.[133]

Throughout, German resentment grew. Not the treaty but Germany's burning resentment of it fostered Hitler's rise. Germany increasingly lost sight of defeat and of any impropriety, including even the violation of Belgium, which German governments had openly acknowledged thrice over. As the national anger grew, fueled by Weimar politicians and much propaganda, so did the sense of injustice and the belief that it was Germany's right to be rid of the entire Versailles treaty. Numerous concessions failed to satisfy the German psyche, which sought not only open Allied renunciation of what remained of the treaty but also public avowal that reparations were morally wrong. By 1929–30, when Germany gained early evacuation of the Rhineland as a reward for accepting the continuance of reparations in sharply reduced form, the national reaction was outrage that any reparations remained at all, as the September 1930 election returns amply demonstrated.

Though Germans believed from the outset that the reparations clauses, especially Article 231, were unfair, British policy did much to reinforce German revisionism and sense of injustice. Lloyd George, who set the pattern and tone of British policy, feared France, sharply overestimating its strength,

---

132 Cecil to Lloyd George, Apr. 4, 1919, F/6/6/25, David Lloyd George papers, House of Lords Record Office, London.
133 The exact figure was 21,448,475,148.75 marks. *FRUS-PPC,* 13:409. In 1932, before totals were complete, the British calculated 20.598 milliard marks. Waley to Foreign Office, June 8, 1932, 371/15911, GB FO, PRO. Schuker (*American,* 106–8) estimates 22.891 milliard marks, of which 6.8 were paid in cash.

and erroneously considered Germany too weak for the European power balance, of which he wanted Britain again to be the fulcrum. In addition, he feared German potential and a war of revenge. These concerns, especially the balance of power, whose long-term underlying reality he badly misread, lay behind Lloyd George's policy from March 1919 until his fall at the end of 1922. Thus he tried to bribe Germany westward, away from Russia, and to induce good behavior by tacit gradual treaty revision at France's expense, never Britain's. Inasmuch as Britain wished to turn away from Europe and the treaty was not self-enforcing, he had no wish to enforce it. Lloyd George also believed German claims that reparation could be paid only by an export drive impacting painfully on Britain's parlous trade figures, and he thought his country had more to gain by trade with Germany than from Britain's modest percentage of reparations, which had to be shared with the dominions.[134] Therefore, he bent his remarkable talents to undoing what he had done at Paris, continuing and even increasing the gap between his public utterances and his private deeds to the extent that on the same day in March 1921 he officially cited the Treaty of Frankfurt to a German delegation and privately assured its leader that if German responsibility for the war were repudiated, the Versailles treaty would be destroyed.[135]

Lloyd George's argument was more true politically than legally. However, the politics of the situation carried more weight than the letter of the law, as France learned when it became legalistic in an attempt to salvage reparations and stave off defeat in the aftermath of deliverance. That policy culminated in the Ruhr encirclement, a final effort to save the treaty and its reparations clauses, wherein France won the battle but lost the war when Britain organized a coalition of erstwhile Allies plus Germany to undo the French victory. The resultant Dawes Plan, which was unquestionably within German capacity,[136] constituted the first major revision of the Versailles treaty as well as a bitterly decisive defeat for France.

134 Lorna Jaffe, *The Decision to Disarm Germany* (Boston, 1985), 164; Corelli Barnett, *The Collapse of British Power* (New York, 1972), 320–7; Thomas Jones, *Whitehall Diary*, ed. Keith Middlemas, vol. 1: *1916–1925* (London, 1969), 1:108–10, 195; Lloyd George to Curzon, Dec. 10, 1919, F/12/2/11, David Lloyd George papers, House of Lords Record Office, London; Scthamer memorandum, Apr. 6, 1920, 2370/4597H/E188141, AA, T-120; Seydoux note #85, n.d. [summer 1921], papers of Jacques Seydoux, file 22, MAE; Seydoux note, Dec. 5, 1921, Seydoux/ 23, MAE; Seydoux to Waterlow, Dec. 20, 1921, Seydoux/11, MAE; Montille to Briand, Nov. 26, 1921, no. 635, file B/32254, archive, Ministère de Finance, Paris; David Lloyd George, *The Truth About Reparations and War Debts* (London, 1932), 15, 43–51, 83. After provision for the dominions, Britain's share of reparations was 18 percent. Occasionally Lloyd George admitted privately that Germany *could* pay. Jones, *Whitehall Diary*, 1:28.
135 DBFP, 1st Series, 15:259; AR, *Das Kabinett Fehrenbach* (Boppard am Rhein, 1972), 510. See also Lentin, *Lloyd George, Woodrow Wilson, and the Guilt of Germany*, 108.
136 Alfred C. Mierzejewski, "Payments and Profits: The German National Railway Company and Reparations, 1924–1932," *German Studies Review* 18, no. 1 (Feb. 1995): 73–4.

Britain's policy of gradual treaty revision, in tandem with Germany's persistent efforts, explains why decisions constantly came unsettled, particularly those pertaining to German liability. For example, a year after the Reparation Commission set the debt, Anglo-German efforts had stimulated an Anglo-American bankers' chorus that reparations must be "settled." Economic uncertainty and political effervescence ensued. Britain's quiet approach to revision failed to satisfy a nation that felt entitled to dramatic open treaty renunciation and renegotiation on a basis of equality and mutuality, but it contributed much to the rapid crumbling of the Versailles treaty, especially the reparations clauses, and to the success of German revisionism. After the United States withdrew, Britain became the crucial power, as the Germans realized by mid-1921.[137] Germany never opposed the Entente when Britain and France spoke in unison; however, they were increasingly easy to split as the crumbling that Brockdorff-Rantzau had hoped for took place and something approaching a reversal of alliances occurred, especially in late 1923 and 1924.

It is difficult to judge the reparations clauses written in Paris in 1919 because they never operated as intended and were revisited and revised so soon and so often. It was planned that the United States preside over the Reparation Commission, since it was the least interested party; with American withdrawal, both the chair and a casting vote went to France, to whom 52 percent of reparations receipts were allocated. Thus the equation was altered from the outset. Perhaps the fundamental criticism of the reparations clauses is that they were unenforceable. It is always unwise to impose heavy burdens on a major power unless it has been brought to acceptance by full awareness of military defeat and unless the instruments to compel obedience are at hand. Neither circumstance pertained in 1919 or thereafter. Enforcement would have been difficult at best in the absence of Russia as an eastern counterweight, but it became impossible when the United States withdrew and Britain chose appeasement. France alone was too weak, as 1923–5 demonstrated. In those years, France, which had never truly been a victor, became a loser as the power balance shifted perceptibly, signaling greater shifts to come.

It is even more difficult to determine what might have happened if Germany had made a conscientious effort to fulfill the reparations clauses, if a treaty had been achieved by negotiation, or if the Allies had accepted the German financial offer, presumably with fewer conditions attached. Either of the latter possibilities would probably have produced a milder treaty but

---

137 Ingrid Schulze-Bidlingmaier, ed., *Die Kabinette Wirth I und II: 10. Mai 1921–26. Okt. 1921–22. Nov. 1922*, 2 vols. (Boppard am Rhein, 1973), 1:240n, 238.

not necessarily one more to German advantage, since the Allies might well then have insisted on its fulfillment. However, speculation on what might have been is futile and quickly descends to counterfactual history. There is also little to be gained by moral condemnation of the highly predictable policies of either side; of course the Allies would attempt to impose at least part of their costs on the loser, and of course Germany would try to evade as much of the burden as possible. Debate over what Germany and the Allies "should" have done tends to be equally profitless.

However, in the realm of the actual, they fought ad nauseam over reparations. If the postwar era proved to be "the continuation of war by other means," reparations were its primary battlefield and propaganda a major weapon. French leaders other than Aristide Briand strikingly lacked any talent in this respect, and the Anglo-German combine easily won the propaganda war – and convinced the historians. Equally, the reparations question remained intensely political throughout, not only in German domestic politics and those of continental receiver countries but also in interwar international politics, notably within the crucial triangle of Britain, France, and Germany. For political reasons, the statesmen at Paris had postponed the unpalatable. Thus so much remained to haggle over through the twenties as differing needs, mentalities, histories, economies, and geographic situations drove the victors apart. In addition, political factors in 1919 had dictated that some clauses contain considerable ambiguity. Thus they could be and were "interpreted" – and reinterpreted – usually without Entente unanimity, which only provided fodder for more arguments, not least over Article 430, the crucial Rhineland sanctions clause.

The fact that reparations were political explains why so much was left unsettled at Paris, why so little was what it seemed, why nothing stayed settled for long, why smoke and mirrors continued to play a role long after the signing ceremony in the Galerie des Glaces,[138] and why Britain's best efforts at treaty revision never satisfied Germany. Because decisions were perpetually deferred or reopened, the issue did not die either diplomatically or politically. Wartime hostility was constantly rekindled, and passions never cooled, especially in Germany and France, until reparations ceased to be. In the thirteen intervening years, however, the perpetual blight of the reparations question plagued Germany, the Entente, and Europe as all those awkward decisions remained to be tackled by a disintegrating Entente, furthering not only its own disintegration but also the interwar destabilization of Europe.

138 Significantly, this was the first major treaty signed in the presence of newsreel photographers. To the disgust of elderly diplomats of the old school, the ceremony was carefully staged for the cameras. Keith Eubank, *Paul Cambon: Master Diplomatist* (Norman, Okla., 1960), 193.

15

The Making of the Economic Peace

ELISABETH GLASER

The fighting in World War I can be described as a composite military, political, and economic effort on all sides. Superior Allied strength from mid-1917 on and final victory resulted in large part from the successful blockade of Germany. Inter-Allied economic cooperation in the control of shipping and raw materials sustained this combined economic campaign. German economic warfare consisted of the submarine counterblockade, the destruction of industries in German-occupied areas, and the transfer of vital food supplies from those areas to Germany. This, combined with the Bolshevik revolution, brought economic havoc to some of the main grain-producing areas in eastern Europe. As a result, 160 million people in Europe were threatened at the end of the war by starvation on a scale unknown since the early nineteenth century. Even for those not directly facing deprivation of necessary foodstuffs, the impending economic crisis – owing to the termination of war production, the ending of price guarantees, and the threat of postwar inflation – meant an existential threat.[1]

In short, the winding up of the economic war proved to be an arduous task. A new economic and political balance of power in Europe seemed to be the precondition for an enduring peace. The peacemakers in Paris faced a double task: to conclude a viable economic peace and at the same time to deal with the most pressing economic problems caused by the end of the war. Those combined problems of economic peacemaking form the subject of this chapter. In the end, the economic clauses of the Versailles treaty emanated from compromises between the different, if not divergent, economic and political goals of the United States and the European Allies. The economic peace consisted not only of the economic clauses of the Versailles

---

1 The wartime blockades are discussed by James Arthur Salter, *Allied Shipping Control: An Experiment in International Administration* (Oxford, 1921); and by Avner Offer, *The First World War: An Agrarian Interpretation* (Oxford, 1989); see also Charles P. Vincent, *The Politics of Hunger: The Allied Blockade of Germany, 1915–1919* (Athens, Ohio, 1985).

371

treaty, but also required stable postwar relations between the United States and the Allies. The contours of such an international system were hammered out between November 1918 and June 1919. During the Paris conference, France depended on helpful relations with the United States and Great Britain. These triangular relations created a constructive economic framework that was predicated, however, on American cooperation after the war in organizations such as the League of Nations and the Reparation Commission. This discussion concentrates on the actual process of making the economic clauses from the time of the Armistice to the signing of the treaty. To be sure, the economic peace derived mainly from political motives and therefore proved unworkable once the political framework changed. Attacked by Germany and John Maynard Keynes, among others, the economic peace figured as the first aspect of the Versailles treaty to undergo revision.[2]

MAIN ECONOMIC PROBLEMS AT THE END OF THE WAR

From 1915 on, Allied demand for foodstuffs and war materials had transformed the United States into the warehouse for the Allied war effort and had thus reversed the prewar flux of world trade. Correspondingly, American trade with the Central Powers decreased and came to a virtual standstill after the United States entered the war. Since the combined blockade likewise covered all neutral countries, it reduced American–Allied exports to the necessary minimum. Simultaneously, French purchasing power of Allied supplies had to be preserved. In 1916 an Anglo-French agreement had pegged the value of the franc to the pound in order to maintain the franc's stability. For the duration of the war, the resulting war-induced loss of British and French foreign trade posed no immediate danger for France. At the same time, Great Britain, though having lost a large part of its foreign trade by virtue of the blockade, found itself in a position of potential absolute control of European trade. In order to compensate for the reduction in exports, Parliament in September 1915 passed the McKenna Tariff, which potentially hurt French, German, and American trade interests.[3]

This reversal of prewar commercial relations and policy coincided with an intensification of inter-Allied economic cooperation during the desper-

---

2 See chapter 19 in this book.
3 Benjamin M. Anderson, *Effects of the War on Money, Credit and Banking in France and the United States,* Preliminary Economic Studies of the War, no. 15 (New York, 1919), 133–40; see also Katherine Burk, *Britain, America, and the Sinews of War, 1914–1918* (Boston, Mass., 1985). Burton I. Kaufman, *Efficiency and Expansion: Foreign Trade Organization in the Wilson Administration* (Westport, Conn., 1974), 172–6, 192–8, provides a sketch of Anglo-American commercial rivalry during the war.

ate war effort in the spring of 1918. In 1916 an Inter-Allied Wheat Executive had pooled Allied wheat purchases and shipping. The Allied Maritime Transport Council began to coordinate Allied shipping and supplies through an executive body as well as through munitions and food councils in March 1918. Thus emerged the first Allied international organization. Its personnel, among them Jean Monnet and Arthur Salter, pursued the concept of international economic planning by means of supranational organizations after the war. The success of the food exports to the European Allies and shipping control in 1918 also resulted to a considerable extent from Herbert Hoover's work as food administrator in the United States. Hoover took the initiative in July 1918 that led to the institution of the Inter-Allied Food Control under American leadership in 1918–19.[4]

Wartime inter-Allied organization by government price and transport regulations functioned well for the time being. Yet it was unclear whether the organizations established for economic warfare would be able to smooth the transition to free trade in peacetime. France forcefully advocated continuation of Allied economic organization after the war; it urgently needed Allied assistance for the realization of its economic war goals.[5] As early as the spring of 1916, Secretary of Commerce Etienne Clémentel had proposed the establishment of a postwar economic bloc to England. Yet the powers that participated in the resulting inter-Allied Paris Economic Conference from June 13–17, 1916, refrained from antagonizing the United States by such a far-reaching endeavor and merely endorsed postwar inter-Allied preferences for supplies of raw materials and denial of most-favored-nation status to the Central Powers. American cooperation, which figured as the essential precondition for any Inter-Allied preferential scheme, was not forthcoming.[6] Shortly after the conference, Walter Hines Page, the American ambassador in London, denounced its results as "an abortion now utterly forgotten here – a mere bag of Australian wind filled by French

---

4 Salter, *Allied Shipping Control*, 134–280; James Arthur Salter, *Memoirs of a Public Servant* (London, 1961), 102–22; Jean Monnet, *Memoirs* (London, 1978), 53–70; Frank M. Surface, *The Grain Trade During the World War* (New York, 1928), 184–211.
5 Ragnhild Fiebig-von Hase and Maria Sturm, "Die transatlantischen Wirtschaftsbeziehungen in der Nachkriegsplanung Deutschlands, der alliierten Westmächte und der USA, 1914–1917," *Militärgeschichtliche Mitteilungen* 51 (1993): 1–34; Georges-Henri Soutou, *L'Or et le sang: Les buts de guerre économiques de la Première Guerre mondiale* (Paris, 1989), 549–57; Erich Bussière, *La France, la Belgique et l'organisation économiques de l'Europe* (Paris, 1991), 1–17. During the war the Dominions gave preference to the United Kingdom as well as to one another. See Department of State, Foreign Trade Adviser's Office, Economic Intelligence Section, undated memorandum on Imperial Preference, F.W. 641.003/1, Record Group (hereafter RG) 256, National Archives, Washington, D.C. (hereafter NA).
6 Soutou, *L'Or et le sang*, 231–71; Fiebig-von Hase and Sturm, "Transatlantische Wirtschaftsbeziehungen." The American opposition to the plans of the Paris Economic Conference is described by Carl Parrini, *Heir to Empire: United States Economic Diplomacy, 1916–1923* (Pittsburgh, 1969).

excitability and an economic absurdity. In fact, after the war we shall be the only people who have anything to sell and the belligerents are bound to buy from us. Nothing is plainer than that."[7] Likewise, England maintained freedom of action for postwar planning. France kept the initiative for an inter-Allied policy of economic cooperation not only on the surface; it also clung tenaciously to the underlying rationale. The results of the Paris Economic Conference foreshadowed the chief motives and constraints of later inter-Allied deliberations about the commercial clauses of the peace treaty with Germany. The chief motive for economic peace planning was France's need to restore its economic independence and security. Yet French decision makers clearly realized that this goal could only be attained through close cooperation with the United States. On the whole, British policy endeavored to accommodate France's wishes for future security without substantially limiting British freedom of action for postwar planning; meanwhile America remained aloof in regard to intergovernmental economic programs. This constellation of assertive French peace plans along with a striking avoidance of commitment from the British and American side shaped inter-Allied deliberations up to the Armistice.

ALLIED AND AMERICAN ECONOMIC PLANS FOR THE PEACE

The close link between the control of Germany's foreign trade and future inter-Allied cooperation determined French economic planning, as Clémentel revised his scheme for a future peace with Germany between July and September 1918. French commercial policy during the war had aimed at abolishing the most-favored-nation clause, the prewar commercial principle that seemingly had guaranteed German domination of the continent's foreign commerce. Following the leadership of Clémentel, the Conseil des Ministres on April 23, 1918, unilaterally abrogated all of France's commercial, transport, and economic conventions. The Ministry of Commerce sought commercial negotiations for eventual bilateral accords with Belgium and Italy in order to isolate the Reich and to counteract wartime imperial preference. According to the minister's plans, Germany would lose most-favored-nation status. Likewise, the Reich's economic and legal power to establish investments in France's key industries was to be curbed. The minister of commerce also wanted to dissolve Germany's new commercial treaties with Eastern Europe, Switzerland, and Italy. A postwar Inter-Allied

Economic Union constituted the complementary aspect of this revisionist scheme. In addition, German reparations would create an international obligation for the Reich and would furnish supplies for inter-Allied reconstruction and economic fortification. Germany would cede coal and other imports to France as reparations in kind. A comprehensive program for industrial expansion and reorganization as well as the establishment of a new energy policy comprised the domestic elements of the ministry's plan. Annexation of the Saar valley and a customs union with an independent Rhineland formed the indispensable territorial prerequisites. Furthermore, France sought to prevent a future customs union between Germany and Austria. Closer French commercial and economic ties with Belgium and Luxembourg would serve to re-enforce this policy of commercial isolation of the Reich. At the heart of Clémentel's design lay the desire to curb Germany's capacity for a future war by curtailing its economic power. This long-term concept for an economic war after the war did not meet a corresponding commitment on the part of the United States and Great Britain.[8]

Compared with France's attempt to reverse permanently long-standing German economic preponderance in Europe, Britain's plans seemed more realistic. True, Lord Milner's report of April 24, 1917, had nominally adopted the Paris design of denying most-favored-nation status to the Central Powers. Yet the report also acknowledged that the entry of the United States into the war seemed likely to upset that scheme. Subsequent British policy sought to reinforce inter-Allied cooperation in wartime food and shipping controls, yet maintained the most-favored-nation principle as the long-term lodestar of British foreign commercial policy. Whitehall thus refrained from any commitment to join a postwar economic union with France. The cabinet instead opted for imperial preference in July 1918, leaving the door open to eventual inclusion of needy Allies. The Board of Trade's memorandum on Economic Considerations for the Treaty of Peace in November 1918 merely suggested withholding most-favored-nation status from the enemy powers for five years or until admission to the League of Nations. During this reconstruction period, the Allied countries would enjoy preference in raw material imports. Allied supplies of potash, coal, gold, and other materials were to be partly guaranteed by German payment of reparations in kind. The thrust of the board's recommendation for eco-

8 See Soutou, *L'Or et le sang,* 528–50, 766–94, and passim, for a recent and full treatment of French planning; Marc Trachtenberg, *Reparation in World Politics: France and European Economic Diplomacy, 1916–1923* (New York, 1980), 1–28; David Stevenson, *French War Aims Against Germany, 1914–1919* (Oxford, 1982), 33–5, 50–1, 82–4.

nomic war goals concerned the shipping question: the Central Powers had to cede their mercantile marine in excess of 1,600 tons to the Allied states in proportion to their wartime losses.[9]

American economic views differed substantially from French and British plans. Throughout the war, the Wilson administration stressed the Open Door as the principal American foreign-commerce guideline. Besides that, widespread American antipathy to governmental schemes of economic redistribution obviated the need for further plans. Thus, Woodrow Wilson's consultations with Edward M. House and the Tariff Commission's economist Frank Taussig in the fall of 1917 emphasized the independent position of the United States in regard to other international foreign-trade regimes. Freedom of the seas and the most-favored-nation clause constituted the main American rules for postwar trade.[10] The Inquiry, in the fall of 1918, subscribed to Taussig's scheme. It refrained from making explicit suggestions in regard to future regulation of Germany's foreign trade.[11]

Yet between the spring of 1918 and the Armistice, American policy makers became more interested in future schemes to control trade in raw materials and to facilitate European reconstruction. After the Russian collapse, House, while continuing to evade any direct commitment to Allied long-term plans, viewed American and Allied control of raw materials as desirable, though he continued to oppose economic schemes discriminating against postwar Germany.[12] In early November, Taussig proposed temporary controls in order to prevent the prices of cotton and other raw materials from collapsing. Shortly before the Armistice, the chairman of the War Industries Board and later member of the American peace delegation, Bernard M. Baruch, suggested to Wilson that any league of nations should enforce a policy of economic equality of opportunity. This included a German obligation to supply Belgium, France, and Poland with raw materials and industrial goods at low prices under machinery set up by American-Allied agreement.[13] Yet a timely arrangement to ensure postwar inter-Allied

---

9 Soutou, *L'Or et le sang*, 478–568; Erik Goldstein, *Winning the Peace: British Diplomatic Strategy, Peace Planning, and the Paris Peace Conference, 1916–1920* (Oxford, 1991), 192–204.
10 Soutou, *L'Or et le sang*, 539–48.
11 Lawrence Gelfand, *The Inquiry: American Preparations for Peace, 1917–1919* (Westport, Conn., 1963), 290–312.
12 Entretien de M. Clémentel avec Sir Albert Stanley, Feb. 8, 1918, with a discussion of House's attitude toward inter-Allied cooperation, F¹² 7798, Archives Nationales, Paris.
13 House to Page, Apr. 13, 1918, ser. I, box 86, EMHP; Arthur Walworth, *America's Moment, 1918: American Diplomacy at the End of World War I* (New York, 1977), 233–4; Taussig to Woodrow Wilson, Nov. 1, 1918, HUG 4823.1.5, Frank W. Taussig papers, Harvard University Archives; Baruch to Wilson, Oct. 23, 1918, in Arthur S. Link et al., eds., *The Papers of Woodrow Wilson* (hereafter *PWW*), 69 vols. (Princeton, N.J., 1966–94), 51:419–20.

cooperation remained impossible, partly because of Herbert Hoover's simultaneous effort to furnish Europe with American food at a guaranteed maximum price for American producers. Hoover incessantly urged complete American postwar independence from Allied economic control. He consented to a temporary scheme of inter-Allied food control only under the condition that he would direct this relief effort. Other materially divisive economic questions included the future disposition of former German property and German ships now under government control, of which the United States held the lion's share.[14]

THE ARMISTICE

American and Allied economic planning for the peace was overtaken by the sudden conclusion of the war. The provisions of the Armistice did not refer directly to economic matters, yet the military and naval terms shaped Europe's future commercial regime: the blockade against Germany and the neutral states continued without any time limit, yet Germany would receive necessary food provisions. Military occupation of the Rhine made control of German trade possible to a large extent. Those provisions came as a result of House's negotiations with the Allies in early November 1918. The colonel had tried to make the Fourteen Points palatable to David Lloyd George, Georges Clemenceau, and Italy's Baron Sidney Sonnino by submitting the Cobb–Lippmann interpretation to his European interlocutors. In the light of this diplomatically correct exegesis of Wilson's statements, freedom of the seas embodied in Point Two was only to be maintained in times of general peace. Even with this limitation, Lloyd George, following cabinet instructions, refused to accept Point Two.[15] Point Three now meant that the removal of all trade barriers only applied to those nations that accepted the responsibilities of membership in the League of Nations. Thus membership remained a precondition for this. Likewise the most-favored-nation clause extended automatically only to members of the League. The Armistice also mandated the delivery of the German merchant fleet now anchored in German and neutral ports for Allied use in the transition period. Admiral Sir Wester Wemyss had expressed doubt during the final negotiations with Germany in Compiègne on November 11 that the fleet would remain German

14 Hoover to Wilson, Oct. 14, Nov. 4 and 7, 1918, in Suda L. Bane and Ralph H. Lutz, eds., *Organization of American Relief in Europe, 1918–1919* (Stanford, Calif., 1943), 26–33; Murray N. Rothbard, "Hoover's 1919 Food Diplomacy in Retrospect," in Lawrence Gelfand, ed., *Herbert Hoover: The Great War and Its Aftermath* (Iowa City, Iowa, 1979), 87–110.

15 Maurice Hankey diary, Oct. 28, 1918, Maurice Hankey papers, HNKY 1/6, Churchill College Archives, Cambridge.

property. The quid pro quo for American acquiescence to these measures of Allied economic control of Germany was, as House cabled to Wilson, an almost free hand for the American relief effort.[16]

The Armistice left England in a comfortable position to attain its most prominent long-standing economic war aim: a hold on German shipping. France obtained temporary control of the Rhine, yet had to refrain from asserting its larger plans for postwar commercial policy. This shift of priorities resulted from Georges Clemenceau's decision to seek American support for France's elementary security goals over all other considerations.[17] Faced with American and British insistence on the continuation of most-favored-nation status, France was threatened with a loss of leverage in future economic negotiations with the Reich. Given that, maintenance of inter-Allied cooperation in shipping and raw materials during the reconstruction period became even more important. In December Clémentel sought to obtain British support for a corresponding plan, yet received little more than a vague assurance of British desire to meet French needs.[18] In their subsequent communications with Americans, the French downplayed their long-term economic goals. Instead, a memorandum handed to David Hunter Miller only demanded continuation of inter-Allied economic control until ratification of the peace treaty, as well as Allied control of German shipping for that period, and rather emphasized French claims for war damages and war costs.[19] In a subsequent internal memorandum, Clémentel stressed that American support for long-term postwar inter-Allied cooperation had become unlikely. French negotiators at the peace conference now sought maximum Allied support for French reconstruction through restitution of industrial stocks and German delivery of raw materials and reparations.[20] Clémentel stated at the end of December that France insisted on German reparations and raw materials deliveries, with or without Allied consent.[21]

16 Telegram from House to Wilson, Oct. 29, 1918, with the Cobb-Lippmann memorandum, *PWW,* 51: 495–504; House to Wilson, Oct. 30, 1918, Nov. 3 and 8, 1918, *PWW,* 51: 511, 569–70, 638–9; Notations concerning the Final Session of the Armistice Commission at Compiègne on Nov. 11, 1918, in Suda L. Bane and Ralph H. Lutz, eds., *The Blockade of Germany* (Stanford, Calif., 1942), 4–5.
17 Jean-Baptiste Duroselle, *Clemenceau* (Paris, 1988), 746–56.
18 Exchange of memoranda between Clémentel and Lord Reading, Dec. 12, 1918, to Jan. 2, 1919, Négociations interalliées sur le régime économique de la période de transition, Papiers d'Agents André Tardieu, vol. 447, Archives Diplomatiques, Ministère des Affaires Etrangères, Paris (hereafter MAE).
19 David Hunter Miller memorandum for House, Dec. 11, 1918, ser. III, box 203, EMHP.
20 Note Clémentel à M. le Président du Conseil au sujet des problèmes économiques qui se poseront au cours des préliminaires de paix, Jan. 20, 1919, Papiers d'Agents André Tardieu, vol. 448; see also chapter 14 in this book.
21 Etienne Clémentel, Avant-projet des clauses economiques des préliminaires de paix, memorandum, Papiers d'Agents André Tardieu, 448: 223.

The pre–Armistice talks, as well as the Armistice itself, foreshadowed the economic diplomacy on which the peacemakers would engage in Paris. The Armistice set up the economic organizations and commissions that would regulate the German economy during the conference. Likewise, substantive economic claims had been staked. As House would put it later, "The peace terms were really written in the Armistice to Germany."[22]

NEGOTIATING THE ECONOMIC PEACE

The task of the diplomats assembled in Paris thus consisted of transforming the terms agreed upon in November 1918 into a viable system of international rules and regulations. First of all, however, a workable plan for organizing the conference needed to be implemented. In early January 1919, the Bureau of the Conference laid down an ambitious scheme for the economic work ahead: procurement of supplies for nations suffering from enemy depredations, international control of trade and transport, and creation of a future basis for economic international relations. In the second half of January, the economic, political, legal, and League of Nations sections of the conference drew up draft economic conventions for freedom of transit and equality of trade. Those conventions paid homage to the American views embodied in the Fourteen Points, yet never became a formal part of the economic clauses of the treaty. In mid–March the American Economic Group approved Baruch's proposal to omit from the treaty any explicit mention of Germany's economic freedom and right to equal trading conditions since the proposed League Covenant contained the appropriate global references. In effect, the foremost champions of commercial equality for all nations had recused themselves from shaping the economic clauses of the treaty.[23] Following Clemenceau's urging, the Council of Four subsequently decided not to admit Germany to League membership immediately. Yet apart from the stipulations of the League Covenant, the Treaty lacked any precise provisions for future German trade equality. This made it appear harsher than it was necessarily intended to be.[24]

---

22 E. F. Wise, memorandum on the Commissions Set Up Under the Armistice with Germany and Their Relation to the Supreme Economic Council, Norman H. Davis papers, box 60, folder: SEC, Finance Section, Library of Congress; House to William G. McAdoo, Nov. 18, 1919, ser. I, box 74, EMHP.

23 Bureau of the Conference meeting, Jan. 13, 1919, RG 256, 185.13/1; note by Secretariat General of Feb. 19 with subsequent notes in Foreign Office (608): Paris Peace Conference 1919–20: Correspondence: FO 608/73; [American] Economic Group meeting of Mar. 19, 1919, Thomas W. Lamont papers, Baker Library, Harvard University, 164–8.

24 Council of Four meeting, June 12, 1919, in *DCF*, 2: 403.

The task of formulating the detailed economic treaty provisions rested with the Economic Commission under the presidency of Clémentel and the secretaryship of Daniel Serruys, the foreign-trade expert at the Commerce Ministry. Subcommissions, such as those on prewar contracts or on economic treaties, prepared the drafts. The Economic Commission consisted of prominent economists or government bureaucrats: Baruch, Thomas Lamont, Allyn A. Young, Sir Hubert Llewellyn-Smith, Jean Morel, and Alberto Pirelli. Most of them subsequently delegated their work to specialists.[25] Members of the Economic Commission and the Reparation Commission frequently corresponded in order to provide the necessary coordination. By the end of February, an Anglo-French agreement had determined the scope of the commission's work. The focus lay on reconstruction and foreign-trade regulations, comprising permanent commercial relations, contracts, property rights affected by the war, and the abrogation or revival of commercial treaties.[26] On the national level, each delegation's economists, notably the American economic group and the British Empire Economic Committee, prepared the Economic Commission's work. The final disposition of the Economic Commission's recommendations rested with the Council of Four. The Economic Commission likewise furnished reports to the Supreme Economic Council (SEC), the highest inter-Allied authority in economic matters under the Armistice, which coordinated the work of Hoover's Supreme Council of Supply and Relief, the Inter-Allied Food Council, the Program Committees, the Allied Maritime Transport Council, and the Superior Blockade Council. In the SEC, Lord Robert Cecil worked most actively for a continuation of inter-Allied economic planning under the League of Nations. Additional inter-Allied military institutions for the occupied areas during the Armistice, such as the Luxembourg Committee, worked under the direct authority of Marshal Ferdinand Foch.[27]

The Economic Commission and its subcommissions began their work in early March and submitted a first report with general rules and regulations on April 1. The commission subsequently dealt with the disposition of German property in Allied countries and other questions of detail. It drafted the final version of its recommendations on April 25, leaving the

25 The minutes of the Economic Commission's meetings can be found in Cabinet papers: Peace Conference and Other International Conferences, vol. 8ff.
26 Memorandum by Norman Davis, Mar. 3, 1919, box 11, Norman H. Davis papers; undated memorandum re: Economic Commission, box 165-4, Lamont papers.
27 Notes on Allied Organizations, in Bane and Lutz, eds., *Blockade of Germany,* 809–41; Allyn Abbott Young, "The Economic Settlement," in Edward M. House and Charles Seymour, eds., *What Really Happened at Paris: The Story of the Peace Conference by American Delegates* (New York, 1921), 291–318.

original stipulations largely intact. In effect, the making of the general commercial clauses preceded the momentous decisions affecting territorial questions or reparations.[28] This lack of coordination also resulted from the fact that the major players were overburdened by a plethora of current problems in running the conference and soothing public opinion at home. Meanwhile, the specialized subcommissions functioned in virtual isolation from each other. As a result, some conference participants, among them House, were shocked when they read the draft treaty in its entirety for the first time. Such reactions helped to intensify the criticisms of the economic clauses once the draft treaty in toto had been presented to the conference. Robert Lansing, Hoover, and James Headlam-Morley held similar views. John Maynard Keynes's strictures appeared more excessive than the others only in that he opted to make them public.[29]

The lack of coordination and supervision in formulating the economic clauses can also be attributed to the fact that the reparations question preoccupied the key decision makers.[30] By comparison, decisions regarding the regulation of international trade and commercial rules seemed unimportant. This change of priorities resulted primarily from the pressing time schedule of the conference combined with the urgency of Clemenceau's and Lloyd George's efforts to arrive at a reparations settlement that would at once satisfy voters at home and command American support. This immediate dilemma rendered all long-term economic issues remote. The shift of attention from foreign-trade planning to reparations as a means to readjust the economic imbalance between the Reich and the Allies likewise reflects the political imperatives of peacemaking. As has been suggested here, after the Armistice little common ground remained between the American, British, and French views on how the world trading system

---

28　Report by H. Llewellyn-Smith about Economic Commission (hereafter EC), Mar. 6, 1919, Great Britain, Cabinet Papers (hereafter GB CAB) 29/9, War Cabinet Paper (hereafter WCP) 202; EC, Draft of Clauses to be inserted in the treaty with Germany, pt. 1, Commercial Relations, Apr. 1, 1919, 185.13/51, RG 256; Council of Four excerpt regarding submission of the EC report, ibid., 181.1702/8.

29　For House's attitude toward the treaty, see his diary entry for May 30, 1919, House diary; compare this with Headlam-Morley's attitude, James Headlam-Morley to Jan Christiaan Smuts, May 19, 1919, in W. K. Hancock and Jean Van der Poel, eds., *Selections from the Smuts Papers*, 7 vols. (Cambridge, 1966), 4: 168–71. For a critique of the economic provisions of the treaty see, e.g., Gordon Auchincloss diary, June 2, 1919, Yale University Archives; John Maynard Keynes, *The Economic Consequences of the Peace* (New York, 1919). The most recent discussion of Keynes's book is D. E. Moggridge, *Maynard Keynes: An Economist's Biography* (London, 1992), 319–47. See also Robert Skidelsky, *John Maynard Keynes: A Biography*, 2 vols. (London, 1983), 1:376–400.

30　E.g., Thomas W. Lamont delegated the work in the EC to A. A. Young and read only the rather condensed reports on economic issues; see, e.g., A. A. Young memorandum to Baruch and Lamont, Apr. 5, 1919, Lamont papers, 165–5.

should be restructured through inter-Allied cooperation. The pre-Armistice agreement on reparations now emerged as the best French option to institutionalize long-term international economic control of Germany with British and American participation. Similarly, the German obligation to pay reparations to France would compensate for the economic imbalance resulting from war-related damages to the mines and industry of northern France and thus enable French industry to compete against the intact German production apparatus.[31] A memorandum sent by the Commerce Ministry at the end of December succinctly articulated this link between reparations, France's need for economic reconstruction and security, and inter-Allied support: "One faces the possibility that France, unsure whether it can count on the guarantees that Inter-Allied cooperation would provide for its restoration and economic recovery, will have to demand from its enemies not merely complete reparation and precautions against new aggression in the economic realm, but also further compensation for the inferiority deriving from its isolation." Thus reparations had taken the place of an inter-Allied economic union in the French quest for economic recovery.[32]

Reparations in kind formed the chief means of immediate economic reconstruction for France and the other Allies. The economic imperative to take materials from current German production thus coincided with Allied needs for compensation of war losses and midrange economic as well as fiscal goals. Yet the pooling of raw materials, one of the chief desiderata of Louis Loucheur, the French minister of industrial reconstruction, was only partly realized, regarding, for example, German delivery of dyestuffs. Treaty provisions for German surrender of its merchant fleet reflected economic self-interest. Germany had to cede to the Reparation Commission all ships over 1,600 tons gross, as well as half the ships between 1,000 and 1,600 tons gross, a quarter of its steam trawlers and fishing boats, a part of its river fleet, as well as a contingent of new ships. Those deliveries served to replace losses from German submarine warfare. The United States had suffered relatively minor losses of 0.43 million tons compared with Great Britain's 8 million tons. The Wilson–Lloyd George Agreement of May 8, 1919, reserved the right of the United States to keep the 0.628 million tons of German merchant ships that had anchored in American harbors during

---

31 For a short and vivid summary of the reparations negotiations from an American perspective, see Edward M. Lamont, *The Ambassador from Wall Street: The Story of Thomas W. Lamont, J. P. Morgan's Chief Executive* (Lanham, Md., 1994), 105–14.

32 Ministère du Commerce, Avant-projet des clauses économiques des préliminaires de paix, Papiers d'Agents André Tardieu, 448: 226; Trachtenberg, *Reparation in World Politics*, 38.

the period of neutrality and that the United States had confiscated upon American entry into the war.[33] This decision did not result from economic considerations but rather from political imperatives, since the United States now commanded an excess of tonnage. As a quid pro quo, the United States accepted Germany's transference of the bulk of its merchant marine to Great Britain, which thus realized one of its main economic war aims. The British government secured French acceptance by reserving for France a part of the new output of British shipyards.[34]

Avoiding Allied interference with confiscated German chemical and industrial holdings in the United States became a prominent goal of American economic diplomacy. Attorney General A. Mitchell Palmer reminded the U.S. delegation:

In any case, action of Custodian here cannot be subject to a review except by American Government, because Custodian, as authorized by acts of Congress, has already sold many properties transferring titles to American citizens and given an account for proceeds in such action. Custodian has particularly endeavored to eliminate enemy businesses improperly menacing American business or competitors. Any attempt to review action of Custodian through discussion of values received by him, or rates of exchange, or currency . . . would create interminable confusion and might result in serious claims against American government.[35]

National egoism and fear of German economic revanchism thus prevented an equitable pooling of German resources for Allied reconstruction needs. Further Allied conflicts of interest, as well as inconsistencies regarding reparations in kind, subsequently became apparent. For example, German deliveries of 20 million tons of reparations coal were certainly necessary to satisfy French, Belgian, and Italian needs, but increased competition for British coal exports. British and American retention of German ships may have helped to overcome the tonnage deficit in the summer of 1919 and to alleviate wartime losses in British exports; yet in the middle run contributed to reviving the German industrial capacity that Great Britain and France

---

33 Discussions about reparations in kind are documented in Paul Mantoux, *Les Délibérations du Conseil des Quatre (24 Mars–28 Juin 1919: Notes de l'officier interprète*, 2 vols. (Paris, 1955), 1:490–9.

34 See, e.g., the statement by Chairman Hipwood at the Section on Permanent Commercial Relations meeting of March 19, 1919, that a satisfactory peace had to include the surrender of the German merchant fleet, GB CAB 29/20, WCP 360. Telegram of Jean Monnet, Nov. 23, 1918, Série F¹² 7798, Archives Nationales, Paris.

35 A. Mitchell Palmer to Baruch, Feb. 25, 1919, RG 256, 185.13/6. The successful American attempts to achieve sole control are documented in the minutes of the Economic Commission, Subcommittee of Permanent Commercial Relations meetings, Mar. 15, WCP 308, GB CAB 29/10; Economic Commission meeting of Apr. 10, WCP 732, GB CAB 29/15.

wanted to curb. Owing to American–Allied disunity, reparations in kind thus only partly fulfilled the French quest for economic recovery through systematic cooperation.[36]

The economic clauses that later became articles 264 to 312 of the Versailles treaty sought to refashion a commercial balance of power. The draft economic provisions regulating German foreign trade adopted in March 1919 provided that Germany would accord the Allied and Associated Powers most-favored-nation status for an unspecified number of years. These clauses barred Germany from discriminating against Allied trade and temporarily forbade a change in the German import tariff. Corresponding clauses extended the antidiscrimination measures to all Allied ships.[37] The draft clauses closely resembled the commercial policy principles laid down by the Board of Trade in November 1918. The British blueprint offered an apt compromise between the widely differing American and French conceptions. Wilson's broad nondiscriminatory policy was embodied in Cecil's equality-of-trade convention. The American government furthermore urged the speedy removal of inter-Allied economic controls. Meanwhile, French members of the Drafting and Economic Committee continued to propose a continuation of inter-Allied economic cooperation as well as quasi-sovereignty over the German economy.[38] A transition phase for the

36 Note sur les clauses à insérer dans le Traité de Paix concernant les mines de houille et la métallurgie, undated, Papiers d'Agents André Tardieu, vol. 447; British Delegation minutes, Notes on reparations in kind, Feb. 20, 1919, Great Britain, Foreign Office Records (hereafter GB FO) 608/75: Memorandum by the Board of Trade on the economic effort of the British Empire during the war, WCP 33a, GB CAB 29/1. For French and American attempts to use reparations as the chief means of economic reconstruction of France, see Extract from Tardieu's Plan of Procedure for the Peace Conference, Jan. 1919, in Philip Mason Burnett, ed., *Reparation at the Paris Peace Conference: From the Standpoint of the American Delegation*, 2 vols. (New York, 1940; reprint, New York, 1965), 1:499; John F. Dulles, Comment on French Project of Principles Governing Reparation for Damages, Feb. 4, 1919, ibid., 522–3. The primordial importance of reparations found reflection in the oft-mentioned necessity to ease trade restrictions on Germany in order to facilitate reparations payments. See, e.g., Wilson's remarks, Council of Four meeting, Apr. 15, 1919, in *PMN,* 1: 70–4. Jan Christiaan Smuts criticized the provision for reparations in kind regarding German ships and dyestuffs as detrimental for British industry; see memorandum by Smuts for Lloyd George, May 5, 1919, Selections from the Smuts papers, 4:148–50. Jacques Bariéty, *Les Relations franco-allemandes après la Première Guerre mondiale* (Paris, 1977), 140–8, and passim, makes a not wholly convincing case for an implicit coal and iron plan embodied in the Treaty of Versailles, yet presents a comprehensive picture of the economic results of German coal deliveries and the transfer of the Saar.
37 Draft commercial clauses communicated by the War Cabinet, Villa Majestic, Mar. 3, 1919, GB FO 608/222, WCP 172.
38 Bernard M. Baruch, *The Making of the Reparations and Economic Sections of the Treaty* (New York, 1920), 79–90, stresses the initial French–American antagonism. For an American interpretation of the commercial clauses, see memorandum by American delegates, Economic Commission, Draft of clauses to be inserted in the Treaty with Germany, Apr. 1, 1919, RG 256, 185.13/51; [U.S.] Economic Group, meeting of Mar. 19, 1919, Lamont papers, 164–8.

first years after the signing of the treaty that accorded unilateral most-favored-nation status to the Allies represented a trade-off between these two lines of thought. The British government supported France's stand by concluding short-term secret bilateral preferential trade conventions.[39]

Remaining bones of contention included the duration of the adjustment period and the free admission of goods from Alsace-Lorraine by Germany. French representatives on the Economic Commission demanded a ten-year period during which those imports should enter Germany free of duty. In the face of American opposition, the French delegation ultimately shortened this transitional regime to five years. At the same time, France persuaded its allies to withhold most-favored-nation status from Germany for a full five years, even though Young and Taussig had repeatedly urged a shorter period.[40] The quid pro quo for this French victory soon became obvious. In early April the British Empire Economic Committee decided to reject any further demands for inter-Allied control of German imports.[41] The American delegation supported that course, but wanted to accord France compensation for industries destroyed during the war. Germany's transfer of the Saar mines became the means to that end. Further treaty provisions enabled the Allied and Associated Powers to abrogate prewar bilateral commercial treaties as well as multilateral conventions with the Central Powers.[42]

Despite this early compromise, the Council of Four waited until the end of April to make its final decision about the commercial clauses. The ongoing deliberations about property regulations was one reason for this delay. As indicated earlier, there existed a close connection between the decisions relating to German property in American and Allied hands and the resulting failure to pool German resources for reparation purposes, as Loucheur had urged.[43] The British and American delegations demanded retroactive approval of vesting and liquidation orders that had enabled their governments to confiscate German property. In particular, American insistence on unilateral control over the proceeds of confiscated property and of ships seized

---

39 Comment by Baruch in the meeting of the [U.S.] Economic Group, Mar. 15, 1919, Lamont papers, 164–8.
40 The Economic Commission decided on the duration of transitional regimes on Mar. 22 and 28; see Economic Commission, Section on Permanent Commercial Relations, Mar. 22 and 28, GB CAB 29/11, WCP 413 and WCP 435, ibid.
41 British Empire Economic Committee, minutes of fifth meeting, Apr. 4, 1919, GB FO 608/75; Sub-Commission on Customs Regulations, Duties and Restrictions, Mar. 28, 1919, RG 256, 185.131/26.
42 Report presented by the Sub-Commission on Economic Treaties, Apr. 8, 1919, GB FO 608/74.
43 British Delegation: Contracts and Claims, Enemy Business Property, Draft Articles, Mar. 8, 1919, GB FO 608/74.

before American entry into the war led the Paris negotiators to abandon the plan to pool German property for reparation purposes.[44] The draft clauses for property regulation of April 5 reserved the right of the Allied and Associated Powers to retain and liquidate all enemy property. In the United States meanwhile, the sale of German property continued, since the Alien Property Custodian had obtained authorization through an extension of the Trading with the Enemy Act. In the end, the treaty pooled reparations in kind only for coal and dyestuffs deliveries and left the disposal of other German property to each power. Owing to French and particularly British apprehension about German industrial competition, the Treaty provided for the in-kind provision of other commodities as an option, not a requirement.[45]

The provisions for German transfer of the Saar mines constituted a major concession to the French quest for economic recovery. Although in principle both the British and American delegations opposed further inter-Allied economic control of Germany, as early as December 1918 the Foreign Office's Political Intelligence Department conceded the legitimacy of increased French coal requirements resulting from the restitution of Alsace-Lorraine.[46] By the beginning of March, the French and British delegation reached an informal understanding about limited French sovereignty over the Saar for the purpose of controlling the coalfields.[47] When the Council of Four began to discuss the Saar in late March, Wilson acknowledged repeatedly the American and Allied economic obligation toward France. Yet a controversy between the president and Clemenceau erupted on March 28 that centered on the French claim to control the German population of the Saar. The upshot was a compromise effectively permitting France to control the Saar for exploitation of the coal mines for a period of

44 Economic Commission, Sub-Commission on Industrial Property, Mar. 15, 1919, GB CAB 29/10, WCP 308; Reparations in Kind, memorandum of conference held Apr. 9, with memorandum by Lord Sumner, Apr. 9, 1919, Vance C. McCormick papers, ser. I, box 7, Yale University Archives.
45 [U.S.] Economic Group, meeting of Apr. 2, 1919, Lamont papers, 164–8; Thomas R. Kabisch, *Deutsches Kapital in den USA: Beiträge zur Wirtschaftsgeschichte* (Stuttgart, 1982), 294–326. For subsequent developments in the property question in the United States, see Elisabeth Glaser-Schmidt, "Von Versailles nach Berlin: Überlegungen zur Neugestaltung der deutsch–amerikanischen Beziehungen in der Ära Harding," in Norbert Finzsch and Hermann Wellenreuther, eds., *Liberalitas: Festschrift für Erich Angermann zum 65. Geburtstag* (Stuttgart, 1992), 319–42. On Loucheur, see Stephen D. Carls, *Louis Loucheur and the Shaping of Modern France, 1916–1931* (Baton Rouge, La., 1993), 162–3.
46 Political Intelligence Department, French Claim to Lorraine-Saar Coalfield, Dec. 21, 1918, GB CAB 29/2, WCP 76.
47 James Headlam-Morley to John Bailey, Mar. 8, 1919, in James Headlam-Morley, *A Memoir of the Paris Peace Conference,* ed. Agnes Headlam-Morley et al. (London, 1972), 47–8. The economic rationale for the French possession of the Saar basin is given in André Tardieu, *The Truth About the Treaty* (Indianapolis, 1921), 257–8.
48 House diary, Mar. 29 and Apr. 3, 1919; notice on Council of Four meeting, Mar. 28, 1919, *PMN,* 58–67. About the conflict between Wilson and Clemenceau, see *PWW,* 56:349, 353–4.

fifteen years.[48] The economic provisions regarding the territorial clauses, however, did not aim at a one-sided transfer of German resources. A final change in the draft treaty during early June allowed Germany to buy coal from Silesia on the same footing as Poland in order to compensate for the loss of Saar coal.[49] By this means the Allies attempted to ensure a fair coal supply for Germany.[50] Thus the temporary German cession of the Saar represents one of the most balanced economic provisions of the treaty.

The economic administration of the occupied Rhineland clearly illustrates the limits of American and British willingness to comply with French demands going beyond the consensus reached during the pre-Armistice negotiations. The Armistice provisions left the economic control of the occupied zones of the Rhineland in the hands of the Luxembourg Commission, an inter-Allied commission under the direction of Marshal Foch. In March, Jacques Seydoux of the Quai d'Orsay submitted a plan that contemplated stringent Allied trade controls for the Rhineland. The Seydoux scheme foresaw the importation only of indispensable raw materials from the rest of Germany in order to keep industrial production in the occupied zones alive. All other imports would originate from England and France. This regime would have created an opportunity for England and France to quickly export surplus supplies to the left bank of the Rhine. This dumping of excess Allied supplies would indeed have fulfilled one of the major economic desiderata of the Empire Economic Committee and the French Ministry of Industrial Reconstruction.[51] Indeed, Minister Loucheur viewed these French exports as an integral part of the scheme for economic recovery. After the loosening of the blockade in April, France in particular, under the direction of Paul Tirard, Foch's controller general for the Rhineland, stepped up its exports. Owing to a subsequent shortage of French currency in the occupied zone and increasing British competition, however, tight economic control of the Rhineland became more and more difficult.[52] Although House backed French economic policy, the British resolved to establish no separate economic regime for the occupied territories and found support among oth-

49 Note on the meeting of the Council of Four, June 3, 1919, *PMN,* 2:278–86; Soutou, *L'Or et le sang,* 802.

50 See note of 2d session of the subcommission to consider the details of the delivery of lignite, etc., from the Left bank of the Rhine to unoccupied Germany, May 13, 1919, GB FO 608, vol. 281, pt. 5, for further evidence.

51 British Empire Economic Committee, meeting of Apr. 4, 1919, GB FO 608/75; Lord Derby, transmitting memorandum by Seydoux of Jan. 28, 1919, GB FO 608/222.

52 Procès–Verbal d'une séance tenue le 20 Juin 1919 au Ministère du Commerce et le l'Industrie, June 20, 1919, folder "Rhénanie," F 12 8044–Rhénanie, Archives Nationales, Paris. Walter A. McDougall, *France's Rhineland Diplomacy, 1914–1924: The Last Bid for a Balance of Power in Europe* (Princeton, N.J., 1978), 90–1, contains a sketch of Tirard's economic plans; see also chapter 12 in this book.

ers in the American delegation. They insisted on the Luxembourg Committee and its metamorphosis into the Inter-Allied Rhineland Commission. Thus economic constraints and British steadfastness undermined the more grandiose French economic ideas.[53]

The economic clauses of the Treaty of Versailles, as has been demonstrated here, constituted a compromise between politically and economically inconsistent Allied and American schemes. All the same, the three Allied victors shared a common vision for postwar Europe insofar as they sought to limit Germany's economic power for the benefit of Poland, Czechoslovakia, and France. The underlying rationale of the treaty was to surround the Reich with an array of economically viable states capable of withstanding future attempts at economic domination. The transition phase of five years provided Germany's neighbors a head start. It weakened the Reich sufficiently so as not to be menacing, yet left it prosperous enough to generate the revenue necessary to sustain the Versailles regime. This required an elaborate balancing act. The commercial rules of the treaty served to reinforce the new postwar order and thus used economic means to achieve political ends.

ECONOMIC PROBLEMS DURING THE PEACE CONFERENCE

The devastation caused by the war and the economic disturbance of the continuing blockade created ongoing practical problems. The negotiators in Paris could not strike a political deal in a vacuum. The following two examples should serve to illustrate the constraints that conditioned their deliberations.

An American-Allied agreement of January 2 led to the establishment of the Inter-Allied Council for Relief under Hoover's direction. Yet despite a manifest lack of foodstuffs in Germany, the revictualing of the Reich remained controversial.[54] From the Armistice onward, the government of

---

53 Minutes of [U.S.] Economic Group, Feb. 26, 1919, box 46, American Economic Group folder, Norman H. Davis papers; note from British Embassy Paris, Apr. 10, 1919, GB FO 608/222; memorandum on the Commission set up under the Armistice with Germany and its relation to the Supreme Economic Council, appendix 77, Supreme Economic Council, minutes of Proceedings, Apr. 5, 1919, found in T 208, Hawtrey papers, Public Record Office; memorandum by S. P. Waterlow, May 17, 1919, GB FO 608/222.

54 The evidence about the effects of the Allied blockade of Germany remains controversial. See, e.g., Reports on Conditions in Germany, Mar. 25, 1919, doc. 58, in M. Dockrill, ed., *British Documents on Foreign Affairs: Reports and Papers from the Foreign Office Confidential Print* (University Publications of America, 1989), ser. I: *The Paris Peace Conference of 1919,* 5:181–9. Gerald D. Feldman, *The Great Disorder: Politics, Economics, and Society in the German Inflation* (New York, 1993), 99–100, underscores the difficulty of arriving at a clear assessment of domestic German food supplies after the Armistice. A revisionist account that stresses the hardships imposed on the German population by the blockade is provided by N. P. Howard, "The Social and Political Consequences of the Allied Food Block-

the United States had forcefully advocated a relaxation of the blockade of the Central Powers and the neighboring neutrals. Americans pointed to the obvious need of Belgium, Yugoslavia, Poland, and Czechoslovakia, as well as the Central Powers, for foodstuffs and their own willingness to furnish them. The American Food Administration had made forward commitments to buy large quantities of grain and meat from domestic producers. After the Armistice, the release of surplus stocks at the prevailing contract prices would avoid a potential political conflict with the farm bloc. The British government initially opposed the American relief effort and refused to lift the blockade. As an American report noted, the British complained that the relief effort would have the indirect result of their having borrowed money in order to "purchase foodstuffs in the United States which are to be dispatched to enemy or ex-enemy territory or [to] finance the supply to such territory of foodstuffs which we are ourselves obtaining from the United States."[55] In view of Hoover's insistence on de facto American direction of the relief effort and the clear indication of American economic self-interest as a moving force behind the effort, British opposition to proposals to lift the blockade grew furious. Cecil Harmsworth, acting director of the British postwar blockade effort, wrote, "I think that our American friends do not in the least realize that the blockade is not an arbitrary and vexatious system established by the European Allies for the purposes of obstructing trade, but that it is in fact an implement of war and now a lever for securing the results of war."[56] The establishment of the Inter-Allied Council for Relief only became possible because the French Foreign Office found it expedient in late December to concur in Hoover's plan.[57]

With the subsequent relaxation of the blockade of neutral countries, Hoover began his food shipments to Germany, only to evoke a cynical comment from Keynes, who visualized the Great Humanitarian sleeping at night with visions of "pigs float[ing] across his bedclothes."[58] Meanwhile,

ade of Germany, 1918–19," *German History* 11 (1993): 161–88. Although the author provides solid statistical evidence of increased civilian deaths in Germany in 1917 and 1918, his case remains ambiguous for 1919. A detailed British report about conditions in the British Zone of the Rhineland shows that the food shortage was partly alleviated by unofficial Allied imports that circumvented the blockade; the shortages seem to have ended with the lifting of blockade restrictions in April. Report by Lieutenant E. F. Strange, Food Commissioner with the British Army of the Rhine and British Delegate to the Inter-Allied Military Food Commission (Mar. 26 to July 2, 1919), July 2, 1919, GB FO 608/279.

55 Hoover to Wilson, Oct. 24, 1918, in Bane and Lutz, eds., *Organization of American Relief*, 27–8; the quotation comes from Oscar T. Crosby to Hoover, Nov. 22, 1918, ibid., 55–6.
56 Cecil Harmsworth to Lord Robert Cecil, Feb. 11, 1919, Cecil Harmsworth papers, GB FO 800/250.
57 House to Stéphen Pichon, Jan. 1, 1919, in Bane and Lutz, eds., *Organization of American Relief*, 138.
58 Keynes memorandum for Sir John Bradbury, Jan. 14, 1919, in *The Collected Writings of John Maynard Keynes* (hereafter *JMKW*), 30 vols. (London, 1971–), 16:392–4.

French resistance to the eventual use of German gold to pay for foodstuffs instead of reparations delayed further progress. February and the first week of March witnessed American alarms about the specter of bolshevism in the Reich and continued French procrastination. The Spa conference deadlocked. At the same time, France tried to use the blockade to channel French food shipments to Bavaria and the Rhineland in order to encourage separatist tendencies there. Both England and France insisted on the surrender of the German merchant marine as a precondition for prolonging the armistice and for food shipments.[59] Owing chiefly to House's and Lloyd George's cajoling of Clemenceau, the American, British, and French delegations arrived at a tentative agreement on March 8 about future relief operations for Germany.[60] The Reich's obstinate refusal to deliver its merchant fleet to the Allies as a quid pro quo for food shipments caused further delay until the Brussels conference began on March 13. There Admiral Wemyss replaced Foch as chief negotiator. With the Allies now eager to resolve the situation, the German delegation gave up its resistance to surrendering its merchant fleet. Limited German trade with its neutral neighboring countries now became possible, and relief goods stored in Allied ports could be delivered to the Reich.[61] Within two months, Germany became the chief recipient of American and Allied food shipments. Despite continued French and Italian opposition, the Reich subsequently transferred gold valued at £34.5 million to neutral banks in order to pay for the food shipments. The British government complained about the American practice of distributing food at prices calculated to afford American producers a profit, yet the program continued until its scheduled end in July.[62]

American–Allied food shipments and the gradual loosening of the blockade constituted the means for a variety of ends. Although Hoover indeed sought to off-load American surplus products, the overriding motive for his

59 Arthur Salter to Jean Monnet, Feb. 18, 1919, F[12] 7809.
60 Commissioners Plenipotentiary of the American Delegation, Mar. 5, 1919, 185.13/17, RG 256; Bureau of the Conference BC–A1, meeting of Jan. 13, ibid., 185.13/2; extracts from minutes of the Supreme War Council, referring to the Spa Conference, Mar. 7, 1919, in Bane and Lutz, eds., *Blockade of Germany*, 198–9; Gordon Auchincloss diary, Mar. 8, 1919; House diary, Mar. 4, 1919.
61 Telegram of Norman Davis for Albert Rathbone, Mar. 9 and 18, 1919, Carter Glass papers, box 130, University of Virginia Library; minutes of a conference held at Brussels on Mar. 13–14, 1919, in Bane and Lutz, eds., *Blockade of Germany*, 249–59. Hans Loewenfeld-Russ, *Im Kampf gegen den Hunger: Aus den Erinnerungen des Staatssekretärs für Volksernährung, 1918–1920* (Munich, 1986), 236–8, states that on Mar. 13, Great Britain, France, and Italy agreed to furnish Austria with a dollar loan of up to $30 million until the coming harvest in order to purchase food.
62 Keynes to Bradbury, May 9, 1919, *JMKW* 16:445–8; report on distribution by Colonel Alvin B. Barber, Aug. 1919, in Bane and Lutz, eds., *Organization of American Relief*, 662; Vance C. McCormick diary, June 13, 1919. For evidence of the high price of Hoover's food deliveries in the Rhineland, see report by Lieutenant E. F. Strange, July 2, 1919, GB FO 608/279.

actions was to fend off penury in Europe. The specter of starvation led the food administrator to deploy his brilliant organizing and propagandistic skills, as well as his less developed diplomatic talents, in order to obtain a relaxation of the Allied blockade. The dispute over food relief for Germany cast a shadow over British and American views of French policy. They starkly exposed French strategy of using economic means to further political and territorial goals.[63] Despite the manifold obstacles that delayed large-scale relief shipments to Germany, the ending of the neutral blockade constituted a momentous achievement for the peace conference. When the Germans threatened not to sign the preliminary treaty in May, Robert Cecil, the former minister of blockade, now in charge of the Foreign Office's League of Nations section, contemplated a re-imposition of the blockade. Yet Wilson refused to accede to this step. The very success of the relief effort had in effect deprived the conference of a credible threat to induce Germany to sign. This substantial concession derived from Hoover's assessment of humanitarian and economic necessities, a sentiment to which economic self-interest was alien.[64]

Accelerated postwar inflation imposed further constraints on the peace negotiations. After the end of the war, France found itself in a position of complete financial dependency on the British and American treasuries. This trying state of affairs grew more dramatic when Great Britain threatened to withdraw its financial support. Like Italy, France subsequently curtailed imports in order to protect its weakened currency. Responding to urgent French requests for assistance, America took the initiative to resolve the question. The United States, France, and England concluded an agreement that provided France with an additional loan of £25 million on March 11.[65] This accord paved the way for the unpegging of the French currency the next day. The franc subsequently depreciated from 5.48 to the U.S. dollar on March 12 to 6.46 to the U.S. dollar on June 25.[66] Although the measure furthered French inflation, it brought immediate relief to the French treasury. This sequence of events suggests that the American–British initiative may have induced France to take a more conciliatory attitude toward relief shipments to Germany. In any case, numerous conference delegates

---

63 Vance C. McCormick diary, May 15, 1919.
64 Meeting of the Council of Four, May 9, 1919, *PMN,* 2:9–11. For a detailed assessment of Hoover's role at the end of the war, see George H. Nash, *The Life of Herbert Hoover: Master of Emergencies, 1917–1918* (New York, 1996).
65 Stevenson, *French War Aims,* 148–9; Lord Robert Cecil, The Economic Situation in Europe, Mar. 2, 1919, GB CAB 29/8, WCP 187; telegrams of the American Mission in Paris to State Department, Mar. 10, Decimal File 851.51/119–121, RG 59, NA.
66 The exchange rates have been obtained from *The Statist,* Jan.–June 1919.

reported a dramatic shift in French willingness to cooperate with the American and British delegations after the agreement came into effect.[67]

Across the yet undetermined border, German inflation proceeded even more rapidly. From November 1918 to June 1919 the dollar-exchange index of the mark (with 1913 = 1.00) increased from 1.77 to 3.34.[68] Apart from gold payments for food, capital flight seemed to have precipitated this steep decline. While German expenditures for food totaled not more than £34.5 million, gold holdings in German banks declined from £113.13 million on December 21, 1918, to £57.57 million on June 21, 1919.[69] Although the Allied blockade had imposed obstacles to German capital exports, it remained possible to find loopholes, such as selling German-owned foreign securities under the pretense of non-German ownership in the Netherlands at a discount.[70] The rapid depreciation fanned French apprehension regarding political motives for the fall of the mark.

The economic problems deriving from the blockade and worsening postwar inflation made a speedy conclusion of the peace necessary. They likewise shaped the economic negotiations themselves. The ending of the blockade and the state of war became ends in themselves. With the conclusion of the peace, American economic diplomacy shifted from immediate material relief to the financial reconstruction of Germany and the Allied countries in order to facilitate a return to stability.[71]

GERMAN REACTIONS

Political elites both within and without the German government agreed on one overriding concern when faced with the preliminary treaty. Above all, the Reich should lose no predominantly German territory. To achieve that goal, Max Warburg, the Hamburg banker and government advisor, proposed that the German delegation should offer substantial economic and financial

67 French gratitude for American assistance in obtaining a further advance from the British Treasury is suggested in the Gordon Auchincloss diary, Mar. 11, 1919; see also Lamont, Strauss, Davis to Albert Rathbone, Mar. 18, 1919, Carter Glass papers, box 130.
68 Carl-Ludwig Holtfrerich, *The German Inflation, 1914–1923: Causes and Effects in International Perspective*, trans. Theo Balderston (Berlin, 1986), 17.
69 The statistical figures about the gold-mark holdings in German banks have been obtained from *The Statist*, Jan.–June 1919.
70 The above-mentioned practice is described in Karl Pelzer to Wilhelm Cuno, Aug. 27, 1919, Bestand HAPAG Lloyd 1480, Staatsarchiv Hamburg. For connections between the German inflation and the German tariff, see comments of Frank Taussig in minutes of the Economic Commission, Section on Permanent Commercial Relations, Mar. 22, 1919, GB CAB 29/11, WCP 413.
71 Stephen A. Schuker, "Origins of American Stabilization Policy in Europe: The Financial Dimension," in Hans-Jürgen Schröder, ed., *Confrontation and Cooperation: Germany and the United States in the Era of World War I* (Providence, R.I., 1993), 377–408.

concessions for the Allies.[72] Nevertheless, the Reich's delegates in Versailles offered a broadside of criticisms of the draft treaty's provisions. Foreign Minister Ulrich Count von Brockdorff-Rantzau's immediate response when he read the draft treaty on May 7 was to deny Germany's sole responsibility for the war in a harsh and undiplomatic manner before calling for cooperation in European economic reconstruction. Brockdorff-Rantzau's speech robbed Germany of the little sympathy remaining in the Allied delegations. As a leading French diplomat wrote afterward: "We pitied them as they entered and were furious as they left."[73] After it became clear that the victors would not revise the main features of the treaty, Brockdorff-Rantzau filed a formal response on May 29, listing German counterproposals. After minimal changes were adopted, the German delegation bowed to Allied-American pressure, including the threat of military occupation, and signed.[74] Despite a tentative reorientation of German foreign trade policy after the end of the war, the Reich did not present credible alternative proposals for the economic clauses. There are several reasons for the failure.

Despite clear evidence to the contrary, the Foreign Office and the Weimar government refused to accept the fact that ultimately peace would be made by America and the Allies. German diplomacy missed the opportunity to enter into constructive negotiations when England and France initiated the Gibson, Massigli, and Haguenin missions in March and April. Instead, the German Foreign Office continued to cling unrealistically to its erroneous interpretation of Wilson's Fourteen Points and the Lansing note. The subsequent German peace proposals demanded reciprocal most-favored-nation treatment, the revival of Germany's prewar commercial treaties, the incorporation of Wilson's Fourteen Points into the League of Nations Covenant, the end of the economic war, and last but not least the right to impose import and export prohibitions. As the commentary to the draft emanating from the German Office for Peace Negotiations (Deutsche Geschäftsstelle für die Friedensverhandlungen) stressed, these proposals were modeled after Wilson's Fourteen Points and were elaborated without

72 Peter Krüger, *Deutschland und die Reparationen 1918/19: Die Genesis des Reparationsproblems in Deutschland zwischen Waffenstillstand und Versailler Friedensschluss* (Stuttgart, 1973), 181–209. For Max Warburg's political role during the war and its aftermath, see Niall Ferguson, *Paper and Iron: Hamburg Business and German Politics in the Era of Inflation, 1897–1927* (Cambridge, 1995).

73 Klaus Schwabe, *Woodrow Wilson, Revolutionary Germany, and Peacemaking, 1918–1919: Missionary Diplomacy and the Realities of Power* (Chapel Hill, N.C., 1985), 330–3; the quotation is from Paul Cambon to his son, May 14, 1919, in Paul Cambon, *Correspondence, 1870–1924*, 3 vols. (Paris, 1946), 3:331–2.

74 See the full account by Klaus Schwabe, *Deutsche Revolution und Wilson Frieden: Die amerikanische und deutsche Friedensstrategie zwischen Ideologie und Machtpolitik 1918/19* (Düsseldorf, 1971), 521–651; also the revised English version, *Woodrow Wilson*, 330–94 (see esp. fn. 66).

considering whether they could prevail in Paris. German diplomats were instructed merely to *use* them during the negotiations. Ernst Schmitt, desk officer at the Bureau of Foreign Commerce in the German Foreign Office, expressed the view that mere tactical considerations lay behind Wilson's principles for a liberal foreign-trade regime.[75] German plans for negotiations in Paris initially did not envision serious economic deliberations; as a result, the Foreign Office missed its chance to influence proceedings in Paris while negotiations about the economic clauses went on. Moreover, German diplomacy did not live up to the liberal ideas that it had opportunistically adopted in the fall of 1918. Instead, the Foreign Office pursued negotiations with Austria about a bilateral customs union that resulted in a draft convention on March 2.[76] This aggressive course ran counter to the Allied attempts to prevent a customs union and resulted in the treaty provision barring an Anschluss.[77]

Brockdorff-Rantzau subsequently urged Chancellor Philipp Scheidemann to turn down a treaty that would impede Germany's economic reconstruction. Out of their own self-interest, according to the foreign minister, Great Britain and America could not allow "Russian conditions" to prevail in Germany.[78] This overconfidence discouraged the submission of realistic German counterproposals to the draft treaty, as Dutch business circles and the Swiss Foreign Office had urged.[79] Indeed, top German businessmen like Hermann Röchling or Wilhelm Cuno shared Brockdorff-Rantzau's belief that a harsh economic peace should be summarily rejected.[80] Röchling's advice to Matthias Erzberger, although also reflecting his apprehension about the Saar question, demonstrated nationalistic ambivalence about the stipulations of the peace treaty:

75 German Office for Peace Negotiations to Foreign Office, Mar. 8, 1919, R 85 [Handelspolitische Abteilung des Auswärtigen Amtes], vol. 890, Bundesarchiv Koblenz; memorandum about discussions on German goals concerning peace negotiations, Mar. 12, 1919, doc. 164, *Akten zur Deutschen Auswärtigen Politik*, vol. A 1 (Göttingen, 1982), 281.
76 Protokoll [über Ergebnis der Verhandlungen zwischen Deutschen und österreichischen Vertretern in der Zeit vom 27.2. bis zum 3.3.1919], Brockdorff-Rantzau papers, Österreichische Anschlussfrage, Politisches Archiv des Auswärtigen Amtes, Bonn; Peter Grupp, *Deutsche Aussenpolitik im Schatten von Versailles, 1918–1920: Zur Politik des Auswärtigen Amtes vom Ende des Ersten Weltkriegs und der Novemberrevolution bis zum Inkrafttreten des Versailler Vertrags* (Paderborn, 1988), 218–25.
77 Stéphen Pichon to French Ambassador in Washington, D.C., Oct. 21, 1918, Papiers d'Agents Stéphen Pichon, vol. 6, MAE.
78 Brockdorff-Rantzau to Scheidemann, Mar. 22, 1919, Akten der Reichskanzlei, R 43/I/1, Bundesarchiv Koblenz.
79 Copy of Reichskanzlei note 4587, Apr. 25, 1919, R 43 I/2; Adolf Müller (Bern) to German Foreign Office, May 9, 1919, ibid.
80 Cuno to Schinckel, June 17, 1919, Hapag Lloyd Bestand, Nr. 21; Hermann Röchling to Erzberger, May 12, 1919, Matthias Erzberger papers, vol. 46, Bundesarchiv Koblenz.

In my view, we can only go in one direction in the present situation: To attempt to declare, by rejecting the treaty as a basis of negotiations, that our national existence does not allow us to negotiate in this manner. . . . At the same time, however, we should make counterproposals, which should amount to offering our total domestic economic and working potential to compensate for the [Allied] debt claims over a 20–30 year period and to subjecting ourselves to any control about the maximum amount we will furnish, consistent with our national honor.[81]

As Röchling's and Warburg's attitudes suggest, widespread apprehension about the draft treaty provisions, once they became known, led German business to urge serious negotiations in Paris. Still, neither the rigid time constraints of the conference nor the prevailing attitude in the German Foreign Office allowed a workable strategy to be designed for technical-level parleys in Paris. Instead, the Foreign Office nurtured the unrealistic hope that the German delegates would be able to strike a deal with the American and British delegations, as the German delegate Walter Simons frankly told his French counterpart René Massigli.[82]

Once it became obvious that this divisive scheme would not work, Brockdorff-Rantzau retreated to the stance of belligerent opposition. Meanwhile, Massigli discussed the draft treaty provisions with Moritz Bonn, August Thyssen, Simons, and other members of the German group in Paris. In contrast to Brockdorff-Rantzau's refusal to acknowledge the reality of an imposed economic peace, Thyssen, upon learning of the territorial stipulations of the draft treaty, coolly called attention to Germany's need for additional fuel. In this way, Massigli's conversations apparently paved the way for a more flexible allotment of Silesia's coal. After Brockdorff-Rantzau cranked up the rhetoric in response to the draft treaty, Simons told Massigli that these harsh reactions, particularly in regard to reparations, had been dictated by the Wilhelmstrasse. Whatever the truth of this claim, the fact that unofficial parleys between the French and German delegations took place underscores the fact that the German delegates in Paris had a sense of Allied economic deliberations in the latter part of the conference. The Germans knowingly rejected the option of more constructive consultation with the Allies. Similarly, members of the French delegation made some effort to counteract the impression

81 Original: "Wir können meines Erachtens in dieser Lage nur einen Weg gehen: den Versuch machen, durch eine Ablehnung des Vertrags als Verhandlungsgrundlage zu erklären, dass wir es mit unserer nationalen Existenz nicht vertragen können, in dieser Form zu verhandeln. . . . Gleichzeitig müssten aber Gegenvorschläge gemacht werden, die dahin gehen, dass wir unsere gesamte innere Wirtschaft und unsere gesamte Arbeitskraft zur Ausgleichung der Schuldforderungen auf 20–30 Jahre zur Verfügung stellen, und dass wir uns jeder, aber jeder mit der nationalen Würde vereinbaren Kontrolle darüber, dass wir das Maximum dessen liefern, was überhaupt möglich ist, unterwerfen."
82 Note of René Massigli, May 13, 1919, Papiers d'Agents Tardieu, vol. 321.

of a unilateral *Diktat* (dictate) imposed on an unsuspecting German delegation. Although France sought to negotiate from a position of strength, it still
aimed to establish pragmatic relations with the new Germany.[83]

The German counterproposals submitted by Brockdorff-Rantzau on
May 29 claimed that the draft treaty conditions would bring economic
havoc to Germany. At the same time, the German foreign minister rejected
the majority of the Allied territorial claims and instead offered yearly German reparation payments amounting nominally to 100 milliard gold marks
over 60 or more years. Brockdorff-Rantzau eschewed promises regarding
immediate cash payments, the most pressing Allied need. His proposal
instead envisioned substantial reparations in kind and vaguely specified assistance for the reconstruction of Belgium and northern France, as well as
Allied use of the German merchant fleet and participation in German coal
mines.[84]

Although Brockdorff-Rantzau held out the seeming prospect of substantial financial concessions, there are strong indications that the offer was
not made in good faith. Since early May, German diplomacy had aggres-
sively tried to stir up public opinion in the United States, England, and
France against the preliminary treaty.[85] It continued its course in Paris by
immediately printing the draft treaty and by making the German edition
available to all comers in Paris as well as in Germany and the neutral countries.[86] The German delegation furthermore sent a sequence of notes to the
American and Allied governments criticizing the economic and territorial
provisions of the draft treaty and outlining the economic consequences in
the blackest colors. As a member of the German delegation to Paris admitted, these notes aimed at alarming the public in the Allied countries.
Brockdorff-Rantzau's counteroffer followed a similar line: "The position
taken in our main response could not be limited to a simple 'unacceptable,'
but had to demonstrate sufficient German responsiveness so that either a
disregard or curt rejection of our propositions would put the enemy governments into a difficult situation before their populations."[87]

The German delegation's attempt to stir up protest achieved a short-lived
success because it reinforced American and British dismay over the discrep-

83 Reports of Massigli, May 12 to June 10, 1919, Papiers d'Agents André Tardieu, vol. 321.
84 Appendix to minutes of the meeting of the Council of Four, May 30, 1919, *PMN,* 2:258–63.
85 Schwabe, *Deutsche Revolution,* 571–84.
86 House diary, May 31, 1919.
87 Dr. von Becker to Erzberger, May 29, 1919, Erzberger papers, vol. 46. Original: "Die Stellung, die
   schliesslich in der Hauptantwort jetzt eingenommen worden ist, konnte sich auch nicht auf das ein-
   fache 'unannehmbar' beschränken, sondern musste so grosses Entgegenkommen zeigen, dass sowohl
   ein Nichteingehen auf die Gegenvorschläge, wie eine schroffe Ablehnung von seiten der feindlichen
   Regierungen ihren eigenen Völkern gegenüber grosse Schwierigkeiten bereiten würde."

ancy between the treaty and the Fourteen Points.[88] Ultimately, however, it backfired. The Council of Four understood the maneuver and took an even more skeptical attitude to the Reich's depiction of doom and gloom. The American–Allied response to Brockdorff-Rantzau's counteroffer noted that the delegation's exaggerated pessimism in itself inflated the crisis at home. The reply coolly pointed out that the Reich could still import food and raw materials it had lost through the territorial provisions of the treaty.[89] A private initiative of Max Warburg met an equally negative reaction. In early June, Warburg wrote to House baldly setting forth preconditions for German reparations payments: retention of Upper Silesia, reduction of the Rhineland occupation, an end to sequestrations of German property, an equal footing for Germany in world trade, and termination of the economic war. Warburg's letter reveals that the German delegation cared more about the commercial clauses of the treaty than its official reactions show. Yet the Hamburg banker only succeeded in reinforcing the prevailing impression that Germany was run by arrogant and unrepentant reactionaries who had no insight into the obligations incurred through Germany's pursuit of the war.[90] Berlin's official diplomacy thus overrode the more conciliatory inclinations of some German business circles. Apart from small modifications in the German-Polish border and the provisions for a plebiscite in Upper Silesia, it failed to effect any substantial changes in the economic clauses.[91]

THE ECONOMIC PEACE: OUTLOOK

German critics remained oblivious of the fact that the economic peace was a provisorium embodying an elaborate compromise between sharply differing aims of the Allies and the United States. The peace settlement accommodated the victor's demands for a transition phase that would maintain economic control over Germany. The rules governing this transition phase formed the core of the economic clauses of the treaty, while the design of a long-term commercial system was relegated to the League of Nations Covenant. In retrospect, it seems fair to say that Wilson's concept of a liberal peace had prevailed at least in its broad lines for the time being. It prevailed not so much because of the American statesman's steadfastness, but

---

88 Vance C. McCormick diary, May 22, 1919. The counterproductive reactions in the French press are described by G. Bernard Noble, *Policies and Opinions at Paris, 1919* (New York, 1968), 353–82.
89 Council of Four meetings, May 14 and 20, *PMN,* 2:69, 120.
90 Max Warburg to House, June 9, 1919, House papers, ser. I, box 114 a. For a scathing criticism of Warburg by Thomas Lamont, see Lamont to Baruch, Apr. 18, 1919, Lamont papers 171–27; now also in Lamont, *Ambassador,* 122–3.
91 Extract from *Headlam-Morley Diary,* June 19, 1919, 149–54.

rather owing to a rough consensus among Wilson, Lloyd George, and Clemenceau.[92] Contrary to Keynes's melodramatic claims, Wilson and his associates understood the economic problems facing them rather well. They did not frame a Carthaginian peace. Instead they preserved the essence of Germany's industrial potential. Maintenance of the Reich's productive capacity formed the logical corollary of the reparations provisions, and, even more, constituted the essence of a liberal vision of a new European economic power balance. The treaty aimed to give Germany's neighbors a head start in postwar reconstruction, but laid out the machinery for a gradual revision of its economic provisions.[93] The treaty provisions relating to the Saar exemplify this liberal concept.

Keynes's assessment of Wilson grossly underrated the latter's command of the economic imperatives of peacemaking. But it was revealing in its way. It underscored the growing rift between the British and Americans during the last weeks of the conference. This rift was precipitated by a combination of factors, starting with the British refusal to furnish France with additional loans, and culminating with British criticism of the American relief effort. Dissension led to disappointment and a loss of personal friendships that had developed during the war.[94] Members of the French and American delegations continued to communicate on reasonably friendly terms; but U.S. delegates reacted with increasing asperity to British complaints about the treaty and American attempts to take the lead in European financial reconstruction. At the end of the conference Thomas Lamont wrote to his wife:

America came over here asking not a dollar and looking for no commercial value. She is maintaining that position all the way through. Great Britain, on the other hand, has been on the make from start to finish. As we figure it, she is going to wind up in a much stronger commercial position than she ever has before. She has let us do the feeding of Europe. America has spent hundreds of millions of dollars in feeding Europe as contrasted with tens on the part of Great Britain, Great Britain maintaining, meantime, that she had not the ability to contribute her share. And now what do we find? We find this: the Hoover organization is winding up its work on July 1st, feeling that harvest time is arriving, and it is possible for the smaller nations to begin to look out for themselves. And now we find that Great Britain, who was too poor to help out in feeding during all this critical time, is writing to the smaller nations that, now that the Hoover organization is quitting on them,

92 For an enlightening exposition of the theoretical concept of historical processes, see Wolfgang J. Mommsen's essay in Christian Meier and Jörn Rüsen, eds., *Historische Methode,* Beiträge zur Historik, vol. 5 (Munich, 1988).
93 Keynes, *Economic Consequences;* Lloyd E. Ambrosius, *Woodrow Wilson and the American Diplomatic Tradition: The Treaty Fight in Perspective* (New York, 1987); Thomas J. Knock, *To End All Wars: Woodrow Wilson and the Quest for a New World Order* (New York, 1992).
94 See, e.g., Vance C. McCormick diary, June 13, 1919.

Great Britain will see about taking care of them, but only in the event that they will do all their business, grant their concessions, &c, &c, to Great Britain. I came over here pro-British, but I go back anything but that.[95]

This rift foreshadowed the difficulties that the negotiators would face in rendering the economic peace workable.[96] The defeat of the treaty in the United States Senate signified the end of the French-American wartime collaboration and of the prospective postwar alliance. This outcome encouraged critics of the treaty in France, such as Raymond Poincaré, to embark on a desperate search for new means to obtain economic security for France. This process played itself out through 1924. The economic peace settlement of 1919 thus contained an unwritten "rebus sic stantibus."

95 Thomas Lamont to Florence Lamont, June 6, 1919, Lamont papers, 165–25; see also Wilson's negative assessment of the British in his discussion with the American Delegation, June 3, 1919, in *PWW,* 60:71.
96 Some of the subsequent developments are discussed in Elisabeth Glaser-Schmidt, "German and American Concepts to Restore a Liberal World Trading System After World War I," in Schröder, ed., *Confrontation and Cooperation,* 353–76.

16

The Balance of Payments Question: Versailles and After

NIALL FERGUSON

On June 5, 1919, the Hamburg banker Max Warburg filled an idle moment by drafting some satirical verses on the Versailles conference, which he was attending as one of the German delegation's financial experts. With characteristic black humor, he gave them the title: "The Villettiade [after the Château Villette, where the German delegation was initially housed], The First Part of a Tragedy."[1] For Warburg, who had just submitted the German delegation's counterproposals to the Allied peace terms, the conference had indeed more than one tragic aspect. As one of the Jewish members of the German delegation, he was condemned – as he had anticipated – to endure vilification for years to come from anti-Semitic critics of the *Schmachfrieden*.[2] His own economic interests were gravely threatened by the terms of the peace, which confiscated the assets of numerous German firms and implied a dramatic increase in direct taxation to finance reparations. Above all, he regarded the peace as a tragedy for Germany, the country to which he remained passionately attached, despite all, until his death in 1946. Shortly after the presentation of the Allied terms, he expressed his bitterness at Germany's treatment in a letter to his wife: "To announce a new era to the world, to speak of love and justice, and then to perpetrate pillage on a global scale, to sow the seeds of future conflicts and kill all hope of better times, is to commit the greatest sin in the world. To experience this at first hand is appalling."[3]

It must be said that not many historians would today agree with Warburg's characterization of the Versailles treaty as "pillage on a global scale."

---

1 Max Warburg papers, M. M. Warburg & Co., Hamburg (hereafter WA), "Jahresbericht 1919," "Labor et Constantia," Max M. W., Versailles, 5 June, 1919, "Die Villettiade (Der Tragödie erster Teil)."
2 WA, "Jahresbericht 1918," Anlage 5, Max Warburg to Fritz Warburg, Oct. 7, 1918; "Jahresbericht 1919," Max Warburg to Alice Warburg, June 20, 1919; Warburg, "Aus meinen Aufzeichnungen," MSS, June 23, 1919. Cf. Max Warburg, *Aus meinen Aufzeichnungen* (Hamburg, 1952), 64.
3 Warburg, *Aufzeichnungen,* 79, quoting letters to his wife of May 8 and 9.

In the past two decades, research in the French, British, and American archives has led to substantial reappraisals of those countries' policies. French policy is now seen by a number of authors as a series of more or less rational stratagems designed to increase French leverage over its eastern neighbor;[4] American policy as an attempt to achieve economic recovery and political stability in Europe through large-scale, though privately organized, capital export;[5] British policy as an unrealistic effort to return to prewar economic conditions and to abandon the wartime "continental commitment" in favor of a remolded empire.[6] The resulting conflicts of interest meant that, by comparison with the ad hoc peace imposed on Germany in 1945, the Versailles peace was relatively lenient.[7] As Andreas Hillgruber has observed, the treaty was "too weak to be a 'Carthaginian' peace."[8] Consequently, some historians have come to view German complaints about the treaty with skepticism. In particular, Sally Marks and Stephen Schuker have sought to demonstrate that the material burdens imposed by reparations were less onerous than the Germans claimed, arguing that Germany "could have paid a good deal more if she had chosen to do so."[9] A view frequently

4 See esp. Walter A. McDougall, *France's Rhineland Diplomacy, 1914–1924: The Last Bid for a Balance of Power in Europe* (Princeton, N.J., 1978); Marc Trachtenberg, "Reparation at the Paris Peace Conference," *Journal of Modern History* (hereafter *JMH*) 51 (1979): 24–55; Marc Trachtenberg, *Reparation in World Politics: France and European Economic Diplomacy, 1916–1923* (New York, 1980); David Stevenson, *French War Aims Against Germany, 1914–1919* (Oxford, 1982); Jon Jacobson, "Strategies of French Foreign Policy After World War I," *JMH* 55, no. 1 (1983): 78–95. See also Stephen A. Schuker, *The End of French Predominance in Europe: The Financial Crisis of 1924 and the Adoption of the Dawes Plan* (Chapel Hill, N.C., 1976).

5 Arno J. Mayer, *Politics and Diplomacy of Peacemaking: Containment and Counterrevolution at Versailles, 1918–1919* (New York, 1967); Carl Parrini, *Heir to Empire: United States Economic Diplomacy, 1916–1923* (Pittsburgh, 1969); Frank Costigliola, *Awkward Dominion: American Political, Economic and Cultural Relations with Europe, 1919–1923* (Ithaca, N.Y., 1984); Werner Link, *Die amerikanische Stabilisierungspolitik in Deutschland, 1921–1932* (Düsseldorf, 1970).

6 Robert E. Bunselmeyer, *The Cost of the War, 1914–1918: British Economic War Aims and the Origins of Reparations* (Hamden, Conn., 1975); Michael L. Dockrill and J. Douglas Gould, *Peace Without Promise: Britain and the Peace Conference, 1919–1923* (London, 1981); Anne Orde, *British Policy and European Reconstruction After the First World War* (Cambridge, 1990).

7 Charles S. Maier, "The Two Postwar Eras and the Conditions for Stability in Twentieth-Century Western Europe," in Charles S. Maier, *In Search of Stability: Explorations in Historical Political Economy* (New York, 1987), 153–84. Cf. Jon Jacobson, "Is There a New International History of the 1920s?" *American Historical Review* 88 (1983): 617–45.

8 Andreas Hillgruber, "Unter dem Schatten von Versailles – die aussenpolitische Belastung der Weimarer Republik: Realität und Perzeption bei den Deutschen," in Karl Dietrich Erdmann and Hagen Schulze, eds., *Weimar: Selbstpreisgabe einer Demokratie: Eine Bilanz heute* (Düsseldorf, 1980), 57; Andreas Hillgruber, "'Revisionismus' – Kontinuität und Wandel der Aussenpolitik der Weimarer Republik," *Historische Zeitschrift* 237 (1983): 587–621; Gerhard L. Weinberg, "The Defeat of Germany in 1918 and the European Balance of Power," *Central European History* 2 (1969): 248–60; Walter A. McDougall, "Political Economy Versus National Sovereignty," *JMH* 51 (1979): 4–23.

9 Sally Marks, "Reparations Reconsidered: A Reminder," *Central European History* 2 (1969): 356–65; Sally Marks, "The Myths of Reparations," *Central European History* 11 (1978): 231–55; Stephen A. Schuker, "American 'Reparations' to Germany, 1919–1933," in Gerald D. Feldman and E. Müller-Luckner, eds., *Die Nachwirkungen der Inflation auf die deutsche Geschichte, 1924–1933* (Munich, 1985), 335–83. But see David Felix, "Reparation Reconsidered with a Vengeance," *Central European History*

expressed, now as then, is that German politicians deliberately set out to sabotage an economically feasible scheme by "working systematically towards bankruptcy."[10] Interestingly, even those historians who take the opposite view of reparations sometimes concede the truth of this. Carl-Ludwig Holtfrerich has suggested that "the progressive depreciation of the mark" was the most effective way of "persuading the rest of the world of the need for a reduction of the reparations burden."[11] Frank Graham said much the same in 1930.[12]

It is certainly not difficult to see *why* German politicians wanted to undermine the Versailles treaty.[13] Reparations aside, the "war-guilt" clause, the disarmament provisions and the losses of territory ensured that the treaty was unpopular across the political spectrum.[14] In this respect, it can even be argued that, paradoxically, Versailles was "the unifying bracket that clamped German politics together."[15] From an economic standpoint, however, the crucial points of the Allied terms related to reparations – to cover

4 (1971): 171–9; Peter Krüger, "Das Reparationsproblem der Weimarer Republik in fragwürdiger Sicht," *Vierteljahrshefte für Zeitgeschichte* 29 (1981): 21–74.

10 Quoted in Gerald D. Feldman, *The Great Disorder: Politics, Economics, and Society in the German Inflation* (New York, 1993), 377. Cf. Charles S. Maier, "Inflation and Stabilization in the Wake of Two World Wars: Comparative Strategies and Sacrifices," in Gerald D. Feldman et al., eds., *Die Erfahrung der Inflation, Beiträge zu Inflation und Wiederaufbau in Deutschland und Europa, 1914–1924*, vol. 2 (Berlin, 1984), 127; Stephen A. Schuker, "Finance and Foreign Policy in the Era of the German Inflation: British, French, and German Strategies for Economic Reconstruction After the First World War," in Otto Büsch and Gerald D. Feldman, eds., *Historische Prozesse der Deutschen Inflation 1914 bis 1924: Ein Tagungsbericht, Einzelveröffentlichungen der historischen Kommission zu Berlin, vol. 21* (Berlin, 1978), 343–61; Carl-Ludwig Holtfrerich, "Die deutsche Inflation 1918 bis 1923 in internationaler Perspektive: Entscheidungsrahmen und Verteilungsfolgen," in ibid., 321–8; Peter Krüger, "Die Auswirkungen der Inflation auf die deutsche Aussenpolitik," in Feldman und Müller-Luckner, eds., *Nachwirkungen*, 297–313; Hans-Jürgen Schröder, "Die politische Bedeutung der deutschen Handelspolitik nach dem Ersten Weltkrieg," in Gerald D. Feldman et al., eds., *Die deutsche Inflation: Eine Zwischenbilanz, Beiträge zu Inflation und Wiederaufbau in Deutschland und Europa, 1914–1924*, vol. 1 (Berlin 1982), 235–51; Hermann J. Rupieper, *The Cuno Government and Reparations, 1922–1923: Politics and Economics* (The Hague, 1976), 32–3; Agnete von Specht, *Politische und wirtschaftliche Hintergründe der deutschen Inflation, 1918–1923* (Frankfurt am Main, 1982), 33, 38.

11 Holtfrerich, "Die deutsche Inflation 1918 bis 1923," 327.

12 Frank D. Graham, *Exchange, Prices, and Production in Hyperinflation Germany, 1920–1923* (Princeton, N.J., 1930), 4, 7–9, 11, 30–5, 248, 321. See also John Maynard Keynes, *The Collected Writings of John Maynard Keynes* (hereafter *JMKW*), 30 vols. (Cambridge, 1971–), 16:365; Knut Borchardt, "Wachstum und Wechsellagen, 1914–1970," in Hermann Aubin und Wolfgang Zorn, eds., *Handbuch der deutschen Wirtschafts- und Sozialgeschichte* (Stuttgart, 1976), 700.

13 Peter Krüger, *Deutschland und die Reparationen 1918/19: Die Genesis des Reparationsproblems in Deutschland zwischen Waffenstillstand und Versailler Friedensschluss* (Stuttgart, 1973), 41–51.

14 See Susanne Miller, *Die Bürde der Macht: Die deutsche Sozialdemokratie, 1918–1920* (Düsseldorf, 1978); Jürgen C. Hess, *"Das ganze Deutschland soll es sein": Demokratischer Nationalismus in der Weimarer Republik am Beispiel der Deutschen Demokratischen Partei* (Stuttgart, 1978); Annelise Thimme, *Flucht in den Mythos: Die Deutschnationale Volkspartei und die Niederlage von 1918* (Göttingen, 1969). Cf. Ulrich Heinemann, *Die verdrängte Niederlage: Politische Öffentlichkeit und Kriegsschuldfrage in der Weimarer Republik* (Göttingen, 1983).

15 Harold James, "Economic Reasons for the Collapse of Weimar," in Ian Kershaw, ed., *Weimar: Why Did German Democracy Fail?* (London, 1990), 54–5.

not only war damage to Belgium and France, but also the costs of war-related pensions and allowances to all the Allied governments.[16] One objection was that, because of the wide differences of opinion among the Allies in the subject, they named no final sum, thus creating a debilitating uncertainty.[17] But the principal objection related to the immediate seizures of German assets on the reparations account: not only the permanent seizure of the ships handed over at Trier, but also substantial amounts of Germany's smaller vessels and rolling stock; German overseas assets confiscated during the war (except those in the United States, whose status was left undecided); all German prewar credits to foreigners, to be offset against money owed by Germans (at prewar exchange rates) through the "clearing" system; and deliveries of coal, up to around 40 million tons a year. These expropriations meant, it was argued, a chronic balance of payments deficit, made still worse by the loss of industrial capacity as a result of territorial changes and the stipulation limiting Germany's right to an independent trade policy. The central theme of German diplomacy from 1919 to 1932 was that this balance of payments problem would have disastrous effects not only for Germany but for the world economy if the terms of the peace were not revised. Even if Germany could be forced to pay reparations, the Allies would not benefit, because Germany would only be able to raise the necessary hard currency to pay such cash payments as the Allies required by running a large trade surplus with the rest of the world.

Although a good deal is known about the balance of payments theory in the contemporary debates of economists, the political origins of this enormously influential line of argument are less well known.[18] A critical role was played in this regard by the Hamburg business community and, in particular, by Max Warburg.[19] As a prominent critic of German wartime diplo-

16 Bruce Kent, *The Spoils of War: The Politics, Economics, and Diplomacy of Reparations, 1918–1932* (Oxford, 1989), 67–77; Dockrill and Gould, *Peace Without Promise,* 45–56; Bunselmeyer, *Cost of the War,* 106–20; Krüger, *Aussenpolitik,* 72–6; Trachtenberg, "Reparation at the Paris Peace Conference," 24–55.
17 Charles S. Maier, *Recasting Bourgeois Europe: Stabilization in France, Germany, and Italy in the Decade After World War I* (Princeton, N.J., 1975), 233.
18 Karl Hardach, "Zur zeitgenössischen Debatte der Nationalökonomen über die Ursachen der deutschen Nachkriegsinflation," in Hans Mommsen, Dietmar Petzina, and Bernd Weisbrod, eds., *Industrielles System und Politische Entwicklung in der Weimarer Republik* (Düsseldorf, 1977), 368–75; Feldman, *Great Disorder,* 399–406.
19 When the German peace delegation arrived in Paris at the end of March 1919, alongside three ministers, a politician, and an academic, Max Warburg's partner Carl Melchior was among its members; and the delegation of "experts" that accompanied them (and that Melchior chaired) included Warburg himself; Franz Witthoefft and Eduard Rosenbaum, the president and secretary, respectively, of the Hamburg Chamber of Commerce; Albert Ballin's successor as general director of the HAPAG (and future chancellor), Wilhelm Cuno, along with his fellow-director Richard Peltzer; as well as the head of the Bremen Norddeutsche Lloyd, Philipp Heineken – an unprecedentedly high representation for Hanseatic interests on a national body of such importance. By comparison, there were only three representatives of heavy industry, and three of non-Hamburg banks. On the German delegation, see Alma

macy whose links with Wall Street and Washington were second to none in Germany, Warburg was identified by both Max of Baden and Friedrich Ebert as a natural choice to represent Germany at the peace negotiations.[20] Initially, he himself demurred when asked by Prince Max to represent Germany at the peace negotiations because "the Entente conditions would doubtless be extremely hard."[21] While other experts talked of reparations demands of 20 billion marks and 30 billion marks, Warburg warned them to brace themselves for an "absurdly high" figure. As he put it to the foreign minister Ulrich Brockdorff-Rantzau, in early April: "We must be prepared for damned hard conditions."[22] He was thus well aware of the opprobrium he was likely to incur if he became involved in negotiating with the Allies. On the other hand, the fact that the Allies had designs on German economic assets — notably, overseas investments and the merchant fleet — gave Warburg and his colleagues in Hamburg a strong personal interest in the peace terms. As Warburg observed, "There has never been as big a business transaction as the peace treaty."[23]

The extent to which Warburg's policies constituted an "alternative" to "traditional" power politics should therefore not be exaggerated.[24] Although he was sincerely attracted to the Wilsonian idea of a league of nations, it was first and foremost economic interest that Warburg believed could bring Germany and the United States together in the postwar world. At the end of December 1918 he recalled how, prior to the Revolution, he had envisaged "close collaboration between America and Germany" after the war.[25] Although such schemes would now have to wait, it remained likely that, in economic terms, America would be the decisive factor in the postwar period. The argument Warburg advanced in early 1919 was that the

Luckau, *The German Peace Delegation at the Paris Peace Conference* (New York, 1941), 188ff.; Leo Haupts, *Deutsche Friedenspolitik: Eine Alternative zur Machtpolitik des Ersten Weltkrieges* (Düsseldorf, 1976), 41, 51, 111, 397–404; Leo Haupts, "Zur deutschen und britischen Friedenspolitik in der Krise der Pariser Friedenskonferenz," *Historische Zeitschrift* 217 (1973): 54–98. Cf. the comments in Klaus Schwabe, "Versailles–nach sechzig Jahren," *Neue Politische Literatur* 24 (1979): 446–75.

20 Hagen Schulze, ed., *Das Kabinett Scheidemann: 13. Februar bis 20. Juni 1919*, Akten der Reichskanzlei, Weimarer Republik (Boppard am Rhein, 1971), 64–96; Krüger, *Reparationen*, 74–5.

21 Ibid., 64.

22 Klaus Schwabe, *Deutsche Revolution and Wilson-Frieden: Die amerikanische und deutsche Friedensstrategie zwischen Ideologie und Machtpolitik, 1918–1919* (Düsseldorf, 1971), 526; Krüger, *Reparationen*, 82, 119; Haupts, *Deutsche Friedenspolitik*, 341. Warburg assumed that Germany would be burdened with reparations for twenty-five years and forty years: WA, Warburg diaries, Jan. 4, 1919 (n.p.); Peter Krüger, "Die Rolle der Banken und der Industrie in den deutschen reparationspolitischen Entscheidungen nach dem Ersten Weltkrieg," in Mommsen et al., eds., *Industrielles System*, 2:577.

23 WA, 19, Gesammelte Vorträge (Warburg speech before economics minister Scholz), Dec. 17, 1920.

24 Schwabe, "Versailles–nach sechzig Jahren," 454.

25 Warburg to Graf Bernstorff, Dec. 30, 1918, in Hans Rothfels et al., eds., *Akten zur deutschen auswärtigen Politik, 1918–1945: Aus dem Archiv des Auswärtigen Amtes*, series A: 1918–1925, 14 vols. (Göttingen, 1982), 1:154–5.

best way to pay reparations was by means of an international – that is, largely American – loan to Germany, which would allow it to pay a fixed capital sum in annuities spread over a period of up to forty years.[26] By April, he was envisaging a loan of 100 billion gold marks, 25 billion of which would be earmarked for the reconstruction of northern France and Belgium.[27] The corollary of such loans was an increase in German exports. To that end, Warburg envisaged a rapid deregulation of German trade and the lifting of exchange controls, to allow German exporters to benefit from the currency depreciation he regarded as inevitable. In an important memorandum of September 1917, his close friend Albert Ballin had already outlined the crucial argument: "[I regard] our gravely ailing currency as an admirable means of dispelling the hatred felt abroad towards Germany, and of overcoming the reluctance to trade with us [likely to be felt] by our enemies. The American who no longer gets for his dollar 4.21 marks' worth of goods from us, but 6.20 marks' worth, will rediscover his fondness for Germany."[28] Warburg had for some time realized that "a short period of a large disagio [on the mark] and even temporarily very high prices on the food and raw material markets" was to be preferred to continued exchange controls.[29] For this reason, he vehemently opposed efforts by Economics Minister Rudolf Wissell to continue and extend wartime controls over trade after the cessation of hostilities.[30] Warburg's starting point was therefore to link the question of German reparations as far as possible to other elements of the German balance of payments: capital imports and exports of goods.

It was a tribute to the ingenuity of these arguments that the Allied representative who proved most receptive to them was John Maynard Keynes, then a young and disaffected Treasury official. Keynes had already suggested as early as October 1918 that the Allies should ask for no more than 20 billion gold marks from Germany in the form of reparations.[31] Admittedly, his final Treasury "Memorandum on the Indemnity Payable by the Enemy Powers for Reparation and other Claims" named a figure twice as high; but the Treasury's arguments were in many ways close to those that the Germans

26 WA, Warburg diaries, Jan. 4, 1919 (n.p.); Warburg, *Aufzeichnungen,* 75; Krüger, "Rolle der Banken," 577; Krüger, *Reparationen,* 119.
27 Haupts, *Deutsche Friedenspolitik,* 337–40; Krüger, *Reparationen,* 128–9.
28 Ballin to Huldermann, Sept. 6, 1917, quoted in Bernhard Huldermann, *Albert Ballin* (London, 1922), 273–4.
29 WA, "Jahresbericht 1916," M. Warburg (untitled memorandum for Reichsbank), Nov. 24, 1916. Cf. "Jahresbericht 1917," Anlage 23; M. Warburg, "Übergangswirtschaft und Devisenregulierung," July 6, 1917; WA, "Jahresbericht 1918," Anlage 2; M. Warburg, "Währung, und Wirtschaftsführung nach dem Kriege," June 15, 1918.
30 Feldman, *Great Disorder,* 142ff., 152–5.
31 *JMKW,* 16:338–43.

intended to advance. More important, the Treasury anticipated an argument that was to become central to German revisionist efforts, by warning against demanding an amount "so large that it cannot be paid without . . . a far-reaching stimulation of the exports of the paying country [that] must necessarily interfere with the export trade of other countries."[32] This coincidence of thought partly explains the strong sympathy that Keynes felt when he encountered Carl Melchior for the first time during the armistice negotiations.[33] There was a similar, though less sympathetic, appreciation of the problems raised by reparations within the American delegation. Although the financial experts Bernard Baruch and Norman Davis envisaged a higher burden than their British counterparts, they fully appreciated that "the problem [was] not so much what Germany can pay but what the Allies can afford to have her pay."[34] However, the efforts of the German financial experts – who had arrived in France on March 28 – to build on these American doubts were less successful than Melchior had been with Keynes.[35]

The terms of the treaty as finally presented to the German delegation are well known, as is the German reaction. Initially, even Warburg was caught up in the febrile mood.[36] His first official response was "dictated . . . in a prolonged rage," and echoed Brockdorff-Rantzau in deploring the "shameless breaches of law" in the treaty.[37] Yet within a matter of days economic considerations had once again come to the fore in his mind.[38] He and Melchior swiftly reached the conclusion that a radical counterproposal was called for: an offer to the Allies of reparations totaling 100 billion gold marks, in exchange for which they hoped to secure major alterations in the peace terms.[39] The proposal has been described as "astonishing," documenting as it did an "honest will to pay" (Melchior's phrase) on the German

---

32 Ibid., 379.
33 John Maynard Keynes, "Dr. Melchior, A Defeated Enemy," in *Two Memoirs* (London, 1949), reprinted in *JMKW,* vol. 10: *Essays in Biography,* eds. A. Robinson and D. E. Moggridge (London, 1972), 415. Cf. R. F. Harrod, *The Life of John Maynard Keynes* (London, 1951), 231–4, 315, 394; Robert Skidelsky, *John Maynard Keynes: A Biography,* 2 vols. (London, 1983), 1:358–63; D. E. Moggridge, *Maynard Keynes: An Economist's Biography* (London, 1992), 301.
34 Rupieper, *Cuno Government,* 2–5.
35 Baker Library, Harvard Graduate School of Business Administration, Thomas W. Lamont papers 171–27, memorandum by Max Warburg for Thomas Lamont, Apr. 16, 1919; Lamont to Baruch, Apr. 18, 1919; memorandum, 30.4.45; National Archives, Washington, D.C. (hereafter NA), Record Group (hereafter RG) 59, 862.00/800, Dresel memorandum, Apr. 20, 1919. Cf. WA, "Jahresbericht 1919"; Warburg, *Aufzeichnungen,* 77; Schwabe, *Wilson-Frieden,* 562, 568, 582.
36 Warburg, *Aufzeichnungen,* 79, quoting letters to his wife of May 8 and 9.
37 Krüger, *Reparationen,* 187.
38 Haupts, *Deutsche Friedenspolitik,* 361.
39 On the origins of this proposal see WA, "Jahresbericht 1919"; Haupts, *Deutsche Friedenspolitik,* 17n.; Krüger, *Reparationen,* 187; Krüger, "Rolle der Banken," 581. The idea may have originated with Keynes and Melchior, but it was Warburg who added the various conditions.

side.[40] In fact, the 100 billion gold marks was not the "present value" of the Warburg-Melchior offer (which Keynes put at closer to 30 billion gold marks), since they envisaged the sum being paid over a prolonged period, beginning in 1926, in annuities of which only a fifth would bear interest. Warburg was, in effect, trying to dress up the estimated cost of reconstructing the damaged areas of Belgium and northern France (for which Germany had admitted liability) in such a way that it appeared sufficient to cover the British claims too; and, in return for this, to "rescue large parts of the East, colonies (albeit only some of them)" in order "to avoid an economic and financial control by the Entente" and "to protect private property."[41] Although the government in Berlin – particularly Finance Minister Bernhard Dernburg – regarded the 100 billion figure with great alarm, Warburg prevailed and the counterproposals were tabled.[42]

The German "offer" began with an attack on the legal basis of the Allied peace terms and made a range of noneconomic demands.[43] However, the central theme remained that the Allied terms implied "the utter destruction of German economic life."[44] The critical arguments were presented in a "Supplement on Financial Questions," probably drafted by Melchior and Warburg, and submitted with the German counterproposals to the Allied terms.[45] Given the economic constraints being imposed on Germany by the peace, the finance experts denied that Germany could pay war damages as defined by the Allies. Attempting to force it to do so by making the Reparations Commission "absolute master of Germany" would have dire consequences – even "death en masse." To pay reparations from current government revenue, it was pointed out, would require drastic cuts in social expenditure that would "destroy" German democracy. But the alternative – financing reparations by borrowing – posed equally grave problems:

In the immediate future it will be impossible to place German state loans in large amounts either at home or abroad, so that compensation [to the owners of assets expropriated for reparations] could be made only by means of large issues of notes. The inflation, already excessive, *would increase constantly if the peace treaty as proposed should be carried out. Moreover, great deliveries of natural products can only take place if the*

40 Haupts, *Friedenspolitik*, 15–16, 368.
41 Warburg to Dernburg, May 19, 1919, in Rothfels et al., eds., *Akten zur deutschen auswärtigen Politik*, series A, 2:56–9; Schulze, ed., *Das Kabinett Scheidemann*, 352n., 355; Krüger, *Reparationen*, 190–1, 195, 198–9, 203–8; Haupts, *Friedenspolitik*, 16n., 363, 370.
42 Warburg, *Aufzeichnungen*, 80–3; Staatsarchiv Hamburg (hereafter StAH), Firmenarchiv Arnold Otto Mayer, I, vol. 10:350, Witthoefft to Warburg, May 26, 1919. According to Warburg, the incensed Dernburg offered to resign and give him the post of finance minister. *Aufzeichnungen*, 82.
43 Text in Luckau, *German Delegation*, 306–406 (doc. 57).
44 Ibid., 319, 377.
45 Luckau, *German Delegation*, 378–91.

state reimburses the producers for their value; this means further issues of notes. As long as these deliveries last, there could be no question of the stabilising of the German currency even upon the present level.

Then came the crucial point: "*The depreciation of the mark would continue. The instability of the currency would affect not only Germany, however, but all the countries engaged in export, for Germany, with her currency constantly depreciating, would be a disturbing element and would be forced to flood the world market with goods at ridiculously low prices.*"[46] In short, the German economic experts predicted that the collection of reparations would lead to a balance of payments crisis, the depreciation of the mark, and a "flood" of German exports into Allied markets. It was this argument that underpinned the strategy of "fulfillment," adopted when it became clear that Germany had no choice but to accept the treaty.[47]

Two developments combined to encourage this approach in the wake of the conference. First, the Hamburg "line" was taken up and publicized internationally by Keynes.[48] Second, the mark slumped against the dollar from 14 marks to 99 marks between June 1919 and February 1920. The principal reason for this was the decision of the new Economics Minister, Robert Schmidt, to lift exchange controls – as Warburg had urged – thus enabling industry to take full advantage of the export premium created as the mark fell faster than domestic prices were rising.[49] As Schmidt put it bluntly: "The tossing out of German goods abroad at slaughter prices . . . will compel the Entente to allow us to bring our exchange into order."[50] The surge of depreciation appeared to confirm the assertion that the Versailles terms had created a balance of payments crisis and an export "fire sale" that only a revision of the treaty and a large international loan could resolve. In the words of Max Warburg: "The German people are . . . firmly resolved to fulfill the treaty as far as it is capable of doing so. If more is demanded, then a disaster will ensue that will affect not only Germany but will have repercussions for all other countries. The financial chaos already visible on the foreign exchange markets will spread."[51]

Yet these predictions of economic disaster turned out, in the all-

---

46 Ibid., 384. Emphasis in original.
47 The term "fulfill" is first used in this sense in the "Appeal of the German Government to the German People" of June 24. Luckau, *German Delegation*, 496–7.
48 John Maynard Keynes, *The Economic Consequences of the Peace* (London, 1919). On the Hamburg group's influence on Keynes, see Niall Ferguson, "Keynes and the German Inflation," *English Historical Review* 110 (1995): 368–91.
49 W. C. Matthews, "The Continuity of Social-Democratic Economic Policy, 1919 to 1920: the Bauer-Schmidt Policy," in Gerald D. Feldman et al., eds., *Die Anpassung an die Inflation*, Beiträge zu Inflation und Wiederaufbau in Deutschland und Europa, 1914–1924, vol. 8 (Berlin, 1986), 485–512.
50 Quoted in Steven B. Webb, *Hyperinflation and Stabilization in Weimar Germany* (New York, 1989), 91.
51 WA, Jahresbericht 1920, 2, Warburg to Lord Parmoor (Fight the Famine Council), Oct. 22, 1919.

important short run, to be wrong. Instead of spiraling inexorably downward, the mark – to the dismay of the pessimists (including Keynes, who had been blithely speculating against it) – suddenly recovered. And instead of collapsing, the German economy started to pick up. True, some American converts were made: John Foster Dulles expressed sympathy with the arguments for revision in the light of his visit to Germany.[52] But when the American ambassador met Max Warburg in July, he was struck by his "complete" pessimism.[53] The failure of the League of Nations international financial conference, which convened in Brussels in December 1920, set the seal on this disillusionment.[54] At Paris in January 1921, the increasingly impatient Allies agreed on scheme for reparations totaling 226 billion gold marks.[55] The German counteroffer of 30 billion gold marks, payable partly by a loan and partly by annuities over 25 years, struck even Lloyd George as risible; and sanctions were duly imposed in the form of the occupation of the Rhine ports and the imposition of the Reparations Recovery Act (a duty on German exports to Britain initially levied at 50 percent). The attempt to avert the threatened occupation of the Ruhr by suggesting a reparations total with a present value of 50 billion gold marks achieved nothing save to bring down the Fehrenbach government.[56] On April 27, the Allies set a definitive total bill of 132 billion gold marks; demanded a first payment of 1 billion gold marks by September; and threatened to occupy the Ruhr if Berlin did not submit.

The first phase of "fulfillment" therefore ended in failure; and for a time the influence of Warburg and Melchior in Berlin unquestionably waned. However, the London Ultimatum, by ending the period of "relative stabilization," did much to restore their credibility. Although all three declined ministerial office in it, Warburg, Melchior, and Cuno again played leading roles in formulating the initial revisionist strategy of the Wirth government.[57] As early as October 1920, Warburg had revealed his continuing belief in the

52 Mudd Library, Princeton University, John Foster Dulles papers, box 3, Dulles, "An Economic Conference?" [May?] 1920: "I do not know the precise condition of Mr. Stinnes's wardrobe now that he has become a billionaire, but I do know that his increased purchases are insignificant compared to the number of shirts and suits which the Germany [sic] worker has had to go without. . . . Europe, by inflating, is destroying its ability to buy from us, and is increasing its ability to compete with us. . . . As the primary cause lies the Reparation unsettlement." See also his speech "What America should know about Germany," Council of Foreign Relations, Jan 11, 1921; and the pro-German article by Paul Warburg published after his visit to Germany. Sterling Library, Yale University, Paul M. Warburg papers, ser. 2, box 11, folder 136, Paul M. Warburg, "Europe at the Crossroads," *Political Science Quarterly* 35 (1920).
53 NA, RG 59, 862.00/1074, Dresel to Secretary of State Colby, July 12, 1920.
54 WA, "Jahresbericht 1920," Blatt 32; "Politische Correspondenz, 1921," Universal Service Radio Interview [transcript], Jan. 1921. Cf. Kent, *Spoils of War*, 119.
55 Maier, *Recasting Bourgeois Europe*, 237–40; Kent, *Spoils of War*, 119, 125ff.
56 Kent, *Spoils of War*, 125ff.; Maier, *Recasting Bourgeois Europe*, 239–48.
57 WA 11, Pol. Corr., Warburg Notiz, June 7, 1921; Maier, *Recasting Bourgeois Europe*, 247; Ernst Laubach, *Die Politik der Kabinette Wirth 1921/22* (Lübeck, 1968), 34.

possibility of achieving revision via currency depreciation: "Even at the risk of sometimes selling our own products too cheaply abroad, the current policy must be abandoned. The world must be made to understand that is it impossible to burden a country with debts and at the same time to deprive it of the means of paying them. . . . The most complete collapse of the currency . . . cannot . . . be avoided if the peace treaty is maintained in its present form. . . . We are on the edge of the abyss."[58] Speaking at Brussels two months later, Cuno backed up his demand for the return of part of the confiscated merchant fleet with similar reasoning: "A factor which was formerly one of our strongest pillars in the balance of trade [i.e., payments] has now been changed from the active to the passive side. [As a result] Germany . . . is a bad buyer and the foreign countries with a high level of their exchange are bad sellers. . . . Political power does not do away with economic facts. If you ignore these facts, Germany must of necessity remain a constant danger for those countries who think they can get on without us."[59]

The London Ultimatum gave these arguments renewed vitality. In a speech drafted in July 1921, Warburg set them out once again:

Only through the greatest trade crisis that there has ever been . . . will we arrive at rational economic conditions. . . . By the end of August it will be clear that this method of pumping us dry is giving rise to an impossible situation in Germany and in the world. As a consequence of the appreciation of foreign currency [and] the depreciation of the mark, the danger exists that we will once again have an export premium, which could call forth an artificial boom in Germany and lead to a flooding of the whole world with [German] goods.[60]

At a dinner a week later with Joseph Wirth, Walter Rathenau, and the British ambassador Viscount D'Abernon, Melchior and Cuno made the same point (though they did not predict such rapid results as Warburg). According to Melchior, Germany might "get through the first two or three years with the aid of foreign loans or possibly of further bank note issues. By the end of that time, foreign nations will have realized that these large international payments can only be made by huge German exports, and these German exports will ruin trade in England and America, so that the creditors themselves will come to us to require modification."[61]

58 WA 19, Gesammelte Vorträge, "Die notwendigen Vorbedingungen für die Gesundung der deutschen Währung," Oct. 26, 1920.
59 HAPAG Archiv, Hamburg, Cuno Nachlass, Cuno speech at Brussels, Dec. 18, 1920.
60 WA 19, Gesammelte Vorträge, Warburg, "Entwurf einer nicht gehaltene Rede anlässlich der Pressetagung in Hamburg," July 4, 1921. Cf. Warburg, *Aufzeichnungen*, 98.
61 Lord D'Abernon, *An Ambassador of Peace: Pages from the Diary of Viscount D'Abernon, Berlin, 1920–1926* (London, 1929), 1:193–4.

Similar warnings of the international consequences of "the progressive decomposition of German economic life" and "cheap German competition" were directed at selected English bankers, as well as at Herbert Hoover.[62] In the words of Max Warburg's American brother Paul: "Every new slump in the reichsmark results in a large volume of foreign orders [and hence] is a menace to competing industrial countries."[63] By the end of 1921, the argument had been taken up by the Hamburg Chamber of Commerce and the Reich Association of German Industry. The Allies, it was argued, would only realize "the impossibility of what they demand as a result of their own sufferings"; already "millions of unemployed" in Britain and America were looking "with sad comprehension at Germany, where almost all factories work in unhealthy activity to earn foreign exchange to pay for reparations."[64] The Reichsbank, too, insisted that "the deterioration of the exchange rate . . . was the explanation for the world economic crisis, i.e., for the production difficulties and unemployment in England and America."[65] The argument was repeated by Melchior in London in February 1922 at a meeting with Sir Robert Horne, the chancellor of the exchequer;[66] and by Max Warburg in a lengthy memorandum entitled "The German Problem," which was widely circulated among business leaders and politicians when he visited the United States in the autumn of 1922.[67]

Again, there were some individuals in Britain and America who were persuaded. Keynes, of course, was already a convert.[68] The need to increase German exports, Keynes argued, posed a direct threat to the recipients of reparations themselves: "If Germany could compass the vast export trade which the Paris proposals contemplate, it could only be by ousting some of the staple trades of Great Britain from the markets of the world. . . . I do not expect to see Mr. Lloyd George fighting a general election on the issue

---

62 StAH, Familiearchiv Sthamer 7, Melchior to Goodenough, July 22, 1921; WA 32, Pol. Corr. 1921, Warburg to Grenfell, Oct. 22, 1921; Sterling Library, Yale University, Paul M. Warburg papers, ser. 1, box 5, folder 63, Melchior memorandum, Aug. 23, 1921.
63 Ibid., Paul Warburg to Hoover, Aug. 29, 1921.
64 Handelskammer zu Hamburg, *Jahresbericht* (1921), 8. Cf. H. Bücher, "Die internationale Wirtschaftslage in ihren Beziehungen zu Deutschland," in *Die deutsche Industrie und die Wiedergutmachungsfrage: Bericht über die dritte Mitgliederversammlung des RdI in München, September 1921* (Berlin, 1921), 21–32. Cf. Specht, *Politische Hintergründe*, 47n.
65 Cit. Specht, *Politische Hintergründe*, 62.
66 WA, Allgemeines 1922, Melchior Report, Feb. 18, 1922; Melchior memorandum, Feb. 20, 1922. According to Melchior, depreciation of the mark was leading to "cheap conditions of labour and great industrial activity, which simultaneously disturbs the industries of competing countries." Cf. ibid., Melchior to Warburg, Apr. 6, 1922.
67 WA, Allgemeines 1922, "The German Problem": "The mark in foreign countries falling so much more rapidly than the purchasing power of the mark in Germany, the latter for four years has been selling her goods much below the price in world markets." Cf. the correspondence between Paul Warburg and Parker Gilbert in NA, RG 39, 6110 (20–4).
68 See John Maynard Keynes, "New Reparations Settlement: Can Germany Pay?" Aug. 21, 1921, in *JMKW,* 17:242–9.

of maintaining an Army to compel Germany at the point of the bayonet to undercut our manufactures."[69] But Keynes was no longer the lone voice he had been in 1919. One of Franz Witthoefft's British contacts quoted former Chancellor of the Exchequer Reginald McKenna as saying that "If Germany could keep up the reparations payments for six months, unemployment in England and America would lead to intolerable conditions."[70] When Rudolf von Havenstein visited London in November 1921, he, too, detected a change in mood.[71] On the other side of the Atlantic, Herbert Hoover argued that if the United States did not "interest itself in the countries struggling with fiscal . . . problems, we must expect to pay many thousand fold in the loss of export markets and in the employment of our people."[72] Nevertheless, such considerations did not suffice to persuade the Allied governments to accede to the twin German requests for a moratorium and an international loan. Wirth's first bid for a moratorium of two or more years at the end of 1921 won only a very limited breathing space: at Cannes, the Allies agreed to postpone the full January and February payments, but still insisted on a continuing transfer of 30 million gold marks every ten days.[73] Indeed, the more doggedly German spokesmen adhered to the balance of payments theory, the more Allied representatives insisted that the problem lay in German fiscal and monetary laxity.[74] When a reduction in the 1922 cash payment to 720 million gold marks was provisionally agreed in March 1922, the Germans were required to raise taxes by 60 billion paper marks; and an extension of that agreement in May was made conditional on eliminating the deficit altogether.[75] Doubts about the German government's fiscal credibility in turn diminished the chances of the international loan. Although the German financial delegates at Genoa won some sympathy from their British counterparts when they argued for a 4 billion gold marks loan, the committee of bankers set up under J. P.

---

69 John Maynard Keynes, "The Economic Consequences of the Paris Settlement," Jan. 31, 1921/Feb. 1, 1921, in *JMKW*, 17:207–13; John Maynard Keynes, "The New Reparations Proposals," May 6, 1921, in *JMKW*, 17:234; John Maynard Keynes, "The New Reparations Settlement: Effect on World Trade," Aug. 28, 1921, in *JMKW*, 17:249–56. Cf. Skidelsky, *John Maynard Keynes*, 2:48, 54, 90. See also Keynes's *A Revision of the Treaty* (London, 1921), in which he proposed a reduction of reparations to 21 billion gold marks.

70 Politisches Archiv des Auswärtigen Amtes, Bonn, SRW FW 16 II, 1105/11 (report of RWR finance policy committee), Oct. 15, 1921. See also the letter from an anonymous "British employer" making a similar point in the *Times* (London), Oct. 20, 1921.

71 Feldman, *Great Disorder*, 377ff.

72 B. Eichengreen, *Golden Fetters: The Gold Standard and the Great Depression, 1919–1939* (New York, 1992), 161n.

73 Laubach, *Kabinette Wirth*, 120–24; Specht, *Politische Hintergründe*, 74–5; Maier, *Recasting Bourgeois Europe*, 249–50, 265ff.; Kent, *Spoils of War*, 173.

74 Kent, *Spoils of War*, 158–65; Maier, *Recasting Bourgeois Europe*, 276ff.

75 Laubach, *Kabinette Wirth*, 157–68, 228–36; Kent, *Spoils of War*, 174–9; Specht, *Politische Hintergründe*, 77–8; Maier, *Recasting Bourgeois Europe*, 282–3; Feldman, *Great Disorder*, 340–5.

Morgan to report on Germany's creditworthiness rejected the idea after two months of deliberation.[76] It was possible, as Rathenau did, to see the Morgan committee's verdict – that a loan to Germany was impossible "unless and until the reparations question was settled" – as "the greatest step forward for the government's policy since the London Ultimatum."[77] But reparations remained, and with them the possibility of increased sanctions rather than revision. A renewed request for a moratorium in July was rejected by the French government in the absence of "productive guarantees."[78] By the time Wirth made his last desperate plea for a three-year moratorium on November 14, 1922, it was clear that French patience had run out. The Cuno government's more confrontational stance thereafter proved no match for military sanctions; and it is impossible to regard the benefit Germany enjoyed in paying no reparations in 1923 as having exceeded the immense social costs of the Ruhr occupation, "passive resistance," and hyperinflation.[79] As for the Dawes Plan: although it is often portrayed as some kind of advance from a German standpoint, from a revisionist perspective it was all but a return to square one. Passive resistance had to be abandoned to break the diplomatic deadlock; the reparations total was unchanged, although there was a "breathing space" of reduced annuities; and the Allied influence over Germany's finances had been somewhat increased by the reform of the Reichsbank.

It is, of course, possible to attribute the failure of the German strategy to factors beyond the control of German policy makers: domestic political forces in France and the United States, in particular. Yet if the revisionist calculation had been correct, these factors would have mattered less. The depreciation of the mark was supposed to lead to a significant boost in German exports at the expense of Allied economies. The German calculation was that this immediate economic pressure would overrule other political considerations, forcing Allied politicians to reduce reparations as a matter of self-interest. In order to understand why this did not happen, an analysis of the macroeconomic impact of "fulfillment" is necessary.

II

In fact, the immediate economic significance of the Versailles treaty for Germany was far less than its critics claimed. Apart from the United States, all

---

76 Kent, *Spoils of War,* 177, 182; Maier, *Recasting Bourgeois Europe,* 284ff.
77 Baker Library, Harvard Graduate School of Business Administration, Thomas Lamont papers, 176–1, J. P. Morgan & Co. Statement, July/Aug. 1922; Specht, *Politische Hintergründe,* 78.
78 Specht, *Politische Hintergründe,* 82; Kent, *Spoils of War,* 185.
79 Feldman, *Great Disorder,* 513–669.

the combatant countries had emerged from the war with heavy losses on their capital accounts – comparably heavy in the case of French loans to Russia.[80] Similarly, although Germany had lost the best part of its merchant fleet, the total losses to world shipping during the war (the better part of them inflicted by Germany) had totaled more than 15 million tons.[81] In any case, the significance of these lost assets should not be exaggerated:[82] shipping in particular was swiftly replaced.[83] Germany's total reparations burden had not yet been determined; but the money owed by the prospective recipients of reparations to the United States already amounted to around 40 billion gold marks.[84] In any case, reparations and inter-Allied debts were problems that could be postponed, pending diplomatic solutions; their impact on economic life in the year after Versailles was negligible. In the short run, the world economy boomed as businessmen rushed to replace inventories and plant run-down during the war, and as trade links were restored that front lines, warships, and submarines had disrupted. By 1920, international trade had recovered to 80 percent of its prewar level.[85] The monetary expansion generated by war finance, which had led to accumulations of cash balances in all the combatant economies, fueled this upswing. It was these underlying strengths that the Cassandras of Versailles had failed to take into account.

In one respect, it is true, the critics of the treaty appeared to be vindicated – namely, with regard to the effect of currency depreciation on German trade. At this point, the historian enters a statistical minefield. German statistics do not record the substantial volumes of goods that passed through the so-called Hole in the West, the customs-free frontier of the occupied zone.[86] The statistics are also incomplete for the second half of 1920 and the first half of 1921; and subsequent figures were often called into question, for reasons to be discussed later in the chapter. Moreover, very different figures can be arrived at for the "real" value of imports and exports depending on

---

80 Gerd Hardach, *The First World War, 1914–1918* (Harmondsworth, 1987), 289.

81 Haniel Archiv, Franz Haniel & Cie. GmbH, Duisberg (formerly Historisches Archiv der Gutehoffnungshütte, Oberhausen), 408213/0 Karl Haniel, "Das Problem des Schiffsraums," May 19, 1919.

82 The real annual losses in invisible income due to the peace terms have been estimated at just 200 million gold marks. Kent, *Spoils of War*, 98–9. However, Kent's figure of 40 million gold marks for the annual income from German foreign securities surrendered to the Allies is too low; the correct figure must be in the region of 800 million gold marks.

83 *Überseedienst*, no. 41, July 23, 1919; *Weserzeitung*, no. 532, Aug. 16, 1919.

84 Friedrich-Wilhelm Henning, *Das industrialisierte Deutschland 1914 bis 1972* (Paderborn, 1974), 45; D. Artaud, "La question des dettes interalliées et la reconstruction de l'Europe," *Revue historique* 261 (1979): 362–82.

85 *Statistisches Jahrbuch für das Deutsche Reich* 54 (Berlin, 1935): 118; Ingvar Svennilson, *Growth and Stagnation in the European Economy* (Geneva, 1954), 292; League of Nations, *Memorandum on Production and Trade, 1923–1926* (Geneva, 1928), 29, 51.

86 Maier, *Recasting Bourgeois Europe*, 67–71; Gerald D. Feldman, *Iron and Steel in the German Inflation, 1916–1923* (Princeton, N.J., 1977), 142.

which deflators are applied to the available paper mark figures: if one uses
the German wholesale price index on both import and export figures, for
example, no account is taken of the substantial fluctuations in the terms of
trade in the period. The distortion is still greater if one simply converts volume figures into 1913 unit values by applying prewar prices to postwar customs data.[87] Using the available monthly figures, three different series of
monthly trade figures can therefore be provided: one expressed in terms of
1913 marks, simply deflating with the wholesale price index; one adjusted
to allow for the divergent tendencies of import and export prices; and one
in volume terms.[88]

Estimated annual figures from the first series show that in 1919 the already wide wartime German trade deficit grew wider still, rising to around
4.13 billion gold marks, or 12 percent of the net national product (NNP);
but fell close to equilibrium in 1920 (see Figure 16.1).[89] Monthly figures
give a more precise indication of the trend, showing the money trade deficit
peaking in July 1919, and thereafter narrowing until March and April 1920,
when a trade surplus was recorded (see Figure 16.2). The surge in imports
in the middle of 1919 was dammed partly by the imposition of customs in
gold marks, so that the value of German imports, which rose sixfold from
178 billion gold marks in March 1919 to a peak of over 1 billion gold marks
in July 1919, fell to just 269 million gold marks in February 1920, whereas
the value of monthly exports fluctuated unsteadily between around 150 and
350 million gold marks, before jumping to more than 650 million gold
marks in July 1920.[90]

---

87 This explains why the annual figures calculated in this way in *Statistik des Deutschen Reiches* (Berlin,
    1924), 317:5, suggest such an improbably low trade deficit for the inflation period as a whole (par-
    ticularly 1922). The figures from this series cannot be reconciled with the evidence discussed below
    for a substantial capital import during the inflation years. This point is overlooked by Webb, *Hyper-
    inflation*, 89–92; Feldman, *Great Disorder*, 600; and V. Hentschel, "Zahlen und Anmerkungen zum
    deutschen Aussenhandel zwischen dem Ersten Weltkrieg und der Weltwirtschaftskrise," *Zeitschrift für
    Unternehmensgeschichte* 31 (1986): 95–9.
88 Statistisches Reichsamt, *Monatliche Nachweise über den auswärtigen Handel Deutschlands 1920, 1921,
    1922, 1923, 1924* (Berlin); Statistisches Reichsamt, ed., *Statistik des Deutschen Reiches*, vol. 310: *Das
    auswärtige Handel Deutschlands in den Jahren 1920, 1921 und 1922 verglichen mit dem Jahre 1913 nach
    Warengruppen: Warengattungen und Ländern* (Berlin, 1924); *Statistisches Jahrbuch für das deutsche Reich
    1923*, 189–90; Costantino Bresciani-Turroni, *The Economics of Inflation: A Study of Currency Depre-
    ciation in Post-War Germany* (London, 1937), 248.
89 Annual figures for the inflation years are arrived at by interpolating the missing months in the
    Monatliche Nachweise series. Slightly higher figures for the trade deficit are given in *JMKW*, 17:251,
    18:48, 54; Karsten Laursen and Jørgen Pedersen, *The German Inflation, 1918–1923* (Amsterdam,
    1964), 69, 90, 101; Webb, *Hyperinflation*, 76, 91.
90 StAH, DHSG II, III C 53 (1919), DHSG 10. Sitzung, Aug. 26 1919; *Hamburger Fremdenblatt*, no.
    458, Sept. 9, 1919. Cf. Carl-Ludwig Holtfrerich, "Deutscher Aussenhandel und Goldzölle 1919 bis
    1923," in Feldman et al., eds., *Anpassung*, 472–84.

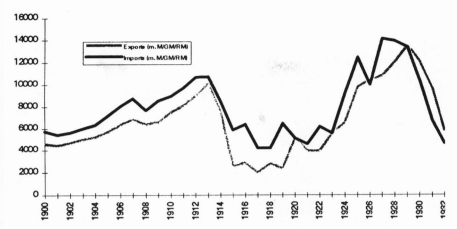

Figure 16.1. German trade (in millions of 1913 marks or reichsmarks), 1900–1932. *Source:* Hoffmann et al., *Wachstum*, 520–1, 524–5; Hardach, *First World War*, 33; *Monatliche Nachweise;* Bresciani-Turroni, *Inflation*, 248.

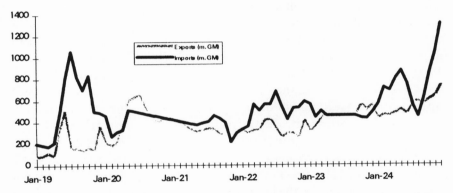

Figure 16.2. German trade in 1913 prices, 1919–1924. *Source:* Bresciani-Turroni, *Inflation*, 248; Graham, *Exchange, Prices, and Production*, 272; *Monatliche Nachweise*.

However, the gold mark figures disguise the significant fluctuations in the relative prices of imports and exports in the inflation years. Export prices did not rise as rapidly as import prices in 1919/20, reflecting above all the extent to which depreciation of the mark outstripped the rise in domestic prices; the deficit may therefore have been rather smaller in "real" terms in 1919/20. Such divergences are best measured by the real exchange rate (the nominal exchange rate divided by the ratio of German to foreign prices), which can be regarded as an index of German competitiveness (see

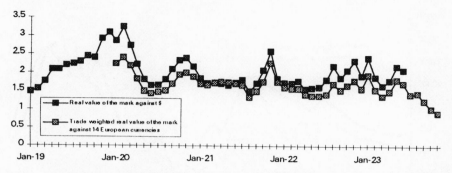

Figure 16.3. German real exchange rates, 1919–1923. *Source:* Bresciani-Turroni, *Inflation,* 446; Holtfrerich, *German Inflation,* 23–4. When index exceeds unity, competitiveness has increased.

Figure 16.3).[91] Comparing this with the figures for trade volumes provides probably the clearest picture of the relationship between exchange rates, prices and merchandise trade.[92] It emerges that the volume of goods exported exceeded the volume of goods imported by some 2.3 million tons in 1919 and 4.9 million tons in 1920 (see Figure 16.4). The figures are all the more remarkable in view of the very high percentage of German imports that took the form of bulky food and raw materials (76 percent in 1920); and the high percentage (84 percent) of German exports that took the form of compact finished goods.[93] It appears therefore that the weak mark did indeed lead to the "dumping" of German exports at "ridiculously low prices," as predicted by the German economic experts at Versailles.

It is clear that the majority of Germans assumed that this depreciation would continue. Max Warburg was not alone in seeking to pay off his firm's foreign currency liabilities, in the belief that they would only appreciate in mark terms.[94] Moreover, the lifting of exchange controls in September 1919 meant that pessimistic Germans could "flee" the mark in favor of foreign

91 Details of computation in Carl-Ludwig Holtfrerich, *The German Inflation, 1914–1923: Causes and Effects in International Perspective,* trans. Theo Balderston (New York, 1986), 22–5.
92 Cf. R. Wagenführ, "Die Industriewirtschaft: Entwicklungstendenzen der deutschen und internationalen Industrieproduktion, 1860–1932," *Vierteljahrshefte zur Konjunkturforschung,* Sonderheft 31 (1933): 26; Holtfrerich, *German Inflation,* 212.
93 Figures for the structure of German postwar trade in Hentschel, "Zahlen und Anmerkungen," 96; *JMKW,* 17:251; Bresciani-Turroni, *Economics of Inflation,* 194; Graham, *Exchange, Prices, and Production,* 214–25; Laursen and Pedersen, *German Inflation,* 101.
94 WA, "Jahresbericht 1919," Melchior to Max Warburg, Aug. 5, 1919; Feldman, *Great Disorder,* 178–9. For similar expectations in industrial circles, see Feldman, *Iron and Steel,* 132–8; Maier, *Recasting Bourgeois Europe,* 68.

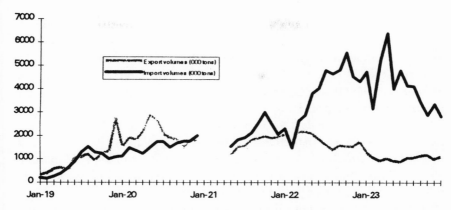

Figure 16.4. German trade volumes, 1919–1923. *Source:* Bresciani-Turroni, *Inflation,* 448; *Monatliche Nachweise.*

currency.[95] Pessimism about the mark manifested itself within Germany in a falling demand for money: cash was moved from savings accounts into current accounts, and transactions were increasingly made by "giro" transfers from one account to another.[96] The effect of such pessimism on the exchange rate was even more pronounced – so long as it was shared by foreign currency speculators: by the end of 1919 the dollar had appreciated against the mark by about 465 percent over the previous year. The more rapid rate of depreciation relative to domestic inflation explains why the price of German exports fell in real terms by about a third – confirming the point made earlier about the "dumping" of German goods on the world market.[97] Yet the expectation of *sustained* depreciation overlooked the strong countervailing tendencies being generated by Germany's economic recovery. According to one estimate, German NNP grew by 10 percent in 1920 and 7 percent in 1921.[98] Although German agriculture continued to languish,[99] indicators of industrial output show a sharp upward trend: up 46 percent in

95 Peter-Christian Witt, "Staatliche Wirtschaftspolitik in Deutschland, 1918–1923: Entwicklung und Zerstörung einer modernen wirtschaftspolitischen Strategie," in Feldman et al., *Zwischenbilanz,* 177–8.
96 Graham, *Exchange, Prices, and Production,* 105.
97 Bresciani-Turroni, *Economics of Inflation,* 200, 248, 446–7.
98 Calculated from Peter-Christian Witt, "Finanzpolitik und sozialer Wandel in Krieg und Inflation 1918–1924," in Mommsen et al., eds., *Industrielles System,* 1:424.
99 Statistics for agricultural output in Bresciani-Turroni, *Economics of Inflation,* 192; Graham, *Exchange, Prices, and Production,* 285; Laursen and Pedersen, *German Inflation,* 135–6; Holtfrerich, *German Inflation,* 182.

1920 and 20 percent in 1921.[100] From a foreign point of view, this combination of rapid growth and a weak exchange rate appeared contradictory.[101]

To some extent, the recovery of foreign confidence in the mark was a
side-effect of Germany's immense appetite for imports in 1919. With export
earnings at such low levels, the inward flow of food and raw materials could
only be sustained by credits from foreign suppliers. In the first instance, this
meant American suppliers: between 1919 and 1921, German imports from
the United States totaled $776 million, according to U.S. figures; Ger-
many's trade deficit with the United States rose from 246 million gold marks
in 1919 to 932 million gold marks in 1920 and 1,226 million gold marks in
1921 – almost equivalent to the entire German trade deficit given in the
official German statistics (see Figure 16.5).[102]

The German commercial community hurried to make contact with
American exporters after the signing of the armistice; and there was no
shortage of interested American firms.[103] However, efforts to create large-
scale channels for American import credits to Germany tended to fall foul
of the U.S. Treasury.[104] The successful negotiation of a 200 million florin
credit from the Dutch state in January 1920 represented a drop in the ocean
of the German trade deficit;[105] and even the specially created International
Acceptance Bank was only able to raise $9 million to finance grain im-
ports.[106] In fact, the greater part of the German deficit in 1919/20 was

100 Calculated from Wagenführ, "Die Industriewirtschaft," 23–8; Bresciani-Turroni, *Economics of Infla-
    tion,* 193–4; Graham, *Exchange, Prices, and Production,* 287, 292; Walther G. Hoffmann, Franz
    Grumbach, and Helmut Hesse, *Das Wachstum der deutschen Wirtschaft seit der Mitte des 19. Jahrhun-
    derts* (Berlin, 1965), 358–9, 383–5, 388, 390–3; Laursen and Pedersen, *German Inflation,* 136; Feld-
    man, *Iron and Steel,* 474–5.
101 On the divergence of foreign and domestic expectations, reflecting partly the fact that foreign spec-
    ulators are staking less than ordinary Germans, see Charles P. Kindleberger, *A Financial History of
    Western Europe* (London, 1984), 318; Holtfrerich, *German Inflation,* 290.
102 Cf. Holtfrerich, *German Inflation,* 214–15; Webb, *Hyperinflation,* 91. Note that 21 percent of Amer-
    ican cotton exports and 30 percent of American copper exports went to Germany in 1921: cf. NA,
    RG 39, G114.2, 17.
103 See, e.g., HAPAG Archiv, Hamburg, Holtzendorff to Vorstand, no. 973, Jan. 5, 1919; no. 976, Jan.
    10, 1919; no. 979, Jan. 10, 1919; Holtzendorff to Cuno, Apr. 10, 1919; NA, RG 39, G111,
    W. C. Tingle (Standard Oil) to Leffingwell, Aug. 13, 1919; Merchants National Bank to Secretary
    of State, Sept. 22, 1919; G114.1, Postau & Son to Glass, Sept. 29, 1919.
104 WA, "Jahresbericht 1920"; Warburg, *Aufzeichnungen,* 93.
105 NA, RG 39, G111, American Embassy the Hague, to State Dept., Sept. 28, 1919; WA, "Jahres-
    bericht 1920"; Warburg, *Aufzeichnungen,* 93. Cf. Hans-Jürgen Schröder, "Die politische Bedeu-
    tung der deutschen Handelspolitik nach dem Ersten Weltkrieg," in Feldman et al., eds., *Zwischen-
    bilanz,* 235–51.
106 On the International Acceptance Bank, which was first conceived of at a meeting between Max
    Warburg, Paul Warburg, and a group of Swiss bankers at St. Moritz in the late summer of 1919:
    WA, "Jahresbericht 1919"; "Jahresbericht 1920," Warburg to Wirth, Dec. 6, 1920; NA, RG 59,
    862.00/1014, Stewart to State Dept., Aug. 23, 1920; Sterling Library, Yale University, Paul M.
    Warburg papers, ser. 1, box 5, folder 62, Paul Warburg to N. M. Rothschild & Sons, London (n.d.);

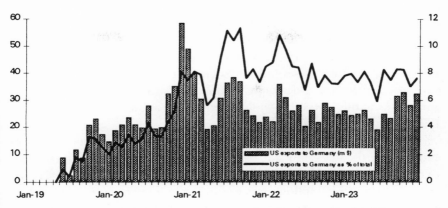

Figure 16.5. American exports to Germany, 1919–1923. *Source:* Holtfrerich, "Germany and the International Economy," 280–3.

financed not by large-scale foreign loans but by numerous, small-scale purchases of paper marks by foreigners. This was a speculative wave much remarked upon at the time. When Benjamin Strong visited Europe in August 1919, he was told by bankers in Amsterdam that "every servant and carpenter in Belgium owned some marks, the poorer people carrying the actual Reichsbank notes, and those of larger means having balances in German banks. The same thing has taken place in Scandinavia and, more striking still, . . . Americans were buying hundreds of millions of marks . . . for speculation."[107] In October, Keynes heard that "the aggregate foreign holdings of marks has now reached the prodigious figure of 20 milliards." "The speculation," he noted three months later, was "on a tremendous scale and was, in fact, the greatest ever known."[108] Recent research confirms these impressions. There was clearly a tendency for foreign visitors to Germany (of which there were many in the early 1920s) or people living in former occupied territory to retain marks in the hope of the currency's recovery. On a larger scale, foreign deposits at the seven Berlin great banks rose from 13.7 billion marks in 1919 to 41.6 billion marks in 1921, and accounted for almost a third of total deposits.[109] Purchases of marks in New York totaled 60 million gold

Eduard Rosenbaum and A. J. Shermann, *M. M. Warburg & Co., 1798–1938: Merchant Bankers of Hamburg* (London, 1979), 159.

107 Federal Reserve Bank of New York, Benjamin Strong papers, 1000.3, "Diary of Trip to Europe," 65ff.

108 John Maynard Keynes, "The Present State of the Foreign Exchanges," in *JMKW,* 17:130–1, 176. See also his later analysis, "Speculation in the Mark and Germany's Balances Abroad," *JMKW,* 17:47–58.

109 Holtfrerich, *German Inflation,* 288.

marks between July 1919 and December 1921.[110] At the same time, mark-denominated bonds became a popular investment, the state of Hamburg leading the way with an unlimited issue of 4½ percent bonds, which raised 48.6 million marks in 1919 alone.[111] Some foreign investors were also attracted by German shares, others by German real estate. As far as can be established, there was a net capital inflow to Germany of about 13 billion gold marks in the years 1919 to 1923, with the lion's share coming in 1919, 1921, and the first half of 1922.[112]

Historians have tended to follow Keynes and other contemporaries in emphasizing the net gain made by the German economy when these loans were rendered worthless by inflation.[113] In the short run, however, the effect of these capital inflows was to fund the German trade deficit, stabilize the German currency, and stop inflation. In March 1920, the mark suddenly ceased falling against the dollar and rallied, rising against the dollar from 99.11 to a peak of 30.13 in June. In the months after March, all the trends of the previous eight months were reversed: export prices rose, and the gap between German prices and world market prices abruptly closed.[114] This development came as a shock in Germany: Max Warburg, hastily rearranging his bank's portfolio, confessed that he could "not understand the

---

110 Webb, *Hyperinflation*, 57.

111 Leo Lippmann, *Mein Leben und meine amtliche Tätigkeit: Erinnerungen und ein Beitrag zur Finanzgeschichte Hamburgs* (Hamburg, 1964), 320. On Berlin's loan of 70.8 million marks, see Feldman, *Great Disorder*, 204.

112 Estimates of this capital inflow include Keynes's (12–15), Graham's (15.6 billion gold marks), and Holtfrerich's (15 billion gold marks). I arrive at the figure of 12.8 billion gold marks by tallying my own extrapolated trade figures with the best available figures on reparations (and including Laursen and Pedersen's modest estimates for the service and gold balances). Keynes and the McKenna committee sought to distinguish between purely speculative purchases of paper marks (2–3 billion or 0.7 gold marks); foreign accounts in German banks (3 or 8 billion gold marks); short-term business credits (0.5–1 billion gold marks); and investment in German securities and real estate (1 or 1.5 billion gold marks). But these figures are little more than guesses. One of the many problems that arise is estimating the real value of any interest and dividend payments made to foreign lenders. For other recent estimates, see Carl-Ludwig Holtfrerich, "Internationale Verteilungsfolgen der deutschen Inflation," *Kyklos* 30 (1977): 271–92; Holtfrerich, "Die deutsche Inflation 1918 bis 1923"; Schuker, "American Reparations."

113 For early comments to this effect, see NA, RG 39, G110 (20–4), F. A. Vanderlip to C. A. Stone, Sept. 8, 1921; Keynes, "Record Depreciation of the Mark," Nov. 9, 1921, *JMKW*, 18:10; Keynes, "Speculation in the Mark and Germany's Balances Abroad," Sept. 28, 1922, *JMKW*, 18:47–58. Cf. Carl-Ludwig Holtfrerich, "Amerikanischer Kapitalexport und Wiederaufbau der deutschen Wirtschaft 1919–1923 im Vergleich zu 1924–1929," *Vierteljahrsschrift für Sozial- und Wirtschaftsgeschichte* 64 (1977): 497–529; Schuker, "American Reparations," passim. Schuker may exaggerate the net gain when he attempts to compare reparations with foreign lending wiped out by inflation (and later by depression). Once allowance is made for German capital flight and repayments, the total "gain" over the whole period (1919–32) is only slightly more than total reparations: 21 billion gold marks compared with 19 billion gold marks. Such calculations obscure the American economy's gain from the high German demand for American exports, and the low cost to Americans of German exports.

114 Cf. Bresciani-Turroni, *Economics of Inflation*, 200, 248, 446–7.

exchange rate movement at all" and attributed it to the speculations of "an extraordinarily powerful group."[115] Nor were the losses confined to German pessimists. Keynes himself lost about £13,125 of his own money and £8,498 of his friends', invested on the assumption that the economic consequences of the peace would be as he had forecast.[116] It was not until some time later that he and Warburg fully grasped what had happened: "The mark is viewed with such incredible confidence abroad – which is more than we can feel. We are living off the credit of earlier decades. The foreigners persuade themselves that we Germans have the industrious character to emerge from all this misery. It is the only explanation for the high mark exchange rate."[117] Or as Keynes put it in September 1922:

[From] itinerant Jews in the streets of the capitals [to] barber's assistants in the remotest townships of Spain and South America . . . the argument has been the same. . . . Germany is a great and strong country; some day she will recover; when that happens the mark will recover also, which will bring a very large profit. So little do bankers and servant girls understand of history and economics.[118]

"History and economics" – and hindsight – might well point to the possibility of further depreciation, irrespective of economic "fundamentals"; but those who had ignored history and economics had been right about the mark in the short run. The result was to stop the export drive in its tracks. As Felix Deutsch of the Allgemeine Elektrizitätsgesellschaft (AEG) put it in late 1920, Germany's "good fortune in the midst of misfortune" had been "our poor currency, which enable[d] us to export on a large scale. If the currency improves externally at a rapid rate, as we saw a few months ago, our exports stop entirely, and our industry is ruined."[119] Although the Economics Ministry took the remarkable step of intervening *against* the mark between March and June 1920, buying substantial amounts of foreign currency to limit the appreciation of the mark, the growth of exports, which had been such a marked feature of the second half of 1919 and the first quarter of 1920, came to a stop.[120] From a peak of 658 million gold marks in July 1920, exports fell to just 193 million gold marks in November 1921.[121]

115 WA, "Jahresbericht 1920," 1, Max Warburg to Fritz Warburg, Apr. 11, 1920. Other evidence of surprise in GHH 300193012/5, Deutsche Werft to Reusch, May 27, 1920; Reusch to Deutsche Werft, May 31, 1920.
116 *JMKW,* 17:131; Harrod, *Keynes,* 288–95; Skidelsky, *John Maynard Keynes,* 2:41.
117 WA, 10, "Pol. Corr. 1921," Warburg (speech before RWM Scholz), Dec. 17, 1920.
118 Keynes, "Speculation in the Mark," 48.
119 Specht, *Politische Hintergründe,* 30, 43n.
120 Gerald D. Feldman, "The Political Economy of Germany's Relative Stabilization During the 1920/21 Depression," in Feldman et al., eds., *Zwischenbilanz,* 180–206.
121 See Figure 16.1.

This helps explain why, in the period immediately after the signing of the Versailles treaty, Germany exerted less effective economic pressure on the Allied economies than Warburg, Keynes, and others had predicted. There was an export boom: but it was snuffed out by the relative stabilization of the mark in 1920/21. However, the London Ultimatum gave new life to the revisionist arguments, not least because it triggered a fresh bout of depreciation. The ultimatum demanded that, beginning at the end of May 1921, Germany pay interest and amortization on "A" and "B" bonds totaling 50 billion gold marks in the form of a 2 billion gold marks annuity, due quarterly. It also specified that, beginning in November 1921, a payment equal to 26 percent of the value of German exports should be made. As German exports in 1920 had been estimated at about 5 billion gold marks, this implied a total annual payment of approximately 3 billion gold marks.[122] When German exports had reached a level sufficient to pay off the "A" and "B" bonds, non-interest-bearing "C" bonds with a face value of 82 billion gold marks would be issued. The 12 billion gold marks still outstanding from the 20 billion gold marks demanded at Versailles were tacitly included in this total, while sums due to Belgium were not, so that the debt outstanding was about 125 billion gold marks. In nominal terms, this was certainly less than had originally been envisaged by some on the Allied side (for example, the Cunliffe Committee's 480 billion gold marks, or Louis-Lucien Klotz's 8 billion gold marks annuity). Moreover, it can be argued that the "C" Bonds were unlikely ever to be collected; or, at least, that their real value would be significantly reduced if German trade was slow to recover. In terms of national income, too, the annuity was less of a burden than Keynes and others claimed at the time: recent estimates of the potential burden on national income of the annuity vary from 5 percent to 10 percent.[123]

Taking the period during which Germany continued to pay reparations as a whole (1919–32), it is clear that the Allies received far less than the 125 billion gold marks demanded at London. About 19 billion gold marks would seem to be a reasonable figure for the total value of unrequited transfers from Germany to the Allies, a relatively small proportion (2.4 percent) of total national income over the period.[124] On the other hand, the extent

122 Maier, *Recasting Bourgeois Europe,* 241–2; Kent, *Spoils of War,* 132–8. Webb suggests that altogether 4 billion gold marks was being demanded because of occupation costs and "clearing" payments; Webb, *Hyperinflation,* 104–5.
123 Charles S. Maier, "The Truth About the Treaties," *JMH* 51 (1979): 56–67; Holtfrerich, *German Inflation,* 148–9; Schuker, "Finance and Foreign Policy," 351; Webb, *Hyperinflation,* 54, 104; Eichengreen, *Golden Fetters,* 129–30.
124 For other recent attempts to compute total payments, see Holtfrerich, *German Inflation,* 147–50; Schuker, "American Reparations," 364–71, 382–3.

of the effort *initially* made by Germany should not be underestimated. At least 8 billion gold marks (and perhaps as much as 13 billion gold marks) were handed over in the period before the Dawes Plan, or between 4 and 7 percent of total national income.[125] There were two fundamental reasons why such a level of unrequited transfers could not be sustained without recourse to inflationary policies. In the first place, the annuity demanded in 1921 put an intolerable strain on the state's finances. Total expenditure under the terms of the Versailles treaty in the years 1920 to 1923 amounted to at least 50 percent of Reich revenue, 20 percent of total Reich spending and 10 percent of total public spending.[126] As Webb has shown, reparations accounted for the lion's share of the Reich deficit in 1921 and 1922 (68 percent and 56 percent of the respective totals); they were thus, in Barry Eichengreen's words, "ultimately responsible for the inflation," meaning that no Weimar government could have raised taxes or cut spending sufficiently to pay reparations *and* balance the budget.[127] Such austerity could only have been achieved by a regime of the sort that was able to extract comparably heavy reparations from the Soviet zone of occupation between 1945 and 1953; or the substantially greater sums transferred from occupied France to the Third Reich between 1940 and 1944.[128]

Even if one imagines a fiscal solution to the problems discussed above, there remained a second obstacle to the payment of reparations, namely, the means whereby reparations in cash could be converted, as the Allies required, into gold or foreign currency.[129] The most straightforward way this could have been achieved was by Germany running a balance of payments surplus, which, in view of the impact of the Versailles treaty on German overseas investments and shipping, effectively meant a trade surplus. Clearly, this did

125 Cf. estimates in Bresciani-Turroni, *Economics of Inflation,* 457; Holtfrerich, *German Inflation,* 147–50; Schuker, "American Reparations," 364–71. I follow Eichengreen in using national income figures in 1913 marks: *Golden Fetters,* 129 n.
126 Calculated from the various figures (ranging between 6.5 and 7.6 billion gold marks) in Bresciani-Turroni, *Economics of Inflation,* 53, 358, 437–8; Graham, *Exchange, Prices, and Production,* 44–5; Peter-Christian Witt, "Tax Policies, Tax Assessment and Inflation: Towards a Sociology of Public Finances in the German Inflation, 1914 to 1923," in Peter-Christian Witt, ed., *Wealth and Taxation in Central Europe: The History and Sociology of Public Finance* (Leamington Spa, 1987), 156–7; Holtfrerich, *German Inflation,* 148–9; Webb, *Hyperinflation,* 33, 37, 108; Eichengreen, *Golden Fetters,* 146.
127 Webb, *Hyperinflation,* 37; Eichengreen, *Golden Fetters,* 141; Feldman, *Great Disorder,* 428, 451.
128 Webb, *Hyperinflation,* 112; A. Milward, *War, Economy and Society, 1939–1945* (Harmondsworth, 1987), 137–44.
129 Not all reparations had to be paid in this way: cash reparations only accounted for about a quarter of total treaty expenses between 1920 and 1922, compared with about 45 percent paid in the form of free goods. However, the net effect on the balance of payments was the same, even if the method of transfer was different: cash transfers required foreign currency to be earned and then handed back, whereas payments in kind simply entailed exporting for nothing. Only treaty expenses such as occupation costs and the loss of state property in ceded territory had no influence on the balance of payments: see Webb, *Hyperinflation,* 108.

not happen. Trade surpluses were recorded in only five years (1920, 1926, and 1930–2) during the Weimar period, and only twice (in 1931 and 1932) exceeded reparations paid. To have turned an average annual deficit of 0.7 billion gold marks into an average annual surplus of 3 billion gold marks a year would have required either a severe contraction in German consumption, implying an acute domestic distributional conflict, or a phenomenal increase in German exports, implying a no less acute international conflict of interests. Of course, the transfer of reparations might notionally have been reconciled with persistent trade deficits if there had been sustained foreign lending to Germany; and, as already mentioned, this did happen on a substantial scale.[130] But this was not a sustainable process. War debts and American domestic politics ruled out large-scale government-guaranteed lending; and the economic and political consequences of reparations – whether of paying them or trying to avoid paying them – tended to erode the confidence of private investors.[131] Moreover, even in an imaginary world without inflation, it seems unlikely that lending to finance reparations would have been sustainable, because of the tendency for the rising burden of debt service on such loans to outweigh their benefits. As it was, the government had increasing difficulty in persuading foreign lenders to provide it with funds, precisely because the London schedule undermined confidence in the Reich's creditworthiness (in that sense, the "B" and "C" bonds *did* matter). Reparations *were* therefore excessive – as the German government claimed. However, it does not necessarily follow from this that the German government was therefore right not to *attempt* to pay them. The principal question addressed here is not whether the transfer was possible, but whether the strategy adopted by the German government after May 1921 was the best way of convincing the Allies that this was so.

The starting point for the strategy for revision through currency depreciation was fiscal imbalance. In order to demonstrate Germany's incapacity to pay in the intended way, the budget deficit had to be maintained; for to attempt to balance it would have amounted to a step toward genuine fulfillment of the London schedule. As Wirth himself put it in arguing against a property levy (or "seizure of real values," in the contemporary catchphrase): "The goal of our entire policy must be the dismantling of the London Ultimatum. It would therefore be a mistake if, by initiating a seizure of real values at this moment, we were [in effect] to declare the Ultimatum to

130 Wolfram Fischer, "Die Weimarer Republik unter den weltwirtschaftichen Bedingungen der Zwischenkriegszeit," in Mommsen et al., eds., *Industrielles System*, 2:26–50.
131 Holtfrerich, *German Inflation*, 154–5.

be 80 percent possible."[132] The domestic debate on financial reform between May 1921 and November 1922 was therefore to some extent a phony debate, as the chancellor himself was not in earnest about trying to balance the budget. This explains why proposals like that for the "seizure of real values" ultimately came to nothing. Such measures had to be discussed partly in order to appease the Reparations Commission and partly to mollify those (notably the officials at the Economics Ministry) who disapproved of the return to inflation; but they were never intended to "close the hole in the budget."[133] The state secretary at the Foreign Office, David Fischer, captured the prevailing mood when he described the Reparations Commission's "wish for a further increase in taxes" as implying a "wish for the economic destruction of Germany."[134] Even local tax collectors believed that "it is in the interests of our people . . . that we do not yet extract all that we can to throw into the mills of the Entente."[135] Significantly, Max Warburg's principal anxiety on the eve of the Genoa conference was that an attempt might be made to impose a "financial control" on Germany.[136]

The Wirth government succeeded, it is true, in cutting the level of real monthly expenditure from a peak of over a billion in the summer of 1921 to between 400 and 500 million gold marks during most of 1922. Indeed, at 24 percent of NNP, total public spending in 1922 was at its lowest level since before the war.[137] But despite a host of new tax measures, real revenue from taxation also fell in the second half of 1921 and rose only slightly in the first half of 1922; so that although the Reich deficit was falling as a percentage of NNP (from 16 percent in 1920 to 12 percent in 1921 and 9 percent in 1922), it remained excessive by modern standards.[138] By the time he visited Berlin in November 1922 as one of Wirth's committee of foreign experts, even Keynes had become disillusioned with the government's financial policy.[139] In the majority report that he signed, and in a subsequent letter to Havenstein, Keynes explicitly repudiated "the point of view which looks first to the balance of trade, and seeks for an improvement there first

132 Specht, *Politische Hintergründe*, 75.
133 Ibid., 69–71; Laubach, *Kabinette Wirth*, 61–6, 145–6; Maier, *Recasting Bourgeois Europe*, 247–55; Kent, *Spoils of War*, 147; Feldman, *Great Disorder*, 350–1.
134 Foreign Office Library, Cornwall House, German Foreign Ministry duplicate series, 3243/D713267, Kabinetsprotokolle, Chefbesprechung, Mar. 23, 1922.
135 Feldman, *Great Disorder*, 349.
136 WA, Allgemeines 1922, Warburg to Melchior, Mar. 20, 1922.
137 Witt, "Finanzpolitik," 424. This partly reflected economies on the railways and cuts in food subsidies: Feldman, *Great Disorder*, 354–76, 577–80. However, the cost of grants to increasingly insolvent municipal authorities continued to rise. Ibid., 561ff., 625–6.
138 Calculated from Webb, *Hyperinflation*, 33, 37; and Witt, "Finanzpolitik," 424.
139 *JMKW*, 18:61ff.; Laubach, *Kabinette Wirth*, 298–306; Specht, *Politische Hintergründe*, 88–91; Kent, *Spoils of War*, 192–3.

of all, or alternatively to the support of foreign loans." "If I felt confident
that I could control the budgetary position," he added pointedly, "I should
not doubt my capacity . . . to control the exchanges. As soon as the supply
of new currency is limited, I do not see how it is possible that the balance
of trade should be adverse."[140]

In the absence of radical fiscal reform, clearly, the German government
could only pay reparations in cash by borrowing foreign currency.[141] As
immediately became clear, however, few investors were willing to lend
foreign currency to a government with a notional external debt of 125 billion gold marks. The first installment of reparations under the London
schedule – 1 billion gold marks, due by August 31 – was only paid with difficulty. Although it proved possible to negotiate short-term credits of about
300 million gold marks from Holland and Italy, the Reichsbank reserves of
foreign currency (accumulated during the 1920 intervention against the
mark) were almost entirely used up.[142] When Havenstein turned to the
Bank of England for 500 million gold marks to help pay the second installment, he was politely refused.[143] Wirth was no more successful when he
appealed to German industry to undertake some kind of "credit action" on
the Reich's behalf.[144] Rathenau attempted at Wiesbaden to reduce the
Reich's need for hard currency by increasing the share of reparations in
kind – direct transfers of goods – in the total reparations bill. But this was
not a real solution. Diplomatically, the bilateral arrangement with France
irritated Britain, without reducing the burden of reparations in the short
run.[145] Economically, it replaced real exports with unrequited transfers,
without evading the tariffs on French imports from Germany. And financially, it was only advantageous if industry was willing to accept less from
the government in paper marks than they would earn from conventional
exports. In fact, reparations in kind only became attractive to industry after
mid-1922 when the gap between German and world prices had closed
(making conventional exports less easy), and the system had been effectively
"privatized" by the Cuntze-Bemelmans and Gillet-Ruppel Agreements.[146]

140 Skidelsky, *John Maynard Keynes*, 2:116–17, 120.
141 Graham, *Exchange, Prices, and Production*, 134. Even if the Reichsbank's entire gold reserve had been
   handed over as reparations, it would not have sufficed to pay for a single year's annuity.
142 Bresciani-Turroni, *Economics of Inflation*, 93ff.; Kent, *Spoils of War*, 142.
143 Ibid., 157–8; Specht, *Politische Hintergründe*, 74–5.
144 Maier, *Recasting Bourgeois Europe*, 264ff.; Kent, *Spoils of War*, 151; Specht, *Politische Hintergründe*,
   72–4; Feldman, *Great Disorder*, 358–76.
145 Maier, *Recasting Bourgeois Europe*, 262–7; Specht, *Politische Hintergründe*, 93ff.; Kent, *Spoils of War*,
   148; Feldman, *Great Disorder*, 356–7.
146 Feldman, *Iron and Steel*, 329, 447; Feldman, *Great Disorder*, 460ff., 479ff.

In short, whether to finance government deficits, buy foreign currency or pay for deliveries in kind, paying reparations meant printing paper marks. The critical question was what effect this inflationary fiscal policy would have on the exchange rate, and what effect the exchange rate would have on trade. The link between the transfer of reparations and the depreciation of the mark was a complex one.[147] The exchange rate depends in the long run upon relative international economic competitiveness, in that this determines the balance of trade (and hence the relative demand for foreign currency to pay for imports and supply of foreign currency from export earnings) and capital flows (purchases of foreign and domestic assets). In the short run, however, it can fluctuate far more rapidly than is justified by changes in competitiveness because of the rapidity with which the expectations of investors change. The post–World War I period was especially volatile in this regard because knowledge and experience of floating exchange rate systems was evolving rapidly from a low point, political instability was very great, and the number of economic agents involved in foreign currency speculation was also rising. Thus the very sharp depreciation of the mark against the dollar between May (62.30) and November 1921 (262.96) was principally due to German flight from the mark: the difficulty of paying the first installment of the London schedule and the loss of Upper Silesia evidently caused more alarm in Germany than abroad, where holders of marks continued to believe in an ultimate recovery of the exchange rate.[148] As Max Warburg observed, it was not necessary to believe in a conspiracy of "influential circles . . . trying forcibly to weaken the currency in order to draw attention to an insolvency that Germany does not actually suffer from, and to force an export that would not otherwise take place."[149] The German speculation against the mark was spontaneous, and required no coordination, because the insolvency was real. It is impossible to know exactly how much capital flowed out of Germany in this way; but clearly there was a movement amounting to several billion gold marks at around

147 Carl-Ludwig Holtfrerich, "Erwartungen des In- und Auslandes und die Geldnachfrage während der Inflation in Deutschland 1920–1923," *Bankhistorisches Archiv* 6 (1980): 3–19; Steven B. Webb, "Fiscal News and Inflationary Expectations in Germany After World War I," *Journal of Economic History* 46 (1986): 769–94. Cf. Holtfrerich, *German Inflation*, 75–6; Webb, *Hyperinflation*, 44–64.

148 On the speculation against the mark in Berlin in September, see Bresciani-Turroni, *Economics of Inflation*, 61, 96–7, 100.

149 WA, Politische Correspondenz 1921, Warburg to Major Sequin, Zurich, Sept. 29, 1921. See the similar comment made by Keynes in November 1921: "I do not believe a word of the silly stories that the German government could be so bold or so mad as to engineer on purpose what will in the end be a great catastrophe for their own people" (Keynes, "Renewed Depreciation of the Mark," Nov. 9, 1921, in *JMKW*, 18:10).

this time.[150] By contrast, Keynes's pessimism about the mark was exceptional among foreign investors, judging by the forward exchange rate against the mark in London, and figures for purchases of marks in New York.[151] A last flicker of foreign hope (ignited by the Cannes Conference) accounts for the temporary halt to depreciation in December–February 1922.

In short, apart from that brief lull, the mark did depreciate rapidly during Wirth's period as chancellor. What effect did this then have on German trade? The theory was that depreciation would, as it had in the second half of 1919, create a gap between German domestic prices and world market prices, because the mark would lose value faster abroad than it did at home. It would thus boost German exports, because hard currency countries would be able to buy German goods at bargain-basement prices. Moreover, it would impede German imports, because German importers would find the prices of foreign goods impossibly high in paper mark terms.[152] For a time, the theory appeared to be working. The Economics Ministry reported that "the fall of the mark . . . though in itself deplorable" was "an unmistakable factor behind the improvement in exports."[153] As if to bear this out, the available export statistics point to a 35 percent increase in the gold marks value of monthly exports (83 percent in volume terms) in the year after May 1921 (see Figure 16.2). Annual figures suggest a two-thirds increase of exports in volume terms.[154] Graham's calculations for forty-three categories of commodities also point to increases in exports.[155] Indeed, it may even be that all

150 In August 1922, the London *Times* estimated German foreign investments at close to their prewar level, but Keynes dismissed this as a gross overestimate, suggesting 1–3 billion gold marks as a plausible figure; Keynes, "Speculation in the Mark and Germany's Balances Abroad," Sept. 28, 1922, *JMKW,* 17:56ff. He later revised this upward to 1.7–3.8 billion gold marks; *The Nation and Atheneum,* Apr. 19, 1924. The McKenna committee ultimately opted for a figure of 5.7–7.8 billion gold marks for total German capital abroad at the end of the inflation period, but this figure was little more than an educated guess. Schuker, "American Reparations," 366. Cf. "Reparations Supplement," *Economist,* Apr. 12, 1924.
151 Keynes, "Will the German Mark Be Superseded?" in *JMKW,* 18:1–6. On the forward exchange rate and foreign holders of marks, see Holtfrerich, *German Inflation,* 73. On foreign purchases of marks in New York, see Webb, *Hyperinflation,* 57. Webb errs in arguing that monetary expansion led to a capital outflow and hence to a trade surplus in 1921/2; ibid., 94. In fact, it is possible to derive a time-path for foreign confidence using (a) the forward exchange rate (ibid., 73) (b) data on foreign purchases of marks abroad (ibid., 57) and (c) data on foreign deposits in German banks (Holtfrerich, "Die deutsche Inflation 1918 bis 1923"). These indicate that confidence only fell in 1922 – and indeed not until July.
152 Graham, *Exchange, Prices, and Production,* 117–33, 174–97, 209, 248.
153 StAH, SK II, III 1 a 1, vol. 1, RWM to RK, "Die Wirtschaftslage," July 21, 1921.
154 Figures from Bresciani-Turroni, *Economics of Inflation,* 194, 235; Wagenführ, "Die Industriewirtschaft," 26.
155 Graham, *Exchange, Prices, and Production,* 214–38, 261. In fact, Graham's results do not quite bear out his interpretation. Only sixteen of his forty-three commodities showed an upward export trend, and only ten showed a downward import trend. Moreover, there was a clear correlation to exchange-rate and price movements in only eight instances. In any case, his use of May 1921–December 1923 without reference to preceding or succeeding periods took the second

these figures are slight underestimates. The Allies claimed that the German government was understating exports to reduce the amount of reparations due, while the Economics Ministry itself accused German firms of understating their foreign sales, in order "to leave the surplus profit abroad."[156] There was also a good deal of smuggling at this time.[157]

However, this tells only a part of the story. In fact, imports substantially outstripped exports – a vital point, since only a trade surplus would have had the intended effect of exerting economic pressure on the Allies. Estimated annual figures point to a trade deficit of about 690 million gold marks in 1921 and more than 2,200 million gold marks in 1922, compared with a tiny surplus in 1920.[158] Monthly figures provide a more precise record: the trade gap widened between May and September 1921; narrowed to record a small surplus in December 1921; and then widened again to reach a peak of 348 million gold marks in July 1922 (see Figure 16.2). The figures for trade volumes tell the same story but suggest an even more dramatic widening of the deficit after February 1922, despite the fact that by this stage the proportion of semifinished and finished goods had risen to a third of all imports (see Figure 16.4).[159] Of the most successful German exports – vehicles, machinery, electrical goods, chemicals, leather goods, silk goods,

depreciation phase out of context. His estimate that Germany suffered a net loss of 10 billion gold marks selling exports too cheaply is curious, since at higher prices fewer exports would presumably have been sold; ibid., 260–76.

156 *JMKW,* 18:48, 54; Graham, *Exchange, Prices, and Production,* 214–15; Feldman, *Great Disorder,* 349, 354ff.
157 On smuggling, see the material in Prussian State Archive (Stiftung Preussischer Kulturbesitz), Berlin-Dahlem, Rep. 84a, 4878/88–93, Wirtschaftsausschuss der deutschen Reederei to Min. Dir. Jonquières, Reichsministerium für Wiederaufbau, 20.8.21; Rep. 84a, 129/196, Zentralverein deutscher Rheder, Rundschreiben, 11.9.22; /249–53, Zentralverein deutscher Rheder, "Schmuggel und Ladungsberaubungen durch der Schiffsmannschaft" (1922).
158 Again, there are a number of quite different calculations to choose from, beginning with Keynes's estimates in *JKMW,* 18:48, 54; *Statistik des Deutschen Reiches,* 317:5; Laursen and Pedersen, *German Inflation,* 68–9, 83, 89–91; Holtfrerich, *German Inflation,* 212; Carl-Ludwig Holtfrerich, "Germany and the International Economy: The Role of the German Inflation in Overcoming the 1920–1 United States and World Depression," in W. Robert Lee, ed., *German Industry and German Industrialisation: Essays in German Economic and Business History in the Nineteenth and Twentieth Century* (London, 1991), 276; Webb, *Hyperinflation,* 91; and Feldman, *Great Disorder,* 600 (citing estimates by R. Pilotti for the Reparations Commission). Though all clearly indicate an increased deficit in 1921, Holtfrerich, Webb, and Feldman follow the *Statistik des deutschen Reiches* in arguing that there was a near balance in 1922. However, the relevant figures are arrived at by converting volume figures into 1913 unit values using the customs schedule of 1913, which makes no allowance for the "dumping" of German exports. My own calculations based on monthly data for value as well as volume suggest that the deficit grew to around 2 billion gold marks in 1922, close to the estimate given by Laursen and Pedersen.
159 Data on the structure of trade in Hentschel, "Zahlen und Anmerkungen," 96; Laursen and Pedersen, *German Inflation,* 99–107; Bresciani-Turroni, *Economics of Inflation,* 194. A substantial part of the volume deficit in 1922 and 1923 was accounted for by the need to import coal, which intensified during the Ruhr crisis: Graham, *Exchange, Prices, and Production,* 214–25; Feldman, *Great Disorder,* 447.

paper, and wood – only vehicles and wood exceeded their 1913 volumes in 1922. By comparison, thirteen categories of import did so: not only food-stuffs and raw materials, but also iron goods (four times the prewar volume) and cotton goods.[160] What is more, these figures may understate the extent of the trade gap. Although Julius Hirsch and others continued to claim that exports were being underestimated and that the deficit in 1922 was negli-gible, there was "complete consensus" in the Reich Statistical Office "that the balance of trade deficit was being significantly underestimated."[161]

The striking point is that, in diametric opposition to the predictions of the architects of the strategy of fulfillment, the trade deficit widened at the times of most rapid nominal exchange rate depreciation (the second half of 1919, May to October 1921, and March to July 1922); and narrowed when the mark stabilized (March 1920 to April 1921 and November 1921 to February 1922).[162] Hence, paradoxically, at a time when Germany was supposed to be putting the Allied economies under pressure from cheap German exports, in reality it was relieving the pressure on them by providing them with an out-let for their exports.[163] In May–September 1921 and March–April 1922 – that is, at critical moments in the diplomacy of fulfillment – Germany's share of American exports rose to peak levels of nearly 12 percent, so that Germany temporarily eclipsed Britain as the largest single foreign market for Ameri-can raw materials.[164] The total U.S. trade surplus with Germany between 1919 and 1923 amounted to about $770 million.[165] Similarly, whereas

160 Calculated from Hentschel, "Zahlen und Anmerkungen," 103–8.
161 Feldman, *Great Disorder,* 484–5, n.
162 Cf. Bresciani-Turroni, *Economics of Inflation,* 83–92, 100–154.
163 Holtfererich, *Inflation,* 213–14. For an opposing view, see Schuker; "Finance and Foreign Policy," 353; Webb, *Hyperinflation,* 89–94. Webb attempts to show that the trade balance narrowed between July 1919 and March 1920, becoming a surplus between December 1919 and March 1920; then returned to deficit during the rest of the period of relative stabilization; and turned positive again from May 1921. This implies that depreciation *did* boost exports. However, these figures are arrived at by applying different deflators to import and export data, hence eliminating changes in the terms (and composition) of trade since 1913. Following the same procedure, I also arrive at a narrow sur-plus for the period November 1921 to November 1922. But what this shows is only that *had Ger-man imports and exports been the same goods as in 1913, valued at 1913 prices,* there would have been a surplus in the fulfillment period. The important point, as the remainder of this section argues, is that even though German exports were to some extent undervalued in historic terms, the gap between German and foreign prices was less pronounced than in 1919/20 because Germany's economy was booming while those of its trading partners were deflating. It was this divergence in economic performance that gave rise to the deficit in dollar (or goldmark) terms; and for the pur-poses of the reparations question, it was the current dollar value of trade that mattered. Webb is in error to conclude that "Germany's efforts to pay reparations punched the mouth they were sup-posed to feed" (ibid., 94); the contrary was true.
164 See Figure 16.4; Cf. Holtfrerich, "Germany and the International Economy," 278ff.; Holtfrerich, *Inflation,* 214–15; and on American cotton exports to Germany – the single largest item in German-American trade, see NA, RG 39, G114.2 (17).
165 Webb, *Hyperinflation,* 91.

between 1904 and 1913, Britain had had a trade deficit with Germany, in the years 1920 to 1923, British exports to Germany exceeded imports from Germany by £83 million – close to 0.5 percent of the United Kingdom's gross national product. The percentage of British exports going to Germany rose from 2.3 percent in 1919 to 6.7 percent in 1923.[166] In fact, it was in politically irrelevant weak-currency countries in the Mediterranean, Scandinavia, and the Far East that German exports were most successful.[167] Fully 37 percent of German exports went to these countries in 1920, compared with 13.6 percent before the war. By contrast, Britain, France, Belgium, Italy, and the United States accounted for 26.3 percent of German exports in 1922, compared with 38.5 percent in 1913; but 44.8 percent of German imports, compared with 35.3 percent in 1913.[168]

All of this, as Holtfrerich has pointed out, was good for the world economy, helping to lift it out of a slump that might otherwise have become a depression; but it was also (and this he overlooks) bad for revisionism.[169] Warburg and others had predicted that if the mark were allowed to depreciate, the pressure of German exports would force the Allies to abandon the London schedule of reparations. Instead, Germany had provided the Allied economies with a booming market for their own exports. The argument that "fulfillment" failed because French and American attitudes did not change is therefore inadequate, since the objective had been precisely to change Allied attitudes by exerting economic pressure. The point is that by doing the opposite – by relieving economic pressure on the Allies – fulfillment removed any need for them to revise the London schedule. As Wirth himself came to realize in October 1922, the Germans had "robbed themselves of one of the most effective propaganda tools in the struggle to relieve our reparations burdens . . . in that the horrifying situation of German foreign trade has remained unknown at home and abroad."[170]

What had gone wrong? According to Theo Balderston, continuing hostility to Germany on the part of its former foes may have negated the price advantage of depreciation, whereas the former neutrals, as Volker Hentschel

---

166 Calculated from figures in Thelma Liesner, comp., *Economic Statistics, 1900–1983: United Kingdom, United States of America, France, Germany, Italy, Japan* (London, 1985).

167 Theo Balderston, *The German Economic Crisis, 1923–1932* (Berlin, 1993), 86–93.

168 Hentschel, "Zahlen und Anmerkungen," 113.

169 Holtfrerich, *German Inflation*, 206–20; Holtfrerich, "Germany and the International Economy," 265–6. Holtfrerich estimates that, if Germany had adopted deflationary policies, imports from the United States would have been reduced by 60 percent, and imports from the United Kingdom by 44 percent. In effect, he suggests, German inflation averted a world depression of the sort experienced a decade later. This point is hard to reconcile with his assertion that inflation was the only way to persuade the Allies of the need for revision after 1921.

170 Feldman, *Great Disorder*, 484–5.

has noted, had accumulated large paper mark balances during the war, which they were eager to exchange for German goods.[171] But a further economic explanation is that although in nominal terms the mark clearly depreciated against the other major currencies, in real terms – allowing for changes in relative prices – there was no significant improvement in German competitiveness (see Figure 16.3). Compared with the gap that had opened up between German prices and world market prices from July 1919 until the relative stabilization of the mark, the gap that opened up after May 1921 was far less significant, all but vanishing in February 1922.[172] The underlying reasons for this can be considered under foreign and domestic headings. Among the former, the most important was the prevailing international economic slump, as a result of which prices, particularly of British and American goods, had fallen sharply since 1919/20. Between 1920 and 1922, British prices fell by 50 percent; American prices by 40–45 percent.[173] Equally important, however, were the domestic factors at work. From one point of view, 1921 and (to a lesser extent) 1922 were among the "golden years" of the Weimar economy. Estimates for NNP suggest growth rates of around 7 percent and 4 percent, while industrial production rose by around 20 percent in 1921 and 8 percent in 1922.[174] Unemployment figures provide the most frequently cited evidence that the era of fulfillment was an era of economic prosperity. Having averaged 3.8 percent for most of 1920, the percentage of trade union members out of work fell from 4.7 percent in February 1921 to just 0.6 percent in June and July 1922, with only a brief increase in January and February of 1922.[175] However, this boom was counterproductive from a diplomatic standpoint. To begin with, Germans now responded with increased alacrity to inflationary signals. Between July 1919 and March 1920, the exchange rate of the mark had plummeted, but domestic prices had lagged some way behind, and wages had altogether stagnated. Thus foreign buyers had been able to buy German goods and German labor at "fire sale" prices, subsidized, in effect, by ignorance and uncertainty. However, things were different when the mark began to slide again in May 1921, as producers, wholesalers, and retailers all struggled to pass on the "*schwarze Peter*" of higher prices. From November

171 Balderston, *Economic Crisis*, 82ff.; Hentschel, "Zahlen und Anmerkungen," 99–112.
172 This had been predicted by Hilferding: "With the increase of the issues [of notes] the balance of trade necessarily becomes passive. In effect, the issues increased internal prices, and that stimulated imports and impeded exports"; Bresciani-Turroni, *Economics of Inflation*, 44n.; Maier, *Recasting Bourgeois Europe*, 251.
173 Liesner, comp., *Economic Statistics*.
174 Witt, "Finanzpolitik," 424; Wagenführ, "Industriewirtschaft," 219.
175 Bresciani-Turroni, *Economics of Inflation*, 449; Graham, *Exchange, Prices, and Production*, 281, 317; Laursen and Pedersen, *German Inflation*, 110; Holtfrerich, *German Inflation*, 199.

1921, Hugo Stinnes and Paul Silverberg pressed for "semiautomatic" adjustment of iron and steel prices via the so-called coal clause; with the result that by the summer of 1922, steel prices were subject to fortnightly revision.[176] Rising import prices, pushed upward by the depreciating currency, were thus closely shadowed by wholesale prices and export prices, with the cost-of-living index (i.e., retail prices) lagging behind – a quite different development from that in 1919-20, when the gap between import prices and all domestic prices persisted. Similar tendencies were detectable in the movement of wages.[177] Two further behavioral changes further reduced the benefits to the economy of currency depreciation. First, it is clear that high levels of employment, although made possible by falling real wages, went hand in hand with falling productivity.[178] Second, there was what might be described as a poor man's consumer boom. In the period 1916-19, indicators of consumption had lagged behind figures for national income, reflecting the extent to which the war had diverted resources from "butter" into "guns." However, in the years 1920-2, at a time when real wages were falling for many groups and real national income increased by no more than 12 percent, consumption appears to have risen sharply. In the absence of proper national accounts, it is hard to know just how far there was an increase in consumption as a proportion of national income. But the statistical evidence confirms that consumer goods production rose faster than that of capital goods: beer production rose by 33 percent, brandy by 53 percent, and sugar by 86 percent.[179]

These, then, were the various economic forces underlying the German economy's failure to generate a trade surplus in 1921/2. On the one hand, foreign prices and demand were depressed, while foreign capital sought a profitable outlet in an apparently booming Germany. On the other hand, prices and wages within Germany adjusted more rapidly than hitherto to currency depreciation, while productivity fell and income was increasingly diverted into consumption. The cumulative effect was to erode the competitiveness of German exports and stimulate imports. The Economic Min-

---

176 Feldman, *Iron and Steel*, 286ff.
177 Between July 1919 and March 1920, employees had experienced drops in real wages of between 50 and 60 percent. However, advances in collective organization made in 1920, combined with the rising demand for labor, meant that almost as soon as depreciation resumed in mid-1921 there was a spate of wage demands. Of course, in real terms, pay rates still fell – by 30 percent on average between May 1921 and December 1922. But repeated increases in nominal pay did mean that real wages followed a saw-tooth path, preventing a collapse of real wage costs such as had occurred in the second half of 1919. Cf. Feldman, *Great Disorder*, 609–21.
178 Graham, *Exchange, Prices, and Production*, 295; Balderston, *Economic Crisis*, 63, 73.
179 Hoffmann, *Wachstum*, 358, 383–5, 388, 390–5; Wagenführ, "Die Industriewirtschaft," 219; Bresciani-Turroni, *Economics of Inflation*, 193–4, 198; Graham, *Exchange, Prices, and Production*, 287, 293, 306.

istry's report on the period June to November 1922 effectively admitted the
bankruptcy of the fulfillment strategy. Previously, it was true, "the depreciation of the mark had had a stimulating effect on domestic manufacturing
activity, . . . because the domestic flight from the mark into real values stimulated demand and the gap [between domestic and foreign prices] acted
as . . . an export premium." But "today a fall in the mark leads, as a rule, to
bottlenecks, because what little available capital there is, given the present
tightness of money, has learnt to flee directly into foreign currency, rather
than into goods; and because . . . the adjustment of the internal value [of
the mark] to its external value happens so quickly that scarcely any time
remains to make sustained use of it."[180]

III

The strategy of revising the London schedule of reparations by means of
depreciation thus failed not solely because of French and American obsti-
nacy, but because it was a misconceived strategy that relieved rather than
increased the pressure on the American and British economies. It therefore
seems legitimate to ask whether an attempt to stabilize the German economy would have been more effective as a diplomatic lever. Higher taxes,
bigger cuts in government spending, a financial "clear-out": none of this
would have sufficed to pay the London schedule. But the braking effect of
such measures on the German economy would, if nothing else, have curtailed the enormous influx of imports into Germany and thereby closed the
export "ventilator" that fulfillment provided. That this is no idle "counterfactual" hypothesis can be demonstrated with reference to subsequent
events.

Under the Dawes Plan, once again, capital inflows offered a temporary
cushion for the German economy. At a rough estimate, the net capital
inflow into Germany between 1924 and 1930 totaled 17.4 billion reichsmarks (the new postinflation currency that was essentially the prewar gold
mark) – over 4.5 percent of NNP in 1924, 1925, 1927, and 1928 – of which
a significant part represented long- and short-term borrowing by local
authorities.[181] Clearly, this repeat of the great speculation of 1919-22 had
certain important advantages, leading some observers to overoptimistic
conclusions about Germany's prospects.[182] The resulting economic stimu-

180 Specht, *Politische Hintergründe*, 87n.
181 Cf. William C. McNeil, *American Money and the Weimar Republic* (New York, 1986).
182 See, e.g., James W. Angell, *The Recovery of Germany* (New Haven, Conn., 1929).

lus in turn meant that the somewhat reduced burden of reparations was relatively easier to shoulder: the total amount paid between 1924 and 1933 did not exceed 11.1 billion reichsmarks – at most about 2 percent of annual NNP.[183] However, interest payments on such loans accounted for some 5 billion gold marks between 1924 and 1932, adding to the burden on the balance of payments. In the absence of a greater reduction in domestic consumption, the German economy showed no sign of achieving the kind of increase in exports that would be necessary in the long run to pay reparations and service the debt. Except in the depressed year of 1926, there was a trade deficit every year between 1924 and 1929, reaching as much as 3.5 percent of NNP in 1924, 1925, and 1927 (see Figure 16.1).

Capital inflows could, of course, be seen as the problem itself.[184] In the new Reichsbank President Hjalmar Schacht's eyes, certainly, they threatened to revive the threat of inflation and undermine German competitiveness. Bound by a fixed exchange rate, a strict minimum ratio between its gold and hard currency reserve and its note-issue, and lacking a proper system of open-market operations, the Reichsbank could not easily prevent an increase in its reserve – as well as in the foreign deposits throughout the banking system – from engendering a corresponding monetary expansion.[185] Schacht struggled somewhat quixotically to limit foreign borrowing by local authorities, but simply drove them from long-term bond issues to short-term borrowing.[186] The difficulty of managing monetary policy under such circumstances was already evident in 1926/7, when reductions in the discount rate designed to stimulate the domestic investment led to capital outflows, which only resumed when interest rates once again rose.[187] But high interest rates tended to worsen the domestic position. By 1928, the dilemma was becoming inescapable: interest rates should have been reduced to boost falling investment but had to be kept up to avoid capital outflows. The balance of payments exerted a further restrictive pressure on fiscal policy. Falling revenues and rising expenditures (notably on unemployment benefits) are inevitable – and indeed desirable as "stabilizers" – in a recession. But the German government was not in a position to fund deficits as large as the 1.4 billion reichsmarks run up by the Reich in 1928:

183 Cf. Harold James, *The German Slump: Politics and Economics, 1924–1936* (Oxford, 1986), 21–3.
184 This was one of the central points at issue between Keynes and Ohlin in their celebrated debate on the "transfer problem." Cf. *JMKW*, 11:451–80; Skidelsky, *John Maynard Keynes*, 1:309ff.
185 See Harold James, *The Reichsbank and Public Finance in Germany, 1924–1933: A Study of the Politics of Economics During the Great Depression* (Frankfurt am Main, 1985).
186 Harold James, "Did the Reichsbank Draw the Right Conclusions from the Great Inflation," in Feldman and Müller-Luckner, eds., *Nachwirkungen*, 211–30.
187 Balderston, *Economic Crisis*, 150ff.

first, because, with the German bond market traumatized by inflation, it could only finance such deficits abroad; and second because it continued to owe a huge sum to foreign creditors in the form of reparations. Rudolf Hilferding's failure to raise a domestic loan, his resort to "second-class" foreign lenders, and the return of reparations to the international agenda at the instigation of Reparations Agent S. Parker Gilbert in September 1928 underlined both points.[188] The outcome of the Young Committee's deliberations closed the circle: not so much because it came up with yet another "final" total (121 billion reichsmarks) and yet another protracted schedule of payments, but because it maintained (indeed in real terms increased) the annual payment of more than 2 billion reichsmarks while offering a loan of just 1.26 billion reichsmarks, two-thirds of which the Reich was obliged to hand over directly to the creditors.[189] This news, and the domestic political furor it precipitated, only served to stimulate further capital outflows.[190]

All of these factors made some kind of fiscal and monetary crisis more or less inevitable. Yet the *degree* of deflation was not predetermined. The Müller government had failed to agree on a minor tax increase; but its successor, under Heinrich Brüning, embarked on a far more radical policy of expenditure cuts and tax hikes.[191] In part, Brüning seems to have believed that deflationary policies would allow him to implement certain constitutional changes. But of equal importance was a foreign policy calculation that, in attempting to achieve reparations revision by instrumentalizing domestic economic crisis, was almost exactly the mirror image of the policies adopted by successive governments in 1919 and 1921/2. The difference was that where the earlier governments had believed that currency depreciation would force the Allies to change their stance, Brüning and his advisers believed that a strict *deflationary* policy would force the Allies to end reparations.[192] In his memoirs, Brüning put the point succinctly: Germany was to "make use of the world crisis . . . to put pressure on all the other powers. . . . We were able to turn our [economic] sickness into our weapon."[193] At the time, Hans Posse (of the Economics Ministry) was more precise. The objectives of German policy should be: "1. To work more defensively for the maintenance of as large a trade surplus as possible, to facilitate the debt payments and to control unemployment; [and] 2. To develop an offensive activ-

188 Ibid., 266–87.
189 Peter Krüger, *Die Aussenpolitik der Republik von Weimar* (Darmstadt, 1985), 541ff.
190 Balderston, *Economic Crisis,* 156–73.
191 Cf. Ilse Maurer, *Reichsfinanzen und Grosse Koalition: Zur Geschichte des Reichskabinetts Müller, 1928–30* (Berne, 1973).
192 Krüger, *Aussenpolitik,* 523–35; 553ff.
193 Heinrich Brüning, *Memoiren, 1918–1934* (Stuttgart, 1970), 193, 221, 309, 367.

ity to avoid the threat of encirclement as a result of the formation of European blocs."[194] This meant a series of trade initiatives such as the German-Austrian Customs Union proposal and proposals for new trade treaties with other Danubian states, accompanied by a sharp reduction in German export prices aimed at "severely damag[ing] the trade of, in particular, the creditor countries."[195] At the same time, creditor fears of default were to be increased by "danger of a national socialist or a bolshevik coup" – exactly as German representatives at Versailles had issued calculated warnings about the dangers of Bolshevism.[196] The culmination of the strategy was the proclamation accompanying the Emergency Decree of 5 June 1931, which declared, in language strongly reminiscent of the declarations of 1919 and 1921: "The continuation of such reparations burdens is not only unbearable for the German economy but must also lead to the ruin of the economy of the whole world."[197] The policy continued even after June 20, when the Americans proposed a one-year moratorium on all reparations and war debts. With capital pouring out of Germany as the Austrian banking crisis spread to Berlin, the government rejected French proposals for a 2 billion reichsmark loan and continued to insist on nothing less than "the whole hog" throughout the Standstill negotiations and the protracted run-up to the Lausanne Conference in June-July 1932.[198]

The attempt to use depreciation to achieve revision between 1919 and 1923 had not only failed: it had precipitated a domestic economic disaster. The attempt to achieve the same end by deflation a decade later had still more deleterious domestic consequences; but it came closer to diplomatic success. Real NNP fell by about 5 percent in 1930, 11 percent in 1931, and 5 percent in 1932; while industrial output fell by 12 percent, 20 percent, and 14 percent, respectively. Unemployment, as is well known, soared to heights not seen since 1923, and then exceeded them, reaching a peak of above 45 percent of union members in 1932. In international terms, however, the aim of an export surplus was certainly achieved in the three years after 1929 – albeit as a result of a 65 percent fall in imports as against a 57 percent fall in exports. The system of reparations did not long survive this.

The conclusion one is driven to is not, of course, that Brüning's revi-

---

194 Krüger, *Aussenpolitik*, 522, 536–9.
195 Ibid., 544.
196 See, e.g., Brüning's comment that the result of the September 1920 Reichstag elections might help "weaken the united front of our creditors." Ibid., 539–40.
197 Edward W. Bennett, *Germany and the Diplomacy of the Financial Crisis, 1931* (Cambridge, Mass., 1962), 116, 128.
198 Krüger, *Aussenpolitik*, 534–46.

sionist strategy was more "rational" than Wirth's. All that can be said is that under Brüning, the policies pursued stood a greater chance of exerting pressure on the Allies than those adopted in the era of "fulfillment," which had a diametrically opposite effect from that intended. But in neither case was the diplomatic achievement in any way worth the domestic economic cost of hyperinflation and "hyperdeflation."

In the final analysis, then, the belief of the 1920s that German economic power could in some way be instrumentalized to restore Germany's international position was a chimera. Perhaps the real tragedy of Versailles was that even men as intelligent as Max Warburg failed to grasp this.

17

A Comment

GERALD D. FELDMAN

The title of this part of the book suggests an optimism and positive attitude in no way justified by its subject matter or content. The chapters here deal with two issues whose outcomes illuminate the failure of European reconstruction at Versailles and the economic and financial disasters of the two miserable decades between the smoke and mirrors surrounding the peace settlement and the explosive and shattering termination marked by the German invasion of Poland. The first of these issues is the territorial settlement; the second is the economic and financial settlement. Both were horrendous failures by any standard one wishes to employ and whatever position one takes on the historical debates surrounding them. At the heart of these debates has been the question of whether the arrangements made were too hard or too easy on Germany. Although most historians would agree that the terms were too hard in relation to the will and mechanisms available to enforce them and too easy to prevent a second German grasp for world power, the quarrel over what might have been done often tends to skirt the overdetermined nature of what actually happened at Versailles.

This is not the case with the contributions here. Whatever position one takes on the specific arguments of these provocative essays, they cannot be charged with presenting counterfactuals that lack historicity and heuristic value. The Owl of Minerva assumes center stage in each one of them. Sally Marks, ever eager to defend the feasibility of the reparations settlement, appears cheerlessly resigned to the hopelessness of the cause in the real world of post-Versailles Europe. Stephen Schuker, the foremost analyst of the loss of French predominance in Europe, virtually outlines the track to France's eclipse at the moment of its victory. Elisabeth Glaser paints a picture of how Allied economic weakness and the division among the victors undermined the cause of economic reconstruction at Versailles. Finally, Niall Ferguson, in a discussion filled with irony, seeks to show that the German policy of fighting reparations with inflation was a misconceived policy

441

and that Germany's ultimate successes in escaping most of the reparations
were bought at the price of political disaster.

The primary issue at Versailles, the common denominator, would seem
to be security, and the paradox is that the quest for security after World War
I produced immense insecurity. As Stephen Schuker argues, the Rhineland
question, insofar as it was a territorial issue involving possible annexations
by France or the creation of a separate state or set of states economically,
militarily, and politically dependent on France, never really was a realistic
option, first, because France's Allies would not allow it and, second,
because the French political leadership was unwilling to listen to military
supporters of annexation and separatism. Whatever the violations of the
principle of national self-determination in eastern Europe, national self-
determination was triumphant in the West, and both the Rhenish solution
of 1815 and the German unification of 1870 seemed irreversible. This leads
me to raise the kind of historicity-lacking counterfactual I was so quick to
criticize at the outset of these remarks. There is more than a hint in
Schuker's analysis that the politicians were responsible for a lost opportunity
to do more on the Rhine. This has its counterpart in Marks's position that
politics and politicians undermined reparations. One wonders in both cases
exactly what success would have meant. Could one really have separated the
left bank of the Rhine from Germany? What would the shape of Europe
have been in the context of so massive a violation of the principle of
national self-determination? What Schuker suggests is that the French military were quite as irresponsible as their German counterpart but were
unable to get their way because of civilian control over the military. To this
domestic political consideration must be added, of course, a diplomatic one.
France was the member of a genuine coalition of great powers and, unlike
Germany, which treated its allies like satellites, could not behave as if political fantasy were reality. Similarly, and I shall return to this theme later, the
playing out of the payment of reparations after Versailles would be an interesting exercise. One wonders how Marks's scenario of fulfillment would
differ from that provided by Niall Ferguson.

The problem of regional arrangements and regional security brings us
back to the Rhine and to the curious fact that none of these chapters
touches on the rather important problem of the linkages between German,
French, Luxembourgeois, and Belgian industry, that is, the regional economic arrangement created by the Schumann Plan, which played so important a role in the economic and security arrangements of Western Europe
after World War II. The recovery of Lorraine by France, after all, may have
righted the wrong done to France in 1870 but also seriously undermined

the coal, iron ore, iron, and steel nexus that had existed before 1914 with very ambivalent results. On the one hand, France's economic potential was greatly increased. On the other, so was its dependence on German coal, while German dependence on minette was much more limited. Hugo Stinnes, with his typical brashness, recognized that the French were in trouble as early as November 1918 when he pointed out that the French would have to come to terms or choke on their minette.[1] As is well known, there were French businessmen and officials who understood the problem and the danger. Not so long ago, Walter McDougall and other new wave historians of French interwar diplomacy were arguing that the ideas of Jacques Seydoux and others for French participation in German industry and regional heavy industrial collaboration as an alternative to reparations presaged the kind of solution to Franco-German difficulties introduced after 1945.[2] They probably were reading a bit too much of the future into the past, but still one wonders why those Frenchmen concerned with the economic side of the Rhineland problem were so ineffective, just as ineffective as Ferdinand Foch and the other military people were with their territorial and separatist plans. Were the Germans lucky in having industrialists with the capacity to bully their government? Were the politicians to blame for the failed victory over Germany here too? What can be said for certain is that the war had tragically put an end to prewar practices of international economic cooperation, corporate multinationalism, and peaceful development of Europe's most important heavy industrial region. The efforts to deal with the region both during and after the war were dominated by hegemonical concerns and nationalist calculations of advantage. One may have tried to restore the gold standard, but little concern was shown for reconstructing the internationalism and globalism on which it had been based.[3]

The politicians, therefore, are certainly to be blamed for failing to establish a viable economic order at Versailles, and Elisabeth Glaser's analysis is an important contribution to this much neglected subject. There was talk during the war of the "economic war after the war," and with good reason. The Germans, of course, had their own plans, although policy makers and eco-

---

1 Gerald D. Feldman, *Iron and Steel in the German Inflation, 1916–1923* (Princeton, N.J., 1977), 84.
2 Walter A. McDougall, *France's Rhineland Diplomacy, 1914–1924: The Last Bid for a Balance of Power in Europe* (Princeton, N.J., 1978); Walter A. McDougall, "Political Economy Versus National Sovereignty: French Structures for German Economic Integration After Versailles," *Journal of Modern History* 51 (1979): 4–23; Marc Trachtenberg, *Reparation in World Politics: France and European Economic Diplomacy, 1916–1923* (New York, 1980).
3 See the suggestive and important essay by Carl Strikwerda, "The Troubled Origins of European Economic Integration: International Iron and Steel and Labor Migration in the Era of World War I," *American Historical Review* 98 (Oct. 1993): 1106–29.

nomic leaders were not in full agreement about them. However they turned out, they would have led to an intolerable German hegemony if put into effect. The French were quite properly worried that even if none of the German plans could be realized because of a happy outcome to the war, the Germans were nevertheless bound to dominate Europe economically unless something systematic was done to prevent it. The territorial changes, formation of economic blocs, and reparations advocated by Etienne Clémentel were designed to produce a decisive shift in the economic balance of power. Once again, however, coalition politics made the realization of French goals impossible, while France's Anglo-American allies were divided themselves and, indeed, in competition with one another for economic and financial leadership of the postwar world. As Glaser convincingly shows, the economic clauses of the treaty were devised in a totally uncoordinated manner, which, however, accurately reflected the absence of a common vision as to what the postwar economic order should be. The end result was an excessive reliance on reparations to redress the balance between Germany and France, combined with a "head-start" program of giving France commercial and territorial advantages for a number of years. Indeed, it is hard not to conclude that reparations were *the* reconstruction program of Versailles and, thanks to the withdrawal of the United States, became the heart of the security program as well.

For Sally Marks, the politicians are certainly to be blamed for what she calls "the perpetual blight of the reparations question," a characterization I find apt, although I suspect for somewhat different reasons than she does. While Marks certainly has done a convincing job of exploring the reparations–war guilt nexus and the manner in which politicians from all sides obscured the issues, her argument that reparations were an eminently political issue involving the balance of power, on the one hand, and that the reparations bills would have been payable if everyone had just been honest and straightforward about it, on the other hand, seems somewhat contradictory. When confronted with such dilemmas, it is best to look for spiritual guidance, and in such instances, one is well advised to turn to types like J. P. Morgan, certainly no pro-German, who put the real issue quite bluntly to the British and French in June 1922:

Broadly speaking, Mr. Morgan appeared to think that the Allies must make up their minds as to whether they wanted a weak Germany who could not pay, or a strong Germany who could pay. If they wanted a weak Germany they must keep her economically weak; but if they wanted her to be able to pay they must allow Germany to exist in a condition of cheerfulness, which would lead to successful business. This meant, however, that you would get a strong Germany, and a Germany that was strong economically would, in a sense, be strong from a military point of view also.[4]

Also sprach J. P. Morgan, and he was right. Indeed, there is absolute continuity in the Allied dilemma since it is well known that David Lloyd George and Georges Clemenceau were both aware of the giant puzzle involved in taking reparations from the Germans while trying to prevent them from becoming a ferocious competitor on world markets. A memorandum by the American Norman Davis, who served on the Reparations Committee of July 5, 1919, contains a lengthy record of the recognition by Lloyd George, Clemenceau, and Woodrow Wilson that they were stuck because of their promises to their peoples and that those who wished to fix a modest final sum – Davis and John Maynard Keynes among them – were right. Davis concluded:

I am also of the opinion that France and England will eventually realize that it is most inadvisable to collect the full amount of Germany's liability even if she is able to pay it, because, in the remote possibility of her being able to do so, it would to a great extent be detrimental to British and French industry. Mr. Lloyd George and M. Loucheur admitted that they would no doubt within two or three years desire to have Germany's bill cut down considerably, because by that time their people would realize that Germany could only pay a very large sum by restricting imports and increasing exports to the extent that Germany would be lost to them as a market and that they would not only become dumping grounds for German exports, but their own exports to other countries would have to give way to those from Germany. The problem is not therefore so much what Germany can pay, but what the Allies can afford to have her pay. While it would have been better to face this fact now and have Germany issue obligations for a reasonable, definite amount which could be used as a basis of credit for the immediate resumption of European industrial life, I am hopeful that the Reparation Commission, which has the power to do so, will adopt a sound policy and a constructive, definite plan within the near future.[5]

Indeed, apparently the only people who really believed that the Germans could fulfill their reparations obligations, the real obligations that is, and not what Marks correctly considers to be the bogus figure of 132 billion gold marks presented by the 1921 London Ultimatum, are some historians. I emphasize *some* historians because I simply do not agree when Marks says, "The scholarly consensus now suggests that paying what was actually asked of it was within Germany's capacity." Peter Krüger does not share this view;

4 Quoted in Gerald D. Feldman, *The Great Disorder: Politics, Economics, and Society in the German Inflation, 1914–1924* (New York, 1993), 446.
5 Norman Davis, "Peace Conference Notes," July 5, 1919, kindly placed at my disposal by Elisabeth Glaser.

neither do I, and neither does Ferguson, that is, one German, one American, and one Englishman.[6] Of course, we all work on Germany, but since the Germans were supposed to pay the money, some attention should be paid to their condition. I will confess that I have a tendency to agree with people who come to the same conclusions I have reached, and I thoroughly agree with Ferguson when he argues that the initial German effort to pay reparations was very substantial (the August 1921 payment in particular), that it produced an immense strain (here there is a consensus among such economic historians as Barry Eichengreen, Steven Webb, and myself), and that to fulfill the London Ultimatum at the pace required, Germany would have had to submit to occupation or a pro-French dictatorship. Although possible dictatorial solutions to Germany's domestic problems were possible in this period, especially in 1923, they were not likely to be pro-French.

What Ferguson does demonstrate, and this is certainly the original contribution of his analysis, is that the smoke and mirrors surrounding reparations were of a different kind from those claimed by Marks. Monetary depreciation in 1919-20 did enable the Germans to dump their products and initially fuel monetary depreciation, but the prediction that monetary depreciation would continue without interruption proved false since German economic activity led to short-run capital inflows, funded the trade deficit, and produced the relative stabilization of 1920-1. The successful dumping policy, therefore, undermined the case for reparation reduction during the crucial period before the London Ultimatum. Similarly, the policy of fulfillment as a mechanism for demonstrating that reparations could not be paid also backfired since both the incapacity and also the unwillingness truly to reduce the deficit and the continuing efforts to maintain the trade offensive and domestic reconstruction led to a vast increase in German imports and a measure of relief for Great Britain and the United States thanks to the overheated German economy. As I understand Ferguson's argument, therefore, the benefits of exporting to Germany outweighed the disadvantages of exported unemployment from Germany. My one question here would be how is one to explain the continued complaints about German dumping and the protectionist measures taken if German imports were proving so stimulating? The British were blaming their unemployment on cheap German exports, but I have not seen much by way of British commentary on their export advantages arising from German business activity.[7]

6 See Peter Krüger, "Das Reparationsproblem der Weimarer Republik in fragwürdiger Sicht," *Vierteljahrshefte für Zeitgeschichte* 29 (1981): 21–47.
7 See Feldman, *Great Disorder,* 332–6.

Nevertheless, I think Ferguson is on to something when he argues that the effort to apply pressure through the combination of fulfillment, increasing inflation, and export underpricing did not succeed because the Allies were not really suffering. One can surmise that if they had been suffering as much as the Germans hoped, they would have done some very unpleasant things about it. Indeed, as we both argue in our respective works, the German balance of trade was even worse than official statistics in 1922 showed and once galloping and hyperinflation set in, German competitiveness was lost, first, because the deflations in the Allied countries had made them more competitive and, second, because Germans began calculating in real values domestically. In short – and here again we come to Ferguson's central point – the often criticized German policy of trying to use inflation to beat reparations is above all to be criticized because it did not work as either Norman Davis in 1919 or the Germans in 1921-22 expected. This leads Ferguson to his intriguing suggestion that the policy of stabilization, which so many historians assume would have enabled Germany to pay reparations, would have been a shrewder policy, not because reparations could have been paid, but because such "good faith" and virtuous behavior would have deprived the Allies of the German export market they enjoyed under an economic regime that combined fulfillment and deficits. Ferguson recognizes that a German stabilization policy prior to 1923 is a counterfactual, and, in his review of my study of the inflation, he argues that the right time was 1920 while criticizing my position that the one realistic chance was during the visit of the international experts in November 1922.[8] The trouble is that the inflation consensus was as strong as ever in 1920 whereas it had broken down by November 1922 when a stabilization consensus was beginning to develop. In the end, of course, the hyperinflation was overdetermined, and reparations were the perpetual blight Marks has called them because they undermined German democracy and were instrumentalized to promote inflation at the beginning of the republic and deflation at its end. In between, they produced domestic conflicts over the use of American money so well described by the late William McNeil.[9] All this served to demonstrate that German recovery as a political power, both economically and territorially, depended in the last analysis on political will. We know who demonstrated that quality at its utmost, and the Treaty of Versailles played no small role in the unhappy way in which the accounts were finally settled.

8 Niall Ferguson, "Your Money or Your Life," *Times Literary Supplement* (Mar. 11, 1994): 3–4. For a full development of his arguments, see his important new study *Paper & Iron: Hamburg Business and German Politics in the Era of Inflation, 1897–1927* (Cambridge, 1995).
9 William C. McNeil, *American Money and the Weimar Republic: Economics and Politics on the Eve of the Great Depression* (New York, 1986).

PART FOUR

The Legacy and Consequences of Versailles

18

The Soviet Union and Versailles

JON JACOBSON

It may be a mistake to refer to Versailles and the other treaties made in Paris in 1919 as a "peace settlement." The real legacy of Versailles was neither peace nor settlement, but rather "a seventy-year crisis" – marked by a continuing European civil war, the rise of communism and fascism as international movements, inflation, depression, the breakdown of the world economy, and a second world war yielding a divided Germany, an occupied eastern Europe, and an international system of bipolar tensions ending only in 1989.[1] The most persistent elements of that crisis were "the German problem" and "the East–West conflict," the seventy years of antagonism between Soviet Russia and the powers that wrote the Versailles treaty. The purpose of this chapter is to reexamine the beginnings of that antagonism – and perhaps to find in those beginnings some indication of why a conflict that ended so quickly lasted so long. It is an effort to look beyond the story of the civil war fought at the time of the Paris peace conference for an answer to this question.[2] The first step is to examine the place of Soviet Russia in "the new world order" that emerged from the great international upheaval that began with the guns of August 1914 and ended with the preliminary treaty of Riga terminating the Soviet–Polish War almost exactly six years later. From there, the discussion moves on to Soviet Russia's stance toward the Versailles order, the challenges that confronted the Union of the Soviet Socialist Republics (USSR) in its relations with the parties to

---

1 Bruce Cumings, "The End of the Seventy-Years' Crisis: Trilateralism and the New World Order," in Meredith Woo-Cumings and Michael Loriaux, eds., *Past as Prelude: History in the Making of a New World Order* (Boulder, Colo., 1993), 15–16.
2 On the Peace Conference and on the problem of Russia, see particularly John M. Thompson, *Russia, Bolshevism, and the Versailles Peace* (Princeton, N.J., 1966), and Arno J. Mayer, *Politics and Diplomacy of Peacemaking: Containment and Counterrevolution at Versailles, 1918–1919* (New York, 1967). Soviet foreign policy during the Revolution and Civil War is examined fully in Richard K. Debo, *Revolution and Survival: The Foreign Policy of Soviet Russia, 1917–1918* (Toronto, 1979); and Richard K. Debo, *Survival and Consolidation: The Foreign Policy of Soviet Russia, 1918–1921* (Montreal, 1992).

the Versailles treaty during the crucial decade from the Paris Peace Conference in 1919 to the advent of the Stalinist system in 1929, and the impact
of this international experience on Soviet foreign relations in subsequent
years.

INTERNATIONAL REVOLUTION AND NATIONAL SECURITY

The USSR emerged from World War I and its civil war in an anomalous and
tenuous position on the international stage. The Bolsheviks now ruled an
empire covering one-sixth of the globe, and the Triple Entente that had
aligned the czarist regime with the imperial governments seated in London
and Paris was not, and could not be, reconstituted. Although Lenin and
Woodrow Wilson seemed like-minded in their opposition to prewar imperialism and had both put forth visions of internationalist and emancipatory
"new world orders," neither they nor their successors could find a common
purpose. Russia did share "a community of fate" with Germany, in that they
were the countries against which the 1918 peace settlement was made, yet
both Berlin and Moscow sought a broader range of diplomatic options than
were available in an exclusive German-Russian "special relationship." Thus,
for reasons of ideology and geopolitics, Soviet Russia would find no "natural allies" within the world order defined at the Paris Peace Conference.

The prevailing Bolshevik attitude toward the postwar order, and toward
the treaty of Versailles in particular, can be seen in the "general line" propounded within the Communist International during the years 1921-4,
with its sustained expectation of a proletarian revolution, even after the failures in Germany, Hungary, and elsewhere, and with its notion that the postwar international situation would inevitably throw capitalism into crisis.
This crisis, as defined at Comintern congresses, would have three distinctive features:[3] (1) The imperialist states would move toward another world
war, which would generate another great revolutionary crisis. The contradictions that would cause that war were the conflicts emerging between the
United States and Great Britain, on the one hand, and between America
and Japan on the other. (2) The initial revolutionary breakthrough would
occur, as it had in 1917, in the country in which the concentration of contradictions, internal and external, produced the greatest explosive charge.
Germany, defeated in the World War, weakened economically, oppressed by
the treaty of Versailles, and possessing the second strongest Communist party

---

3 The analysis here depends on Fernando Claudin, *The Communist Movement: From Comintern to Com-
   inform* (New York, 1975), 65–7; original Spanish edition: *La Crisis del Movimiento Comunista* (Paris,
   1970).

affiliated with the Communist International, would perform the role Russia had played in 1917. (3) Following the breakthrough in Germany, socialist revolution would spread to the other links in the imperialist chain – the industrialized nations, the dependent countries, and the colonies. This time the revolution could count from the beginning on the support of a proletarian state with military resources at its disposal. For that reason, while the proletariat of the industrialized Europe remained the activator of global socialist revolution, protecting, conserving, and strengthening the Russian bastion of socialism was fundamental to its success.

This "general line," with which Georgii Zinoviev has been primarily identified, was introduced in "Theses on the World Situation" and "Theses on Tactics" adopted by the Third Comintern Congress in June–July 1921. The Treaty of Versailles was at the center of the analysis of the revolutionary situation presented there, and, at the Fourth Congress in November–December 1922, member parties were directed to work for its abolition. The nuances of the anti-Versailles analysis were elaborated by Karl Radek, chief Comintern tactician and a member of the Presidium of the Comintern Executive Committee (ECCI) during the years 1921-1925, in his report to the Third ECCI Plenum in July 1923 during the crisis of the Ruhr occupation.[4] This postwar-crisis "general line" persisted through the Fourth Congress of June–July 1924. The Fifth Plenum of the ECCI in March–April 1925 assimilated the full effect of the failures of Communist-led uprisings in Germany, Bulgaria (and Estonia), the end of German inflation, and the adoption of the Dawes Plan. There, the Comintern "general line" took on a much more "pessimistic" tone. The phrase "partial stabilization of capitalism" came into usage, thereby acknowledging that the Europe of Versailles had made an undeniable recovery from the postwar crisis. The Sixth ECCI Plenum in February–March 1926 introduced the notion that this "international capitalist stabilization" was "temporary" and "precarious," a line that persisted essentially unchanged at the Seventh ECCI Plenum of November–December 1926 at which Nikolai Bukharin and Josef Stalin assumed leadership of the organization. However, no reference to "international capitalist stabilization" was made in the resolution on "The Tasks of the Communist International in the Struggle Against War and the Danger of War" adopted by the Eighth ECCI Plenum six months later in May 1927. That resolution stated, rather, that the "relative equilibrium" which had existed to that time had given way to an international situation in which war

---

4 Karl Radek, *Der Kampf der Kommunistischen Internationale gegen Versailles und gegen die Offensive des Kapitals* (Hamburg, 1923).

could break out at any time, and one in which "open military conflict" had already begun in China.[5]

Lenin was the first Bolshevik to depart from the reassuring reassertions of the 1921–1924 "general line." In what were his final writings – five short articles composed in January–February 1923, between his first and second strokes, and a body of work referred to as his "Political Testament"[6] – he turned his attention to the future of global international relations. In the last of those articles, "Better Fewer, but Better," he divided the world into two groups of countries, the "haves" and "have nots" of the postwar settlement.[7] One group was composed of the prosperous nations that had emerged victorious from the World War. The other included the colonial and semi-colonial countries, revolutionary Russia, and those European nations that had succeeded the empires defeated in the World War. The nations of Group I held the advantage, not only militarily but economically, Lenin thought. Both extending and modifying the analysis put forth in his 1916 writings, he maintained that the imperialist countries that had emerged victorious from the war were able to dominate their colonies militarily, to exploit them economically, to utilize the profits to compensate their metropolitan proletariat, and to delay revolution within industrialized capitalist society.[8] Among the nations of Group II, on the other hand, were Russia, which was in economic ruin and without large-scale industry, and Germany, which was at the mercy of the victorious powers. For these reasons, Lenin regarded the immediate prospects for successful international proletarian revolution with extreme caution and prudence – even pessimism.

In this, his final prognostication of the effects of international politics on international revolution, Lenin did not construct "world revolution" as the inevitable consequence of the postwar crisis, as set out in the Comintern "general line." Nor did he attempt to define exactly the process leading to it. By 1923 the next world crisis had become for him a future eventuality rather than a product of present circumstances. His supposition was that it would take the form of a "military conflict between the counterrevolutionary imperialist West and the revolutionary and nationalist East." The outcome of this East–West conflict was beyond doubt, he thought. Group II

5 Alan Adler, ed., *Theses, Resolutions, and Manifestos of the First Four Congresses of the Third International* (London, 1980), 184–203, 274–99, 383–8; see also Kermit E. McKenzie, *Comintern and World Revolution, 1928–1943: The Shaping of Doctrine* (London, 1964), 51–2.
6 See Moshe Lewin, *Lenin's Last Struggle* (New York, 1968).
7 V. I. Lenin, "Better Fewer, but Better," *Collected Works* (hereafter *CW*), 45 vols. (Moscow, 1960–70), 33:487–502.
8 Lenin, "Imperialism, the Highest Stage of Capitalism," *CW*, 22:185–304, and "The Socialist Revolution and the Rights of Nations to Self Determination," *CW*, 22:143–56.

would prevail because it was united against imperialism, while the advanced industrial nations were incapable of harmonizing their international economic relations because of the contradictions inherent in imperialism. Moreover, the countries of Asia, which Lenin called "the peoples of the East," were becoming radicalized through increasing involvement with the imperialist system. Their population added to that of the Soviet Union resulted in a geopolitical entity that Lenin referred to as "Russia, India, China, etc." Because that entity comprised the vast majority of the world's demographic resources, its revolutionary success was ensured, he believed. And within Group II the world revolutionary role of Russia was defensive, he asserted. It was that of *proderzhatsiia* or "holding out," of "prevent[ing] the West European counterrevolutionary states from crushing us," until the great battle between East and West took place.[9] Thus, as it became evident to him that the 1917 breakthrough in Russia had exhausted the revolutionary potential of the World War, Lenin came to a conception of international relations that differed significantly from his earlier formulations. The completion of what would come to be termed "the world revolutionary process," he now believed, would involve the maturation of the peoples of Asia into a revolutionary force and culminate, not in the second interimperialist war forecast in Comintern theses, but in an East–West struggle, an armed conflict between the forces of European imperialism and those of Asian revolution.

In terms of actual foreign relations, the Bolsheviks approached the global international system of the post–Versailles era with foreign policies based on not one but two fundamental doctrines. One stated that the revolution begun in Russia could be continued by organizing and promoting a coordinated international Communist movement modeled on the Bolshevik example and aligned with mass-based, noninsurrectionary proletarian organizations in Europe and with anti–imperialist, nationalist movements in Asia. The other doctrine, equally fundamental, stated that the survival of Soviet Socialist Republics in the lands of the former Russian Empire and the consolidation of the revolution there depended on protecting those states against further intervention by the capitalist powers – both military and economic – and on creating in Russia a national economy out of the devastation of warfare and famine. To achieve that security and reconstruction, the leadership of Soviet Russia sought to obtain the technology of the advanced industrial countries, to construct zones of protection on the frontiers of the USSR made up of independent states having friendly relations with Moscow, and to prevent the

9 Lenin, "Better Fewer, but Better," *CW,* 33:500–502.

formation of coalitions of capitalist powers hostile to Soviet Russia. To these ends, those who made the October Revolution formed conventional commercial and diplomatic relations with the governments of the capitalists of Europe and of the authoritarian modernizers of Asia, some of which they continued to attempt to subvert, and none of which were at all sympathetic to the international Communist movement.[10]

Neither doctrine could be renounced. No Bolshevik believed – even after the doctrine of "socialism in one country" had come to prevail among some of them in 1924–6 – that the regime could survive what they termed "hostile capitalist encirclement," and neither diplomacy nor revolution could be dispensed with as a means of overcoming it. The USSR would find durable security through a "world revolution," which would bring forth socialist republics in Europe and anticolonial nationalist states in Asia. The diplomacy of "peaceful coexistence" afforded the USSR security and trade until then. Both consolidation of the revolution in Russia and support for revolutionary movements in Europe and Asia became the essentials of "the anti-imperialist struggle," and in the 1920s that struggle formed the basis of the regime's legitimacy. Consequently, while the Foreign Commissariat announced that socialism and capitalism could exist side by side to their mutual benefit, Comintern manifestos proclaimed the violent demise of capitalism and the inevitability of proletarian revolution in Europe.

The foreign policies of the war's victors were the product of a double doctrine as well. In London, Paris, and Washington, doctrines of détente and intransigence coexisted and alternated. Those who regarded the Russian market as essential to the recovery of the world economy, who wanted to do business with the Bolsheviks, and who were ready to grant the Soviet government de jure recognition contended with ideological "die-hards" who opposed any measures that might give legitimacy and stability to a regime that murdered monarchs, renounced debts, and spread sedition.[11]

---

10 This particular formulation of the duality of Soviet foreign relations is from Jon Jacobson, *When the Soviet Union Entered World Politics* (Berkeley, Calif., 1994), 274–5. George F. Kennan, *Russia and the West Under Lenin and Stalin* (Boston, 1961), is usually credited with the first careful analysis of the dual policy. For a discussion of the security imperatives of Soviet foreign relations between the wars, see Teddy J. Uldricks, "Russia and Europe: Diplomacy, Revolution, and Economic Development in the 1920s," *International History Review* 1 (1979): 55–83; see also Teddy J. Uldricks, "Soviet Security Policy in the 1930s," in Gabriel Gorodetsky, ed., *Soviet Foreign Policy, 1917–1991: A Retrospective* (London, 1994), 65–74. The drive for trade and credits is examined in Michael Jabara Carley, "Five Kopecks for Five Kopecks: Franco-Soviet Trade Negotiations, 1928–1939," *Cahiers du Monde russe et soviétique* 33 (1992): 23–58; Christine A. White, *British and American Commercial Relations with Soviet Russia, 1918–1924* (Chapel Hill, N.C., 1992); and Andrew J. Williams, *Trading with the Bolsheviks: The Politics of East–West Trade, 1920–1939* (Manchester, 1992).

11 For a discussion of persistent anti-Bolshevism in London and Paris during the interwar years, see Michael J. Carley, "Down a Blind-Alley: Anglo–Franco–Soviet Relations, 1920–39," *Canadian Journal of History* 29 (1994): 147–72; and Michael J. Carley, "End of the 'Low, Dishonest Decade': Failure of the Anglo–Franco–Soviet Alliance in 1939," *Europe-Asia Studies* 45 (1993): 303–41.

This duality would continue to be a feature of the foreign policies of the capitalist powers toward the USSR for as long as there was a Soviet Union. In the immediate post-Versailles period, it combined with Russia's dislocation within the Versailles world order and the Bolsheviks' own "dual policy" of "world revolution" and "peaceful coexistence" to produce a chronic instability in the relations between Russia and the West and lead the USSR to become virtually isolated within the postwar order.

THE CHALLENGES OF THE POST-VERSAILLES DECADE

Soviet Russia's unstable and isolated world position was evident in the three international challenges that confronted the Bolsheviks during the period from the Paris peace conference in 1919 to what has been called "the great turn" toward Stalinism ten years later. The first emerged in 1919–1921 when, contrary to expectations, successful proletarian revolutions in central and western Europe did not follow forthwith from the October Revolution in Russia.[12] Soviet Russia and the other socialist republics in the former czarist empire remained the first and only socialist states in a world order dominated by capitalist powers whose policies toward the USSR ranged from strict nonrecognition and some willingness to deal with the USSR, but only on terms that undermined the results of the revolution there, to a reluctant toleration of the new regime. Therefore it was only slowly and unevenly that those powers established normal relations with Soviet Russia. Not until 1929, when Great Britain renewed diplomatic relations with the USSR after a two-year break, and exchanged representatives at the ambassadorial level for the first time, did the Soviet Union have functioning diplomatic relations with all the powers present at the peace conference. Belgium and the United States remained the exceptions, establishing relations in the 1930s.

The second challenge came in 1924–6 when the international relations of Europe and America were stabilized through a series of arrangements in which the USSR did not participate. The most significant of them were the Dawes Plan, the treaties of Locarno, and the incorporation of Germany into the League of Nations.[13] These agreements enabled the governments of England and France to reconcile their most outstanding differences over how

---

12 On Anglo–Soviet tensions, see Stephen White, *Britain and the Bolshevik Revolution: A Study in the Politics of Diplomacy, 1920–1294* (London, 1979); and Gabriel Gorodetsky, *The Precarious Truce: Anglo–Soviet Relations, 1924–1927* (Cambridge, 1977).
13 Stephen A. Schuker, *The End of French Predominance in Europe: The Financial Crisis of 1924 and the Adoption of the Dawes Plan* (Chapel Hill, N.C., 1976); Jon Jacobson, *Locarno Diplomacy: Germany and the West, 1924–1929* (Princeton, N.J., 1972); Christoph M. Kimmich, *Germany and the League of Nations* (Chicago, 1976).

to implement the treaty of Versailles. Germany managed a rapprochement with the war's victors. The United States underwrote western European arrangements with advances of capital. In contrast, the USSR had established relatively well–defined diplomatic and commercial relations with only one of the major Versailles signatories, Germany. The evolution of the Dawes/ Locarno/Geneva stabilization not only dramatically underscored Soviet isolation from the Versailles world order, but it also went directly against the very premise underlying the Soviet approach to foreign relations since the October 1917 Revolution – namely, that conflicts among the imperialist powers could be counted on to keep Soviet Russia safe from what were presumed to be the numerous and various diplomatic, economic, and military dangers to be feared from a united coalition of capitalist powers.

The third challenge became evident by 1926. By that time, the economies of the industrialized nations of Europe had recovered from the devastation of the war and from the dislocations of the postwar inflation. Industrial production in the United States had expanded well beyond prewar levels through the extensive introduction of new technologies. Whereas both Europe and America had surpassed prewar production levels, however, Russian industrial production had by the same date barely recovered to the level of 1913.[14] The policy questions inherent in these three challenges were unmistakable. How could a revolutionary socialist country be safe in a world dominated by major capitalist states that were not being transformed by proletarian revolution, were becoming relatively and absolutely more prosperous and powerful, were being integrated into a more stable world order, and, with the exception of Germany, were not concluding with the USSR the political and economic agreements deemed vital to both its security and its economic development?

THE IMPASSES OF THE "DUAL POLICY" AND THE PROSPECTS FOR A RUSSIAN PEACE SETTLEMENT

Soviet Russia's two-pronged approach to the challenges of isolation and instability created persistent foreign relations problems during the post-Versailles decade. On the one hand, how were commercial and diplomatic relations with the Versailles powers, and with the powers of the Western Entente in particular, to be initiated and conducted without jeopardizing the precepts on which the international Communist movement was based? After all, to the parties of the Comintern, recognizing and trading with the

---

14 Robert W. Davies, *The Soviet Economy in Turmoil, 1929–1930* (Cambridge, Mass., 1989), 37–42.

governments of the capitalist powers could be considered collaboration with the enemy, and relations with the enforcers of Versailles in particular could be regarded as an expression of doubt about the notion that the crisis of capitalism would emerge directly out of the postwar international situation produced by Versailles. On the other hand, how could Comintern connections to revolutionary movements abroad be kept from being held hostage to favorable diplomatic relations with the capitalist powers – particularly as governments signing recognition and trade treaties with Moscow in the postwar period required that the Soviet government pledge not to promote revolutionary activities in their countries and their colonies?

To be sure, in considering the problem of making Soviet Russia secure while continuing the revolution on an international scale, Lenin did articulate a concept of foreign relations in which the two projects operated dialectically.[15] In the conduct of actual foreign relations, however, the dialectic worked clumsily. Internationalizing the October Revolution in Asia and Europe threatened capitalist stabilization internally and internationally while the search for trade and loan agreements presupposed a stable and prosperous order of capitalist states ready to transfer technology and advance credits. The ideological opposition in which their commitment to global revolution placed the Bolsheviks posed an immediate and formidable obstacle to the efforts of Soviet diplomacy to establish political and economic relations with the states of Europe and America. And efforts to sharpen social conflict in Europe and nationalist conflict in Asia, and thereby to promote the global revolution on which the security of socialist revolution was presumed ultimately to depend, directly increased the isolation and insecurity of the Soviet state. In particular, the financial aid dispatched to the general strike in England and the ideological encouragement, the political advice, and the military assistance given to the Nationalist Revolution in China in 1923–1927 were rendered at the expense of stable diplomatic and commercial relations with Great Britain, the major foreign power in China, and the state from which most of the other governments of the world had taken their lead in relations with the Soviet Union up to that time. And it provoked Soviet Russia's most severe foreign relations emergency during the twenty-year period between the end of the civil war in 1921 and the German invasion in 1941 – the war scare of 1927. Thus, normalizing relations with European capitalists and Asian nationalists while internationalizing and institutionalizing the October Revolution seriously complicated the efforts of the Soviet party and state elite to cope with the Versailles world order. No

15 Jacobson, *When the Soviet Union Entered World Politics*, 48–9.

sure way was found, therefore, both to participate in and to overthrow capitalist international relations.

It was with regard to the Germany of Versailles that Bolshevik attempts to increase the level of social conflict undermined long-term Soviet security most significantly. The strategy of revolution in Europe articulated in Comintern theses and resolutions during the early 1920s was designed both to sharpen the contradictions among the imperialist states by supporting Germany in opposition to the war's victors and to increase class antagonisms by encouraging the German proletariat in revolutionary opposition to the bourgeoisie of both Germany and western Europe. In both instances Comintern rhetoric was deployed against Versailles. It was represented as the instrument by which the working class of Germany was exploited through reparations and the entire German people oppressed by the reparations-collecting Entente powers. However, this attack on Versailles could not but encourage nationalist and revanchist forces in Germany, and thereby undermine the peace settlement, diminish the prospects for international stability in Europe, and eventually undo what elements of a security system Soviet diplomats attempted to construct during the years 1926–35. At the same time, Comintern strategists failed to recognize and to grasp the opportunity for strategic, as opposed to tactical, "united front" collaboration with the forces of social democracy in Europe against the threat posed by fascism. Instead, from 1924 to 1934, Comintern spokesmen from Radek, Trotsky, and Zinoviev to Stalin and Bukharin associated the two forces within the doctrine of "social-fascism."[16] The result again was to undermine those forces most favorable to the durable peaceful stability in Europe essential both to Soviet national security and to the construction of socialism in Russia.

Thus, while neither the drive for trade and security nor the revolutionary project of early Soviet foreign relations could be renounced, the two could not be integrated into a coherent grand strategy either. Nor, despite

16 Zinoviev and Stalin first associated social democracy and fascism in January 1924 in the reaction against the Communist-Socialist "united front from above" that took place in the wake of the abortive Communist revolution in Germany the previous November. Stalin stated then that "there had occurred a major shift of the petty bourgeois social-democratic forces to the side of the counterrevolution, into the fascist camp." From this he concluded that the best tactic for the Comintern to adopt was "not a coalition with social democracy but lethal battle against it, as the pillar of fascisized power" (quoted by Fridrikh I. Firsov in "Nekotorye voprosy istorii kominterna," _Novaia i noveishaia istoriia_ 2 [1989]: 89). At the Fifth Comintern Congress in June–July, the leadership of the Russian Communist Party led a chorus of denunciation of Social Democracy that would last for years. Zinoviev: "The Fascists are the right hand and the Social Democrats are the left hand of the bourgeoisie." Stalin: "Social Democracy is objectively _the moderate wing of Fascism_" (both quoted in Claudin, _Communist Movement_, 152–3). The exact term _social-fascism_ was first used in April 1929 in an editorial in _Kommunisticheskii Internatsional;_ see Firsov in "Nekotorye voprosy istorii Kominterna," 89.

the repeated efforts of Georgii Chicherin (people's commissar for foreign affairs, 1918–30), were the revolutionary mode and the diplomatic mode of Soviet foreign relations effectively separated, either institutionally or rhetorically. From the initial effort of the Foreign Commissariat (NKID) at détente with Europe and America in 1921 until the eve of his retirement in 1930, Chicherin petitioned the Politburo to disjoin the two modes and to separate the activities, the personnel, the instruments, and the policies of Comintern from those of the Soviet government. Lenin supported him, insisting in 1921 that the Politburo adopt an official ban on foreign policy statements by party leaders without Chicherin's prior consent, and Lenin himself ceased to lump together the policies of the government and those of the Comintern in his public speeches. Moreover, he directed Soviet diplomatic representatives not to engage in propaganda and agitation: "We have the Comintern for such purposes," he stated.[17] Trotsky openly derided these principles on several occasions, especially at the Fourth Comintern Congress in 1922, however, and, as it was, Politburo members sat on the Executive Committee of the Comintern (ECCI); leading diplomats had Comintern connections; embassies abroad housed Comintern emissaries throughout the 1920s. The credibility of the campaign for "peaceful coexistence" conducted by the NKID in London, Paris, and Rome was accordingly undermined.

But it was the public pronouncements of Comintern leaders that troubled Soviet diplomacy most of all. They not only affected diplomatic relations with the war's victorious powers, but also with the defeated nations NKID regarded as the best candidates for resistance to possible anti-Soviet coalitions. The foreign relations conducted by the NKID during the period of Georgii Chicherin's effective leadership as commissar for foreign affairs (1918–28) were based on favorable relations with Weimar Germany and Kemalist Turkey. These successor states to the defeated Central Powers were the anchors of his foreign policy in Europe and Asia, respectively, and promoting favorable relations with them was the major achievement of his career. He was therefore particularly sensitive to damage caused by the Communist International to diplomatic relations with either government. Following a series of statements made in late 1926 and early 1927 by Bukharin, at that time leader of the Comintern, Chichérin addressed a letter to Bukharin directly: "Would you please stop equating Chiang Kai-shek with Kemalism. This is absolutely ridiculous and spoils our relationship

---

17 Vladlen G. Sirotkin, "Ot grazhdanskoi voiny k grazhdanskomu miru," in Iu. N. Afanasèva, ed., *Inogo ne dano* (Moscow, 1988), 384.

Jon Jacobson

with Turkey. Isn't spoiling our relationship with Germany enough for you?
. . . Now you are definitely spoiling our relations with Turkey!"[18]

Given the strongly contradictory tendencies within the dual policies of
both the USSR and the powers of what was coming to be called "the capitalist camp," what prospects were there for a comprehensive post-Versailles
East–West settlement? Hypothetically, one might have been reached through
either of two routes. One route was through the potential inherent within
the preparations made for the Genoa Conference in 1921–2 for a multilateral East–West settlement and a general treaty of peace between Russia, the
Entente powers, and Germany.[19] That route was blocked by the complexity
of the issues involved, disagreement on all sides over what debts of the Russian past were to be paid, and reciprocal ideological antagonism. The other
route was through complete bilateral settlements on the model of the treaties
of Rapallo and Berlin with Germany.[20] The features intrinsic to the Rapallo
model included full diplomatic recognition followed by a treaty of neutrality, mutual cancellation of pre-1918 debts and reparations, a commercial
agreement and medium-term credits, and tacit willingness to forgo punishing the Soviet government for Communist insurrections. In the decade following Versailles, relations on this basis remained *special* to Weimar Germany
and Soviet Russia. No corresponding complete bilateral settlements were
made with London and Paris – despite the fact that the USSR was recognized diplomatically as the successor to the regime of the czars by most of
the nations of Europe, Asia, and Latin America during the years 1924-6.[21]
While London and Paris recognized the Soviet regime at this time, subse-

18 Quoted in S. Iu. Vygodskii, *Vneshniaia politika SSSR, 1924–1929* (Moscow, 1963), 292. For other
  NKID complaints about the Comintern, see Carley "Blind Alley," 156.
19 On Genoa, see Carole Fink, *The Genoa Conference: European Diplomacy, 1921–1922* (Chapel Hill,
  N.C., 1984); and Stephen White, *The Origins of Détente: The Genoa Conference and Soviet Western
  Relations, 1921–1922* (Cambridge, 1985).
20 A significant portion of E. H. Carr's *A History of the Soviet Union* for this period is devoted to
  Soviet–German relations: *The Interregnum, 1923–1924* (New York, 1954), chaps. 5, 7, 9; and E. H.
  Carr, *Socialism in One Country, 1924–1926* (New York, 1958–64), 3:46–62. Martin Walsdorff, *West-
  orientierung und Ostpolitik: Stresemanns Russlandpolitik in der Locarno Ära* (Bremen, 1971), 29–42,
  broke through toward a fuller understanding of Soviet policy. Gunter Rosenfeld's *Sowjetrussland und
  Deutschland, 1917–1922* and *Sowjetunion und Deutschland, 1922–1933* (both Cologne, 1984) are
  based on archival sources in the former Soviet Union and the former German Democratic Republic and on printed sources published in German, Russian, and English. Although the work utilizes
  "bourgeois" as well as "socialist" scholarship, it sustains a pervasive Marxist-Leninist interpretation.
  The Soviet work in the field is A. A. Akhtamsian, *Rapallskaia politika: sov. ger. diplomat. otnosheniia
  v 1922–1932 gg* (Moscow, 1974). The author's glasnost publications based on unpublished archival
  sources are significant contributions to understanding Soviet intentions: "Sovetsko-germanskie eko-
  nomicheskie otnosheniia v 1922–1932 gg," *Novaia i noveishaia istoriia*, no. 4 (1988): 42–56 and
  "Voennoe sotrudnichestvo SSSR i Germanii v 1920–1933 gg," *Novaia i noveishaia istoriia* (1990:5):
  3–24.
21 Carr, *Interregnum*, 243–53.

quent negotiations with England and France never got beyond the no–debt-payment/no–loan impasse that had fatally undermined the Genoa Conference.[22] Thus neither the Genoa model nor the Rapallo model became the basis for a comprehensive postwar East-West settlement. Indeed, despite the flood of de jure recognitions, the USSR remained in relative diplomatic isolation during the 1920s. As the victors and the defeated of the Versailles order resolved their outstanding postwar conflicts and regularized their relations with the United States, the governments of Great Britain, France, and Germany suspended postrecognition negotiations with the Soviet Union or kept them on a strictly tentative basis until after the Locarno treaties were signed.[23] And when Germany and the Allied Powers assembled at The Hague in 1929–1930 to arrange what was called at the time "the final liquidation of the war," the USSR was not invited.

"The international stabilization of capitalism" was the phrase used in reports on the international situation addressed to congresses of the Comintern and of the Soviet Communist Party to denote the Bolshevik consensus view of the international order of 1924–6 – an order in which economic and political stability was restored to bourgeois Europe with American capital and at the cost of the economic and political subordination of Great Britain and the continent to the United States and an order from which the USSR was excluded. Agreement among the leadership of the party that capitalism had stabilized on an international level influenced strongly the development of the Soviet experiment. It was as the relations among the leading powers that had been present at the Paris peace conference were regulated, without Soviet participation, that the crucial debates within the party leadership on the construction of industrial socialism in Russia took place. Dawes, Locarno, and Geneva constituted the international situation in which a Central Committee majority formed around Stalin and Bukharin and asserted officially that the achievement of socialist industrialization in Russia did not depend on either the proletariat or the capitalists of Europe – although the assistance of neither was conclusively renounced.

---

22 On the bilateral negotiations in London and Paris, see Francis Conte, *Un Révolutionnaire-diplomate: Christian Rakovski: L'Union soviétique et l'Europe (1922–1941)* (Paris, 1978); Stuart R. Schram, "Christian Rakovskij et le premier rapprochement franco–soviétique," *Cahiers du Monde Russe et Soviétique* 1 (1960): 205–37, 584–626 (two parts); Carley, "Five Kopeks," in Gorodetsky, *Precarious Truce*, 13–35.
23 Jacobson, *When the Soviet Union Entered World Politics*, 152–75.

The adoption of this doctrine of development, termed "socialism in one country," is the best-known feature of the crucial period of Soviet history that began in late 1924 and culminated in late 1926.[24] What is less well known is that "socialism in one country" was not a declaration of independence from Europe, either economically or politically. Instead, in one of the heretofore least understood developments in the history of early Soviet foreign relations, the expectation of quick breakthroughs to comprehensive settlements, either on the multilateral Genoa model or on the bilateral Rapallo model, was abandoned in favor of a search for piecemeal arrangements, including foreign trade agreements designed to establish, improve, or restore not only economic but also political relations with the major capitalist powers, bilateral nonaggression pacts with states adjacent to the USSR in Europe and Asia,[25] exploratory participation in instruments of multilateral international cooperation such as the Disarmament Conference, and a downgrading of the Rapallo "special relationship" with Germany in favor of treating evenhandedly the major capitalist powers – Great Britain, France, the United States, and Germany. Current evidence suggests that in 1926 Soviet foreign relations were reevaluated and reformulated for the first time since the introduction of the New Economic Policy (NEP) in 1921 and the consolidation of a foreign relations consensus among the Lenin-led party leadership at that time.

The assumptions, the doctrine, and the concept of foreign relations on which this reformulation was based can be briefly summarized here.[26] (1) As was the strategy of the industrialization drive, also adopted by the party leadership in 1926, foreign relations were now premised on the notion that proletarian rule in the USSR had achieved internal stability and that socialism could and would evolve out of the conditions of NEP in a gradual and relatively gradual manner. Soviet relations with the capitalist powers would improve in the same evolutionary and incremental way. In diplomatic circles, Stalin's emergence as leader of the party was taken to be evidence of this stability and pragmatism. He was seen as cautious and moderate,

24 Stephen F. Cohen, *Bukharin and the Bolshevik Revolution: A Political Biography, 1888–1938* (New York, 1975), 147–8, 162, 186, 188; Richard B. Day, *Leon Trotsky and the Politics of Economic Isolation* (Cambridge, 1973), 3–16, 98–101; Robert Tucker, *Stalin as Revolutionary, 1879–1929: A Study in History and Personality* (New York, 1973), 377–94.

25 Rolf Ahmann, "'Localization of Conflicts' or 'Indivisibility of Peace': The German and the Soviet Approaches Towards Collective Security and East-Central Europe, 1925–1939," in R. Ahmann, Adolf M. Birke, and Michael Howard, eds., *The Quest for Stability: Problems of West European Security, 1918–1957* (New York, 1993), 209.

26 For a fuller discussion, see Jacobson, *When the Soviet Union Entered World Politics,* 197–205.

whereas Zinoviev and Trotsky, against whom Stalin and Bukharin contended, were regarded as ideological and volatile. (2) Foreign policy was based on a doctrine of international stabilization emphasizing that the world order was currently characterized by "a prolonged period of respite" from imperialist warfare during which a restabilized system of capitalist states could and would continue to coexist with stabilized "proletarian power" in the USSR for an indefinite period of time. (3) The reformulation of policy was accompanied by the elements of a "debate," or at least differences of opinion, within both Narkomindel and Comintern regarding the most fundamental of foreign relations doctrines. Maksim Litvinov (deputy people's commissar for foreign affairs, 1921–30), on the one hand, and Bukharin, on the other, openly challenged the concept put forth by Lenin five years earlier, namely, that Soviet security depended on the antagonisms within the Versailles order and on utilizing the divisions among the capitalist powers to align the USSR with Germany against Great Britain and France. They each put forth elements of a "peace is indivisible" foreign relations doctrine, including the notions that (a) Germany was an imperialist power just as were Great Britain and France; (b) Germany was, moreover, not the victim of an oppressive Versailles order but rather a revisionist and revanchist power, the country most likely to bring on a second twentieth-century general European war; and (c) a second such war would prove even more destructive than the first, bringing an unacceptable level of damage to the USSR as well as to Europe, and detrimental to the future of socialism as well as that of capitalism.[27] The implications of this doctrine were significant. The national security of the USSR, and the future of socialism, depended on preventing a second imperialist war, and to that end abandoning the Leninist strategy of exploiting the antagonisms among the imperialist powers and, insofar as it encouraged those antagonisms, the Rapallo "special relationship" with Germany as well.

"THE GREAT TURN" AND FOREIGN RELATIONS

A "prolonged period of respite" during which socialism would evolve gradually in Russia while relations with Europe and America improved in an evolutionary and incremental manner was not in the offing, however. A

---

27 Anna di Biagio, "Bukharin's International Alternative," in A. Kemp-Welch, ed., *The Ideas of Nikolai Bukharin* (Oxford, 1992); Hugh D. Phillips, *Between the Revolution and the West: A Political Biography of Maxim M. Litvinov* (Boulder, Colo., 1992).

series of crises beginning with a dramatic war scare in the spring and summer of 1927 and continuing with the grain procurement crisis the following winter profoundly affected the post–Lenin struggle for leadership within
the party and the course of national economic development.[28] By early
1929 these crises resulted in the adoption of the maximum version of the
Five-Year Plan and "the great turn" into rapid industrialization, coerced
agricultural collectivization, preemptive state terror, and the cult of the
leader. The influence of the international situation on the course of this
"leap forward" and the effects of the leap in turn on Soviet policy regarding
the Versailles order and relations with the Versailles powers have not been
well understood and are among the many problems of early Soviet foreign
relations deserving of archival research. At present the crucial developments
seem to have been as follows:

1. The supposition, closely associated with the Sixth Comintern Congress of
    1928 where it was adopted as a thesis, that the temporary stabilization of cap-
    italism was ending and international relations were entering "a new era of wars
    and revolutions" that would bring about capitalism's further demise seems to
    have been first propounded by Georgii Zinoviev at the beginning of the Chi-
    nese Nationalist Revolution in the spring of 1926. However, it was during the
    war scare crisis of 1927 that the Central Committee majority's official foreign
    policy conception was transformed from one centered on an indeterminate
    period of international stability and respite from immediate foreign threat to
    the USSR's security to one proclaiming the approach of a new imperialist war
    and a mounting foreign threat to the USSR.[29] And it was in the immediate
    aftermath of that crisis that alarm over the "foreign threat" was joined to the
    prosecution of internal class enemies in a campaign of preemptive terror against
    foreign engineers and Soviet citizens in what was the regime's most open defi-
    ance to that time of internationally accepted humanitarian and democratic
    norms.[30]

2. It was also as a result of the war scare that Stalin publicly stated elements of the
    view of the international situation he had begun to express secretly beginning
    in early 1925. Rejecting implicitly the tentatively advanced notion of an "indi-
    visible peace," with its hope that a second imperialist war might be avoided, he
    reaffirmed the more strictly Leninist view that the capitalist world order was

28 Michael Reiman, *The Birth of Stalinism: The USSR on the Eve of the "Second Revolution"* (Blooming-
    ton, Ind., 1987).
29 Sheila Fitzpatrick, "The Foreign Threat During the First Five Year Plan," *Soviet Union/Union Sovié-
    tique* 5 (1978): 26–35, finds in "the foreign threat" the beginnings of mass mobilization; L. N.
    Nezhinskii, "Byla li voennaia ugroza SSSR v kontse 20-kh – nachale 30-kh godov?" *Voprosy istorii*,
    no. 6 (1990): 14–30 concludes from an examination of the international situation in the years
    1927–33 that the menace of a war against the Soviet Union did not exist.
30 Kendall Bailes, *Technology and Society Under Lenin and Stalin: Origins of the Soviet Technical Intelligentsia,
    1917–1941* (Princeton, N.J., 1978), 69–121.

incapable of extended stabilization and that the security of the USSR depended on the ability of Soviet diplomacy to utilize the antagonisms among what he now called "imperialist groups of states" and on the modernization and expansion of Soviet armed forces.[31]

3. The drive for socialist industrialization aimed from the beginning for the creation of a military-industrial complex that would manufacture for Soviet armed forces weapons of modern warfare, and the industrialization drive and the armaments program developed hand in hand. Plans for both crystallized in the spring of 1926; both were actually launched at the time of the 1927 war scare.[32] And with the adoption of the maximum version of the First Five-Year Plan, the heavy industrial basis for arms manufacture was given first claim on Soviet national income and natural resources.

4. The autarchical and isolationist tendencies of Soviet foreign relations during the period of "the great turn" were not as strong as was at one time thought. The doctrines of "the foreign threat," "the internal class enemy," and "the new era of wars and revolutions" did not signal an abrupt change in Soviet diplomatic relations with the Versailles powers. Instead, spokesmen for the Foreign Commissariat and the Council of Peoples Commissars continued to issue pronouncements in line with the course adopted in 1926. And the search for foreign trade agreements with the capitalist powers was sustained. The obvious reason was that accelerated industrialization under the Five-Year Plan increased rather than decreased the need for foreign technology and capital. Consequently, the formal announcement of the adoption of the Five-Year Plan did not in itself set the USSR on a course of autonomous economic development any more than had the doctrine of "socialism in one country" a few years earlier. Not until the collapse of international trade in 1932 did Soviet economic planning shift over to the path of autarchy.[33]

5. Most significantly, within ten years of the end of the civil war, what would remain for decades the basic foreign policy orientation and the fundamental doctrines and institutions of Soviet national security had taken rudimentary form. Those policies, doctrines, and institutions were not fully inherent in the prerevolutionary ideology of the Bolsheviks; nor were they established completely as a direct result of the revolution itself. They evolved fully only in the course of the international relations of the post-Versailles decade. Their principal goals were to follow a course of economic development directed at once toward catching up to the advanced capitalist societies and toward emancipating Russia from dependence on them; assign priority to forming a military-industrial complex committed to developing modern weapons technology and

31 Stéphane Courtois, "Le système communiste international et la lutte pour la paix, 1917–1939," *Relations internationales* 53 (1988): 7–10.

32 Jacobson, *When the Soviet Union Entered World Politics,* 206–15, 233–4.

33 Michael R. Dohan, "The Economic Origins of Soviet Autarky, 1927/28–1934," *Slavic Review* 35 (1976): 603–35; Michael R. Dohan, "Foreign Trade and Soviet Investment Strategy for Planned Industrialization, 1928–1938," in Robert W. Davies, ed., *Soviet Investment for Planned Industrialization, 1929–1937: Policy and Practice: Selected Papers from the Second World Congress for Soviet and East European Studies* (Berkeley, Calif., 1984).

to constructing the heavy-industrial base for it above all other social, environmental, and human goals; militarize Soviet society;[34] and develop slogans of "anti-imperialist struggle" to accompany the state's class war doctrine of international relations.

Both the doctrine and the slogans – the latter deployed to give the regime legitimacy, direction, and reassurance – remained continuous elements of Soviet foreign relations until *perestroika*. By the time of "the great turn," the class war doctrine of international relations had reaffirmed Lenin's post–Civil War description of the international system as one in which the imperialist powers were hostile to Soviet Russia, but presented a direct threat mainly if united in agreement regarding how and when to implement that opposition. This doctrine dictated the distinguishing precepts of Soviet foreign relations. On the one hand, no matter whether the country's strategy of economic development was autarchical or integrative, the USSR would be more secure if involved in the international politics of the capitalist world order and preventing anti-Soviet coalitions than it would be in diplomatic isolation. On the other hand, because of the continued hostility ascribed to the capitalist powers, any rapprochement between the two camps stopped at the point of the "peaceful coexistence" standoff, something that placed heavy burdens on any efforts at détente until the late 1980s.

34 Mark von Hagen, *Soldiers in the Proletarian Dictatorship: The Red Army and the Soviet Socialist State, 1917–1930* (Ithaca, N.Y., 1990), 333–9.

19

Versailles and International Diplomacy

WILLIAM R. KEYLOR

Shortly after receiving an invitation from the German Historical Institute to attend the stimulating meeting that later transpired in Berkeley in the spring of 1994, I happened to be lecturing on the Paris Peace Conference in my undergraduate course on the history of international relations. After the class, a student sauntered into my office and put to me a question that coincidentally pertained directly to the subject of the essay for that meeting that I was just beginning to compose in my mind: Had Woodrow Wilson been able to withstand the pressures from what the student called the "vindictive" European statesmen in 1919 to impose what he characterized as a "Carthaginian" peace on defeated Germany, did I not think that the world would have been spared the agony of the Great Depression, the rise of Nazism, World War II, and the Holocaust?

As is my custom, I replied with a question of my own. Where had he learned the term "Carthaginian"? To my surprise he reeled off a thoroughly competent summary of the peace settlement after the Third Punic War. (It turned out that he had taken a survey course in ancient history.) But when I probed his knowledge of the more recent, metaphorical connotation of the word, the conversation took a distinctly more nebulous turn. Had he read Keynes? No. Ray Stannard Baker? Who? In the end it proved impossible to identify the specific source of this evocative adjective that had somehow found its way into the young man's mind. He had simply picked it up somewhere in the general historiographical literature. It somehow seemed to be the natural modifier for the noun "peace" with reference to the Treaty of Versailles.

I decided to explore a bit further. What did he think was "vindictive" about the policies of the European leaders at the Paris Peace Conference, and what did he consider "Carthaginian" about the treaty provisions that they had allegedly been able to bamboozle the naive American president into accepting? His reply contained indistinct allusions to the very topics that I had been pondering, and that in fact were to become the three themes in the discussion that follows. He muttered something about the "old diplomacy" without appearing to understand precisely what the phrase meant, except that it represented an odious practice that should have been, but was not, abandoned in 1919. He mentioned millions of Germans deprived of their nationality, but supplied none of the relevant geographical details. There were also, of course, the ritualistic references to the "astronomical" reparations burden imposed by the victors on the vanquished and the notorious "war-guilt clause" by which this had been justified.

This exchange during office hours was not an isolated incident. On the contrary, it was merely the most recent variation of a running conversation that I have had with my brightest students whenever the subject of the Versailles treaty arose. But its serendipitous recurrence as I prepared my contribution to the forthcoming conference prompted me to focus on a question that had periodically occurred to me as I regularly encountered negative references to the Versailles treaty in general works of history: Whence derives the captious attitude among the educated public, particularly widespread in the English-speaking world, toward the peace settlement of 1919? The answer to such a question would have been obvious in the years immediately after the conference. The profound sense of disillusionment that afflicted so many of those sensitive souls in the American and British peace delegations who elected to write about their experience in Paris virtually foreordained that the early verdict would be a decidedly negative one. As the United States rapidly extricated itself from European entanglements and Great Britain reverted to its prewar policy of focusing on imperial and commercial concerns while promoting a Franco-German balance on the continent, it is scarcely surprising that Anglo-American assessments of the peace conference turned out to be as uncharitable as they did.

What I have found particularly striking, however, is the *persistence* of that critical assessment long after the early texts of historical revisionism had begun to gather dust on library shelves. This extraordinary record of endurance is all the more remarkable in light of the findings of monographic research based on the British and French records of the peace conference that had not been accessible to scholars until the 1960s and 1970s, respectively. Without committing the opposite sin of idealizing the role of the peacemakers or of exaggerating the achievements of the diplomatic settlement that they fashioned in 1919, much of this subsequent historical work has challenged the overwhelmingly critical evaluation of earlier generations. Rejecting the Manichean conception of a virtuous Wilsonism crashing on the shoals of the reactionary, imperialist, militaristic policies of

America's European associates in the Great War, it offers a much subtler, more complex historical analysis. What emerges from this recent multi-archival research is a much more nuanced portrait of statesmen and diplomats striving, with a remarkable degree of flexibility, pragmatism, and moderation, to promote their nation's vital interests as they interpreted them in the face of potent public pressures from electorates inflamed by four years of slaughter on the Western front and sacrifice on the home front. Yet in spite of these scholarly correctives the original indictment has remained firmly set in the public consciousness, retaining its authority even (as in my experience) among today's undergraduates.

It was with this interesting historiographical phenomenon in mind that I undertook the large assignment from the German Historical Institute to assess the Paris Peace Conference and the Versailles Treaty in the context of international diplomacy. In so doing I have chosen to concentrate on what seems to me to be the three radical innovations in statecraft that assured the Paris Peace Conference of 1919 its distinctive niche in the history of international relations. The first was a purely procedural matter, which, though it proved in retrospect to be of entirely ephemeral significance, was hailed at the time by many of President Wilson's most enthusiastic supporters as the key to the new world order that he had gone to Paris to forge. This was the famous principle of "open diplomacy." The other two were substantive contrivances of much greater consequence for the future of Europe and the world: one was the concept of national self-determination, which was to replace the balance of power as the criterion for the postwar redistribution of territory; the other was the redefinition of the traditional concept of a war indemnity as reparation of damage to persons and property. Since the last of these three topics has been treated at considerable length elsewhere in this book by eminent specialists in the field, I will merely adumbrate the subject of reparations in the hope of stimulating further reflection about what is unquestionably the most misunderstood legacy of the Versailles settlement.[1]

It may seem perverse to omit consideration of the League of Nations in a discussion purporting to assess the place of the Versailles treaty in the history of international diplomacy. The reason for doing so is my belief that the significance of the League has been vastly exaggerated by historians of the peace conference. The idea was the brainchild of two eccentric Englishmen, the high church lawyer Walter Phillimore and his political ally, Lord Robert Cecil (who rebelled against the Realpolitik practices of his prime minister father, Lord Salisbury, which he hoped to replace with

---

1 See chapters 14, 15, and 16 in this book.

moral authority). Once Wilson belatedly appropriated it as the centerpiece of his peace program, David Lloyd George and Georges Clemenceau were obliged to pay lip service to the concept for fear of offending the American president from whom they needed to ask so much. But the European leaders never took it seriously (except as a bargaining chip with which to obtain from Wilson the concessions that really mattered to them), nor did their foreign offices or military advisers.[2]

It is no exaggeration to characterize the Paris Peace Conference as a unique episode in the annals of international diplomacy. Whether measured by objective criteria such as the number of nations represented, the size of the participating delegations, the rank of the plenipotentiaries, and the duration of the proceedings, or by more qualitative yardsticks such as the complexity of its agenda and the appalling difficulties with which it had to cope, it is safe to assert that the world had seen no postwar summit conference like it before and has seen nothing like it since.[3] Twenty-seven national delegations, accompanied by hundreds of political advisers, military aides, clerks, servants, and journalists, descended on the French capital in early January 1919 and remained for half a year (save for Wilson's month-long respite from mid-February to mid-March) until the German treaty was signed and sealed at the end of June.[4] The four leaders of the coalition of states that had waged

2 A succinct summary of the origins of the League idea and the Allied prime ministers' skepticism of it appears in Paul Johnson, *Modern Times: The World from the Twenties to the Eighties* (New York, 1983), 30–2.

3 In assessing the complex set of multilateral negotiations for a Middle East peace settlement that U.S. Secretary of State James Baker had orchestrated in 1992, the authors of the authoritative annual summary of world affairs *Strategic Survey* observed (with a considerable degree of hyperbole) that "the Arab–Israeli peace process was now a multi-track, multi-state operation – perhaps the most complex peace effort since Versailles." International Institute for Strategic Studies, *Strategic Survey, 1991–1992* (London, 1992), 94.

4 Among the American participants, Admiral Cary T. Grayson, Wilson's personal physician (who was at his side almost continuously in Paris) has left the most vivid, evocative descriptions of the atmosphere surrounding the peace conference. From her more restricted vantage point, Mrs. Wilson's secretary, Edith Benham Helm, was able to observe and record much of great interest. Ray Stannard Baker's irritating prolixity, together with his anxious striving to burnish the public image of his chief even in his private, handwritten jottings, detracts from his diary's utility. The record of Colonel Edward House's daily attempts to manipulate the statesmen who lined up outside his door at the Hôtel Crillon to seek his assistance in "fixing" this or that problem, dictated each evening to his faithful secretary "Miss Fanny" Denton, has proved invaluable as a documentary record of decision making. But it suffers from the very absence of attentiveness to the behavior of others that permitted the colonel to continue to imagine himself "the governor's" closest confidant long after Wilson had lost all confidence in him. Copious extracts from the Grayson diary during the peace conference appear in Arthur S. Link et al., eds., *The Papers of Woodrow Wilson* (hereafter *PWW*), 69 vols. (Princeton, N.J., 1966–94), vols. 53–61. The complete Helm diary (selections of which are also reproduced in ibid.) is in the Papers of Edith Benham Helm (hereafter EBHP), box 1, Library of Congress, Manuscript Division (hereafter LCMD). The Baker diary is in the Papers of Ray Stannard Baker (hereafter RSBP), reel 4, LCMD. The House diaries for the peace conference are in the Papers of Edward M. House (hereafter EMHP), cartons 15–16, Sterling Library, Yale University, Manuscripts Department (hereafter SLMD).

and won the Great War engaged in face-to-face negotiations of unprecedented length and intensity to fashion a new international order out of the
wreckage of postwar Europe amid an agitated atmosphere of political, social,
and economic crisis, not to speak of an epidemic of contagious diseases that
at one time or another afflicted most of the participants.[5]

In preparing for the conference, European officials who combed their
national archives in search of instructive precedents for protocol and procedure found that the only manifest model for peacemaking on such a grand
scale, the Congress of Vienna, offered few useful guidelines for officially terminating the present state of war.[6] For the aristocratic peacemakers of 1814–
15 had operated on the basis of two firmly held premises that were wholly
unsuited to the political atmosphere that prevailed in the aftermath of "the
war to make the world safe for democracy." The first of these was the assumption that peace treaties could and should be devised by diplomats on the basis
of private deliberation and rational calculation, without reference to the
wishes or requirements of the populations concerned. The second was
the conviction that power – political, economic, and military – determined
the relations between states, and that the future stability of the international
system depended on the restoration of the balance of power that had been
disturbed by the recently defeated aggressor.

It was already well known that these two commonplaces of what had
come to be disdained as the "old diplomacy" were anathema to the American president, whose novel conception of international relations was unveiled to the world in his notable address to a joint session of Congress
on January 8, 1918, which specified in the form of fourteen "points" his

5 "Everybody has the flu or has just had it or is just going to have it," lamented Hugh Gibson, at the
   time an aide to Herbert Hoover in Paris. Gibson to Lou Henry Hoover, Feb. 25, 1919, Pre-Commerce File, box 5, folder "Hoover, Lou Henry," Papers of Herbert Hoover, Herbert Hoover Library,
   West Branch, Iowa (hereafter HHP). For additional evidence of the pervasivness of illness in Paris
   during that dreary winter of 1918–19, see folder "White House Notes. Trip to Paris," Feb. 1, 1919,
   container 7, Irwin H. Hoover papers (MDLC) (hereafter IHHP). It is well known that the influenza
   epidemic of 1918–19 claimed more victims than the war itself. But apart from the voluminous literature on Wilson's medical problems and their effect on his behavior (beginning with Edwin A. Weinstein, *Woodrow Wilson: A Medical and Psychological Biography* [Princeton, N.J., 1981]), little scholarly
   attention has been devoted to the effects of illness on other participants in the conference.
6 The British historian Charles K. Webster had prepared a handbook summarizing the diplomatic procedures followed at the Congress of Vienna for the Foreign Office; the French commentator André
   Géraud ("Pertinax") publicly reminded the French delegation of the Metternichian precedents; the
   Quai d'Orsay had already presented the State Department with the results of its exhaustive study of
   the Vienna procedures. See Charles K. Webster, *The Congress of Vienna, 1814–15* (London, 1919);
   Pertinax, "L'Exemple du Congrès de Vienne," *Echo de Paris*, Dec. 18, 1918; Jusserand to Lansing, Nov.
   29, 1918, with enclosure, *PWW*, 53:292–8. See also the unsigned "Note sur le Congrès de la Paix,"
   Nov. 19, 1919, which reviewed the precedents of the congresses of Vienna (1814–15), Paris (1856),
   and Berlin (1878), in carton 6N72, Fonds Clemenceau, Service Historique de l'Armée de Terre, Vincennes (hereafter SHA).

country's principal war aims. The memorable phraseology of the first point, "Open covenants of peace, openly arrived at," had a precise referent: the notorious series of "secret treaties" contracted among the European allies before the American intervention, whose texts the Russian Bolsheviks had recently discovered in the czarist archives and published in an effort to expose the cynical annexationist ambitions of the capitalist imperialist powers.[7] But the singular nature of the Wilsonian slogan, with its melodramatic biblical imagery that was so typical of his rhetorical style, was interpreted by Wilson's admirers everywhere in a much broader sense: In their eyes it became a solemn admonition that the American president would not tolerate, at the peace conference after the present war, the familiar type of clandestine, high-level horse-trading that had characterized European diplomacy in the past. It has been widely remarked in Wilson's defense that he did not mean to imply that diplomacy ought to be conducted in public session with the entire world as spectators, but rather that the *results* of such negotiations must be given the broadest possible publicity. But this interpretation ignores the phrase "openly arrived at" that Wilson inserted in the draft of the speech on the fourteen points just prior to its delivery.[8] In any case, that was the interpretation that public opinion and the Wilsonian press gave it. Exposed to the bracing blast of public sentiment, the process of peacemaking would reflect the pacific, altruistic will of the people rather than the bellicose, parochial machinations of the statesmen.[9]

Another casualty of Wilson's wartime rhetoric was the traditional presumption of power as the foundation of the international system and the confidence in the balance of power as the most reliable guarantee of that system's stability. In his formulation, this discredited relic of a bygone era would be superseded by the concept of "right" in general, and the right of

7 Though Wilson later denied knowledge of these agreements prior to his arrival in Paris and there is no conclusive evidence that he ever actually read them, it is inconceivable that he was unaware of their contents. British Foreign Secretary Arthur Balfour had sent him copies of the "secret treaties" on May 18, 1917, and they were widely publicized in American newspapers after the Bolshevik government published them. Lincoln Colcord, the liberal correspondent for the *Nation*, recalled "dozens of conversations with Colonel House about the secret treaties" before the Armistice. The *Nation*, Aug. 30, 1919, 272–5, Sept. 13, 1919, 364; see also Walter Lippmann to Ray Stannard Baker, Jan. 2, 1922, Oswald Garrison Villard to Baker, Feb. 28, 1922, container 31, RSBP; Arno Mayer, *Wilson vs. Lenin: Political Origins of the New Diplomacy, 1917–1918* (Cleveland, Ohio, 1964), 330–1.

8 The original draft read "Open covenants of peace, *after which* there shall be no private international understandings of any kind" (italics added for emphasis). See the Jan. 7, 1918, insertion in Wilson's handwriting of "openly arrived at" after the comma on the typed draft of the fourteen points address in *PWW,* 55:511.

9 An unsigned article in the *New Republic* entitled "Censorship and the Peace Conference" warned shortly after the Armistice that "the reactionary and conservative minority in Europe" would strive to "destroy the influence of the popular majorities there which might otherwise give success to the President's policy. . . . [H]e gets more ready sympathy and support from the European peoples than he can sometimes [get] from the governments" (*New Republic,* Nov. 16, 1918, 61–2).

"national self-determination" in particular. Though the meaning of this term remained imprecise, it was widely interpreted by Wilson's European admirers to imply that each nationality group – defined by a common cultural tradition, history, and, above all, language – deserved to constitute its own political unit and to conduct its own affairs without interference from powerful, predatory neighbors.[10]

It is important to note that such an interpretation did not accurately reflect the American president's original design. There was no reference to the concept of self-determination in the Fourteen Points address. Its first public airing came three days later before a hastily arranged joint session of Congress in the context of Wilson's assessment of the Central Powers' reply to his peace terms. There was nothing in this declaration indicating a belief that newly drawn political boundaries could or should coincide precisely with ethnic frontiers.[11] On the contrary, his subsequent negotiations with Vienna reflected an inclination to grant some form of autonomy to its subject nationalities rather than an insistence on shattering the Austro-Hungarian Empire into its constituent ethnic components. Once the disintegration of that multinational empire became a fait accompli at the end of the war, his reluctance to endorse the multitude of petitions from disgruntled ethnic groups that inundated the peace conference revealed his lack of enthusiasm for self-determination based on ethnicity. The essence of Wilson's conception of self-determination was his faith in popular sovereignty, in government through the consent of the governed, without any connotations of ethnicity.[12]

---

10 The abundant theoretical literature on nationalism and ethnicity has recently been enriched by several important studies, among which Liah Greenfeld, *Nationalism: Five Roads to Modernity* (Cambridge, Mass., 1993), and Kamal S. Shehadi, "Ethnic Self-determination and the Breakup of States," *Adelphi Papers* (1994): 283, have proved particularly useful to me in preparing this section.

11 It is worth reproducing the original text to convey the spirit of caution that inspired Wilson's original public utterances on the subject: "This war had its roots in the disregard of small nations and of nationalities which lacked the union and the force to make good their claim to determine their own allegiances and their own forms of public life," the president declared in his message to the German and Austrian governments. He then proceeded to add four additional "principles" to the fourteen "points" already adduced. These four principles held that "peoples and provinces are not to be bartered about from sovereignty to sovereignty as if they were mere chattels and pawns in a game, even the great game, now forever discredited, of the balance of power," and insisted instead that "every territorial settlement involved in this war must be made in the interest and for the benefit of the populations concerned, not as a part of any mere adjustment or compromise of claims amongst rival states." The fourth principle stated that "all well defined national aspirations shall be accorded the utmost satisfaction that can be accorded them without introducing new or perpetuating old elements of discord and antagonism that would be likely in time to break the peace of Europe and consequently the world" ("An Address to a Joint Session of Congress," Feb. 11, 1918, in *PWW,* 46:321–3).

12 I am indebted to Lloyd E. Ambrosius and Betty Miller Unterberger for engaging me in stimulating conversations about the complicated subject of Wilson's theory of self-determination, from which some of these insights were gleaned. Some of Professor Unterberger's observations on the subject were included in her comments on my paper – a greatly abbreviated version of this chapter –

Nevertheless, the very idea of popular sovereignty, when applied to the crazy quilt of heterogeneous populations in postwar Europe, inevitably acquired an ethnic dimension in spite of Wilson's original intent. His ambiguously defined principle of self-determination became the miraculous means of salvation in the eyes of discontented folk all across the continent who were struggling against those whom they regarded as their oppressors (and who not coincidentally spoke a different language and practiced different customs). Secretary of State Robert Lansing had recognized the danger of such misinterpretations of Wilson's wartime rhetoric and grumbled about them in his customary private manner. "When the President talks of 'self-determination,' what unit has he in mind?" he wondered as the preparations for the peace conference proceeded. "Does he mean a race, a territorial area or a community? Without a definite unit which is practical, application of this principle is dangerous to peace and stability."[13] Wilson unwittingly contributed to the type of misinterpretations that disturbed his secretary of state through his ritualistic denunciation of the Congress of Vienna as a repellent precedent for the treatment of claims to self-determination.[14] What had represented for the architects of the Vienna system (and many latter-day Metternichians in the Allied governments) dangerous threats to international stability against which the postwar international order must be insulated – the power of public opinion and the unbridled force of national sentiment – were hailed by "Wilsonians" on both sides of the Atlantic as the essential bases of a just and lasting peace.

Once the American chief executive had decided (against the advice of his closest associates at home and contrary to the wishes of his apprehensive counterparts in Europe) to attend the peace conference in person and to remain in Paris as an active participant in its sessions, his idiosyncratic conception of diplomacy could not be ignored by those charged with the responsibility of devising a new international system after the Great War.[15]

entitled "The Versailles Settlement After Seventy-Five Years: A Retrospective Assessment," which was presented at the conference of the Society for Historians of American Foreign Relations, June 24, 1994, Bentley College.

13 "Certain Phrases of the President Contain the Seeds of Trouble," typewritten copy dated Dec. 20, 1918, in Pre-Commerce File, box 10, folder "Lansing," HHP.

14 "The method the German Chancellor [Hertling] proposes is the method of the Congress of Vienna. We cannot return to that," Wilson declared in response to the German government's polite refusal to apply Wilsonian principles to the negotiations with Russia at Brest-Litovsk. "What we are striving for is a new international order based upon broad and universal principles of right and justice." "An Address to a Joint Session of Congress," Feb. 11, 1918, *PWW,* 46:320.

15 For expressions of opposition to Wilson's participation in the peace conference, see House to Wilson, Nov. 14, 1918, box 121, folder 1214291, EMHP; The Diaries of Robert Lansing, Nov. 12 and 16, 1919, Papers of Robert Lansing (hereafter RLP), LCMD; Clemenceau cable to Lloyd George, Nov. 15, 1918, Fonds Clemenceau, 6N72, folder "Négotiations de Paix," SHA.

Indeed, in light of the two trumps that Wilson held in his hand on the eve of the end of the war, it seemed inevitable that his publicly articulated war aims – which at his behest had been incorporated (with a British and French reservation) in the armistice terms accepted by Germany and America's European associates – would exercise a commanding influence on the forthcoming deliberations.[16]

The first of these advantages was the extraordinary financial leverage over the European victors that he retained in the form of the "stick" represented by Allied indebtedness to the U.S. Treasury as well as the "carrot" represented by the possibility of future U.S. financial assistance for Europe's postwar reconstruction. Wilson fully appreciated the latent diplomatic utility in Paris of those Allied government securities stacked securely in the Treasury vaults in Washington (which, by the terms of the liberty- and victory-loan legislation, were legally payable on demand).[17] Equally advantageous to the American negotiating position at the peace conference was the prospect of future U.S. government credits to finance purchases of the products of American farms and factories that the European countries desperately required for their postwar reconstruction. The option of compelling Allied acceptance of his principal diplomatic goals through an explicit threat to call in the war debt, or abruptly to terminate the flow of credits to the European allies from the unexpended portion of the $10 billion appropriated by Congress, represented – to shift the metaphor from bridge to poker – Wilson's ace in the hole.[18]

But by brandishing this potentially efficacious financial weapon, Wilson would have risked alienating public opinion in the Allied countries, shattering the unity of the victorious wartime coalition, and encouraging German resistance. It was a blunt instrument that proved wholly unsuitable to the task at hand. As it turned out, the United States delegation in Paris refrained from pursuing a strategy that Henry Kissinger would later designate as "linkage": the imposition of financial penalties on foreign powers in retaliation for objectionable policies or the provision of financial favors as a reward for good behavior. Treasury officials had decided before the peace conference opened that they were not prepared to press the Allies to take up the question of converting the demand obligations into long-term bonds

---

16 For Great Britain's preparations for the Armistice, see chapter 2 in this book.
17 On the Allied war debts, see Denise Artaud, *La Question des dettes interalliés et la reconstruction dé l'Europe (1917–1929)*, 2 vols. (Paris, 1978); and Ellen Schrecker, *The Hired Money: The French Debt to the United States, 1917–1929* (New York, 1979).
18 For the official statement of France's reconstruction needs accompanied by the urgent request for postwar credits from the U.S. Treasury, see Tardieu to Leffingwell, Nov. 4, 1918, F30 750, folder 7, Archives du Ministère des Finances, Paris.

in Paris. This reticence was prompted not by heartfelt sympathy for the debtors plight, but rather by the fear – an entirely justifiable one, by the way – that the Europeans would jump at the occasion to press the case for cancellation or attempt to link the inter-Allied debts to the entirely unrelated matter of German reparations.[19] Washington continued to respond promptly and sympathetically to each request for credits from the financially strapped Allies throughout the peace conference, even during periods of the most acrimonious disputes between Wilson and one or another of his colleagues in the Council of Four.[20]

A second trump held by the American president was much less tangible but much more playable: This was the enormous reservoir of popularity that he enjoyed – or was led to believe that he enjoyed – among the populations of the Allied countries. In the latter stages of the war and during the preparations for the peace conference, Wilson's agents in Europe had confidently assured him that public opinion in Great Britain, France, and Italy – in sharp contrast to the ruling elites of those countries – enthusiastically endorsed the project of a moderate peace that he had outlined in his wartime addresses.[21] The rousing reception that he received from the euphoric citizens of Paris, London, and Rome on his whirlwind tour of those Allied capitals in December 1918 furnished dramatic confirmation of his advance men's assurances and emboldened him to exploit this public support to win acceptance of his peace program.[22]

After the official opening of the peace conference on January 18, 1919, however, it rapidly became evident that the soundings of his advisers had been inaccurate and the adulation of the crowds deceptive. As his preliminary proposals encountered the anticipated resistance from the Allied prime ministers, he was dismayed to learn that their recalcitrance stemmed less from personal conviction than from attentiveness to political realities at

19 McAdoo cable to House, Dec. 10, 1918; Rathbone cables to Crosby, Dec. 11 and 17, 1918; Glass cable to Davis, Jan. 14, 1919; container 7, Russell C. Leffingwell papers (hereafter RCLP), LCMD; Ministry of Finance to de Billy, Jan. 17, 1919, Rathbone to de Billy, Mar. 8, 1919, Série Amérique, 1918–29, sous-série Etats-Unis, vol. 226, Archives du Ministère des Affaires Etrangères (hereafter MAE).
20 See the periodic requests from the French and Italian financial representatives for credits and the Treasury Department's approval (without any political conditions) during the winter and spring of 1919 in container 7, RCLP.
21 See the reports from William Buckler in London to House, box 5, folder 9, William Buckler papers, Sterling Library, Yale University. Ray Stannard Baker, after testing public opinion in Italy and France, assured House that the European people would rally to Wilson's cause against "the reactionary and imperialist leaders of all the Allied nations – including our own." Baker to House, Nov. 1, 1919, container 30, RSBP.
22 For evocative eyewitness descriptions of this euphoria, see Irwin H. Hoover, the head White House usher, "White House, Notes, Trip to Paris," container 7, IHHP; Diary of Cary T. Grayson, Dec. 14 and 26, 1918, Jan. 3, 1919, *PWW,* 53:382–3, 508–12, 595–7.

home. Imbued with the progressive's optimistic faith in human nature, Wilson had arrived in Europe fired with determination to mobilize the beneficent power of popular opinion in the Allied countries to bolster his campaign to impose a peace of reconciliation on the narrow-minded defenders of national interest whom he expected to confront in the peace negotiations. What he discovered instead was incontrovertible evidence of European populations far more exigent and vindictive than their elected spokesmen who sparred with him at the conference table. On a number of occasions it became evident that Lloyd George and Clemenceau had assumed what Wilson regarded as uncompromising positions not because of their own vengeful proclivities but because they feared the domestic political consequences of leniency toward the defeated powers.[23]

This state of affairs could not have come as a surprise to such an astute observer of the European political scene as Woodrow Wilson. In the absence of scientific opinion polls, the only reliable barometers of public sentiment at the time were the electoral returns and the legislative votes of confidence to which the heads of parliamentary governments were periodically obliged to submit. The "Khaki" election in Great Britain on December 14, 1918, produced a stunning victory for the governing coalition of Unionists and Lloyd George Liberals, whose campaign rhetoric had bristled with demands for severe measures against Germany.[24] Proponents of conciliatory peace terms similar to those proposed by Wilson, such as former Liberal Prime Minister Herbert Asquith and future Labour Prime Minister Ramsay MacDonald, were prominent victims of the Conservative landslide.[25] A day

---

23 Clemenceau was under intense pressure from a variety of domestic interest groups that demanded financial relief from Germany. See, e.g., the poignant entreaties contained in hundreds of petitions from farmers and shopkeepers in the "devastated regions" of the northeast. Fonds Clemenceau, carton 80, folder "Traité de Paix, Réparations," SHA; and handwritten letters from frantic mayors complaining about the primitive living conditions in their villages, in carton C7769, Chambre des Députés, Commission des Régions Liberées, folder "Sous-Commission des Finances," Archives Nationales. Although spared the ire of refugees returning to ruined towns, Lloyd George had to cope with demands from organized business groups such as the Federation of British Industries and the Associated Chambers of Commerce that Germany indemnify Britain for the costs of the war. 23/42, Great Britain, Cabinet Papers, Public Record Office.

24 House had confidently predicted that "the General Election in England will afford us an opportunity to nail down the British Government more securely to the President's program." On learning of the results, the colonel lamented that Lloyd George would be "much less likely to agree with our views." House diary, Nov. 4 and Dec. 28, 1918, box XIV, EMHP.

25 On the "khaki election", see Mayer, *Politics and Diplomacy of Peacemaking,* 133–66; and Robert E. Bunselmeyer, *The Cost of the War, 1914–1919: British Economic War Aims and the Origins of Reparation* (Hamden, Conn., 1975), 121–70. The most vengeful (and memorable) piece of campaign rhetoric ironically emanated from one of the most moderate members of the Lloyd George government, whose conciliatory stand on reparations had antagonized his Cambridge constituency. It was in response to this public outcry that First Lord of the Admiralty Sir Eric Geddes struggled to demonstrate his patriotic credentials with the notorious declaration: "The Germans, if this government is returned, are going to pay every penny; they are going to be squeezed as a lemon is squeezed – until the pips squeak." The other notorious sample of anti-German bombast also came from another mod-

after the British electoral results were announced, French Prime Minister Georges Clemenceau faced a vote of confidence in the Chamber of Deputies. After unabashedly extolling the traditional precept of the balance of power and firmly pledging to protect France's security interests at the peace conference, he easily defeated his "Wilsonian" critics on the Socialist left by the lopsided margin of 386 to 88.[26] Far from endorsing the Wilsonian peace program, the populations of America's two principal European allies had registered – either directly (as in the British case) or indirectly (as in the French) – their firm support for political representatives who had expressed explicit reservations about the axioms of the "new diplomacy" as enunciated by the American head of state.

A similar interpretation may be given to the results of the congressional elections of November 5 in Wilson's own country. Though sectional domestic issues such as the high price of wheat in the Midwest played an important role in the outcome,[27] the Republican electoral victory in this first nationwide test of public sentiment since the U.S. intervention in the war may also have reflected popular support for the insistent demands from Senator Henry Cabot Lodge, former President Theodore Roosevelt, and other political adversaries of Wilson for unconditional surrender at the armistice negotiations then underway and stringent measures against Germany at the forthcoming peace conference.[28] Whatever the true cause of the Democratic debacle, Wilson would arrive in Paris repudiated by his own electorate to face two wily diplomatic adversaries who had just won resounding votes of confidence from theirs.

erate in the coalition, the Labourite George Barnes, whose offhand remark on the hustings that "I am for hanging the Kaiser" contrasted sharply with his consistent advocacy of lenient terms for Germany as a delegate to the peace conference. Bunselmeyer, *The Costs of the War*, 133, 155–6, 173. For evidence of Barnes's moderation, see Barnes to Lloyd George, Apr. 2, May 6, May 15, 1919, F/4/3/9, 14, 15, LGP.

26 *Journal Officiel de la République Française,* Chambre des députés, Dec. 29, 1918, 3732–6.
27 Thomas J. Knock notes that Roosevelt, Lodge, and Republican national chairman Will H. Hays, the three architects of the Republican campaign strategy in the November 1918 election, exploited such parochial issues while concentrating on two nationwide themes: the threat to free enterprise posed by the administration's centralization of power during the war, and the danger that Wilson would pursue a compromise rather than a dictated peace with Germany. Thomas J. Knock, *To End All Wars: Woodrow Wilson and the Quest for a New World Order* (New York, 1992), 168–9.
28 The well-connected Republican lawyer Chandler P. Anderson remarked (a bit too optimistically) to a British friend that "the only effect it [the November 1918 midterm election] would have on the war would be to prevent any peace short of [Germany's] unconditional surrender." Anderson diary, Nov. 6, 1918, reel 2, container 2, Chandler P. Anderson papers, LCMD. House fretted that the American and British elections and the vote in the French Chamber represented "about as bad an augury for the success of progressive principles at the Peace Conference that we could have.... [T]he situation strategically could not be worse." But he realized "how very fortunate it was that we got the American terms written into the German armistice. Without that, I am afraid we would have but little chance of accomplishing the things we have so much at heart." House diary, Dec. 30, 1918, EMHP.

Such inauspicious political signals shook Wilson's confidence in public opinion as a check on Allied belligerence at the beginning of the peace conference. It was possible to explain away these unforeseen manifestations of illiberal sentiment across the Atlantic by ascribing them to the iniquitous influence of the jingoist press in Paris and London.[29] But whatever the source, the consequences were unmistakably ominous for his vision of a just and judicious peace. The pursuit of "open covenants of peace, openly arrived at" would manifestly run the risk of codifying the un-Wilsonian spirit of malevolence toward defeated Germany that gripped the Allied publics in the frenzied political atmosphere of postwar Europe.

Wilson's mounting apprehension about the potentially deleterious effects of public opinion on the peace negotiations prompted him to join his European colleagues in sacrificing the cherished principle of open diplomacy before the negotiations began. The world press became the chief victims, and eventually the harshest critics, of this change of heart. The thankless task of maintaining liaison with the hundreds of American newspaper correspondents who had accompanied Wilson to Paris was assigned to Ray Stannard Baker, the muckraking journalist who had served as the president's advance man in the Allied countries during the war by mobilizing support among liberal and socialist leaders and their constituencies for his patron's peace program.[30] It became the paradoxical duty of this ardent proponent of "open diplomacy" to bear the brunt of the newspaperpersons' howls of rage as the veil of secrecy descended around the deliberations with Wilson's full approval.[31] Representatives of the press were invited to witness the long-winded, tedious palaver of the plenary sessions at the Quai d'Orsay, where all seventy plenipotentiaries of the twenty-seven delegations were periodically herded into the stuffy Salle de l'Horloge to debate and ratify the decisions already reached in absolute secrecy by the Council of Ten.[32] The

29 Most particularly, the Parisian dailies *L'Echo de Paris* and *Le Matin* and the Northcliffe press (especially the *Daily Mail*) in London.
30 House diary, Nov. 5, 1918, EMHP; Ray Stannard Baker, notebook entry, Aug. 14, 1918, reel 4, RSBP.
31 See the protest signed by Herbert Bayard Swope et al., enclosed in Baker to Grayson, Jan. 14, 1919, *PPW*, 54: 59–60. The *Nation* had already denounced the secrecy of the armistice negotiations as a blatant violation of Wilsonian principles, expressing "indignation" that the American public was not informed of the peace terms before they had been communicated to the Germans. The liberal journal worried that such secret methods would result in "accomplished facts" which "no pressure of public opinion can modify." Whereas "the only guarantee of [a just and lasting peace] is open diplomacy," the Allied leaders "hope to turn the Conference of Versailles into another Congress of Vienna." Before the formal opening of the conference, the *Nation* (represented in Paris by the indomitable Oswald Garrison Villard, the probable author of these anonymous observations) lamented that "Even Mr. Wilson can no longer be counted among the supporters of open diplomacy. . . . [T]he web of secrecy has already been spun about the peace conference." *Nation,* Nov. 9, 1918, 544; Nov. 30, 1918, 636; Dec. 7, 1918, 191; and Dec. 28, 1918, 792–3.
32 The Council of Ten comprised the heads of government and foreign ministers of the five "Principal Allied and Associated Powers" – the United States, Great Britain, France, Italy, and Japan.

rule of confidentiality was subsequently extended to the fifty-eight specialized committees that were formed to do much of the important spadework
for the peace treaties.[33]

But the diligence of the thwarted reporters, the public's thirst for information about the impending peace agreement, and the temptation for the
plenipotentiaries to manipulate the media for their own purposes gave rise
to numerous breaches of confidence. The heavily censored Parisian press
became a propaganda vehicle in Clemenceau's increasingly bitter contest
with Wilson on a variety of issues.[34] Lloyd George and his staff did not hesitate to manipulate correspondents of the London dailies to promote the
British position in various controversies. The decision to initiate private
conversations among the Council of Four at Wilson's residence on March
25, though prompted in large part by the necessity for a more efficient
decision-making process than had been possible in the unwieldy Council of
Ten, also reflected the American president's mounting irritation at the self-
serving leaks from the Allied delegations.[35] So concerned was Wilson about
preserving the confidentiality of these high-level exchanges that he declined
to appoint an American secretary to accompany him,[36] preferring to rely on
the trusty and tactful head of the British secretariat, Sir Maurice Hankey –
"man of secrets," as his biographer aptly dubbed him[37] – to record the discussions and decisions taken.[38] Although Hankey's procès-verbal was circu-

33 Harold Nicolson, *Peacemaking 1919* (New York, 1965), 124.
34 John Foster Dulles diary, Jan. 29, 1919, box 278, John Foster Dulles papers (hereafter JFDP), Fire-
    stone Library, Princeton Library; House diary, Feb. 11, 1919, EMHP; Polk to Auchincloss, Feb. 12,
    1919, Auchincloss to Polk, Feb. 13, 1919, included in Auchincloss diary, Feb. 13, 1919, series 1,
    box 2, Gordon Auchincloss papers (hereafter GAP), SLMD. On the role of propaganda and public
    opinion during the peace conference, see George Bernard Noble, *Policies and Opinions at Paris* (New
    York, 1935); Pierre Miquel, *La Paix de Versailles et l'opinion publique française* (Paris, 1972); William
    R. Keylor, "'How They Advertised France': The French Propaganda Campaign in the United
    States During the Breakup of the Franco–American Entente, 1918–1923," *Diplomatic History* 17
    (Summer 1993): 351–73.
35 Even before the formal opening of the conference, Wilson had expressed to his wife's secretary his
    annoyance at French press leaks. Edith Benham Helm diary, Jan. 14, 1919, box 1, EBHP.
36 Lawrence E. Gelfand, "Where Ideals Confront Self-Interest: Wilsonian Foreign Policy," *Diplomatic
    History* 18 (Winter 1994): 132.
37 Stephen Roskill, *Hankey: Man of Secrets*, 3 vols. (London, 1970–4).
38 It was Lord Riddell, Lloyd George's liaison with the British press, who had suggested to his chief
    that he insinuate "Hankey-Panky" into the deliberations of the Big Four. *Lord Riddell's Intimate Diary
    of the Peace Conference and After, 1918–1923* (hereafter Riddell diary) (New York, 1934), Mar. 24,
    1919. House noted in his diary that while he and Wilson were in conference "[Sir William] Wise-
    man telephoned asking if the President objected to having a [British] secretary in at the meetings of
    the Council of Four. It seems that Lloyd George had told his people that the reason they could not
    sit in was because of the President's objections. The president readily consented to having one."
    House later criticized "the President's almost childish action in going into conference with Lloyd
    George and Clemenceau without having any of our secretaries to make a proces verbal [*sic*]. He relies
    entirely on Mantoux and Hankey." House diary, Apr. 18 and 26, 1919.

lated to the British and French delegations, Wilson adamantly refused to permit copies to reach his colleagues (including even his confidant, Colonel Edward House) on the American Peace Commission.[39] Lloyd George played his cards characteristically close to the vest, prompting even his publicity agent Lord Riddell (with whom he had earlier shared many an indiscretion on the golf course or around the piano in his apartment) to complain that "no four kings or emperors could have conducted the conference on more autocratic lines. . . . [E]very day I have received a dole [of information] from the P.M. or [his secretary, Phillip] Kerr on his behalf, which I have passed on to the press, but there has been no systematic issue of information, and the doings of the Council of Four have been shrouded in mystery."[40] The sphinx-like Clemenceau was equally secretive, sharing nothing with the top officials at the Quai d'Orsay and confiding only in his hand-picked aide André Tardieu in much the same way that Lloyd George relied on Kerr and Wilson on House until their parting of ways.[41] The military brass was kept entirely in the dark until the work on the treaty was completed.[42]

Woodrow Wilson had traveled a long path from his wartime exhortations on behalf of "open diplomacy" to an obsession with security that bordered on paranoia at the peace conference. Convinced that the members of his household staff in Paris were spies for Clemenceau, he avoided discussing sensitive matters in their presence and meticulously filed all important doc-

39 "I have never seen a copy of it," House complained. "Hankey proposed sending it down to me, but the President vetoed it by saying he was afraid to let it come to the Crillon because there were so many newspaper men around." House diary, May 31, 1919.

40 Riddell diary, Apr. 9, 1919.

41 "All problems are referred to the Council of Four without documentation or criticism," French Foreign Ministry official Philippe Berthelot complained. "[In] a very brief discussion they examine them and instruct Hankey to prepare an English text and the procès verbal (which is not communicated to us). We learn what has happened in the newspapers. . . . Pichon [the foreign minister] himself knows nothing" about the deliberations in Wilson's library. Berthelot to Camille Barrère (French ambassador to Italy), June 14, 1919, box 1, no. 28, Papiers d'Agents, Papiers Camille Barrère, MAE.

42 Foch was reduced to commiserating over tea with General Sir Henry Wilson, Chief of the Imperial General Staff, about their exclusion from the deliberations by the detestable "frocks" (as Wilson contemptuously referred to the diplomats). As recorded in General Wilson's diary, the two military chiefs were merciless (and in Wilson's case, shockingly insubordinate) in their private evaluation of what General Wilson regularly referred to as "the two Bolshevists, Lloyd George and Woodrow Wilson" (entry of Jan. 18, 1919). "Foch agrees with me that Wilson is both Boche and Bolshevik" (Jan. 26). "Foch has a hatred of Wilson and a supreme contempt for . . . such idiodic ideas as the League of Nations, mandataries, etc. I cordially agree with him" (Feb. 23). "Saw Foch. We discussed the Frocks who he says are 'pitoyable,' and Foch and I are absolutely of one mind about the coming crash [of the peace conference]" (Mar. 21). When the two military chiefs arrived at the conference to discuss the strategic significance of the Polish frontier and were dismissed after being told by President Wilson ("my cousin," General Wilson arrogantly called him) that the drawing of borders was not a proper topic for military advisers to address, Foch turned to the Chief of the Imperial General Staff and muttered "Eh bien, Henri, ils sont fous les Messieurs là et puis Henri ils sont très, très, très malade" (Mar. 19). Microfilm of Diary of General Sir Henry Wilson, 8 (1918–19), Imperial War Museum, London.

uments in a locked strong box.[43] At the conclusion of the conference he adamantly insisted that the absolute confidentiality of Hankey's minutes of the meetings of the Big Four be preserved, in the face of Clemenceau's protestation that French political practice obliged him to turn them over to his successor.[44] Perhaps the most notorious incident in this saga of secret covenants secretly arrived at was the fate of the text of the Versailles treaty after its presentation to the German delegation on May 7. While American officials were returning home from Paris with souvenir copies stuffed in their luggage[45] and entrepreneurs were hawking translations on the streets of German cities, Wilson forbade the publication of the treaty in the United States or even its informal presentation to the Senate until the official signing ceremony on June 28.[46]

Delighted at the opportunity to derive political advantage from the controversy, Wilson's enemies on Capitol Hill feigned outrage at being denied access to a document they would be called upon to ratify that was being avidly perused by private citizens in New York and Berlin.[47] *The New Republic, The Nation,* and other organs of the American Left that had taken at face value Wilson's pledge of open diplomacy assailed their erstwhile idol for betraying the precious principles of progressivism. These disillusioned devotées of a democratic peace would join the Republican Right in opposing, albeit for entirely different reasons, the compromise package that Wilson later brought home from Paris.[48] Before the opening of the peace con-

43 Benham diary, Mar. 29, Apr. 18 and 19, 1919, box 1, EBHP; Grayson diary, Apr. 8, 1919, *PWW,* 57:100. "Ike" Hoover, the head of the president's household staff, and the chief secret service agent determined that none of the French servants understood more than a few words of English but were unable to allay the president's anxieties. See Hoover's handwritten memoir, "The Facts About President Wilson's Illness," container 7.

44 Meeting at Versailles, June 28, 1919, in Paul Mantoux, *The Deliberations of the Council of Four (March 24–June 28, 1919): Notes of the Official Interpreter,* trans. and ed. Arthur S. Link, with the assistance of Manfred F. Boemeke, 2 vols. (Princeton, N.J., 1992), 2:599–601.

45 See the unsigned, undated note by Henry Davison, and Elihu Root to Davison, June 9, 1919, box 17, folder 50, Dwight Morrow papers, Frost Library, Amherst College.

46 House observed that "The Germans are giving us an example of open diplomacy. They print the treaty as soon as it is given to them." House diary, May 31, 1919, EMHP.

47 Henry Cabot Lodge indignantly informed the Senate that he had first seen a copy of the treaty during a trip to New York City. *New York Times,* June 3, 1919. Similar complaints emanated from members of parliamentary committees in France, whom Clemenceau refused to supply with copies even after they were published in Germany. See the protest by the Socialist deputy Marcel Sembat in Chambre des Députés, Commission du Budget, Procès-Verbaux, séance du 16 mai 1919, carton C7555, Archives Nationales.

48 It was that unholy alliance of liberals opposed to the "Carthaginian" features of the German treaty and conservatives opposed to the seemingly limitless foreign obligations embodied in the League Covenant that doomed the Versailles settlement in the court of American public opinion. Lloyd E. Ambrosius, "Wilson, the Republicans, and French Security After World War I," *Journal of American History* 59, no. 2 (Sept. 1972): 341–52; William R. Keylor, "'Lafayette, We Have Quit!' Wilsonian Policy and French Security After Versailles," in Nancy L. Roelker and Charles K. Warner, eds., *Two Hundred Years of Franco–American Relations* (Newport, R.I., 1981), 44–75; William R. Keylor, "The

ference, Lansing had presciently predicted that the president's careless rhetoric about "open diplomacy" would come back to haunt him. "Of course everyone who has had any experience knows that negotiations cannot be conducted like a town meeting," he observed. "It is silly to declare a doctrine like that, because it never will work and I am sure that the President will not attempt to follow it himself, and he will be criticized and ridiculed for not doing so."[49]

If, as the foregoing suggests, Wilson and his colleagues in Paris prudently shelved the *procedural* principle of open diplomacy in the interests of securing their objectives, what can be said about the fate of the two other *substantive* tenets upon which the American president had hoped to base the peace settlement: the principle of national self-determination in territorial affairs, and the commitment to a moderate reparation settlement? It is worth remarking that it was the putative violation of these two Wilsonian precepts by the peacemakers of 1919, after all, that prompted the guilty verdict that has been rendered against them in the court of historiographical opinion.

The ink was scarcely dry on the treaty of Versailles when it became the object of the most intense kind of criticism from youthful "insiders" in the American and British delegations who felt that they had witnessed at first hand the betrayal of Woodrow Wilson's august principles. The oral indictment presented to the Senate Foreign Relations Committee even *before* the ink was dry by the resentful William Bullitt, whose mission to Russia in search of peace terms with the Bolsheviks had been disavowed by Wilson and Lloyd George, set the censorious tone.[50] The jeremiad from the pen of Maynard Keynes expressed the smoldering resentment of the British Treasury's self-appointed specialist on reparations at seeing his authority usurped by the deaf little Australian prime minister, William Hughes, and the detestable "heavenly twins," Lords Cunliffe and Sumner.[51] It also may have

Rise and Demise of the Franco–American Guarantee Pact, 1919–1921," *Proceedings of the Annual Meeting of the Western Society for French History* 15 (1988): 367–77.

49 Robert Lansing, "Certain Phrases of the President Contain the Seeds of Trouble," Dec. 20, 1918, in Pre-Commerce File, box 10, folder "Lansing," HHP. Before taking Lansing's complaint at face value, however, the reader should consider House's recollection that the day before the fourteen points address (in which the principle of open diplomacy was first enunciated) Wilson and House called in the secretary of state to review the revised draft of the speech and "Lansing accepted it in toto, although he made several suggestions as to words which the President adopted" (*PWW,* 45:507).

50 U.S. Senate, Committee on Foreign Relations, *Treaty of Peace with Germany: Hearings,* doc. 106 (Washington, D.C., 1919), 1161ff. Bullitt's seething rage at Wilson, which boiled over in his incendiary testimony before Lodge's committee, found another outlet much later in the form of a half-baked "psychohistory" of the American president coauthored with Dr. Freud himself: William C. Bullitt and Sigmund Freud, *Thomas Woodrow Wilson* (Boston, 1967).

51 "Keynes got sore because they wouldn't take his advice, his nerve broke, and he quit," grumbled an indignant Thomas Lamont (who, as an American delegate to the Reparation Commission, had observed the young British Treasury official attempt in vain to win acceptance of his views in the spring of 1919). Lamont to Edward Grenfell, Dec. 23, 1919, in Pre-Commerce Files, box 10, folder

reflected his sense of guilt at having worked in the Treasury during the war while his pacifist chums in Bloomsbury, such as Lytton Strachey and his former lover Duncan Grant, chose conscientious objection and let him know of their disapproval.[52] The powerful sentiment of affection – a mélange of sympathy, respect, and eroticism – that he had developed for the German financial delegate Dr. Carl Melchior as they commiserated about Germany's food shortages in early March, possibly had an effect as well.[53] So, too, may his intense dislike of the French in general and his nemesis, the French finance minister, Louis–Lucien Klotz, in particular.[54] Whatever the psychological forces that drove him to put pen to paper on his return to Cambridge, *The Economic Consequences of the Peace*[55] was begun even before the peace treaty was signed, completed in four months of feverish writing, and rushed into print in December 1919 – two months after the final chapters reached the publisher.[56] Owing to the timely intervention of his new friend and fellow disillusioned Wilsonian, Felix Frankfurter, Keynes secured an American publisher that promptly disseminated the book widely in the United States in time for it to play a role in the ultimate rejection of the treaty by the Senate in the spring of 1920.[57] Its savage portrait of a well-meaning but artless American leader outwitted at every turn by his crafty European counterparts – complete with barbed allusions to Don Quixote and Blind Man's Bluff – remains one of the most unforgettable caricatures of a public figure. Unfortunately for the proponents of the peace settlement,

"Lamont, Thomas," HHP. Lamont's uncharitable characterization is corroborated by Keynes's churlish announcement to Lloyd George of his decision to wash his hands of the whole business: "I ought to let you know that on Saturday I am slipping away from the scene of nightmare. I can do no more good here. I've gone on hoping even through these last dreadful weeks that you'd find some way to make the treaty a just and expedient document. But now it's apparently too late. The battle is lost. I leave it to the twins [Cunliffe and Sumner] to gloat over the devastation of Europe." Keynes to Lloyd George, June 5, 1919, F/7/2/32, LGP.

52 Robert Skidelsky, *John Maynard Keynes: A Biography*, vol. 1: *Hopes Betrayed, 1883–1920* (New York, 1986), 322–6.

53 "I looked across the table at Melchior. He seemed to feel as I did. Staring, heavy-lidded, helpless, looking, as I had seen him before, like an honourable animal in pain. . . . I was quivering with excitement, terrified out of my wits at what I was doing, for the barriers of permitted intercourse had not then begun to crumble. . . . In a sort of way I was in love with him." "Dr. Melchior, A Defeated Enemy," in John Maynard Keynes, *The Collected Writings of John Maynard Keynes*, 30 vols. (Cambridge, 1919), 10:413–15.

54 Howard Elcock, "J. M. Keynes at the Paris Peace Conference," in Milo Keynes, ed., *Essays on John Maynard Keynes* (Cambridge, 1975), 167; Skidelsky, *John Maynard Keynes*, 1:359, 362.

55 John Maynard Keynes, *The Economic Consequences of the Peace* (London, 1919; reprint, New York, 1920).

56 Skidelsky, *John Maynard Keynes*, 384.

57 The *New York Times* Washington correspondent spoke to several U.S. senators on whom Keynes's critique of the economic provisions of the treaty had made "a deep impression" in the months prior to the final vote on the treaty. *New York Times*, Feb. 19, 1920. By the spring of 1920 nearly 70,000 copies had been sold in the United States. Skidelsky, *John Maynard Keynes*, 381, 394.

it was to become what Keynes's biographer has aptly characterized as "one of the most influential books of the twentieth century."[58]

The presidents' defender's rushed to their typewriters in an effort to redeem the reputation of their ailing, incommunicado chief (though not in time to enhance the prospects of the third term that Wilson coveted in his dotage).[59] The first "Wilsonian" reply to Keynes issued from Bernard Baruch in the spring of 1920 in a work that was largely drafted by the young attorney John Foster Dulles,[60] both of whom were in a better position to comment on the confidential work of the reparation specialists in Paris.[61] The Baruch–Dulles rejoinder caused Keynes some embarrassment by exposing the hypocritical role of his friend, the South African statesman Jan Christiaan Smuts, in pressing for the inclusion of pensions in the reparation bill even as he condemned the treaty's harshness. But Dulles's wooden style, aggravated by his preoccupation with arcane financial details, proved a poor match for the gossipy informality of Keynes's trenchant character sketches. The book consequently had little impact on public opinion. Wilson himself had intended to write his own apologia on leaving the White House, but his physical and mental condition obliged him to engage the services of a reliable surrogate. The natural choice for the assignment was Ray Stannard Baker, an accomplished literary figure with impeccable "Wilsonian" credentials who, as American press chief at the peace conference, had met daily with the president and kept a copious record of his observations.

After obtaining unrestricted access to the president's private file of peace conference papers for ammunition, Baker composed a ringing defense of his patron's diplomacy in Paris that paradoxically supported the case against the Versailles settlement for which Wilson had vainly sought senatorial consent. Sparsely footnoted, save for sporadic citations of his own diary or occasional references to the "Secret Minutes, Council of Four" that Wilson had turned over to him, Baker's hagiographic portrait of Wilson as the courageous advocate for humanity at large against the grasping, parochial Allied statesmen and their bellicose military chiefs was serialized in the *New York Times* before becoming a best seller.[62] Its haunting evocation of Wilson's courageous attempts to forge a just and durable peace amid the sordid atmosphere of diplomatic intrigue in Paris assumed the aspects of a moral-

58 Skidelsky, *John Maynard Keynes*, 384, 394. Within half a year of its publication, the book had recorded world sales of over 100,000 and had been translated into eleven foreign languages.
59 Lloyd E. Ambrosius, *Woodrow Wilson and the American Diplomatic Tradition: The Treaty Fight in Perspective* (Cambridge, 1987), 268–70.
60 Skidelsky, *John Maynard Keynes*, 395–6.
61 Bernard Baruch, *The Making of the Reparation and Economic Sections of the Treaty* (New York, 1920).
62 Ray Stannard Baker, *Woodrow Wilson and the World Settlement*, 2 vols. (Garden City, N.Y., 1922–3).

ity play. The villains were "the reactionary group [in France] led by Foch and Poincaré," who pressured Clemenceau into adopting intransigent positions on reparations, the Rhineland, and other matters.[63] The hero of the two-volume narrative struggled valiantly for the cause of "permanent world peace based upon sound moral principles" while his antagonists thought only of "French security, French reparations, French expansion."[64] At the beginning of the peace conference the president had hoped to collaborate with the British, "for he felt that the ideals that he had set forth were truly Anglo-Saxon ideas." But Lloyd George spurned the advice of "clear-sighted liberals" such as Smuts, Cecil, and Keynes in favor of "a group of bitter old lords, men like Cunliffe and Sumner, who looked backward to the old order of cut-throat economic rivalry," and who favored a vindictive peace.[65] Had the British prime minister "stood by Wilson at Paris, even half-heartedly," Baker concluded, "the story might have been different."[66] As it was, the moderation of the extreme French demands (which, if accepted, would have led to "the bankruptcy of our system of civilization") was due to "the determined fight made by President Wilson."[67] The tone of condescension and ridicule that had suffused Keynes's uncharitable portrayal of Wilson in Paris as a gullible victim of Old World chicanery gives way in Baker's sketch to the heroic image of the lonely campaigner for justice and right who salvaged as much as he could of his visionary plan for the future of mankind. The common thread linking both of these early and influential studies of the peace conference is the devastating representation of the European allies in general, and the French in particular, as avaricious, aggressive, reactionary powers no more deserving of American sympathy or support in the postwar period than the recently defeated enemy.

Baker's spirited exoneration of Wilson and condemnation of Clemenceau and Lloyd George, appearing in 1922 on the heels of Keynes's earlier indictment of all three, reinforced the Anglo-American tendency in the 1920s to view Versailles as a fatally flawed peace settlement from which the United States should remain aloof and which Great Britain should seek to revise. In the fateful year 1933 these two early exposés of the peace conference were succeeded by a belated lamentation from another disenchanted participant, who recollected his six-month Parisian sojourn with a melancholy regret of opportunities missed as he surveyed the wreckage of the new international order he had played a minor part in creating. "We came to Paris convinced

63 Ibid., 2:31, 79. Poincaré had become prime minister a few months before the appearance of Baker's work and was already on a collision course with the Weimar Republic over reparations that would end with the French occupation of the Ruhr in Jan. 1923.
64 Ibid., 3.   65 Ibid., 47, 281.   66 Ibid., 53.   67 Ibid., 82, 302.

that the new order was about to be established," recalled Harold Nicolson, a midlevel official in the British Foreign Office who had worked on East European and Balkan affairs. "We left it convinced that the new order had merely fouled the old. We arrived as fervent apprentices in the school of President Wilson: we left as renegades. . . . We arrived determined that a Peace of justice and wisdom should be negotiated: we left it, conscious that the Treaties imposed upon our enemies were neither just nor wise." As he gazes out a window in the Palace of Versailles at the Big Four basking in the adulation of the crowd after the signing ceremony, he encounters an associate "standing miserably in the littered immensity of the Galerie des Glaces. We say nothing to each other. It has all been horrible." Then, after returning to British headquarters at the Hôtel Majestic: "To bed, sick of life."[68]

Brimming with titillating gossip and vivid character sketches gleaned from the peripatetic young clerk's sporadic encounters with plenipotentiaries from all of the major delegations, Nicolson's *Peacemaking, 1919,* rapidly took its place alongside the Keynes and Baker volumes on the shelf of "inside stories" by peripheral participants that shaped public perceptions and memories of the conference. Bids by the principal *dramatis personae* themselves to defend their handiwork in print were marred either by a didactic style or a self-serving tone that reduced their effectiveness.[69] As a consequence, the image that succeeding generations have retained of the peace conference has to a large extent remained the dreary one first sketched by the minor players in the drama who wrote so evocatively of their disappointing experience in Paris. What one is tempted to call the "demonology of Versailles" continued well into the era of the Cold War, when a new school of historians traced the Western world's obsession with

---

68 Nicolson, *Peacemaking 1919,* 186, 370–1. This language of bleakness and despair may have reflected Nicolson's bitter memories of his turbulent marital situation at the time. While he labored at the peace conference, his wife, Vita Sackville-West, was conducting a torrid and entirely public love affair in Monte Carlo with Violet Trefusis (the model for the Russian princess Sasha in Virginia Woolf's *Orlando*), with whom she later eloped for a brief Bloomsbury-type "marriage." As their son later observed with characteristic understatement, "his narrative of those days in *Peacemaking* makes poignant reading when one knows the concurrent drama in his private life." Nigel Nicolson, *Portrait of a Marriage* (New York, 1973), 139.

69 Charles Seymour and Edward M. House, eds., *What Really Happened at Paris* (New York, 1921). André Tardieu, *The Truth About the Treaty* (Indianapolis, 1921); Robert Lansing, *The Peace Negotiations: A Personal Narrative* (Boston, 1921); David Lloyd George, *The Truth About the Peace Treaties,* 2 vols. (London, 1938). Old Clemenceau's mordant memoir was a moving *cri de coeur,* written shortly before his death after he had witnessed the demolition of much of the protective shield that he thought he had erected against Germany. It was full of rancor and recrimination, mainly against Foch (who, on reading the text of the draft submitted to the Germans, had snarled with uncanny prescience that "this is not a treaty. It's a twenty-year truce." Georges Clemenceau, *Grandeur and Misery of Victory* (New York, 1930).

suppressing Communist revolution to the latter stages of the Great War and the peace conference that terminated it.[70]

A common theme pervading most of this literature is the supposed determination of the European victors in general, and the French in particular, to impose a "Carthaginian peace" – to repeat Keynes's hackneyed historical allusion – on a defeated, demoralized, but staunchly democratic Germany that was desperately struggling to survive amid the twin threats of bolshevism from the left and militarism from the right.[71] As noted earlier, the territorial and reparation provisions of the Versailles treaty bore the chief burden of this accusation. Never far from the surface of this critique was the accusation that the peacemakers at Paris had missed a golden opportunity to offer moderate peace terms to the defeated power that would have proved beneficial to victor and vanquished alike. The ineluctable implication of such analyses was that the peacemakers' forbearance in territorial and reparation matters would have resulted in a stable, peaceful international order: An enlightened territorial settlement eschewing immoderate amputations of territory inhabited mainly by German-speaking peoples would have reinforced the democratic, pacific tendencies in postwar Germany. The fledgling Weimar republic would have been induced to settle the ancient quarrel with France, to discover means of coexisting peacefully with the new Habsburg successor states to the east, and eventually to rejoin the family of nations on the basis of an unequivocal commitment to respect the new territorial arrangements. Similarly, a moderate reparation agreement would have facilitated the economic rehabilitation of Germany, which in turn would have inoculated that country against the plague of xenophobic, *völkisch* nationalism later personified by Hitler while promoting the economic recovery of Europe as a whole.[72]

To what extent is this severe historiographical assessment of the territorial and reparation clauses of the Versailles treaty justified? How credible is

70 Arno J. Mayer, *Politics and Diplomacy of Peacemaking: Containment and Counterrevolution at Versailles, 1918–1919* (New York, 1967).
71 Mayer's juxtaposition of the "forces of movement" and the "forces of order" revived categories earlier employed by Baker, on whom Mayer relies heavily for his analysis of Wilson's policies at the peace conference. Mayer, *Politics and Diplomacy of Peacemaking.* A similar assessment is offered in N. Gordon Levin Jr., *Woodrow Wilson and World Politics: America's Response to War and Revolution* (New York, 1968). See also Lloyd E. Ambrosius, "The Orthodoxy of Revisionism: Woodrow Wilson and the New Left," *Diplomatic History* 1 (Summer 1977): 199–214.
72 Antony Lentin traces this disillusionment with the treaty in Great Britain and connects that mood to the appeasement of the 1930s in *Lloyd George, Woodrow Wilson, and the Guilt of Germany: An Essay in the Pre-history of Appeasement* (Baton Rouge, La., 1985), chap. 6. For a discussion of the Anglican clergy's denunciation of the Versailles treaty as "un-Christian" and its subsequent support for appeasement in the 1930s, see Catherine Ann Cline, "Ecumenism and Appeasement: The Bishops of the Church of England and the Treaty of Versailles," *Journal of Modern History* 61 (Dec. 1989): 683–703.

the alluring counterfactual proposition sketched above as the representation of an excellent opportunity tragically missed?

One might begin to address these questions by considering the implications of the scrupulous application of the celebrated doctrine of national self-determination to the particular geopolitical configuration of postwar Europe. Let us postulate the volition of the inhabitants as the chief criterion for the disposition of disputed territory. Let us further assume that individuals, if given the option, would be inclined to choose citizenship in a state that accorded preferential status to their native tongue rather than in one which relegated them to the category of a linguistic minority.[73] In the absence of scientific opinion polls and reliable censuses for the period, it is impossible to speak with authority about the popular preferences and ethnic-linguistic composition of those disputed territories of postwar Europe that were not permitted to hold plebiscites. But one is certainly entitled to doubt that the citizens of Danzig and West Prussia, had they been afforded the opportunity, would have voted to relinquish their German nationality in favor of citizenship in a free city under the League of Nations or annexation by Poland, respectively.[74]

As for Alsace-Lorraine, Clemenceau's adamant insistence on the recovery of the "lost provinces" of 1870 without a plebiscite – endorsed by Wilson and incorporated in the armistice agreement – betrayed a certain apprehension about putting the true inclinations of their heterogeneous populations to the test of a popular vote.[75] And for good reason. The original report on Alsace-Lorraine that the Inquiry had submitted to Wilson recognized the strong possibility that a combined plebiscite held in both provinces would favor Germany and a separate polling in each would reveal

---

73 For lack of space I shall merely mention here two alternative solutions to the problem of ethnically heterogeneous political units. The first is the brutal (but effective) policy of compulsory population transfers, either by treaty (as with the relocation of Greeks from Asia Minor after the Greco–Turkish conflict of 1920–2) or under the duress of war (as with the emigration of Germans from Silesia and the Sudetenland after World War II and Palestinians from Israel after the Arab–Israeli war of 1948–9). The second is the noble (but ineffective) attempt by the League of Nations to enforce protective measures on behalf of minorities that had been written into the peace treaties of 1919–20, a subject on which Carole Fink has worked and which she addresses in chapter 11 in this book.

74 Louis L. Gerson, *Woodrow Wilson and the Rebirth of Poland, 1914–1920* (Hamden, Conn., 1972), 121–36. Kay Lundgreen-Nielson, *The Polish Problem at the Paris Peace Conference,* trans. Alison Borch-Johansen (Odense, 1979), 197–204, 233–45. The German census for 1910 showed a substantial German majority for the Corridor and Danzig combined. Sir Robert Donald, *The Polish Corridor and Its Consequences* (London, 1930), 23. See also chapter 13 in this book.

75 In preparing for the armistice, French military planners warned that liberated Alsace should be occupied by French troops alone "because American soldiers . . . could be impressed by its Germanic character." They also urged that the French occupation begin immediately after the armistice to prevent appeals for a plebiscite by Alsatian citizens. "Conditions d'Armistice, 28 octobre 1918 [unsigned, for Clemenceau]," Fonds Clemenceau, box 6N70, SHA.

opposition in Alsace to French annexation.[76] The map of Alsace-Lorraine employed by the American specialist on the subject (Wilson's former Johns Hopkins colleague, the Harvard medievalist Charles Homer Haskins) showed the vast majority of districts with at least 75 percent German speakers.[77] While the linguistic and ethnic composition of every other disputed region was the subject of detailed analysis by the American experts attached to the Inquiry, Haskins's recommendation concerning France's lost provinces was brief and to the point: "The restoration of Alsace-Lorraine to France, with the boundaries of 1870, may be assured as settled by the acceptance of President Wilson's eighth point and of the terms of the Armistice of November 11, 1918. No discussion necessary."[78]

The once privileged German-speaking elite of the defunct Habsburg Empire predictably shuddered at the prospect of minority standing in the Bohemian borderlands of the new state of Czechoslovakia, or of economic deprivation in a rump Austria shorn of its prewar markets and sources of food and raw materials. The Germans of Bohemia favored inclusion in what was universally referred to as "German Austria"[79] while inhabitants of the latter state petitioned the peacemakers for *Anschluss* with the German Reich, both on impeccably Wilsonian grounds.[80]

The satisfaction of these ethnic aspirations at the peace conference would have had the paradoxical consequence of significantly strengthening the German state by authorizing it to expand its national territory far beyond the frontiers of Bismarck's Reich. Indeed, with a postwar redistribution of territory based purely on considerations of nationality or ethnicity, Germany's penalty for its military defeat would have been the acquisition of *Lebensraum* more extensive than the vast terrain acquired by Hitler through diplomatic intimidation by the beginning of 1939. In any case, specula-

---

76 Lawrence E. Gelfand, *The Inquiry: American Preparations for Peace, 1917–1919* (New Haven, Conn., 1963), 140.

77 Charles Homer Haskins papers, box 13, Mudd Library, Princeton University.

78 Undated memorandum [probably mid-Jan. 1919] entitled "The Franco–German Frontier," and subsequent drafts with identical language dated Feb. 4 and 6, 1919, box 12, ibid. The internal discussions concerning Alsace-Lorraine in the French delegation always focused on security, economic, and historical considerations rather than the principle of self-determination. See, e.g., Foch's "Note sur l'Alsace. Etat Definitif," Nov. 21, 1919, in Fonds Clemenceau, box 6N73, folder "Alsace-Lorraine," SHA.

79 Johann Wolfgang Brügel, *Tschechen und Deutsche* (Munich, 1967), 75–6; Elisabeth Wiskemann, *Czechs and Germans: A Study of the Struggle in the Historic Provinces of Bohemia and Moravia* (London, 1967), 84–5.

80 Alfred D. Low, *The Anschluss Movement, 1918–1919,* Memoirs of the American Philosophical Society, vol. 103, pt. 10 (Philadelphia, 1963). The term "German Austria" was employed throughout the peace conference in all documents. See the French case for the prohibition of *Anschluss* and the denial that such a policy violated the Wilsonian principle of self-determination in "Note Relative à l'Autriche allemande. Proposition française," Fonds Clemenceau, box 6N75, folder "Autriche," SHA. The adjective "allemande" was subsequently crossed out in pencil on many of the documents in this collection.

tion about the systematic application of the principle of national self-determination to postwar Europe must remain a purely academic exercise. Woodrow Wilson himself, not to speak of his more hard-boiled interlocutors (who had been skeptical of the doctrine from the very beginning), was prepared to sacrifice that goal whenever competing principles or interests claimed a higher priority.

The judicious abrogation of the nationality principle in deference to overriding strategic concerns (such as Czechoslovakia's requirement of a defensible frontier)[81] or economic considerations (such as Poland's need for a commercial outlet to the Baltic)[82] in the drafting of the German treaty went hand in hand with similar concessions in the peace agreements with Germany's chief wartime ally. Italy's claim to the southern Tyrol at Austria's expense, which had received the endorsement of France and Great Britain in the Treaty of London of 1915, was plainly spurious on ethnic grounds.[83] Yet Orlando enjoyed the consistent support of Clemenceau and Lloyd George at the peace conference – except for the Italian claim to Fiume, which had not been assigned to Italy in the Treaty of London – because the competing principle of the sanctity of written engagements bound them to the prior promises of territorial gain that had been required to secure Italy's intervention in the war.[84] While refusing to recognize the validity of the Treaty of London, President Wilson nonetheless awarded the Brenner line to Orlando in spite of its unmistakable incompatibility with the ninth of his fourteen points, which read: "A readjustment of the frontiers of Italy should be effected along clearly recognizable lines of nationality." Though he later disingenuously claimed to have mistakenly consigned some 200,000 German-speaking Tyrolese to Italian citizenship through a misreading of the map of the disputed frontier, this concession to Orlando appears to have been consciously tendered for the higher purpose of securing the Italian premier's support for the League of Nations.[85]

81 See the record of the heated discussion between Jules Cambon and Robert Lansing on the question of basing the Czechoslovak-German frontier on strategic considerations in Procès-verbal du Conseil des Ministres des Affaires Etrangères, Troisième Séance, Apr. 1, 1919, Fonds Clemenceau, box 6N74, SHA.
82 Lundgreen-Nielsen, *Polish Problem,* 203, 269–73.
83 René Albrecht-Carrié, *Italy at the Paris Peace Conference* (Hamden, Conn., 1966), 90–4.
84 See the memorandum entitled "Fiume and the Peace Settlement," Apr. 23, 1919, signed by Clemenceau and Lloyd George. After noting that 200,000 German-speaking Tyrolese and 750,000 Slavs had been included within the new Italian frontiers, the two prime ministers nevertheless affirmed that they were "bound by the Pact of London," and promised that "any demand for a change in that pact which is adverse to Italy must come from Italy herself." Fonds Clemenceau, box 6N76, folder "Italie," SHA.
85 Charles Seymour, "Woodrow Wilson and Self-Determination in the Tyrol," *Virginia Quarterly Review* 38 (Autumn 1962): 582–5; Sterling J. Kerneck, "Woodrow Wilson and National Self-Determination along Italy's Frontier: A Study of the Manipulation of Principles in the Pursuit of Political Interests,"

In the world beyond Europe, of course, the question of national self-determination for the inhabitants of Germany's former colonies simply never arose. The acquisition of German possessions in Africa and the Pacific by various Allied claimants, though furnished with the cloak of moral respectability represented by the mandate system of the League, transpired without reference to the wishes of the indigenous populations concerned.[86] Smuts, widely hailed as the progressive architect of the League whom Wilson admired more than any other official of the British Empire, rapaciously pressed for the annexation of German South West Africa by his own country and the German Pacific islands by the other dominions.[87] When that proved impossible for the American president to swallow, the shrewd South African statesman devised the mandate scheme in order to achieve the same result by more "Wilsonian" means. There was never any intention of preparing the Class B and C mandates in Africa for independence, despite respectful pleas by distinguished representatives of African-American groups.[88] As the American expert on colonial matters, Professor George Louis Beer of Columbia, put it: "The negro race has hitherto shown no capacity for progressive development except under the tutelage of other peoples."[89] Similarly, the security concerns of Australia, New Zealand, and Japan dictated the disposition of the former German islands in the Pacific.[90] On the mainland of Asia, Wilson readily sacrificed China's ethnically unimpeachable claim to the former German concessions on its Shantung peninsula to the higher priority of securing Japan's endorsement of, and membership in, his precious League.[91] The American delegation turned a deaf ear to Korean protests of Japanese repression on the peninsula and ignored a "declaration of independence" by militant Korean patriots for the same reason.[92]

As for the non-Turkish possessions that had been severed from the disintegrating Ottoman Empire by fiat of the victors, British appreciation for

Proceedings of the American Philosophical Society 126 (Aug. 1982): 255–64; Arthur Walworth, *Wilson and His Peacemakers* (New York, 1986), 54–5. Baker, *Woodrow Wilson and the World Settlement*, 2:146.

86 Brian K. Digre, *Imperialism's New Clothes: The Repartition of Tropical Africa, 1914–1919* (New York, 1990), 157–72.

87 Smuts to Lloyd George, Jan. 14, 17, 20, 1919, F/45/26, 27, 28, LGP; Diary of Lord Robert Cecil, Jan. 22, 1919, Papers of Viscount Cecil of Chelwood, Add. 51113, British Library, London.

88 W. E. B. Du Bois to Tumulty, Nov. 27, 1918, with enclosure entitled "Memoranda on the Future of Africa," *PWW*, 53:236–8.

89 George Louis Beer, *African Questions at the Paris Peace Conference* (New York, 1923), 179.

90 Russell H. Fifield, "Disposal of the Carolines, Marshalls, and Marianas at the Paris Peace Conference," *American Historical Review* 51 (Apr. 1946): 472ff.

91 Despite the plaintive plea of the Chinese representative, V. K. Wellington Koo, reproduced in "Hankey's Notes of Two Meetings of the Council of Ten," Jan. 28, 1919, *PWW*, 54:314–18; Apr. 22, 1919, ibid., 57: 614–26.

92 Walworth, *Wilson and His Peacemakers*, 365, 372.

Arab cultural achievements together with residual chagrin at having to repudiate wartime promises of self-rule yielded a privileged status for the Arabic-speaking lands south of Anatolia within the mandate system: as Class A mandates, the newly established political units with predominately Arab populations – Mesopotamia (later Iraq), Palestine, Syria, and Lebanon – were to be prepared for early independence because their populations were thought to have reached a higher stage of development than the former German colonies in Africa and the Pacific. But the inhabitants of Syria would not be consulted about their wishes concerning a French mandate (to which Lloyd George had previously committed himself), since their opinion in the matter was both predictable and unacceptable.[93] Nor would Great Britain hazard a plebiscite in Palestine on the question of its wartime pledge to establish a Jewish "home" in a region where non-Jews constituted 90 percent of the population at the end of the war. In the latter case, the historic right to reoccupy territory relinquished in the distant past took precedence over contemporary claims of nationality.[94] The nearest thing to a plebiscite in the former Ottoman domains was the investigation of the King-Crane Commission, which toured the region in the summer of 1919 and found widespread opposition to a French mandate in Syria and to a Jewish home in Palestine. But the report (which Wilson probably never saw) was suppressed until 1922, after the British and French mandates had been assigned, and was thereafter entirely forgotten.[95]

Having denied the newly emancipated subjects of the German and Ottoman Empires recourse to the prerogative of national self-determination, the Allies could hardly have been expected to proffer it to the residents of their own overseas possessions, protectorates, or spheres of influence. Spokespersons for anticolonialism within the British and French Empires, such as the Egyptian nationalist leader Zaghlul Pasha and the young Vietnamese militant later known by the pseudonym Ho Chi Minh, failed to obtain a hearing. Lloyd George and Clemenceau, both subject to intense political pressure from their colonial lobbies, were not about to permit such incendiary topics on the agenda.[96] The United States delegation obtained British and French approval of the informal American protectorate in

---

93 A plea for self-determination by the hapless Kurds, inhabiting then as now a territory divided among Mesopotamia (later Iraq), Persia (later Iran), Turkey, and Syria also went unheeded. See the Kurdish petitions in Fonds Clemenceau, 6N74, folder "Revendications Diverses," SHA.

94 The Zionist case was movingly presented in Julian W. Mack, Louis Marshall, and Stephen S. Wise, "Enclosure II" [To Woodrow Wilson], Mar. 1, 1919, *PWW,* 55:381–5.

95 Harry N. Howard, *The King–Crane Commission: An American Inquiry in the Middle East* (Beirut, 1963), 224–5, 258; Henry C. King to Ray Stannard Baker, May 6 and 23, 1922, container 31, RSBP.

96 Walworth, *Wilson and His Peacemakers,* 509; Jean Lacouture, *Ho Chi Minh,* trans. Peter Wiles (Harmondsworth, 1969), 26.

Liberia, though the Americans balked at permitting the use of the imperialist-sounding term in the records.[97] Potentially embarrassing questions about the political status of the Philippines, or about the Roosevelt Corollary to the Monroe Doctrine, the Platt Amendment, and other instruments of United States hegemony in the Western Hemisphere, never arose.

In sum, it may be recorded that the principle of national self-determination was applied with great selectivity at the peace conference that was expected to enshrine it as the foundation of the "new" diplomacy. "Wilsonians" who acknowledged in theory the right of nationality groups to shape their own destiny sacrificed that precept with equanimity when it clashed with more compelling considerations of strategic and economic interest, historic right, or the sanctity of contracts. In spite of these shortcomings, it must be conceded (as H. Stuart Hughes has observed) that "the boundaries drawn in 1919 conformed more closely to linguistic frontiers in Europe than any before or since."[98]

The result was a territorial settlement on the old continent marked by a notable paradox which, in the eyes of some observers, did not bode well for the stability of the new international system: The treaty of Saint Germain-en-Laye with Austria certified the dissolution of the weakest member of the Germanic coalition into its constituent ethnic components while the treaty of Versailles preserved the territorial integrity of the strongest. The Reich's territorial cessions were the source of considerable inconvenience and much irritation. But the peacemakers did not tear asunder what Bismarck had joined, as some French proponents of an authentic "Carthaginian peace" had ardently hoped. "German Unity Consecrated at Versailles," the royalist commentator Jacques Bainville ruefully proclaimed on reviewing the details of the territorial settlement. From the callous perspective of this devotée of the balance of power, the peace settlement was fatally flawed. The preservation of a centralized and potentially powerful Germany, embittered by its territorial losses and bounded on the east by a collection of fragile new nation-states with discontented German-speaking minorities in their midst, represented the worst possible combination of the carrot and the stick: "Une paix trop douce pour ce qu'elle a de dur."[99]

In turning to the topic of reparations one encounters the provision of the peace settlement that has engendered more historiographical misconcep-

---

97 Emily S. Rosenberg, "The Invisible Protectorate: The United States, Liberia, and the Evolution of Neocolonialism, 1909–1940," *Diplomatic History* 9 (Summer 1985): 198–9.

98 H. Stuart Hughes, *Contemporary Europe: A History* (New York, 1971), 123.

99 *Action Française*, May 8 and 9, 1919. For Bainville's more extended assessment of the Versailles treaty, see Jacques Bainville, *Les Conséquences politiques de la paix* (Paris, 1920); and William R. Keylor, *Jacques Bainville and the Renaissance of Royalist History in Twentieth-Century France* (Baton Rouge, La., 1979), 137–45.

tions and popular myths than any other.[100] At the end of previous wars, the victors had required tribute (in the form of war costs) from the vanquished on the basis of the antediluvian claim to the just deserts of military triumph.[101] The most recent instance of such a transaction in Europe was the 5-billion-franc indemnity extracted from defeated France by the newly united Germany after 1871. The idea of requiring compensation for specified damages caused by armies in the field never entered the deliberations that produced the Treaty of Frankfurt, for an obvious reason: no German soil had been devastated by the French military forces, which had been intercepted at the frontier, defeated in battle, and compelled to capitulate on their own territory.[102] A similar outcome in the summer of 1940 likewise resulted in a stiff financial exaction from defeated France, this time in the form of the wholesale requisitioning of manufactured goods, raw materials and labor, though there was (as yet) no war-related damage in Germany to repair.[103]

In this respect the Great War had represented something of an anomaly in modern military history: the four years of ruinous combat on all fronts had paradoxically been confined to the territory of the eventual victors. The defeated power had sagaciously surrendered before the ravages of modern warfare had reached its frontiers. There was also some evidence, though its credibility has not gone unchallenged,[104] that the wholesale destruction or removal of machinery, equipment, manufactured goods, and raw materials by the German army in the occupied territory represented deliberate industrial sabotage aimed at crippling France as a postwar commercial competitor.[105] Whatever the motivation for this depredation, the consequences

100 A succinct, sensible summary of the controversy at the peace conference, blessedly free of the customary cant, may be found in Alan Sharp, *The Versailles Settlement: Peacemaking in Paris, 1919* (New York, 1991), 77–101.

101 Lord Sumner reminded the reparation experts on February 10, 1919, that war costs had been demanded by the Allies from France in 1815, Prussia from Austria in 1866, and Prussia from France in 1871, and concluded that "The reimbursement of war costs is the constant practice of international law." Quoted in Tardieu, *Truth About the Treaty,* 287.

102 The 1871 precedent was reviewed in detail by Sumner and John Foster Dulles, British and American delegates to the Reparation Commission, respectively: Commission des Réparations, 5e séance, 13 février 1919; 9e séance, 19 février 1919, Dossiers Klotz, box 87, Bibliothèque de Documentation Internationale Contemporaine, Nanterre, France (hereafter Dossiers Klotz).

103 The Germans used the pretext of "occupation costs" to extract the equivalent of 631,866,000,000 francs from the occupied zone, a figure which represented 58 percent of the Vichy government's income during the occupation. Robert O. Paxton, *Vichy France: Old Guard and New Order, 1940–1944* (New York, 1972), 143–4.

104 Georges-Henri Soutou, "Les Buts de guerre économiques des grandes puissances de 1914 à 1919," Ph.D. diss., Université de Paris I, 1985, 2305–8.

105 Klotz had presented the evidence of this premeditated destruction for postwar commercial purposes to the Peace Conference in February. Tardieu, *Truth About the Treaty,* 280–4. Thomas Lamont, the Morgan partner and one of the American experts on the Reparation Commission, was persuaded that Germany had tried to "cripple particular French industries" so that France would

of the asymmetrical wartime experience of these two antagonists were plain: Defeated Germany's industrial heartland in the Ruhr, the Rhineland, and Westphalia had survived the war unscathed, while the industrial centers of victorious France in the northeastern départements lay in ruins. Already surpassed by Germany according to all important indices of economic achievement before the war, France faced a bleak prospect of even more pronounced industrial inferiority vis-à-vis her neighbor across the Rhine in the years to come.[106]

Only two possible means of escaping this cruel and paradoxical fate loomed on the horizon: One was artificially to enhance French productivity through the retention of the wartime preferential trade arrangements among the Allied and Associated Powers while pressing for a massive dose of financial assistance from Washington, two policies that were doggedly championed by French Commerce Minister Etienne Clémentel[107] and Finance Minister Louis-Lucien Klotz,[108] respectively. The other was to harness German industrial productivity to the cause of France's postwar recovery through the reparation scheme.[109] Once the Wilson administration had abruptly decided to terminate American participation in the inter-Allied economic bodies[110] and announced the end of U.S. Treasury advances to

be "unable to compete with Germany after the war." See his undated note entitled "Devastated Areas," box 166, folder 3, Thomas W. Lamont papers, Baker Library, Harvard University Business School (hereafter TWLP).

106 There are two schools of thought concerning France's postwar economic plight and its prospects for recovery. Schuker maintains that France emerged from the war with manageable financial difficulties that could have been overcome with relatively modest lending from U.S. banks. Silverman paints a much darker picture of the postwar French situation and poses the rhetorical question: "Why should the French have been satisfied with 'modest' economic recovery while the United States and Britain sought to restore Germany to its predominant economic position on the continent?" See Stephen A. Schuker, *The End of French Predominance in Europe: The Financial Crisis of 1924 and the Adoption of the Dawes Plan* (Chapel Hill, N.C., 1976), 13; and Dan P. Silverman, *Reconstructing Europe After the Great War* (Cambridge, Mass., 1982), 6.

107 Clémentel, "Entente économique entre les Alliés, l'arme économique: le contrôle des matières premières, série Y, International," carton 213, MAE; Clémentel, "Avant-projet des clauses économiques des préliminaires de paix," Dec. 31, 1918, Ministère de Commerce et de l'Industrie, sous-série F12, carton 8104, Archives Nationales.

108 Archives du Sénat, Procès-verbaux de la Commission des Affaires Etrangères, audition de M. Klotz, Feb. 27, 1919, 1695ff.

109 Préliminaires de Paix. Proposition du Ministère des Finances, Nov. 18, 1918, Fonds Clemenceau, carton 80, folder "Negotiation de Paix," SHA.

110 As the end of the war approached, a difference of opinion emerged within Wilson's small coterie of economic and financial advisers concerning the wisdom of retaining the inter-Allied organizations. "The plans [for the pooling of raw materials and shipping] that they have instituted cannot be cut off the moment the war is over, as you know, and are likely to continue for some time anyway," Lamont declared in a private meeting with Wilson in early October 1918. "Why not try to work out some scheme for their permanent continuance, a sort of international socialism on a grand scale," To which Wilson replied, "A very interesting suggestion." "Memorandum of a Talk with the President at the White House," Oct. 4, 1918, box 118, folder 1, TWLP. Hoover, on the other hand, confidently (and accurately) predicted to his aide in London shortly before the Armistice that "this government will not agree to any program that even looks like inter-Allied

America's wartime partners, the alternative of "l'Allemagne paiera"[111] remained the only viable option for French postwar planners intent on bridging the Franco–German productivity gap in the postwar years.[112]

The tangled question of reparations has generated a monumental scholarly literature ever since Keynes launched the historiographical debate. The controversy has traditionally been divided into three interrelated categories: The first is the ethical and juridical justification for the reparation liability. The second is the amount owed and the correlative question of how much of that total Germany could reasonably have been expected to pay in light of its available financial resources. The third is the supposedly technical question of how such cash payments as were required could have been effected through the transfer of Germany's national assets into the currencies of the recipient countries without unduly disrupting foreign exchange markets and international trade. Each of these three aspects of the reparation imbroglio has received exhaustive treatment by competent specialists who have exploited the relevant primary sources.[113] As noted above, this growing body of monographic scholarship appears to have had very little impact on general studies of twentieth-century history, and therefore on popular attitudes. As a consequence, the shop-worn pronouncements of Keynes have stood the test of time. As the great British economist's biographer put it in his evaluation of the long-term significance of *The Economic Consequences of the Peace*, "Of the dozens of accounts of the Treaty which appeared in the 1920s it is the only one which has not sunk without a trace."[114]

control of our economic resources after peace." Hoover to Joseph Cotton, Nov. 7, 1918, Pre-Commerce File, box 3, folder "Joseph Cotton," HHP.

111 A phrase long attributed to Klotz. I have been unable to find any evidence in the French sources that Clemenceau's much maligned Finance Minister ever uttered those words. Trachtenberg also doubts that Klotz ever said them. Marc Trachtenberg, *Reparation in World Politics* (New York, 1980), 41.

112 I lack the space here to discuss the French interest in postwar economic collaboration with, rather than coercion of, Germany (especially in the metallurgical sector based on the complementarity of Lorraine iron ore and Ruhr coke). Suffice it to say that this important topic, which has been addressed by a number of important monographs, has been almost totally neglected by general histories of the period. See Gerald D. Feldman, *Iron and Steel in the German Inflation, 1916–1923* (Princeton, N.J., 1977); Jacques Bariéty, *Les Relations franco-allemandes après la première guerre mondiale* (Paris, 1977), 126–71; and Walter A. McDougall, "Political Economy Versus National Sovereignty: French Structures for German Economic Integration After Versailles," *Journal of Modern History* 51 (Mar. 1979): 4–23.

113 In addition to the chapters in this book that address the topic, see the brief but splendid synopsis (though written before the pathbreaking research of the 1970s) by Sally Marks entitled "Reparations Reconsidered: A Reminder," *Central European History* 2 (1969): 356–65, and her substantial contribution "The Myth of Reparations," *Central European History* 17 (1978): 231–55.

114 Skidelsky, *John Maynard Keynes*, 399. The same may be said of the 1940s, when two works much more sympathetic to the Versailles settlement that were composed during World War II had minimal effect and are seldom cited. Paul Birdsall's *Versailles Twenty Years After* (New York, 1941) was written entirely from secondary sources. Etienne Mantoux's *The Carthaginian Peace, or the Economic Consequences of Mr. Keynes* (New York, 1952), a posthumously published polemic by the son of Paul

The issue of German responsibility – as specified in the notorious article 231 of the peace treaty – has given rise to the most egregious popular misconceptions about the reparation settlement that have persisted down through the decades. The truth of the matter is that this provision had been inserted at the behest not of some French or British hard-liner (such as the devious "Klotzkie," the bombastic "Billy" Hughes, or the obdurate "heavenly twins"), but rather of the American representatives on the Reparation Commission, Norman Davis and John Foster Dulles. The courtly southern gentleman and the stolid Wall Street lawyer had been conscientiously seeking diplomatic language that would mollify the British and the French while reducing the amount of Germany's financial obligation were it held liable for the totality of war costs, as Clemenceau and Lloyd George had been frantically demanding in order to satisfy their publics' insistence on integral repayment. By affirming (in what was to become article 231) Germany's *moral responsibility* for the war and its *legal liability* for the damage to persons and property, while implicitly acknowledging (in what was to become article 232) her *financial incapacity* to pay the enormous bill that was certain to result from an objective inspection of the devastated regions of France and an actuarial projection of pension costs,[115] Davis and Dulles thought that they had devised a brilliant solution to the reparation dilemma: Here was a means of furnishing what Arthur Walworth has aptly called a "psychological sop"[116] to Allied public opinion as compensation for the loss of the huge German payments that Allied leaders knew could and would never be made.[117] As Vance McCormick, another one of Wilson's economic advisers in Paris, summarized the matter, "I think the preamble is useful. We are adopting an unusual method in not fixing a definite sum. The pream-

---

Mantoux (the interpreter for the Council of Four at the peace conference) who was killed in action during the liberation of France at the end of World War II, has been largely dismissed as special pleading based on insufficient economic data.

115 The inclusion of claims for pensions and separation allowances did not increase the total sum owed by Germany but merely affected the proportion that each Allied claimant would receive by increasing the share allocated to Britain (with little damage to repair but a substantial unfunded pension liability). This modification of the original reparation scheme therefore operated at the expense of the other allies rather than of the defeated power. It nevertheless became, in the eyes of the treaty's many critics, a major example of the piling on of indefensible reparation claims.

116 Walworth, *Wilson and His Peacemakers*, 288.

117 House diary, Mar. 19, 1919; memorandum entitled "For Mr. Baruch from Mr. Dulles," Feb. 26, 1919, box 2, folder "Baruch," JFDP. See also the various other Dulles drafts combining the principles of German responsibility and limited liability in box 2, folder "Reparation Commission II"; *DCF,* 1:147–8. When Gordon Auchincloss, House's secretary and son-in-law, sent the draft of what was to become article 231 of the Versailles treaty to the State Department, he remarked that "you will note that the President's principles have been protected in this clause" (Auchincloss to Polk, Apr. 9, 1919, Auchincloss diary, Apr. 9, 1919, GAP). Trachtenberg, *Reparation and World Politics,* 56–7.

ble tends to explain this, and, further, prepares the public mind for disappointment as to what actually can be secured."[118]

What the well-intentioned American experts had unwittingly established instead was a pretext for subsequent German opposition to the entire reparation obligation on the paradoxical grounds that its justification rested entirely on the indefensible moral judgment that Germany was "guilty" of launching a war of aggression.[119] Whereas scholarly specialists such as Marc Trachtenberg and Antony Lentin[120] together with a few generalists, such as Hajo Holborn,[121] have dutifully debunked the myth of the "war-guilt clause," it continues to crop up in most general histories of twentieth-century Europe. The most eminent members of the profession are not exempt from the temptation to perpetuate the misconception. James Joll speaks of "the notorious 'war guilt clause'" which "suggested that a degree of moral blame attached to Germany from which, by implication, her opponents were free. . . . Germany's guilt was assumed. . . . [T]he emphasis was not on making a new start, but rather on the stern exaction of moral and material penalties."[122] H. Stuart Hughes, citing Keynes's "masterly polemic," concludes that "the reparations imposed on Germany were both unjust and impossible to collect, and the 'war guilt' statement which sought to justify them was a radical distortion of the actual origins of the conflict."[123]

The other two critical components of the reparation controversy – the question of Germany's capacity to pay and the so-called transfer problem – were raised but not resolved at the peace conference, so I will not address them in any detail here.[124] Suffice it to say that both issues have suffered a

---

118 Memorandum of a conference held Apr. 3, [1919], 3 P.M., at the [French] Ministry of Finance, Paris, in J[ohn] F[oster] D[ulles], "Record of Informal Confidential Memoranda and Conferences Dealing with Reparation Clauses of Conditions of Peace With Germany," copy in HHP, separately filed.

119 Twenty years after the event, Dulles recorded his "surprise" that article 231 "could plausibly be, and in fact was, considered to be a historical judgment of war guilt. . . . [T]he profound significance of this article of the Treaty came about through accident, rather than design" (John Foster Dulles, "Forward, Philip Mason Burnett," *Reparation at the Paris Peace Conference from the Standpoint of the American Delegation*, 2 vols. [New York, 1940], 1:xii).

120 Trachtenberg, *Reparation and World Politics*, 56–67; Lentin, *Lloyd George, Woodrow Wilson, and the Guilt of Germany*, 101–2. While remarking that the clause was "a bill of costs, not a moral indictment," Lentin takes a somewhat different position: "The moral imputation [in article 231] arose, as it were accidentally, through the inadvertence and the immediate preoccupations of the Big Three; but once it impinged itself on their consciousness, they did not disclaim it."

121 Hajo Holborn, *A History of Modern Germany, 1840–1945* (New York, 1969), 564–5.

122 James Joll, *Europe Since 1870* (New York, 1973), 277.

123 Hughes, *Contemporary Europe: A History*, 123.

124 For the preliminary airing of these two issues at the peace conference, see Commission des Réparations des Dommages, Deuxième Sous-Commission, Etude de la Capacité Financière des Etats Ennemis et des Moyens de Paiement et de Réparation. Procès-Verbaux. Dossiers Klotz, box 94a. See also the exhaustively documented assessment by Niall Ferguson in chapter 16 in this book.

historiographical fate similar to that of the infamous war–guilt controversy; to wit, the prevalence of a popular mythology that has survived in spite of scholarly refutations based on archival sources that became accessible in recent years. Charles Maier and Trachtenberg have demonstrated that the relatively moderate sum of 132 milliard gold marks (or roughly $33 billion) specified in the London Schedule of Payments of May 1921, which approximated the amount that had been recommended by the American delegates to the Reparation Commission at the peace conference,[125] would not have been unmanageable had the Wirth government in Berlin pursued a politically courageous fiscal policy.[126] Stephen Schuker has detailed the means by which the Weimar Republic ended up paying no net reparations at all, employing the proceeds of American commercial loans to discharge its reparation liability and finance its own economic recovery in the second half of the twenties before defaulting on its foreign obligations in the early thirties.[127] Finally, Keynes's early verdict on the "transfer problem" has also been persuasively challenged by studies solidly grounded in economic theory as well as archival research. These have shown that a relatively moderate increase in taxation and reduction in consumption in the Weimar Republic would have yielded the requisite export surplus to generate the foreign exchange needed to service the reparation debt.[128]

Yet the presumption has endured to our own day that the reparation section of the Versailles treaty (even as modified by the London Schedule of

125 Lamont, who represented the U.S. on the second subcommittee of the Reparation Commission (charged with recommending a total figure), originally (and tentatively) suggested $1.5 billion per year for thirty-five years, for a total of $52.5 billion without interest. 2d Sub-Commission, 6th meeting, Feb. 21, 1919, Dossiers Klotz, box 93. Norman Davis told the Big Four on Apr. 5, 1919, "Regarding the capacity to pay, we have made estimates which varied, at least in the American delegation, between a minimum of 25 billion dollars and a maximum of 35 billions." *DCF,* 1:157. It must be noted that most of the sums bandied about at the peace conference represented the total of all payments including compound interest, whereas the 132 billion gold marks of the London Schedule represented the present value of the debt. On the other hand, the sum specified in the London Schedule was deceptive, since about half of the total was represented by the so-called "C bonds that no one expected ever to be paid." Stephen A. Schuker, "Origins of American Stabilization Policy in Europe: The Financial Dimension, 1918–1924," in Hans-Jürgen Schröder, ed., *Confrontation and Cooperation: Germany and the United States in the Era of World War I, 1900–1924* (Providence, R.I., 1993), 396–7.
126 Charles S. Maier, *Recasting Bourgeois Europe: Stabilization in France, Germany, and Italy in the Decade After World War I* (Princeton, N.J., 1975), 249–53; Trachtenberg, *Reparation in World Politics,* 213–23; Schuker, "Origins of American Stabilization Policy," 397. For a contrary interpretation, see David Felix, *Walther Rathenau and the Weimar Republic: The Politics of Reparations* (Baltimore, 1971), 25–40; and Peter Krüger, "Das Reparationsproblem der Weimarer Republik in fragwürdiger Sicht," *Vierteljahrshefte für Zeitgeschichte* 29 (1981): 21–47.
127 Stephen A. Schuker, *American "Reparations" to Germany, 1919–33* (Princeton, N.J., 1988).
128 Useful discussions of the theoretical literature on the transfer problem appear in Maier, *Recasting Bourgeois Europe,* 250–3, and Trachtenberg, *Reparation in World Politics,* 72–84, 337–42. See also Schuker, *End of French Predominance,* 15–16.

1921) was entirely unworkable owing not only to the "huge," "mountain-ous," "enormous," "heavy," "burdensome," "astronomical," "unjust" amounts required but also to the technical impossibility of converting them into the currencies of the creditors without upsetting the exchanges and hobbling international trade.[129] The familiar corollary of this judgment is the conviction that the misguided attempt to collect these vast sums contributed significantly to Europe's subsequent descent into barbarism, or, as Keynes's biographer put it, "Had Keynes's 1919 programme been carried out, it is unlikely that Hitler would have become German Chancellor."[130] On Armistice Day thirteen years ago, a highly respected commentator on world affairs could not restrain himself from blaming the tragic events of 1933–45 in Europe on "the vindictive madness of the French and British peace terms" of 1919.[131]

That the more positive assessment of the Versailles settlement offered by recent archive-based scholarship has yet to be incorporated into the general historiography and the public consciousness may in part be attributable to the modern world's memory of the terrible events that followed the collapse of the international order created by the peace treaties of 1919. The emotional need to embrace a credible explanation for those subsequent calamities may be an important element in that motivation. Which brings us back to the counterfactual proposition of my student interlocutor mentioned at the beginning of this paper. What if the peace deliberations had been thrown open to public scrutiny, instead of being conducted behind closed doors? What if the head of the German delegation, Ulrich Graf Brockdorff-Rantzau, had been invited to participate in the drafting of the treaty, instead of having been required to sign on the dotted line after the essential features of the agreement had been hammered out without German participation? What if the Weimar Republic had been permitted to retain or acquire those contiguous territories with predominantly German-speaking inhabitants who wished to join it? What if the reparation obligation had been scaled back to the modest sum envisioned by Keynes? What if the war-guilt clause had been expunged from the treaty in recognition of the fact that all belligerents bore an equal share of the blame? What if the Rhineland had escaped the humiliation of foreign military occupation? In short, what if the

---

129 George Moss, *America in the Twentieth Century* (New York, 1989), 89–90; Mortimer Chambers et al., *The Western Experience,* 5th ed. (New York, 1991), 3:1110; Carter V. Findley and John A. M. Rothney, *Twentieth-Century World,* 2d ed. (Boston, 1990), 76–7; George Lichtheim, *Europe in the Twentieth Century* (New York, 1972), 111; Hughes, *Contemporary Europe: A History,* 123, among dozens of other highly respected history and political science texts that could be cited.

130 Skidelsky, *John Maynard Keynes,* 399.

131 George F. Kennan, in the *New York Times,* Nov. 11, 1984.

spirit of Keynes's broadside, combined perhaps with that of Lloyd George's Fontainebleau memorandum,[132] had been incorporated into the German treaty in lieu of its putatively malignant features? Consider how many lives would have been spared, how much property protected, how much human suffering averted!

It should be evident from the foregoing analysis that I am skeptical about deriving such a conclusion from the documentary record of the peace conference. On the contrary, I would propose instead that we strive to obviate this type of counterfactual speculation by clearing away once and for all the thick underbrush of mythology that has grown up around the Versailles treaty during the past seventy-five years and concealed from public view some important features of the settlement of 1919.

In so doing, let us remind our students, readers, and textbook authors of the following verities:

(1) The "Wilsonian" notion that international negotiations should transpire in the full glare of publicity and that the negotiators should be held directly and immediately accountable to their national constituencies did *not* become the defining characteristic of the "new diplomacy" of the twentieth century. It proved instead to be the last gasp of a noble but evanescent aspiration that gave way to a "new diplomacy" of utmost secrecy, from the Churchill–Stalin percentages agreement of 1944 to the Oslo Declaration of an Israeli–Palestinian peace arrangement of our own decade.

(2) The celebrated principle of national self-determination that was ambiguously defined and selectively applied to postwar Europe in 1919 has proved to be no panacea for the world's ills (as many "Wilsonians," though not Wilson himself, earnestly believed). It is therefore altogether inappropriate to condemn the peacemakers for failing to ensure its universal application.

(3) There was no war-guilt clause in the treaty of Versailles. The provision with which that chimera has long been confused was inserted at the suggestion of the most moderate members of the Reparation Commission representing the only country that had no reparation claims as part of their strategy to protect Germany from the economic ruin that would surely have resulted from the requirement that it pay for the entire cost of the war.

(4) The French finance minister probably never asserted that the sole solution to his country's postwar economic difficulties could be summarized in the phrase "Germany will pay," and, even if he had, his government pursued a much more cautious and moderate reparation policy than is expressed in that memorable historical allusion.

(5) The British politicians who indulged in reckless electoral rhetoric about executing the Kaiser and squeezing the German lemon were not devising a strategy for the peace conference but rather were struggling to establish their patri-

132 "Some considerations for the Peace Conference before they finally draft their terms," Mar. 25, 1919, conveniently reprinted in *PWW,* 56:259–70.

otic bona fides in the eyes of an electorate momentarily in the grip of a post-war jingoism that would rapidly fade before the end of the negotiations.

In sum, let us affirm that the Versailles settlement was far from a Carthaginian peace, compared not only with the fate of ancient Carthage itself but more recently with the brutal treatment of defeated Germany at the end of World War II in the form of both territorial amputations and reparations.

Having advanced this proposition, however, I am realistic enough to anticipate that the reputation of the Versailles treaty is unlikely to recover soon from the severe indictment originally issued by disaffected Wilsonians in the interwar period and perpetuated in subsequent generations in the United States and Great Britain. When the German Historical Institute commemorates the centennial of the treaty in 2019, however, it will be exceedingly interesting for those present to review the current state of the field. Will the new scholarly discoveries and interpretations of the 1970s and 1980s finally have been incorporated into the general historiography, and therefore the public memory, of the Versailles settlement? Or will the conventional wisdom continue to embrace the condemnatory verdict of those embittered, angry young men in the American and British delegations at Paris who had briefly glimpsed the promised land – or so they thought – only to see it recede from view as the grim realities of national interest, power, and politics inconveniently intruded into the negotiations to produce a less-than-perfect, that is to say, human, pact of peace?

20

The League of Nations:
Toward a New Appreciation
of Its History

ANTOINE FLEURY

Of all the questions on the agenda of the 1919 peace conference, the project to create a League of Nations was at once the most promising and the most innovative. It was also the matter to which Woodrow Wilson, the president of the peace conference, attached the greatest importance. In Wilson's eyes, the formation of a League of Nations, which he had proposed in his Fourteen Points war-aims address on January 8, 1918, would represent the most crucial contribution that the statesmen meeting in Paris could make to building the new international order. In effect, the League of Nations would form the keystone of the arch. It was to be a whole new concept for eliminating the recourse to war in international relations and ensuring the peace to which people fervently aspired after having been battered and shaken by the greatest martial conflict that humanity had yet known.

THE PEACE CONFERENCE AND THE LEAGUE OF NATIONS

The task of creating a League of Nations was not in itself half as complicated as resolving the other questions that the peace conference faced. Certainly the decisions adopted on this issue required a strong commitment over the long term. But there were no immediate disputes or conflicts of interest among the founding states of the League. No doubt these nations had quite different ideas about the structure the League should take, the optimum degree of engagement, and the powers that should be assigned to this or that branch of the new organization. But at that point everyone's attention was on the innovative nature of the scheme – and on other more pressing issues of the peace conference. Some of the negotiators present at Paris were not

This chapter was translated from French by Stephen A. Schuker.

particularly struck by the idea, however, for they did not think such a league could play an important role or had much of a future. As is well known, it took all of President Woodrow Wilson's persuasive powers to ensure that the League Covenant was introduced as a preamble in the several treaties drawn up at the peace conference. In Wilson's view, none of the arrangements agreed on in Paris should contravene the general principles embodied in the covenant. This implied in turn that all applications of the peace settlements should accord with the spirit of equity that would henceforth prevail in international negotiations and the arrangements proceeding from them. Of course, certain clauses of the Versailles treaty – notably those dealing with the delicate question of reparations – could be interpreted as contravening the principles of the covenant. Indeed, the enforcement of that treaty was placed outside the purview of the League. However, other questions that fell within the League's competence (such as the stipulations governing the Saar, the Free City of Danzig, minorities, mandates, and disarmament) ensured that in the final analysis certain aspects of the Versailles treaty would be grappled with in Geneva.

All the same, this initial bending of the League's founding principle clearly suggested that all those who had assembled at the peace conference were allowing the new international forces of realpolitik to carry the day instead of pursuing the path toward order and a universal solidarity. The contradictions and inconsistencies present at the creation of the League clearly account for many of its weaknesses, the most notable being the lack of universality implied at the start in the decision to exclude Germany from membership. This action led many to complain that the new international organization was merely going to be an instrument for the use of the victorious powers. This departure from the organization's original intent, as inscribed in the covenant and proposed to the public, created considerable consternation among the neutral chancelleries, which saw it as a maneuver by the Allied states.[1] But it also profoundly divided and troubled the public, especially in countries that had initially expressed strong support for the concept.[2]

THE TRANSFORMATION OF INTERNATIONAL POLITICS

With the adoption of the League of Nations Covenant, international politics embarked on a completely new course. Henceforth, nations would

---

1 Cf. *Documents diplomatiques suisses*, 15 vols. (Berne, 1979–88), vols. 7–8.
2 For insights into the attitudes of certain pacifist circles after World War I, see Jacques Bariéty and Antoine Fleury, eds., *Peace Movements and Initiatives in International Policy, 1867–1928* (Berne, 1987), 153ff.

commit themselves to the revolutionary idea of collective security and international solidarity, as embodied in Article 10 of the covenant: "The members of the League undertake to respect and preserve as against external aggression the territorial integrity and existing political independence of all members of the League. In case of any aggression or in case of any threat or danger of such aggression the Council shall advise upon the means by which this obligation shall be fulfilled."

The idea of such a pact in 1919, by comparison with the bilateral alliances and coalitions of the pre-1914 era, and indeed the period of World War I itself, represented a major step forward in international affairs. Indeed, the principle of collective security and solidarity is so important a concept that it figures prominently in the United Nations Charter. Seventy-five years ago, however, the method of guaranteeing the collective security set forth in the Covenant was still in its infancy and many weaknesses still had to be ironed out before the ideals of peace could take hold and discourage the use of force in concrete international relationships. Even some of the states belonging to the League (Japan and Italy) could not be dissuaded from resorting to force. Their clear violation of the covenant demonstrated the inadequacy of its system of collective security and consequently the insufficiency of the measures adopted to guarantee the peace.

It was above all this unfortunate experience in the realm of peacekeeping that discredited the entire League of Nations enterprise, not merely among those who in 1918 were dreaming of a world at peace, but also many who came after.

The second major step forward embodied in the covenant was the idea of institutionalizing mechanisms for international cooperation in every aspect of life – economic, social, scientific, technical, and cultural – which might otherwise generate interstate conflict but under the League would reinforce universal solidarity. From the vantage point of the late twentieth century, when the notion of the *global village* has become a commonplace, one can fully appreciate the visionary spirit of the architects of the League Covenant, as well as of certain of their collaborators within the permanent Secretariat established at Geneva. Very early on, those visionaries saw that mutual interdependence among states and increasingly among societies was a result of the profound forces in play since the beginning of the century that were conducive to an international, rather than a purely national, perspective. It was of great merit to the authors of the covenant that they recognized those great forces entrusted their management to the fledgling League of Nations.

Certainly, at first glance, one might conclude that the sense of international cooperation had still eluded the statesmen and experts who set them-

selves the task of crafting the rules of the new international order. It was
only in Article 23 that they enumerated six areas in which member states
should undertake obligations to cooperate. At the time, all those activities
appeared prosaic, or for the most part within the jurisdiction of technical
services attached to diverse state administrations. Nevertheless, one of those
dimensions began straightaway to assume the greatest importance, namely,
the social question referred to in clause A of Article 23. That clause stipu-
lated: "The Members of the League will endeavor to secure and maintain
fair and humane conditions of labor for men, women, and children both in
their own countries and in all countries to which their commercial and
industrial relations extend, and for that purpose will establish and maintain
the necessary organizations."

The treatment of the social question would lead to a surprising development at the peace conference designed to thwart the propagation of the
communist model that Lenin sought to impose on the laboring masses and
humanity. To counter the League of Nations, which Lenin deemed the
instrument of bourgeois capitalist states, he created the Third International
in March 1919.[3]

Negotiators at the peace conference attached such urgency to the measures to be taken in this domain that they proposed that an entire section
entitled "Labor" be included in the Versailles treaty. That section, recapitulated in the other treaties of peace, comprised the forty articles forming Part
XIII of the treaty. This imposing ensemble would serve as the charter for
the International Labour Organisation (ILO), which was set up by the first
international labor conference held in Washington, from the end of October to December 1919. Some of its clauses remain in effect today.

The statesmen assembled in Paris thus confirmed the importance of the
social dimension in international relations. The preamble to Part XIII
expressly states that "the League of Nations has as its aim the establishment
of universal peace, and that such a peace can only be founded on the basis
of social justice." Note that President Wilson, the moving force behind the
League, had not even mentioned the social question in his Fourteen Points.

Here is a dimension of policy that would see universal and uninterrupted
development from 1919 to the present, thanks to the ILO, whose activities
during its first era were marked by close proximity and complementarity
with the League of Nations. This organization, formally named in the
League Covenant and the Versailles treaty, could be the first of the existing
international organizations to associate itself with the United Nations,

---

3 Arno J. Mayer, *Politics and Diplomacy of Peacemaking: Containment and Counter-Revolution at Versailles*
   (New York, 1967).

which would acknowledge its status as a *specialized institution*. In this area, it would be inaccurate to speak of failure or of ephemeral results, even though it has proved difficult to persuade national states to endorse objectives set forth by the ILO at the outset, and even though certain objectives remain far from universally accepted today.

In the other areas in which international cooperation was proposed to under Article 23, the results would prove less significant. Some of those areas – such as the treatment of women and children, traffic in opium and other drugs – were entrusted to appropriate services within the Secretariat, which had only meager financial resources. Later, the United Nations would take responsibility for those services and transform them into UN bureaus. Meanwhile, cooperation in fighting disease (Article 23 F) would be transferred in 1948 to the World Health Organization (WHO). The WHO thus emerged as the successor to the International Office of Hygiene created in 1904, and the International Office of Public Health, created in 1907 and integrated with the League in 1920. In other words, in the struggle against epidemics and infectious disease, the League reinforced measures conceived by a few states before 1914 and helped to apply them universally. The results obtained in the field of health have been notable, thanks to cooperative efforts coordinated by the League during the entire interwar period and by the WHO since 1948. These efforts have contributed to humanity far beyond what those founding statesmen could ever have imagined in 1919.

Another task assigned to the League under Article 23, Clause D, concerned collaboration in the control of arms trafficking. In this case, the League Secretariat met with enormous difficulty gaining support for its proposals for conferences to negotiate arms reductions. When it finally succeeded in organizing the World Disarmament Conference at Geneva in 1932, the confluence of international events proved inauspicious.[4] A world economic crisis had wreaked havoc on societies everywhere, leaving them in political and social disarray. In Germany, Hitler had begun rising in power and encouraging Germany to free itself from the "servitude" that had made it inferior to other powers. From that time on, the Germany disposed to cooperate began to disappear. The disarmament talks seemed destined to break down, not because of any lack of preparation, or qualified delegates.

4 Cf. Naoum Sloutzky, *La Société des Nations et le contrôle du commerce international des armes de guerre, 1919–1938* (Geneva, 1969); Maurice Vaïsse, *Sécurité d'abord: la politique francaise en matière de désarmement, 1930–1934* (Paris, 1981); Maurice Vaïsse, "La SdN et le désarmement," in *The League of Nations in Retrospect: Proceedings of the Symposium, 6–9 November 1980* (Berlin, 1982), 245ff.; see also Antoine Fleury, "La Suisse et la question de désarmement dans l'entre-deux guerres," in Alessandro Migliazza and Enrico Decleva, eds., *Diplomazia e storia delle relazioni internazionale: Studie in onore di Enrico Serra* (Milan, 1991), 303–20.

Rather it was due to the deliberate obstruction by a power that wished to remain free to rearm and be free to do so in time to resort to war should its international policy objectives demand it. Hitler's radical opposition to the "spirit of Geneva" and indeed to the very philosophy of the League of Nations was well known, not only from *Mein Kampf,* but also from his speeches.

Finally, under subsection E of Article 23, the covenant specified that the powers would "make provision to secure and maintain freedom of communications and of transit and of equitable treatment for the commerce of all Members of the League. In this connection, the special necessities of the regions devastated during the war of 1914–1918 shall be borne in mind."

This brief paragraph embodies the spirit of two propositions figuring in President Wilson's original Fourteen Points. Wilson's Point 2, calling for "absolute freedom of navigation upon the seas, outside territorial waters," is replaced here by "freedom of communications and of transit." And Wilson's Point 3, proposing the removal of all economic barriers and the establishment of equal trade conditions, was incorporated almost word for word in Article 23 E of the covenant.

President Wilson and the American delegation to the Paris Peace Conference attached great importance to the gradual removal of all obstacles to commercial exchanges, to the dismantling of war economies, and to freedom of communication, which, for the Americans, boiled down essentially to freedom of the seas. Under this final rubric, the League of Nations succeeded in establishing a program of intensive activity that bore its first fruits at the May 1921 Barcelona Conference on communications and transit. The Barcelona meeting established a convention and a set of rules for regulating waterways of international interest. Those activities would be pursued under the auspices of the League of Nations section on communications and transit with a view to promoting multilateral consultation in the fields concerned. As early as the 1920s, League proponents had urged the establishment of a radio institution designed to promote information exchange between the Secretariat and the various member states, and more particularly to hasten consultation and relief activities in the event of an international crisis. However, the League Assembly did not adopt the plan for the creation of a radiotelegraph transmitter with a worldwide range until September 24, 1929. The League of Nations radio station finally began operating on February 2, 1932, but by then the League itself had already begun its decline.[5]

5 See Antoine Fleury, "La Suisse et Radio-Nations," in *League of Nations in Retrospect,* 126–230. On this question, see also *Documents diplomatiques suisses,* vols. 8–11, under rubric, "Switzerland and the League of Nations."

The Paris Peace Conference was unable to spend much time discussing the removal of economic barriers and the establishment of the new economic order called for by President Wilson in January 1918. That question was forced to yield to others that assumed more importance in the calculations of the victorious powers, which were bent, above all, on the political recasting of the continent, and the determination of complex frontiers, which bore a direct relation to certain economic objectives. In any case, it would have been difficult to push ahead with the discussion of a new economic order inspired by Wilsonian ideas without blocking all negotiation on the economic clauses of the Versailles treaty, for the governing principle of reparations stood in contradiction to the Wilsonian principle of the equal treatment of all nations. After all, the economic clauses of the Versailles treaty were calculated precisely to ensure that Germany, deprived of its key resources, would no longer have the means to launch a new war on its neighbors.[6]

These considerations explain why the new economic order, which speeches before and during the peace conference had described as one of the essential ingredients of a political peace, was dispensed with in a few words in Article 23 E, while the economic clauses of the Versailles treaty were set down in fuller detail. Obviously, the founders, by limiting themselves to recognizing the principle of equal trade conditions among nations, failed to give the League even a modicum of authority. Another important factor to mention here is that the majority of statesmen, diplomats, and experts still thought that reconstruction needs at the end of the war would suffice to restart the economy and that it would not take long to return to the production levels and practices of the prewar period. It is true enough that an upsurge of production took place in various countries during 1919. But beginning in 1920, discussion again focused on overproduction, the absence of markets, and crisis. The financial underpinnings for recovery were nowhere to be seen. The commercial networks that had existed before 1914 had been broken almost beyond repair broken in Europe. New economic entities, with a distinctly limited commercial and financial purview, had replaced the large-scale arrangements of the prewar era. This unforeseen situation led the League of Nations Council, as early as February 1920, to hold a conference designed "to study the financial crisis and seek the means of overcoming it or attenuating its dangerous consequences."[7] This would be the international financial conference that met in Brussels from September 24 to October 8, 1920.[8]

6 See chapter 15 in this book.
7 *Journal Officiel de la Société des Nations: Procès-verbaux du Conseil II, 6ème séance* (Geneva, 1920), 24.
8 See Marie-Renée Mouton, "Société des Nations et reconstruction financière de l'Europe: la con-

The important result of that conference, to which Germany was invited, was to create a committee, embracing both a financial and an economic section. That committee, as a note from the League Council to member governments intimated, would be charged with making proposals for dealing with this "extremely complex problem whose solutions required the continuity of a long effort pursued in common."[9] In the first instance, the conference anticipated entrusting the permanent staff of this provisional committee to the care of the League Secretariat, before the constitution of a permanent economic and financial organism attached to the League of Nations. The permanent civil servants and experts of the League had counted on this Brussels meeting, for which they had laid the groundwork in London, to revive some of the inter-Allied cooperative mechanisms that had worked so well during the war.[10] But the tangible result, which led to the creation of an economic and financial organization attached to the League, would permit those very experts to impose their solutions, without always succeeding, save in the notable case of the economic and financial rescue of Austria, in securing the approval of the various governments. Had the governments implemented the experts' recommendations, one could have "spared Europe from twenty years of stagnation and another war." The team at the League Secretariat had the conviction of pioneers. They felt as though they were "developing the habits of cooperation among peoples who had earlier known no relations but force."[11]

Unfortunately, it seems that the national representatives were not yet experienced enough to recognize that the best way to safeguard their long-run national interests was to undertake multilateral negotiation. The main concern of the country delegates was to find solutions that respected national interests. To be sure, the rule of unanimity led to the development of a spirit of cooperation in negotiation, but by the same token that rule held each state back from sacrificing its immediate national interest on the altar of universal solidarity.

That is why international conferences tended to end up doing a great deal of talking but little signing. Nevertheless, by dint of perseverance things gradually changed. The international economic conference held at Geneva in May 1927 not only offered a precise diagnosis of the health of the world

férence de Bruxelles (24 septembre–8 octobre 1920)," *Relations internationales*, no. 39 (Autumn 1984): 309–31. See also Marie-Renée Mouton, *La Société des Nations et les intérêts de la France (1920–1924)* (Berne, 1995).

9 Archives de la Société des Nations, Palais des Nations, Geneva, R 443; see also R 503–4.
10 Jean Monnet, *Mémoires* (Paris, 1976), 131. Monnet served as deputy secretary general of the League of Nations from 1919 to 1922.
11 Ibid.

economy, still disfigured from economic nationalism, despite the new spirit of cooperation resulting from the Locarno accords and the German entry into the League; it also proposed a program of negotiations leading to the abolition of prohibitions and restrictions on imports and exports. A new dynamic was set in motion. As early as October 1927, a follow-up conference to promote economic action met in Geneva.[12]

Certain positive results were obtained in the form of conventions and protocols aiming to reduce customs duties and, as economic recession spread over the world, to check and even to forbid new protectionist measures that countries had a tendency to adopt unilaterally. But despite all those negotiations aimed at developing a progressive program to reduce trade barriers they could not resist the strength of unilateral measures adopted by the Great Powers (that is, the Smoot-Hawley Tariff of May 1930 and then, in 1932, the inauguration of a preferential economic zone linking the members of the British Commonwealth through the Ottawa accords).

The World Economic Conference of London sought a remedy for this general panic in June–July 1933. But given the depth of antagonisms and the lack of faith in multilateral negotiation, it met with little success. The effort at international economic cooperation within the framework of the League lost all its significance. With the defeat of the Briand Plan for a European federal union, failure was registered both on a world scale and also within the more circumscribed nambit of Europe.[13]

From the foregoing events, it seems clear that the framework for international economic cooperation was still too fragile, its results still too precarious, to withstand the protectionist storm soon to be coupled with a nationalist hubris that would once again pit the peoples of the world against each other. But it would be erroneous to blame the League of Nations for the breakdown of economic negotiations. Quite the contrary, the activities of the League in the economic sphere, although neither anticipated nor wished for by its founders, appeared with the passage of time to constitute a contribution to the fashioning of the contemporary world.[14]

12 For the details of this conference and the commercial negotiations that followed, see Antoine Fleury, "Un sursaut antiprotectionniste dans le contexte de la crise économique de 1929: le projet d'une trêve douanière plurilatérale," *Relations internationales*, no. 39 (Autumn 1984): 333–54.

13 See *Le Plan Briand d'union fédérale européene: Documents* (Geneva, 1991); see also *Le Plan Briand d'union européene: Actes du Colloque de l'Association Internationale d'Histoire Contemporaine tenu à Genève (19–21 septembre 1991)* (Berne, forthcoming).

14 For a comprehensive view of the League's achievements in this area, see *La politique commerciale dans le monde d'après-guerre: Rapport des Comités économique et financier* (Geneva, 1945), C31.M31.1945.IIA. For other references, see Antoine Fleury, "Un sursaut antiprotectionniste"; see also Eric Bussière, "L'Organisation économique de la SdN et la naissance du régionalisme économique en Europe," *Relations internationales*, no. 75 (1993): 301–13.

In a sense, the economic experience of the League of Nations can be compared to an apprenticeship in international economic cooperation. As in any apprenticeship, it takes time to develop the necessary skills, but time was not always available to the League of Nations. Since the end of World War II, however, the apprenticeship in international economic cooperation has continued to build on those early experiences, among them a plan proposed during World War I for a central organization to institutionalize international economic cooperation. However, it was not until very recently, on December 15, 1993, following the negotiations of the Uruguay Round in the General Agreement on Tariffs and Trade (GATT), that an agreement was reached to set up a World Trade Organization.[15] That agreement superseded an older GATT adopted provisionally on October 30, 1947, which had remained in force until recently because of the objections to an International Trade Organization, elaborated at a U.N. Conference on Commerce and Employment in May 1948, but not ratified by many countries, including the government of the United States, which refused even to submit it to Congress.

If this development, after decades of almost constant multilateral trade negotiations, signifies that nations will never resort again to war for economic reasons, then it can be said that one of the major objectives of the League's founding fathers has indeed been achieved. As already mentioned, the members of the League Secretariat never once stopped hoping that international economic relations would some day, through multilateral negotiations, arrive at compromises satisfactory to all partners over the long term. Often they came up against national egos and the nationalist utopias embraced by most of the political leaders of the interwar generation. Those leaders, alas, still believed in the supremacy of the nation–state and of national interest without regard for the transnational dimension, whether regional or on a world scale.

Viewed from this perspective, the League of Nations can be said to have been the harbinger of a new world order based on international cooperation. It embodied the new ideas that characterized the twentieth century. But one must also recognize the precariousness of those ideas and acknowledge the provisional failure of the experience between 1930 and 1945. Yet those early efforts brought with them a vision that would be recast in the framework of the United Nations. Then between 1948 and 1989 the Cold War would divide the whole world into two opposing blocs, thereby pre-

15 The World Trade Organization was established after the ratification of the Uruguay Round accords on April 15, 1994, in Marrakesh.

venting nations from arriving at any truly global solutions to the great problems of humanity. Yet, one need not be too pessimistic about the history of
the twentieth century now coming to a close. One can hope that the ideal
of a world at peace – the ideal animating the League's founders and leading
its collaborators in the 1920s to elaborate mechanisms of consultation and
cooperation applicable in the event of bilateral as well as multilateral men-
aces – will become the dominant feature of the twenty-first century. This
justifies a renewed close study of the League of Nations' accomplishments,
for the League represents a milestone in the long process required to establish multilateral diplomacy on a world scale.

Within the community of historians and among numerous commentators on
international organizations, the consensus has long been that the League of
Nations was a failure and a group unworthy of serious study. The matter
seemed self-evident.[16] The general works devoted to the subject have stressed
the political dimension of the League. They have analyzed the major issues
and political conflicts of the interwar period in order to highlight the incapacity of the League's machinery to solve them. By contrast, numerous specialized studies have dealt with the institutional questions (the covenant, the
assembly, the council, the secretariat) and the administrative functioning of
the new international organization.[17] On the occasion of the League's sixti-
eth anniversary, in 1980, an international colloquium meeting in Geneva
outlined the results of research on particular aspects of the League's work
emphasizing the innovations that it had made in specialized aspects of international relations while in a large measure confirming earlier judgments.[18]

However, with the passage of time and almost half a century's experience
with the United Nations, that organization, too, has now and then failed to
attain its declared objectives of 1945. In fact, the disrepute into which the
United Nations has fallen is scarcely less today than that suffered by the
League of Nations before its official interment at Geneva in April 1946. Yet

16 One may cite, as a recent example of synthesis, Paul M. Kennedy's *The Rise and Fall of the Great Powers: Economic Change and Military Conflict from 1500 to 2000* (New York, 1987). Kennedy devotes but
   two paragraphs and a few scattered references to the League, mostly in order to emphasize the political reasons for its failure. He goes so far as to venture this summary judgment: "Ironically . . . the
   League's actual contribution turned out to be not deterring aggressors, but confusing the democracies" (290).
17 For a detailed guide to this abundant literature of varying quality, see V. Y. Ghebali, ed., *Bibliographical Handbook of the League of Nations*, 3 vols. (Geneva, 1980).
18 See *League of Nations in Retrospect.* Note that the fifty-year rule for consultation of the League of
   Nations Archives has served, until recently, to discourage thorough historical research.

have historians not been too quick to lose interest in the achievements of the League of Nations, just as they have taken insufficient notice of the contributions of the United Nations, not merely to the history of international relations but to the history of the contemporary world? René Girault recently asked why historians have shied away from the subject.[19]

> Perhaps unconsciously, historians have felt reluctance to study these centers of decadence. They have preferred to concern themselves with the Powers, the real actors in international relations. The illusions and the rude awakenings that surrounded the life of the League of Nations have doubtless helped to discredit all international organizations. What good does it do to analyze an institution that in practical terms failed to find a solution to the disputes existing at the time? The black legend of the League of Nations was born; one would soon forget Geneva and its sterile debates.[20]

Actually, much recent research and work in progress takes a different approach to the League experience. Many current investigators are introducing a long-term perspective into the study of the emergence and deepening of the transnational dimension in the field of international relations. Such a perspective restores a sense of pride to the League and its activities. New inquiries allow the reconstruction of the distant origins or lines of development of existing institutions; they permit a new inventory of certain international realities and actions. Through these studies, as Girault has rightly noted, "the traditional view of a decadent League of Nations is challenged, not in respect to its immediate political results; but rather regarding its influences on current international life." In fact, there is more continuity between the world before and after 1945 than is usually acknowledged. World War II functions not as a caesura, but rather as an accelerator of preexisting tendencies.[21]

This chapter does not propose to discuss all new research in the field, which on many points brings forth fresh perspectives if not additional substantive knowledge.[22] Because of the limited scope of this discussion, I can only touch on a few of the recent contributions that deal with questions that

---

19 *Relations internationales,* no. 75 (Autumn 1993).
20 Ibid., 273.
21 Ibid., 274. On this particular point, see also Georg Kreis, "Entre deux étapes de la diplomatie multilatérale permanente: réflexions et jugements sur la Société des Nations au moment de la fondation des Nations Unies," *Relations internationales,* no. 39 (Autumn 1984): 373–87. See also a recent reappraisal of collective security in the twentieth century: see the special issue of *Relations internationales* (no. 86, Summer 1996), edited by Antoine Fleury, *The League of Nations, 1920–1946: Organization and Accomplishments: A Retrospective of the First Organization for the Establishment of World Peace* (Geneva, 1996).
22 For a first appraisal of promising new studies or work in progress, see the special issue of *Relations internationales* (no. 75, Autumn 1993) devoted to the League of Nations.

preoccupied the leaders of the League of Nations and that remain today or have again become the salient issues of international politics.

Gabriel Carette, in his study of League efforts to create an international police force, analyzes the difficulties that arose at the Peace Conference and later in the League in attempting to endow the latter with an armed force that would serve as the "secular arm of an international organization, whose decisions it could enforce on a military level."[23] The failure to achieve this in the 1920s, unhappily confirmed in the 1930s, turned out to be only provisional. The concept would be revived in the United Nations Charter, although there, too, and even up to the present, practical application has met with difficulty and still encounters grave difficulties that perhaps can at last be surmounted now that the Cold War has come to an end.

Eric Bussière emphasizes the importance of investigating the "economic organization of the League." He offers a detailed analysis of the attempts to promote economic regionalism in Europe between 1925 and 1932, and thus focuses on the intense labor that served as the source of the future progress of European economic integration after 1945.[24] Bussière calls attention to the progress in economic cooperation within the League, from the universalist approach that still prevailed in 1927, at the time of the International Economic Conference, to a regional approach designed to amalgamate the European states into a Continental economic entente. It was indeed within the League Secretariat that the plans for a United States of Europe were hatched, whether the particular formulations were those of Arthur Salter, director of the economic and financial section, or those of his deputy Pietro Stoppani.[25] These experts in international cooperation, in contrast to the politicians, were convinced in 1929–30 that "the creation of a great European market was a long-term objective that would only be achieved in 50 years or at any rate after several decades."

This long-term planning took into account the problems of economic organization and harmonization as they had been perceived since 1927, that is to say before the Great Crash of October 1929. The new difficulties that the Great Depression brought about merely reinforced efforts already under way to solve the problems of the European economy. In his analysis of solu-

23 See Gabriel Carette, "La force internationale de police dans le cadre de la Société des Nations: concepts et réalités au seuil des années vingt," *Relations internationales,* no. 75 (Autumn 1993): 293.

24 Ibid., 301ff.

25 Arthur Salter, *The United States of Europe and Other Papers* (London, 1983), 82–104; Pietro Stoppani, "Mémorandum relatif à l'dée d'un accord collectif pour une meilleure organisation des relations internationales en Europe," League of Nations Archives, R 2867. Excerpts from these two documents have been published in Michel Dumoulin and Eric Bussière, eds., *Les cercles économiques et l'Europe au XXe siècle* (Louvain-la-Neuve, 1992), 53–80.

tions considered in the Study Commission for the European Union, created in the wake of the Briand memorandum for a European federal union in May 1930, Bussière notes the effort that went into "the creation of a Europe with variable geometry," including "communities of interest" that would permit the achievement of economic unity on a progressive basis.[26] It was the "political circumstances in Europe after 1933 and the development of the world economic crisis" that compelled the postponement until much later of the first practical results of those ideas.[27]

Indeed, it is precisely the present difficulties of organizing Europe – whether the modalities of integration and the enlargement of the European Community, or the European Union and the nature of relations between that union and nonsignatory European states – that makes it especially important to obtain in-depth knowledge of the debates, plans, and failures of the interwar era. The interest in doing so becomes all the greater when one scrutinizes more closely the role of professional associations and their relation to wider organization of the economy, as well as the executives of such groupings, many of whom after 1945 became the key shapers of the reorganized European economy. The works of Peter Krüger, in a very similar spirit, shed light on those efforts at economic cooperation during the 1920s that could serve as precursors for European integration plans after 1945.[28] Krüger quite correctly raises some questions about the prevailing interpretation, according to which the German authorities and other concerned circles followed a fundamentally negative and destructive policy during the 1920s.[29]

To tell the truth, this area of research is immense and practically untouched. It awaits the historian who wishes to focus precisely on the respective positions of different groups in the diverse countries concerned with the economic issues placed on the agendas of the League study committees and the economic conferences that it organized.

One additional realm has suffered from the disrepute into which the League has fallen. That is the system for protecting minorities. The Great Powers, conscious of having cut up the frontiers during the peace conference, knew that certain national claims could disturb the general peace, and

---

26 Bussière, "L'Organisation èconomique," 313.
27 Ibid.
28 Peter Krüger, "Die Ansätze zu einer europäischen Wirtschaftsgemeinschaft in Deutschland nach dem Ersten Weltkrieg," in Helmut Berding, ed., *Wirtschaftliche und politische Integration in Europa im 19. und 20. Jahrhundert* (Göttingen, 1984), 1490–68.
29 See Matthias Schulz, "Die deutsche Aussenwirtschaftspolitik im Rahmen der multilateralen Wirtschaftskonferenzen des Völkerbunds, 1927–1933," Ph.D. diss., University of Hamburg, 1997.

they entrusted the League with the protection of minorities. Marie-Renée Mouton presents a global analysis of the system, draws up a balance sheet, and shows how ultimately Nazi Germany abused the principle of nationality to vitiate all results achieved in Europe.[30] Carole Fink's published studies and works in progress on European national minorities underscore the extent to which the modest actions undertaken by the League fulfilled an essential function in promoting equitable treatment among populations of diverse origin, culture, and religion within a single state and between neighboring states.[31] As is well known, the great powers that founded the United Nations – the United States and the Soviet Union – were allergic to any sort of international statutory regime for minorities. Nevertheless, current events challenge the received wisdom on the League experience. The breakup of the Soviet Union, Yugoslavia, and Czechoslovakia, not to speak of minority problems in the great countries of Asia and Africa, demonstrate how much more effectively regional peace, indeed world peace, could be guaranteed if a system for the protection of minorities were adopted. And this is so, notwithstanding all the unwillingness that several powers have expressed, today as in the aftermath of World War I, to abandon one iota of their sovereignty for the sake of a juridical solution.

CONCLUSIONS

It is impossible in the space of this short chapter to recount the League of Nations' contribution to contemporary history. Yet the League has had many achievements in matters of technical diplomacy whose effects impose themselves over the very long term. Nor can one adumbrate the attainments in the field of multilateral economic diplomacy, which exceeded by far what seemed possible before 1914. Nor, finally, can one do justice to political diplomacy in the area of conflict resolution.

The essential thing is to provide a long-term perspective on the principal contributions of the League to contemporary international relations. This chapter has called attention to a few such contributions, too long forgotten or even condemned by diplomats and too often used by historians merely as pegs on which to hang negative references to what one should not do in international affairs.

Recent developments in the international situation, especially in Europe,

---

30 Marie-Renée Mouton, "La Société des Nations et la protection des minorités nationales en Europe," *Relations internationales*, no. 75 (autumn 1993): 315–28.
31 See also chapter 11 in this book.

marked by the breakup of states, the plotting of new frontiers, and unprecedented changes in the reorganization of economic and social systems, has lent sudden immediacy to these questions, and to solutions that hark back both to the 1919 Peace Conference and to the activities and proposals of the League. Let unbiased historians rediscover the models, means, and objectives suggested, elaborated, and more or less happily put into practice by the League of Nations. Such a rediscovery would doubtless constitute a salutary contribution to the studies now under way with a view to reorganizing Europe and the world on equitable bases acceptable to all the populations concerned.

21

A Comment

DIANE B. KUNZ

Winston Churchill was once asked: What are the desirable qualifications for any young man who wishes to become a politician. He replied: "It is the ability to foretell what is going to happen tomorrow, next week, next month and next year. And to have the ability afterwards to explain why it didn't happen." To comment on the legacy and consequences of the Versailles treaty, one must be willing to take up Churchill's challenge. I will do my best to live up to this task.

The three chapters in this section cover the entire gamut of the Versailles treaty. First, William Keylor calls attention to the Paris Peace Conference as a unique episode in the annals of international diplomacy.[1] Had it been successful, a conference and five associated treaties that attempted to redraw the map of over half the world's continents, change the nationalities of millions of people, redo economic relations, create a formula for the abolition of war, and even reframe the basic concepts of morality in international relations would have had immeasurable importance. Ironically, the fact that the conference was by and large a failure increased its influence in the years to come. It is to the failures that so much time and study have been devoted: as events in and of themselves, as cause and effect on the road to the next war, and finally as guideposts to our future, which eerily resembles the world the Versailles peacemakers saw.

Above all, the Versailles treaty failed to create a brave new world order, and it "triggered" World War II. However, the treaty itself, representing, in Piotr Wandycz's description, the peacemakers' attempt to achieve "equity and political reality," was not the real culprit.[2] In actuality, the guilt associated with the treaty, rather than the treaty as such, helped spark World War II. As Keylor explains, even though historians have successfully refuted the

1 See chapter 19 in this book.
2 See chapter 13 in this book.

myth of war guilt and the view that reparations were an intolerable burden, these ideas rapidly became accepted wisdom and remain so now.[3] Most people "know" that the Versailles treaty helped precipitate World War II and they "know" that reparations were wrong. Many statesmen came to believe, as John Maynard Keynes wrote in *The Economic Consequences of the Peace,* that reparations could never have worked, indeed, as the British Treasury official and banker put it, that they jeopardized the "order of Government and Society for which [the French government] stands."[4] Moreover, it became a basic part of the weltanschauung of the chattering classes during the interwar era that these payments lay buried in a treaty the wrongs of which needed to be redressed.

Looming largest was the "war-guilt clause" – the provisions of Article 231 of the Versailles treaty stating that Germany was theoretically responsible for the entire expenditures arising out of the war but would actually be liable only for the costs specifically enumerated. Rather than being seen as an American lawyer's clever attempt to limit actual German financial responsibility by buying off French politicians and their public with the sop of a piece of paper, this clause became an easily exploitable open sore.[5] During the interwar era, the increasingly prevalent view that the Versailles treaty had brought about, in Harold Nicolson's phrase, a peace that was "neither just nor wise" stoked traditional anti-French prejudice in Britain while giving German revisionists potent ammunition.[6]

Reparations, a time-honored part of the postwar settlement process, most recently exacted by the German government from the infant Soviet state in the Treaty of Brest-Litovsk, became universally excoriated under the Weimar republic. British leaders, following Keynes, also rejected the premises that British Prime Minister David Lloyd George had utilized in Paris. Few in London or Berlin stopped to consider that without reparations the French and Belgians, not the Germans, would be paying the price for the First World War.[7] As Keylor points out, rather than having been saddled with a Car-

---

3 See chapter 19 in this book.
4 John Maynard Keynes, *The Economic Consequences of the Peace* (New York, 1920), generally and 131. See also David Lloyd George, *The Truth About Reparations and War Debts* (Garden City, N.Y., 1932; reprint, New York, 1970). Lloyd George, the British prime minister and chief negotiator for His Majesty's Government at the Versailles Conference, details in this 1932 volume his original position in favor of reparations and his shift to a Keynesian revisionism in the intervening decade.
5 The clever lawyer in question was John Foster Dulles, nephew of Woodrow Wilson's secretary of state, Robert Lansing.
6 See chapter 19 in this book.
7 On the reparations question, see Stephen A. Schuker, *American "Reparations" to Germany, 1919–1933: Implications for the Third-World Debt Crisis* (Princeton, N.J., 1988); and Stephen A. Schuker, *The End of French Predominance in Europe: The Financial Crisis of 1924 and the Adoption of the Dawes Plan* (Chapel Hill, N.C., 1976); Marc Trachtenberg, *Reparation in World Politics: France and European Economic Diplomacy, 1916–1923* (New York, 1980), generally and 50–1.

thaginian peace, Germany "could easily have managed the payments with but a moderate reduction of domestic consumption."[8]

The long-life span of inaccurate beliefs concerning pivotal historical events is undeniable. A parallel situation arose after the American Civil War. Abraham Lincoln's promise of "with malice toward none" resembles Woodrow Wilson's Fourteen Points. Southern whites, left to their own devices, reenacted in the black codes many of their antebellum restrictions on African-Americans. Had the seceding states been readmitted to the Union on the basis they sought, the Confederacy would have won the Civil War. Southern states would have gained significantly more representation in Congress at the same time as they preserved "the southern way of life" – the total subservience of African-Americans to white rule and regimentation.[9] Yet it soon became received wisdom that Congress's attempt to provide the freed slaves with their due rights was little short of criminal and that justice triumphed only after radical Reconstruction ended in the aftermath of the 1877 electoral compromise. In the 1960s, however, Kenneth Stampp and other revisionists successfully challenged this view.[10] Today no one would dream of citing historians such as Claude Bowers or Merton Coulter to back up an assertion concerning Reconstruction.[11] Perhaps not enough time has yet passed for the renunciation of Versailles myths. Keynes still wins out despite thirty years' work to the contrary by the distinguished scholars contributing to this collection and elsewhere.

Keynes's ideas about reparations, particularly his fixation on transfer problems, left important legacies for World War II peacemaking and also undermined Western confidence during the oil shocks of the 1970s. The ghosts of Versailles helped configure the Bretton Woods agreements (in which Keynes himself had a serious hand), and they bolstered Anglo-American resistance to Soviet demands for reparations. Western leaders exhibited little sympathy for Moscow's expectations that Nazi slash-and-burn tactics would be redressed. Everyone "knew" that reparations would be bad for the postwar economic world order. As the battle over German reparations played a major role in the mushrooming hostility between the victorious powers, the con-

8 William R. Keylor, *The Twentieth Century World: An International History*, 2d ed. (New York, 1992), 94.
9 Blacks now would be counted on the basis of one person, one vote instead of as three-fifths of a person as the Constitution had required.
10 Kenneth M. Stampp, *The Era of Reconstruction, 1865–1877* (New York, 1965).
11 Yet traces of earlier views remain, e.g., in this description of the effect of Abraham Lincoln's death on the course of Reconstruction found in the Week in Review section of the *New York Times* of November 12, 1995: "Without him, Northern Republicans brought vengeance down on the South with a ferocity that was alien to Lincoln, putting it under military rule." See, e.g., Claude G. Bowers, *The Tragic Era* (Boston, 1929); E. Merton Coulter, *The South During Reconstruction, 1865–1877*, vol. 8: *A History of the South*, ed. Wendell Homes Stephenson and E. Merton Coulter (Baton Rouge, La., 1947).

tribution to the Cold War of Versailles-era misconceptions cannot be gain-said. During the oil shocks the specter of Keynes's prognostications of the evil effects of massive monetary transfers, in this case from oil-consuming nations to oil producing-states, on the world economy visibly hovered over many discussions. Yet just as Keynes had overestimated the problem of mon-etary transfers in the interwar period, the dire prognostications of diplomats and bankers during the 1970s never came to pass.

The next failure of the Versailles peacemakers concerns the national bor-ders that they created and their treatment of the question of national self-determination. The postwar division of the territories of the German Reich, the Ottoman Empire, and Austrian-Hungarian Empire can easily be criticized. Piotr Wandycz shows how the Polish delegates to Versailles used their ethnic strength to legitimize the reemergence of the "Polish question" from a matter of antiquarian interest to an agreed-upon item for the agenda of Versailles peacemakers. His dissection of diplomatic strategies, Polish, German, and Allied, provides a guide to the antecedents, actuality, and aftermath of conference diplomacy.[12] Poland, albeit with different borders, has stood the test of time; Czechoslovakia and Yugoslavia, presenting far more difficult issues for the diplomats to consider, have dissolved. Wandycz's discussion offers some reasons for why this was so.

As Keylor points out, Wilsonian self-determination was a more limited notion than is commonly thought.[13] Furthermore, Versailles peacemakers did not cause the fission of the nineteenth century – they had been disinte-grating for decades. Rather, the importance of the Versailles and associated treaties was that they gave a modern imprimatur to ethnically pure nation states. Manufactured nationalist movements of the nineteenth century simultaneously received Great Power validation and tangible victories. Yet the Versailles and other treaties required new states to draft minority rights' provisions that if adhered to would have extended significant protection to members of the minorities now included in states aspiring to ethnically or religiously pure populations.

But the Versailles peacemakers left vague the major questions inherent in Wilsonian ideals of self-determination: Whose nationalism will count, where will it count, when will it count, how will it count? The situation in Kosovo today makes it all the more urgent to address these issues. Within the region, the population has a clear Albanian majority. But the region is located inside Serbia, which for historical and present-day reasons refuses to

12 See chapter 13 in this book.
13 See chapter 19 in this book.

recognize the Tito-era autonomy that Kosovo's citizens seek to retain. Nationalism to the *n*th degree dictates that the only viable states will be ethnically or religiously homogenous states. This is the lesson eastern European nations themselves applied to German minorities in the aftermath of World War II. Attempts to institute such racially pure nations contributed to the Yugoslavian wars of succession and the continuing conflict between Armenia and Azerbaijan. Radical nationalism had triggered the First World War; in the treaty ending the conflict, the Versailles peacemakers gave further impetus to nationalist fervor. During the Cold War, however, the long arm of the Soviet Union placed a lid on the boiling pot of central and eastern European nationalism. This quiescence, combined with the increased economic and political integration of western Europe, led many to conclude that European nationalism was withering away. But with the end of the Cold War and the removal of Communist antinationalist pressure, nationalism was resurrected into one of the dominant forces driving eastern European developments. Prognostications concerning the future of Europe that ignore this factor do so at their peril.

The failure of Versailles diplomats to create a stable world economic order represents another count in the indictment. Undeniably, their task was large. Faced with an economic sea change of major proportions, the negotiators attempted to find their moorings. Financial power had shifted from Europe to the United States, a nation with a very different economic worldview from that of the previous financial behemoth. The primacy of laissez-faire theory in the United States, its self-sufficiency and vast internal markets, its hegemonic economic interests without having the government play a correspondingly large role in the economy produced a unique system of economic governance and a confused set of national priorities. A limited desire to export without a corresponding need to import mirrored the split in American business circles between a small number of vocal, internationally oriented companies and the bulk of manufacturers concerned only with the domestic market.

French leaders, for their part, attempted to cope with their nation's impoverishment while in London diplomats dealt with Britain's economic decline and their own fears about the future.[14] Reparations, for all their problems, provided the only available solution to Allied economic woes

14 On French policy, see, e.g., Schuker, *End of French Predominance;* on British policy, see Paul M. Kennedy, *The Realities Behind Diplomacy: Background Influences on British External Policy, 1865–1980* (London, 1981), 223–312; Diane B. Kunz, *The Battle for Britain's Gold Standard in 1931* (London, 1987).

that did not require the British, French, and the American governments to construct a political compromise, something that would have been impossible to achieve. Most important, they allowed the United States to receive war debt repayments as long as reparations continued. It was only on this basis that any economic cooperation could have been expected from the United States in the interwar years. For better or worse, Americans agreed with Calvin Coolidge that "they hired the money, didn't they?" Washington's waiver of war debts was simply not in the postwar political cards.

Had German leaders accepted in good faith the need to live up to the reparations deal struck in Paris, as quantified at the later London Conference, a stable world economic system might have materialized during the interwar period. The German government's decision not only to sabotage the Versailles treaty but to manipulate its economy for short-term political gain triggered the financial chaos of this period. But it also led to a determination in London and Washington to avoid what were seen as the mistakes of Versailles-era international economic management after World War II. The result was the Bretton Woods system, which enabled the government of the United States to play a responsible role in the international financial order. Although the Bretton Woods agreements feel short of their architects' intentions, they provided a framework that nurtured the unprecedented postwar prosperity in the West.

With economic power much more diffused than it was after World War II, statesmen today are facing difficulties not unlike those that the Versailles peacemakers confronted. To a large extent, the decisions of politicians in the G-7 countries determine the path of international economic actions, and these politicians have begun seriously questioning the importance of the free and fair trade regime that has governed international financial relations among non-Communist nations for fifty years. At the same time, they are facing the task of integrating the former Communist countries into the global financial system. Most important, it is clear that the political framework is what governs economic stability – not the other way around. A stable and responsive government can withstand the slings and arrows of economic fortune, whereas a sinking government all too often finds an economic crisis to be the last straw, as events in czarist Russia and Weimar Germany have amply demonstrated. By the same token, a successful international system can withstand the downside of the economic cycle. International economic stability therefore requires a strong political framework, both on a macro-basis (among states) and on a micro-level (within states). The successful workings of the Western economic order between 1945 and

1989 was a stroke of luck. It depended on the existence of a bipolar conflict that both ensured constant American involvement and excluded the Soviet sphere from its aegis. The failure of the men of Versailles may ultimately be our own.

The inability of the peacemakers to create a League of Nations that would "afford mutual guaranties of political independence and territorial integrity to great and small nations alike" was another problem. It is true that the emphasis on the security aspects of the Versailles treaty have overshadowed the important role played by the League of Nations, particularly its contributions to the European integration learning curve. But the security side – the questions of life and death – of the responsibilities given to the League of Nations presented the most meaningful test of its efficacy. The failure to address these issues adequately rendered the League of Nations a failure. During World War II planners and the public alike hoped that a United Nations organization would rectify the mistakes made by the preceding generation. With the United States and the Soviet Union both charter members, hopes ran high for the new world body. This attempt at reincarnation demonstrated the Versailles legacy of elevating institutions over substance. It ignored the reality that if countries agree on the substance of issues, they do not really need multilateral institutions. If they do not agree, institutions will not fill the vacuum. During the Cold War, the global conflict's structure rendered the United Nations irrelevant. For that reason, the myth of its potential effectiveness continued to flourish. Pundits waxed lyrical: once the bipolar world collapsed, the United Nations, working as intended, would provide international security for all at a nominal price. The Persian Gulf conflict appeared on first examination to prove this assumption. What it actually showed was that collective security works only when, first, big powers care about an issue and, second, they either agree or abstain from disagreeing with the goal in question. The Yugoslavian wars have demonstrated what happens when one or both conditions do not apply to the case at hand.

The failure to find a proper place for the Soviet Union in the international world order constitutes another weakness of the Versailles treaty. Jon Jacobson is very persuasive in his delineation of Soviet foreign policy during the 1920s. The Versailles treaty reflected the empty-chair attitude of Britain and the United States toward the Soviet Union and its leaders. Jacobson shows that the Soviet Union quickly reciprocated Wilsonian hostility while also sharing the American president's confusion about the proper course of postwar policy. Each side wondered: Should its diplomats attempt to nurture coexistence or work toward competition?[15] Just as Soviet leaders waffled between confrontation or conciliation, Western leaders could not decide what was the true nature of the Soviet Union: Was it a potential member of the family of nations or an outlaw state? Jacobson also corrects a common misconception about the Soviet Union, namely, that it enjoyed the same freedom as the United States to avoid European diplomatic questions during the 1920s. Rather, the Bolshevik state, attacked by Poland and having lost its "near abroad" was, for better or worse, part of Europe. Jacobson clearly defines the various diplomatic maneuvers used by the Soviet Union as it tried to cope with interwar developments. A crucial question raised by him, which becomes more important in the aftermath of the Cold War, is the precise nature of Soviet foreign policy: how much of it derived from Communism, how much was determined by particular leaders, and how much represented a continuation of traditional Russian policies? Fortunately, the continuing release of Soviet archives will provide some of the answers.

Not including the United States in the Versailles settlement was one of the treaty's most important failings, and one of its most important legacies. American diplomats and historians have viewed this legacy differently in the seventy-five years since it was drafted. During the 1930s, American politicians attempted to undo U.S. participation in World War I.[16] The messy aspects of the treaty negotiations and the flaws in the final documents became a shibboleth wielded against those who sought to increase U.S. involvement abroad. By contrast, as victory in World War II drew closer, American internationalist-interventionists became convinced that their task was to assure U.S. membership in the United Nations.[17] They drew the lesson that Americans had paved the way for the rise of Adolf Hitler and World War II by not joining the League. During the Cold War the belief that the United States needed to act as the world's policeman dominated American political debates. European states, left to their own devices, could not keep the peace – Washington would have to do it for them.[18] These simple lessons provided the United States with effective guidelines for its foreign policy in the simplistic arena of post-1945 diplomacy. Unfortunately, the fall of the Berlin Wall ren-

15 See chapter 18 in this book.
16 See, e.g., Robert Dallek, *Franklin D. Roosevelt and American Foreign Policy, 1931–1945* (New York, 1979).
17 See, e.g., Randall Woods, *A Changing of the Guard: Anglo-American Relations 1941–1946* (Chapel Hill, N.C., 1990).
18 See, e.g., John Lewis Gaddis, *Strategies of Containment: A Critical Appraisal of Postwar American National Security Policy* (New York, 1982); Melvyn P. Leffler, *A Preponderance of Power: National Security, the Truman Administration, and the Cold War* (Stanford, Calif., 1992).

dered these lessons obsolete, leaving American politicians and the public thoroughly confused about the appropriate diplomatic road to take thereafter. Moreover, this country's geographic isolation and bountiful riches have allowed Americans to have the luxury of debating whether they should have a foreign policy at all. In the six years since the Cold War ended, Americans have not yet questioned what kind of foreign policy they should have. The history of both World War II and the Cold War apparently demonstrates that only a war or warlike threat will bring the United States into a full involvement abroad. This track record bodes ill for international stability.

The final and most important failure of the Versailles peacemakers was their inability to fathom the contradiction that commonly exists between democracy and peace. Keylor highlights Wilson's abiding faith in public opinion.[19] Yet public opinion often supports war, nationalist feuds, and territorial aggrandizement. Wilson predicated his faith in the principles of self-determination and covenants openly arrived at on the assumption that information and democracy will lead to peace and freedom. But the gap between democracy and peace bedeviled diplomacy in the interwar years. It has become equally striking since the Cold War ended. Ironically, the Cold War period nurtured the growth of a romantic neo-Wilsonian faith in "the democracy of the people" as being benign and right thinking. Vietnam-era notions of the moral importance of peace and the immorality of war heightened the continuing significance of Wilsonian views. In the aftermath of that divisive confrontation, American politicians recognized that they needed to sell their foreign policy in moral terms. Unfortunately, the moral terms of the majority may not be moral at all. This contradiction becomes even more important in an era of instant media coverage. One picture may din out a thousand thoughtful words leading to an outpouring of misguided reaction, or worse. Since 1989 further evidence of the depth of this fallacy has come to light. How today's peacemakers will deal with this problem will be of the greatest importance to the structure of the newest world order.

Thus far, the emphasis in this discussion has been on the failures of Versailles diplomats. But their one successful legacy should not be forgotten – they provided the framework and vocabulary of international relations. Partly because historians helped formulate the Versailles treaty and then founded schools, think-tanks, and journals to hammer home their legacy, the ideas spawned between 1919 to 1921 remained enormously influential. American policy during the Cold War further strengthened this legacy;

---

19 See chapter 19.

Washington's diplomats used Wilsonian rhetoric to cover anti-Wilsonian realpolitik strategy. Since the immediate issues were entirely different from the ones statesmen faced in the interwar period, the rhetorical exercise was of no real consequence. Unfortunately, today the world is saddled with a Versailles-era framework and Versailles-style rhetoric as it again confronts a Versailles-era reality. The problems that became so evident in the aftermath of the First World War have re-emerged. Perhaps then, this success was a failure as well.

PART FIVE

Antecedents and Aftermaths: Reflections on the War-Guilt Question and the Settlement

22

Max Weber
and the Peace Treaty of Versailles

WOLFGANG J. MOMMSEN

The following observations are intended as a modest contribution to a subject that is of undiminished political significance even today, namely, the
historical assessment of the Treaty of Versailles and its repercussions in German political and historical consciousness.[1] The impetus for these remarks
is the recent discovery of new sources during research on the collected
works of Max Weber.[2] The scope of these new sources is not great, but they
are grounds for a reassessment of the treaty from the perspective of recent
German history.

During the 1920s, the Treaty of Versailles was viewed by all German parties, with only minor exceptions, as a "dictate of shame," the conditions of
which were designed exclusively to keep Germany permanently in punitive
bondage and to prevent it for the foreseeable future from rebuilding itself into
a European superpower. The conclusion, recorded unmistakably in the
treaty, that the German Reich was to blame for the outbreak of the war was
viewed as far more intolerable than the admittedly extremely harsh material
conditions. It touched upon a point of honor that was all the more sensitive
since the great majority of Germans had rushed to arms in 1914 in the sincere personal conviction that they were fighting a war of self-defense. Moreover, German misery in the period between the wars, particularly the inflation and later severe economic and social crisis of the early 1930s, was, and
still often is, generally considered to be the main cause of the collapse of the
Weimar Republic. Certainly the most effective weapon of the German

This chapter was translated from German by Sally E. Robertson of Arlington, Virginia.

1 Wolfgang J. Mommsen, "Betrachtungen zum Friedensvertrag von Versailles," in Ferenc Glatz, ed.,
  Modern Age – Modern Historian: In Memoriam György Ránki (1930–1988) (Budapest, 1990), 249–56.
2 Wolfgang J. Mommsen, ed., in collaboration with Wolfgang Schwentker, *Max Weber-Gesamtausgabe*,
  vol. I/16: *Zur Neuordnung Deutschlands: Schriften und Reden 1918–1920* (hereafter MWG I/16)
  (Tübingen, 1988), 562–7.

Right, most notably the National Socialists, against the "system," as it was derisively called, was the agitation against the Treaty of Versailles. The repercussions of this manner of thinking can be found even in present-day discussions of recent German history, for example, at the 1986 Römerberg dialogue in Frankfurt am Main at the outset of the *Historikerstreit* when Michael Stürmer stated that "Versailles [was] a fatal error by the Allies."

Putting aside the question of how the Treaty of Versailles should be assessed historically or politically, one thing is certain. Whereas the Germans in 1918–19 were not internally prepared to come to terms with their defeat and soberly face the facts, this was not the case after 1945, after a war with an outcome that was not even sanctioned by a peace treaty and that brought not only considerable reduction in the territory of the Reich, as in 1919–20, but also the complete destruction of national unity and, at least initially, the loss of sovereignty. A bitter conflict over the Treaty of Versailles cast a shadow over the political development of the Weimar Republic from the very beginning. In all political camps, there was a tendency to attribute anything that did not go as desired to the oppressive political, military, and particularly economic conditions of the peace treaty. This was completely different in the years after 1945. The rebuilding of western Germany and the establishment of a democratic order of liberal capitalism were presumably possible only because the Germans were willing to close the door on the past and begin anew.

This experience has had a significant influence on the way recent research has assessed the Treaty of Versailles and, above all, the German handling of the negotiations.[3] At the time of the singing of the armistice, and even in the spring of 1919, the greater part of the German public assumed, on the basis of the "Fourteen Points" of American President Woodrow Wilson, that they could expect a relatively tolerable peace settlement, despite what turned out to be certain territorial losses in the east and the west. From the fact that the armistice negotiations had begun with express reference to Wilson's Fourteen Points, German diplomats concluded that the Fourteen Points were a binding prerequisite of international law for the impending peace negotiations and that the tendencies of the Allied powers to make demands beyond the Fourteen Points were therefore without any

3 Peter Krüger, *Deutschland und die Reparationen 1918/19* (Stuttgart, 1973); Peter Krüger, "Die Reparationen und das Scheitern einer deutschen Verständigungspolitik auf der Pariser Friedenskonferenz im Jahre 1919," *Historische Zeitschrift* 221 (1975); Peter Krüger, *Die Aussenpolitik der Republik von Weimar* (Darmstadt, 1985); Hagen Schulze, *Deutschland, 1917–1933* (Berlin, 1983); Udo Wengst, *Graf Brockdorff-Rantzau und die aussenpolitischen Anfänge der Weimarer Republik* (Berne, 1973); Ulrich Heinemann, *Die verdränge Niederlage: Politische Öffentlichkeit und Kriegsschuldfrage in der Weimarer Republik* (Göttingen, 1983).

legal foundation. Only gradually did it become clear that the war had really been lost and that there was no chance for substantive negotiations, even from a position of reduced legal standing.

When the German peace delegation to Versailles, under the leadership of Count Ulrich Brockdorff-Rantzau, was presented with the conditions for peace by the Allied and Associated Powers on May 7, 1919, the first impression was crushing. Social Democratic chancellor Philipp Scheidemann aptly expressed popular sentiment when he exclaimed before the Constituent Assembly that the hand that signed this treaty must wither. Stunned by the speech of French Prime Minister Georges Clemenceau, the chairman of the peace conference, Count Brockdorff-Rantzau, the leader of the German delegation, set aside his draft response of moderate tone and instead made a fierce reply. This treaty, he said, "departs in decisive points from the agreed-upon foundation of the legal peace." For any country that valued its honor, he continued, the treaty was intolerable and virtually impossible to fulfill. Furthermore, Brockdorff-Rantzau expressly protested the underlying assumption of the entire document, namely the premise that the German Reich bore all the guilt for the outbreak of the war.[4]

Recent research has been by and large unanimous in judging that it was Brockdorff-Rantzau's fierce and uncompromising conduct of affairs at Versailles, rather than his personal arrogance, that did the most to damage the chances for mitigating the conditions of the treaty in the negotiations with the Allied and Associated Powers.[5] Other defeated nations, notably Austria and Hungary, understandably paid no attention to this aspect of the draft treaty, a strategy that served them well. It is certain, however, that it was not the original intention of the German government to appear completely intransigent toward the representatives of the Allied powers in Versailles. The German peace delegation was initially prepared to make significant concessions on at least two important points, the payment of reparations and the reduction in the authorized strength of the German army, as a prelude to concrete negotiations with the Allies on the details of the treaty.

Before the Versailles negotiations began, the German government took the position that it would be inadvisable in any case for the Germans to elevate the question of war guilt to a subject of negotiation. In fact, it was only at the last minute that Brockdorff-Rantzau decided to disregard the repeated explicit decisions of the Reich cabinet and launch a frontal attack on the Allies' position regarding war guilt, which was the formal basis for

4 Count Brockdorff-Rantzau, *Dokumente und Gedanken um Versailles* (Berlin, 1925), 70–3.
5 Fritz Dickmann, "Die Kriegsschuldfrage auf der Friedenskonferenz von Paris 1919," *Historische Zeitschrift* 197 (1963): 75ff.; Krüger, *Die Aussenpolitik der Republik von Weimar,* 72–3.

the claims to reparations. In Berlin at the time, top-level government officials were apparently aware that Germany's position on this matter was not nearly so favorable as the imperial government had led the German public to believe during the war. In any event, it was justifiably felt that nothing would come of raising this issue.

Count Brockdorff-Rantzau apparently held a different opinion on this point from the very beginning. He saw in the war-guilt clause of § 231 a point of honor that he considered out of the question to evade. He also felt that the issue must be addressed head-on because it was the foundation on which the structure of reparations was built. It was essentially to this end that Brockdorff-Rantzau sought the assistance of four prominent scholars associated with the Arbeitsgemeinschaft für Politik des Rechts (Heidelberger Vereinigung) (Heidelberg Association for a Policy of Justice) created by Prince Max von Baden and Kurt Hahn. He hoped that their international reputation would help persuade the negotiators to modify the accusation of war guilt.[6] In vain, the Reich cabinet warned that raising the war-guilt issue would impede the slim chances of ever sitting down at the table with the Allies for the substantive negotiations on which everything hinged, given the circumstances at the time.[7]

In light of the numerous public pronouncements of Max Weber on the issues raised by the impending peace treaty and his clear position on the question of war guilt, which was echoed widely by the German public, it was logical to enlist him as an expert adviser to the peace negotiations, despite the fact that he was unfamiliar with the specific political and diplomatic problems. His decisive stand against German self-incrimination on the war issue, which he viewed as bordering on "undignified" behavior, was entirely consistent with Brockdorff-Rantzau's views.[8] His interpretation of the events of July 1914, placing the primary blame for the war on czarist Russia, was by and large in line with that of the German Foreign Office. In addition, through his work in the Heidelberger Vereinigung, Max Weber was engaged in various efforts to improve Germany's moral standing in the

---

6 On the history leading up to the enlistment of Hans Delbrück, Albrecht Mendelssohn-Bartholdy, Count Max Montgelas, and Max Weber for the peace negotiations in Versailles, and the production of the four-man memorandum on the war-guilt issue, see MWG I/16, 23–31.

7 See the "Richtlinien für deutsche Friedensunterhändler" adopted by the Cabinet, Politisches Archiv des Auswärtigen Amtes, Bonn (hereafter PA-AA Bonn), Bernhard Wilhelm von Bülow Nachlass, vol. 2, and the minutes of the cabinet meetings of May 21 and 27, 1919, reprinted in Hagen Schulze, ed., *Das Kabinett Scheidemann: 13. Februar bis 20. Juni 1919,* Akten der Reichskanzlei, Weimarer Republik (Boppard am Rhein, 1971), 359, 384.

8 See his article "Zum Thema der 'Kriegsschuld,'" MWG I/16, 179ff.

impending peace negotiations by exerting appropriate influence on public opinion in the neutral countries.[9]

The full extent of Max Weber's role in the peace negotiations in Versailles has only very recently been discovered. He is generally known only for his collaboration on the "professorial memorandum" on the issue of Germany's war guilt, which was written to rebut the premise of the Allied Commission on War Guilt. The memorandum was written by the Commission of Four, consisting of Max Weber, Albrecht Mendelssohn-Bartholdy, Hans Delbrück, and Count Max Montgelas. In fact, however, Weber participated much more extensively in the Versailles peace negotiations. For example, in the period preceding the Versailles negotiations, he was recruited by a special commission of the Arbeitsstelle zur Vorbereitung der Friedensverhandlungen (Agency to Prepare for the Peace Negotiations) at the Foreign Office in Berlin as an adviser on territorial issues. However, little is known about Weber's actual role in these preparatory proceedings, which subsequently turned out to be largely superfluous.[10]

The invitation to Max Weber to participate as an expert adviser in the negotiations of the peace delegation in Versailles was issued on the understanding that he would be asked to take a position on questions of war guilt. However, immediately after his arrival in Versailles, he was recruited into the discussion of possible strategies for fighting off demands for surrender of eastern territory. At first, this consisted of writing a special "Note über die Ostfragen" (Notes on the Eastern [European] Issues) intended to protest the provisions of the peace treaty for the surrender of German territory in the east. The peace delegation was entirely aware of the gravity of the situation. In order to save Upper Silesia, Danzig, and the connection to East Prussia, it would be necessary to offer considerable territorial concessions in Posen and West Prussia. In contrast to the Reich cabinet, which was unwilling to surrender German territory under any circumstances without a plebiscite, the peace delegation felt that plebiscites must be avoided at any cost. If anything, they felt, the Germans would have to appeal to the fact that the territories in question had historically always belonged to the German Reich, but the double-edged sword of a plebiscite must be avoided. There is reason to believe that it was partly at Max Weber's instigation that the eastern experts in the peace delegation to Versailles addressed an appeal to the chancellor of the Reich on May 18, 1919. Citing the highly uncertain outcome, the appeal expressly warned against a plebiscite in the eastern territories on

9 Ibid., 196ff.   10 Ibid., 254ff.

whether these territories should remain in the Reich. Weber, at any rate, was one of the signers of this appeal.[11] Instead, the delegation weighed the possibility of accommodating the Allies on other matters, particularly the payment of reparations and the size of the future German army, as long as this would enable them to keep the territorial concessions within acceptable limits.

Max Weber apparently did not think much of this approach. He demonstrated significant irritation at the extent of the accommodation that other experts, including Carl Melchior and Max Warburg, were willing to accept if necessary. In his view, all of this went much too far. At this point, Weber, at any rate, probably felt the only realistic option open to the German government was to refuse to sign the peace treaty. Even in the preliminary discussions in Berlin, he had raised questions regarding the conditions under which a strategy similar to that of Trotsky in Brest-Litovsk could be pursued: "If I am a personal proponent of the idea of saying, 'We reject the treaty; occupy Germany and see how you can get your money' then it is because certain conditions are such that, in the event of rejection, we will inescapably suffer the most extreme consequences and that, in the event of acceptance, we will suffer those consequences anyway in the coming years. This alone must be the determining viewpoint."[12] In his view, the government of the Reich had to get used to this possibility from the outset and had to "be completely clear, before taking such a step, what administrative, domestic political and other measures it intended to implement immediately in order to be able to handle this situation so that it could be tolerated as a long-term solution if necessary."[13]

In Versailles, Max Weber apparently leaned fairly early toward this alternative of rejecting the treaty. On the other hand, the majority of the peace delegation, led by a number of prominent businessmen, wagered that accommodation in certain important matters, particularly disarmament and possible reparations by Germany, would lead to detailed negotiations in which they would have to try to avert the worst of the conditions. Thus, the peace delegation was initially considerably more conciliatory than the government in Berlin, which was committed to a relatively firm course, primarily for domestic political reasons. The German peace delegation set out to enter substantive negotiations on the details of the treaty, thereby simultaneously influencing world opinion in favor of the German position. They worked feverishly on a major memorandum summarizing the Ger-

---

11 The appeal appears in ibid., 297; see also files of the Reichskanzlei, Pol. 8a, Polen, in Schulze, ed., *Das Kabinett Scheidemann,* 395.
12 Ibid., 260.   13 Ibid.

man counterproposals. In the process, it became apparent that the delegates, even the majority of the experts, including such heavyweights as Melchior and Warburg, were willing to make significant concessions to the Allied and Associated Powers on a number of points.

Within the delegation, despite hefty resistance, the view that eventually prevailed was that the Germans could and should accommodate the Allies in economic and military matters in order to obtain favorable concessions on the territorial issues, which were considered by far the most important matter. If the goal was to "limit concessions in the territorial realm to a minimum," the peace delegation believed, then "extensive sacrifice in the financial and economic realms [was] possible and necessary."[14] Accordingly, a proposal was made to acknowledge in principle the German obligation to pay reparations for war damages, up to the sum of 100 billion gold marks specified in the draft treaty, with the proviso that the annual burden would be kept bearable by means of appropriate interest and repayment terms and that the actual payments would begin only after a rather lengthy grace period. There was also some talk of accepting a reduction in the authorized strength of the German army to 100,000 as long as a sufficient transition period was allowed. It was the cabinet in Berlin that considered such a degree of accommodation to be inappropriate, just as, on the issue of territorial arrangements in the east, it clung stubbornly to the principle that not a single piece of land would be surrendered without a plebiscite, whereas the delegation, as mentioned earlier, had concluded that, under the circumstances, the plebiscite was a double-edged sword that was better avoided.[15] The German delegation was thus initially prepared to accept a purely protectorate status for the German Reich and to trust the League of Nations to preserve the peace in Europe.[16]

Max Weber, on the other hand, was among those who considered the concessions envisioned by the delegation to be much too far-reaching. He chose the unusual step of writing a letter to the peace delegation in order to explicitly protest the concessions that the delegation had detailed in a telegram to the government of the Reich:

The present dispatch to Berlin is inconsistent with yesterday's discussions [by the experts – W.J.M.] inasmuch as

---

14 Telegram from the German peace delegation to the Foreign Office on May 19, 1919, PA-AA Bonn, German Peace Delegation in Versailles, Pol. 13, vol. 2, in Schulze, ed., *Das Kabinett Scheidemann*, 354–5.

15 For more detailed documentation, see MWG I/16, 293–5, 560–1.

16 See ibid., 563f., and Krüger, *Deutschland und die Reparationen*, 187–8.

(1)   60 billion – 20 in 1926 and the rest only on a very long-term, interest-free payment
      schedule – was described as the maximum, if a specific amount was to be mentioned at
      all (against which many of us had serious reservations),
(2)   the absolute precondition /for this/ was to be the absence of any kind of suppression
      of the economy, the return of all private property and restoration of the critical
      colonies,
(3)   the opponents were to be told (that) an absolute precondition would be authorization
      of a real army (Swiss militia system) of a much larger size (the figure of 250,000 was
      named), since there would otherwise not be the least guarantee against the possibility
      of such a "squeezing" of Germany.[17]

So as not "to indirectly share responsibility," he said, he felt obliged to formally protest the views of the peace delegation expressed in the aforemen-
tioned dispatch. Of course, this all turned out to be immaterial, since the
anticipated negotiations never occurred and the above counterproposals
were reduced to wastepaper.

There was clearly a connection between these developments and the fact
that the plan for a German memorandum on the war-guilt question became
acute after all, despite the opposition of the Reich cabinet. Brockdorff-
Rantzau felt that the intransigence of the Allied and Associated Powers left
him no other option. Unlike the cabinet, once it was clear that there would
be no detailed negotiations anyway, Brockdorff-Rantzau considered it
essential to lodge a formal protest against the war-guilt memorandum of the
Allied Powers, to which Clemenceau had explicitly referred in rebutting
Brockdorff-Rantzau's declaration on the war-guilt issue, although that
memorandum was described by the Allies as an "internal document" that
had not even been made available to the German peace delegation. The
basis for this response would be a memorandum with extensive appended
documentation that had been written in Berlin by Bernhard von Bülow,
director of the war-guilt section at the Foreign Office.

The members of the Commission of Four were originally supposed to
issue this memorandum in their own names without committing the German government; it was thought that their academic reputation would lend
the document credibility in the eyes of the Allies and the world community. Brockdorff-Rantzau saw it as a tactical advantage that this opinion on
the war-guilt issue would be coming from an independent source, and the
resistant government of the Reich would therefore not necessarily have to
be identified with it. The experts were not even fully informed of all of the
facts. The Austrian files available at that time in Berlin were intentionally

withheld from them. Likewise, they were not even given a straight story about the differences between Brockdorff-Rantzau and the Reich cabinet on procedural questions.

Thus the starting point for the work of the German experts was more than confused, and they were allowed little latitude from the very beginning. Nonetheless, Montgelas, Mendelssohn-Bartholdy, Delbrück, and Max Weber set to work immediately, but the memorandum looked quite different by the time they had finished. It distinctly disavowed the responsibility of the German Reich for the First World War and portrayed czarist Russia as the power actually responsible for bringing about the war. The "Rückblickende Betrachtungen" (retrospective reflections), which sprang largely from the pen of Max Weber, expressly stated that "there was no honorable means by which Germany [could have avoided] armed conflict with the apparently imperturbable czarist system."[18] Moreover, "Czarism [had been] the most horrible system of subjugation of human beings and nations ever devised – until the peace treaty which has now been proposed." The defensive war against czarism had therefore been justified, he concluded.[19] Accordingly, the arguments in the memorandum culminated in a direct challenge to the Allied Powers. It was obviously not well suited to smooth the way for the detailed negotiations that the peace delegation still desired. It is therefore not surprising that some members of the peace delegation considered the memorandum one-sided and unsuitable for delivery to the Allies and in general found it to be too harsh.[20] The experts were therefore asked to revise the memorandum once again, and to soften its tone. To what extent this actually was done is not known because only the final, revised version has survived in the archives. Even this version aimed massive, though largely indirect criticism at the Allied Powers. Only after significant hemming and hawing was it then finally delivered to the Allies, against the direct instructions of the Reich cabinet. Its immediate effect was virtually none.

Max Weber apparently held the opinion, more or less from the beginning of the negotiations in Versailles, that it was far better not to sign the peace treaty, notwithstanding all the consequences thereof, than to accept a "rotten peace." In particular, he saw the economic conditions for peace as so crushing that even limited acceptance of them would be irresponsible. "The closer one examines the economic conditions," he wrote to Marianne Weber on May 19, "the more terrible and complex they are, so that, even

18 MWG I/16, 349.   19 Ibid., 350.
20 See the editorial foreword in ibid., 311.

if we were to accept only half of them, we would see before us only a dark hole, without even the most distant beam of light."[21] Weber was skeptical of the efforts of the peace delegation to adopt a relatively conciliatory position in order to achieve substantial modification of the treaty provisions in detailed negotiations. Nevertheless, he was asked, albeit along with other members of the peace delegation, to draft a "cover note" to accompany the German counterproposals. Max Weber undertook this task with a heavy heart; he considered it essentially an imposition. He reported to his wife afterward that he had "done it in such a way that I knew it would be rejected."[22] Accordingly, it is not surprising that Weber's draft, which has not survived, did not prevail. The final version was written primarily by Walter Schücking.

Of course, matters then took a turn in a different direction when the Allied and Associated powers soon thereafter demanded acceptance of the peace treaty with no ifs, ands, or buts. Fourteen days after the German counterproposals of May 29 were delivered, the treaty was returned to the peace delegation with only minimal amendments, requested by David Lloyd George. The treaty was accompanied by a note stating that the Allies were unwilling to engage in further negotiation, and that the treaty must be accepted in its entirety. This made Max Weber's protests against excessive concessions to the Allies immaterial.

After all this, it is not surprising that Max Weber returned to Heidelberg from Versailles deeply frustrated and embittered. For a time, he avoided all political activity and buried himself in scientific research. This can be seen, in part, as an attempt to retreat from all engagement in the politics of the day. In addition, he was now convinced that the peace treaty should be rejected, despite all the consequences thereof, including a potential military occupation of parts of the Reich and the temporary loss of the unity of the Reich. In this, he was moved primarily by considerations of the domestic political implications that would otherwise result. As early as 1917, he had reflected on the fatal connection between democratization and defeat with which Germany was threatened: "Germans of the future will say, 'The foreign powers forced democracy upon us.' It is a sad story."[23] He now felt this danger looming large on the horizon. At the same time, however, he hoped that such a step would lead to an "awakening of [domestic] national resistance."[24]

21 Letter of May 19, 1919, Max-Weber-Schäfer collection, privately owned.
22 See introduction to MWG I/16, 33.
23 Letter of July 13, 1917, to Marianne Weber; copy in Weber Nachlass, Rep. 92, Geheimes Staatsarchiv, Berlin.
24 See letter to Marianne Weber of July 1, 1919, in Wolfgang J. Mommsen, *Max Weber und die Deutsche Politik, 1890–1920* (Tübingen, 1974), 343 n. 144.

He anticipated that the army in the east would abandon its allegiance to the government if the treaty were signed.[25] "The Ostmark will take up arms and refuse to obey the government of the Reich."[26] In retrospect, rejection of the Versailles peace treaty might have been the only way to prevent the noxious debate of the following years that ultimately contributed significantly to the fall of the Weimar Republic and the rise of National Socialism.

During these months, a passionate debate unfolded in the German Reich, within government and public circles, on the question of whether Germany should reject the treaty, even at the risk of an invasion by Allied troops, or whether Germany should bow to force and submit to the inevitable. Max Weber himself continued to support rejection of the treaty, yet he became less and less certain that this path remained feasible given the critical state of the domestic situation.[27] He feared that a rejection would bring about serious conflicts and that the treaty would eventually be accepted after all.

The position of the Big Four at the peace conference is, of course, well known by now. However, it is not certain whether given the widespread fear of a Bolshevization of Germany, failure to reach a peace might not indeed have led to more favorable conditions which the German public might have then been able to grit its teeth and accept. This scenario, among others, was carefully subjected to scrutiny by the leadership of the Reich at the time.[28] No one in Germany at the time was willing to place the fate of the Reich in the hands of the victorious powers as Max Weber had suggested. In the end, Matthias Erzberger won out with his sober argument that, in the event of rejection, followed by invasion of Allied troops, the unity of the Reich would be lost and the Allies would ultimately conclude even more oppressive treaties with a series of German ministates.[29]

A wave of emotional protest against the treaty far exceeding the bounds of rationality had long been building in the German public. One example is cited in the journals of Thomas Mann (under the date May 10, 1919): "The headlines over the discussion of the treaty of entente read 'The Monstrosity' or some such remark. The specifics, particularly the more detailed ones, inspired by a sadistic infamy, a considered intention to disgrace Germany

25 See Mommsen, *Max Weber,* 343, especially the letter to Marianne Weber on July 1, 1919, cited in ibid., note 144, as well as in MWG I/16, 32f.
26 See Mommsen, *Max Weber,* 341.
27 Ibid., 343f.
28 See Horst Mühleisen, "Annehmen oder Ablehnen: Das Kabinett Scheidemann, die Oberste Heeresleitung und der Vertrag von Versailles im Juni 1919," *Vierteljahrshefte für Zeitgeschichte* 35 (1987): 438ff.
29 Ibid., 465.

forever, to rob her of even the memory of glory, which poisons the blood – which is the whole purpose. Contrived in the sleepless nights of a dangerous old man."[30] Such attempts at a sober, rational assessment of the actual situation, which were present initially in Versailles as well and had determined the stance of the more moderate politicians, now disappeared completely. Henceforth, the public debate was ruled by a purely emotional nationalism obsessed especially with the points of honor, since concessions on these would indeed have threatened the psychological prerequisites for restoring a militarist and monarchic order. To this extent, Max Weber was all too right to be concerned that acceptance of the treaty would have devastating effects on the domestic situation and would severely burden the new democratic order. In his famous speech on "Politik als Beruf" (Politics as a Vocation) on January 28, 1919, he predicted that "a polar night of icy darkness and austerity" awaited the Germans; "in ten years, for a variety of reasons, the reaction [will] long since [have] set in."[31] And that, with a slight delay, is exactly what happened.

30 Cited in Peter de Mendelssohn, ed., *Thomas Mann: Tagebücher, 1918–1921* (Frankfurt am Main, 1979), 233.
31 Wolfgang J. Mommsen and Wolfgang Schluchter, eds., in collaboration with Birgitt Morgenbrod, *Max Weber-Gesamtausgabe,* vol. I/17: *Politik als Beruf/Wissenschaft als Beruf: Schriften und Reden 1919* (Tübingen, 1992), 250–1.

23

The Construction of the American Interpretation: The Pro-Treaty Version

WILLIAM C. WIDENOR

Reviewing "Ten Years of Peace Conference History" in the *Journal of Modern History* in 1929, Robert C. Binkley complained that American historiography of the Paris Peace Conference was formulated "around personalities on the one hand and high-sounding generalities on the other." The result was history as morality play or melodrama in which Woodrow Wilson was pitted against Georges Clemenceau, a new shining order vied with an old hackneyed one, and a just peace struggled to prevail over a militaristic or imperialistic peace. Binkley railed particularly against a history cast in terms of heroes and villains and "against elucidating motives without understanding circumstances and coloring narratives with ethical judgments." The requisite antidote was a history that stressed analysis, common denominators, and addressed the atmosphere of the conference in terms of social psychology.[1]

I suppose we might congratulate ourselves on the extent to which we have been able to do precisely those things, though lest we fall into complacency we need always to keep in mind Marc Trachtenberg's 1982 admonition that the older views have remained strikingly intact and that the diplomacy of 1919 remains "over-schematized."[2] If that problem persists, another and perhaps even greater one may lie not so much in our growing sophistication but rather in the fact that we know too much, that the intervening tragedies have so colored our point of view that the mind set of those who sought to make peace in 1919 increasingly eludes us. There was wisdom in the remark of one of the American participants, David Hunter Miller, when first recorded in 1921 and it remains a useful admonition

---

1 Robert C. Binkley, "Ten Years of Peace Conference History," *Journal of Modern History* 1 (1929): 607–29.
2 Marc Trachtenberg, "Versailles After Sixty Years," *Journal of Contemporary History* 17 (1982): 487–506.

today, namely, that "the moral qualities of an act are to be judged as of its date and not from subsequent events."[3]

For that very reason I decided it might be helpful to take a fresh look at the histories of, and the commentaries on, Versailles that were written in the United States in the immediate aftermath of events. My purpose, consequently, is twofold: first, I intend to analyze the various official and semiofficial histories of the conference written by Americans in the 1920s – often by people who had played important roles in the conference – to the end of arriving at a better understanding of the foundations of the American national historiographical school with respect to the negotiation of the Versailles treaty and, second, to ascertain if those accounts might not yet provide some additional insight into the whole panoply of problems attendant to the American approach to the making of peace in 1919.

I have spent a good deal of my life working the other side of the street, studying the critics of Wilsonian foreign policy. I shall not consider them here; they have received adequate attention elsewhere. Moreover, whether emanating from the conservative end of the political spectrum (such as Henry Cabot Lodge's _The Senate and the League of Nations,_ which emphasizes Wilson's personal interests and ambitions) or from the more radical end (such as Harold Stearns's _Liberalism in America_ and William Bullitt's testimony before the Senate Foreign Relations Committee, which like John Maynard Keynes's _Economic Consequences of the Peace_ provide a literature of personal betrayal), the early critiques fit the terms of Robert Binkley's indictments even more obviously than do many of the works written in defense of Wilson's actions.[4]

My primary concern here is with the accounts of members of the American delegation and of the Inquiry (the advisory body, composed largely of academicians, that Wilson established, outside the reaches of the State Department, to prepare the American peace program) and with those written by members of the administration or persons otherwise close to Wilson. Wilson never had the opportunity to provide his own account, but he gave his papers to Ray Stannard Baker (who had been the American delegation's press chief in Paris), consulted with him extensively and certainly was fully apprised of the interpretive tack Baker intended to take.[5] Consequently,

3 David Hunter Miller, "The Adriatic Negotiations at Paris," _Atlantic Monthly,_ Aug. 1921, 269.
4 See Henry Cabot Lodge, _The Senate and the League of Nations_ (New York, 1925), 74 and 98–9. Lodge, revealingly, had practically nothing to say about the settlement as a whole and focused all his ire on Wilson and on the League. See also Harold Stearns, _Liberalism in America_ (New York, 1919), 143–4, and William C. Bullitt, _The Bullitt Mission to Russia_ (New York, 1919), 96–7.
5 See, e.g., Arthur S. Link et al., eds. _The Papers of Woodrow Wilson_ (hereafter _PWW_), 69 vols. (Princeton, N.J., 1966–94), 66:537, 544–5, and 67:7, 15–16. Whereas the absence of Wilson's own account of the peace conference is certainly lamentable, it is not at all clear that, had his health permitted, he

Baker's accounts head my list.[6] Also included are the interpretations of Colonel Edward House, Joseph Tumulty, George Creel, and Bernard Baruch.[7] I also decided to include Robert Lansing who, though a strong critic of Wilson's course, nevertheless supported ratification of the treaty, which is the one common thread tying together all the accounts I have considered.[8] Representing "The Inquiry" are the works of David Hunter Miller, a volume coauthored by Charles Homer Haskins and Robert Howard Lord, and a collection of defenses of various aspects of the American proceedings edited by Colonel House and Professor Charles Seymour.[9] I have also included a number of additional academic and journalistic accounts which tend to buttress the semiofficial interpretations or to clarify the differences with which Americans approached the peace conference and the ratification issue – the philosophical differences respecting the proper role for the United States and the nature of the problems that beset the American delegates throughout their efforts.

It would be both tedious and unproductive to review these various accounts seriatim, for what remains of primary interest are the tensions and contrasts among them and their relation to the manner in which the American delegates tended to approach their task. A number of fault lines seem rather revealing and may be worthy of further attention.

AMERICAN ALTRUISM AND AMERICAN EXCEPTIONALISM

In his most recent book, Henry Kissinger claims, referring to the United States, that "no other nation has ever rested its claim to international leadership on its altruism."[10] Though the claim is debatable (one can cite at the very minimum a number of British and Russian exceptions), there is no

would have provided us with the kind of statesmanlike account likely to satisfy Professor Binkley's criteria. Those familiar with his romanticized and idealized account of the "Redemption" of the South after Reconstruction in volume 5 of his *History of the American People* (New York, 1902) have reason to be skeptical.

6 Ray Stannard Baker, *What Wilson Did at Paris* (Garden City, N.Y., 1919), and Ray Stannard Baker, *Woodrow Wilson and World Settlement*, 3 vols. (Garden City, N.Y., 1922–3).

7 Charles Seymour, ed., *The Intimate Papers of Colonel House*, 4 vols. (Boston, 1926–8) (hereafter *IPCH*); Joseph P. Tumulty, *Woodrow Wilson as I know Him* (Garden City, N.Y., 1921); George Creel, *The War, the World, and Wilson* (New York, 1920); and Bernard M. Baruch, *The Making of the Reparation and Economic Sections of the Treaty* (New York, 1920).

8 Robert Lansing, *The Peace Negotiations: A Personal Narrative* (Boston, 1921), and Robert Lansing, *The Big Four and Others of the Peace Conference* (Boston, 1921).

9 David Hunter Miller, *The Drafting of the Covenant*, 2 vols. (New York, 1928); Charles Homer Haskins and Robert Howard Lord, *Some Problems of the Peace Conference* (Cambridge, Mass., 1920); and Edward Mandell House and Charles Seymour, eds., *What Really Happened at Paris: The Story of the Peace Conference, 1918–1919* (New York, 1921).

10 Henry Kissinger, *Diplomacy* (New York, 1994), 46.

gainsaying the fact that Progressive generation Americans tended to insist on their altruism and to define America's role as one of moral leadership.[11] Prevalent was the kind of confusion of purpose reflected in Wilson's claim that "America had the infinite privilege of fulfilling her destiny and saving the world." In the formulation of Ray Stannard Baker, this was the very essence of the American approach – "an idea of national service to the world." As the intellectual historian Ernest Tuveson once remarked, this kind of thinking had hoary roots in the American past, but in a more secular and somewhat less religious mode, it was almost irresistible to Progressives.[12] Where one might see in Wilson's formulation a profound confusion between serving selfish national interests and world service, let alone world salvation, Progressive-generation Americans (and not just Wilsonians) were susceptible to the mind trick of perceiving of the United States as a nation in the forefront of the march of human progress and therefore believing that to serve its interests was also to serve mankind. Moreover, for many American progressives national interests were to be excoriated just as much as corporate interests. Hence, the pains that Ray Stannard Baker took to establish the fact that Wilson "was never used by anybody or any interest at the Peace Conference."[13] Wilson's remarks to the American peace delegation while crossing the Atlantic claiming that Americans "would be the only disinterested people" in Paris became a prominent and standard feature of semiofficial American accounts and found its way into most journalistic accounts as well. There the formulation was usually that the United States came with "clean hands" and wanted only peace and justice and, hence, served as a check on those who wanted "to make the Paris Conference nothing better than the Congress of Vienna."[14]

Implicit, if not explicit, in most early American accounts was the idea of American exceptionalism – that the United States was different from other countries and that "different" was only another way of saying better. The classic juxtaposition was "innocent nation, wicked world," but whereas innocence had previously been viewed as a product of the protection afforded by isolation it was now seen as the badge of an activist moral superiority. The cultivation of Wilson's and America's moral reputation was an

11 I am indebted to my colleague, Paul W. Schroeder, for an enlightening discussion on this point.
12 Baker, *Wilson and World Settlement,* 1:265. Ernest Lee Tuveson, *Redeemer Nation: The Idea of America's Millennial Role* (Chicago, 1968), 210–14. Wilson is quoted on the frontispiece.
13 Baker, *What Wilson Did,* 62.
14 *IPCH,* 4:280; and Baker, *Wilson and World Settlement,* 1:10. See also Harry Hansen, *The Adventures of the Fourteen Points* (New York, 1919), 369; and David Lawrence, *The True Story of Woodrow Wilson* (New York, 1924), 262.

almost ubiquitous concern of both participants and commentators. In Charles Seymour's account, one reads of Frank Cobb's preoccupation with Wilson "remaining the great arbiter of human freedom."[15] In George Creel's account, Wilson was "the noblest figure in Paris"; in Joseph Tumulty's, Americans were variously characterized "as infinitely better than the others," as "the most idealistic people in the world," and, quoting Wilson, as "crusaders" who "saved the liberty of the world."[16] Baker recurred to this and similar themes almost ad nauseam. Wilson "set the allied cause on a new moral plane"; he "alone held up the moral tone of the Conference"; and it was Wilson who "expressed the soul of America at its noblest and truest."[17] Even outside official and semiofficial circles one confronts repeated variations on the same overriding theme. History Professor John Spencer Bassett claimed for America the "position as the champion of high moral ideas" and Political Science Professor Lindsay Rogers upped him by stating that "the United States is now the moral arbiter of the world."[18] In the more prosaic world of American journalism, Wilson was portrayed as "just an honest, straightforward American statesman who had faced a gigantic task without flinching and had performed a man's work in the world," but the message was basically identical.[19] The pervasiveness of this mind set is perhaps best cemented by the fact that Lansing, writing even after his dismissal, nevertheless claimed that "Wilson was on a higher ethical plane than that of any of his colleagues" at Paris.[20]

Now any American diplomatic historian will say that it has always been easiest for Americans to define their role in opposition, that is, when they had a well-defined enemy. So it was during the negotiation of the Versailles treaty and in its aftermath. Since talk of a conflict of interests was not admissible, events had to be defined in terms of a conflict of principles and of personalities. Most American Progressives held to a moral rather than a political theory of conflict.[21] As historian John Mulder has recently recalled, Wilson himself was prone to make simplistic divisions between right and wrong and to use military and moral imagery to describe political issues; the

---

15 *IPCH,* 4:210.
16 Creel, *War, the World, and Wilson,* 239; and Tumulty, *Wilson As I Know Him,* 368, 373, 450.
17 Baker, *What Wilson Did,* 63; Baker, *Wilson and World Settlement,* 1:2; and Baker, *The Versailles Treaty and After* (New York, 1924), 27.
18 John Spencer Bassett, *Our War with Germany* (New York, 1919), 332; Lindsay Rogers, "The League of Nations and the National State," in Stephen Duggan, ed., *The League of Nations: The Principle and the Practice* (Boston, 1919), 95.
19 Hansen, *Adventures of the Fourteen Points,* 362.
20 Lansing, *The Big Four,* 129.
21 Trachtenberg, "Versailles After Sixty Years," 494.

result was that his speeches had all the trappings of a moral and religious crusade.[22] Moreover, he was encouraged by the often sycophantic Colonel House to see himself as the prophet of a new order overcoming an older order of statesmen.[23]

As a result, there was a marked tendency among those closest to Wilson to depict the Paris negotiations in the kind of Manichean terms that were a standard of Progressive historiography in general. Baker told Wilson of his plans to depict the negotiations as "the first really great clash of America and American ideals with world affairs" and to endeavor to write from the American point of view.[24] The chances of Baker writing a morally neutral account were no better than if the writer had been Vernon Louis Parrington or Charles Beard. In order to defend Wilson and the treaty, Baker wove a tale that contained precisely those elements that Robert Binkley had so vigorously complained about in 1929. Baker depicted a struggle of personalities (Wilson against Clemenceau and Lodge, and even Arthur Balfour for that matter) and a battle of abstract principles and generalities. The forces of light were pitted against the forces of darkness, it was democracy versus autocracy, justice versus imperialism and the new order versus the old, and Wilson had been forced to "'go down on the mat' with each of the great powers in turn."[25] In a review in *Foreign Affairs,* the journalist Simeon Strunsky complained that Baker in order to justify Wilson had found "it necessary to use a great deal of Rembrandt black on the European background" and that he had depicted a Europe motivated by perversity rather than by experience.[26] Nor were the Europeans the only targets. Baker's conceptual scheme and his defense of Wilson led him on to attack the Republicans and then Lansing and finally Colonel House for undermining Wilson's negotiating position.[27] To protect Wilson's moral stature, it was necessary to impugn the motives of everyone else.

The dangers of such an interpretation are manifest. They led Charles Seymour to the admonition that while "it is easy to dramatize the difference between the American and the European point of view regarding the peace settlement" (and he found such differences "real and inevitable"), "the his-

---

22 John Mulder, "A Gospel of Order," in John Milton Cooper Jr. and Charles Neu, eds., *The Wilson Era: Essays in Honor of Arthur S. Link* (Arlington Heights, Ill., 1991), 227.

23 Ibid., 257.   24 *PWW*, 67:15.

25 The instances are too frequent to list, but see Baker, *What Wilson Did,* 68; Baker, *Wilson and World Settlement,* 1:235 and 302, and 2:127, as well as Baker, *The Versailles Treaty and After,* 19, for examples.

26 Simeon Strunsky, "Wilsoniana," *Foreign Affairs,* Sept. 1923, 159–60.

27 See Baker, *Wilson and World Settlement,* vol. 1, chap. 17: "While Wilson Was Away" and chap. 18: "American Criticism of the Covenant." The targeting of the premiers of Europe and of the Republicans followed the pattern already set in Creel, *War, the World, and Wilson,* 309.

torian must be careful not to exaggerate it in order to gain a picturesque heightening of contrasts." He thought it more appropriate to argue that the Europeans and Wilson were seeking the same end – "a stable and just peace."[28] But Baker's scheme would not permit that. Moreover, it led, just as did Wilson's own interpretive framework, as French historian Jean-Baptiste Duroselle has complained, to a point of view that was not only ultranationalistic but also derogatory of other leaders and nations.[29] Baker's account, like that of Creel, sometimes bordered on the xenophobic. The Europeans were "greedy imperialists" determined to divide up the world; their diplomatic dealings had been "slimy"; the French were so "monumentally stupid" that "French fear may prove to be as dangerous to world peace as German greed."[30] Creel's writing, which had a more obvious and immediate political intent, actually encouraged American xenophobia by drawing attention to "the intense dislike for America and Americans that dominates the average Englishman" and then using that claim for a political end by linking his dual villains and alleging that the Republicans (Lodge and his group) "had been acting throughout in British interests."[31] American journalists were prone to the same invidious contrasts. To Charles Grasty the problem lay in the fact that while the Americans went about "making peace with an eye to the ultimate good of the world" the Europeans were selfish. To David Lawrence the problem lay in the fact that public opinion was not made in Europe in the same manner as it was formed in America.[32] The import of such suggestions was clearly that Europeans, the product of an inferior moral milieu, had no business opposing the plans of the United States.

Such an interpretive framework, antiforeign in its most basic assumptions, may also help to explain actual events, such as the rejection of the treaty by the Senate and the "Red Scare" of 1919–20. There can be little doubt that it served to strengthen the forces of isolationism and xenophobia at home. American opinion in the aftermath of Versailles was not unrelated to the opinion the journalist Walter Weyl had so tellingly described in the America of 1914:

Believing thus in our intrinsic peacefulness, it was in no spirit of humility that we met the outbreak of the Great War. We did not put ourselves in the place of the

28 *IPCH*, 4:158.
29 Duroselle quoted in Robert Crunden, *Ministers of Reform* (New York, 1982), 249.
30 Creel, *War, the World, and Wilson*, 208; Baker, *Wilson and World Settlement*, 1:79 and 2:8; Baker, *Versailles Treaty and After*, 9.
31 Creel, *War, the World, and Wilson*, 187 and 342.
32 Grasty quoted in Bassett, *Our War with Germany*, 363. Lawrence, *True Story of Wilson*, 265.

fighting nations, and acknowledge that in their circumstances we too might have been struggling in the dust. Rather we boasted of our restraining democracy, and of our perfect co-operative union, which protected us from the European anarchy. We, a people unassailed, talked loudly of our superior merit, and, as we looked over the broad oceans and saw no enemy, thanked God that He had not made us as other nations. Our compassion for the peoples of Europe was tinged with a bland, self-righteous arrogance.[33]

American entry into the war, of course, changed all that and seemingly dramatically. It brought with it an American crusade against all things German, except supposedly the German people themselves. But such distinctions were difficult to maintain when speaking of German iniquities in the war. As Simeon Strunsky once wrote, many Americans became quite "savage in speaking of the crime against Belgium," but then seemed to have no compunction about turning right around after the war and deploring the Allied "crime of Versailles."[34] It is not merely ironic that the defenders of Wilsonian internationalism contributed to this state of affairs; their internationalism had always had a fragile quality, based as it was on the willingness of the rest of the world to accept America's supposedly disinterested ideals. In their disappointment they castigated their enemies, and for those progressives who could not bring themselves to criticize either Wilson or American diplomacy, there seemed no alternate but to blame ungrateful Europe. Just as Wilson himself became embittered and railed against the French and Italians for having "made waste paper of the treaty of Versailles," so too did one of his foremost defenders. David Lawrence, in the very same volume that perpetrated this "Americanist" interpretation, concluded that things had come to such a pass that even if the United States had joined the League, "there had developed in the United States [such] a reaction against all things European" as to prevent the United States from exercising any considerable influence in European affairs for the foreseeable future.[35]

There is an additional characteristic of early official and semiofficial American interpretations of Versailles that is not quite so obvious, but is perhaps of equal importance. It is a corollary of the abiding emphasis on American altruism. This was a generation of Americans who viewed the writing of history as prescription more than as description of what actually happened. Their America was transforming itself, and so had little need for its admittedly checkered past. In fact, I searched in vain for any reference at all to the country's diplomatic history. A little self-knowledge might have

33 Walter E. Weyl, *American World Policies* (New York, 1917), 32.
34 Strunsky, "Wilsoniana," 155.
35 Lawrence, *True Story of Wilson,* 306. Wilson quoted on 354.

lent some much needed perspective. While Progressives applauded the idea of extending the Monroe Doctrine to the whole world, they seemed (willfully or not) to ignore the idea that the Monroe Doctrine had always represented a claim to special privilege and status on the part of the United States and therefore derogated from the rights of other states. Equally surprising is that for all their talk about a New Diplomacy, they seemed to know nothing of the fate of the Model Treaty of 1776 (the actual Franco–American Alliance Treaty of 1778 represented a painful accommodation to the international realities of the day) or of the "Young America" movement of the 1850s (which though aimed at world reform had more to do with domestic politics than with foreign policy). The great assertions of American prerogatives over against Europe such as those contained in Secretary Daniel Webster's letter to the Chevalier Huelsemann, Secretary William Seward's despatches to Napoleon III, and Secretary Richard Olney's communications to Lord Salisbury went unmentioned and unacknowledged. Only in such an atmosphere could the mythology of American altruism flourish and flourish at the expense of an understanding that America had interests just like everyone else, economic interests to be sure but also an interest, as Walter Lippmann only later came to see it, in finding allies to support America's now vast commitments.[36]

CONTRASTING INTERPRETATIONS OF THE FOURTEEN POINTS AND OF THE LEAGUE COVENANT

Though there was general agreement on the proposition of American moral superiority, when it came to more specific manifestations of same, as with respect to the value and significance of the Fourteen Points and the League Covenant, American opinion, even within Wilson's community, tended to divide and in some revealing ways. Apropos the Fourteen Points, there were disputes both as to whether they constituted an effective peace program and as to whether they had been incorporated in the treaty. The inner circle was fairly steadfast, but the further one moved from it the more doubts were entertained. From Ray Stannard Baker's perspective, a just peace was not only definable and achievable; the Fourteen Points were perfectly clear, were without ambiguity and had been accepted by the Allies in their entirety. That last theme was invoked often enough to make it appear as if Baker was trying to convince himself, just as he obviously was when he accepted Wilson's explanation respecting point one, arguing that "open

---

36 Walter Lippmann, *U.S. Foreign Policy: Shield of the Republic* (Boston, 1943), 39.

covenants openly arrived at" did not mean what it so obviously said, but rather only the abolition of secret treaties.[37] But even Baker, in the face of the many criticisms emanating from his friends, could not claim that the treaty was totally based on the Fourteen Points. He found it much more comfortable to take refuge in the arguments that the treaty was "the best arrangement for peace that could be made at a moment still dominated by the spirit of war" and that the greater triumph was Wilson's when one considered "that he had largely discounted the terms of the treaty in advance and pinned his faith to the League."[38] The journalist Simeon Strunsky, in a review of Baker's work, was so exasperated by Baker's thus giving away so much of the game (at his writing an apology rather than an apologia) that he was led to insist that "the zeal with which liberals will stress those of the Fourteen Points which fell by the wayside is only equalled by their assiduity in forgetting the larger number that were vindicated."[39]

George Creel was at such pains to counter the arguments of John Maynard Keynes that he could only set his own obvious falsehoods against those he thought proffered by Keynes:

Mr. Keynes has caught up and expressed every attack, misrepresentation, distortion and malignance. His book – jerked into notoriety by those who hate the President, endowed with scriptural values by every German, Austrian and Hungarian, copied extensively by reactionary and radical publications, and hailed with joy by the semi-intelligent as a short cut to statecraft – has done more than any other thing to poison the wells of public opinion. . . . Taken up one by one, and compared with the terms of the Peace Treaty, it is seen that the Fourteen Points were not only *not* repudiated, but were put into effect as solemnly and effectively as though each had been worded with the legal precision of a contract. . . . Let there be an end to the lie – circulated by malignants and accepted by the half-baked – that the Fourteen Points were "thrown into the discard." Everyone of them was written into the treaty, and the result will stand for all time as a monument to the courage and faith of Woodrow Wilson.[40]

But when not carried away by his own propaganda, even Creel could admit that the Fourteen Points were "in no sense a definitive practical formula, but [rather] a broad announcement of principles," more "articles of faith" than anything else.[41] Likewise, though cast in somewhat different terms, the friendly journalist Harry Hansen, in his book *The Adventures of the Fourteen Points,* while proclaiming that the Fourteen Points were a "standard Amer-

37 See, e.g., Baker, *Wilson and World Settlement,* 1:89, 138.
38 Ibid., 173, 313.
39 Strunsky, "Wilsoniana," 157.
40 Creel, *War, the World, and Wilson,* 229, 301, 309.
41 Ibid., 150, 301.

ica has formulated for the world," "definite principles of justice and fair dealing to all men," could still admit that in enunciating them Wilson was establishing a policy "and preaching a sermon all in one."[42]

Those who were involved in the actual negotiations were more circumspect. In the careful formulation of Bernard Baruch, the economic clauses of the treaty were not "unjustly onerous upon Germany" nor were they "in derogation of the letter or the spirit of any of President Wilson's Fourteen Points."[43] Inquiry members Charles Haskins and Robert Lord thought the treaty "an honest effort to secure a just and durable settlement" and that "substantial results" had been achieved.[44] When it came down to specifics, David Hunter Miller thought point three respecting economic equality was a sound diplomatic "counter move against both the German notion of economic domination of other countries and the ideas of the Allies of 1916," but he also found it necessary to record that "the practical difficulties in the way of any *general* agreement on the question were almost insuperable."[45] Isaiah Bowman claimed that the Fourteen Points received almost universal approval only "because they were put into general terms" and that they did not provide a guide to specific settlements.[46] Another Inquiry member, Manley O. Hudson, observed that the Fourteen Points did not provide a simple principle for action, and drew particular attention to the vagueness of the principle (point five) of an impartial adjustment of all colonial claims based on the idea that the interests of the populations concerned must have equal weight with the equitable claims of the governments contending for title.[47] Such noble sentiments could never entirely mask the fact that where interests clashed hard choices were inevitable and needed to be faced soberly.

Both because of the fact that time usually lends perspective and because their early edited work (*What Really Happened at Paris*) recognized these problems, one might have expected a similar line of argument in Charles Seymour's *The Intimate Papers of Colonel House*. But actually there was only a particularly revealing tension, almost a contradiction in Seymour's interpretation. That the vagueness of the Fourteen Points initially "unfitted them for service as a peace programme" was now freely admitted, but of

42 Hansen, *Adventures of the Fourteen Points*, 241, 385.
43 Baruch, *Making of the Economic Sections*, 89.
44 Haskins and Lord, *Some Problems of the Peace Conference*, 31–2.
45 Miller, *Drafting of the Covenant*, 19.
46 Isaiah Bowman, "Constantinople and the Balkans," in House and Seymour, eds., *What Really Happened at Paris*, 142.
47 Manley O. Hudson, "The Protection of Minorities and Natives in Transferred Territories," in House and Seymour, eds., *What Really Happened at Paris*, 224.

course respect for the diplomatic reputation of Colonel House (a stance which tends to mar *The Intimate Papers* throughout) led Seymour to stress that House had not only successfully codified them but had won a great diplomatic victory in securing their acceptance by the Allies. House was even quoted as having recorded in his diary that the exceptions made by the Allies were not that important substantively, because they served to emphasize their overall acceptance of the Fourteen Points.[48]

Though the establishment of a League of Nations to preserve the peace was called for in Wilson's fourteenth and last point, the League deserves separate consideration because it served as the axis around which so many interpretations revolved.

Similarly interesting differences in interpretation surround early American writing on the subject of the League. Opinion diverged both as to the League's overall importance in the treaty and as to whether it was sure to work. Once again the publicists (those who were at home in the realm of publicity and politics) were much more prone than were the academicians to see the League in a salvationist mode rather than as an experiment. To a Progressive journalist like Charles Thompson, it was sufficient to mouth Wilson's claim that the League was a definite guarantee of peace – a guarantee against all future aggression.[49] George Creel found that an emphasis on what the League would be able to do and on the dire nature of the alternative to it (namely huge military establishments) solved many of his interpretive problems.[50] This was even more obvious in Baker's case. He saw the League of Nations as the symbol of Wilson's triumph, as evidence that the "New Diplomacy" had finally vanquished the "Old." He identified himself completely with those who felt, like General Smuts and Wilson himself, that the League was such a force that it would be able to amend the peace of the statesmen and substitute a "real peace of the Peoples."[51] Tumulty, writing always with a hand on the pulse of political trends in the United States, could not resist, as Wilson himself on his Western tour could not resist, portraying the covenant in the very isolationist tones to which it was the supposed antithesis; adoption of the League meant no Americans would ever have to fight again.[52]

These somewhat apocalyptic versions of the League Covenant aside, there was another conception of the League current among many of the

48 *IPCH*, 4:152 and 188.
49 Charles T. Thompson, *The Peace Conference Day by Day* (New York, 1920), 204.
50 Creel, *War, the World, and Wilson*, 6–7.
51 Baker, *Wilson and World Settlement*, 1:235 and 2:520.
52 Tumulty, *Wilson As I Know Him*, 360. See also Lawrence's account of Wilson's Western tour in the *True Story of Wilson*, 276.

Americans who had been in Paris or who wrote for more academic audiences. The argument that Wilson, in his defiance of the Senate by making the League and the treaty inseparable, could never get quite right was well articulated by others. Inquiry member Charles Haskins, quoting the British account edited by Harold Temperley, approved of the argument that it was unlikely that the conflicting national interests involved could ever have been reconciled (a good example of this was the Saar question) without there being the facilitation of settlement provided by the incipient machinery of the League.[53] Arthur Pearson Scott, Assistant Professor of History at the University of Chicago, likewise argued that because there was a need for some organization to carry out its terms, "the League really facilitated the Treaty."[54] A similar line of thought was reflected in Bernard Baruch's careful emphasis on the importance of the on going processes for adjudication established by the treaty.[55]

I must confess to being quite impressed by the analytical mode adopted by those Americans who had had an opportunity to study international organization. Foremost among them was Francis B. Sayre, Wilson's own son-in-law, assistant professor of law at Harvard, who was allegedly not taken to Paris because the President feared the charge of nepotism. Sayre in his book *Experiments in International Administration* approached the subject of international organization historically and clinically and demonstrated a good understanding of how deleterious unanimity requirements had been in previous international accords.[56] Similarly, Stephen P. Duggan, director of the Institute of International Education at the College of the City of New York, introducing a collection of essays by leading American figures in the fields of history, law and political science, urged the adoption of the League as a first step, but warned that the war had strengthened nationalism, that the League was not yet a world league and that it represented little more than increased international administration.[57] Perhaps my favorite account, unmatched in its simplicity and lack of pretension, was that of Isaiah Bowman, written as an introduction to his text, *The New World: Problems in Political Geography*. Bowman argued matter-of-factly that there would always be war, that the danger had now increased because of the many additional miles of international boundaries created by the treaty, and that the

53 Charles Homer Haskins, "The New Boundaries of Germany," in House and Seymour, eds., *What Really Happened at Paris*, 61.
54 Arthur P. Scott, *An Introduction to the Peace Treaties* (Chicago, 1920), 70.
55 Baruch, *Making of the Economic Sections of the Treaty*, 8.
56 Francis B. Sayre, *Experiments in International Administration* (New York, 1919), 150–8.
57 Stephen P. Duggan, ed., *The League of Nations: The Principle and the Practice* (Boston, 1919), 6, 13, 15 and 17.

League was in the nature of an "experiment" and that not too much should initially be expected of it.[58]

An interesting debate also arose as to the centrality and importance of Article X. Whereas Wilson never wavered from his insistence that such a provision was essential to the very conception of a league, Lansing, who had never liked it, described it as the real obstacle to ratification by the Senate. Claiming that the issue was not the creation of a league but rather the means that it would employ, Lansing insisted that there would have been no problem at all if his idea of providing in Article X only a negative guarantee (having states merely pledge not to pursue aggression) had been adopted.[59] More complicated was the reasoning of David Hunter Miller, who favored the covenant with or without Article X. To him, such a commitment was implicit in the setting up of the League, but it need not necessarily be written into its constitution. A possible alternative to Lansing's proposal was a positive guarantee coupled with a member state's unlimited right of withdrawal, which would of course have weakened such a guarantee.[60]

Again, as with respect to the Fourteen Points, one might have expected to see these efforts to deglorify and desanctify the League reflected in Seymour's reconstruction of the role of Colonel House. There was some understanding of the League's limitations (that its successful operation was dependent on the continuation of U.S.–British cooperation) and a firm reiteration of the view that the League facilitated the settlement ("If it had not been for the existence of the League, to which control of these problems might be and was turned over, agreement upon the treaties would have been postponed indefinitely").[61] But once again analysis was sacrificed to a cultivation of House's reputation, thus serving only to personalize the issue once again. Seymour's whole approach to the League was colored by his attempt to refute Baker's charges that the problems attendant to the treaty's deviations from the standards of perfection long advocated by Americans were the result of House's acquiescence, in Wilson's absence, to the demands of the greedy European imperialists.[62] In the Seymour version, the problem lay not with House, but rather with Wilson, who, in his preoccupation with securing the League he wanted, had to pay a heavy price in compromises with the Europeans, all of which detracted from the perfection of the treaty. The final indictment could hardly have been more severe: "but to compro-

58 Isaiah Bowman, *The New World: Problems in Political Geography* (Yonkers-on-Hudson, N.Y., 1921), 1, 3, and 11.
59 Lansing, *Peace Negotiations*, 31, 45, 52, 78, and 125.
60 Miller, *Drafting of the Covenant*, 31–2.
61 *IPCH*, 4:181 and 322.
62 Baker, *Wilson and World Settlement*, 1:295–313 and 2:140 and 169.

mise with the Europeans on the treaty and then fail to secure the Senate's endorsement of the League, meant not only disaster for his whole policy, but the bankruptcy of the liberal movement in the United States of which he had been the leader."[63] Wilson's lapses may have been primarily tactical, but what is all too obvious here is that in historiography just as in politics, the key to victory was seen to be in holding the supposedly more moral and upright ground.

THE OVERALL ASSESSMENT: WHAT THE TREATY DID AND DID NOT ACHIEVE

Differences over the realization of the Fourteen Points and over the importance of the League were integral to one's overall assessment of the treaty – of the extent to which it was deserving of ratification and of being upheld. Again the reactions were very mixed and revealed some important philosophical divisions within American Progressivism.

Perhaps the differing evaluations of the treaty can be traced back to contrasting conceptions of the opportunities presented by the war and the making of peace. Exactly how high were the stakes? Some Americans saw American foreign policy in a redemptive and millennial mold. Wilson himself viewed the gathering in Paris as "the supreme conference in the history of mankind," as a "great world enterprise, which after all is the enterprise of Divine mercy, peace and good will."[64] Baker felt on the eve of the conference that the world was in more of a "plastic state" than ever before, that the forces of reform were on the verge of a great opportunity.[65] Such millennial hopes could lead only to disappointment or to a posture of closing one's eyes to what one did not want to see. For a propagandist like Creel, the latter disposition was endemic; he had no trouble whatsoever in touting the treaty's "amazing justice."[66] Wilson himself, even after the treaty's defeat, still saw the League as "their real hope, their last chance, perhaps, to save civilization!"[67] Baker's task was more difficult. He had trouble hiding his disappointment and sometimes it resurfaced as tragedy, but more often than not he simply steeled himself, trying to convince everyone (himself included) that:

63 *IPCH*, 4:409–10.
64 Quoted in Lawrence, *True Story of Wilson*, 255; also in Tumulty, *Wilson As I Know Him*, 336.
65 Baker quoted in John A. Thompson, *Reformers and War: American Progressive Publicists and the First World War* (New York, 1987), 234.
66 Creel, *War, the World, and Wilson*, 299.
67 Wilson quoted in Tumulty, *Wilson As I Know Him*, 455.

if the ordinary reasonable American could have sat in at those conferences of the fourteen nations in Colonel House's office at the Crillon Hotel day after day – or failing that, had had the proceedings presented so dramatically and vividly that he could really understand – he would have seen all the forces at work against the lurid background of a suffering Europe; would have seen why, with such warring ideals and interests, there had to be much give and take – much of what the President calls "accommodation" – and would no doubt have come out about where the Commission came out and would have adopted much the same kind of covenant.[68]

It was probably better to have started with one's feet more firmly planted on the ground. By that route the road to acceptance and to giving the League a try lay more readily open. Professor Arthur Scott posed a telling question: "Is the peace settlement of 1919 so different from those of the past that more may be expected of it?"[69] In a similar vein, Inquiry members Charles Haskins and Robert Lord wrote, "The congress could not create a new heaven and a new earth; it could at best only make some sort of advance on the road thither and show the way along which further advance lay."[70] From this more modest start flowed a better understanding of limitations and a more tempered judgment as to what had been achieved. Haskins and Lord thought the treaty "an immense gain for the cause of liberty and nationality"; Baruch looked favorably on Wilson's role and declared that "the treaty may not embrace all he desired, but I believe that it embodies all that could have been obtained"; and Clive Day of Yale, chief of the Balkan Division of the American Peace Commission, managed to be upbeat without being apocalyptic, writing that "when compared with similar bodies in the past . . . the Paris Peace Conference faced vastly greater problems, studied its problems in a more scientific way, and sought more earnestly to harmonize its settlement with the principles of justice."[71] By this route one could readily support ratification of the treaty and even its enforcement. Lansing, for all his difficulties with Wilson, thought that the treaty's defects were not sufficient to warrant a refusal to ratify.[72] Professor Scott strongly supported ratification in the present coupled with work to modify the treaty in the future.[73] Professor Archibald Cary Coolidge of Harvard, looking back in 1927 from the perspective of "Ten Years of War and Peace", admon-

68 Baker, *What Wilson Did at Paris*, 17.
69 Scott, *Introduction to the Peace Treaties*, 1.
70 Haskins and Lord, *Some Problems of the Peace Conference*, 7.
71 Ibid., 287; Baruch, *Making of the Economic Sections of the Treaty*, 8; Clive Day, "The Atmosphere and Organization of the Peace Conference," in House and Seymour, eds., *What Really Happened at Paris*, 36.
72 Lansing, *Big Four*, 8.
73 Scott, *Introduction to the Peace Treaties*, vi.

ished his readers to remember that "whatever its imperfections, it [the Treaty of Versailles] is now an important integral part of the public law of Europe."[74]

There remains an important question. Was the Versailles treaty an American peace? Professor Coolidge, without raising the question of morality, answered yes without compunction: "It was based on propositions laid down in advance by the United States and in the main adhered to."[75] But, writing from the same perspective in time, Charles Seymour did not agree. He still complained about those who saw the conference as a clear-cut conflict "between the evil of the old European diplomatic System and the virtue of the new world idealism." From his perspective:

In reality the Peace Conference was not nearly so simple. It was not so much a duel as a general melee, in which the representatives of each nation struggled to secure endorsement for their particular methods of ensuring the peace. The object of all was the same to avoid a repetition of the four years of world devastation; their methods naturally were different, since each was faced by a different set of problems.

Inevitably each nation put forward a solution which was colored by self-interest. This was, in a sense, just as true of the United States as of France, Italy, or Great Britain. We sacrificed very little in announcing that we would take no territory (which we did not want), nor reparations (which we could not collect). Our interest lay entirely in assuring a regime of world tranquillity; our geographic position was such that we could advocate disarmament and arbitration with complete safety. Wilson's idealism was in line with a healthy *Realpolitik*. But American methods did not fit so perfectly the peculiar problems of European nations, dominated as they were by geographical and historical factors. According to the American programme, we ourselves gave up nothing of value, but we asked the European nations to give up much that seemed to them the very essence of security.[76]

Interestingly, the question for Coolidge and for Seymour was not so much any longer one of whether the American peace program had actually prevailed or not. Seymour, when he was not having to deflect charges against the diplomatic reputation of Colonel House, was capable of considerable perspective and insight. What was important for both was that Americans develop a heightened sense of self-awareness in the hope that this would lead to a heightened sense of responsibility. It was as if they were saying that the kind of morality play favored by the Progressive publicists had already had too long a run and needed to be shut down.

Historian Robert Crunden once remarked that the treaty fight was "the last great battle within progressivism," a battle between Wilsonians and the

74 Archibald Cary Coolidge, *Ten Years of War and Peace* (Cambridge, Mass., 1927), 165.
75 Ibid., 113.   76 *IPCH*, 4:377–8.

Irreconcilables, the latter led by two of the most progressive men in Washington.[77] That fissure still has a tendency to overshadow all others, and it may have caused us to neglect another and perhaps equally important one. Ray Stannard Baker once tried to argue that a "real peace," the kind of peace Wilson envisaged, had to have two supports: "It must be inspired by a new moral purpose and be directed by dispassionate scientific inquiry."[78] That those two principal supports had different philosophical underpinnings and were often not reconcilable seemed to escape Baker entirely. No one today would think of arguing that Wilson was not strongly influenced by the vast array of experts he took with him to Paris, but that contention tends to mask the fact that there were severe tensions between those who thought that wisdom would flow from knowledge and expertise and those who thought that changes in international politics could be effected only by means of moral regeneration. The same tensions that beset the American Progressive approach to the conduct of foreign policy abide with us still. And, if there is any consolation at all to be derived from revisiting the early American attempts to interpret what went on in Paris, it is only to be found in the knowledge that the American approach to the making of peace in 1919 was more variegated and less overweening than it was at first made to appear.

77 Crunden, *Ministers of Reform*, 265.
78 Baker, *Wilson and World Settlement*, 1:181.

24

British Revisionism

MICHAEL GRAHAM FRY

For revisionism to occur, an orthodoxy of some vitality, political and intellectual, must exist. In the case of the 1919 settlement with Germany, revisionism of a certain kind emerged within the British Empire delegation and its epistemic community of experts sufficiently early and with enough credibility and vigor to affect what became the most tenuous of orthodoxies, the final treaty. Then and since, in British official and scholarly circles, revisionism has flourished to an extent that it has virtually institutionalized paradox – to defend the 1919 settlement would be revisionist. This state of affairs has come to pass, moreover, without there being a satisfactory account of British policy at the Paris Peace Conference.

I

Revisionism about the 1919 peace treaty has ranged in scope from the most abstract to the most pointed, instrumental level of analysis. It took two forms – political and historical – both driven by competitive interpretation. The former preceded and grounded the latter, and then recruited it. The distinction between them was, initially, sharp and clear; it became less so over time. Statesmen and officials, David Lloyd George, the prime minister, and Harold Nicolson, Foreign Office official, for example, became historians of a kind; historians, like economists and lawyers, populated temporarily officialdom. In some cases one can trace change – E. H. Carr the liberal idealist of 1919, expecting so much of Lloyd George and then turning, disillusioned, on him, and becoming the ultimately celebrated realist of 1939 – in others dogged consistency and determined defense of self.

Political revisionism had, in 1919, two strands, one realist, that is, tactical, the other ideological. Neither strand was homogeneous. Lloyd George, unavoidably, stood at the center of the British debate in Paris. He found nothing of merit in ideological revisionism, if only because the enragés threatened the essences of his handiwork, and thus his political stature. Indeed, Lloyd George developed a level of proprietary commitment to the draft treaty that represented, in his view, principally the result of his collaboration with Woodrow Wilson, without either alienating Georges Clemenceau or destroying Allied unity, that made it difficult for him finally to accept elements of tactical revisionism. Senior colleagues found him reluctant and difficult to convince. Lloyd George, in a word, was caught between the necessities of revisionism and a stubborn preference to defend his creation. Tactical revisionism, however, led him ultimately, logically, to orthodoxy. Lloyd George set out both the mature case for tactical revision in the Council of Four and, in his statements to the House of Commons on June 30, and July 3 and 21, 1919, in defense of the peace treaty, the first articulation of orthodoxy. It then became, predictably, as historian, a matter of defending the treaty, revised as it had been, to the death. In 1923, 1932, and 1938 Lloyd George defended the treaty, and himself, while finding fresh grounds for the defense. It was entirely characteristic of Lloyd George to play such an involved role. He was, and it was a defining characteristic of his intellectual makeup and his reasoning, an instrumentalist, full of how great men, relatively free of structural constraints, shape history and face its judgment. Like Woodrow Wilson, he had a sense of opportunity, of unfettered choice between alternative courses of action, of the possibility of change. Yet he felt the pull of constraints, international and domestic, of power, ideas and politics. Nothing makes him more controversial.

Both Lloyd George's tactical revisionism and his preparation to defend the treaty began in mid-April. They were underpinned by the Fontainebleau memorandum, and very much bound by context. Naval affairs marred Anglo-American cooperation; Syria kept Lloyd George and Clemenceau apart; and Belgian, Japanese, and Italian policies, with Vittorio Emanuele Orlando, the Italian prime minister, sobbing his way toward empire, threatened Allied unity. But conditions in, and the policies of, Germany and Russia were the keys to the context, for there lay costs and risks to the Allies of major proportions. Between April 16 and May 7, when the draft terms were presented to Germany, the uncertainties with regard to Germany and Russia – would the German government sign the treaty, survive its signature, and implement the treaty faithfully, making a resumption of the war or the reimposition of the full blockade unnecessary, and would the anti-Bolshevik elements succeed militarily and restore a friendly, liberal Russia – seemed to have diminished if not evaporated. The German government would sign and survive; Lenin would fall. Risk, however, had two faces – of policy failure and political vulnerability – and Lloyd George, judging every issue in part in terms of domestic politics, saw every reason to produce peace rather than invite a resumption of the war, even if the Allies triumphed decisively as they most certainly would. Buoyed by the assessment of Walter Long, First Lord of the Admiralty, of the state of opinion at home, Lloyd George spoke of a treaty flawed but containing a mode of correction – the League – of a treaty that was just but not vindictive, stern but not revengeful, severe but a vindication of justice. To avoid a repetition of the war the draft treaty contained deterrents – war crimes trials and reparations – both underpinned by disarmament. The settlement would have an intrinsic legitimacy for there would be no sense of wrong, no need to seek redress, no point to revisionism. The League, in fact, would preside over a state of general order, of permanent security. Tactically, Lloyd George left the door open to concessions on secondary issues, refused to add irritants, and wanted the draft treaty kept secret so as to protect it from critics at home and enemies of peace, spartacists and nationalists, in Germany.[1]

Some of his colleagues were far less sure. Robert Cecil, handling League affairs, launched biting criticism of the reparations clauses – full of uncertainty and indefinite liability, and leaving ample room for French mischief, they would deny Germany loans, give undue power to the Reparations Commission, hamper Germany's economic recovery, create financial uncertainty and imperil Europe's economic revival. It was an error to seek £1,000 million by May 1921, to seize Germany's merchant fleet and to require Germany to build merchant ships for the Allies. Andrew Bonar Law, Lord Privy Seal, felt that Germany would not sign. Louis Botha, the South African prime minister, distrusted French policy and did not support the treaty of guarantee of France. The prose of Henry Wilson, the chief of the Imperial General Staff (CIGS), claiming to speak for George Barnes, the Labour member of the cabinet and the British delegation, Robert Borden, the Canadian prime minister, and Cecil, could not have been more preemptive – they were in a "vile mess," the terms, "flung together," were a "mass of contradiction, inconsistency and nonsense," which Germany

1 Lloyd George speech, Apr. 16, *Parl. Deb.* (H.C.), 5th ser., 114: 2936–56: and Long to Lloyd George, Apr. 20 and 29, LGP, F/33/2/30 and 36. Long also warned of public uncertainty over reparations, Italy and excessively lenient treatment of Germany. See also Council of Four, Apr. 20, 21, 23, and 24, and May 1, 5, and 6, in Paul Mantoux, *The Deliberations of the Council of Four (March 24–June 28, 1919): Notes of the Official Interpreter,* (hereafter DCF), trans. and ed. Arthur S. Link, with the assistance of Manfred F. Boemeke, 2 vols. (Princeton, N.J., 1992), 1:290–7, 309–10, 339–42, 353–7, 442–6, 486 and 488–9; and British Empire delegation, May 5, 1919, LGP, F/126. Lloyd George wanted to reduce Allied interference in Germany's internal affairs and eliminate certain "pinpricks." How well Lloyd George and his colleagues, from their various sources, understood the state of the German political economy remains unanswered. One can begin to judge the quality of their intelligence on Germany from Great Britain, Foreign Office Records (hereafter BB FO) 608/131.

would shred. There was widespread unease because the empire delegation
had not seen and thus could not grasp the cumulative impact of the draft
terms in their entirety. Barnes, uneasy about French policy, the army of
occupation and the failure to name the accused German war criminals,
wanted the minor demands removed. Given the news of suffering in Germany, they would foster pro-German sympathies among labor across
Europe. Moreover, Barnes argued, some of the proposed terms were out of
step with popular expectations. The denial of self-determination to Austria
invited trouble and the reparations clauses, in view of Germany's reduced
resources, required reexamination. Barnes was already crossing the line
between tactical and ideological revisionism. Yet Lloyd George agreed
merely that Bonar Law and Jan Smuts, the South African delegate, could
have two days to comb the treaty for flaws.

Smuts, speaking privately of a world crisis in which governments that
followed rather than educated and led public opinion were floundering in
the face of anarchy, and of peacemakers devoid of plan and vision, themes
that he shared with John Maynard Keynes, the principal Treasury official,
produced his caveats on May 5. Without challenging the basic structure of
the treaty, he recommended amendments principally in eight areas – that is,
in the territorial terms (Danzig and the Saar), the military, air, aerodromes,
and reparations clauses, the punishment of war criminals, the rivers and railways provisions, and, "the most shocking of all," the fifteen-year occupation
of the left bank of the Rhine. Keynes, close ideologically to Smuts, moved
by Carl Melchior, head of the German financial commission, more sympathetic to German distress than French injury, his prose as intemperate in its
own way as that of Henry Wilson – "Heaven give me escape from this Paris
nightmare" – was horrified. The reparations clauses were unworkable and
folly, Germany would challenge the territorial and military terms,the economic clauses were spiteful, those on waterways humiliating and intrusive,
and, on war crimes, an affront to German honor. The Rhineland occupation was likely to bring abuse and thus friction. Keynes felt Germany would
not sign this "outrageous and impossible" treaty but argued that a German
signature would in fact produce the worst possible outcome – collapse, revolution, and a "morass of destruction." Folly and wickedness were rampant.
The U. S. delegation had rejected his scheme for European economic
reconstruction, linking reparations to the cancellation of war debts.
Woodrow Wilson was "the greatest fraud on earth."[2]

---

2 Cecil diary, Apr. 13, and May 1 and 9; H. Wilson diary, Apr. 20 and 23, and May 2, 3, and 4; Cecil
   to Lloyd George, Apr. 30 and May 5 and Lloyd George to Cecil, May 2, LGP, F/16/6/38 and 41;
   Long to Lloyd George, May 8, Long papers, 747/746; Smuts to Lloyd George, May 5, LGP,

Lloyd George's guarded optimism about Russia remained substantially intact throughout May, although his doubts about Allied unity increased. Germany did not respond fully to the draft terms until May 29. In those three weeks, between May 7 and 29, the evidence about German policy was neither clear nor consistent, nor uniformly credible – Germany would sign after haggling; Germany would reject the terms, ally with Russia and attack Poland; Germany would refuse to sign, risk an Allied invasion and then sign under protest; Germany would sign in bad faith and, as the government collapsed, the state fragmented and the socialists seized power, evade implementing the treaty, and force an Allied invasion. Credible Allied responses, amid diminishing military capability, in the face of German defiance – resume the war and march on Berlin, a limited military advance, and reimposition of the full blockade – all had their drawbacks. Perhaps the threat of coercion would bring Germany to heel? Lloyd George, now being referred to in the French press as "L'insaissisable Gallois," was as militant as anyone. "They must convince the Junkers that they were beaten." "It must be rammed into their heads" that a refusal to sign would mean the resumption of general war in which the Poles and the Czechs would welcome participation.[3] At home, five by-elections were held between February and April. The coalition government retained two of the seats but three were lost to the Liberals, and a percentage swing against the coalition occurred in all of them.

In response to this higher level of uncertainty, Lloyd George went in both directions. On a limited set of issues he added firmness to coercion. Germany could not be allowed to challenge the legal and moral validity of either the peace process or the treaty as a whole; the military and naval terms must be enforced; Germany must surrender its merchant fleet; articles 231 and 232 were not negotiable, and a failure to pay reparation would

---

F/45/9/33; Nicolson diary, May 14, Harold Nicolson, *Peacemaking 1919* (London, 1933), 336; Barnes to Lloyd George, May 6 and 16, 1919, LGP, F/4/3/14 and 15, and Milner to Kerr, Apr. 24, 1919, Lothian papers, GD/40/17/1176. Milner, as an interim step toward creating a de-Prussianized Germany, actually spoke of partition so as to detach liberal west Germany from Prussia. See also Keynes to Bertrand Russell, Apr. 12, 1919, Bertrand Russell papers, correspondence files, and Robert Skidelsky, *John Maynard Keynes: A Biography*, 2 vols. (London, 1983), 1:370–2.

3 Council of Four, May 9, 10, 14, and 19, in DCF, 2:12–13, 17–24, 64–5, 100–3; H. Wilson diary, May 8 and 12; Riddell diary, May 11, 28 and 30, in J. McEwen, ed., *The Riddell Diaries* (London, 1986), 276–7; W. Steed memorandum, May 18, Steed papers, file 1910–19; Cecil to Lloyd George, May 14, LGP, F/6/6/45; Lloyd George address, May 31, ibid., H/113/48; Lothian to Bonar Law, May 14 and 23, Lothian papers, GD/40/17/1198 and 1199; and Lloyd George to Borden, May 9, Borden papers, vol. 294, reel C-4469. Bonar Law and Long kept Lloyd George abreast of domestic discontent and urged him to stay in touch with those of his colleagues who were in touch with the people, that is, his Tory colleagues. (Bonar Law to Lloyd George, May 13 and 17, Bonar Law papers, 101/3/65 and 73, and Long to Lloyd George, May 28, 1919 LGP, F/33/2/46).

warrant an Allied occupation of German territory under article 429. On other issues, Lloyd George favored concessions. He continued to oppose publication of the proposed terms but on different grounds – publication would lock them in, prevent them from making reasonable amendments, from improving the treaty, and open them up to public charges of weakness or betrayal if they made concessions. Germany must be given additional time to respond, from May 22 to 29, and "I would not like to sign a treaty which will deliver to foreigners all the colonies, the entire merchant fleet of my country." They must also correct German misperceptions and educate German opinion. There was, Lloyd George suggested, merit in some of Germany's interim responses – that states violating the covenant pay the costs of the resulting war; accepting the principle of disarmament; questioning the Saar and Danzig terms; that the proposed 100,000-man army would leave Germany defenseless against the well-armed, greedy and aggressive Poles; and that the Allied occupation of the west bank of the Rhine was unwise. There must be, moreover, no additional demands, no new pinpricks, no fresh irritants, this in response to Clemenceau who could see improving the draft terms by tightening them.[4] In beginning to explore this tactical revisionism, while defending his handiwork, Lloyd George was following his instincts and judgment, giving full rein to his anger at the Poles (a complex theme, for he admired the Germans more as a race and found striking a balance between Polish aspirations and German necessities difficult), and responding, visibly irritated, to criticism from within the empire delegation, which he viewed as somewhat of a low blow, and against which the lavish praise of Borden was little comfort.

Winston Churchill, secretary of state for war, and H. A. L. Fisher, president of the Board of Education, speaking perhaps for cabinet colleagues Edward Shortt and Christopher Addison, made the case for tactical revision of the treaty. Barnes, Smuts, and Cecil, the latter two drawing on Keynes's utter disillusionment and the growing dissatisfaction of Nicolson, grew more ideological. Keynes, Nicolson recorded, found the draft treaty immoral and incompetent. Germany would gain nothing from signing it, and lose nothing by refusing to sign. Both Keynes and Nicolson, with

4 Council of Four, May 8, 9, 10, 13, 15, 17, 19, 20, 21, 22, 23, 24, 26, 28, 29, and 30, in *DCF,* 2:3–8, 11–12, 24, 49–50, 80, 84, 105, 120–2, 126, 128, 153–4, 158–60, 161–3, 165–8, 182–7, 191, 195, 196–200, 207, 237–8, 251–4, and 255–7; Lloyd George notes on U.S. draft response on reparations, May 9, LGP, F/214/2/1; Kerr to Bonar Law, May 27, Lothian papers, GD/40/17/1200; Headlam-Morley minute, Apr. 24, GB FO 608/62; Nugent to Foch, May 16, de Wiart to Balfour, May 23 and Balfour to Wyndham, May 19, GB FO 608/62; Gen. N. Malcolm reports, n.d., H. Wilson diary, May 12, Winthrop-Bell report, May 19, GB FO 608/143, Basil Thompson to Lord Drogheda, May 8, GB FO 608/134, and Nicolson diary, May 20, 1919, Nicolson, *Peacemaking 1919,* 345.

regard to reparations, wanted to save Austria from Germany's fate, a fate constructed to please the House of Commons, and quite impossible to impose on a Germany that was left without hope. The draft treaty was worth only what it was printed on – the *Daily Mail*. The foreign secretary, Arthur Balfour, apparently, could bring himself at this stage neither to defend nor attack the draft treaty. Colleagues identified Lord Milner, colonial secretary, as a critic, but precisely on what grounds was not clear.[5]

Churchill's advice, which Henry Wilson endorsed, was crisp, lyrical, and palatable, and not unconnected with his Russian policy – negotiate with patience and goodwill, compromise promptly with Germany, reap the harvest of victory, and protect the empire's vital eastern interests. "Agree with thine adversary whilst thou art in the way with him." Ensure that Germany signed and implemented a treaty that represented its own defeat and the empire's victory. Beware, Churchill warned, of "Latin ambitions and hatreds." "Settle now while we have the power," and remove the need to invade and occupy Germany "or lose perhaps forever the power of settlement on the basis of a military victory." Fisher agreed, assuring Lloyd George of full Liberal support for those concessions needed to purchase a

---

5 Smuts memorandum, May 17, and Smuts to M. C. Gillett, May 19, Smuts papers, in Jan Christiaan Smuts, ed., *Selections from the Smuts Papers*, ed. W. K. Hancock and Jean van der Poel, 7 vols. (London, 1966), vol. 4; Smuts to Lloyd George, May 14 and 22, LGP, F/45/4/34 and 35; Milner diary, May 17 and 20; H. Wilson diary, May 13 and 19 and Barnes memorandum, May 19, Great Britain, Cabinet Papers (hereafter GB CAB) 29/15; Barnes to Lloyd George, May 18, LGP, F/4/3/16, Cecil to Lloyd George, May 8, 15, and 27, ibid., F/6/6/43, 46 and 47, and GB FO 608/166; Churchill to Lloyd George, May 20, LGP, F/8/3/55; T. Jones to J. T. Davies, May 23, and Fisher to Lloyd George, May 28, ibid., F/23/4/69/ and F/16/7/39; Fisher to Gilbert Murray, May 12, and Fisher to wife, May 13, Fisher papers, box 7; Cecil diary, May 26; Keynes memorandum, May 10, Lothian papers, GD/40/17/70; Crowe minute, May 21, and Hardinge minute, n.d., GB FO 608/143; J. Headlam-Morley minutes, May, and E. Howard minute, May 28, 1919, GB FO 608/131. Crowe found droll the sight of a "liberal" Germany demanding a Wilsonian peace. Hardinge wanted Germany kept down until it embraced democracy. Headlam-Morley and Howard were tactical revisionists, but Howard was less comfortable with concessions being made at Poland's expense. Headlam-Morley told Smuts in May that the draft treaty was both indefensible and unimplementable. It resulted from the preferences of the French military and from the failure of everyone to read the terms as a whole and thus to have the ability to gauge its cumulative impact. While the territorial terms must stand, the financial, reparations, commercial and military clauses could be amended, particularly if Germany were admitted to the League. They should, therefore, accept those German modifications that were fair and reasonable, including on the Saar, and omit Article 38 with its threat of coercion. The Board of Trade preferred, however, to reject what it regarded as Germany's grossly exaggerated claim that it could not, in view of the proposed territorial losses, meet the demands for coal deliveries. In losing Alsace-Lorraine and the Saar, Germany forfeited equally consumption and production. Upper Silesia would not be a disastrous loss. German coal shortages would be purely temporary (H. Llewellyn-Smith memorandum, May 20, LGP, F/45/8/6). See also Nicolson diary, May 20 and 28, 1919, and Nicolson to Vita Sackville-West, May 28, 1919, in Nicolson, *Peacemaking 1919*, 345–51, and Borden to Lloyd George, Apr. 29 and May 13, and Lloyd George to Borden, May 9 and 13, 1919 LGP, F/5/3/44, 54, 61, and 62.

prompt peace, concessions that did not include returning Germany's colonies. Those who opposed such amendments were in a minority. The public would rebel against renewing the war and balk at imposing the hardships of total blockade. Fisher found the Polish terms, largely Woodrow Wilson's fault, to be most objectionable. Unlike Churchill, he made specific suggestions – accept German claims on its borders with Poland, and to Memel, although he was unsure about Upper Silesia. Lloyd George was, he enthused, "within view of a brilliant peace,"and, even if he conceded all of Germany's demands, the settlement "will be in fact beyond the dreams of avarice." Bonar Law found the terms too stiff, especially those on German disarmament. The German government would need 120,000 men to police Berlin alone. He joined with Fisher in anticipating Prussian irredentism and a German–Polish war – "not a golden outlook."

Smuts, however, contrasted a statesman's, that is a reactionary, peace for which Lloyd George, with his "unrivaled power and influence" could still make amends with a peace that conformed to public wisdom, convinced as he was that the combined effect of the territorial and reparations clauses made it virtually impossible for Germany to implement the proposed treaty. Lloyd George must take up the challenge of effecting drastic revision to produce a treaty that all people of good sense and sound conscience preferred. "Democracy is looking to you who have killed Prussianism – the silent masses who have suffered mutely appeal to you to save them from this fate to which Europe seems now to be lapsing." The occupation of the Rhineland and the transfer of German territory on its western and eastern frontiers to "historic enemies," the two cardinal errors, meant war not peace. Privately, however, Smuts was complaining that Woodrow Wilson, not really a great man, was failing him. Clemenceau was proving too strong for Wilson and the "mercurial and tricky" Lloyd George. The draft treaty was a work of sand not of brass, a tin of poison gas that would asphyxiate the League. The Big Three were "wrapped in their delusions."

On May 22, at Lloyd George's request, Smuts spelled out the indispensable amendments – delete the occupation clauses while retaining the treaty of guarantee of France; amend the Saar terms to ensure automatic return of the region to Germany after fifteen years; retain the principal and general thrusts of the reparations terms (Germany must pay), including the Reparations Commission, and assist Germany's economic recovery so that it could pay, but scrap the objectionable and unworkable features (seeking £1,000 million in the first two years, the bonds scheme, the excessive coal deliveries, demanding merchant ship construction, and the looting of industrial machinery); as the Polish settlement was "a house of sand," likely

to collapse when Germany and Russia revived, revise Poland's proposed
frontiers; leave Upper Silesia and all German territory in Germany; reduce
the territory of the free city of Danzig and place it administratively, with
German not Polish suzerainty, under the League; limit the demand for war
crimes trials "to a definite, reasonable, short list" of persons guilty of major
crimes; increase the size of the 100,000-man army, and allow Germany to
retain quotas of tanks and military and naval aircraft, and aerodromes close
to its border; amend the proposed administration of the internationalized
German rivers and railways; remove all "pinpricks," galling, wounding,
spiteful, unworthy and provocative as they were; and, to ensure that Germany sign "a fair and good treaty," willingly and not under coercion, one
that the German people would not repudiate, negotiate fairly with the German delegation. In that way, Smuts argued, the treaty would have moral
authority and thus be binding, and constitute an honorable end to the war
in the eyes of both German and world opinion.

Barnes, privy to labor criticism, had weighed in on May 19 both on matters of process and substance. The empire delegation was inadequately
informed. The reparations clauses went beyond those of the pre-armistice
agreements and gave Germany merely the right to appeal the length of the
period of payment, but not the total sum that would ultimately be fixed.
The proposed thirty years of payment, was, in any case, too long, mere
wishful thinking in fact, and to allow Germany to extend the period of payment was to prolong the period when German labor would be "in pawn."
Surely the Reparations Commission should be allowed to reduce the total
sum as well as extend the payment period. The cost of the army of occupation of the Rhineland would be the first charge on reparations received,
yet its size was not determined. They must, Barnes insisted, determine its
size. Moreover, a list of indicted war criminals must be published before the
treaty was signed. It must be a final and definitive list. No addition should
be made subsequently. Such a revised treaty, Barnes argued, the current,
laudable German government would sign. No alternative government
would be required to demonstrate to the German people the enormity of
the offenses of their former rulers. Peace would follow.

Cecil, already jousting with Lloyd George on economic issues and reparations, went further, claiming affinity with radical opinion in Britain and
the United States. The cumulative effect of the draft treaty, Cecil insisted,
was almost overwhelming; awarding Poland the Corridor and Upper Silesia, and the Saar provisions, were indefensible. The economic and financial
items made Germany's economic recovery impossible. Germany could not
pay £1,000 million in the first two years. The Polish, Saar, and reparations

clauses, moreover, defied the published war aims of Britain and the United States. Thus, if their enumerated war aims were sound and likely to bring about lasting peace, the proposed treaty was not and could not. The empire's gains, Lloyd George's jewels, did not, Cecil argued, compensate for the treaty's gross defects. The people wanted a lasting peace and a league. They doubted whether the treaty provided for either, the clamor to make Germany pay and to punish the Kaiser notwithstanding.

Furthermore, Cecil argued, the treaty threatened Anglo-American accord. The Atlanticist relationship, Cecil conceded, had prospered at Paris, the only blemish, blithely ignoring the naval battle, coming over reparations. The U.S. delegation had trusted and followed British judgments, even when they seemed severe, all the time retaining its faith in Britain's sense of justice, in its innate generosity toward the enemy. If, however, members of the U.S. delegation felt misled and concluded that the treaty was neither generous nor fair, they would defend themselves, blaming Britain for preventing leniency and obstructing moderation. That could lead to a U.S. reaction against the League and a burst of Germanophilia, developments that could threaten Anglo-American relations. Britain's greatest asset, Cecil pontificated, typified in Edward Grey, exemplified in 1914 and an incalculable boon in the war, was the widely held belief in its devotion to justice. But during the peace conference, Britain's moral stature had suffered greatly. Indeed, the draft treaty suggested moral bankruptcy, and neutral opinion was disillusioned. In consequence, Cecil warned, the moral leadership of the world might pass from Britain to the United States, a disastrous prospect.

This must have been very hard for Lloyd George to take. Perhaps the credibility of the messenger undermined the message. His differences with Cecil were many, his relationship with Smuts, in despair at Lloyd George's sheer flippancy, distinctly cool. Indeed, Smuts, citing Keynes, was about to deliver an angry lecture on the outright folly of policy toward Austria.[6] But the issue was less the specific areas of distance or common ground, and there were both, and more the evidence of the effective distinction between tactical and ideological revisionism. That distinction had reverberations in London. In the shadow of by-election results, radical, liberal, and socialist opinion, sections of the press, prestigious clerics, and those Lloyd George called "intellectuals," were calling for moderation, even generosity. Public opinion was difficult to judge. On the other hand, the Northcliffe press was as devoted as ever to opposing leniency and to seeing the fulfillment of elec-

6 Smuts to Lloyd George, May 26 and 27, and Lloyd George to Smuts, May 26, 1919, LGP, F/45/9/36, 37, and 38.

tion pledges. Extremist elements in the Commons were unrepentant and irrepressible.[7]

Lloyd George's immediate reaction to the German reply of May 29 focused on Silesia, which, he asserted, had been German not Polish for some 700 years. He was inclined to accept Germany's claims; Silesia had no truly Polish history. The Polish Commission had been excessively sympathetic to Poland, and, indeed, its first draft report had been "scandalous."[8] Generally, quite in line with his position throughout May, without the need for a *volte-face,* he was willing to give the German counter due consideration. If Germany had identified inconsistencies where the Allies had used the Fourteen Points selectively, that is, when they favored their own case, they must correct the discrimination. But Lloyd George was not bent on major revision. He was, Cecil recorded, "prepared to loosen the screws a bit," probably on Germany's eastern borders, but "curiously reluctant" to touch reparations. In any case it was time to consult his senior colleagues, some coming in from London.[9]

Most accounts of the inadequately documented meetings that took place in Paris between May 30 and June 1 speak of unanimity. Certainly, everyone involved found merit in the German response and criticized the terms offered on May 7 as flawed, hastily constructed, and never examined as a whole, some to the point of declaring the German response unanswerable. There emerged, however, ever more distinctly, the two groups – the tactical and the ideological revisionists, the realists and the enragés. Lloyd George led the former, politically but not intellectually, Smuts the latter, protesting vehemently against the prime minister's interpretation of the proceedings. Both groups tampered neither with what the empire was about to pocket – the disarmament of Germany with a gesture toward general arms limitation, and Germany's colonies – nor, except perhaps Barnes, with

7 Churchill to Lloyd George, May 20, LGP, F/8/3/55; and Bonar Law to Lloyd George, May 9, 1919, Bonar Law papers, 101/3/60. The German response actually appeared in the London press on May 28, irritating Lloyd George, and causing dismay in Liberal circles.

8 Council of Four, May 29 and 30, 1919, in *DCF,* 2:251–8.

9 BED, May 30 and June 1, LGP, F/126; Cecil diary, May 30 and 31; H. Wilson diary, May 31 and June 1; Milner diary, June 1; Riddell diary, May 30, 1919, in McEwen, *Riddell,* 277; also L. D. Waley, *Edwin Montagu* (London, 1964), 211–12; David Lloyd George, *The Truth about the Peace Treaties* (London, 1938), 684–720; and Fisher diary, May 22, 28, and 31 and June 1 and 2, 1919. Montagu, assuming that a resumption of the war was virtually unavoidable, accompanied Fisher and Churchill on May 31. At a dinner that evening, lasting until midnight and attended by Lloyd George, Barnes, Balfour, Cecil, Chamberlain, Churchill, Fisher, Kerr, Montagu, Smith, Smuts, and Henry Wilson, Smuts went on the attack. The debate continued at the morning session of the empire delegation on June 1; decisions were reached at the afternoon session. Lloyd George dined that evening with Churchill, Fisher, Kerr, Montagu, and Smith, and at breakfast on June 2, along with Fisher, Kerr, and Montagu, reported the decisions to Bernard Baruch of the U.S. delegation.

German national as well as elite responsibility for the war, the guarantees against future German aggression, and the principle of reparations, although certain modifications to the reparations terms were deemed desirable.

The tactical revisionists – Balfour, less inclined than most to listen to German "lamentations and misfortunes," and rejecting the legally binding nature of the Fourteen Points and the pre-armistice agreements, Botha, leery of French policy, Bonar Law, Austen Chamberlain (chancellor of the exchequer), Churchill, Fisher, William Massey, New Zealand prime minister Milner, Edwin Montagu (secretary of state for India), F. E. Smith (the attorney general), Joseph Ward (New Zealand delegate), and Henry Wilson[10] – asked what concessions would induce Germany to sign the treaty, while preserving its essence. Politically, they wanted to be able to demonstrate to the British public that, if Germany did not sign, they had done everything possible to secure peace. They were, with varying degrees of inner doubt, willing to leave the case for concessions in Lloyd George's hands. They estimated that a plebiscite in Upper Silesia, modest rectifications in Germany's favor of its eastern borders with Poland, and perhaps of the status of Memel, more ample use of plebiscites, reducing the size of the force and the duration of the occupation of the west bank of the Rhine to one or two years, making provision for Germany's prompt admission into the League, tactical amendments to the reparations clauses, and removing some of the pinpricks would induce Germany to sign a treaty that was both "expedient as well as just," and to carry it out in good faith and thus ensure its durability. Such a treaty should head off a German–Polish war.

Some – Bonar Law, the CIGS, Fisher, Milner, and Churchill – would have gone further – on the Saar, Memel, Danzig and the Corridor, war crimes and German access to raw materials. Henry Wilson predicted on May 31 that only considerable modifications would induce Germany to sign a peace treaty. He warned against undue risk-taking, that is, a German government signing under protest after Allied coercion, or an alternative government signing but then evading the treaty, calling for passive resistance and appealing to world revolutionary sentiment. Concessions, Wilson argued, were required in the east, not the west, so as to avoid a German–Polish war, which Germany would win and which would then present the Allies with the predicament of either acquiescing in a German victory or assisting the Poles. In addition, he would allow Germany a 200,000- man army, with a six- not

10 Bonar Law to Lloyd George, May 31, Bonar Law papers, 101/3/93 and LGP, F/30//3/71; Ward to Lloyd George, June 2, ibid., F/36/4/17; and Kerr to L. Curtiss, June 3, 1919, Lothian papers, GD/40/17/461. Ward stood with Churchill, against Bolshevism and in fear of a Russo-German alliance.

twelve-year period of service (with six years in the reserves), and six months to hand over war materiel and destroy fortifications. Bonar Law found the Rhineland occupation useless and irrelevant. He tied reparations to Upper Silesia – they could neither deprive Germany of coal and expect it to recover industrially and pay reparations, nor make Germany an importer of coal and yet demand coal as part of reparations. He wanted a final reparations sum established, even £5,000 million, despite a predictable outcry at home, and an end to seizures of food. He told Lloyd George flatly that demanding the surrender of German citizens for war crimes trials conducted in Allied courts was impossible. He was ready for private negotiations with the Germans.

Others, including Lloyd George, with his eye on the House of Commons and Allied unity, and consulting Lords Sumner and Cunliffe on reparations, were more cautious, even reluctant. Lloyd George, as he had been throughout, was determined to avoid a premature, unsatisfactory reparations settlement that was politically damaging to him personally. The experts and the hard economic facts should extricate him from election rhetoric. Lord Derby, the ambassador to France, reported that Lloyd George had asked him to assess what support in France the Poles enjoyed in their defiance of the Allies. The prime minister remained impressed, however, with the German case on Silesia and felt there must be a plebiscite. Philip Kerr, Lloyd George's private secretary, and Sir Maurice Hankey, head of the secretariat, may have joined Churchill in his argument for splitting the difference with Germany on contested issues, and Fisher in recommending concessions, especially with regard to Poland, still leaving Lloyd George with "the greatest triumph in the history of the world." Fisher found Balfour's attempt to defend the Polish terms "amusing."[11]

In summation, Lloyd George claimed a mandate to demand concessions on Upper Silesia, the German–Polish frontier, early (perhaps within two years) admission of Germany to the League on evidence of fulfillment of its obligations, a reduction in the size and duration of the army of occupation, and modifications to the reparations clauses so as to make progress toward

11 Derby to Balfour, May 31, Balfour papers, Add 49744; H. Wilson memorandum, May 31, GB CAB 29/15; H. Wilson to Hankey, June 1, H. Wilson papers, box 73/1/6, file 6; H. Wilson to Allenby, June 6 and 10, H. Wilson to G. T. M. Bridges, June 19, ibid., box 73/1//13/ files 33 and 35A; H. Wilson diary, June 6, 1919. The evidence on Milner is very thin. His most recent biographer, A. M. Gollin, ignores the issue, as does Churchill's principal biographer, M. Gilbert, writing a form of prehistory. Cecil recorded that Churchill and Fisher, on May 31, argued that Germany should pay no reparations in the first year and that a final sum of £5,000 million be set. See also Sumner memorandum, May 31, LGP, F/213/5/36; Cunliffe memorandum, June 1, Lothian papers, GD/40/17/62; and Long to Lloyd George, June 11, 1919, LGP, F/33/2/51.

fixing a definite and final sum.[12] The realists predicted French but not U.S. opposition and gave Lloyd George a mandate to threaten that unless these concessions were made Britain would participate neither in a resumption of the war nor in the reimposition of a full blockade, so as to coerce Germany. It was unlikely, however, that Lloyd George would use the treaty of guarantee of France as a lever unless it was to reinforce the case against the army of occupation.

Smuts, for the enragés, denouncing the "French" peace as a breach of faith and the Saar terms as "indefensible," asked what terms constituted a principled peace, a Wilsonian settlement, one consistent with the Fourteen Points. Free of Barnes's guile, not rising to Lloyd George's bait, undeterred if not unembarrassed by the less than clear distinction between restricted and substantial amendments, and between inducing Germany to sign a treaty and reintegrating her into the family of nations, by his own role in adding pensions to the reparations bill, and by his acquiescence in the unavoidable decision to leave the negotiations in Lloyd George's hands and to rely on him effectively to manage Clemenceau, Smuts was less concerned with punishment and more with legitimacy, healing and integration. He demanded a "very drastic course," the recasting and transformation of the "impossible draft" treaty so as to make it "more in accord with our solemn undertakings, our public declarations, and the requirements of a reasonable and practical policy." The draft treaty, possibly fitting in the seventeenth and eighteenth centuries, was "entirely opposed to the spirit of our times" and likely to prove disastrous. Specifically, initially and then in response to Lloyd George's interrogation, Smuts insisted on Germany's immediate entry into the League, no occupation of the Rhineland, the removal of all terms not consistent with "the Wilson formulas" – on the Saar, Danzig, and Memel, that is, "indisputably German territories" – and all pinpricks, a "thorough revision" of the terms for Germany's eastern frontiers, skeptical as he was of Poland's viability, plebiscites for all contested areas on Poland's proposed frontiers, fixing "a reasonable though high amount" for reparations (£5,000 million) and counting Germany's contribution to the restoration of devastated areas toward the total bill, ensuring that French and Belgian claims for physical damage (limited to £2,000 million) did not squeeze out claims for pensions, and thoroughly revising the powers of the Reparations Commission so as to prevent a "serious invasion of German sovereignty."

---

12 Two schemes were examined—Germany would repair and restore all physical damage and then pay a fixed sum, or Germany would sign a treaty containing the reparations clauses as drafted and offer a fixed sum within three months.

Smuts dismissed Lloyd George's jibe on South West Africa – it was "as dust in the balance compared to the burdens now hanging over the civilized world." He and his people were concerned with civilized behavior, moderation and fair play, not "a bit of desert." He concluded on a characteristically elevated note. The choice before them was between good and evil. It was a matter of conscience and faith, for the proposed treaty "breathes a poisonous spirit of revenge which may yet scorch the fair face – not of a corner of France but Europe."[13] Smuts, in a word, forecasted the opposition of all of mankind to the proposed treaty. No one had done more to differentiate the ideological from the realist position. While the realists asked what concessions would induce Germany to sign, Smuts asked what principled peace would Germany honor because of its legitimacy. He would negotiate face to face with Germany; the realists would not. Smuts would ransack the draft treaty, not merely amend it. Whereas the realists predicted French opposition to concessions, Smuts predicted the revulsion of mankind to a treaty merely amended for reasons that were patently tactical.

Lloyd George finessed Smuts procedurally and substantively. He ignored Cecil who argued that the League should be allowed to renegotiate the Rhineland terms and remove humiliating minor clauses, and warned again that the treaty would fail without fundamental revision of the reparations provisions. Barnes demanded that British policy be in step with the "international solidarity of the democratic forces," and, like Keynes, that there be international financial cooperation to promote German and European economic recovery. Most uncomfortable about the Polish corridor, he threatened not to sign the treaty unless the Rhineland occupation, useless, superfluous, dangerous, in violation of the pre-armistice agreements and looking like a reparations collection agency, was reduced to a period of five years. Like Cecil, Barnes wanted to see Germany admitted immediately to the League of Nations and the League to exorcise all unnecessary humiliations and "milch cows." Lloyd George locked him into a debate on reparations and the reparations commission that Barnes could not win and would not want publicized. Barnes turned then on Woodrow Wilson, the "villain of the Peace . . . a child in the hands of Clemenceau."[14] Lloyd George was

13 Smuts to Lloyd George, June 2, Lloyd George to Smuts, June 3, and Smuts to Lloyd George, June 4, 1919, LGP, F/49/9/39, 40, and 41.
14 Cecil to Lloyd George, June 7 and 10, ibid., F/6/6/54; Cecil memorandum, June 3, GB FO 608/241; Barnes to Lloyd George and replies, June 2, Barnes to Lloyd George, June 3, LGP, F/4/3/17, 18, 19, 20, and 21, and Barnes memorandum, June 10, GB FO 608/142. Cecil felt let down by what he judged to be Lloyd George's failure to secure German access to the League. Whether Barnes put much stock in intelligence reports on the campaign of Ramsay Macdonald and other European socialists against the treaty is not clear. His report to Lloyd George on the condition of Ger-

willing to risk politically embarrassing but not debilitating resignations, and even a public campaign against the treaty. Indeed, Lloyd George saw the value of such dissent in handling Clemenceau. Fisher's views would, presumably, impress Woodrow Wilson, and both would weigh the fact that only Balfour and Massey had joined him in defending the draft treaty.

Keynes walked away from "this scene of nightmare," from a treaty he judged to be neither just nor expedient, from a battle lost over reparations, leaving "the twins to gloat over the devastation of Europe." Keynes had no doubts to whom Lloyd George would turn on reparations, and offered to join Smuts in public protest. Lloyd George passed off Keynes's resignation as an artifact of intraexpert conflict, with no sense of the political consequences. Keynes, full of moral indignation, indulging his ego as well as his conscience, repaired to England and, urged on by Smuts, Cecil, and the "Squiffs," wrote *The Economic Consequences of the Peace,* published in December 1919. Keynes did not mend fences with Lloyd George until 1926.[15]

Lloyd George, informed by Bernard Baruch of the American delegation that the United States would not fund a march on Berlin, went to the Council of Four on June 2 both to secure amendments to induce Germany to sign a treaty and to retain the essentials of the draft treaty. He put on the negotiating table Upper Silesia (and now spoke of a plebiscite favoring the Poles), the Polish–German border (though whether Germany or Poland constituted the imminent threat to those borders was not clear), Memel, reparations, Germany's admission to the League, the army of occupation

many suggested that Germany could pay considerable reparations. (Barnes to Lloyd George, June 22, LGP, F/4/3/22.) He had denounced the Reparations Commission as being able to hold German life and labor at its mercy for two generations, yet suggested a fixed sum of £7,000–8,000 million, free of interest, to be paid in ten years (or £3,000 million at 5 percent for fifteen years producing £6,000 million, which, if payments were made for more than fifteen years, would produce £7,000 million to £8,000 million) and an agreement on its distribution between the Allies that would give Britain 20 percent. That would impress the Commons. If Clemenceau balked, Lloyd George could threaten to refuse to prop up the people of the "non-American" world indefinitely. Barnes blamed Billy Hughes, prime minister of Australia, and Lords Sumner and Cunliffe for the reparations fiasco (Thomas Jones diary, July 2, 1919, in Thomas Jones, *Whitehall Diary* [Oxford, 1969], 1:85–6).

15 Keynes to Lloyd George, June 5, 1919, LGP, F/7/2/32; Skidelsky, *John Maynard Keynes,* 1:373–402; H. Elcock, "J. M. Keynes at the Paris Peace Conference," in Milo Keynes, ed., *Essays on John Maynard Keynes* (Cambridge, 1975), 162–76; Austen Chamberlain to Keynes, Dec. 22, and reply, Dec. 28, Austen Chamberlain papers, AC/35/1/9; S. Roskill, *Hankey: Man of Secrets* (London, 1972), 2:96; Keynes to the *Times* (London), June 13 and 18; and Lloyd George to the *Times* (London), June 19, 1923, LGP, F/238. Chamberlain chastised Keynes for writing the book but agreed that he was correct on reparations, if too pessimistic. He derived a certain "malicious pleasure" from the attack on Wilson, a man duped by his own words. He felt that it was wrong to blame Lloyd George rather than Sumner and Cunliffe. "How could Lloyd George or anyone else definitely reject advice tendered on such high authority?" Wilson's Fourteen Points were an orgy of rhetoric, neither a legal contract nor a guide for the peace conference and quite unsuited for submission to Germany before the armistice. It was deplorable of Wilson to have done so.

and various pinpricks, but not the Saar. He intended to confirm Germany's responsibility for the war so as to justify reparations and to ensure public support should it prove necessary to resume hostilities, and to stand firm on war crimes trials.[16] In pursuing this dual strategy, he set the agenda of June, with an eye to Allied unity and to avoiding unmanageable problems at home. He earned unstinting praise from Nicolson. That Long was satisfied and full of advice was equally significant. Continued uncertainty about Germany's intentions, Count Ulrich von Brockdorff-Rantzau's resignation, and the fall of the German government served the first purpose; Scapa Flow and flag burning in Berlin the second. The fact that the news from Russia had turned sour, that the anti-Bolshevik elements were failing both militarily and politically, re-enforced the case for inducing Germany to sign a treaty. The prospect of defeating Lenin's government lived on in Churchill's fervid imagination, but, as early as June 9, the evidence to the contrary seemed compelling. It could also have served Smuts's purposes, but Smuts's opportunity had passed. China, not Japan, now threatened Allied unanimity and Lloyd George was willing to threaten Italy as he had Belgium.

As Lloyd George pursued this dual strategy, he found himself locked in dispute with both Clemenceau and Wilson, but not equally so. That meant, however, that his ability to secure amendments to the draft treaty was circumscribed. In any case, he turned the morality play over to Kerr. His script, of June 12, set out the preliminary version of official orthodoxy, wrapping punishment and deterrence of, and hardship for, Germany (its people were not to be reprieved by a tardy and convenient revolution) in principle, justice and right. Germany was responsible for "having planned and started the war" and for "the savage and inhuman manner in which it was conducted." In that way, confirming the legal and moral justification for collecting reparations for agreed categories of damage was becoming, under Kerr's pen, and then because of the necessities of German politics, war guilt. The victors were not settling merely for a convenient peace. Eventually, however, "reconciliation and appeasement" would come as recognition of the essential legitimacy of the treaty united with the reign of law.[17]

16 Council of Four, June 2, in *DCF,* 2:268–77; Lloyd George to Clemenceau, n.d. LGP, F/51/1/27; Riddell diary, June 3, in McEwen, *Riddell,* 277–8; and Paton memoranda, June 2 and 3, 1919, GB FO 608/165.
17 Council of Four, June 3, 12, and 13, in *DCF,* 2:278–93, 402–3, 405–15, 442, and 445–7; Nicolson diary, June 5, 6, and 19, and Nicolson to father, June 8, 1919, Nicolson, *Peacemaking 1919,* 358–9. Lloyd George was "fighting like a little terrier all by himself," tackling Clemenceau with no help from Wilson and fighting off the *Times* (London) and the French press. Nicolson described the terms as punitive, not merely stern, and the reparations clauses as "immoral and senseless"; but, if Lloyd George won, Germany would sign. Cecil misinterpreted Lloyd George's position on Upper Silesia (Cecil diary, June 7, 1919). Long reported that public feeling was still hostile toward Germany, but

Lloyd George, principally in the speech in the House of Commons on July 3 that was below par oratorically, with a particularly limp peroration, but astute enough politically, built on Kerr's justification.[18] His explanation rested on four pillars – that the treaty was stern but just, just and wise in that it was not made up of terms that individually were fair but cumulatively constituted a crushing burden, that the treaty did not punish Germany for the crimes of its rulers, and that the guarantees of implementation ensured that the treaty would not become a mere scrap of paper.

The stern but just argument rested first on a general claim – they had imposed "terrible" terms because of Germany's "terrible" deeds and the especially dire consequences that would have followed from a German victory. Specifically, the treaty was stern but just because it disarmed Germany, ensuring that it retained only defensive capability, because it stripped Germany of its colonies thus ending its thoroughly reprehensible imperial record (he then applauded the mandate system), because it would bring to trial in London the Kaiser, personally and primarily responsible for plotting and planning the war and for violating treaties, because it would bring to trial officers accused of violating the laws of war and committing atrocities, and because it would more than double Germany's war debt in order to pay reparations (and there was justifiable moderation here in that they had allowed Germany's limited capacity to pay to amend a perfectly just claim for the full cost of the war.)[19] The treaty's territorial clauses on Alsace-Lorraine, Schleswig-Holstein, Poland (without creating a new Alsace-Lorraine) and Danzig, the negation of the treaties of Brest-Litovsk and Bucharest, and putting major rivers under international control were stern but just measures.[20] Justice, Lloyd George argued, was fairness and fair play,

---

that it would support concessions to Germany if they were made on their merits and not out of pity. Despite labor unrest and a Northcliffe plot to destroy him and make Churchill prime minister, Lloyd George had a free hand. He was stronger politically than before the election, and the Unionists were loyal. Lloyd George should follow Sumner and Cunliffe on reparations, and indict the Kaiser. Because Germany's capacity to pay was undetermined, Lloyd George should insist on the entire reparations bill and reduce it only when it became clear that Germany could not pay in full.

18 Lloyd George response, June 30, *Parl. Deb.* (H.C.) 5th ser., vol. 117: cols. 620–1; speech, July 3, 1919, ibid.: cols. 1211–32, and statement, July 21, 1919, ibid., vol. 118: cols. 1039–55, 1070, 1074, 1085, 1093, 1116–17, 1127, and 1128.

19 Lloyd George claimed to occupy the middle ground on reparations, between excessive harshness and unnecessary leniency. Britain would receive substantial amounts. Germany had, legally and morally, accepted its responsibility for the costs of the war, but every expert recognized its limited capacity to pay – hence the compromise, the undetermined sum, that was fair to both France and Germany.

20 The Alsace-Lorraine analogy produced a lengthy explanation of his battle to keep Germans out of Poland and Poles out of Germany. The Polish corridor divided east from west Prussia but violated neither history nor ethnographic justice. The peoples of the corridor would vote for union with Poland in a plebiscite. The Prussias were amply linked by sea and rail. The clauses on Danzig and Marienwerder were equally just.

the absence of undue harshness. He challenged anyone to identify a single act of injustice.

Lloyd George's refutation of the charge that the treaty was cumulatively crushing, that is, his assertion that the treaty was just and wise, led him to examine three possible ways to have responded to Germany's crime, i.e., war guilt, which, had Germany triumphed, would have meant the end of liberty and the victory of militarism in Europe. They could have forgiven Germany, saying "go and sin no more," in effect handing an unscathed Germany a physical and moral victory. They could have dictated a Carthaginian peace of punishment and partition, what Prussia had handed out to Poland, or taken the path they had, the just and wise path, one of "discouragement" (he meant deterrence), where reparations and war crimes trials would ensure that Germany did not repeat its crime.

To the charge that the treaty punished Germany for the crimes of its rulers, Lloyd George insisted that "the nation approved, the nation applauded," in unity and enthusiastically, a war of aggression. The Germans must learn; they must know what was in store for them if they ever risked war again. The guarantees in the treaty, he suggested, were ample and comprehensive – a disarmed Germany on land and sea, the treaties guaranteeing France against "wanton German aggression" (not likely to be activated for "Germany has had enough"), the army of occupation on the Rhine, and "the greatest guarantee of all," the League, "that great and hopeful experiment," worthwhile if it prevented one war, if it gave peace to one generation, all underpinned, crucially, indispensably, by disarmament.[21] Germany would join the League when it had earned the right, broken with its past, and was free of militarism, Junkers, and the Hohenzollerns.

In sum, British official orthodoxy rested on the claim that the treaty would help exorcise the horror of war, especially if war was stripped of its romance and seen as a crime, and its perpetrators indicted as felons. The treaty, Lloyd George conceded, was not perfect but it had the League to remedy, repair, and redress, to adjust the "crudities, irregularities, and injustices." They had redressed many old wrongs and, to shouts of "Shantung," he "could not think of any new ones we have created." They had restored territory where restoration was justified, imposed reparation for damage and injury, created guarantees against future wars, and disarmed and punished so as to show that states could not trample on rights, flout liberties, and break treaties. The treaty "will be like a lighthouse in the deep, warn-

---

21 France was fully justified in demanding the British and U.S. guarantee treaties until the League was proved effective. The deterrent value against further German transgression was undeniable.

ing nations and the rulers of nations against the perils on which the German Empire shattered itself."

Pointedly, Lloyd George thanked every dominion leader but Smuts. Smuts had agonized over whether to sign this "rotten thing of which we shall all be heartily ashamed in due course, this thoroughly bad peace – impolitic and impracticable in the case of Germany and absolutely ludicrous in the case of German Austria." He signed the treaty. He had done what he could, from the inside, to provide some openings of hope. The League was the most promising of them, along with the destruction of Prussian militarism. Peace along with growing public awareness of "what it all means" might, with God's help, produce "a great revulsion" and create a favorable atmosphere in which the public would "scrap this monstrous instrument." The people, responding to their better instincts, their generosity, humanity and preference for reconciliation, would "bring us out of darkness." The people's peace, real peace, the peace animating the League, would replace the statesmen's peace. The real work of making peace would begin, in fact, only when the treaty was signed. Only then would progress be made toward a new international order, a "fairer and better world," a "real and lasting appeasement," a triumph of the spirit, of the moral over the material. They faced a "ruined and broken world," "the collapse of the whole political and economic fabric of Central and Eastern Europe," a Europe "threatened with exhaustion and decay." "Russia has already walked into the night" and the rest of Europe might easily follow. Yet Germany must fulfill its obligations under the treaty to the extent that it could if it was to be welcomed into the community of nations. Germany was the most formidable of the European powers, and there could not be a stable Europe without a stable Germany. Both were necessary for a prosperous Britain. Only the Russians could save Russia, along with the removal of the blockade and a posture of friendly neutrality and impartiality by the Allies. If the result was "a sobered purified Soviet system," so be it; it was preferable to czarism.[22]

II

Of the tactical revisionists, the realists, only Churchill and Lloyd George wrote at length.[23] Churchill, in 1929, asked that the treaties be judged by

22 Smuts to Keynes, n.d., in Hancock and Van der Poel, *Smuts,* 532–3; Smuts to C. P. Scott, June 26, in Trevor Wilson, *The Political Diaries of C. P. Scott, 1911–1928* (Ithaca, N.Y., 1970), 374–5; Smuts to J. L. Garvin, June, Garvin papers, box 13; Nicolson diary, June 24, in Nicolson, *Peacemaking 1919,* 364; and Smuts's statements, June 29 and July 3, 1919, in H. W. V. Temperley, ed., *A History of the Peace Conference of Paris* (London, 1920), 3:74–80.
23 Winston S. Churchill, *The World Crisis,* vol. 2: *The Aftermath* (London, 1929), 202–6, 214–16, 222–31.

the territorial settlement in Europe. They reflected, he claimed, "the methodical application of a principle, the universally revered principle of self-determination." True enough, ethnicity had competed with geography, history, economics, politics, and strategy, but, to the credit of the peace-makers, "probably less than 3 percent of the European populations are now living under governments whose nationality they repudiate; and the map of Europe has for the first time been drawn in general harmony with the wishes of its peoples." There were difficulties and anomalies, but "a fair judgment upon the settlement," Churchill concluded, "cannot leave the authors of the new map of Europe under serious reproach." "The fundamental principle which governed the victors was honestly applied within the limits of their waning power."

Germany, moreover, judged by "Gladstonian standards," had benefited from the war and the peace. They had brought "domestic self-determination" in place of the imperial system, parliamentary government, the abolition of conscription, disarmament, and freedom from entirely superfluous colonial responsibilities. Many segments of German society had suffered economically and financially, but the "absurd and monstrous economic and financial chapters of the Treaty" had been swept away. Germany's economic future seemed assured. Finally, Churchill observed, Britain and its empire, through victory, had escaped a German peace, one he identified with financial ruin, national decline, and perhaps even "final extinction."[24]

Lloyd George, delayed by politics, ill health, and travel, turned to serious writing in 1932. Bent on self-vindication more than money, determined to destroy his critics, living and dead, unfailingly ignorant as they were, or had been, reliving his years of power, fighting battles long past, dispensing truth while meting out justice, and warning against recent errors and current dangers, he published six volumes of war memoirs by January 1937 and two volumes on the peacemaking by December 1938.[25] The first volume of the war

24 Austen Chamberlain contrasted his handiwork, i.e., the Locarno treaties – negotiated, voluntary, promoting reconciliation, even-handed and pointed at no particular state – with the 1919 treaty in his memoirs (*Down the Years* [London, 1935]). Kerr did not write at length and in a formal way on the treaty. Hankey made detached references to it in his *Diplomacy by Conference* (London, 1946). In his *The Supreme Control at the Paris Peace Conference* (London, 1963), he criticized the war crimes clauses and the time wasted on Italy and the Near East. He saw the clash between the Fourteen Points and the secret treaties as damaging, and U.S. rejection of the League and the Russian problem as undermining the treaty. But, on balance, he remained sympathetic toward the settlement.

25 David Lloyd George, *The Truth About the Peace Treaties,* 2 vols. (London, 1938). Hankey, Frances Stevenson, E. D. Swinton, A. J. Sylvester, Malcolm Thomson, and Basil Liddell-Hart assisted him generally. Smuts, Lord Reading, Eric Geddes, Lord Lee, Sir Joseph Maclay, Sir John Stavridi, Chaim Weizmann, Ivan Maisky, and Sir Bernard Pares made specific contributions. See Michael Graham Fry, *Lloyd George and Foreign Policy,* vol. 1: *The Education of a Statesman, 1890–1916* (Montreal, 1977), 1–9. Before then, Lloyd George had published *Is It Peace?* (London, 1923) and *The Truth About Reparations and War Debts* (London, 1932). He was particularly incensed by the publication of the Henry Wilson diaries in 1927. See also Lloyd George's article, "Clemenceau," Nov. 26, 1929,

memoirs relieved Germany and the Kaiser of war guilt, without referring to the 1919 treaty. The volumes on 1919 were to serve four purposes. First, they would document Lloyd George's contributions to the treaty, perhaps to the point of making him the principal architect. Second, at Hankey's bidding, they would illuminate the process of decision, in part to lay to rest revisionist criticism – decisions were not taken hastily under emotional stress or the strain of recurrent crises; the sterner peace terms were not crafted in the delirium, frenzy, and intoxication of victory; moderation was neither forced on them from outside, nor was it the preserve of Wilson's "noble mind"; and the main outlines of the treaty were, in fact, under public, neutral, and U.S. scrutiny, defined in the war not in the flush of victory, by statesmen who had remained dedicated to the pursuit of victory. The decisions made in Paris in 1919 were crafted from lengthy, careful and consultative discussions involving the Allies and the empire delegation.

Third, an unrepentant Lloyd George returned to defend the treaty. Generally, it met the test of "the highest standard of right" and did not contravene "the principles of equity and wise statesmanship." Specifically, Germany's territorial losses and reparations payments were a vindication of international right. The emancipation of subject races, the overthrow of despotisms, fixing boundaries on the principle of government with the consent of the governed, and the plebiscites made the treaty a "charter of freedom" for oppressed nations. The disarmament of Germany, and the expectation of general disarmament, struck at the principal cause of war. The reparations and war crimes clauses had made war a crime against international society and both punished the perpetrators and deterred their successors. An authoritative League of Nations was meant to replace war with the rule of law. The International Labour Organisation (ILO) was a triumph for labor throughout the world; the mandates system altered imperial relationships for the better. The League was to revise all unjust and unworkable items, all "crudities and injustices," understandable and inadvertent as they were.

Finally Lloyd George joined, even anticipated, what became a classic debate between those who saw the 1919 treaty, imperfect as it was, as giving Europe a chance at peace and order, only to be wrecked by circumstance, the march of events and betrayal, and those who saw it so funda-

LGP, H/143; Lloyd George to Kingsley Martin, Mar. 28, 1936, ibid., G/14/2/3; Hankey to Lloyd George, July, 11, 1938, ibid., G/8/18/39; and Lloyd George to Noel Buxton, Apr. 17, 1941, ibid., G/15/11/8. Privately, in 1922, he had blamed Wilson's moral collapse and Clemenceau, making private deals with Wilson, seizing control of the conference while he was away in London, for the problems at Paris (Herbert Lewis diary, Feb. 20, 1922, Herbert Lewis papers, file 231).

mentally flawed as to give Europe a mere twenty years' armistice before an inevitable, second great war, a debate recently reexamined by P. M. H. Bell. Lloyd George insisted that Europe's dangerously fragile condition was due not to any inherent defect in the treaty but entirely to the neglect and abuse of it, to broken pledges and breaches of faith, principally by the victors. "A broken Treaty is like a broken pitcher – it no longer holds water." The justice of the treaty, he insisted, was beyond question. But the victors had refused to follow Germany and disarm, thus ensuring an arms race. They had failed to protect the lesser states from aggression, permitted the shameless disregard of minority rights, and ignored the revisionary powers vested in the League. Inept second-raters, lacking every attribute of statesmanship, had doomed the treaty and brought the once-mighty democracies "shivering and begging for peace on the doorsteps of the European dictators."

Fate, Lloyd George conceded, in the form of dual tragedies, had played its hand – the defeat of Clemenceau opening the door of power to Raymond Poincaré, "a rather sinister little man," vindictive and arrogant, whose policies (perverting the League and rearming) had prompted the Nazi revolution, and, second, the collapse of Woodrow Wilson, physically and politically, leaving the League in the wrong hands, undermining disarmament and altering the complexion of the Reparations Commission. He made no mention of the 1929 crash. America's retreat and Europe's treachery had denied the 1919 treaty a fair trial. Characteristically, those who had failed Europe blamed the architects of the treaty. Churchill, describing the first volume of the peace conference memoirs as "a marvel," concluded "all now thrown away – not even by traitors – only muffs and boobies."[26]

Of the ideological revisionists, Smuts never wrote, Barnes wrote inconsequentially, and Cecil contented himself with homilies on the League.[27] Keynes, writing in 1919 also for Smuts, modifying his analysis somewhat in his *A Revision of the Treaty* published in 1922, proceeded to argue from three axioms – that economic rationality precedes political order and is the only barrier to disorder; that the international economic order of the nineteenth century, with Germany as its pivot, a system of free trade, the unfettered movement of investment capital, industrial growth, and low inflation, linking Europe and the Americas in mutual prosperity, was a golden age; and the liberal belief in progress through education. Keynes put the treaty to two tests – its justice and its wisdom and expedience. Justice rested on the validity of German war guilt, which Keynes made relative and then finessed

26 Churchill to Lloyd George Oct. 17 and Dec. 10, 1938, LGP, G/4/5/33 and 34.
27 Viscount Cecil, *A Great Experiment* (London, 1941), and Viscount Cecil, *All the Way* (London, 1949); and G. N. Barnes, *From Workshop to War Cabinet* (London, 1924).

with a sermon on looking to the future not the past, distinguishing between rulers and peoples, and calling for magnanimity not hatred, wisdom not revenge, humility not moral arrogance, and on the nature of the pre-armistice agreements. The latter were, he claimed, a binding contract, not the preface to unconditional surrender, demanding, mandating, a Wilsonian peace devoid of annexations, "contributions," and punitive damage. The treaty was, therefore, a breach of contract with regard to reparations, the Saar, tariffs, and rivers. The claim for pensions and allowances was illegitimate. In that way, Keynes disavowed those like Balfour who had claimed that the Fourteen Points and the pre-armistice agreements were not contractually binding, and those who insisted that the treaty conformed substantially to the Wilsonian design. He also dismissed a series of what he felt were spurious arguments (Germany, in victory, would not have kept faith; the Allies could have forced unconditional surrender on Germany; Wilson had exceeded his powers; and Lloyd George and Clemenceau had registered convincing reservations to the Fourteen Points).

To trash claims that the treaty was wise and expedient, Keynes made three arguments – that the treaty, in its territorial clauses, in its attempts to provide France with security, ignored Europe's economic unity; that it sought by intent to impoverish and deindustrialize Germany, deny it food, work, and recovery, and destroy its economy, and thus threatened Europe's economic health; and that, in making impossible demands on Germany, the treaty would defy and destroy itself, or invite noncompliance, and thus compound not solve the problems caused by the war. Either way, Europe risked the same fate as Russia. Political bolshevism would follow from economic bolshevism, and a form of civil war would erupt to challenge both progress and civilization.

The Carthaginian peace Keynes found in clauses destroying Germany's trade, depriving it of its merchant fleet, colonies, foreign investments, merchant networks, coal, iron, and transportation and tariff systems, and in dishonorable pettiness. Reparations and coal were at the core of the impossible demands that settled nothing and made the treaty a menacing impostor. Given Germany's principal responsibility for the war, "legal" reparations, for direct physical damage, looting and so forth, were permissible if not necessarily expedient. "Illegal" reparations for pensions and allowances were neither. From there, Keynes went to his statistics – on legal claims, between £1600 million and £3000 million, probably £2000 million; on the "illegal" bill that could bring the total to an impossible £8000 million; on soaring annual payments with compounded interest after paying £1000 million by May 1921; and on Germany's capacity to pay, given its reduced resources, conveniently put at £2000 million, with £100 million being the maximum annual payment from its trade surplus. Keynes argued both that Germany could not pay beyond its capacity and would not pay beyond the limit of "legal" reparations.

The treaty as a whole, he concluded, should be revised at once and fully, not incrementally, removing all trace of indictment and punishment of the German people. Specifically, the total reparations bill should be set at £2000 million, loans should flow to Germany and Europe, intra-Allied war debts should be cancelled, and European free trade reconstituted. Germany, in the logic of history, should be encouraged to help revive and reorganize Eastern Europe, including Russia.

At the root of the folly and injustice, Keynes suggested, lay flawed states-men, giving precedence to politics, strategy, ethnicity, punishment and the balance of power, and ignoring economics – food, coal, and transportation. Flawed character accompanied flawed ideas. Clemenceau was least con-demnable. Wilson, "the eponymous hero," the enigmatic theologian, deceived by European tricksters and deceiving himself, was very much responsible. Lloyd George, unprincipled and irresponsible (the equivalent of Smuts's charge of sheer flippancy) and seducing Wilson was beyond redemp-tion. The treaty, "child of the least worthy attributes of each," was "without nobility, without morality, without intellect."[28]

Harold Nicolson was almost as close to Smuts as was Keynes in 1919 but differed from Keynes on at least two counts when he wrote.[29] He was less critical of the Big Three and then more critical of the slow-minded, exces-sively sensitive Wilson, an arid revivalist, a prophet not a philosopher, than of the quick-witted and "gloriously pachydermatous" Lloyd George and Clemenceau.[30] He denied that the peace conference should be seen as a clear-cut struggle between light and dark, old and new, in pursuit of a Carthaginian or Wilsonian peace. Rather, the conference was a constant interaction between inconsistent elements and pressures, which wrapped it in "exhaustion, disability, suspicion, and despair." That reasoning led him to

28 John Maynard Keynes, *The Economic Consequences of the Peace* (London, 1919); *The Revision of the Treaty* (London, 1922); *Essays in Persuasion* (London, 1931); and *Essays in Biography* (London, 1933). See also Skidelsky, *John Maynard Keynes*, 1:376–402.

29 Nicolson, *Peacemaking 1919*.

30 Nicolson admired Lloyd George in 1919, despite his frailties, and took positions in 1933 that Lloyd George's detractors still find hard to swallow. Nicolson, for example, defended and praised Lloyd George's election conduct, dismissed his supposed ignorance, and applauded his insistence on delay-ing fixing a final reparations sum (a claim Lloyd George had made himself in 1932) and on the com-position of the Reparations Commission. Nicolson took the revisionary provisions of the treaty seri-ously, and concluded that Lloyd George did not win the war only to lose the peace. Nicolson thus provided a foundation for reconciliationist history.

what he described as his main thesis, which Lloyd George pointedly rejected in 1938, that the treaty reflected confusion, turmoil, stress, exhaustion, overwork, despair and the pressure of time constraints, that Paris was the "scurrying cacophony," a "riot in a parrot house," that the atmosphere and passion made it impossible to devise a peace of moderation and righteousness. Nicolson concluded, in fact, that only hypocritical compromise flourished between a Carthaginian and a Wilsonian peace, which, despite its accomplishments, was worse than what would have resulted from either of the polar opposites.

To explain the compromise, which he elsewhere in the book represented as more unavoidable and less the result of hypocrisy, as much inadvertent as calculated, amid inescapable misfortunes, avoidable mistakes, and the corrosive influence of the Italian question, Nicolson traced a course of human tragedy. The peace treaty was the result of a descent from high aspiration to fixing things, from a moral and intellectual deterioration, from a loss of idealism and a dimming of moral awareness. The peacemakers wanted a New Europe of peace and produced disorder, that is, a new order that "merely fouled the old." They were in search of justice and wisdom and produced a treaty that was neither just nor wise. They wanted a Germany reintegrated and pacific, and produced a Germany punished and full of revenge. The "fervent apprentices" of Wilsonism left Paris as renegades. The treaty, as Keynes claimed, scarcely conformed to what they had venerated – the Fourteen Points. It was a case of a bad treaty now rather than a better treaty later, of an imperialistic peace under the surplice of Wilsonism, of vindictiveness cloaked in "unctuous sophistry." The treaty's greatest fault was its "sanctimonious pharisaism."

This tragedy, Nicolson claimed, rested in "falsity," present at the outset, deepening and leading the peacemakers into being false. Falsity began with Germany accepting the original version of the Fourteen Points as the basis of the peace, and the Allies turning to Edward House's interpretation of them of October 29, 1918, with Germany claiming, quite rightly, a contractual agreement and the Allies denying its existence. The idealism that accompanied the uncertainty as to the war's outcome became the ruthlessness of victory. Falsity gathered strength as democratic diplomacy, "riddled with imprecision," came face to face with realism, as new competed with old, as Wilsonian theology confronted the practical needs of empire, and as the expectations of electorates jousted with expert reason. Finally, and more profound than Wilsonism confronting Europe, Nicolson returned to duality of purpose, to inner contradictions – Britain the imperial power championing self-determination, the United States, moral abroad and discriminatory at home. There had also been a pervasive, mutual distrust – the U.S. delegation of Europe, the Latin mind of the Anglo-Saxon, and Europe's profound, subterranean conviction that it should not abandon its ways because the United States would be the first to betray its own ideals, that Wilson's signature was worthless. So deep ran the falsity.

III

Nicolson called the six volumes edited by H. W. V. Temperley "the standard history." Written by Temperley and an Anglo-American team of historians and participants, published between 1920 and 1924, they were not strictly speaking a history of the peace conference at all. They were meant to be independent, objective, moderate, detached, and impartial, steering a course between "official apologetics" and "unofficial jeremiads." They were, in fact, initially essentially an endorsement of official orthodoxy, and then became laced, but not excessively so, with elements of revisionism.[31] Temperley and his essayists, all identified, Dr. Lord and Mr. Paton for example on Poland, found much to applaud in the treaty and those who had framed it, and ample explanation and excuse for the failures and compromises. The Allies, in sharp contrast to all that Germany stood for, were imbued with a sincere and lofty idealism, rooted in Wilsonianism. At Paris, they set out to replace force with the rule of law (volume one).

The Big Three, the "commanding personalities," were justifiably pragmatic and thus effective (volume one). The territorial settlement was "defensible on the basis of the Fourteen Points," preventing purely strategic considerations from ruling. The plebiscites were "unique in their fairness to the defeated nations." Germany could not mount an effective critique of the territorial clauses, except perhaps on Danzig, the Saar and the denial of Anschluss. The war guilt and reparations clauses were understandable if not entirely defensible, and the transit, transportation, and communications terms desirable. There seemed little reason to question the military and naval terms, the colonial settlement, and the denial of Belgium's claims. The creation of the League to deter, punish and protect, the greatest result of the conference, was beyond criticism (volume two). Indeed, Temperley, while respecting Smuts, did not follow him, except in praise and expectation of the League. In describing the deliberate provision for amendment of the treaty as the Big Three's "greatest claim to the gratitude of posterity," he set

---

31 The volumes are, in that sense, a reflection of what John Fair called Temperley's pro-establishment views and his liberal idealism. See John D. Fair, *Harold Temperley* (Newark, Del., 1992), 147–9.

the tone. Much of the treaty was "obviously provisional," its penal sections were "deliberately temporary." Its architects had recognized the need for continued, peaceful revision, and that process would provide the opportunity for public opinion to influence the course of revision.

Volume four coupled a defense of the Austrian treaty, against Cecil and Asquith, with an evasive discourse on justice. The justice of the German treaty depended on its conformity with Wilsonian principles and the pre-armistice agreements, but justice was a vague concept not a legal term, a relative matter and capable of several definitions – justice for France *and* Germany, for the great *and* the small, punishment of wrongdoing, prevention of wrongdoing in the future, and even-handed, impartial treatment of friend and enemy. Perhaps the League would devise a standard of international justice? Volume five, on economic issues, asked for indulgence – the treaties could not settle everything, and had focused correctly on problems arising from the war. The commercial clauses, uneven rather than harsh, had not delayed economic recovery. It also applauded the attempt to protect minority rights. Volume six, published in 1924, lavished almost as much praise on Poland as on the League. Both were "great constructive experiment(s)." It showered advice on the former to help it survive, and further praise on the latter as the vehicle of adaptation and for representing the Anglo-American view of the world. The ILO joined the mandate system and the protection of minorities as thoroughly laudable constructs. The volume contrasted the "principled behavior" of the men of 1919 with the "patched up fumbling expedients" of their successors.

Each volume diluted praise with relativism and excuse, and, ultimately, by 1924, forthright criticism, much of it revisited in Nicolson's misfortunes and mistakes, most of it revealing the problem of maintaining consistency of argument through six edited volumes. The Council of Four was good and bad; the League was flawed and so were the Polish and reparations clauses. The peacemakers were fettered by the secret treaties, compelled to balance the sanctity of treaties against the Fourteen Points, handcuffed by the need for unanimity, and bound by differing experiences. The Supreme War Council was a flawed model. The conference lacked preparation, coordination and organization, experts were used poorly, explaining in part the unjust and unworkable terms. Indeed, conference diplomacy itself might well be deeply flawed. The Big Four were correct to dismiss the complaints of the small powers but wrong in handling them cavalierly. While the influence of public opinion might have helped avoid error the press was both irresponsible and narrow. Were the victors' claims that the treaty was based on Wilsonian principles, that the Fourteen Points were the foundation of the treaty in the moral if not legal sense, that they had accepted the moral obligations implied in them, and that they had constructed a treaty based on "broad-visioned justice and mercy," valid? Had they resolved adequately the conflict between ethnicity and security, and between ethnicity, economics, and geography, even with the plebiscites? At best there had been compromise. Perhaps Lloyd George was correct – the treaty was the minimum France would accept. In any case, criticism should be laid more at the door of U.S. than British policy.

The outright defects that Temperley blamed principally on "passion" and secondarily on "confusion," the lack of creativity of the statesmen and their failure to consult experts, were several – excessive secrecy, the cumulative heavy burden of the various sections of the treaty drawn up without coordination, that the reparations clauses did in fact violate the pre-armistice agreements and the final sum demanded (in 1921) was exorbitant, that undesirable, even fatal compromises had emerged from the presence of the secret treaties and vagueness of the Fourteen Points, the failure to negotiate with Germany, and the violation of the pledge of open diplomacy. Clearly, by 1924 a somewhat different perspective prevailed from that of 1920.

IV

It does not do any great injustice to historians – Commonwealth, U.S., and British (except Arno Mayer and Seth Tillman) – to suggest that not a great deal was added before the opening of the British archives in the 1960s.[32]

---

32 Paul Birdsall, *Versailles Treaty Years After* (New York, 1941); T. E. Jessop, *The Treaty of Versailles: Was it Just* (London, 1942); W. M. Jordan, *Great Britain, France, and the German Problem, 1918–1939* (London, 1943); F. S. Marston, *The Peace Conference of 1919: Organization and Procedure* (London, 1944); Lewis Namier, *Diplomatic Prelude* (London, 1948); and Lewis Namier, *Europe in Decay* (London, 1950); Hajo Holborn, *The Political Collapse of Europe* (New York, 1951); Charles Seymour, *Geography, Justice, and Politics at the Paris Conference of 1919* (New York, 1951); and Etienne Mantoux, *The Carthaginian Peace, or the Economic Consequences of Mr. Keynes* (New York, 1952). Arnold Toynbee's publications from the RIIA were, doubtless, a systematic critique of the settlement. In his *Acquaintances* (London, 1967), he made a pointed attack on Smuts for his role, and his pathetic defense of that role, in the matter of reparations. Lord Hardinge used his discussion of the peace conference to present the Foreign Office version, in intemperate, derogatory prose aimed at Lloyd George. The amateur dictators in the Council of Four, ignoring the experts, blundered on in their ignorance and ineptitude, the Central European settlement being particularly deplorable. Lloyd George, delightful but dangerous, Hardinge concluded, was principally responsible for the debacle and actually embarrassing when he went in search of concessions in June 1919 (Lord Hardinge, *Old Diplomacy* [London, 1947]). Robert Vansittart's private reservations about the treaty, coupled with a blasting of Keynes, are far more sensible (Robert Vansittart, *The Mist Procession* [London, 1958]). See also Norman Rose, *Vansittart: Study of a Diplomat* (London, 1978). It is not inappropriate to include A. J. P. Taylor, *The Origins of the Second World War* (London, 1963) here, and, indeed, to suggest that Sally Marks's "1918 and After: The Postwar Era," in Gordon Martel, ed., *The Origins of the Second World War Reconsidered* (London, 1986), 17–48, is far more illuminating on this subject.

594 Michael Graham Fry

E. H. Carr, a complicated man, not untouched by Nicolson, judged the treaty as he pronounced on the interwar years, bringing a fresh dimension to the debate over a Wilsonian as opposed to a Carthaginian, French peace. The 1920s witnessed the collapse of utopianism, of excessive idealism; the 1930s the moral failure and political challenge of realism unleashed and unrestrained, of unadulterated realism. Carr saw the 1919 settlement as riddled with absurdity and hypocrisy (Nicolson's falsities?), failing both because of being utopian, that is, ignoring the realities of power, and for imagining itself to be utopian despite its reliance on and abuse of power. The victors

attempted to build up a new international morality on the foundation not of the right of the stronger, but of the right of those in possession. Like all utopias which are institutionalized, this utopia became the tool of vested interests and was perverted into a bulwark of the *status quo*. It is a moot point whether the politicians and publicists of the satisfied Powers, who attempted to identify international morality with security, law and order and other time-honored slogans of privileged groups, do not bear their share of responsibility for the disaster as well as the politicians and publicists of the dissatisfied Powers, who brutally denied the validity of an international morality so constituted. Both these attempts to moralize international relations necessarily failed.

Thus the 1919 treaty failed, crucially for Carr, to find the middle ground of peaceful change, the ground between rampant Social Darwinism and the natural harmony of interests, between what was good for nation states and the world community, between idealism and the exigencies of power. Yet Carr did not specify how much "realism" should have been usefully inserted into the treaty, and acknowledged that a settlement resting on power would unavoidably be challenged from an alternative source of power.[33]

Gordon Wright, in 1979, wrote of a "swarm of revisionists" descending on the carcass of Europe of the 1920s.[34] He found them, the Americans, young, talented, and on the whole persuasive. The generation of partici-

33 E. H. Carr, *The Twenty Years' Crisis, 1919–1939* (London, 1939); Seth Tillman, *Anglo-American Relations at the Paris Peace Conference of 1919* (Princeton, N.J., 1961); Arno J. Mayer, *Political Origins of the New Diplomacy, 1917–1918* (New Haven, Conn., 1959); and Arno J. Mayer, *Politics and Diplomacy of Peacemaking: Containment and Counterrevolution at Versailles, 1918–1919* (New Haven, Conn., 1967). Tillman ranged over the whole field of Anglo-American relations, taking the analysis as far as the U.S. archives could. Mayer, in Hegelian style, gave substance to the theme of the peacemaking as a counter to alien ideologies – Prussian militarism and Bolshevism – separately and yet simultaneously, and to the perceived threat of a Russo – German alliance that Japan, Turkey, Hungary, and even Italy might exploit.
34 Walter A. McDougall, "Political Economy versus National Sovereignty: French Structures for German Economic Integration after Versailles," *Journal of Modern History* 51, no. 1 (Mar. 1979): 4–23, Marc Trachtenberg, "Reparations at the Paris Peace Conference," ibid., 24–55, Charles S. Maier, "The Truth About the Treaties?" ibid., 56–67, Klaus Schwabe, "Comment" ibid., 68–73, Wright, "Comment," ibid., 74–7, and replies by McDougall and Trachtenberg, ibid., 78–85.

pant-historians had expired. The opening of the archives offered a golden opportunity to revisit the more compelling of the earlier debates, to confirm, overturn, retain, and discard, and to reconcile, and, above all else, to approach the new evidence with fresh questions, to set the subject on new paths. Their British counterparts, Howard Elcock, Michael Dockrill, Douglas Goold, Anthony Lentin, Alan Sharp, and Erik Goldstein rose to the challenge, without the guiding hand of a deductive theory, except the balance of power, scarcely pausing, rightly, to wait for the intelligence dimension.[35] Most of them, revisiting one of Lloyd George's earliest themes on which Nicolson had elaborated, make something of the emotional and political atmosphere, the context of near chaos, the massive agenda of global issues, Lloyd George's whirlwind raging in Eastern Europe and beyond, the changing military balance, and the unfortunate site. It brought, a point Lloyd George and Hankey had never conceded, along with time constraints and inadequate information, the challenge of overwhelming tasks, awesome responsibilities, decision making under enormous pressure, and mental and physical exhaustion. Together, when coupled with differing perceptions, principles, standards and goals, and the need, for example, to reconcile history, geography, economics, strategy, and ethnicity in determining frontiers, they resulted, understandably, unavoidably, in a quilt of compromise.

That line of reasoning pointed in three other directions – an attempt, albeit rudimentary, to assess the constraints, domestic and international, on the Big Three and a half: an understanding of the drama of a race between peace and anarchy, of a choice between not a Wilsonian and a compromise peace, but between compromise and the specter of no peace; and finding a fair balance between the argument that the peacemakers had achieved all

35 Howard Elcock, *Portrait of a Decision* (London, 1972); Michael Dockrill and J. Douglas Goold, *Peace Without Promise: Britain and the Peace Conference, 1919–1923* (London, 1981); Antony Lentin, *Lloyd George, Woodrow Wilson, and the Guilt of Germany: An Essay in the Pre-history of Appeasement* (Leicester, 1984); Alan Sharp, *The Versailles Settlement: Peacemaking in Paris, 1919* (New York, 1991); and Erik Goldstein, *Winning the Peace* (Oxford, 1991). See also Anne Orde, *British Policy and Reconstruction After the First World War* (Cambridge, 1990); and Agnes Headlam-Morley, *Sir James Headlam-Morley: A Memoir of the Paris Peace Conference, 1919* (London, 1972). Headlam-Morley, of the Political Intelligence Department, and then historical adviser to the Foreign Office, was the most influential British official at Paris on territorial matters and minority rights. His minutes in GB FO/608 must be read to capture both his views of Lloyd George and the peace process. What Lloyd George had accomplished on the Rhineland, for example, he described as in the best traditions of foreign policy and consistent with British war aims. Headlam-Morley opposed the war guilt clause, and was convinced that the worst features of the treaty would collapse or be amended. He agreed with Keynes that the pre-armistice note of Nov. 5, 1919, was binding on all parties, legally and morally, but was appalled at the shoddiness of Keynes's subsequent political analysis. The reparations section of his unpublished official history of the peace conference was, in its way, a more profound indictment than that of Keynes. Hankey took him severely to task for it. Headlam-Morley to Sylvester, Jan. 25 and Mar. 25, 1924, Headlam-Morley to Hankey, 23 July 1924, and Headlam-Morley to Lloyd George, Jan. 14 and 15, 1925, LGP, G/257.

that could reasonably be expected of them and had, genuinely, provided for the revision of an admittedly flawed treaty, and that which indicted them for constructing an edifice of mere devices and shallow compromise, institutionalizing error and folly in a treaty which, nevertheless, could, momentarily in Lloyd George's case, be sold to attentive publics.

From there they moved to assess overall the Big Three and the treaty, and more. Elcock judged the Council of Four to be both essential and effective, its secrecy justified. He is critical of, but sympathetic toward Wilson, very critical of House, understanding of Clemenceau, capturing nuances of compromise that Keynes missed, and sympathetic toward Lloyd George, the authentic voice of moderation, managing the British delegation effectively. Above all, Elcock argues, British policy was marked by clarity, coherence, and a unity of purpose, and made Lloyd George the dominating figure in shaping the unavoidably polyglot treaty. Goldstein, in part in the footsteps of Nicolson, concludes with a paradox – Britain, befitting its superb preparation, its competent officials, and Lloyd George's skill, securing its aims, attaining the maximum possible in the circumstances, but so many of its officials leaving Paris profoundly dissatisfied. The reference to Lloyd George is well placed and welcome. What is so often missed, particularly by those misled by the Foreign Office version, is his appropriate use of experts and his determination, entirely justified, not to tolerate what Clemenceau, Orlando, and even Wilson could not prevent – damaging disloyalty. Goldstein's book on British preparations generally, and the Political Intelligence Department specifically, is now the basis for assessing the role of Lloyd George's epistemic community.

Lentin's "essay on the pre-history of appeasement," bearing the mark of Keynes and Nicolson, goes in a different if not novel direction. As Lentin examined war guilt, reparations, and indicting the Kaiser, Clemenceau emerged as understandable and honest, Wilson as a deeply flawed and tragic apologist for a hero, and Lloyd George, at center stage, as an enigma being himself, fulfilling his own personality. A liar, an opportunist, a vulgarian, and a clever fixer, pandering to but not understanding the public mood, the treaty was another of his stopgap devices, a "convenient improvisation," a breathing space, a fleeting moment of stability that could be defended and then revised. Lloyd George from 1919 to 1922 attempted, unsuccessfully, to undo the damage he had done. Entirely in character, he became infatuated with Hitler and dreamed of becoming Britain's Pétain. Sharp is more restrained. He finds Clemenceau formidable and pessimistic, dominating the conference, Wilson full of pathos and self-delusion, and Lloyd George fascinating, elusive, a mix of admirable and deplorable qualities, on balance a liar, always requiring from those who judge him the "and yet" factor.

Lentin, seeing the treaty as the worst of compromises, falling between familiar stools, and Sharp, concluding that the peacemakers attempted to arrange a settlement that brought peace and order, and failed, accept the judgments of European scholars, refined from the classic Carthaginian–Wilsonian confrontation – a treaty, when touched by Clemenceau, too harsh to conciliate Germany and prejudging the health of German democracy, and thus contributing to its failure; a treaty, when touched by Wilson, too moderate, too feeble to constrain, weaken and deter Germany and thus force compliance; a treaty too mild for its severity, riddled with punitive clauses that were distasteful but not fatal, leaving Germany humiliated not crippled, full of anger, contempt and hatred; and a treaty bearing the marks of incrementalism, each clause seemingly justifiable, the whole being deplorable, something Lloyd George had always denied. The war had damaged France; the treaty left Germany relatively stronger than in 1914, able to recover and challenge for hegemony, and thus violated the realities of power.

From there Lentin and Sharp diverge. The former concludes that Smuts and Keynes were wrong – the treaty was neither Wilsonian nor Carthaginian; it would have been better had it been either. What it was seen to be, a Carthaginian peace snatched from Wilsonianism, was then defied, undermined and overthrown, not defended, because it was legally and morally indefensible. Liberals and radicals fed on Keynes, devouring his cleverness while spitting out Lloyd George's ingenuity, and, joined by the apostate Kerr, ashamed, disgusted, guilt-ridden, wrote the tainted treaty off. The treaty, explicitly from the outset providing for and requiring revision, was doomed by its image. In that way the peace settlement spawned appeasement and contributed to the origins of the Second World War.

Sharp examined how Wilson and Lloyd George, against Clemenceau's instincts, envisioned a Germany democratic and stable, essential to the revival of trade, peaceful but with reduced capabilities, reasonable but not hegemonic, no longer a colonial competitor or a world rival but a check on Russia and France. It was a vision of a self-regulating, self-enforcing peace, reflected in the relatively few clauses in the treaty providing for enforcement. It proved to be a chimera as the treaty was both attacked and not defended. In that way the flawed treaty bore part of the responsibility for the Second World War. There was, however, after all, Hitler, the ultimate revisionist, reveling in revisionism.

Elcock, applauding the attempt to create new rules for managing the
international system, and endorsing Churchill's verdict on the territorial
settlement, finds merit in Lloyd George's contention that events (the 1929
crash), error (U.S. responses to the treaty), and radical, liberal revulsion,
inspired by Keynes, undermined a defensible treaty. Goldstein goes much
further – Britain won both its war and the peace. Dockrill and Goold, however, conceding that by the test of narrow self-interest Britain did well out
of the treaty, conclude otherwise. Britain was merely one of the Pyrrhic
victors, its gains made at terrible cost. The peace was "without promise" and
made a prophet out of Marshal Ferdinand Foch, the commander of the
Allied armies in 1919 – there would be merely a twenty-year armistice.

                                    V

Lloyd George had gone to Paris expecting to be the transcendent man at the
peacemaking. He had left the peace conference convinced that he had
earned and achieved that status. He expected to wield commensurate influence in the postwar era.[36] British policy toward Germany in 1919 was, then,
operationally if not intellectually, Lloyd George's preserve. Beyond serving
essential national and imperial interests it rested essentially on the dual concepts of deterrence, which embraced punishment, and legitimacy, looking
back to concert principles as it looked forward to the League, underpinned
by one public good – arms limitation. Lloyd George believed it appropriate
to punish, constrain, and deter Germany. Reparations and war crimes trials
were, for him, part of deterring Germany and other would-be aggressors,
but deterrence rested also on more conventional features – disarming Germany and establishing guarantees against German aggression (the occupation
of the Rhineland and the British and U.S. guarantees of France, which,
beyond their provisions, would demonstrate the unity and resolve of the free
peoples).[37] Deterrence was, moreover, combined with the reduction of

36 Bonar Law, Balfour, Hankey, naturally, and even Derby concurred. Derby actually told Curzon that
   he was full of admiration for the way Lloyd George had conducted the empire's case at the peace
   conference. He had kept the nation's interests to the fore. The French and the Americans were complaining that the treaty was a British peace. Derby to Curzon, June 30, 1919, Curzon papers, box
   22, F/6/2.
37 Lloyd George assured Botha that the treaty of guarantee committed Britain to assist France only in
   the case of clear, unprovoked, and premeditated aggression as had been the case in 1914. Britain
   would be the judge of that and would not be drawn into controversies that did not concern it. Irresponsible French policies would not activate the commitment. The dominions individually would
   be free to judge any situation and would not be committed by British policy. Lloyd George felt that
   France, because of its sacrifices, deserved security; Germany, still the potential hegemon, must be
   deterred. Lloyd George to Botha, June 26, 1919, LGP, F/5/5/14.

German resources, capabilities, and potential, that is, its territorial, economic, and population losses. Punishing and constraining Germany was, in Lloyd George's view, not only appropriate but also just.

He also believed, a view that took on greater validity as the peace conference progressed, that German unity must be preserved, unequivocally, that German democracy must be given every opportunity to succeed, and that the German economy, a major British export market, must be revived. In that way, Lloyd George was attempting to reintegrate Germany, politically, economically, and ideologically into the European state system, into the core of the family of nations. These considerations gave the treaty its legitimacy, a treaty already revised, not excessively punitive, tough but just, and surely subject to further revision at the margin by way of the League or conference diplomacy. Germany would accept the essence of the treaty and negotiate on change in good faith. Enforcing the treaty, French style, against Germany's will would be unnecessary. Legitimacy provided the basis from which to begin to drain the pathology from the international system, to promote general arms limitation en route to order and peace. To begin to exorcise the threat of German aggression was to begin to exorcise aggression *per se* from the system. To guard against a repetition of the German war was to guard against war itself. Germany and, by inference, all irredentist states, would harbor less of a sense of being wronged, have no need and no way of reaching beyond peaceful change, beyond ordered revision. Germany with its seventy million people, with the distribution of resources between it and its neighbors altered but not decisively, and given the unstable state of affairs in Eastern Europe, remained the potential hegemon. But Germany could become a benign hegemon, a trading partner, an informal ally, a barrier to Bolshevism. As David Stevenson pointed out, Lloyd George was asking a punished, chastened, but still powerful Germany to cooperate in its own containment and to play a new role in Europe. It must accept for the near future the fact that its political boundaries were not its strategic frontiers. Clearly, the situation to the east was most dangerous. But German minorities outside Germany would be protected, other states would limit their arms, and the reparations commission under a U.S. chairman would produce, in time, a moderate and acceptable settlement. Lloyd George's expectations of France were no less. France, secure, sobered, must not seek to use its temporary advantage, must not attempt to exploit a victory that was not France's to exploit. The Great War with all its sacrifice was not to have been fought in vain.

There would emerge, in Lloyd George's scheme of things, in Paul Schroeder's phrase about the nineteenth century, a balance of satisfactions. It would make less threatening the still unequal distributions of power in Europe, less likely that Germany would seek to take unwarranted advantage of the sources of disorder that existed as the New Europe turned to state-building – rampant nationalism exploited by unstable and unreliable governments; militarism and aggressive expansionism conveniently in league with or posing as the enemy of Bolshevism, exploiting its threat even as they were threatened by it. Indeed, as the whirlwind roared, as peace bred war, as claims to justice bred extremism not moderation, as competitive justices confronted one another, as the principle of national self-determination threatened order, the menacing threats to the New Europe came principally, exasperatingly, from within, and, if from without, from the Soviet Union rather than from Germany. It was a disconcerting fact, moreover, that the Allies, with dwindling military power and their reliance progressively on economic weapons, could more easily bring Germany to heel than either the East European states that flouted their decisions or the Soviet Union.

The balance of satisfactions would replace the balance of power as *the* theory of state behavior. It would, crucially, reduce Britain's continental commitments, making them less necessary, even redundant, and Britain's involvement in European wars, as it made more vital, even indispensable, Britain's leadership of Europe diplomatically. British grand strategy would then serve, as it must, the cause of imperial security for the empire was the antidote to relative decline. Lloyd George was, in that way, seeking to break with pre-1914 practice. The balance of power had meant standing aloof from European diplomacy, but, on occasions, intervening decisively in Europe's wars. It had been, therefore, a certain path to periodic involvement in war, most recently, most tragically, in 1914, involvement that was the blood-stained monument to the absence of forthright and effective British leadership, to the failure of British statecraft. Lloyd George felt he could do better than that. He could fashion a self-regulating system for Europe that would leave the empire as the unit of action, enjoying prosperity and security. Statesmen should not be embarrassed to defend this first, remarkable in the circumstances, step toward European order that the 1919 treaty was meant to be.

This perspective on British policy carries with it certain consequences. It suggests that the political and scholarly debate that has rested on contrasting a Wilsonian with a Carthaginian peace, and then on the refinements of the contrast, must, to some extent, give way to other approaches. If the 1919 treaty was essentially a British construct, then the Trade Union speech of January 1918, Britain's role in constructing the armistices, British preparations for the peace conference, political and bureaucratic, the Fontainebleau memorandum of March 1919 (Temperley put the peace treaty to the test of the Fontainebleau memorandum in volume vi), and Lloyd George, creative, resilient, dominating the agenda and the tempo, expecting to collaborate to the end with Woodrow Wilson, willing to slake Clemenceau's thirst but not that of French officialdom, becomes the focus of analysis. Just as Wilson ultimately preferred something other than a Wilsonian peace, just as a Carthaginian peace was not exclusively a French peace, so a Georgian peace was, by political conception and circumstance, by intent and bargaining, a compromise, intellectually, politically, and even morally. Lloyd George sensed the relationship between the ideal and the feasible, that what was intellectually conceivable and even morally desirable was not always politically possible. He understood paradox and irony, that liberals demanded that democratic opinion influence diplomacy only to become bewildered when it did not prefer moderation. More presidential than Wilson, for him every policy had a political dimension. The legitimation imperative, the need to explain and justify policy or risk deception and secrecy, ruled, unavoidably and to excess. This was 1919 not 1815, but Lloyd George had both feet in the media age before the age had dawned. He was both dominant and accountable.

It follows that Lloyd George should be judged when the structural constraints on his freedom of action are weighed, by those willing to follow him, issue by issue, across each phase of the conference, as Klaus Schwabe followed Wilson. Lloyd George can be held accountable for what he brought about, defensible and indefensible, prescient and merely convenient, acceptable when none could forecast the outcome, deplorable when drift, neglect, and worse took hold. One can start with the central proposition – the balance of satisfactions as a theory of state behavior. The peace treaty, through a series of devices, had amended the state of affairs that was the unequal distribution of power between France and Germany, and between Germany and Eastern Europe, but not decisively and perhaps only temporarily, and, some would say, artificially and dangerously. Germany was not as strong as in 1914 but the Russian problem remained unresolved and Bolshevik Russia presented more opportunities to Germany than to France. What had been done had damaged Germany more politically and psychologically than physically (and some elements of German society were ready to exploit the damage), the most dangerous of conditions. French behavior would be a critical factor. One need not be a pessimist to argue, therefore, that the balance of power would reassert itself as *the* theory of state behavior. Germany, in harness with Russia, Hungary, Turkey, and even Japan, some felt, would one day challenge the construct of 1919. The issue became could Lloyd George and his colleagues manage the postwar system in ways that meant that the postwar years did not become the interwar years?

25

Woodrow Wilson's Image of Germany, the War-Guilt Question, and the Treaty of Versailles

MANFRED F. BOEMEKE

I have always detested Germany. I have never gone there. But I have read many German books on law. They are so far from our views that they have inspired in me a feeling of aversion.
        –Woodrow Wilson, c. June 14, 1919

If German nationalists during the Weimar Republic could have overheard what Woodrow Wilson told the British prime minister, David Lloyd George, two weeks before the signing of the Treaty of Versailles, it would have confirmed what they had believed all along: it was Wilson's deep-seated hatred of Germany that had led him deliberately to deceive and betray the German people by promising them a "peace without victory" and imposing upon them a treaty of infamy.[1] This verdict, born of the furious passions of the immediate postwar years, became one of the hallmarks of a spate of popular and pseudoscholarly books and articles in Germany during the 1920s and 1930s, but even as late an account as Howard J. Elcock's *Portrait of a Decision* has maintained that Wilson's driving force at

---

1 For incisive analyses of the fierce denunciations of Wilson in post–World War I Germany, see Ernst Fraenkel, "Das deutsche Wilsonbild," *Jahrbuch für Amerikastudien* 5 (1960): 66–120, and his untitled contribution in Arthur S. Link et al., *Wilson's Diplomacy: An International Symposium* (Cambridge, Mass., 1973), 45–78. The reactions of German-Americans to the Versailles settlement are discussed in Lloyd E. Ambrosius, "Ethnic Politics and German–American Relations after World War I: The Fight over the Versailles Treaty in the United States," in Hans L. Trefousse, ed., *Germany and America: Essays on Problems of International Relations and Immigration* (New York, 1980), 29–40.

Paris was his profound hatred of Germany that was akin to Georges Clemenceau's but was irrational and inexplicable in its origin.[2]

Although most serious studies have thoroughly discredited this largely propagandistic view and have instead explained the discrepancy between Wilson's avowed liberal principles and his acquiescence in a harsh settlement by the objective need for a compromise with the Carthaginian demands of the European Allies, a number of recent works have again called attention to the punitive aspects that were clearly inherent in Wilson's peace program. N. Gordon Levin and Klaus Schwabe, for example, have both pointed out the dichotomy between Wilson's long-range objective of integrating a democratized Germany into a new world order and his short-range goal of subjecting Germany to severe punishment;[3] Marc Trachtenberg, on the other hand, has denied any contradiction between these two considerations and has emphasized the integral role that the punitive component played in the liberal peace agenda in general.[4]

These analyses have convincingly shown that it is no longer tenable to claim that all Wilson desired at Paris was a moderate peace of reconciliation and understanding. However, none of them, it seems, has adequately explained the rationale behind Wilson's insistence on a harsh treatment of Germany, a treatment, moreover, that he continued to advocate even after the German people had heeded his implicit demand to overthrow their militaristic rulers and had apparently joined the family of democratic nations. Although it is clearly too simplistic to see Wilson's endorsement of severe peace terms as nothing but the inevitable result of his emotional anti-German bias, it can nevertheless be argued that the punitive undercurrent of Wilson's policies had its origin in his image of Germany and the German people, as well as in his passionate, if somewhat naive and self-righteous, sense of retributive justice.

There is no reason to doubt that Wilson's private, off-hand remark to Lloyd George, picked up and recorded by chance by the French interpreter in the Council of Four, represented his true feelings toward Germany at the time. And yet, despite its categorical tone and its implication of a lifelong

2 Howard J. Elcock, *Portrait of a Decision: The Council of Four and the Treaty of Versailles* (New York, 1972). See also Sigmund Freud and William C. Bullitt, *Thomas Woodrow Wilson, Twenty-eighth President of the United States: A Psychological Study* (Boston, 1967), 163, 168–9, 192–3.

3 N. Gordon Levin, *Woodrow Wilson and World Politics: America's Response to War and Revolution* (New York, 1968), 123–82; Klaus Schwabe, *Woodrow Wilson, Revolutionary Germany, and Peacemaking, 1918–19: Missionary Diplomacy and the Realities of Power* (Chapel Hill, N.C., 1985), 393–402, and Klaus Schwabe, "Die USA, Deutschland und der Ausgang des Ersten Weltkrieges," in Manfred Knapp et al., eds., *Die USA und Deutschland, 1918–75: Deutsch–amerikanische Beziehungen zwischen Rivalität und Partnerschaft* (Munich, 1978), 11–59.

4 Marc Trachtenberg, "Versailles after Sixty Years," *Journal of Contemporary History* 17 (1982): 487–506.

antipathy toward Germany, Wilson's statement cannot be taken at face value. For, if he "detested" Germany in 1919, it can hardly be said that he had "always" done so. Although one of Wilson's most characteristic features throughout his life was his marked Anglophilism and his intense interest in British affairs, his early views on other nations, including Germany, were far less pronounced and do not add up to a coherent picture.[5] As a graduate student at Johns Hopkins and in his career as a political scientist, he was strongly influenced by the traditions of German scholarship, and, at one point, actually did consider spending a year or two in Berlin to improve his knowledge of the German language.[6] As a teacher and writer, he depended to an extraordinary degree on German sources, both for his factual knowledge and his ideas.[7] In fact, those German books on law that later inspired in him such a "feeling of aversion" were the very foundation of *The State*, the book that has been described as "perhaps his greatest scholarly achievement"[8] but parts of which have also been shown to constitute little more than "rather thinly veiled plagiarism."[9]

Wilson's early assessment of German society and institutions was, on the whole, rather positive, particularly if compared with the stinging criticism he leveled at French public affairs.[10] The development of German institutions, he argued, had benefited from the salutary influence of Prussian "students of government" like Stein, Hardenberg, and Gneist, who had steered the country in a direction that was "conservative and carefully observant of historical conditions."[11] Moreover, Wilson perceived a certain affinity between the British institutions that he so admired and those of Germany, due in part to what he called the "pan-Teutonic" heritage of the two nations. Thus, in a lecture on the municipal government of Berlin, in

---

5 For detailed discussions of the strong British influences on Wilson's early life, see Arthur S. Link, *Wilson: The Road to the White House* (Princeton, N.J., 1947), 1–35; John M. Mulder, *Woodrow Wilson: The Years of Preparation* (Princeton, N.J., 1978), 32–102; and Ray Stannard Baker, *Woodrow Wilson: Life and Letters*, 8 vols. (Garden City, N.Y., 1927–39), 1:64–5.

6 See Wilson to Richard Heath Dabney, Nov. 7, 1886, in Arthur S. Link et al., eds., *The Papers of Woodrow Wilson* (hereafter *PWW*), 69 vols. (Princeton, N.J., 1966–94), 5:383–6.

7 See, e.g., the bibliographies in *PWW*, 6:563–611, and 8:124–37. See also Henry Wilkinson Bragdon, *Woodrow Wilson: The Academic Years* (Cambridge, Mass., 1967); and Mulder, *Years of Preparation*.

8 Link, *Road to the White House*, 21.

9 Mulder, *Years of Preparation*, 103; see also Niels Aage Thorsen, *The Political Thought of Woodrow Wilson, 1875–1910* (Princeton, N.J., 1988), 92; and the editorial note in *PWW*, 6:244–52.

10 A disciple of Edmund Burke, Wilson condemned French revolutionary philosophy as "radically evil" and argued that no state could ever be administered on its principles. It was precisely because of their revolutionary heritage, he claimed, that the French people had never learned the art of self-government, that their politics were characterized by "carnage and fierce convulsions," and that the bourgeoisie lacked any civic consciousness. See, e.g., "Self-Government in France," c. Sept. 4, 1879, in *PWW*, 1:515–39; "Commemorative Address," Apr. 30, 1889, ibid., 6:180–1; and *The State* (Boston, 1889); see also Link, *Road to the White House*, 32–3.

11 Woodrow Wilson, *The State: Elements of Historical and Practical Politics*, rev. ed. (Boston, 1901), 279.

which he praised the civic-mindedness of the population and its wide participation in the administration of the city, he maintained that the case of the German capital was "not a foreign example, strictly speaking," but "just as truly an English example."[12] At the same time, however, he noted the strong democratic influences and traditions in England and their virtual absence in Germany. For example, in comparing Elizabeth and Frederick the Great as builders of their respective nations, he emphasized the early existence of the "full machinery of constitutional government" in England, while Prussia, which treated its subjects "like servants rather than like citizens of a great state," had nothing but a "dependent bureaucracy" that did not derive its power from the people and did not represent their interests.[13]

That same autocratic tradition Wilson found perpetuated in the German Empire, which was ruled by an "irresponsible constitutional monarch," governed by a "virtually supreme head of state," and characterized overall by the almost total absence of parliamentary responsibility on the part of the imperial administration.[14] The German emperor, in fact, was "the most powerful ruler of our time,"[15] although, as early as 1890, Wilson found "the latest Hohenzollern" less of a divine king than a "bumptious young gentleman slenderly equipped with wisdom or discretion."[16] Coming, as it did, only two months after the dismissal of Bismarck, this comment undoubtedly reflected Wilson's great respect for the Iron Chancellor, whom he had previously described as "the centre and soul of European politics" and "that genius now so greatly feared and so justly admired."[17]

In fact, one of his earliest published writings was a biographical essay on Bismarck, composed in 1877. It discussed the creation of the German Empire in terms of pure power politics as a great Prussian military triumph; dismissed the "fear-begotten bitterness of the French"; and, in words that would have surely embarrassed him forty years later, portrayed the Franco-Prussian War as "a campaign of almost unrivalled brilliancy" that "brought proud France to the feet of Prussia" and rewarded it with the "smiling fields of Alsace and Lorraine."[18] Yet, with Bismarck's dismissal, Wilson found that the "deliberation" and "restraint" that had characterized the policies of the German Empire under its first chancellor were giving way to a more aggres-

---

12 Newspaper Report of a Lecture on Municipal Government, Jan. 18, 1889, in *PWW,* 6:52–7.
13 Constitutional Government, *PWW,* 18:90–3.
14 Wilson, *The State,* 253–4, 260–1, 264.
15 Ibid., 254.
16 Quoted in Harley Notter, *The Origins of the Foreign Policy of Woodrow Wilson* (New York, 1965), 100; see also "Leaders of Men," *PWW,* 6:660.
17 "Speech on Bismarck," Dec. 6, 1877, *PWW,* 1:325; "Prince Bismarck," *PWW,* 1:308.
18 Ibid., 1:311.

sive posturing. As a result, one can detect in Wilson some apprehension about the way Germany employed its military power in the Caribbean.[19] And its eagerness to seize the Philippines in 1898 convinced him that Germany was fast becoming the chief rival of the United States in the Pacific.[20]

On the whole, however, during the decade or so before he assumed the presidency, Wilson talked and wrote as if the world outside the United States did not exist. As Arthur S. Link has pointed out, Wilson was curiously ignorant of and unconcerned with foreign affairs, and neither the recurrent crises in Europe nor the growing tensions among the major powers after the turn of the century elicited as much as a single public or private response from him.[21] Nor did Wilson pay much attention to or learn anything about European affairs during his first year in the White House, so that, in his annual message to Congress in December 1913, he could report on the "many happy manifestations . . . of a growing cordiality and sense of community of interest among the nations" that were "foreshadowing an age of settled peace and good will."[22] Although six months later, his closest friend and adviser, Colonel Edward M. House, graphically conveyed to Wilson the firsthand impressions of an impending cataclysm in Europe that he had gained during his consultations with the German and British governments, it is small wonder that the outbreak of hostilities caught the president completely unprepared and sent him into shock and consternation.[23]

Wilson's initial reaction was intensely personal, purely emotional, and completely in line with his deep affection for England. "Every thing that I love most in the world is at stake," he told the British ambassador, who thereupon quoted a few lines from Wordsworth about English freedom that brought tears to the president's eyes.[24] In these early days of the war, House heard Wilson inveigh against everything German – from government to people to what he called "selfish" German philosophy, which was lacking in spirituality. He was bitter about the destruction of Louvain, scornful of Germany's disregard of treaty obligations, and indignant at Bethmann Hollweg's designation of the Belgian Neutrality Treaty of 1839 as a "scrap of paper." A German victory, Wilson felt, would imperil the United States,

19 See, e.g., "Mr. Cleveland as President," *PWW,* 10:117.
20 News Report, Nov. 2, 1898, *PWW,* 10:62–6.
21 See Arthur S. Link, *Wilson the Diplomatist: A Look at His Major Foreign Policies,* 2d ed. (New York, 1974), 8–11.
22 "Annual Message to Congress," Dec. 2, 1913, *PWW,* 9:3.
23 For a discussion of House's mission, which was intended to draw the United States, Britain, France, and Germany into an informal entente and bring about a reduction of military and naval armaments, see Arthur S. Link, *Wilson: The New Freedom* (Princeton, N.J., 1956), 314–18.
24 See Sir Cecil Arthur Spring Rice to Sir Edward Grey, Sept. 3, 1914, *PWW,* 30:472, and Sept. 8, 1914, ibid., 31:13–14.

force the country to give up its liberal ideals, and turn it into a vast military camp.[25] Clearly, the impartiality in thought and the "fine poise of undisturbed judgment" that he asked his fellow Americans to observe were not part of Wilson's own emotional response to the European conflagration:[26] Prussian militarism, which had been the very foundation of the German Empire but had been held in check during Bismarck's reign, had run stark mad under the "foolish" policies of William II, who had created a "powder magazine" and had deliberately risked an explosion.[27]

Strict neutrality, however, was the only feasible and wise official course for the United States to take, not least because it was the prerogative for Wilson's most cherished role, that of a mediator between the warring parties. And, in due time and with greater perspective, Wilson's own initial emotional reactions, too, gave way to a more detached and balanced view. Although his basic perception of the autocratic and militaristic nature of the German government never changed, he no longer automatically absolved the Western democracies from any responsibility for the outbreak of hostilities. The elements of the war, he wrote in October to the American ambassador in London, were too vast to be yet comprehended,[28] but, as he told a friend, he now "so obviously felt that all the wrong was not on one side."[29] A few weeks later, he spelled out his new understanding in detail in a confidential interview with a reporter for the *New York Times*. "It will be found before long," he observed, "that Germany is not alone responsible for the war, and that other nations will have to bear a portion of the blame in our eyes." To be sure, he believed, the German government might have to be "profoundly changed" to bring back the self-restraint that was characteristic of its policies during Bismarck's times and that was evident, for example, in the chancellor's perspicacious advice not to annex Alsace-Lorraine. But since neither side was entirely free of blame in starting the war, the most advantageous outcome would be a deadlock in which no nation would win a decision by arms and be able to enforce its will upon others.[30] What a German victory would look like, Wilson sketched out some time later: annexation of territories, huge indemnities, and the military subjugation of all of Europe. An Allied triumph, similarly, would result in the partition of German colonies, the breakup of Austria-Hungary, and the control of the

25 Diary of Edward M. House, Aug. 30, 1914, ibid., *PWW,* 30:462–3.
26 Appeal to the American People, Aug. 18, 1914, *PWW,* 30:393–4.
27 Diary of Edward M. House, Aug. 30, 1914, *PWW,* 462.
28 Wilson to Walter Hines Page, Oct. 28, 1914, *PWW,* 31:242–3.
29 Memorandum by Mary Eloise Hoyt [early Oct. 1914], quoted in Arthur S. Link, *Wilson: The Struggle for Neutrality, 1914–15* (Princeton, N.J., 1960), 52.
30 Memorandum by Herbert Bruce Brougham, Dec. 14, 1914, *PWW,* 31:458–60.

seas by British "navalism." An enduring peace on these foundations, he concluded, was "the empty talk of partisan dreamers."[31] Only a stalemate, Wilson argued, would make it possible to settle the differences among the powers according to the principles of right and justice and to establish a just and
equitable peace, the only peace that could last.[32]

Here, then, was the central theme that Wilson would expound over and
over again throughout the next few years: the settlement that was to end this
war, whatever else it might be, had to be just. Wilson's passionate, all-
consuming, almost pathological sense of justice had its roots in his deep
Christian faith, his Calvinist heritage that made him reduce all issues to
well-defined moral categories, and his belief in a moral universe, the laws
of which governed the conduct of nations as well as men.[33] "Justice, and
only justice," he had declared in his inaugural address, "shall always be our
motto," a justice that was absolute, indivisible.[34] To be sure, the leaders of
the European belligerents also claimed to be fighting for justice, to have
God on their side; but in Wilson's mind, his concept of justice was different: it was pure, it was an end in itself, it did not serve merely as a rationale
for the achievement of material gains.[35]

In any event, since both sides, in one way or another, were responsible for
the war and both were pursuing selfish war aims, it followed that a just settlement would be a negotiated peace that avoided "exemplary triumph or
punishment."[36] This, in essence, was the policy toward the belligerents that
Wilson pursued throughout the period of American neutrality. As late as
October 1916, he still believed that the origins of the war had never been
disclosed, that it would take "the long inquiry of history" to establish its
causes.[37] The logical consequence of this policy, then, was his call, in January 1917, for a "peace without victory," a peace among equals – a call that
the German government answered a week later with conditions for a settlement that amounted to a crushing victor's peace and with the inauguration
of unrestricted submarine warfare around the British Isles. The subsequent

---

31 Prolegomenon to a Peace Note, c. Nov. 25, 1916, *PWW,* 40:68–9.
32 Memorandum by H. B. Brougham, Dec. 14, 1914, *PWW,* 31:458–60.
33 For detailed discussions, see Mulder, *Years of Preparation;* and Arthur S. Link, "Woodrow Wilson and
    His Presbyterian Inheritance," in Arthur S. Link, *The Higher Realism of Woodrow Wilson and Other
    Essays* (Nashville, Tenn., 1971), 3–20.
34 Inaugural Address, Mar. 4, 1913, *PWW,* 27:151.
35 See, e.g., Address in Philadelphia to Newly Naturalized Citizens, May 10, 1915, *PWW,* 33:149; see
    also Wilson to Robert Lansing, Sept. 19, 1915, *PWW,* 34:438; Remarks to the Clerical Conference
    of the New York Federation of Churches, Jan. 27, 1916, *PWW,* 36:5; Address in Pittsburgh on Pre-
    paredness, Jan 29, 1916, *PWW,* 36:27; Address to the League to Enforce Peace, May 26, 1916,
    PWW, 37:115; and Nonpartisan Address in Cincinnati, Oct. 26, 1916, *PWW,* 38:542.
36 Memorandum by H. B. Brougham, Dec. 14, 1914, *PWW,* 31:459.
37 Address in Omaha, Oct. 5, 1916, *PWW,* 31:347.

submarine attacks on American shipping and the pseudo-Machiavellian machinations revealed in the Zimmermann telegram convinced Wilson that, as he told House, "Germany was 'a madman that should be curbed.'" Although he was still not entirely convinced of the justice of the Allied cause,[38] he concluded that only by accepting belligerency could the United States assure a just peace and prevent a German victory that would mean domination and conquest.[39] "He sees red when he thinks of the Imperial government," Count von Bernstorff, the German Ambassador, reported, and correctly pointed out the earliest beginning of Wilson's changed attitude toward Germany that contributed to the tragedy of Versailles.[40]

In his war message of April 2, 1917, Wilson declared that belligerency had been forced upon America by "Prussian autocracy," which had never been and could never be a friend of the United States. While he still did not identify with the Allied position as to the responsibility for the outbreak of the war in 1914, he made it clear that he now regarded Germany as the last great foe of universal peace. However, in explicit references that were to be characteristic of his views throughout much of the rest of the war, he absolved the German people from any guilt for the policies of their government – an approach that came all the more natural to him, since he had always emphasized the autocratic nature of German society. The German people, Wilson observed, had never known, let alone approved, the designs of their rulers, but had been used as mere "pawns and tools." The United States was, in fact, fighting for their liberation, too.[41]

Wilson continued to talk about his great goal of a just peace, but it became increasingly clear that he ruled out any "peace without victory" with the present German government of military autocrats. Whereas, only a short time ago, he had maintained that the causes of the war were too vague to make any judgment, he now became fully convinced that it was "begun by the military masters of Germany." In his Flag Day Address of June 14, for example, he drew a picture of German designs that reads like an outline of the Fischer thesis: the deliberate, planned, carefully executed

38 See, e.g., Henri Bergson to the French Foreign Ministry, Mar. 3, 1917, *PWW,* 41:317: "Le Président Wilson m'a paru en tous cas faire siens les principes pour lesquels nous nous battons, mais il considère l'Angleterre comme luttant uniquement pour sa prépondérance commerciale qu'il ne semble pas soucieux d'assurer."

39 For detailed discussions of the events leading to the break between Germany and the United States, see Reinhard R. Doerries, *Imperial Challenge: Ambassador Count Bernstorff and German–American Relations, 1908–1917* (Chapel Hill, N.C., 1989), 191–231; and Arthur S. Link, *Wilson: Campaigns for Progressivism and Peace, 1916–17* (Princeton, N.J., 1965), 220–431.

40 Johann Heinrich Graf von Bernstorff, *Deutschland und Amerika: Erinnerungen aus dem fünfjährigen Kriege* (Berlin, 1920), 370–1.

41 Address to a Joint Session of Congress, Apr. 2, 1917, *PWW,* 41:519–27.

conquest of Europe and Asia "from Berlin to Bagdad." "From Hamburg to the Persian Gulf," he maintained, "the net is spread."[42] To Wilson, the moral issues had become clear-cut: the German leaders and the entire German political system were the embodiment of evil, "a Thing without conscience or honor or capacity for covenanted peace." A compromise with evil, a negotiated peace, was clearly out of the question, a just accommodation of interests impossible. Instead, justice demanded that this "menace of combined intrigue and force" be "crushed"; if it could not be entirely defeated, it had to be at least punished by excluding it from the comity of nations.[43]

Indeed, Wilson's wartime speeches and notes, while not endorsing in any way the war aims of the Allies, were full of contempt for the notion of a compromise peace with Germany's military rulers. At the same time, however, he continued to absolve the German people from any responsibility for the aggression of their government, paid generous tribute to their peacetime achievements and saw them as victims of rather than participants in the German drive for world domination. In his Fourteen Points Address, he demanded to know who was speaking for the German people, their military leaders who insisted upon conquest and subjugation or the "liberal leaders and parties" who had professed a spirit of moderation and conciliation in the peace resolutions of the Reichstag in 1917.[44] To the latter, he held out the olive branch of a peace based on "generosity and justice," if they would but rid themselves of their ruthless and duplicitous masters and set up a government that was truly representative of the popular will and that could be trusted.[45] Apparently, Wilson had believed even before the United States entered the war that the German people had "their bellies full," were "weary of Prussian militarism and perhaps of the imperial regime," and would soon overthrow their government.[46] Now, in his wartime speeches, Wilson was encouraging the Germans, and particularly the Majority Socialists, to do just that, hoping that, once military autocracy had yielded to responsible government, once the German people were free to determine their own destiny, they would be naturally impelled toward honest and fair cooperation.

42 Flag Day Address, June 14, 1917, *PWW,* 41:498–504. See also his Address to the American Federation of Labor, Nov. 12, 1917, *PWW,* 45:11–17.
43 Annual Message, Dec. 4, 1917, *PWW,* 45:194–9.
44 Address to a Joint Session of Congress, Jan. 8, 1918, *PWW,* 65:535. See also his Four Points Address, Feb. 11, 1918, *PWW,* 45:318–24.
45 See, e.g., Flag Day Address, June 14, 1917, *PWW,* 42:500; and Annual Message, Dec. 4, 1917, *PWW,* 45:196; and Wilson's reply to the papal peace note, Aug. 23, 1917, *PWW,* 44:33–6 (draft), 57–9.
46 See the account by Henri Bergson of an interview with Wilson in February 1917, summarized in *PWW,* 41:316; and Henri Bergson to Aristide Briand, Mar. 3, 1917, *PWW,* 41:315: "Il croit que les Allemands sont las du miltarisme prussien et peut-être du régime impérial."

The acid test, as it were, and the answer to his question came at Brest-Litovsk. In January 1918, strikes in Berlin and other German cities seemed to indicate the high level of discontent among the German people. In addition, a detailed analysis of the German internal situation by William C. Bullitt emphasized that the leaders of the Majority Socialists, among others, were prepared to oppose an annexationist settlement with Russia.[47] However, when the rapacious terms of Brest-Litovsk revealed what a German peace would look like, and when the Majority Socialists failed to vote against them, it showed to Wilson that the military extremists were still the true masters of the empire and that no civilian politicians were able or willing to challenge them. "Force, Force to the utmost, Force without stint or limit," was his answer, "the righteous and triumphant Force that shall make Right the law of the world, and cast every selfish dominion down in the dust."[48]

Brest-Litovsk not only caused Wilson to drastically step up America's military contribution to the war, it also had an effect that, in the long run, was far more fateful for Germany. The failure of the Majority Socialists to fight the annexationist peace terms seems to have convinced him that even the civilian opposition, if not most of the German people, had been inculcated with the spirit of militarism. Thus, when he subsequently called for the "destruction of every arbitrary power" that could menace the peace of the world, he no longer exempted the German people from blame for the deeds of their rulers.[49] On the contrary, he had come to believe that, in the final analysis, the German people themselves were behind German militarism. It was amazing to him, he told a group of foreign correspondents in April 1918, to realize that a lot of German people liked the government they were living under. "It took me a long time to believe it," he added.[50] That same summer, he pointed out that, yes, there were "genuine liberal elements" even in Germany, who sincerely desired a peace of understanding, but they were "too small a minority to have any influence at present on the people, as a whole." "The German people," he continued, "must be made to hate war, to realize that no military machine can dominate the world today."[51] And how were the Germans to be turned into good pacifists? There seemed to be only one way: by "disciplining Germany."[52]

47 Memorandum by William C. Bullitt, Jan. 31, 1919, *PWW,* 46:183–93.
48 See his Address at the Opening of the third Liberty Loan Campaign, Apr. 6, 1918, *PWW,* 47:267–70.
49 Address at Mount Vernon, July 4, 1918, *PWW,* 48:516.
50 Remarks to Foreign Correspondents, Apr. 8, 1918, *PWW,* 47:288.
51 Sir William Wiseman to Arthur Cecil Murray, Aug. 30, 1918, *PWW,* 51:399.
52 Notes of a Conversation with Wilson by William Emmanuel Rappard, Nov. 20, 1918, *PWW,* 63:626 (emphasis in original).

Thus, by the end of the war, Wilson had in essence reverted to a view about German war guilt that he had held during the first days of the European conflict. But, whereas in 1914, his reactions had been purely emotional, by the end of 1918, he had arrived at this position by a reasoned judgment and long experience, after four years of direct dealings with the German government. What this meant, of course, was that a "peace without victory," even with a newly democratized Germany, was impossible, that it would not be a peace among equals, that its terms would be dictated. Although Wilson insisted on the removal of Germany's "military masters" and "monarchical autocrats" as a precondition for the consideration of any peace overtures (since they were so obviously beyond the pale), it essentially did not matter who would represent the Germans at Versailles, because the people, not just their leaders, would be on trial.[53]

And a trial the peace conference was, according to Wilson. He would later remind his colleagues in the Council of Four, that they were "sitting as judges," charged with the "great task to establish justice and right."[54] Justice, the central theme of Wilson's policies that he affirmed over and over again: justice demanded that, on the one hand, the excessive demands of the Allies be curbed, that Germany remain as a viable nation-state, that it was not saddled with unbearable burdens; it required, on the other hand, that the Germans be punished for their crimes. Thus, he fought long, hard, and often heroically to establish a peace as close as possible to the principles of his Fourteen Points, and without his valiant efforts, Versailles might have truly been a Carthaginian peace. But it was precisely on those questions that the Germans objected to most vigorously – questions that had a punitive character and involved national honor and prestige, such as exclusion from the League of Nations, the trial of the emperor, the delivery of war criminals, and, of course, the war-guilt clause of Article 231 – that Wilson was not to be moved.

What Wilson refused to admit, however, was that one man's justice might be another man's abomination, that his claim to have served justice even to the Germans might not be reciprocated by them. For Wilson, justice was absolute, not relative. How did he know what was just and right? He usually referred to such amorphous arbiters as "world opinion" or "the will of the people," but his embittered secretary of state, Robert Lansing may have been correct for once when he pointed out, somewhat acerbically: "Why, he knew it, and that was the best reason in the world."[55] Obviously, Ger-

53 Robert Lansing to Friedrich Oederlin, Oct. 23, 1918, *PWW,* 63:416–19.
54 Diary of Cary Travers Grayson, Mar. 25, 1919, *PWW,* 56:248.
55 Robert Lansing, "The Mentality of Woodrow Wilson," in John Braeman, ed., *Wilson* (Englewood Cliffs, N.J., 1972), 87.

many was guilty, it was self-evident; the more the Germans disputed their war guilt, the more they convinced him of it; the more they pointed out the many violations of the Fourteen Points, the more they exasperated and alienated him and simply proved to him that they had learned nothing, that they were unwilling to atone for their sins, that they deserved to be punished. Wilson truly believed that the treaty was just, and his many later references to this fact were neither hypocritical, nor were they a mere rationalization and self-deception, nor simply intended to "sell" the treaty to the American public – arguments that have all been advanced.

Thus, it was not Wilson's emotional anti-German prejudice or his capitulation to Allied, and particularly French, demands (or, one may add, his medical problems that have lately been blamed for some of his compromises) that account for his endorsement of harsh and punitive peace terms.[56] Rather, it was due to his conviction of the guilt of the German people and his insistence on a just settlement. As he remarked in discussing the German protests to the terms of the treaty:

The question that lies in my mind is "Where have they made good in their points?" "Where have they shown that the arrangements of the treaty are essentially unjust?" Not "Where have they shown merely that they are hard?," for they are hard – but the Germans earned that. And I think it is profitable that a nation should learn once and for all what an unjust war means in itself.[57]

56 See the appendix, "Wilson's Neurological Illness at Paris," in *PWW,* 58:607–40.
57 Discussion with the American Delegation, June 3, 1919, *PWW,* 60:67.

26

A Comment

GORDON MARTEL

A "last word" on anything may only repeat the first word ever
said about it. . . .

—A. P. Thornton, Minneapolis, 1977

Before the ink had dried on the Treaty of Versailles, the movement to tinker
with its terms, to renegotiate its most controversial provisions or to destroy it
altogether had begun. This was hardly a novel phenomenon: those who had
"lost" at Frankfurt am Main in 1871, at Paris in 1856, at Vienna in 1815, had
immediately contrived to place renegotiation or revision of the peace terms
at the top of the diplomatic agenda. The "winners," the Metternichs, the
Palmerstons, and the Bismarcks, would have been surprised had it been otherwise; they began to make their plans for how they would uphold the postwar political system even as they were creating it. This posture was mimic-
ked by Woodrow Wilson, David Lloyd George, and Georges Clemenceau:
they did not expect the Germans to submit without complaint to the imposition of the new order and would have been astonished had they done so.
The Big Three thought they had created new rules, new techniques, new
mechanisms that would uphold the integrity of the system that they had
designed. It might be argued that the leaders of the Entente constituted the
first wave of revisionists: those who believed that once the Germans had been
disciplined and democratized that they would become a part of the system,
and, becoming a part of it, could mend it to match their new morality.[1]

But it is seldom the Big Three that one pictures when images of "aftermath" are evoked: each of them was politically – if not literally – dead

---

1 See Antony Lentin's *Lloyd George, Woodrow Wilson, and the Guilt of Germany: An Essay in the Pre-history of Appeasement* (Leicester, 1984), 134–6; and Michael Graham Fry's comments on what he refers
to as Lloyd George's "tactical" revisionism in this book.

within a few years of their meetings in Paris. When one thinks of the postwar years, one thinks of "revisionism," of the *Kriegschuldfrage,* of the march – or stumble – toward Locarno and a new era.[2] The faces one associates with revisionism are less familiar, easily forgotten by anyone who is not a specialist in the subject: Charles Beard, Harry Elmer Barnes, C. Harley Grattan, Walter Millis, Charles Tansill, Goldsworthy Lowes Dickinson, H. N. Brailsford, E. D. Morel, Max Montgelas. Unfamiliar faces, but champions of a familiar cause: their purpose was to disprove the contention contained in Article 231 that Germany had been responsible for the outbreak of war in 1914. In proving this article to be faulty, they would remove the keystone of the treaty, which depended on it for its legitimacy. Who says that history is written by the winners? One of the many ironies of twentieth-century diplomatic history is that the Big Three are vividly remembered, but as failures, whereas the revisionists are by and large forgotten, although they were the winners.

By 1933 comments such as those found in *The Intelligent Man's Review of Europe Today* were unexceptional and testify to the extent of the revisionist victory: "The Peace Treaties and the European settlement which emerged from them . . . were, and remain, unjust in themselves. . . . [and] the vested interests and nationalistic sentiments which they have entrenched have permeated Europe to-day with a spirit of militarism."[3] The most widespread view of the roots of the injustice referred to by G. D. H. and Margaret Cole is neatly encapsulated in the comments in one popular textbook in twentieth-century history:

The primary misconception which dominated the thought of many millions of people in 1919 was the belief that a few wicked men in high places had planned the war . . . the persistent and effective propaganda of the Allied publicists fastened the dire responsibility for the catastrophe upon the Kaiser, the German and Austrian military leaders, and German industrial magnates. . . . It was easier to accept this "devil theory" of war, to blame it on a handful of power-mad militarists in Berlin and Vienna than to face the somber truth.[4]

The conference held at Berkeley in April 1994 demonstrated, if nothing else, how the revisionist agenda still organizes our discussions of Versailles. Warnings of a decade of disasters, or a twenty-year crisis or a century of backwardness began to be issued only months after the armistice of November 1918. A young William Bullitt, an attaché to the American commission

2 See Selig Adler, "The War Guilt Question and American Disillusionment, 1918–28," *Journal of Modern History* 23 (Mar. 1951): 1–28.
3 G. D. H. and Margaret Cole, *The Intelligent Man's Review of Europe Today* (London, 1933), 821.
4 Geoffrey Bruun and Victor S. Mamatey, *The World in the Twentieth Century,* 4th ed. (Boston, 1962).

to negotiate peace, resigned his position in May 1919, and in doing so wrote directly to President Wilson:

I was one of the millions who trusted confidently and implicitly in your leadership and believed that you would take nothing less than "a permanent peace" based upon "unselfish and unbiased justice." But our Government has consented now to deliver the suffering peoples of the world to new oppressions, subjections, dismemberments – a new century of war.[5]

The revisionists foresaw an international system made unworkable because of its illegitimate foundation, a series of states in which democracy could not take root and grow because these new regimes were associated with the *Diktat* of Versailles, a new world order that was bound to breed unrest everywhere because it was organized and operated by the militarists, capitalists, and conservatives of the old order that had already led Europe to Armageddon in 1914.[6] Thus did the revisionists have prescience on their side. And their story, which has been condensed and repeated *ad infinitum* for the last fifty years has now become "common knowledge": how the world had been given the opportunity to rebuild itself along new lines of justice and morality at Paris in 1919; how the wicked triumphed over the weak; how Versailles poisoned the Weimar Republic and made possible the rise of Hitler; how Hitler then pushed the world into another nightmare, even more horrifying than the last. Every textbook tells this story, and the bulk of historical research for the last seventy-five years has sought to explain how this happened by filling in the details missing from the outlines sketched by the revisionists of the 1920s:[7]

The Germans had been required to change their political system by the victorious Allies, and the Republic was always associated with defeat. It was also inextricably tied up with the onerous Treaty of Versailles. The treaty not only brought loss of territory and heavy financial payments, but in the eyes of most Germans an impairment of German honor, for they refused to recognize the so-called war-guilt clauses of the treaty. German honor also seemed challenged because Germany was not considered civilized enough to act as a mandatory power under the League and

5 Bullitt to Wilson, May 17, 1919. Cited in Sigmund Freud and William C. Bullitt, *Thomas Woodrow Wilson: A Psychological Study* (Boston, 1967), 271.
6 The Independent Labour Party of Britain quickly enunciated its official position: the Treaty of Versailles was "a capitalist, imperialist and militarist imposition. It aggravates every evil which existed before 1914. It does not give the world peace, but the certainty of other and more calamitous wars" (cited in Kenneth E. Miller, *Socialism and Foreign Policy* [The Hague, 1967], 93).
7 Cyril E. Black and Ernst C. Helmreich, *Twentieth-Century Europe: A History*, 4th ed. (New York, 1972), 446; see also Walter L. Langsam, *The World Since 1914* (New York, 1933), 730: "The task of the republic was made the harder, finally, by its inability to achieve more substantial treaty revision than it did; thus it was unable to meet the challenge of the extreme nationalists who clamored for ever more international concessions. All these things and others paved the way for the onward march of Nazism."

was forced to accept a policy of unilateral disarmament. The financial burdens exacted by the treaty weighed down every cabinet from the moment it came to power. . . . Had Chancellor Bruening obtained the changes in reparations for which he begged and which were eventually made, and had the Allies granted to him the slightest measure of equality in armament, many observers believe that he might have been able to stay in office.

The essays by Michael Fry, William Widenor, Wolfgang Mommsen, and Manfred Boemecke, while testifying to the continuing pressure that the revisionist perspective exerts on those who contemplate the Treaty of Versailles, also suggest some interesting new avenues of approach, some new ways for historians to grapple with an old problem. First, I would suggest that the essays by Boemecke and Mommsen add up to testimony for something that might (with a nod to Fritz Fischer) be termed *Der Frieden der Illusionen*. Second, I would argue that by highlighting the reminiscences, diaries, and autobiographies of those who participated in the peace process on the victorious side, the essays by Fry and Widenor have succeeded in illuminating that aspect of the "aftermath" that accounts for how the victors came to view their victory as a failure. Finally, I wish to propose several ways in which these new approaches may be extended.

I

The illusion with which we have had to learn to live is that World War I was "the war to end wars" – a phrase that has been used by every hack novelist, moviemaker, songwriter and textbook-writer. This turns the awful, complicated, and perplexing story of the war into an easily digested tale of tragedy: all those wonderful young men, the "flower of our youth," "the best and the brightest," going off to fight, to suffer and to die, in order to build a better world, to "make the world safe for democracy" were cheated by the duplicity of an older generation who used the ideals of the young in order to manipulate them into serving as pawns for their own devious, petty interests. The propaganda phrase coined by H. G. Wells neatly fused with the Fourteen Points put together by Woodrow Wilson to embody the aspirations of what the Allied and Associated Powers were supposed to be fighting for. Thus, the litmus-test by which the peace settlement would be judged was drawn up well in advance of the conference in Paris: Did it embody the principles laid down by the president? Did it promise to prevent wars in the future?

Few have been surprised by the revisionist phenomenon in Germany in the aftermath of the war, nor should they be. Losers complain. It may be graceless to do so, but it is not unexpected. Wolfgang Mommsen has, however, added something to the growing body of literature that testifies to the extent that the new German republic was in the business of sponsoring historians and other "disinterested" scholars in dismantling the moral foundation on which the edifice of Versailles had been erected. The activities of Max Weber are most illuminating in two respects. First, they show the extent to which German reaction focused on the Fourteen Points as the hinge on which the treaty turned. Second, they show how the kind of "good German" to whom Wilson and Lloyd George – and the Anglo-American liberals who supported them – had hoped to appeal instead regarded Versailles as a mortal blow to their hopes for a new, democratized Germany. A new régime that was, in essence, imposed upon the Germans by the victors was doomed from the start, particularly when it had to live with the *Diktat* of Versailles. German scholars in the aftermath of the war sought to disprove the charge that Germany was responsible for its outbreak while they proved that the peace failed to live up to the promise of the Fourteen Points.

Manfred Boemecke follows in the tradition of the German revisionists. He argues that the real Woodrow Wilson was the one who stood up in Paris, not the one who had enunciated the famous points to Congress on January 8, 1918. In spite of the occasional positive reference to things German, Wilson was a dyed-in-the-wool anglophile whose first instinct when war broke out in 1914 was to blame the Germans and help the British. Thus, "peace without victory" was a posture, a temporary aberration. At bottom, he believed that the autocratic militarism of Prussian-dominated Germany was the real cause of war, and that it would have to be destroyed if America – and democracy – were to be safe in the future.[8] Although this view is not a new one, it is certainly a minority opinion within the body of Wilsonian scholarship.[9] It is, however, well grounded in fact and goes far to explain Wilson at Paris: that he was not innocent, not a dupe, not incompetent.[10]

8 Thus, Wilson's own pre-settlement rhetoric contained in such speeches as his Flag Day address of 1917. The war, he declared, had been launched by "the military masters of Germany." The German government was, by this time, ready to make peace only in order to buy its "pound of flesh"; if these "military masters" succeeded they would be entrenched in power, but if they failed "a government accountable to the people" would be established in Germany: "If they succeed they are safe and Germany and the world are undone; if they fail Germany is saved and the world is at peace" (cited in H. F. C. Bell, *Woodrow Wilson and the People* [Garden City, N.Y., 1945], 221).

9 For an early version of this approach, see, e.g., Harley Notter, *The Origins of the Foreign Policy of Woodrow Wilson* (Baltimore, 1937), 42, 93, 100.

10 See Harold Nicolson, *Peacemaking 1919* (London, 1933), 198: "Wilson's vision had been narrowed by the intensive ethical nurture which he had received: he possessed, as he himself admitted, 'a one-track mind.' This intellectual disability rendered him blindly impervious, not merely to human character, but also shades of difference. He possessed no gift for differentiation, no capacity for adjustment to circumstances. It was his spiritual and mental rigidity which proved his undoing."

By the time of the peace conference, Wilson had returned to his Calvinist roots: to be improved, the Germans must be disciplined and punished. Max Weber's sense of betrayal would have been less dramatic had he been familiar with the Wilson portrayed by Boemecke.

Michael Fry's Lloyd George is as callous and even more formidable than Boemecke's Wilson. His defense of the treaty in the House of Commons in July was postulated on the premise that Germany had committed a crime in pushing the world into war in 1914. The militaristic tradition of Prussia, the autocratic régime of the Hohenzollerns, must be obliterated if the world were to be safe in the future; the German people, who had "approved and applauded" the war of aggression, must learn to be peaceful and democratic. No one who knew Lloyd George ever portrayed him as a New-World innocent: he was clever and underhanded; his part in creating a "terrible" peace was more cynical and less forgivable.

These essays almost succeed in restoring the faded, wrinkled, and shrunken triptych of the Big Three at Paris. Except that Clemenceau is missing. But Clemenceau – at least in Anglo-American scholarship – is not mysterious and in no need of revision. His role, consistent and explicable, has never been questioned, and is the one factor at Paris that is taken as a "given" in all historical equations. He had no interest in reforming or improving the German people; had no illusion that democracy on the left bank of the Rhine would mean safety for those who lived on the right of it. His role at Paris was to outfox the Americans and the British – a role that he performed brilliantly.[11] Revisionism in France during the aftermath was almost unknown, and what there was of it was bought and paid for by the German government.[12] The French defended the terms of the treaty, had no difficulty supporting Clemenceau's part in designing it and sought to have it enforced:

The name of the danger is German militarism. To defend ourselves against militarism and its consequences we waged war and we made peace. If we want the peace to last – Germany must be made to understand that peace is a sacred thing. . . . Every weakness that encourages German imperialism stimulates complications. Every division among the Allies sows the seed of future war. And as France and America both want peace, America must help us to enforce it – there is no other way of making the world safe.[13]

11 Or at least in the eyes of Anglo-American participants at the time and commentators since; at home he faced the criticism of Foch that he had failed to find the solution to the German threat. See Jere Clemens King, *Foch Versus Clemenceau: France and German Dismemberment, 1918–1919* (Cambridge, Mass., 1960). For Clemenceau's defense of his policy, see his introduction to André Tardieu, *The Truth About the Treaty* (Indianapolis, 1921).
12 This is the argument André Kaspi made in his presentation to the Berkeley conference.
13 Tardieu, *Truth About the Treaty*, 472.

The challenge for historians is how to explain the collapse of support in the United States and Britain, where "revisionism" quickly became the dominant mode of political discourse.

One of the favorite words used to describe the atmosphere that distinguished the aftermath of World War I is "illusion." In Britain, this was an "Age of Illusion" and the British foolishly enjoyed "The Long Week-End" between the wars; Europe suffered as a result of the Great Powers having created "The Illusion of Peace." Taking up the suggestive work of William Widenor and Michael Fry, I would propose to extend this approach and to examine the roots of illusion on which much of the peace settlement was postulated, and which gave rise to so much of the disillusionment in the aftermath.

Anglo-American officials and propagandists created a dream-world during the course of World War I, a castle in the air that was most alluring because it was constructed from materials of their own design, brought together from their own experience, and cemented by their most deep-seated beliefs about themselves, the nature of progress and the meaning of civilization.[14] They dreamed that European history could be brought to a close. They dreamed that world history could, and should, begin, would begin if the war were properly perceived as an opportunity to turn Europeans into Americans or Englishmen. What was missing in central and eastern Europe were the institutions and the traditions of democratic government.[15] Democracy stimulated progress by reducing privilege; progress stimulated civilization by increasing education, opportunity and the numbers of citizens who could take advantage of them. Americans had, after all, once been Europeans – but they had gotten over it; Englishmen had once been conquered and oppressed by foreigners – but they had recovered from it.[16]

Democracies were ipso facto peaceful. The ordinary citizen had no wish to take up arms, had no interest in doing so. Autocracies were other. Wherever a privileged elite controlled social and political institutions – even in the German Empire, which had the trappings of democracy, but not the reality – they retained their privileges by militarism. The young Walter Lipp-

14 For an excellent survey of one aspect of this phenomenon, see John A. Thompson, *Reformers and War: American Progressive Publicists and the First World War* (Cambridge, 1987).

15 And war, it was believed, would stimulate the transition if only because governments were being forced to appeal to their publics by the need to raise funds: "The government can only mitigate the resultant bitterness through granting the respective classes a fair share in determining the distribution of burdens. But this means constitutional reform. Barring the miracle of colossal military indemnities, autocratic government in Germany is doomed" (*New Republic* 4 [Oct. 30, 1915]: 325–6).

16 See Henry May, *The End of American Innocence* (New York, 1959); and David W. Noble, *The Paradox of Progressive Thought* (Minneapolis, 1958).

mann had sketched the outlines of this paradigm soon after the outbreak of war in 1914, but a full two years before the U.S. entered the conflict:[17]

It is in time of peace that the value of life is fixed. The test of war reveals it. That is why democracies tend to be peaceful. In them the importance of each person has been enlarged, and the greater the equality, the less able are small groups able to use their fellows as brute instruments. Democracies are compelled to look toward peaceful adjustments because the cost of war is too tremendous for them. . . . There is, perhaps, the most important relation between social reform and the problem of peace. The aggressors of the future are likely to be the nations in which life is cheap, and the hope of international order rests with those countries in whom personality has become too valuable to be squandered. This is why the whole world waits the democratization of Germany, Russia and Japan.

When victorious, they could bribe their people with the bounty they had won (as the Prussians did after 1871); when losing, they might try to convince their people that defeat could be avenged and honor restored by becoming more militaristic, not less. Herein lay the formula that satisfied almost every liberal-minded progressive-thinking Anglo-American: no enduring peace without a democratic world, no democratic world without peace.[18]

War between democracies had become unthinkable. The war within a democracy that had raged within the United States from 1861 to 1865 had broken out because of the "peculiar institution" that dominated southern society; once slavery – the most profoundly undemocratic institution imaginable – had been abolished, Americans had finally begun to realize the dreams of the founders.[19] Was there any question that the power and the wealth of the United States had grown exponentially in the half-century since? But these triumphs could be jeopardized if America, threatened by a powerful, militarized state, were forced to militarize in order to defend itself; the militia of independent, armed citizens would no longer suffice.[20]

17 From "Life Is Cheap," *New Republic* (Dec. 19, 1914), reprinted in Walter Lippmann, *Early Writings* (New York, 1970), 17.
18 Thus, Herbert Hoover in a speech of July 28, 1919: "We went into the war to destroy autocracy as a menace to our own and all other democracies. If we had not come into the war every inch of European soil today would be under autocratic government" (cited in Herbert Hoover, *The Ordeal of Woodrow Wilson* [New York, 1958], 267). This postsettlement view was perfectly in accord with the pre-intervention view of George Creel: "It is autocracy that is at bay – the whole infamous theory of the divine right of kings that now has the sword at its throat" (*Harper's Weekly* 59 [Aug. 29, 1914]: 197; cited in Thompson, *Reformers and War,* 92).
19 See Wilson's own treatment of the Civil War in his *Division and Reunion, 1829–1889* (New York, 1893), in which he argued that the United States did not become a nation until after the conflict.
20 It is illuminating to look at the establishment of two internationalist organizations in the United States following 1914 that were specifically devoted to combating the spread of the militarist spirit at home: the American League to Limit Armaments and the American Union Against Militarism. See C. Roland Marchand, *The American Peace Movement and Social Reform, 1898–1918* (Princeton, N.J., 1972).

The reason why the French were so thoroughly resented in the aftermath of the war, why francophobia became a dominant characteristic of Anglo-American liberalism, was that French determination to keep the Germans down, to impose the harshest possible interpretation of the terms agreed at Versailles, would certainly have the effect of stimulating the appetite for revenge.[21] Once this appetite increased, democracy would disappear and militarism would mount another charge. A thread that ran throughout the fabric of postwar revisionism was the attack on French intransigence, both in formulating the terms of Versailles and then in implementing them. France, it was argued, was still playing the old game of the old world, sticking to the outworn, unworkable, and immoral idea of the balance of power, promoting political and minority discontent wherever it served French interests, accumulating strategically and financially valuable properties whenever possible.[22]

Nowhere was this difference between Anglo-American and French views more apparent than in their attitude toward the League of Nations. At Paris itself, André Tardieu acted at the most outspoken advocate of a League that would act as a policeman (or *gendarmerie*) to enforce the treaty. This created resentment at the time, conflicting directly with the views of those members of the U.S. and British delegations who saw themselves as responsible for formulating the ideas behind a League and for putting it on the peacemaking agenda through their publicity campaign during the war. They interpreted the French maneuvers as an attempt to kidnap their creation. Although most of the League's proponents could accept the formula that only democratic states should be eligible for membership in the organization, they anticipated that the Germans would soon take their place at the table – unless the French succeeded in creating a League that was reminiscent of the post-Vienna Congress system employed by Metternich as a de facto alliance of the reactionary victors.

---

21 "One could not help feeling [in traveling through the Saar Valley] that in a moment all that has happened in the last 50 years was wiped away: the French soldiers were back again in the place where they used to be under the Monarchy and the Revolution: confident, debonair, quick, feeling themselves completely at home in their historical task of bringing a higher civilisation to the Germans. . . . Again and again one finds the same thing: the French Departments of State and the inferior people seem completely defective in all sense of justice, fair play or generosity" (Headlam-Morley to Bailey, May 10, 1919, Headlam-Morley manuscript. Wilson himself, in his only radio broadcast, condemned France [and Italy], on November 10, 1923, for making "waste paper" of the Treaty of Versailles. Thomas A. Bailey, *Wilson and the Peacemakers* [New York, 1947], 349–50).

22 See the superb treatment of this theme in W. M. Jordan's *Great Britain, France, and the German Problem, 1918–1939: A Study of Anglo-French Relations in the Making and Maintenance of the Versailles Settlement* (London, 1943). In many ways this study has yet to be surpassed. But on French imperial designs, see Christopher M. Andrew and A. S. Kanya-Forstner, *France Overseas: The Great War and the Climax of French Imperial Expansion* (London, 1981).

The fear of reaction was the dominant mood of the Anglo–American delegates at Paris, a concern that was reflected in both their criticism and their defense of the peace settlement. William Widenor, in considering the defense of the treaty mounted by Charles Seymour, provides valuable insight into the relationship between reaction and revision. He admires Seymour's pragmatism, his rendition of the difficulties facing the peacemakers; but most important, he shows how even a clear-headed defender of the settlement looked to the League of Nations as the most important institutional mechanism for overcoming the defects of the treaties. In other words, the League, in the eyes of most of its adherents, was, from the beginning, an instrument of revision. If the French were to have their way, it would be a weapon of reaction instead. Even those who did not walk away from Paris as disenchanted officials, as John Maynard Keynes and Bullitt did, would soon join the parade of those who felt that things had gone terribly wrong and that some new way would have to be found to build the new world order that they had dreamed of in the final years of the war.[23]

Historians have hitherto used the diaries, memoirs, autobiographies, and fragmentary recollections of officials as materials for writing the history of "what really happened" at Paris. For most of the period between the wars these were the only sources that historians could draw upon in their quest to explain what had happened – with the mostly unspoken assumption that this consisted of identifying what had gone wrong. But there is a different use to which these sources may be put: to study the officials themselves.[24] There was not much interest in such a subject between the wars; then, after the experience of World War II, it seemed to be even more apparent that Versailles had been fundamentally flawed, that it led to Nazism, the war, and the Holocaust; therefore, such interest as there was continued to revolve upon the axis of failure, the reason for the American retreat from Europe – a mistake that must never be repeated. So even in the later period the only good reason for studying officials was in order to evaluate the perspicacity of their criticisms: Was the absence of realism or morality more fatal? Was there too much expertise or too little? Was there too little consultation or too much? Was public opinion too influential or was it ignored?

By refocusing attention on the officials who were involved in the process of defining and promoting war aims and then in the drama of attempting to

---

23 James T. Shotwell, e.g., who remained a staunch internationalist, concluded that "the supreme attribute of statesmanship, magnanimity, was lacking at Paris. . . . [Wilson] accepted retribution for ill-doing as a part of the moral order of the world, and believed that it applied to nations as well as to individuals" (*At the Paris Peace Conference* [New York, 1937], 51).

24 I am using "officials" in a broad sense here, for want of a better word. I mean to include both career civil servants and those who labored on behalf of their governments (sometimes without pay) during the war, and thus can be considered part of the "official" war effort.

accomplish them at Paris, historians can get a much clearer sense of why the treaty, or the defense of it, failed. Instead of beginning with the assumption that it was wicked – and then piling up the footnotes to demonstrate its departures from the Fourteen Points – they ought to be asking why its progenitors failed to defend it successfully. Asking what it was that they approved and disapproved of is to take their views less seriously and more meaningfully. Many of the men mentioned by Widenor and Fry had been active in "The Inquiry" or in the compilation of the "Peace Handbooks." Wilson and Lloyd George, both of whom had overcome tremendous odds to become successful politicians, understood the importance of having articulate and dedicated supporters among the intellectual elite.[25] And they had successfully harnessed that support in the way in which they had gone about formulating war aims. Thus did these men at Paris (and many more of their friends who stayed at home but kept in touch) feel personally responsible for the peace settlement. Their sense of the meaning of Versailles ranged from disenchantment to betrayal.[26]

In this approach, the question of how legitimate the complaints of these critics were is beside the point: by making these secondary characters the subjects of our investigation their opinions become, by definition, meaningful and significant. And we must begin by integrating the zeal of the war-aims process with the disillusionment of war-guilt revisionism; to put it another way, we must force a marriage between Lawrence Gelfand and Warren Cohen.[27] And we must remind ourselves that we are looking not for an explanation of the treaty's weaknesses, but for an explanation of how those involved in its creation failed to become responsible for its defense. Other major peace settlements have had their flaws and their critics, but none of them had their flaws magnified in this manner, none of them failed to find articulate and convincing advocates.

No one has seriously studied the deterioration in public support for the treaty of Versailles.[28] The underlying assumption has long been that,

25 See Laurence W. Martin, *Peace Without Victory: Woodrow Wilson and the British Liberals* (New Haven, Conn., 1958).

26 "I am afraid everybody in Germany will be feeling hopeless about the indemnity; there is no end to it . . . the more I study it [the treaty] the more I feel that we have absolutely broken the pledge we made in November, under which we induced the Germans to disarm." Alfred Zimmern to mother, May 19, 1919, Zimmern manuscript, box 9, folder 100, Bodleian Library, Oxford; "I think I agree with you about the Treaty of Peace. The cumulative effect of it is to put on Germany disabilities of such a nature that no nation could be expected to acquiesce in them" (Headlam-Morley to Saunders, May 12, 1919, Headlam-Morley manuscript, Churchill College, Cambridge).

27 Warren I. Cohen, *The American Revisionists: The Lessons of Intervention in World War I* (Chicago, 1967).

28 There is a pioneering work on public opinion, R. B. McCallum's *Public Opinion and the Last Peace* (London, 1944). Although full of insight and interesting suggestions, it is actually very thin on "public opinion" and is more illuminating as a primary document in the genre of "personal history." See

because the settlement was both unrealistic and immoral, the enthusiasm of the public for it in Britain and the United States was bound to erode as it slowly become evident how badly the peacemakers had bungled. But it is exceedingly difficult to believe that there was anything inevitable about this, that it could have been predicted that the people of Britain and the United States would cease to regard Germany as responsible for the war, that they would no longer accept the premise that Germany ought to bear the brunt of the costs of the war, that they would fail to agree that territories must be taken and military restrictions instituted in order to safeguard against a German attempt to renew the conflict, that they would fail to approve of the proposition that Germany must demonstrate that she had become democratic and willing to abide by the rules of the new international system before it could take its place at the League of Nations.[29]

That public support did deteriorate has been assumed, but not tested. Once the "treaty fight" ends in the United States and the "retreat into isolation" begins (a concept that a later generation of New Left revisionists would challenge) the interest of American historians in the peace settlement evaporates.[30] In Britain, widespread opposition to the French occupation of the Ruhr is taken as evidence of the public's unwillingness to uphold the reparations clauses or to support the provisions for enforcement of the treaty's terms; but this is, for the most part, an untested hypothesis. What is readily demonstrable in both cases is the decline in support for the treaty amongst those who had had a part in its creation. During the war Wilson and Lloyd George had succeeded in mobilizing an unprecedented degree of progressive, liberal support among the intellectual elite of their two countries; by 1922 both were out of office and their reputations in tatters.[31] As the essays by Widenor and Fry show, none of their supporters were able to mount more than a lukewarm defense of Versailles – and many of the defenses consisted of arguing that its best and most innovative feature was in keeping the door open to revision. Even Wilson, in his fruitless campaign for ratification of the treaty, and Lloyd George, in his memoirs, took this line. And, as the multivolume history of the conference edited by

also Catherine Ann Cline, "Ecumenism and Appeasement: The Bishops of the Church of England and the Treaty of Versailles," *Journal of Modern History* 61 (1989): 683–703.

29 *The Spectator*, e.g., declared on May 10, 1919: "The Peace is a good peace; it is what it ought to be – a dictated peace." For a survey of French views, see Pierre Renouvin, *Les Crises du XXe Siècle*, vol. 1: *de 1914 à 1929* (Paris, 1957), chaps. 7 and 9.

30 For the New Left view of the interwar years, see William Appleman Williams, *The Tragedy of American Diplomacy* (New York, 1959), chap. 4; and Joan Hoff Williams, *Ideology and Economics: U.S. Relations with the Soviet Union, 1918–1933* (Columbia, Mo., 1974).

31 See Charles B. Forcey, *The Crossroads of Liberalism: Croly, Weyl, Lippmann, and the Progressive Era, 1900–25* (New York, 1961).

Harold Temperley shows, the line became less supportive, more critical as each succeeding volume appeared.[32]

How do we explain this phenomenon? I would suggest that we begin by returning to the publicity campaigns during the war itself, with special attention to the activities of those who would turn up at Paris in 1919. Although there has been a good deal of work on the propaganda of World War I, it has consisted, for the most part, of high-minded hatchet jobs.[33] The purpose of studying it is to condemn it, to show how even civilized, educated, and liberal people could perpetrate a series of frauds in order to whip up the support necessary to continue the slaughter. Few are inclined to take the views of the propagandists seriously, as evidence of real belief in the principles they enunciated, of true commitment to the destruction of the wickedness they claimed to be fighting. But if we were to suspend our disbelief for a time and instead treat them as something other than knaves or fools, scoundrels or dupes, we might see that there was a consistency in their attitudes that led them from outspoken support for the war, to the formulation of war-aims, to a belief in a new international system, to disillusionment and pessimism in the aftermath of the war. William A. White, one of the Progressive publicists recruited to serve in the war effort, explained this succinctly to his friend (and Wilson's official biographer) Ray Stannard Baker: "We had such high hopes of this adventure; we believed God called us, and now at the end we are put to doing hell's dirtiest work, starving people, grabbing territory – or helping to grab it for our friends; standing by while the grand gesture of revenge and humiliation links this war up with the interminable chain of wars that runs back to Cain!"[34]

If nothing else, such an approach would rescue a vast literature that has gone largely unexamined.[35] Attention ought to be focused particularly on

32 See chapter 24 in this book and the superb article by George Egerton, "The Lloyd George *War Memoirs*: A Study in the Politics of Memory," *Journal of Modern History* 60 (1988): 55–94.

33 For leading examples of this genre, see Peter Buitenhuis, *The Great War of Words: British, American, and Canadian Propaganda and Fiction, 1914–1933* (Vancouver, B.C., 1987); and Stuart Wallace, *War and the Image of Germany: British Academics, 1914–1918* (Edinburgh, 1988). This is not to suggest that there have not been some very good scholarly studies of the propaganda campaign, although these have more frequently concentrated on the organization of the effort and personnel involved than they have on the arguments and the ideas contained within the publicity. See Stephen Vaughn, *Holding Fast the Inner Lines: Democracy, Nationalism and the Committee on Public Information* (Chapel Hill, N.C., 1980); and Michael Sanders and Philip M. Taylor, *British Propaganda During the First World War, 1914–18* (London, 1982).

34 White to Baker, June 3, 1919. Quoted in Thompson, *Reformers and War*, 239–40. Equally pertinent to our discussion here is White's reluctant decision to campaign on behalf of treaty ratification, "but I shall say that the only hope of the world is in . . . the common people turning out their governments and putting in new governments which will void that treaty and make over the League of Nations."

35 And the mass sales/circulation of some of these productions certainly merits closer consideration. According to George Creel, the first significant publication sponsored by the Committee for Pub-

the structure of the propagandistic arguments, on the link between perceptions of the causes of the war and the objectives for which it was being
fought.[36] These are so numerous and varied that it is impossible to summa-
rize them here; virtually every imaginable argument had its adherents and
almost all were marshaled in the effort to maximize support. And this was
part of the problem. Some, for example, argued that the underlying cause
of the war was nationalism: that individual liberties had been abrogated in
the drive to create a powerful nation whose purpose it was to promote and
expand its culture, its language, its faith. The remedy for this was a series of
restraints on the authority of the state within the national boundaries, and
the creation of an international authority outside them. Others argued the
opposite, that the roots of the war were to be found in the suppression of
nationalism, that most of the conflicts in Europe since 1815 had arisen from
nationalities struggling to be free, and that this had certainly been the
immediate cause of the outbreak of war in 1914. The remedy for this was
the creation of a series of new states based upon the principle of national
self-determination. During the war, such contradictory assumptions could
be ignored; but during the peace process they could not, and as war-aims
came to be formulated some of the cracks and fissures began to be evident;
by the time that the terms of peace were laid down in black and white, it
was almost impossible to conceal such differences.[37]

Institutions like the League of Nations and innovations like the Minority Treaties were designed to bridge the gaps in Anglo-American thinking.
The "nationalists" were to be satisfied with the creation of newly independent states in eastern and southern Europe; the "internationalists" were to
be assured that the rights of linguistic and religious minorities would be
protected against the intrusion of powerful, centralized states and that the
League would enforce this protection.[38] The adherents of both sides found
the arrangements unsatisfactory: self-determination was a sham that had not
been fairly applied; the protections of minorities were inadequate and the

---

lic Information, "How the War Came to America," sold six and one-quarter million copies. *How We
Advertised America* (New York, 1920).

36 E.g., the liberal-pacifist philosopher John Dewey was converted to the interventionist position
largely because of the conclusion he had reached concerning the underlying cause of the war: "German lust for spiritual and political monopoly." The remedy, as he saw it, was to impose American
values on them. "Fiat Justitia, Ruat Collum," *New Republic* 12 (Sept. 29, 1917): 238.

37 To cite just one example of this phenomenon, G. P. Gooch, an active publicist and propagandist
throughout the war, worried that the "balkanization" of the Austro-Hungarian Empire would
inevitably lead to irredentist grievances and thus to a series of "Ulsters." See his pamphlet, *The Races
of Austria-Hungary* (London, 1917), written on behalf of the Union of Democratic Control.

38 See Agnes Headlam-Morley, Russell Bryant, and Anna Cienciala, eds., *Sir James Headlam-Morley:
A Memoir of the Paris Peace Conference, 1919* (London, 1972).

League was too feeble to enforce them. The wounds went deeper because those who had publicized, propagandized, and fought for their interpretation of the ills that had caused the war found it impossible to agree that they had been wrong. Mobilizing the historians, the geographers, the classicists, and the social scientists of all varieties was tremendously successful during the war, but the price was paid in the aftermath.

One more example of this phenomenon will have to suffice. A thread of the propagandistic ephemera now consigned to the scrap-heap of British history contains within it both "imperialist" and "anti-imperialist" strands. Although both sides of this debate saw the war as essentially an Anglo-German conflict, one argued that it was caused by German envy, the other by British predominance. The first maintained that Britain, as a seafaring island and as a trading nation, had legitimately founded an empire that was morally defensible because huge numbers of people were having their lives materially improved while being instructed in the lessons of responsible, democratic government; Germany, as a continental state in the center of Europe, had no business in building a high-seas fleet, and when they did seize non-European territories they exploited them against the interests of the inhabitants and brought with them the immoral institutions of a militarist autocracy. The second maintained that imperialism was in and of itself wicked and a cause of war: a small elite of special-interest groups were the only ones to profit from imperial expansion, but they inevitably came into conflict with similar interests in other states; apart from this elite, imperialism did no one any good: not the ordinary citizen at home, not the native abroad. And yet, during the war, both these groups were able to support the war effort and to publicize their particular interpretation of its causes and their remedies to prevent its renewal.[39]

This wartime alliance was bound to unravel once it came time to make peace. And to many it appeared that the imperialists were clear winners: the German fleet was scuttled and the German overseas empire was seized. Even more territory – and certainly more valuable – was taken from the Turks. The anti-imperialists, the Cobdenite liberals, and the Hobsonian laborites were able to argue that the peace settlement represented a policy of "grab" on the part of the victors, and that this symbolized the moral bankruptcy of the treaty.[40] But the imperialists were able to counter that the

39 It is illuminating to follow the career of J. A. Hobson from his famous prewar *Imperialism: A Study* to his wartime aspirations in *The Fight for Democracy* (London, 1917).
40 And such became the official policy of the Labour Party in the 1920s. As Charles Trevelyan put it, "The imperialist war had ended in Imperialist peace." See John F. Naylor, *Labour's International Policy* (London, 1969).

system of mandates by which Britain, France and Italy were to act as "trustees" under the League of Nation, symbolized the new era; their complaint was that too much had been given to the French, who would now be in a position to revive their old competition with the British overseas.[41]

This kind of debate, which raged in the immediate aftermath of the war, continued throughout the interwar period. And there is much to discover about the groups involved, their ideas, their activities, and their support by returning to their propaganda efforts during the war. Such an approach may also highlight the distinctive political culture of each of the combatant states; certainly the United States, France, and Germany had very different views concerning the role of imperialism in causing the war, which were the guilty parties, and how this state of affairs was to be remedied. One vivid thread running throughout the fabric of German propaganda was the complaint that Entente powers had "encircled" Germany in order to prevent it from taking its rightful place as one of the world powers (with the attendant right to empire that this status conferred). But this is a much more interesting theme and worthy of further investigation; German liberals, for instance, complained that this encirclement forced Germany into a position of relying upon the Habsburg Empire, which then succeeded in dragging Germany into a war that served Austro-Hungarian, not German, interests; German socialists took a line similar to that of the anti-imperialists in the Labour Party and the Progressives in the United States. The complicated and contradictory indignation and sense of betrayal that characterized the aftermath of the war had its roots in the war itself.[42]

As Lawrence Gelfand and Erik Goldstein have shown, both within this collection of essays and in work elsewhere, many of those who propagandized their point of view during the war were involved in formulating war aims or in negotiating the terms of peace.[43] This activity gave rise to many a guilty conscience after the war. An interesting, and largely unexamined,

41 The *Round Table* was the leading exponent of this view in the aftermath of the war; on the theme of trusteeship and francophobia, see Gordon Martel, "The Origins of the Chatham House Version," in Edward Ingram, ed., *National and International Politics in the Middle East: Essays in Honour of Elie Kedourie* (London, 1986).

42 This is not the place to review the vast secondary literature on German propaganda and publicity, but some useful studies are: Otto Eichenlaub, ed., *Deutsche Propaganda im Weltkrieg: Festgabe für Wilhelm Waldkirch* (Ludwigshafen, 1940); Wolfram Selig, *Paul Nikolaus Cossmann und die "Süddeutschen Monatshefte" von 1914–1918: Ein Beitrag zur Geschichte der nationalen Publizistik im Ersten Weltkrieg* (Osnabrück, 1967); Gotthart Schwarz, *Theodor Wolff und das "Berliner Tageblatt": Eine liberale Stimme in der deutschen Politik (1906–1933)* (Tübingen, 1968); and Heinz-Dietrich Fischer, *Pressekonzentration und Zensurpraxis im Ersten Weltkrieg* (Berlin, 1973).

43 Lawrence E. Gelfand, *The Inquiry: American Preparation for Peace, 1917–1919* (New Haven, Conn., 1963); Erik Goldstein, *Winning the Peace: British Diplomatic Strategy, Peace Planning, and the Paris Peace Conference, 1916–1920* (Oxford, 1991).

aspect of the experience of war is the impact of propaganda on the propagandists. Most interesting is the effect on those who saw themselves as liberal, progressive reformers and threw themselves into the war effort in order to prevent the militarists and the reactionaries from using it to extend their power.[44] Their exertions frequently caused them to be embarrassed or ashamed once the war was over: they were aware of how often they had exaggerated the sins of the enemy or distorted the record of history in order to manipulate public opinion; they came to see themselves as having been manipulated by politicians who used them for their own purposes.[45] And when the peace turned out to be less than perfect, they turned against it with a vengeance. The conference in Paris had been "a soul-destroying affair," Arnold Toynbee told his mother; to a friend he explained, "that pathetic illusion of building something up, which we all cherished during the war, in self-defence, whatever we were doing, seems for the moment to have fallen flat. . . . One had made believe during the war that one was building something up, and not merely assisting at a catastrophe, and now it has all fallen flat, and one sees the war for what it is – pure destruction. One had the pathetic delusion that because it wasn't one's fault one ought to be able to make some good come of it."[46]

We know something of the activities of those involved in the Committee for Public Information, the Inquiry, the Department of Political Intelligence, at Wellington House. References are made to the arguments and opinions they expressed in the *New Republic* and *Nation,* in the *New Europe* and the *Round Table* – although we have not examined their ideas carefully enough. But we know very little about how this experience was connected with their activities in the aftermath of the war. Men like James Shotwell, Charles Homer Haskins, Isaiah Bowman, William Westerman, and R. H. Lord in the United States, like Arnold Toynbee, James Headlam-Morley, Lewis Namier, R. W. Seton-Watson, and Alfred Zimmern in Britain did not simply disappear after the war. If anything, they were more active polit-

---

44 Witness, e.g., the outspoken position of Harold Laski, referred to by Michael Howard as the intellectual leader of the Hobson-Leninist theorists: "Foreign investment begat imperialism; imperialism begat militarism; militarism begat war. . . . Once the imperialistic phase has arrived, the relationship between capitalism and war is inescapable" (Quoted in Michael Howard, *War and the Liberal Conscience* [London, 1978], 88–9).

45 Charles Beard, whose outspoken revisionism is well known, is less well known for his interventionism in 1917: "Personally I favor more drastic action than the President has taken up to date. I have thought for some months that this country should definitely align itself with the Allies and help eliminate Prussianism from the earth" (cited in Cohen, *Revisionists,* 5).

46 July 21, 1919, Toynbee manuscript, Bodleian Library, Oxford; Toynbee to Robert Darbyshire, July 21, 1919, ibid. And thus, Laurence Martin in the conclusion to *Peace without Victory:* "Liberals who had been the most fervent of Wilson's supporters were bitterly disappointed and outraged by the Treaty. Some were surprised and shocked; others considered their gloomy warnings vindicated" (204).

ically after the war than they had been before it. Each of them became, although usually in distinctive and often in conflicting ways, a "revisionist." Each of them could find something to detest in the peace settlement; each of them felt a sense of personal responsibility for its shortcomings; each of them continued to work toward that better world for which they had strived during the war.[47]

The aftermath of the war was characterized by a proliferation of new organizations dedicated to a "scientific" understanding of international relations, to raising awareness of international issues, and to facilitating communication across national boundaries. Most of those who were in the vanguard of organizations such as the Council on Foreign Relations or the Royal Institute of International Affairs had been involved in propaganda or peacemaking, and frequently in both. The seeds of these two organizations had, in fact, been sown at the peace conference, where a large group of Americans and British agreed that a *non*national organization dedicated to the promotion of international cooperation in general and Anglo-American harmony in particular was badly needed. That this objective was soon lost and the organization split into its national components says much about the atmosphere of the aftermath.[48]

In the British Isles, important new chairs for the study of international relations were established: the Woodrow Wilson at the University of Wales (occupied by peacemaking veterans Alfred Zimmern and E. H. Carr); the Stevenson at the University of London (occupied by propagandist and peacemaker Arnold Toynbee); the Burton at Oxford (occupied again by Zimmern and then by James Headlam-Morley's daughter, Agnes). These men used the prominence of their new positions to promote their views of what a new international system should consist of. The men of 1919 did not simply disappear: they launched a relentless attack on Lloyd George and what they regarded as his treachery at Paris. The Wilsonians in the United States followed a similar path – although they did not have the man himself to kick around any more – occupying important places in new departments and schools created for the study of international relations. An organization such

47 See, e.g., George B. Noble's *Policies and Opinions at Paris, 1919: Wilsonian Diplomacy, the Versailles Peace, and French Public Opinion* (New York, 1935). Attached to the American Commission to Negotiate Peace in 1919, Noble explained at the beginning of his book that "The ills of present-day Europe, if not the world, can in large measure be ascribed to the devastation and dislocation of the World War, and to the failure of the peacemakers of 1919 to reestablish a viable international order" (v).

48 See Gordon Martel, "From Round Table to New Europe: Some Intellectual Origins of the Institute of International Affairs," in Andrea Bosco and Cornelia Navari, eds., *Chatham House and British Foreign Policy, 1919–1945: The Royal Institute of International Affairs During the Inter-war Period* (London, 1994), 13–40.

as the League of Free Nations Association, founded by Charles Beard and Herbert Croly in order to educate the American public on foreign affairs and to promote the League of Nations, was transformed into the Foreign Policy Association, and soon had an influential membership in excess of 10,000 and published the weekly *Foreign Policy Bulletin* (joining the Council on Foreign Relations' *Foreign Affairs* and the Royal Institute of International Affairs' *Annual Survey of International Relations*). Charles Levermore helped to organize the American Association for International Cooperation in 1922 and the League of Nations Non-Partisan Association in 1923. Internationalism did not die after 1919, but it did take on new forms and turned into some surprising shapes; it was distinctively different from the free-trade internationalism of Cobden and Bright, from the international socialism of Marx and Engels, and from the pacifism of the prewar evangelicalists.

Charting the course followed by the men of 1919 in the period between the wars is no easy task. The "movement" was fissiparous and fragmentary; its records are diverse and difficult. They engaged in journalism and produced scholarly studies; they gave speeches and talked on the radio; they trained students and briefed experts. They disputed one another's theories in public and feuded in private. Perhaps the only thing on which they could all agree was that the peace settlement had not lived up to the promises of wartime; they were all, in some sense "revisionist" – although what they thought it was essential to revise varied greatly.[49] In the United States, some of the old Wilsonians remained as deeply internationalist as ever: Shotwell[50] and Seymour, for example; while others, like Beard and Barnes, became isolationist.[51] In Britain, the differences became most obvious during the era of appeasement, with old friends and colleagues such as Arnold Toynbee and R. W. Seton-Watson attacking one another in public, largely over the question of how, when, and where to revise the treaties of 1919.

But I also wish to suggest that students of international history would do well to extend the meaning of "revisionism." If we are to understand the political culture of the world that emerged from the war and the peace, we need to extend our studies beyond that of the politicians, the experts and the intellectuals who were, for a time, part of the official world. Revisionism in

---

49 On the theme of "persistence," see Otis L. Graham Jr., *An Encore for Reform: The Old Progressives and the New Deal* (New York, 1967).

50 James Shotwell, who continued his academic career at Columbia, also served as a director for the Carnegie Endowment for International Peace.

51 To the point that both opposed intervention in World War II, even after the bombing of Pearl Harbor. Harry Elmer Barnes, *The Chickens of the Interventionist Liberals Come Home to Roost* (New York, 1973).

634   *Gordon Martel*

Germany, France, Italy, Britain, the United States and elsewhere became a cultural phenomenon in which the very *mentalité* of Western civilization was shaken and stirred. Cultural revisionists paid little attention to the Treaty of Versailles in the aftermath of the war; if they referred to it at all it was in the form of a literary shorthand in which "Versailles" stood for everything that was wrong with the world. To them, the war and its settlement together symbolized the bankruptcy – or the death – of Western culture.

In this view, the rocks upon which nineteenth-century civilization had been erected turned out to be nothing more than shifting sand. Industrialization? What did it mean except an enormous capacity to kill human beings with their own machinery at an unprecedented rate? Rationalism? What did it amount to in the trenches, where men wore charms, chanted incantations, and believed that ghostly platoons haunted no-man's land? Progress? Was it anything more than a *bourgeois* veneer that could be stripped away in an instant when men were taken out of their comfortable surroundings and forced to confront death?[52]

Revisionism ran like a tidal wave through the West in the aftermath of the war. Spengler discovered that civilizations are no more enduring than any organism, that they will all wither and die. Freud discovered that he had been wrong, that there was something even more elemental than sex in the human psyche: the death-wish. Jung discovered that all human beings were connected through a "collective unconscious": the history of man goes back hundreds of thousands of years, and "a mere fifty generations ago many of us in Europe were no better than primitives. The layer of culture, this pleasing patina, must therefore be quite extraordinarily thin in comparison with the powerfully developed layers of the primitive psyche. But it is these layers that form the collective unconscious." It is at this point that Jung parted company with Freud and Adler in their reduction of everything psychic to primitive sexual wishes: "But these specifically Jewish doctrines are thoroughly unsatisfying to the Germanic mentality; we still have a genuine barbarian in us who is not to be trifled with, and whose manifestation is no comfort for us and not a pleasant way of passing the time. Would that people could learn the lesson of the war!"[53]

---

52 Witness, e.g., the disillusionment of the historian Carl Becker, who had served on the Creel Committee during the war and written the CPI pamphlet *America's War Aims and Peace Program*. The war, he wrote, was "the result of some thousands of years of what men like to speak of as 'political, economic, intellectual, and moral Progress.' If this is progress, what in Heaven's name would retardation be!" (Cited in Burleigh Williams, *Carl Becker* [Cambridge, Mass., 1961] 132).

53 "Über das Unbewusste," *Schweizerland: Monatshefte für Schweizer Art und Arbeit* 4 (1918), trans. by R. F. C. Hull in *Civilization in Transition* (New York, 1964).

The development of a new anthropology after the war provides vivid illustration of the extent of revisionist thinking that swept through Europe. W. H. R. Rivers discovered that the laws of progressive evolution that had been superimposed on all societies by prewar anthropologists were crude, oversimplified, and misleading.[54] Malinowski articulated a view of culture in which myths performed a vital function in all societies at all times: the reactions of "civilized" Europeans at war, he argued, were no different from those of the most "primitive" beings – both conjured up myths as necessary, "born from the innermost and emotional reaction to the most formidable and haunting idea" – death.[55] Malinowski's study of the Trobriand islanders led him to question the superiority of the West and the right of colonialist administrators to determine what was best for natives.[56]

Everywhere the same fanatical zeal to prune, uproot, make an *auto-da-fé* of all that shocks our own moral, hygienic or parochial susceptibilities, the same ignorant and stupid lack of comprehension of the fact that every item of culture, every custom and belief, represents a value, fulfils a social function, has a positive, biological significance. . . . There is a good deal which is already undermined by missionary teaching and by indispensable claims of European interests and European prejudices. When, therefore, the legislator and administrator, in a burst of uncalled-for reformatory zeal, further prune and uproot much of the native's tree of life – is there no urgent need to stop and think?

Perhaps the West was no better than the East; perhaps primitives were superior to moderns. The world was being turned upside-down.

All of the Victorian verities came under attack in the aftermath of World War I: progress was a myth, rationality a veneer, industry a mistake. No one in authority was to be trusted; politicians and generals had turned lying into an art form; mothers and fathers would patriotically send their sons off to die. Nothing in the newspapers was true; it was all propaganda, all facts were invented. Revisionism fused with modernism, which fused with surrealism, which fused with expressionism, which fused with futurism, which fused with fascism, which fused with. . . .

54 He declared that he and the new movement in anthropology regarded the prewar approach "with its main supports of mental uniformity and orderly sequence as built upon sand" (*History and Ethnology* [London, 1922] 5). Most intriguing for the theme of "revisionism" is his method for introducing new concepts to his readers: he imagines a Melanesian islander setting out for Europe to test the principles by which the history of his own people has been formulated. This was turning things upside-down and very difficult to imagine before the war and the consequent disillusionment with Western civilization.
55 "Myth in Primitive Psychology" (1925), in Ivan Strenski, ed., *Malinowski and the Work of Myth* (Princeton, N.J., 1992), 89.
56 "Ethnology and the Study of Society" (1921), in Strenski, ed., *Malinowski,* 46–7.

Making sense of these vastly complicated phenomena and showing how they intruded into the "real" world of politics, strategy, and diplomacy is an arduous agenda. But if we are to avoid the temptation of repeating ourselves forever, of revising the revisionists or repeating the first words ever uttered on this subject, we must extend our field of vision in ways that move characters from the background to the foreground, that highlight new connections and which expand the definition of "international history."

Bibliography

Abramsky, Chimen, *War, Revolution, and the Jewish Dilemma* (London, 1975).

Adam, Magda, *The Little Entente and Europe (1920–1929)* (Budapest, 1993).

Adler, Selig, "The Congressional Election of 1918," *South Atlantic Quarterly* 37 (Oct. 1937): 447–65.

Adler, Selig, "The War Guilt Question and American Disillusionment, 1918–28," *Journal of Modern History* 23 (1951): 1–28.

Albrecht-Carrié, René, *Italy at the Paris Peace Conference* (Hamden, Conn., 1934).

Ambrosius, Lloyd E., "The United States and the Weimar Republic, 1918–1923: From the Armistice to the Ruhr Occupation," Ph.D. diss., University of Illinois, 1961.

Ambrosius, Lloyd E., "Wilson, the Republicans, and French Security After World War I," *Journal of American History* 59 (1972): 341–52.

Ambrosius, Lloyd E., "The Orthodoxy of Revisionism: Woodrow Wilson and the New Left," *Diplomatic History* 1 (1977): 199–214.

Ambrosius, Lloyd E., "Secret German-American Negotiations During the Paris Peace Conference," *American Studies/Amerikastudien* 24 (1979): 288–309.

Ambrosius, Lloyd E., *Woodrow Wilson and the American Diplomatic Tradition* (Cambridge, 1987).

Ambrosius, Lloyd E., *Wilsonian Statecraft: Theory and Practice of Liberal Internationalism During World War I* (Wilmington, Del., 1991).

Anderson, B. M., "Effects of the War on Money, Credit and Banking in France and the United States," *Preliminary Economic Studies of the War,* no. 15 (New York, 1919).

Artaud, Denise, *La Question des dettes interalliés et la reconstruction de l'Europe (1917–1929),* 2 vols. (Paris, 1978).

Aycoberry, Pierre, Jean-Paul Bled et al., eds., *Les Conséquences des traités de paix de 1919–1920 en Europe centrale et sud-orientale* (Strasbourg, 1987).

Baden, Max von, *Erinnerungen und Dokumente* (Stuttgart, 1927).

Bailey, Thomas A., *Woodrow Wilson and the Great Betrayal* (New York, 1945).

Bailey, Thomas A., *Woodrow Wilson and the Lost Peace* (Chicago, 1944).

Bainville, Jacques, *L'Allemagne* (Paris, 1949).

Bainville, Jacques, *Journal, 1901–1918* (Paris, 1939).

Bainville, Jacques, *Journal, 1919–1926* (Paris, 1948).

Baker, Ray Stannard, *Woodrow Wilson, Life and Letters,* 8 vols. (Garden City, N.Y., 1927–39).

Baker, Ray Stannard, *Woodrow Wilson and World Settlement,* 3 vols. (New York, 1922).

Baker, Ray Stannard, *What Wilson Did at Paris* (Garden City, N.Y., 1919).

Bane, Suda L., and Ralph H. Lutz, eds., *Organization of American Relief in Europe, 1918–1919* (Stanford, Calif., 1943), 26–33.

Bane, Suda L., and Ralph H. Lutz, eds., *The Blockade of Germany* (Stanford, Calif., 1942).

Barbier, Jean, *Un Frac de Nessus* (Rome, 1951).

Bariéty, Jacques, "Le Rôle de la minette dans la sidérurgie allemande après le Traité de Versailles," *Centre des recherches relations internationales de l'Université de Metz* 3 (1973).

Bariéty, Jacques, "Les Réparations allemandes, 1919–1924: objet ou prétexte à une politique rhénane de la France?" *Bulletin de la Sociéte d'Histoire Moderne* 72 (May 1973): 21–33.

Bariéty, Jacques, "Das Zustandekommen der Internationalen Rohstahlgemeinschaft 1926 als Alternative zum misslungenen 'Schwerindustriellen Projekt' des Versailler Vertrags," in Mommsen, Petzina, Weisbrod, eds., *Industrielles System,* 552–68.

Bariéty, Jacques, *Les Relations franco-allemandes après la Première Guerre Mondiale, 11 novembre 1918–10 janvier 1925: de l'exécution à la négociation* (Paris, 1977).

Bariéty, Jacques, and Antoine Fleury, eds., *Peace Movements and Initiatives in International Policy, 1867–1928* (Berne, 1987).

Barnett, Louise, *British Food Policy During the First World War* (London, 1985).

Barnett, Correlli, *The Collapse of British Power* (London, 1984).

Barrès, Maurice, *La Politique rhénane* (Paris, 1922).

Bartlett, Ruhl, *The League to Enforce Peace* (New York, 1944).

Baruch, Bernard M., *The Making of the Reparation and Economic Sections of the Treaty* (New York, 1920).

Bassett, John Spencer, *Our War With Germany* (New York, 1919).

Baumgart, Winfried, "Brest-Litovsk und Versailles: Ein Vergleich zweier Friedensschlüsse," in Bosl, ed., *Versailles,* 49–76.

Baumgart, Winfried, *Deutsche Ostpolitik 1918: Von Brest-Litovsk bis zum Ende des Ersten Weltkrieges* (Vienna, 1966).

Baumont, Maurice, *La Faillite de la paix, 1918–1939,* 2d ed. (Paris, 1946).

Beau de Loménie, E., *Le Débat de ratification du Traité de Versailles à la Chambre des Députés et dans la presse en 1919* (Paris, 1945).

Bell, Archibald C., *A History of the Blockade of Germany* (London, 1937).

Bell, H. C. F., *Woodrow Wilson and the People* (Garden City, N.Y., 1945).

Beneš, Edvard, *Souvenirs de guerre et de révolution,* 2 vols. (Paris, 1928–9).

Berg, Manfred, *Gustav Stresemann und die Vereinigten Staaten von Amerika: Weltwirtschaftliche Verflechtung und Revisionspolitik, 1907–1929* (Baden-Baden, 1990).

Berghahn, Volker R., *Germany and the Approach of War in 1914* (New York, 1973).

Bergmann, Carl, *Der Weg der Reparationen* (Frankfurt am Main, 1926).

Berle, Adolf, *Navigating the Rapids, 1918–1971: From the Papers of Adolf A. Berle,* ed. Beatrice B. Berle and Travis B. Jacobs (New York, 1973).

Bessel, Richard, "The Great War in German Memory: The Soldiers of the First World War, Demobilization, and Weimar Political Culture," *German History* 6 (1988): 20–34.

Bessel, Richard, *Germany After the First World War* (New York, 1993).

Binkley, Robert C., "Ten Years of Peace Conference History," *Journal of Modern History* 1 (1929): 607–29.

Birdsall, Paul, *Versailles Twenty Years After* (London, 1941).

Birke, Ernest, "Die französische Osteuropa-Politik, 1914–1918," *Zeitschrift für Ostforschung* 3 (1954): 321–35.

Blatt, Joel, "France and the Franco-Italian Entente, 1918–1923," *Storia delle Relazioni internazionali* 6 (1990): 173–97.

Bloch, Camille, and Pierre Renouvin, "La Genèse et la signification de l'article 231 du traité de Versailles," *Revue d'histoire de la guerre mondiale* 10 (1932): 1–24.

Blociszewski, Joseph, *La Restauration de la Pologne et la diplomatie européene* (Paris, 1927).

Boll, Friedhelm, *Frieden ohne Revolution? Friedensstrategien der deutschen Sozialdemokraten vom Erfurter Programm 1891 bis zur Revolution 1918* (Bonn, 1980).

Bonsal, Stephen, *Suitors and Suppliants: The Little Nations at Versailles,* 2d ed. (New York, 1969).

Bosl, Karl, ed., *Versailles – St. Germain – Trianon: Umbruch in Europa vor fünfzig Jahren* (Munich, 1971).

Bowman, Isaiah, *The New World: Problems in Political Geography* (Yonkers-on-Hudson, N.Y., 1921).

Brockdorff-Rantzau, Ulrich K., *Dokumente und Gedanken um Versailles* (Berlin, 1925).

Brügel, Johann Wolfgang, *Tschechen und Deutsche* (Munich, 1967).

Buitenhuis, Peter, *The Great War of Words: British, American and Canadian Propaganda and Fiction, 1914–1933* (Vancouver, 1987).

Bullitt, William C., *The Bullitt Mission to Russia* (New York, 1919).

Bullitt, William C., and Sigmund Freud, *Thomas Woodrow Wilson* (Boston, 1967).

Bunselmeyer, Robert E., *The Cost of War, 1914–1919: British Economic War Aims and the Origins of Reparations* (Hamden, Conn., 1975).

Burk, Katherine, "Diplomacy and the Private Banker: The Case of the House of Morgan," in Gustav Schmidt, ed., *Konstellationen internationaler Politik* (Bochum, 1983).

Burk, Katherine, *Britain, America, and the Sinews of War, 1914–1918* (Boston, 1985).

Burnett, Philip Mason, *Reparation at the Paris Peace Conference from the Standpoint of the American Delegation,* 2 vols. (reprint, New York, 1965).

Bussière, Éric, *La France, la Belgique et l'organisation économique de l'Europe* (Paris, 1991).

Butler, Harold, *The Lost Peace* (London, 1941).

Calder, Kenneth J., *Britain and the Origins of the New Europe, 1914–1918* (Cambridge, 1976).

Callwell, C. E., *Field Marshal Sir Henry Wilson: His Life and Diaries,* 2 vols. (London, 1927).

Cambon, Jules, "La Paix (notes inédites, 1919)," *Revue de Paris,* Nov. 1, 1937.

Campbell, F. Gregory, "The Struggle for Upper Silesia, 1919–1922," *Journal of Modern History* 42 (1970): 361–85.

Carley, Michael J., *Revolution and Intervention: The French Government and the Russian Civil War, 1917–1919* (Kingston, Ont., 1983).

Carls, Stephen, *Louis Loucheur and the Shaping of Modern France, 1916–1931* (Baton Rouge, La., 1993).

Carsten, Francis L., *The Reichswehr and Politics, 1918–1933* (Oxford, 1966).

Chatelle, Albert, *La Paix manquée?* (Paris, 1936).

Chatfield, Charles, *For Peace and Justice: Pacifism in America, 1914–1941* (Knoxville, Tenn., 1971).

Chernow, Ron, *The Warburgs: The Twentieth-Century Odyssey of a Remarkable Jewish Family* (New York, 1993).

Christoph, Jürgen, *Die politischen Reichsamnestien, 1918–1933* (Frankfurt am Main, 1989).

Churchill, Winston S., *The World Crisis* (London, 1929).

Cienciala, Anna M., and Titus Komarnicki, *From Versailles to Locarno: Keys to Polish Foreign Policy, 1919–1925* (Lawrence, Kans., 1984).

Cienciala, Anna M., "The Battle of Danzig and the Polish Corridor at the Paris Peace Conference of 1919," in Paul Latawski, ed., *The Reconstruction of Poland, 1914–1923* (London, 1992).

Clemenceau, Georges, *The Events of His Life as Told by Himself to His Former Secretary Jean Martet* (Paris, 1930).

Clemenceau, Georges, *Grandeurs et misères d'une victoire* (Paris, 1930).

Cline, Catherine Anne, "Ecumenism and Appeasement: The Bishops of the Church of England and the Treaty of Versailles," *Journal of Modern History* 61 (Dec. 1989)

Cohen, Warren I., *The American Revisionists: The Lessons of Intervention in World War I* (Chicago, 1967).

Coolidge, Archibald Cary, *Ten Years of War and Peace* (Cambridge, Mass., 1927).

Cooper, John M., "The British Response to the House-Grey Memorandum: New Evidence and New Questions," *Journal of American History* 59 (1973): 958–71.

Cooper, John M., *The Warrior and the Priest: Woodrow Wilson and Theodore Roosevelt* (Cambridge, Mass., 1983).

Cooper, John M., and Charles E. Neu, eds., *The Wilson Era: Essays in Honor of Arthur S. Link* (Arlington Heights, Ill., 1991).

Costigliola, Frank, *Awkward Dominion: American Political, Economic, and Cultural Relations with Europe, 1919–1933* (Ithaca, N.Y., 1984)

Craig, Gordon A., and Felix Gilbert, eds., *The Diplomats* (Princeton, N.J., 1953).

Creel, George, *How We Advertised America* (New York, 1920).

Creel, George, *The War, the World, and Wilson* (New York, 1920).

Crunden, Robert, *Ministers of Reform: The Progressives' Achievement in American Civilization* (New York, 1982).

Curry, G., "Woodrow Wilson, Jan Smuts, and the Versailles Settlement," *American Historical Review* 66 (1961): 968–86.

Dahlin, Ebba, *French and German Public Opinion on Declared War Aims* (Stanford, Calif., 1933).

Dallin, Alexander et al., *Russian Diplomacy and Eastern Europe, 1914–1917* (New York, 1963).

Davies, Norman, "The Poles in Great Britain, 1914–1919," *Slavonic and East European Review* (1972): 63–82.

Davis, Joseph S., "Recent Economic and Financial Progress in Germany," *The Review of Economic Statistics* 3, no. 6 (1921).

Day, Clive, "The Atmosphere and Organization of the Peace Conference," in House and Seymour, *What Really Happened at Paris.*

Debo, Richard, "The Maniulskii Mission: An Early Soviet Effort to Negotiate with France, August 1918–April 1919," *International History Review* 8 (1986):214–35.

Debo, Richard K., *Revolution and Survival: The Foreign Policy of Soviet Russia, 1917–1918* (Toronto, 1979).

Debo, Richard K., *Survival and Consolidation: The Foreign Policy of Soviet Russia, 1918–1921* (Montreal, 1992).

de Groot, Gerard, *Blighty: British Society in the Era of the Great War* (London, 1996).

Demm, Eberhard, "Propaganda and Caricature in World War I," *Journal of Contemporary History* 28 (1993): 163–92.

Dickmann, Fritz, *Die Kriegsschuldfrage auf der Friedenskonferenz von Paris 1919* (Munich, 1964).

Digre, Brian K., *Imperialism's New Clothes: The Repartition of Tropical Africa, 1914–1918* (New York, 1990).

Dmowski, Roman, *Polityka polska i odbudowanie pa stwa* (Warsaw, 1925).

Dockrill, Michael, and Zara Steiner, "The Foreign Office at the Paris Peace Conference in 1919," *International History Review* 2 (1980): 55–86.

Dockrill, Michael, and J. Douglas Goold, *Peace Without Promise: Britain and the Peace Conferences, 1919–1923* (London, 1981).

Dodd, William E., *Woodrow Wilson and His Work* (Garden City, N.Y., 1920).

Donald, Robert, *The Polish Corridor and Its Consequences* (London, 1930).

Dorten, J. A., "Le Général Mangin en Rhénanie," *Revue des deux mondes* (July 1937): 39–67.

Dorten, J. A., *La Tragédie rhénane* (Paris, 1945).

Duggan, Stephen P., ed., *The League of Nations: The Principle and the Practices* (Boston, 1919).

Duroselle, Jean-Baptiste, *Clemenceau* (Paris, 1988).

Duroselle, Jean-Baptiste, "Clemenceau a sacrifié la réalisation complète de son programme au maintien d'une alliance – garanties comprises – qu'il croyait plus solide qu'elle n'était en effet," in *Clemenceau et la Justice* (Paris, 1983).

Duroselle, Jean-Baptiste, *La France et les Français, 1914–1920* (Paris, 1972).

Duroselle, Jean-Baptiste, *La Grande Guerre des Français; l'incompréhensible* (Paris, 1995).

Ebert, Friedrich, *Schriften, Aufzeichnungen und Reden* (Dresden, 1926).

Egerton, George W., "The Lloyd George Government and the Creation of the League of Nations," *American Historical Review* 79 (1974): 419–44.

Egerton, George W., *Britain and the Creation of the League of Nations: Strategy, Politics, and International Organization, 1914–1919* (Chapel Hill, N.C., 1978).

Egerton, George W., "Britain and the 'Great Betrayal': Anglo-American Relations and the Struggle for United States Ratification of the Treaty of Versailles, 1919–1920," *Historical Journal* 21 (1978): 885–911.

Egerton, George W., "The Lloyd George War Memoirs: A Study in the Politics of Memory," *Journal of Modern History* 60 (1988): 55–94.

Eisterer, Klaus et al., eds., *Tirol und der Erste Weltkrieg* (Innsbruck, 1995).

Elcock, Howard, "Britain and the Russo-Polish Frontier, 1919–1921," *Historical Journal* 12 (1969): 137–54.

Elcock, Howard, *Portrait of a Decision: The Council of Four and the Treaty of Versailles* (London, 1972).

Elcock, Howard, "J. M. Keynes at the Paris Peace Conference," in Milo Keynes, ed., *Essays on John Maynard Keynes* (Cambridge, 1975).

Epstein, Klaus, *Matthias Erzberger and the Dilemma of German Democracy* (Princeton, N.J., 1959).

Erdmann, Karl-Dietrich, *Adenauer in der Rheinlandpolitik nach dem Ersten Weltkrieg* (Stuttgart, 1966).

Erdmenger, Katharina, *Neue Ansätze zur Organisation Europas nach dem Ersten Weltkrieg (1917–1933): Ein neues Verständnis von Europa* (Sinzheim, 1995).

Eschenburg, Theodor, "Das Problem der deutschen Einheit nach den beiden Weltkriegen," *Vierteljahrshefte für Zeitgeschichte* 5 (1957): 107–34.

Eubank, Keith, *Paul Cambon, Master Diplomatist* (Norman, Okla., 1960).

Farrar, Lancelot L., *Divide and Conquer: German Efforts to Conclude a Separate Peace, 1914–1918* (Boulder, Colo., 1978).

Fair, John D., *Harold Temperley* (Newark, N.J., 1992).

Feldman, Gerald D., *The Great Disorder: Politics, Economics, and Society in the German Inflation, 1914–1923* (New York, 1993).

Feldman, Gerald D., *Iron and Steel in the German Inflation, 1916–1923* (Princeton, N.J., 1977).

Feldman, Gerald D., "Economic and Social Problems of the German Demobilization, 1918–1919," *Journal of Modern History* 47 (1975): 1–47.

Feldman, Gerald D., "Die Demobilmachung und die Sozialordnung der Zwischenkriegszeit in Europa," *Geschichte und Gesellschaft* 9 (1983): 156–77.

Feldman, Gerald D., Eberhard Kolb, and Reinhard Rürup, "Die Massenbewegungen der Arbeiterschaft in Deutschland am Ende des Ersten Weltkrieges (1917–1920)," *Politische Vierteljahrsschrift* 13 (1972): 84–105.

Felix, David, "Reparations Reconsidered with a Vengeance," *Central European History* 4 (1971): 171–9.

Fellner, Fritz, "Die Friedensordnung von Paris 1919–1920," in Isabella Ackerl, Walter Hummelburger, and Hans Mommsen, eds., *Politik und Gesellschaft im alten und neuen Österreich: Festschrift für Rudolf Neck zum 60. Geburtstag*, 2 vols. (Vienna, 1981), 2: 39–54.

Fellner, Fritz, *Vom Dreibund zum Völkerbund: Studien zur Geschichte der internationalen Beziehungen, 1882–1919* (Munich, 1994).

Ferguson, Niall, *Paper and Iron: Hamburg Business and German Politics in the Era of Inflation 1897–1927* (Cambridge, 1995).

Ferguson, Niall, "Keynes and the German Inflation," *English Historical Review* 110/436 (1995): 368–91.

Ferro, Marc, *The Great War, 1914–1918*, trans. N. Stone (London, 1973).

Fest, Wilfried B., "British War Aims and German Peace Feelers During the First World War (December 1916–November 1918)," *Historical Journal* 15 (1972): 285–308.

Fest, Wilfried B., *Peace or Partition: The Habsburg Monarchy and British Policy, 1914–1918* (London, 1978).

Fiebig-von Hase, Ragnhild, and Maria Sturm, "Die transatlantischen Wirtschaftsbeziehungen in der Nachkriegsplanung Deutschlands, der alliierten Westmächte und der USA, 1914–1917," *Militärgeschichtliche Mitteilungen* 51 (1993): 1–34.

Fink, Carole, Isabel V. Hull, and MacGregor Knox, eds., *German Nationalism and the European Response, 1890–1945* (Norman, Okla., 1985).

Fink, Carole, Axel Frohn, and Jürgen Heideking, eds., *Genoa, Rapallo, and European Reconstruction in 1922* (New York, 1992).

Fischer, Fritz, *Germany's Aims in the First World War* (London, 1967).

Fischer, Fritz, "Twenty Years Later: Looking Back at the 'Fischer Controversy' and Its Consequences," *Central European History* 21 (1988): 207–23.

Floto, Inga, *Colonel House in Paris: A Study of American Policy at the Paris Peace Conference, 1919* (Aarhus, 1973).

Foglesong, David S., *America's Secret War Against Bolshevism: United States Intervention in the Russian Civil War, 1917–1920* (Chapel Hill, N.C., 1995).

Foltz, David A., "The War Crimes Issue at the Paris Peace Conference, 1919–1920," Ph.D. diss., American University, 1978.

Forcey, Charles B., *The Crossroads of Liberalism: Croly, Weil, Lippmann, and the Progressive Era, 1900–1925* (New York, 1925).

Fortuna, Ursula, *Der Völkerbundsgedanke in Deutschland während des Ersten Weltkrieges* (Zurich, 1974).

Foch, Ferdinand, *Mémoires pour servir à l'histoire de la guerre de 1914–1918*, 2 vols. (Paris, 1931).

French, David, *The Strategy of the Lloyd George Coalition, 1916–1918* (Oxford, 1995).

French, David, *British Strategy and War Aims, 1914–1916* (London, 1986).

Fridenson, Patrick, *The French Home Front, 1914–1918* (Providence, R.I., 1992).

Fry, Michael G., "The Imperial War Cabinet, the United States, and the Freedom of the Seas," *Journal of the Royal United Services Institution* 110/640 (1965): 353–62.

Fry, Michael G., "Britain, the Allies, and the Problem of Russia, 1918–1919," *Journal of Contemporary History* 2 (1967): 62–84.

Fry, Michael G., *Illusions of Security: North Atlantic Diplomacy, 1918–1922* (Buffalo, N.Y., 1972).

Fry, Michael G., *Lloyd George and Foreign Policy* (Montreal, 1977).

Gajda, Patricia A., *Postscript to Victory: British Policy and the German-Polish Borderlands, 1919–1925* (Washington, D.C., 1982).

Garraty, John, *Henry Cabot Lodge* (New York, 1953).

Gatzke, Hans W., *Germany's Drive to the West: A Study of Germany's Western War Aims During the First World War* (Baltimore, 1950).

Gatzke, Hans W., "Russo-German Military Collaborations During the Weimar Republic," *American Historical Review* 63 (1958):565–97.

Geiss, Immanuel, *Der polnische Grenzstreifen, 1914–1918: Ein Beitrag zur deutschen Kriegszielpolitik im Ersten Weltkrieg* (Lübeck, 1960).

Gelfand, Lawrence E., "Where Ideals Confront Self-Interest: Wilsonian Foreign Policy," *Diplomatic History* 18 (winter 1994).

Gelfand, Lawrence E., *The Inquiry* (New Haven, Conn., 1963).

Gelfand, Lawrence E., ed., *Herbert Hoover: The Great War and Its Aftermath, 1914–1923* (Iowa City, Iowa, 1979).

George, Alexander L., and Juliette L. George, *Woodrow Wilson and Colonel House: A Personality Study* (New York, 1956).

Gerard, Jolyon R., *Bridge on the Rhine: American Diplomacy and the Rhineland, 1919–1923* (Ann Arbor, Mich., 1977).

Gerson, Louis L., "The Poles," in Joseph P. O'Grady, ed., *The Immigrants' Influence on Wilson's Peace Policies* (Lexington, Ky., 1967), 272–86.

Gerson, Louis L., *Woodrow Wilson and the Rebirth of Poland, 1914–1920* (Hamden, Conn., 1972).

Gilbert, Charles, *American Financing of World War I* (Westport, Conn., 1970).

Glaser-Schmidt, Elisabeth, "Von Versailles nach Berlin: Überlegungen zur Neugestaltung der deutsch-amerikanischen Beziehungen in der Ära Harding," in Norbert Finzsch and Hermann Wellenreuther, eds., *Liberalitas: Festschrift für Erich Angermann* (Stuttgart, 1992), 319–42.

Glaser-Schmidt, Elisabeth, "German and American Concepts to Restore a Liberal World Trading System After World War I," in Schröder, ed., *Confrontation and Cooperation*, 353–76.

Goldstein, Erik, *Winning the Peace: British Diplomatic Strategy, Peace Planning, and the Paris Peace Conference, 1916–1920* (Oxford, 1991).

Gorlow, Sergej, "Die geheime Militärkooperation zwischen der Sowjetunion und dem deutschen Reich, 1920–1933," *Vierteljahrshefte für Zeitgeschichte* 44 (1996): 133–65.

Gräber, Gerhard, and Matthias Spindler, *Revolverrepublik am Rhein: Die Pfalz und ihre Separatisten: 1. November 1918–November 1923* (Landau, 1992).

Grayson, Cary T., "The Colonel's Folly and the President's Distress," *American Heritage* 15 (Oct. 1964): 4–7, 94–101.

Grigg, John, *Lloyd George: From Peace to War, 1912–1916* (London, 1985).

Grupp, Peter, "Vom Waffenstillstand zum Versailler Vertrag: Die aussen - und friedenspolitischen Zielvorstellungen der deutschen Reichsführung," in Karl Dietrich Bracher, ed., *Die Weimarer Republik, 1918–1933* (Düsseldorf, 1988).

Grupp, Peter, *Deutsche Aussenpolitik im Schatten von Versailles, 1918–1920* (Paderborn, 1988).

Hadler, Frank, "Peacemaking 1919 im Spiegel der Briefe Edvard Beneš' von der Pariser Friedenskonferenz," *Berliner Jahrbuch für osteuropäische Geschichte* 1, no. 1 (1994): 213–55.

Hankey, Maurice, *The Supreme Control at the Paris Peace Conference* (London, 1963).

Hankey, Maurice, *Diplomacy by Conference* (London, 1946).

Hanna, Martha, *The Mobilization of Intellect: French Scholars and Writers During the Great War* (Cambridge, Mass., 1996).

Hanotaux, Gabriel, *Carnets (1907–1925),* ed. Georges Dethan et al. (Paris, 1982).

Hansen, Harry, *The Adventures of the Fourteen Points* (New York, 1919).

Hardach, Gerd, *The First World War* (London, 1977).

Hardinge, Charles, Lord, *Old Diplomacy: The Reminiscences of Lord Hardinge of Penshurst* (London, 1947).

Harris, José, "Bureaucrats and Businessmen in British Food Control, 1916–1919," in Katherine Burk, ed., *War and the State: The Transformation of British Government, 1914–1919* (London, 1982).

Haskins, Charles Homer, "The New Boundaries of Germany," in House and Seymour, eds., *What Really Happened at Paris.*

Haskins, Charles Homer, and Robert Howard Lord, *Some Problems of the Peace Conference* (Cambridge, Mass., 1920).

Haupts, Leo, "Zur deutschen und britischen Friedenspolitik in der Pariser Friedenskonferenz: Britisch-deutsche Separatverhandlungen im April-Mai 1919?," *Historische Zeitschrift* 217 (1973): 64–5.

Haupts, Leo, *Deutsche Friedenspolitik, 1918–19: Eine Alternative zur Machtpolitik des Ersten Weltkrieges* (Düsseldorf, 1976).

Haupts, Leo, *Graf Brockdorff-Rantzau: Diplomat und Minister im Kaiserreich und der Republik* (Göttingen, 1984).

Hawley, Ellis W., *The Great War and the Search for a Modern Order: A History of the American People and Their Institutions* (New York, 1979).

Heater, Derek, *National Self-Determination: Woodrow Wilson and His Legacy* (London, 1994).

Heideking, Jürgen, "Vom Versailler Vertrag zur Genfer Abrüstungskonferenz: Das Scheitern der alliierten Militärkontrollpolitik gegenüber Deutschland nach dem Ersten Weltkrieg," *Militärgeschichtliche Mitteilungen* 28 (1980): 45–68.

Heideking, Jürgen, *Areopag der Diplomaten: Die Pariser Botschafterkonferenz der europäischen Hauptmächte und die Probleme der europäischen Politik, 1920–1931* (Husum, 1979).

Herman, Sondra, *Eleven Against War: Studies in American Internationalist Thought, 1898–1921* (Stanford, Calif., 1969).

Herwig, Holger H., "Admirals vs. Generals: The War Aims of the Imperial German Navy, 1914–1918," *Central European History* 5 (1972): 208–33.

Hildebrand, Klaus, *Das vergangene Reich: Deutsche Aussenpolitik von Bismarck bis Hitler, 1871–1945* (Stuttgart, 1995).

Hogan, Michael J., "The United States and the Problem of International Economic Control: American Attitudes Toward European Reconstruction, 1918–1920," *Pacific Historical Review* 44 (1975): 84–103.

Hogan, Michael J., *Informal Entente: The Private Structure of Cooperation in Anglo-American Economic Diplomacy, 1918–1928* (Columbia, Mo., 1977).

Hogenhuis-Seliverstoff, Anne, *Les Relations franco-soviétiques, 1917–1924* (Paris, 1981).

Holborn, Hajo, *The Political Collapse of Europe* (New York, 1951).

Holtfrerich, Carl-Ludwig, *Die deutsche Inflation, 1914–1923* (Berlin, 1980).

Hölzle, Erwin, *Die Selbstentmachtung Europas: Das Experiment des Friedens vor und im Ersten Weltkrieg* (Frankfurt am Main, 1975).

Hoover, Herbert, *The Ordeal of Woodrow Wilson* (New York, 1958).

Horak, Stephen, *Poland and Her National Minorities, 1919–1939* (New York, 1961).

Horne, John N., *Labour at War: France and Britain, 1914–1918* (Oxford, 1991).

House, Edward M., and Charles Seymour, eds., *What Really Happened at Paris* (New York, 1921).

Houston, David F., *Eight Years with Wilson's Cabinet, 1913–1920*, 2 vols. (New York, 1926).

Hovi, Karlevo, *Cordon sanitaire ou barrière de l'est? The Emergence of the French East European Alliance Policy, 1917–1919* (Turku, 1975).

Hovi, Karlevo, *Alliance de revers: Stabilization of France's Alliance Politics in East Central Europ, 1919–1921* (Turku, 1984).

Howard, Esme, *Theatre of Life* (Boston, 1935–6).

Howard, N. P., "The Social and Political Consequences of the Allied Food Blockade of Germany, 1918–1919," *German History* 11 (1993): 161–88.

Hudson, Manley O., "The Protection of Minorities and Natives in Transferred Territories," in House and Seymour, eds., *What Really Happened at Paris*.

Iancu, Carol, *Les Juifs en Roumanie (1866–1919): de l'exclusion à l'émancipation* (Aix-en-Provence, 1978).

Jacquot, Paul, *General Gérard und die Pfalz*, ed. Ritter von Eberlein (Berlin, 1920).

Jaffe, Lorna S., *The Decision to Disarm Germany: British Policy Towards Postwar German Disarmament, 1914–1919* (London, 1985).

Jardin, Pierre, "La Politique rhénane de Paul Tirard (1920–1923)," *Revue d'Allemagne* (Apr.–June 1989).

Jessop, T. E., *The Treaty of Versailles: Was It Just?* (London, 1942).

Johansson, Rune, *Small State in Boundary Conflict: Belgium and the Belgian-German Border, 1914–1919* (Lund, 1988).

Johnson, Paul, *Modern Times: The World from the Twenties to the Eighties* (New York, 1983).

Joll, James, *The Origins of the First World War* (New York, 1984).

Jones, Thomas, *Whitehall Diary, 1916–1925*, ed. Keith Middlemas (London, 1969).

Jordan, W. M., *Great Britain, France, and the German Problem, 1918–1939: A Study of Anglo-French Relations in the Making and Maintenance of the Versailles Settlement* (London, 1943).

Joyce, James A., *Broken Star: The Story of the League of Nations (1919–1939)* (Swansea, 1978).

Kabisch, Thomas R., *Deutsches Kapital in den USA: Beiträge zur Wirtschaftsgeschichte* (Stuttgart, 1982).

Karski, Jan, *The Great Powers and Poland, 1919–1945: From Versailles to Yalta* (Lanham, Md., 1985).

Kaspi, André, *Les Temps des Américains: Le concours américain à la France en 1917–1918* (Paris, 1976).

Kaufman, Burton I., *Efficiency and Expansion: Foreign Trade Organization in the Wilson Administration* (Westport, Conn., 1974).

Keiger, J. F. V., *Raymond Poincaré* (Cambridge, 1997).

Kennan, George F., *American Diplomacy* (Chicago, 1951).

Kennan, George F., *Russia Leaves the War* (Princeton, N.J., 1956).

Kent, Bruce, *The Spoils of War: The Politics, Economics, and Diplomacy of Reparations, 1918–1922* (Oxford, 1989).

Kern, Werner, *Die Rheintheorie der historisch-politischen Literatur Frankreichs im Ersten Weltkrieg* (Saarbrücken, 1973).

Keylor, William R., "Rise and Demise of the Franco-American Guarantee Pact, 1919–1921," *Proceedings of the Annual Meeting of the Western Society for French History* 15 (1978): 367–77.

Keylor, William R., *Jacques Bainville and the Renaissance of Royalist History in Twentieth-Century France* (Baton Rouge, La., 1979).

Keylor, William R., " 'Lafayette, We Have Quit!': Wilsonian Policy and French Security After Versailles," in Nancy L. Roelker and Charles K. Warner, eds., *Two Hundred Years of Franco-American Relations* (Newport, R.I., 1981), 44–75.

Keylor, William R., " 'How They Advertised France': The French Propaganda Campaign in the United States During the Breakup of the Franco-American Entente, 1918–1923," *Diplomatic History* 17 (Summer 1993): 351–73.

Keynes, John Maynard, *The Economic Consequences of the Peace* (London, 1920).

Keynes, John Maynard, *The Revision of the Treaty* (London, 1922).

Keynes, John Maynard, *Essays in Persuasion* (London, 1931).

Keynes, John Maynard, *Essays in Biography* (London, 1933).

Keynes, John Maynard, *Two Memoirs* (London, 1949).

Kimmich, Christopher M., *The Free City: Danzig and German Foreign Policy, 1919–1934* (New Haven, Conn., 1968).

Kimmich, Christopher M., *Germany and the League of Nations* (Chicago, 1976).

King, Jere C., *Generals and Politicians: Conflict Between France's High Command, Parliament, and Government, 1914–1918* (Berkeley, Calif., 1951).

King, Jere C., *Foch versus Clemenceau: France and German Dismemberment, 1918–1919* (Cambridge, Mass., 1960).

Kitchen, Martin, *The Silent Dictatorship: The Politics of the German High Command under Hindenburg and Ludendorff, 1916–1918* (London, 1976).

Klein, Fritz, *Die diplomatischen Beziehungen Deutschlands zur Sowjetunion, 1917–1932* (Berlin, 1953).

Klein, Fritz, "Der Erste Weltkrieg in der Geschichtswissenschaft der DDR," *Zeitschrift für Geschichtswissenschaft* 42 (1994): 293–302.

Kleine-Ahlbrandt, W. Laird, *The Burden of Victory: France, Britain, and the Enforcement of the Versailles Peace, 1919–1925* (Lanham, Md., 1995).

Klümpen, Heinrich, *Deutsche Aussenpolitik zwischen Versailles und Rapallo: Revisionismus oder Neuorientierung?* (Münster, 1992).

Klotz, Louis-Lucien, *De la Guerre à la Paix, souvenirs et documents* (Paris, 1924).

Knock, Thomas J., *To End All Wars: Woodrow Wilson and the Quest for a New World Order* (New York, 1992).

Koenen, Gerd, "Überprüfung an einem 'Nexus': Der Bolschewismus und die deutschen

Intellektuellen nach Revolution und Weltkrieg, 1917–1924," *Tel Aviver Jahrbuch für deutsche Geschichte: Deutschland und Russland* 24 (1995): 359–91.

Kolb, Eberhard, "Internationale Rahmenbedingungen einer demokratischen Neuordung in Deutschland, 1918–19," in Lothar Albertin and Werner Link, eds., *Politische Parteien auf dem Weg zur parlamentarischen Demokratie in Deutschland: Entwicklungslinien bis zur Gegenwart* (Düsseldorf, 1981).

Kreis, Georg, "Entre deux étapes de la diplomatie multilatérale permanente: Réflexions et jugements sur la Société des Nations au moment de la fondation des Nations Unies," *Relations internationales* 39 (1984): 373–87.

Krüger, Peter, *Deutschland und die Reparationen, 1918–19: Die Genesis des Reparationsproblems in Deutschland zwischen Waffenstillstand und Versailler Friedensschluss* (Stuttgart, 1973).

Krüger, Peter, "Die Reparationen und das Scheitern einer deutschen Verständigungspolitik auf der Pariser Friedenskonferenz im Jahre 1919," *Historische Zeitschrift* 221 (1975): 326–72.

Krüger, Peter, "Das Reparationsproblem der Weimarer Republik in fragwürdiger Sicht: Kritische Überlegungen zur neuesten Forschung," *Vierteljahrshefte für Zeitgeschichte* 29 (1981): 21–47.

Krüger, Peter, *Die Aussenpolitik der Republik von Weimar* (Darmstadt, 1985).

Krüger, Peter, *Versailles: Deutsche Aussenpolitik zwischen Revisionismus und Friedenssicherung* (Munich, 1986).

Krüger, Peter, "German Disappointment and Anti-Western Resentment, 1918–1919," in Schröder, ed., *Confrontation and Cooperation*, 323–36.

Kuehl, Warren F., *Seeking World Order: The United States and International Organization to 1920* (Nashville, Tenn., 1968).

Kunz, Hans Beat, *Weltrevolution und Völkerbund: Die schweizerische Aussenpolitik unter dem Eindruck der bolschewistischen Bedrohung, 1918–1923* (Berne, 1981).

Lacroix-Riz, Annie, "Le Vatican et les buts de guerre germaniques de 1914 à 1918: le rêve d'une Europe allemande," *Revue d'Histoire moderne et contemporaine* 42 (1995): 517–55.

Lamont, Edward M., *The Ambassador from Wall Street: The Story of Thomas W. Lamont, J. P. Morgan's Chief Executive* (Lanham, Md., 1994).

Lansing, Robert, *The Peace Negotiations: A Personal Narrative* (Boston, 1921).

Lansing, Robert, *The Big Four and Others of the Peace Conference* (Boston, 1921).

Lapradelle, A. de, ed., *La Paix de Versailles*, 13 vols. (Paris, 1930–2).

Laroche, Louis-Pierre, "L'affaire Dutasta: Les dernières conversations diplomatiques pour sauver l'empire des Habsbourg," *Revue d'Histoire Diplomatique* 108 (1994).

Latawski, Paul, "The Dmowski-Namier Feud," *Polin* 2 (1987): 37–49.

Lawrence, David, *The True Story of Woodrow Wilson* (New York, 1924).

Lentin, Antony, *Lloyd George, Woodrow Wilson, and the Guilt of Germany: An Essay in the Pre-History of Appeasement* (Leicester, 1984).

Lentin, Antony, "Philip Kerr e l'aggressione della Germania'," in Giulio Guderzo, ed., *Lord Lothian: Una Vita per la Pace* (Florence, 1986).

Lentin, Antony, *Die Drachensaat von Versailles: Die Schuld der "Friedensmacher"* (Leoni am Starnberger See, 1988).

Lentin, Antony "The Treaty That Never Was: Lloyd George and the Abortive Anglo-French Alliance of 1919," in Judith Loades, ed., *The Life and Times of David Lloyd George* (Bangor, Me., 1991), 115–28.

Lentin, Antony, "Several Types of Ambiguity: Lloyd George at the Paris Peace Conference," *Diplomacy and Statecraft* 6, no. 1 (Mar. 1995): 223–51.

Levene, Mark, "Nationalism and its Alternatives in the International Arena: The Jewish Question at Paris, 1919," *Journal of Contemporary History* 28 (1993): 511–31.

Levin, N. Gordon, *Woodrow Wilson and World Politics: America's Response to War and Revolution* (New York, 1968).

Lhopital, René Michel, *Foch, l'armistice, et la paix* (Paris, 1938).

Link, Arthur S., *Wilson, the Diplomatist: A Look at His Major Foreign Policies* (Baltimore, 1957).

Link, Arthur S., *President Wilson and His English Critics* (Oxford, 1959).

Link, Arthur S., *Wilson: The Struggle for Neutrality* (Princeton, N.J., 1960).

Link, Arthur S., *The Higher Realism of Woodrow Wilson and Other Essays* (Nashville, Tenn., 1971).

Link, Arthur S., *Wilson's Diplomacy: An International Symposium* (Cambridge, Mass., 1973).

Link, Arthur S., *Woodrow Wilson: Revolution, War, and Peace* (Arlington Heights, Ill., 1979).

Link, Arthur S., ed., *Woodrow Wilson and a Revolutionary World, 1913–1921* (Chapel Hill, N.C., 1982).

Link, Werner, *Die amerikanische Stabilisierungspolitik in Deutschland, 1921–1932* (Düsseldorf, 1970).

Lippmann, Walter, *U.S. Foreign Policy: Shield of the Republic* (Boston, 1943).

Livermore, Seward, *Politics Is Adjourned: Woodrow Wilson and the War Congress, 1916–1918* (Middletown, Conn., 1966).

Lloyd George, David, *The Truth About Reparations and War Debts* (London, 1932).

Lloyd George, David, *Memoirs of the Peace Conference*, 2 vols. (New Haven, Conn., 1939).

Lloyd George, David, *The Truth About the Peace Treaties* (London, 1938).

Lloyd George, David, *War Memoirs* (London, 1938).

Lodge, Henry Cabot, *The Senate and the League of Nations* (New York, 1925).

Łossowski, Piotr, *Między wojną a pokojem* (Warsaw, 1976).

Loucheur, Louis, *Carnets secrets, 1908–1932* (Brussels, 1962).

Louis, William Roger, *Great Britain and Germany's Lost Colonies, 1914–1919* (Oxford, 1967).

Low, Alfred D., *The Anschluss Movement, 1918–1919, and the Paris Peace Conference* (Philadelphia, 1974).

Luckau, Alma, *The German Delegation at the Paris Peace Conference* (New York, 1941).

Lundgreen-Nielsen, Kay, *The Polish Problem at the Paris Peace Conference: A Study of the Great Powers and the Poles, 1918–1919* (Odense, 1979).

Lundgreen-Nielsen, Kay, "Woodrow Wilson and the Rebirth of Poland," in Link, ed., *Woodrow Wilson and a Revolutionary World*.

Lundgreen-Nielsen, Kay, "The Mayer Thesis Reconsidered: The Poles and the Paris Peace Conference, 1919," *International History Review* 7 (1985): 68–102.

Macartney, C. A., *National States and National Minorities*, 2d ed. (London, 1968).

Maddox, Robert, *The Unknown War with Russia: Wilson's Siberian Intervention* (San Rafael, Calif., 1977).

Mangin, Charles, "Lettres de Rhénanie," *Revue de Paris* (Apr. 1936): 481–526.

Mangin, L.-E., *La France sur le Rhin* (Geneva, 1945).

Mantoux, Etienne, *The Carthaginian Peace or the Economic Consequences of Mr. Keynes* (New York, 1952).

Marchand, C. Roland, *The American Peace Movement and Social Reform* (Princeton, N.J., 1972).

Marder, Arthur J., *From the Dreadnought to Scapa Flow: The Royal Navy in the Fisher Era, 1904–1919: Victory and Aftermath (January 1918–June 1919)* (Oxford, 1970).

Marechal, Evert, "De belgisch-russische betrekkingen, 1917–1920," *Studia diplomatica* 46 (1993): 35–58.

Margulies, Herbert F., *The Mild Reservations and the League of Nations Controversy in the Senate* (Columbia, Mo., 1989).

Marks, Sally, "Reparations Reconsidered: A Reminder," *Central European History* 2 (1969): 356–65.

Marks, Sally, "The Myth of Reparations," *Central European History* 11 (1978): 231–55.

Marks, Sally, *Innocent Abroad: Belgium at the Peace Conference of 1919* (Chapel Hill, N.C., 1981).

Marks, Sally, "Ménage à trois: The Negotiations for an Anglo-French-Belgian Alliance in 1922," *International History Review* 4 (1982): 524–52.

Marks, Sally, "1918 and After: The Postwar Era," in Martel, ed., *Origins of the Second World War Reconsidered,* 17–48.

Marks, Sally, *The Illusion of Peace* (New York, 1989).

Marston, Frank S., *The Peace Conference of 1919: Organization and Procedure* (London, 1944).

Martel, Gordon, ed., *The Origins of the Second World War Reconsidered: The A. J. P. Taylor Debate After Twenty-Five Years* (London, 1986).

Martel, Gordon, "The Revisionist as Moralist – A. J. P. Taylor and the Lessons of European History," in Martel, ed., *Origins of the Second World War Reconsidered.*

Martel, Gordon, "From Round Table to New Europe," in Andrea Bosco and Cornelia Navari, eds., *Chatham House and British Foreign Policy, 1919–1945: The Royal Institute of International Affairs During the Interwar Period* (London, 1994), 13–40.

Martin, Laurence W., *Peace without Victory: Woodrow Wilson and the British Liberals* (New Haven, Conn., 1958).

Marwick, Arthur, *The Deluge: British Society and the First World War,* 2d ed. (London, 1991).

Maurras, Charles, *Les Trois Idées du Président Wilson* (Paris, 1919).

May, Henry, *The End of American Innocence* (New York, 1959).

Mayer, Arno J., *The Political Origins of the New Diplomacy, 1917–1918* (New Haven, Conn., 1959).

Mayer, Arno J., *Politics and Diplomacy of Peacemaking: Containment and Counterrevolution at Versailles, 1918–1919* (London, 1968).

Mayer, Karl, *Die Weimarer Republik und das Problem der Sicherheit in den deutsch-französischen Beziehungen, 1918–1925* (Frankfurt am Main, 1990).

McCallum, R. B., *Public Opinion and the Last Peace* (London, 1944).

McCrum, Robert, "French Rhineland Policy at the Paris Peace Conference, 1919," *Historical Journal* 21 (1978):623–48.

McDougall, Walter A. "Political Economy versus National Sovereignty: French Structures for German Economic Integration After Versailles," *Journal of Modern History* 51 (1979): 4–23.

McDougall, Walter A., *France's Rhineland Diplomacy, 1914–1924: The Last Bid for a Balance of Power in Europe* (Princeton, N.J., 1978).

Melchionni, Maria Grazia, *La Vittoria Mutilata: Problemi ed incertezze della politica estera italiana sul finire della grande guerra (ottobre 1918–gennaio 1919)* (Rome, 1981).

Mermeix, Gabriel Terrail, *Le Combat des trois* (Paris, 1922).

Messerschmidt, Manfred, "German Military Effectiveness Between 1919 and 1939," in

Alan R. Millett and Williamson Murray, eds., *Military Effectiveness: The Interwar Period* (Boston, 1988).

Miller, David Hunter, *My Diary at the Conference of Paris,* 21 vols. (New York, 1924).

Miller, Susanne, *Die Bürde der Macht: Die deutsche Sozialdemokratie, 1918–1920* (Düsseldorf, 1978).

Miller, Steven E., Sean M. Lynn-Jones, and Stephen Van Evera, eds., *Military Strategy and the Origins of the First World War* (Princeton, N.J., 1991).

Miller, David Hunter, *The Drafting of the Covenant,* 2 vols. (New York, 1928).

Miquel, Pierre, *Poincaré* (Paris, 1961).

Miquel, Pierre, *La Paix de Versailles et l'opinion publique française* (Paris, 1972).

Moggridge, Donald E., *Maynard Keynes: An Economist's Biography* (London, 1992).

Mommsen, Hans, *Die verspielte Freiheit: Der Weg der Republik von Weimar in den Untergang* (Berlin, 1990).

Mommsen, Hans, Dietmar Petzina, and Bernd Weisbrod, eds., *Industrielles System und politische Entwicklung in der Weimarer Republik* (Düsseldorf, 1974).

Mommsen, Wolfgang J., ed., *Die Organisierung des Friedens: Demobilmachung, 1918–1920* (Göttingen, 1983).

Mommsen, Wolfgang J., ed., *Kultur und Krieg: Die Rolle der Intellektuellen, Künstler und Schriftsteller im Ersten Weltkrieg* (Munich, 1996).

Monnet, Jean, *Memoirs* (London, 1978).

Mordacq, Jean Jules Henri, *Le Ministère Clemenceau: journal d'un témoin,* 4 vols. (Paris, 1930).

Mordacq, Jean Jules Henri, *L'Armistice du 11 novembre 1918: récit d'un témoin* (Paris, 1937).

Morgan, Kenneth, *Consensus and Disunity: The Lloyd George Coalition Government, 1918–1922* (Oxford, 1979).

Morgenthau, Hans, *In Defense of the National Interest: A Critical Examination of American Foreign Policy* (New York, 1951).

Mulder, John, "A Gospel of Order," in Cooper and Neu, eds., *The Wilson Era.*

Nadler, Harry E., *The Rhenish Separatist Movements During the Early Weimar Republic, 1918–1924* (New York, 1987).

Namier, Lewis, *Diplomatic Prelude* (London, 1948).

Namier, Lewis, *Europe in Decay* (London, 1950).

Nelson, Harold I., *Land and Power: British and Allied Policy on Germany's Frontiers, 1916–1919* (London, 1963).

Nelson, Keith L., "What Colonel House Overlooked in the Armistice," *Mid-America* 51 (Apr. 1969): 75–91.

Nelson, Keith L., *Victors Divided: America and the Allies in Germany, 1918–1923* (Berkeley, Calif., 1975).

Nicolson, Harold, *Peacemaking 1919* (London, 1933).

Nielson, Jonathan M., *American Historians in War and Peace: Patriotism, Diplomacy, and the Paris Peace Conference 1919* (Dubuque, Iowa, 1994).

Noble, George Bernard, *Policies and Opinions at Paris* (New York, 1935).

Northedge, F. S., *The Troubled Giant: Britain among the Great Powers* (London, 1966).

Notter, Harley, *The Origins of the Foreign Policy of Woodrow Wilson* (Baltimore, 1937).

O'Brien, Francis William, ed., *The Hoover-Wilson Wartime Correspondence* (Ames, Iowa, 1974).

Offer, Avner, *The First World War: An Agrarian Interpretation* (Oxford, 1989).

Oppeland, Torsten, *Reichstag und Aussenpolitik im Ersten Weltkrieg: Die deutschen Parteien und die Politik der USA, 1914–1918* (Düsseldorf, 1995).

Orde, Anne, *British Policy and Reconstruction After the First World War* (Cambridge, 1990).

Osgood, Robert E., *Ideals and Self-Interest in America's Foreign Relations* (Chicago, 1953).

Parrini, Carl, *Heir to Empire: United States Economic Diplomacy, 1916–1923* (Pittsburgh, 1969).

Parsons, Edward B., "Why the British Reduced the Flow of American Troops to Europe in August-October 1918," *Canadian Journal of History* 12 (1977–8).

Paul, Vincent C., *The Politics of Hunger: The Allied Blockade of Germany, 1915–1919* (Athens, Ohio, 1985).

Pedroncini, Guy, *Pétain: Général en chef, 1917–1918* (Paris, 1974).

Pegg, Carl H., *The Evolution of the European Idea, 1914–1932* (Chapel Hill, N.C., 1983).

Petricioli, Marta, ed., *A Missed Opportunity? 1922: The Reconstruction of Europe – Une occasion manquée? 1922: La reconstruction de l'Europe* (Berne, 1995).

Pingaud, A., *Histoire diplomatique de la France pendant la Grande Guerre*, 3 vols. (Paris, 1938–40).

Pogge von Strandmann, Hartmut, "Deutscher Imperialismus nach 1918," in Dirk Stegmann, Bernd-Jürgen Wendt, and Peter-Christian Witt, eds., *Deutscher Konservatismus im 19. und 20. Jahrhundert: Festschrift für Fritz Fischer zum 75. Geburtstag und zum 50. Doktorjubiläum* (Bonn, 1983).

Poincaré, Raymond, *Au Service de la France: à la recherche de la paix 1919* (Paris, 1974).

Poincaré, Raymond, *Au Service de la France: neuf années de souvenirs* (Paris, 1974).

Reimer, Klaus, *Rheinlandfrage und Rheinlandbewegung (1918–1933): Ein Beitrag zur Geschichte der regionalistischen Bestrebungen in Deutschland* (Frankfurt am Main, 1979).

Renouvin, Pierre, *Les Crises du XXe Siècle: De 1914 à1929* (Paris, 1957).

Renouvin, Pierre, "Les buts de guerre du gouvernement français, 1914–1918," *Revue historique* 235 (1966): 1–37.

Renouvin, Pierre, *L'Armistice de Rethondes, 11 novembre 1918* (Paris, 1969).

Renouvin, Pierre, *La Traité de Versailles* (Paris, 1969).

Rhodes, Benjamin D., "Reassessing Uncle Shylock: The United States and the French War Debt, 1917–1929," *Journal of American History* 55 (1969): 787–803.

Riddell, Lord, *Lord Riddell's Intimate Diary of the Peace Conference and After, 1918–1923* (London, 1933).

Ritter, Gerhard, *Staatskunst und Kriegshandwerk: Das Problem des Militarismus in Deutschland*, 4 vols. (Munich, 1968).

Rochester, Stuart I., *American Liberal Disillusionment in the Wake of World War I* (University Park, Pa., 1977).

Rogers, Lindsay, "The League of Nations and the National State," in Stephen Duggan, ed., *The League of Nations: The Principle and the Practice* (Boston, 1919).

Rose, Norman, *Vansittart: Study of a Diplomat* (London, 1978).

Roskill, Stephen, *Hankey: Man of Secrets*, 3 vols. (London, 1970–4).

Rössler, Helmut, ed., *Ideologie und Machtpolitik 1919: Plan und Werk der Pariser Friedenskonferenzen 1919* (Berlin, 1966).

Rössler, Helmut, *Die Folgen von Versailles, 1919–1924* (Göttingen, 1969).

Rossini, Daniela, "Wilson e il patto di Londra nel 1917–1918," *Storia contemporanea* 22 (1991): 473–512.

Rossini, Daniela, *L'America riscopere l'Italia: L'Inquiry di Wilson e le origini della questione adriatica, 1917–1919* (Rome, 1992).

Rothbard, Murray N., "Hoover's 1919 Food Diplomacy in Retrospect," in Gelfand, ed., *Herbert Hoover: The Great War and Its Aftermath,* 87–110.

Rothwell, Victor H., *British War Aims and Peace Diplomacy, 1914–1918* (Oxford, 1971).

Rudin, Harry R., *Armistice 1918* (New Haven, Conn., 1944).

Rupieper, Hermann-Josef, "Die freien Gewerkschaften und der Versailler Vertrag, 1919–1923," *Geschichte in Wissenschaft und Unterricht* 29 (1978): 482–99.

Salter, Arthur J., *Allied Shipping Control: An Experiment in International Administration* (Oxford, 1921).

Salter, Arthur J., *Memoirs of a Public Servant* (London, 1961).

Sanders, Michael, and Philip M. Taylor, *British Propaganda During the First World War, 1914–1918* (London, 1982).

Sayre, Francis B., *Experiments in International Administration* (New York, 1919).

Schattkowsky, Ralph, *Deutschland und Polen von 1918–19 bis 1925: Deutsch-polnische Beziehungen zwischen Versailles und Locarno* (Frankfurt am Main, 1994).

Scherer, J., and A. Grunewald, eds., *L'Allemagne et les problèmes de la paix pendant la Première Guerre Mondiale,* 4 vols. (Paris, 1966–78).

Schiff, Victor, *The Germans at Versailles, 1919* (London, 1930).

Schmidt, Gustav, "Politische Tradition und wirtschaftliche Faktoren in der britischen Friedensstrategie, 1918–1919," *Vierteljahrshefte für Zeitgeschichte* 29 (1981): 131–88.

Schmidt, Royal, *Versailles and the Ruhr: Seedbed of World War II* (The Hague, 1968).

Schmitt, Hans A., ed., *Neutral Europe Between War and Revolution, 1917–1923* (Charlottesville, Va., 1988).

Schrecker, Ellen, *The Hired Money: The French Debt to the United States, 1917–1929* (New York, 1979).

Schröder, Hans-Jürgen, ed., *Confrontation and Cooperation: Germany and the United States in the Era of World War I, 1900–1924* (Providence, R.I., 1994).

Schüddekopf, Otto-Ernst, "Deutschland zwischen Ost und West: Karl Moor und die deutsch-russischen Beziehungen im Jahre 1919," *Archiv für Sozialgeschichte* 2 (1962): 223–63.

Schuker, Stephen A., *The End of French Predominance in Europe: The Financial Crisis of 1924 and the Adoption of the Dawes Plan* (Chapel Hill, N.C., 1976).

Schuker, Stephen A., "Finance and Foreign Policy in the Era of German Inflation," in Otto Büsch and Gerald D. Feldman, eds., *Historische Prozesse der deutschen Inflation, 1914–1924* (Berlin, 1978), 343–61.

Schuker, Stephen A., "The End of Versailles," in Martel, ed., *Origins of the Second World War Reconsidered,* 17–48.

Schuker, Stephen A., "Origins of American Stabilization Policy in Europe: The Financial Dimension, 1918–1924," in Schröder, ed., *Confrontation and Cooperation,* 377–408.

Schuker, Stephen A., *American "Reparations" to Germany, 1919–1933* (Princeton, N.J., 1988).

Schuker, Stephen A., "Woodrow Wilson vs. American Public Opinion: The Unconditional Surrender Movement of 1918," in Guido Müller, ed., *Germany, Western Europe, and the United States: Festschrift für Klaus Schwabe* (Stuttgart, 1998).

Schulte-Nordholt, J. W., *Woodrow Wilson: Een leeven for de wereldvrede* (Amsterdam, 1990).

Schulz, Gerhard, *Revolutions and Peace Treaties, 1917–1920* (London, 1972).

Schwabe, Klaus, *Wissenschaft und Kriegsmoral: Die deutschen Hochschullehrer und die politischen Grundfragen des Ersten Weltkrieges* (Göttingen, 1969).

Schwabe, Klaus, *Deutsche Revolution und Wilson-Frieden: Die amerikanische und die deutsche Friedensstrategie zwischen Ideologie und Machtpolitik, 1918–1919* (Düsseldorf, 1971).

Schwabe, Klaus, "Die amerikanische und die deutsche Geheimdiplomatie und das Problem eines Verständigungsfriedens im Jahre 1918," *Vierteljahrshefte für Zeitgeschichte* 19 (1971): 1–32.

Schwabe, Klaus, "Versailles nach sechzig Jahren," *Neue Politische Literatur* 24 (1979).

Schwabe, Klaus, "Die USA, Deutschland und der Ausgang des Erste Weltkrieges," in Manfred Knapp et al., eds., *Die USA und Deutschland, 1918–1975* (Munich, 1978), 11–61.

Schwabe, Klaus, "Äussere und innere Bedingungen der deutschen Novemberrevolution," in Michael Salewski, ed., *Die Deutschen und die Revolution* (Göttingen, 1984).

Schwabe, Klaus, *Woodrow Wilson, Revolutionary Germany, and Peacemaking, 1918–1919: Missionary Diplomacy and the Realities of Power* (Chapel Hill, N.C., 1985).

Schwabe, Klaus, "U.S. Secret War Diplomacy, Intelligence, and the Coming of the German Revolution in 1918: The Role of Vice-Consul James McNally," *Diplomatic History* 16 (1992): 175–200.

Schwarz, Benjamin, "Divided Attention: Britain's Perception of a German Threat to Her Eastern Position in 1918," *Journal of Contemporary History* 28 (1993): 103–22.

Schwarz, Hans-Peter, *Adenauer: Der Aufstieg, 1876–1952* (Stuttgart, 1986).

Schwarz, Marvin, *The Union for Democratic Control in British Politics During the First World War* (Oxford, 1971).

Schwengler, Walter, *Völkerrecht, Versailler Vertrag und Auslieferungsfrage: Die Strafverfolgung von Kriegsverbrechen als Problem des Friedensschlusses, 1919–1920* (Stuttgart, 1982).

Scott, Arthur P., *An Introduction to the Peace Treaties* (Chicago, 1920).

Selsam, John P., *The Attempts to Form an Anglo-French Alliance, 1919–1924* (Philadelphia, 1936).

Seehusen, Ellen A., "Der öffentliche Meinungsbildungsprozess zur Schleswigfrage in den Vereinigten Staaten nach dem Ersten Weltkrieg und Präsident Wilsons Friedensvorschläge," Ph.D. diss., Christian-Albrechts Universität Kiel, 1987.

Seton-Watson, Hugh, and Christopher Seton-Watson, *The Making of a New Europe: R. W. Seton-Watson and the Last Years of Austria-Hungary* (London, 1981).

Seymour, Charles, *Geography, Justice and Politics at the Paris Conference of 1919* (New York, 1951).

Sharp, Alan, "Britain and the Protection of Minorities at the Paris Peace Conference, 1919," in A. C. Hepburn, ed., *Minorities in History* (London, 1978), 170–88.

Sharp, Alan, "Britain and the Channel Tunnel, 1919–1920," *Australian Journal of Politics and History* 25 (Aug. 1979): 210–15.

Sharp, Alan, "'Quelqu'un nous écoute:' French Interception of German Telegraphic and Telephonic Communications During the Paris Peace Conference, 1919: A Note," *Intelligence and National Security* 3 (Oct. 1988).

Sharp, Alan, *The Versailles Settlement: Peacemaking in Paris, 1919* (London, 1991).

Sharp, Alan, "Standard-bearers in a Tangle: British Perceptions of France After the First World War," in David Dutton, ed., *Statecraft and Diplomacy in the Twentieth Century* (Liverpool, 1995).

Shartle, Samuel G., *Spa, Versailles, Munich: An Account of the Armistice Commission* (Philadelphia, 1941).

Shaw, Bernard, *Peace Conference Hints* (London, 1919).

Shotwell, James T., *At the Paris Peace Conference* (New York, 1937).

Silverman, Dan P., *Reconstructing Europe After the Great War* (Cambridge, Mass., 1982).

Sirinelli, Jean-François, *Génération intellectuelle: Khâgneux et Normaliens dans l'entre-deux-guerres* (Paris, 1994).

Skidelsky, Robert, *John Maynard Keynes: A Biography,* 2 vols. (New York, 1983–6).

Sloutzky, Naoum, *La Société des Nations et le contrôle du commerce international des armes de guerre, 1919–1938* (Geneva, 1969).

Smith, Gaddis, *Woodrow Wilson's Fourteen Points After 75 Years* (New York, 1993).

Snell, John L., "Wilson's Peace Programme and German Socialism, January–March 1918," *Mississippi Valley Historical Review* 38 (1951): 187–214.

Soutou, Georges-Henri, "L'Impérialisme du pauvre: la politique économique du gouvernement français en Europe centrale et orientale de 1918 à 1929," *Relations internationales* 7 (1976).

Soutou, Georges-Henri, "Guerre et économie: le premier projet français de nouvel ordre économique mondial," *Revue universelle* 31 (Apr. 1977).

Soutou, Georges, "La France et les marches de l'est , 1914–1919," *Revue historique* 578 (1978): 341–88.

Soutou, Georges-Henri, "L'Alliance franco-polonaise (1925–1933) ou comment s'en débarrasser?" *Revue d'Histoire diplomatique* 95 (1981).

Soutou, Georges-Henri, "Le Luxembourg et la France en 1919," *Hémecht* 39 (1987).

Soutou, Georges-Henri, "Briand et l'Allemagne au tournant de la guerre (septembre 1916–janvier 1917)," in *Media in Francia . . . Recueil de mélanges offerts à Karl Ferdinand Werner à l'occasion de son 65ème anniversaire* (Paris, 1989).

Soutou, Georges-Henri, *L'Or et le sang: les buts de guerre économiques de la Première Guerre mondiale* (Paris, 1989).

Soutou, Georges-Henri, "La France et l'Allemagne en 1919," in J. M. Valentin, J. Bariéty, and A. Guth, eds., *La France et l'Allemagne entre les deux guerres mondiales* (Nancy, 1987).

Soutou, Georges-Henri, "Jean Pélissier et l'Office Central des Nationalités, 1911–1918: Renseignement et influence," *Relations internationales* 78 (1994).

Specht, Agnete von, *Politische und wirtschaftliche Hintergründe der deutschen Inflation, 1918–1923* (Frankfurt am Main, 1982).

Stearns, Harold, *Liberalism in America* (New York, 1919).

Steel, Ronald, *Walter Lippmann and the American Century* (Boston, 1980).

Steinbach, Lothar, *Revision oder Erfüllung: Der Versailler Vertrag als Faktor der deutsch-britischen Beziehungen, 1920–1921* (Freiburg im Breisgau, 1972).

Steinmeyer, Gitta, *Die Grundlagen der französischen Deutschlandpolitik, 1917–1919* (Stuttgart, 1979).

Stevenson, David, "French War Aims and the American Challenge, 1914–1918," *Historical Journal* 22 (1979): 877–94.

Stevenson, David, *French War Aims Against Germany, 1914–1919* (Oxford, 1982).

Stevenson, David, "Belgium, Luxembourg, and the Defence of Western Europe, 1914–1920," *International History Review* 4 (1982): 504–23.

Stevenson, David, *The First World War and International Politics* (Oxford, 1988).

Stevenson, David, "The Failure of Peace by Negotiation in 1917," *Historical Journal* 34 (1991): 65–86.

Stone, Ralph A., ed., *Wilson and the League of Nations: Why America's Rejection?* (New York, 1967).

Strikwerda, Carl, "The Troubled Origins of European Economic Integration: International Iron and Steel and Labor Migration in the Era of World War I," *American Historical Review* 98 (Oct. 1993): 1106–29.

Strunsky, Simeon, "Wilsoniana," *Foreign Affairs* 2, no. 1 (Sept. 1923): 147–60.

Surface, Frank M., *The Grain Trade During the World War* (New York, 1928).

Sutterlin, Siegfried, *Munich in the Cobwebs of Berlin, Washington, and Moscow: Foreign Policy Tendencies in Bavaria, 1917–1919* (New York, 1995).

Tardieu, André, *La Paix* (Paris, 1921).

Tardieu, André, *The Truth About the Treaty* (Indianapolis, 1921).

Taylor, A. J. P., *The Origins of the Second World War* (London, 1963).

Taylor, Philip, and Michael Sanders, *British Propaganda During the First World War, 1914–18* (London, 1982).

Temperley, H. W. V., ed., *History of the Peace Conference of Paris*, 6 vols. (London, 1920).

Thompson, Charles T., *The Peace Conference Day by Day* (New York, 1920).

Thompson, John A., *Reformers and War: American Progressive Publicists and the First World War* (Cambridge, 1987).

Thompson, John M., *Russia, Bolshevism, and the Versailles Peace* (Princeton, N.J., 1966).

Tillman, Seth P., *Anglo-American Relations at the Paris Peace Conference* (Princeton, N.J., 1961).

Timmermann, Heinrich, *Friedenssicherungsbewegungen in den Vereinigten Staaten von Amerika und in Grossbritannien während des Ersten Weltkrieges* (Frankfurt am Main, 1978).

Tirard, Paul, *La France sur le Rhin: Douze années d'occupation rhénane* (Paris, 1930).

Tomlinson, R., "The Disappearance of France, 1896–1940: French Politics and the Birth Rate," *Historical Journal* 28 (1985): 405–15.

Toynbee, Arnold J., "The So-Called Separatist Movement in the Rhineland," *Survey of International Affairs* (1928).

Toynbee, Arnold, *Acquaintances* (London, 1967).

Trachtenberg, Marc, "'A New Economic Order': Etienne Clémentel and French Economic Diplomacy, 1916–1923," *French Historical Studies* 10 (1977): 315–41.

Trachtenberg, Marc, "Reparation at the Paris Peace Conference," *Journal of Modern History* 51 (1979): 24–55.

Trachtenberg, Marc, *Reparations in World Politics: France and European Economic Diplomacy, 1916–1923* (New York, 1980).

Trachtenberg, Marc, "Versailles After Sixty Years," *Journal of Contemporary History* 17 (1982): 487–506.

Trachtenberg, Marc, "The Meaning of Mobilization in 1914," in Miller, Lynn-Jones, and Van Evera, eds., *Military Strategy and the Origins of the First World War*, 195–225.

Trask, David F., *The United States in the Supreme War Council: American War Aims and Inter-Allied Strategy, 1917–1918* (Middletown, Conn., 1961).

Trask, David F., *The AEF and Coalition Warmaking, 1917–1918* (Lawrence, Kans., 1993).

Traversay, Guy de, "La Première Tentative de République rhénane," *Revue de Paris* (Nov.–Dec. 1928): 404–31, 586–614.

Troeltsch, Ernst, *Spektator-Briefe: Aufsätze über die deutsche Revolution und die Weltpolitik, 1918–1922* (Tübingen, 1924).

Tumulty, Joseph P., *Woodrow Wilson As I Know Him* (Garden City, N.Y., 1921).

Tuomainen, Tuuliki, *Versailles'sta maailmanherruuteen: Versailles'n rauhansopimus johtavien kansallissosialistien propagandassa 1919–1923 ja Hitlerin ulkopoliittisessa konseptiossa* (Jyvaskyla, 1988).

Turner, John, *British Politics and the Great War: Coalition and Conflict, 1915–1918* (New Haven, Conn., 1992).

Ullmann, Richard H., *Anglo-Soviet Relations, 1917–1921: Britain and the Russian Civil War, November 1918–February 1920* (Princeton, N.J., 1968).

Unterberger, Betty Miller, *The United States, Revolutionary Russia, and the Rise of Czechoslovakia* (Chapel Hill, N.C., 1989).

Utkin, Anatolii I., *Diplomatiia Vudro Vil'sona* (Moscow, 1989).

Van Evera, Stephen, "The Cult of the Offensive and the Origins of the First World War," in Miller, Lynn-Jones, and Van Evera, eds., *Military Strategy and the Origins of the First World War,* 59–108.

Vansittart, Robert, *The Mist Procession* (London, 1958).

Viefhaus, Erwin, *Die Minderheitenfrage und die Entstehung der Minderheitenschutzverträge auf der Pariser Friedenskonferenz 1919* (Würzburg, 1960).

Villepin, Patrick de, *Victor Margueritte* (Paris, 1991).

Volkogonov, Dmitri, *Lenin: Life and Legacy* (London, 1994).

Wagemann, Christiane, *Das Scheitern des grossen Friedens: Eine Fallstudie zum praktischen Scheitern der Weltfriedenskonzeption Wilsons: Die Südtirol-Frage* (Neuried, 1985).

Waite, Robert G., *Vanguard of Nazism* (Cambridge, Mass., 1952).

Wallace, Stuart, *War and the Image of Germany: British Academics, 1914–1918* (Edinburgh, 1988).

Wallach, Jehuda L., *Uneasy Coalition: The Entente Experience in World War I* (Westport, Conn., 1993).

Walters, Francis Paul, *A History of the League of Nations* (London, 1952).

Walworth, Arthur, *America's Moment, 1918: American Diplomacy at the End of World War I* (New York, 1977).

Walworth, Arthur, *Wilson and His Peacemakers: American Diplomacy at the Paris Peace Conference, 1919* (London, 1986).

Wandycz, Piotr S., *France and Her Eastern Allies, 1919–1925: French-Czechoslovak-Polish Relations from the Paris Peace Conference to Locarno* (Minneapolis, 1962).

Warburg, Max, *Aus meinen Aufzeichnungen* (Glückstadt, 1952).

Warman, Roberta, "The Erosion of Foreign Office Influence in the Making of Foreign Policy, 1916–1918," *Historical Journal* 15, no. 1 (1972): 133–59.

Watson, David Robin, *Georges Clemenceau: A Political Biography* (London, 1974).

Weikardt, Charles Richard, "Das Rheinland in den deutsch-britischen Beziehungen, 1918–1923: Eine Untersuchung zum Wesen der britischen Gleichgewichtspolitik," Ph.D. diss., University of Bonn, 1967.

Weill-Raynal, Etienne, *Les Réparations allemandes et la France,* 3 vols. (Paris, 1947).

Wein, Franziska, *Deutschlands Strom, Frankreichs Grenze: Geschichte und Propaganda am Rhein, 1919–1930* (Essen, 1992).

Weinstein, Edwin A., *Woodrow Wilson: A Medical and Psychological Biography* (Princeton, N.J., 1981).

Wengst, Udo, *Graf Brockdorff-Rantzau und die aussenpolitischen Anfänge der Weimarer Republik* (Frankfurt am Main, 1973).

Weygand, Maxime, *Mémoires: mirages et réalité* (Paris, 1957).

Weyl, Walter E., *American World Policies* (New York, 1917).

Wheeler-Bennett, John W., *Brest-Litovsk, the Forgotten Peace* (New York, 1971).

Widenor, William E., *Henry Cabot Lodge and the Search for an American Foreign Policy* (Berkeley, Calif., 1980).

Williams, John M., "German Foreign Trade and the Reparations Payments," *Quarterly Journal of Economics* 36 (1922): 483–502.

Williamson, David G., *The British in Germany, 1918–1930: The Reluctant Occupiers* (New York, 1991).

Willis, J. F., *Prologue to Nuremberg: The Politics and Diplomacy of Punishing War Criminals of the First World War* (Westport, Conn., 1982).

Wilson, Edith Bolling, *My Memoir* (Indianapolis, 1938).

Wilson, Henry, *The Military Correspondence of Field Marshal Sir Henry Wilson, 1918–1922,* ed. Keith Jeffery (London, 1985).

Wilson, Trevor, *The Myriad Faces of War: Britain and the Great War, 1914–1918* (Oxford, 1986).

Winkler, Heinrich August, *Von der Revolution zur Stabilisierung: Arbeiter und Arbeiterbewegung in der Weimarer Republik, 1918–1924* (Berlin, 1985).

Winkler, Heinrich August, "Die Revolution von 1918–19 und das Problem der Kontinuität in der deutschen Geschichte," *Historische Zeitschrift* 250 (1990): 303–19.

Winkler, Heinrich August, *Weimar, 1918–1933* (Munich, 1993).

Wiskemann, Elisabeth, *Czechs and Germans: A Study of the Struggle in the Historic Provinces of Bohemia and Moravia* (London, 1967).

Woodward, David R., *Trial by Friendship: Anglo-American Relations, 1917–1918* (Lexington, Ky., 1993).

Wormser, Georges, *La République de Clemenceau* (Paris, 1961).

Wormser, Georges, *Clemenceau vu du près* (Paris, 1979).

Wüest, Erich, *Der Vertrag von Versailles in Licht und Schatten der Kritik: Die Kontroverse um seine wirtschaftlichen Auswirkungen* (Zurich, 1962).

Wulf, Peter, "Die Vorstellungen der deutschen Industrie zur Neuordnung der Wirtschaft nach dem 1. Weltkrieg," *Zeitschrift für Unternehmensgeschichte* 32 (1987): 23–42.

Yates, Louis R., *The United States and French Security, 1917–1921* (New York, 1957).

Young, Allyn Abbott, "The Economic Settlement," in House and Seymour, eds., *What Really Happened at Paris,* 291–318.

Zarusky, Jürgen, *Die deutschen Sozialdemokraten und das sowjetische Modell: Ideologische Auseinandersetzung und aussenpolitische Konzeptionen, 1917–1933* (Munich, 1992).

Zechlin, Egmont, *Die Deutsche Politik und die Juden im Ersten Weltkrieg* (Göttingen, 1969).

Zeman, Z. A. B., *A Diplomatic History of the First World War* (London, 1971).

Zivojinovic, Dragoljub R., *America, Italy, and the Birth of Yugoslavia (1917–1919)* (Boulder, Colo., 1972).

Index

844479

Printed in Great Britain by
Amazon.co.uk, Ltd.,
Marston Gate.